WHAT THE BIBLE TEACHES

General Editors
TOM WILSON
KEITH STAPLEY

Contributors

ERNEST WILSON

T. Ernest Wilson was born in 1902 in Belfast, N. Ireland into a Christian home. At 21 years of age he was commended to the work of the Lord in Central Africa. His service of the next 40 years is graphically described in his book *Angola Beloved.* On leaving Africa he went to reside in U.S.A. and commenced a ministry of Bible teaching, travelling extensively. He is also the author of several books including *Mystery Doctrines of the New Testament* and a devotional book on the Psalms.

THOMAS SMITH

Born and brought up on Merseyside, T.W. Smith has been associated with Wirral assemblies for the past 35 years. Now retired from the civil service, he travels throughout the British Isles teaching the Word of God.

JAMES ALLEN

An Ulsterman by birth, Jim Allen went to Malaysia first in 1955 in government service. He returned there in 1968 as a commended missionary. In latter years he has resided in N. Ireland is engaged in preaching the Gospel and in ministry to the saints at home and abroad.

JAMES BAKER

Having spent his early life in Liverpool, J. R. Baker has lived in Scotland for the past 20 years. In addition to professional life, he travels widely conducting Bible Readings and ministering the Word of God. He is also a member of the Editorial Panel of *Believers' Magazine,* in which he has conducted the Question Page for a number of years.

DAVID WEST

Brought up in Essex, David E. West has been engaged for the past 20 years in education at Leicester. He is known for his oral ministry throughout the British Isles, and for his contribution to assembly periodicals.

WHAT THE BIBLE TEACHES

with

Authorised Version

of

The Bible

IN NINE VOLUMES
COVERING THE NEW TESTAMENT

JOHN RITCHIE LTD
KILMARNOCK, SCOTLAND

ISBN 0 946351 03 1

WHAT THE BIBLE TEACHES
Copyright © 1983 by John Ritchie Ltd.
40 Beansburn, Kilmarnock, Scotland

Printed at The Bath Press, Avon

CONTENTS

ABBREVIATIONS

AV	Authorised Version or King James Version 1611
JND	New Translation by J.N. Darby 1939
LXX	Septuagint Version of Old Testament
Mft	New Translation by James Moffat 1922
NASB	New American Standard Bible 1960
NEB	New English Bible 1961
Nestle	Nestle (ed.) Novum Testamentum Graece
NIV	New International Version 1973
NT	New Testament
OT	Old Testament
Phps	New Testament in Modern English by J.B. Phillips 1962
RSV	Revised Standard Version 1952
RV	Revised Version 1881
TR	Textus Receptus or Received Text
Wey	New Testament in Modern Speech by R.F. Weymouth 1929

PREFACE

They follow the noblest example who seek to open the Scriptures to others, for our Lord Himself did so for those two dejected disciples of Emmaus (Luke 24:32). Whether it is the evangelist "opening and alleging that Christ must needs have suffered and risen from the dead" (Acts 17:3) or the pastor-teacher "expounding... in all the Scriptures the things concerning Himself" (Luke 24:27) or stimulating our hope "through the patience and comfort of the Scriptures" (Rom 15:4), he serves well in thus giving attendance to the reading of the Scriptures (1 Tim 4:13).

It is of course of equal moment to recognise in the exercise of able men, the continued faithfulness of the risen Head in giving gifts to the Church, in spite of her unfaithfulness. How good to recognise that "the perfecting of the saints... the work of the ministry... the edifying of the body of Christ" need not be neglected. Every provision has been made to ensure the well-being of the people of God. And every opportunity should be taken by the minister of Christ and those to whom he ministers to ensure that the saints "grow up unto him in all things which is the Head, even Christ" (Eph 4:15).

At various times in the post-apostolic period, certain teachers have come to prominence, sometimes because they succumbed to error, sometimes because in faithfulness they paid the ultimate price for the truth they had bought and would not sell. Some generations had Calvin and Luther, others Darby and Kelly, but in every generation God's voice is heard. It is important that we hear His voice today and recognise that He does speak through His servants. The contributors to this series of commentaries are all highly-respected expositors among the churches of God. They labour in the Word in the English-speaking world and have been of blessing to many throughout their years of service.

The doctrinal standpoint of the commentaries is based upon the acceptance of the verbal and plenary inspiration of the Scriptures so that their inerrant and infallible teachings are the only rule of conscience. The impeccability of Christ, His virgin birth, vicarious death and bodily resurrection are indeed precious truths worthy of the Christian's defence, and throughout the volumes of this series will be defended. Equally the Rapture will be presented as the Hope of the Church. Before the great Tribulation she will be raptured and God's prophetic programme will continue with Jacob's trouble, the public manifestation of Christ and the Millennium of blessing to a restored Israel and the innumerable Gentile multitude in a creation released from the bondage of corruption.

May the sound teaching of these commentaries be used by our God to the blessing of His people. May the searching of the Scriptures characterise all who read them.

The diligience of Mr. J. Ferguson and Professor J. Heading in proof-reading is gratefully acknowledged. Without such co-operation, the production of this commentary would not have been expedited so readily.

T. WILSON
K. STAPLEY

1 THESSALONIANS

T.E. Wilson

1   THESSALONIANS

Introduction

1. Authorship

The Pauline authorship of 1 Thessalonians has been confirmed by competent scholars who have carefully investigated the evidence. During the last century, objections to its genuineness were raised by critics, but these have all been satisfactorily answered.

2. The City of Thessalonica

The place is first mentioned in history under the name of Therma on account of the warm mineral springs in the area. Thessalonica was founded by Cassander in BC 315. He chose the place for its excellent location and named it after his wife Thessalonica, who was a half-sister of Alexander the Great. Cassander was a Greek general under Alexander. When the Romans conquered the area in BC 168 they divided Macedonia into four districts and named Thessalonica the capital of one of them. In 146 BC the Romans reorganised Macedonia and made Thessalonica the capital of the new province which was composed of all four of the older districts. It was declared a free city with important rights of self-government enjoying autonomy in all its internal affairs. Although there was a provincial governor resident there he had no civil authority, the city being ruled by politarchs as Luke accurately describes them in Acts 17:6. Under Roman rule it became an important centre and, with a population of about 200 000, was one of the greatest cities along the Egnatian Road, the great military highway linking Rome with the Orient.

Its location, at the north-western corner of the Aegean Sea midway between the Adriatic and the Hellespont, and its sheltered harbour contributed to its importance. As a result of its flourishing commerce, it attracted many wealthy Romans and Jewish business men (Acts 17:4). Being a seaport, ships and sailors coming and going from all over the Mediterranean congregated there, bringing it a reputation for immorality and licentiousness.

In contrast to Philippi where Jewish worshippers had only a *proseuchē*, an open-air meeting place for prayer by a riverside (Acts 16:13), at Thessalonica the Jews had an important synagogue, indicating their numbers and influence (Acts 17:1). The city, now called Salonica, is still one of the busiest ports of the Aegean with a population of about 300 000. In World War 2, it was reported that 60 000 Jews were arrested there, and later executed by the Nazis.

The country which we now call Greece, in Paul's day comprised two territories, the northern called Macedonia, in which were located Philippi, Thessalonica and Berea, the southern Achaia with its chief cities Athens and Corinth. These are places mentioned in Acts 16-18 as being evangelised by Paul and his fellow-workers on his second missionary journey.

3. The Founding of the Church at Thessalonica (Acts 17:1–10)

The narrative recorded in the Acts of how the Gospel first reached Europe is one of the most graphic and exciting stories in the annals of missionary work. Paul, accompanied by Silas and Timothy, on this second missionary journey revisited the churches which had been planted in Syria, Cilicia and Galatia, establishing and encouraging the believers. Then by a series of divine interventions they were guided north-west to the historic seaport town of Troas. While there, Paul received a vision of a man of Macedonia beseeching him, "Come over into Macedonia and help us". It was evidently the guiding voice of the Holy Spirit and they immediately obeyed. They were the first pioneers with the Gospel in Europe. Landing at Neapolis in Macedonia, they headed for the important colonial city of Philippi. Their first converts were a few women who met at a prayer meeting at a riverside. After healing a demon-possessed girl, Paul and Silas, who were Roman citizens, were arrested on flimsy charges, brutally scourged and thrown into the maximum security prison, their feet shackled in the stocks. Instead of weeping and bemoaning their plight, in the middle of the night they prayed and sang praises to God. God sent an earthquake and released them from their bonds. When the jailor heard that they were Roman citizens he was terrified for his own safety, and, recognising God's intervention in the earthquake, he cried, "What must I do to be saved?" Paul's answer was "Believe on the Lord Jesus Christ and thou shalt be saved, and thy house". Paul then had the joy of pointing him and all that were in his house to the Lord. After baptising them and being hospitably entertained in the house of Lydia, they comforted the brethren and departed.

It is a distance of approximately 100 miles from Philippi to Thessalonica. The converted jailor had bathed their bleeding backs, but the wounds and weals resulting from the flogging must have only partially healed as they walked the four or five days' journey to the capital city. Luke takes up the story in Acts 17: "Now when they had passed through Amphipolis and Apollonia, they came to Thessalonica, where was a synagogue of the Jews. And Paul, as his manner was, went in unto them and three sabbath days reasoned with them out of the Scriptures, opening and alleging that Christ must needs have suffered and risen again from the dead, and that this Jesus, whom I preach unto you, is Christ". As a result of the preaching, some of them (presumably Jews) believed, and consorted with Paul and Silas, "and of the devout Greeks a great multitude, and of the chief women not a few". Paul's message, as related by Luke, consisted of two main points: the OT predicted a suffering, dying, resurrected Messiah; these prophecies were fulfilled in Jesus of Nazareth. Three words are used of Paul's method of preaching: Reasoning, the word meaning to marshall arguments and dispute; Opening, opening the mind and the Scriptures (Luke 24:32,45); Alleging, not only expounding but explaining, setting his teaching alongside the Scriptures. The great theme of his messages was Jesus Christ and Him crucified and risen.

Obviously the record of Paul's preaching at Thessalonica is concise and not detailed. The doctrine unfolded in his two epistles shows that it must have covered a wide range. Many commentators feel that Paul must have stayed much longer at Thessalonica than three weeks. Three sabbath days are mentioned in Acts 17:2, but this could refer to the duration of his teaching in the synagogue. He tells us twice that he worked with his hands night and day so that he would not be a burden to anyone (1 Thess 2:9; 2 Thess 3:8). While he was there he received at least two fellowship gifts from the church at Philippi (Phil 4:15-16). During his stay a considerably-sized church was established and their faith and good reputation spread abroad, not only in Macedonia and Achaia but also in every place (1 Thess 1:8). These facts seem to indicate a stay longer than three weeks. Again, in 1 Thess 5:12 the church is exhorted "to know them which labour among you and are over you in the Lord". Some time must have elapsed for leaders to have been raised up able to admonish and recognised as such. In any case there had been a real movement of the Spirit of God. Their enemies described it as having "turned the world upside down". It caused serious opposition which, fomented by the Jewish element, developed into a riot. Apparently Paul was staying in the home of Jason. The mob assaulted the house expecting to find the preachers, but failing in this they dragged the occupants before the rulers of the city. The charge was a political one, that of revolutionary propaganda against Caesar and the Roman government. They were said to be announcing another king, Jesus. It was the same charge brought by the Jewish leaders against the Lord Himself and for which He was condemned and crucified as the King of the Jews. Apparently the magistrates could see through the trumped-up charge against the preachers, and taking bail of Jason for good behaviour, they let him go. This may have been the reason that Paul was prevented from returning to Thessalonica for some time (1 Thess 2:18). It is evident that Jewish fanatical opposition continued after the preachers had left. Paul's two epistles to the church mention affliction and persecution repeatedly (1 Thess 1:6; 2:14; 3:3; 2 Thess 1:4,6).

After the riot at Thessalonica, the movements of Paul, Silas and Timothy are not absolutely clear, but the following reconstruction seems fairly probable. All three went to Berea (Acts 17:10,14). Then Paul left for Athens, Silas and Timothy (v.14) remaining to carry on the work; later they too came to Athens (vv.15-16). From Athens Paul sent back both, Timothy to Thessalonica (1 Thess 3:1-2) and Silas to Macedonia, probably to Philippi (Acts 18:5). Paul himself went on from Athens to Corinth. Silas rejoined Timothy on the return journey from Macedonia, and both followed Paul to Corinth, perhaps bringing financial aid (2 Cor 11:9; Phil 4:15). Paul, encouraged by their reports, redoubled his energies (Acts 18:5) and wrote the first epistle to the Thessalonians (cf. 1 Thess 1:1 with Acts 18:5). So from his lodging in the home of Aquila and Priscilla, where he worked night and day with his hands weaving goats' hair cloth for making tents, and in the intervals between meetings in the house of Justus, Paul wrote these great letters to the church at Thessalonica, the first of his written ministry and among the first of the NT writings.

4. Paul's Purpose in Writing

The fact that Paul and his companions had to be smuggled out of Thessalonica in the midst of a riot, and a court case ensued in which his friends and recent converts had suffered severely, meant that his mind must have been torn with anxiety. When, after his experiences at Berea and Athens, he finally arrived at Corinth, he must have worried constantly about the recently-formed church and the new believers. The pioneer evangelists had been only a comparatively short time at Thessalonica and naturally they would wonder whether the believers would be able to face up to the persecution and fanatical opposition of their enemies. In his anxiety to know what was happening, Paul sent Timothy back to Thessalonica from Athens to comfort them and to establish them in the faith (1 Thess 3:1-5). When Timothy returned with his report, there was news which filled Paul's heart with joy. The saints were standing fast in the midst of trial and were spreading the good tidings of salvation both at home and further afield. But the enemy was also at work, seeking to undermine Paul's character and motives (1 Thess 2:1-10). Paul felt it was his duty to answer and repudiate these insinuations.

As well as their reaction to trial and persecution, the apostle was concerned about their personal lives and behaviour in the midst of a wicked and licentious environment. Ch.4:1-12 deals with this. Soundness in faith and doctrine must always be accompanied by purity and holiness of life.

One of the most important matters which called for this first epistle of Paul, was the subject of resurrection and the second coming of Christ. Apparently some of the believers had died, and the bereaved families were anxious to know some details about the present condition of their loved ones. This letter gives the first great revelation concerning this glorious subject. It is the result of Timothy's encouraging report to Paul of the internal condition of the church at Thessalonica and the answer to some of their problems.

5. The Time and Place

References in Acts 17:1-10 and 18:1 as well as in 1 Thessalonians make it clear that Paul wrote this epistle in Corinth, evidently shortly after his arrival in that city. Conservative scholars date the epistle between AD 50 and AD 54. The approximate date has been confirmed by an archaeological discovery which has given us a definitely fixed reference-point for Paul's stay in Corinth. An inscription found at Delphi shows that Gallio was proconsul of Achaia in AD 52. The account of Paul's trial before Gallio (Acts 18:12-17) suggests that Gallio had recently come to office. Since Paul had already been there eighteen months (Acts 18:11), it is likely that he came to Corinth about AD 50. 1 Thessalonians was written by Paul in Corinth as shown by internal evidence in the epistle. It is likely that it was written within a short time of his arrival, probably in AD 50-51.

6. Paul's Written Ministry

Paul's epistles are thirteen in number and fall into four groups.

1. *The Advent Epistles:*   1 & 2 Thessalonians, written in Corinth in AD50-51. They were designed to steady the faith of a persecuted and afflicted infant church in view of the Lord's return.
2. *The Gospel and Church Epistles:*   Galatians, 1 & 2 Corinthians, and Romans, written between June 53 and March 57 in Ephesus and Corinth. They are occupied with the Jewish controversy between law and grace; the great doctrines of the Gospel and practical procedure in the local church.
3. *The Prison Epistles:*   Philippians, Ephesians, Colossians and Philemon, written in Rome between November 60 to about January 62.
4. *The Pastoral Epistles:*   1 Timothy, Titus, and 2 Timothy. They were penned respectively in Colosse, Corinth and Rome between the Spring of 83 and the Autumn of 67. "They represent the ripened tenderness of a master-shepherd" (H. St. John).

The two epistles to the Thessalonians are the first writings of the NT, with the possible exception of the Epistle to the Galatians. Paul had been a Christian for seventeen or eighteen years when he wrote 1 Thessalonians, and had been a missionary for seven or eight years. It was twenty-two years after our Lord's ascension, four years before writing the Epistle to the Romans, and about fifteen years before his death by martyrdom. His written ministry covered a period of approximately sixteen years.

7. Analysis and Outline of 1 Thessalonians

I.	*Salutation and Greetings*	1:1
II.	*Thanksgiving and the Reasons for it*	1:2–10
	1. Their work of faith	1:3a,4-5
	2. Their labour of love	1:3b, 8
	3. Their patience of hope	1:3c, 6-7
	4. Their election by God	1:4
	5. Their outreach with the Gospel	1:5-8
	6. Its effect in their own lives	1:9-10
III.	*Paul's Personal Character and Work*	2:1-20
	1. His suffering at Philippi	2:1-2
	2. Motivation in his preaching	2:3-6
	3. Attitude to his converts	2:7-12
	4. Results in the believers	2:13-14a
	5. Fierce Jewish persecution	2:14b-16
	6. Paul's desire to see them again	2:17-20
IV.	*Timothy's Mission and his Report*	3:1-13
	1. Timothy's commendation and mission	3:1-5
	2. Timothy's encouraging report	3:6-9
	3. Paul's prayer	3:10-13
V.	*Exhortation to Holy Living*	4:1-12
	1. Personal purity	4:1-8
	2. Brotherly love	4:9-10
	3. Attitude to the world	4:11-12
VI.	*Revelation of the Rapture*	4:13-18
	1. Certainty instead of ignorance	4:13
	2. The basis of the hope	4:14
	3. Participants in the Rapture	4:15-17
	4. Three sounds at the Rapture	4:16

8. Bibliography

Hogg, C.F. and Vine, W.E. *The Epistles of Paul the Apostle to the Thessalonians.* Reprint. Grand Rapids: Kregel Publications, 1959.

Hendriksen, William. *1 & 2 Thessalonians. New Testament Commentary.* London: Banner of Truth Trust, 1972.

Ryrie, Charles Caldwell. *First and Second Thessalonians. Everyman's Bible Commentary.* Chicago: Moody Press, 1968.

Walvoord, John F. *The Thessalonian Epistles.* Grand Rapids: Zondervan Publishing House, 1958.

Morris, Leon. *The Epistles of Paul to the Thessalonians. The Tyndale New Testament Commentaries.* Grand Rapids: Wm. B. Erdmans Publishing Co., 1957.

Lees, Harrington C. *Thessalonians.* London: Marshall Brothers, 1905.

Pentecost, J. Dwight. *Thessalonians.* Philadelphia: A. J. Holman Co., 1960.

Findlay, George G. *The Epistles to the Thessalonians. Cambridge Bible for Schools and Colleges.* London: Cambridge University Press, 1891.

Kelly, William. *The Epistles of Paul the Apostle to the Thessalonians.* London: C. A. Hammond, 1953.

Ironside, H.A. *Addresses on the First and Second Epistles to the Thessalonians.* New York: Loizeaux Brothers, 1947.

Constable, Thomas L. *1 Thessalonians. The Bible Knowledge Commentary.* Wheaton, Ill: Victor Books, 1983.

Macdonald, William. *Letters to the Thessalonians.* Kansas City, Kansas: Walterick Publishers, 1969.

Vine, W. E. *An Expository Dictionary of New Testament Words.* New Jersey: Fleming H. Revell Co., 1966.

Vincent, Marvin R. *Word Studies in the New Testament*. Grand Rapids: Wm. B. Erdmans Publishing Co., 1946.

Robertson, Archibald Thomas. *Word Pictures in the New Testament*. New York: Harper Brothers, Publishers, 1931.

Lineberry, John. *Vital Word Studies in 1 Thessalonians*. Grand Rapids: Zondervan Publishing House, 1960.

Hogg, C.F. and Vine, W.E. *Touching the Coming of the Lord*. London: Oliphants Ltd., N.D.

Text and Exposition

I. Salutation and Greeting   (1:1)

> v.1   "Paul and Silvanus, and Timotheus, unto the church of the Thessalonians, which is in God the Father and in the Lord Jesus Christ; Grace be unto you, and peace, from God our Father, and the Lord Jesus Christ".

1   Paul does not use the title "apostle" in this salutation as he does in 1 and 2 Corinthians where his apostolic authority was being questioned. His attitude to his beloved children in the faith at Thessalonica was one of love, affection and concern. He also includes his two esteemed fellow-workers, using the formal form of their names, Silvanus instead of Silas and Timotheus instead of Timothy. He was careful about honour and courtesy in mentioning those associated with him; cf. Prisca instead of Priscilla in 2 Tim 4:19 and the names in Rom 16. Love and appreciation are seen but no undue familiarity.

Paul's name means "little". It was the common practice at this time among the Jewish people to give a child both a Jewish and a gentile name. His Jewish name was Saul, meaning "asked for". It was the name of the first king of Israel who was a Benjamite. Paul too came from the same tribe (Phil 3:5) and possibly he may have been named after him. Paul was a Roman citizen (Acts 22:25-28). His Jewish name Saul is used in the Acts until he commenced his missionary work among the gentiles (Acts 13:9). After that his gentile name, Paul, is consistently used.

Silvanus (Silas) was also a Jew and a Roman citizen (Acts 16:37). He was a leading member of the church at Jerusalem and a prophet (Acts 15:22,23). His name is Latin, meaning "wood or woods" (cf. English "sylvan"). He had the honour with the apostle Paul of planting the first assembly in Europe (Acts 16). His association with Paul seems to have terminated with the second missionary journey, but he is probably the Silvanus mentioned in 1 Pet 5:12. If so, there is a link with Peter and Mark.

The name Timotheus (Timothy) means "honouring God", composed of *timaō* (to honour) and *Theos* (God). He lived at Lystra, a city in Lycaonia about

11

18 miles south of Iconium. He had a Greek father and a Jewish mother. Saved under Paul's preaching (1 Tim 1:2), he became a fellow-labourer with the apostle. He was invited by Paul to join him on his second missionary journey (Acts 16:1-3) and was associated with him until the end of Paul's life. His name is linked with Paul's in 1 and 2 Thessalonians, 2 Corinthians, Philippians, and Colossians. At the close of his life, Paul wrote two inspired letters to his beloved and "dear child Timothy".

The form of address used in the two letters to the Thessalonians is unique: "unto the church of the Thessalonians, which is in God the Father, and in the Lord Jesus Christ"; he never employs it again. It indicates Paul's special interest in each individual member of the church and their exalted standing in Christ. His usual address is: "unto the church of God which is at Corinth" or "to the saints which are at Ephesus", emphasising their location on earth. But here it is "in God the Father, and in the Lord Jesus Christ". Thus at the beginning of Paul's written ministry we meet his Christology. He at once uses the full title, Lord Jesus Christ, and puts Him in the same category with God the Father. He speaks about Jesus as "the Lord" or "our Lord" about twenty-five times in 1 Thessalonians. This company of persecuted believers was not only gathered in a definite location in Macedonia, but they were enfolded, encompassed, and shielded by two Persons of the Holy Trinity, God the Father and the Lord Jesus Christ. In v.6 we are told that they were full of the joy of the Holy Ghost.

The salutation ends with greeting; grace (*charis*) and peace (*eirēnē*) are two of the greatest words in the NT. "Together they sum up the Gospel" (Hogg and Vine). "Grace is God's favour towards man, free and unmerited; peace is the result to all who receive that favour in Christ". In the salutation, Paul speaks of their exalted position in relation to the Godhead, but in the greeting he reminds them of their daily blessing of grace and peace. It has been suggested that the words seem to combine the greetings current among the Greeks and the Jews (*chairein, shalom*), but as Paul uses them, the words have a fuller and deeper meaning. He defines grace in 2 Cor 8:9, "For ye know the grace of our Lord Jesus Christ, that, though he was rich, yet for your sakes he became poor, that ye through his poverty might be rich". Nothing could be fuller or deeper than that. Then our Lord's first greeting to the disciples gathered in the upper room after His resurrection was: "Peace be unto you" (John 20:19,21,26).

II. Thanksgiving and the Reasons for it (1:2-10)

v.2   "We give thanks to God always for you all, making mention of you in our prayers;

v.3   Remembering without ceasing your work of faith, and labour of love, and patience of hope in our Lord Jesus Christ, in the sight of God and our Father;

v.4   Knowing, brethren beloved, your election of God.

> v.5 For our gospel came not unto you in word only, but also in power, and in the Holy Ghost, and in much assurance; as ye know what manner of men we were among you for your sake.
>
> v.6 And ye became followers of us, and of the Lord, having received the word in much affliction, with joy of the Holy Ghost;
>
> v.7 So that ye were ensamples to all that believe in Macedonia and Achaia.
>
> v.8 For from you sounded out the word of the Lord not only in Macedonia and Achaia, but also in every place your faith to Godward is spread abroad; so that we need not to speak anything.
>
> v.9 For they themselves show of us what manner of entering in we had unto you, and how ye turned to God from idols, to serve the living and true God;
>
> v.10 And to wait for his Son from heaven, whom he raised from the dead, even Jesus, which delivered us from the wrath to come."

2 The present tense, "We are constantly giving thanks", denotes continuous action. With Paul, thanksgiving was not a spasmodic exercise, but a habit of life (2 Thess 2:13). He includes his fellow-workers by using the plural form. Did the three missionaries have daily prayer meetings for the saints at Thessalonica? Ch.3:10 informs us that they engaged in thanksgiving and intercession night and day for them. In every epistle except Galatians, the apostle's first words are of thanksgiving and praise for those to whom he is writing. In ch.5:18 of this epistle he exhorts "in every thing give thanks" and he practised what he preached. The remaining verses of ch.1 outline the sixfold reason for his thanksgiving.

1. *Their Work of Faith*

3a This goes back to their conversion, saving faith manifested by good works. Paul emphasises faith without works as the means of justification (Rom 5:1), but in his letter to Titus he insists that good works are the accompaniments of a living faith (Titus 2:7,14; 3:1,8,14). James is very emphatic that faith without works is dead (2:17-26). Paul and James do not contradict one another but are complementary in their teaching. The hymn-writer has put it simply and beautifully:

> "I would not work my soul to save;
> For that my Lord has done.
> But I would work like any slave,
> For love to God's dear Son. "

2 *Their Labour of Love*

3b A faith that works, leads on to a labour of love. Labour (*kopos*) means "intense labour united with toil, even to the point of fatigue". Love (*agapē*) is divine, self-sacrificing love. Here we see the motive spring of a godly, spiritual life, issuing in devoted service for Christ and mankind. This is evidenced in their outreach with the Gospel in an increasingly wide area.

3. *Their Patience of Hope*

3c "Patience" (*hupomonē*, from *hupo*, under, and *menō*, to remain, abide) means "endurance even under the greatest trial and suffering". "Hope" *(elpis)* has the definite article before it. It is *the* hope, one of the main subjects of 1 Thessalonians, and referred to by Paul in Titus 2:13, "Looking for that blessed hope, and the glorious appearing of the great God and our Saviour Jesus Christ".

The three great Christian graces, faith and love and hope, are found together in 1 Thess 5:8; Rom 5:2-5; Gal 5:5-6; Col 1:4-5; Heb 6:10-12; 1 Pet 1:21-22 and especially 1 Cor 13:13. In Rev 2:2 the three attributes of works, labour and patience are mentioned in the commendation of the church at Ephesus, but the fundamentals of faith, love and hope are noticeably missing. Perhaps this is the reason that they had drifted from their early devotion to Christ. They had left their first love. At Thessalonica these graces characterised the three tenses of the believers' Christian testimony, past, present and future, and were the rock foundation of their consecration.

4. *Their Election by God*

4 Another reason for thanksgiving was God's choice of these people for salvation and blessing. The RV and JND translate the verse "Knowing, brethren beloved by God, your election". The word used for "knowing" *(oida)*, "intimates that this knowledge came not by revelation, nor by intuition, but by observation" (Hogg and Vine). How did Paul know that they were elect? Paul's knowledge of their election came from what he had seen among them and what he had heard about them. After a comparatively brief stay at Thessalonica, the missionaries were convinced by the change in the lives of these new converts, that they were genuine trophies of grace, and that they were God's chosen ones. They had responded affirmatively and quickly to the Word as it was preached, for it came to them in power, in the Holy Ghost and in much assurance. They also had brought forth the fruit of faith in works of faith, labours of love, and patience of hope. Thus it is that we know the elect in any time and age.

The doctrine of election is clearly taught in the Bible. The word *eklogē* means, choice, selection. Election has been defined as "the sovereign act of God in grace, by which from eternity certain are chosen from the human race for Himself" (see John 15:9; Eph 1:4). In the OT the term "elect" is used of:

The Servant of Jehovah, the Messiah, the Lord Jesus (Isa 42:1);
The nation of Israel (Isa 65:9,15,22).

In the NT the doctrine of election occurs in the following passages: Acts 9:15; Rom 9:11; 11:5,7,28; Eph 1:4; 1 Thess 1:4; 1 Pet 1:10. Election may be corporate as in the case of the nation of Israel (Isa 45:4), or the Church (Eph 1:4), or individual (1 Pet 1:2). Election is based on God's foreknowledge (1 Pet 1:2; Rom 8:29). "Foreknowledge of God is the basis of His foreordaining counsels. God's foreknowledge involves His electing grace, but this does not preclude human will. He foreknows the exercise of faith which brings salvation" (W.E.Vine). God's sovereignty is consistent with His love, mercy, compassion, justice and holiness. His sovereign choice of individuals and companies to salvation and blessing, and man's free will and consequent responsibility, are both taught in Holy Scripture, sometimes in the same verse (e.g. John 6:37). To our finite minds these may seen irreconcilable. The truth lies in holding both in equal balance. To exaggerate or push either to an extreme leads to error. A comment of Dean Alford is worthy of note. Writing on Romans 11:28 he says: "On the one side GOD'S SOVEREIGNTY, on the other, MAN'S FREE WILL is plainly declared to us. To receive, believe, and act on these, is our duty and our wisdom ... But all attempts to bridge over the gulf between the two are futile in the present imperfect condition of man". The capitals are Alford's. The lesson is for us.

5. *Their Outreach with the Gospel*

5   First of all, we are reminded of the threefold character and dynamic of the preaching. It was the sharp sword of the Word of God, clothed in the power of the Holy Spirit. It was also the trumpet sound of the herald with no uncertain note, but with the authority of God behind it. It was directed to the heart, mind and conscience of the hearers and demanded the response of the will. Along with the character of the preaching was the character of the preachers; their manner of life corresponded with the message they proclaimed. Paul elaborates on this in ch.2 and refers to it again and again. The preacher must be a walking example of what he preaches.

6-8   As a result of the preaching there was a threefold dramatic result in the lives of the new converts at Thessalonica.

1.   They became followers (*mimētai* from *mimeomai*, to imitate) of us. The word is much stronger than "followers" and is used only six times in the NT: 1 Cor 4:16; 11:1; Eph 5:1; 1 Thess 1:6; 2:4; Heb 6:12. They became imitators, not only of the preachers, but of the Lord (v.6). The ultimate model was the Lord Himself, and as the missionaries followed Him, they sought to follow them. It was not a case of imitating their mannerisms, but their manner of life. All of this was in the midst of severe affliction and persecution which dated back to their first reception of the Gospel (Acts 17:6) and continued both while the apostle was with them (2:14) and after he had left (3:2-3).

2.   They were "ensamples" (*tupos*, a type) to all that believe in Macedonia and
     Achaia. They became models of what a Christian should be. So the chain
     reaction of Christian character is first the perfect Model, the Lord Himself;
     then His servant, the Gospel preacher; then the convert spreading the
     testimony far and wide.
3.   They were heralds of the message of the Gospel: "For from you sounded
     out the word of the Lord". "Sounded forth (*exēcheomai*) commonly refers
     to the sounding of a herald's trumpet" (Hogg and Vine). We recognise it in
     the English word echo. The verb is in the perfect tense. It indicates action
     completed in the past, having existing results. The message of the Gospel
     through them reverberated and echoed in the whole region like a roll of
     thunder.

6. *Its Effect in their Own Lives*

9   Here again there is a dramatic threefold effect of the impact of the Gospel on
a community. A turning to God from idols indicates true repentance and faith.
These were the two main themes of Paul's preaching of the Gospel (Acts 20:21).
Repentance is a complete change of mind about God, self and sin, and is followed
by a turning to God for salvation through faith in the Person and work of the
Saviour. It involved turning their backs on the old life of sin and idolatry. Among
the converts were both Jews and Greeks (Acts 17:4). Outside the city, like a
backdrop on the horizon, was Mount Olympus with its snow-clad peak, the
supposed heaven of the dark pagan world of idolatry. On the one hand was the
world of satanic Greek mythology, and on the other hand the Jewish synagogue
with its prejudice and fierce persecution of the messengers of a crucified but
risen-from-the-dead Messiah. But outside of it all was the company of Jews and
Greeks and chief women who had been illuminated by the Holy Spirit and had
taken their place with a rejected and glorified Christ. That was their conversion
in the past. Now their present occupation was to serve the living and true God.
"To serve" (*douleuo*) is "to serve as a slave, a bond-servant". The word is used of
Christ Himself (Phil 2:7) and of Paul (Rom 1:1). The idea of a bond-servant is
probably taken from Exod 21:1-6, which describes the voluntary slave motivated
by love. His pierced ear was an indelible mark of his devotion and lifetime
servitude to his master. The Thessalonian believers served the living and true
God in contrast to the dead and false gods of the heathen world. It was a
continuous and lifelong occupation.

10   "To wait for his Son from heaven" is the future tense of the Christian life.
The hope of the return of the Lord Jesus Christ is the prominent theme of the
two epistles to the Thessalonians. The word "wait" is in the present tense. They
had turned to God in one act. But day by day they were in constant expectation
of the Lord from heaven. "Whom he raised from the dead, even Jesus"
introduces the resurrection of Christ, the foundation stone of the Gospel which

Paul preached. Here is its first mention in his written ministry; it is later expounded in detail in 1 Cor 15. In this passage it is significantly linked with the human name "Jesus", that of the Saviour.

It is important to notice that the names and titles of our Lord are not used at random in the NT writings. The choice of names in every verse where the Lord is mentioned has a definite meaning consistent with the context. The personal name "Jesus" was given to the Son of God at His incarnation in obedience to the command of the angel to Joseph the husband of His mother, Mary (Matt 1:21). It is the Greek rendering of the Hebrew "Joshua", which itself is a contraction of Jehoshua, "Jehovah is Salvation". It is the name appointed by God the Father, not only for the brief time of our Lord's sojourn upon earth, but to enshrine and express the mystery of His Person, and the wonder of His redeeming grace. In the Gospels the Lord is referred to narratively by the name "Jesus" about 600 times, yet remarkably, there is no record of anyone addressing Him by it, not even His own disciples. They never adopted towards Him an attitude of familiarity, but always addressed Him with titles of reverence and respect such as "Lord" or "Master". In the whole range of the epistles the name "Jesus" occurs only twenty-two times. It never occurs by way of narrative and there is always a special reason for its use.

The full title, the Lord Jesus Christ, is used more frequently in the Thessalonian epistles than anywhere else in the NT. "In the eight chapters it is found twenty-four times" (Morris). This brings into high relief the uniqueness of the phrase in this verse, "whom He raised from among the dead, Jesus, our deliverer from the coming wrath" (JND). Jesus is the name of God who became Man; it declares His true humanity; it expresses all that was contained within the OT "Immanuel", Himself truly Man albeit very God. In resurrection He has ascended to the throne in that glorified humanity as our Advocate and High Priest. This is the main theme in the Epistle to the Hebrews, where the human name "Jesus" occurs eight times. In that name He is crowned with glory and honour (2:9); is our great high priest (4:14); the Forerunner (6:20); the surety of a better covenant (7:22); access into the holiest is by His blood (10:19); the Author and Finisher of our faith (12:2); and the Mediator of the new covenant (12:24). All of this is based on His atoning death and resurrection glory. "Which delivered us from the wrath to come" is literally "our Deliverer from the coming wrath". "The same word in the same tense (it is an articular present participle) is found only in Rom 11:26, where it is translated 'the deliverer' in the RV as it surely should have been translated in 1 Thess 1:10 also. It thus becomes clear that the reference is not to the Cross and the deliverance from guilt accomplished there, but to the deliverance from wrath at the coming of the Lord in power and glory" (C.F. Hogg).

The word "wrath" is found many times in the NT. It was used by John the Baptist in addressing the Jewish unbelievers of his day, "Who hath warned you to flee from the wrath to come?" (Matt 3:17). The wrath of God abides on the Christ rejector (John 3:36). The word is used seven times in Rom 1-9 concerning

God's wrath against sin and unrighteousness. Then there is the great promise of the Gospel, "We shall be saved from wrath through him" (Rom 5:9).

In Rev 6-19 the word wrath (*orge*) is used five times of the Great Tribulation (7:14 JND), that period of unparallelled judgment poured out on the ungodly world. The relevant passages are:

"And said to the mountains and rocks, Fall on us, and hide us from the face of him that sitteth upon the throne, and from the wrath of the Lamb" (6:16).

"For the great day of his wrath is come and who shall be able to stand?" (6:17).

"And the nations were angry, and thy wrath is come, and the time of the dead, that they should be judged, and thou shouldest give reward unto thy servants the prophets . . . and shouldest destroy them which destroy the earth" (11:18).

"And great Babylon came in remembrance before God, to give unto her the cup of the wine of the fierceness of his wrath" (16:19).

"And out of his mouth goeth a sharp sword, that with it he should smite the nations; and he shall rule them with a rod of iron; and he treadeth the winepress of the fierceness and wrath of Almighty God" (19:15).

Another five references use the word *thumos* for wrath.

"The same shall drink of the wine of the wrath of God, which is poured out without mixture into the cup of his indignation" (14:10).

"And the angel thrust in his sickle into the earth, and gathered the vine of the earth, and cast it into the great winepress of the wrath of God" (14:19).

"And I saw another sign in heaven, great and marvellous, seven angels having the seven last plagues; for in them is filled up the wrath of God" (15:1).

"And one of the four beasts gave unto the seven angels seven golden vials full of the wrath of God, who liveth for ever and ever" (15:7).

"And I heard a great voice out of the temple saying to the seven angels, Go your ways, and pour out the vials of the wrath of God upon the earth" (16:1).

Thumos (wrath) is to be distinguished from *orge* in this respect that *thumos* indicates a more agitated condition of the feelings, an outburst of wrath from inward indignation, while *orge* suggests a more settled or abiding condition of mind, frequently with a view to taking revenge. *Orge* is less sudden in its rise than *thumos* but more lasting in its nature. *Thumos* expresses more the inward feeling, *orge* the more active emotion" (*An Expository Dictionary of New Testament Words*, W.E.Vine).

In consideration of these quotations, there does not seem to be any doubt that the reference to the coming wrath in the verse under consideration is a reference to that period of wrath on earth subsequent to the Rapture of the church. It is one of the great promises that the completed church, the body of Christ, will be with Christ in glory when "the wrath" is poured out on apostate Christendom during the Great Tribulation.

Paul expounds this in more detail in 2 Thess 2. After outlining the order of events on the earth after the Rapture of the church and the features of the Day of the Lord (which includes the Great Tribulation) he says: "But we are bound to give thanks for you brethren, because God hath from the beginning chosen you to salvation through sanctification of the Spirit and belief of the truth". The salvation in the context is deliverance from the dread judgments of the Day of the Lord. Many years later this was reinforced and confirmed by our Lord's promise to the church at Philadelphia: "Because thou hast kept the word of my patience, I also will keep thee from the hour of temptation, which shall come upon all the world, to try them that dwell upon the earth. Behold, I come quickly; hold that fast which thou hast, that no man take thy crown" (Rev 3:10-11).

Note

1   Ch.1 is stamped with the number three.

Three authors are named; three verbs govern vv.2,3; three graces are named in v.3: faith that rests upon the past, love that labours in the present, hope which looks to the future. Then in vv.6-8 three striking words are used to describe Paul's converts: imitators, types and heralds. Finally three stages can be seen in a pattern conversion; first there is a turning to God from idols (vv.9-10); secondly, the redeemed become the bondslaves of Him whose service is perfect freedom; finally, for the rest of life we await the Deliverer, even Jesus.   Adapted from H. St. John.

2   Illustrations of faith, love, and hope are found in Noah (Heb 11:7):

Work of faith: "By faith Noah, being warned of God";

Labour of love: "prepared an ark to the saving of his house";

Patience of hope: he waited and worked and witnessed for 120 years.

3   A wealth of fundamental doctrine lies in ch.1:

The Holy Trinity	vv.1,5,6
The Deity and Humanity of Christ	vv.1,10
The Death and Resurrection of Christ	v.10
The Lordship of Christ	vv.1,3,6
Election	v.4
The Gospel	v.5
The Second Coming of Christ	v.10
Divine Judgment	v.10

4   The coming of Christ is mentioned at the end of each chapter in 1 Thessalonians:

ch.1   Salvation assured.

ch.2   Service reviewed.

ch.3   Glory manifested.

ch.4   Loved ones united.

ch.5   Sanctification perfected.

III. Paul's Personal Character and Work (2:1-20)

1. *Paul's Suffering at Philippi*
   2:1-2

> v.1   "For yourselves, brethren, know our entrance in unto you, that it was not in vain.
>
> v.2   But even after that we had suffered before, and were shamefully entreated, as ye know, at Philippi, we were bold in our God to speak unto you the gospel of God with much contention."

1 Paul refers to "our entering in unto you" (ch.1:9). There it resulted in genuine conversions and the planting of a local assembly. Here (2:1) he says that it was not "in vain" or empty. The words "in vain" are used four times in 1 Cor 15 in connection with the preaching of the Gospel (vv.2,10,14,17). Three Greek words are used to define three different conditions.

In v.2, "unless ye have believed in vain", the word is *eikē*, meaning "without success or effect", "at random". It would indicate some who had made a profession without reality.

In vv.10,14 it is *kenos*, "empty" with special reference to quality, "to make void", "of no effect", "endeavours which result in nothing", "fruitless". "Both Paul's preaching and their faith are empty if Christ be not raised" (A. T. Robertson).

V.17 has a much stronger word, *mataios*, "devoid of truth, a lie". Ye are yet in your sins. If the resurrection of Christ is not believed, then there is empty preaching, empty belief and empty faith. It is a spurious Gospel, a travesty of the truth.

The second of these words is the one used here. There was nothing "empty" about the preaching at Thessalonica. It was a full-orbed Gospel and had solid and lasting results. Some have suggested that the words could mean "empty-handed". (See Grimm-Thayer *Greek-English Lexicon to the NT*, p.343 under *kenos*.)

When the messengers arrived, the local population might wonder, "What brought them here?" The country was full of wandering philosophers, jugglers and charlatans begging for money. But the preachers of the Gospel came not to get but to give. Their hearts and their hands were full of the love of Christ which they came to dispense without cost. The pioneer missionary today is often faced with the same situation. The native population cannot understand why a person should travel thousands of miles and settle in an uncongenial environment dangerous to his health and life and limb. Is he looking for gold or diamonds or oil? It takes time and patience and love to convince them that the only motive is their spiritual welfare. He does not come empty-handed.

2 When the preachers arrived at Thessalonica after their three days' journey from Philippi, they still bore the marks of the beating at the hands of the jailor. It rankled in Paul's mind. The suffering was not only physical but mental. As a Roman citizen he should have been immune to the indignity of a public flogging. The insult at Philippi did not close Paul's mouth but had precisely the opposite effect: "We were bold in our God to speak unto you the gospel of God with much contention". The word "bold" means "with freedom of speech, a public declaration". After their treatment at Philippi, diplomacy might have suggested going softly, approaching interested people one by one and not arousing antagonism. But that was not Paul's method. Note, he says "bold in our God". It was not mere natural courage or enthusiasm but divine enablement. Some claim to be secret disciples but as Walvoord remarks "secret believers do not lead people to Christ".

Then it was "the gospel of God" that they preached. The Scriptures speak of "the gospel of the kingdom" (Matt 4:23) and "the gospel of the grace of God" (Acts 20:24). Then in Rev 14:6 we find the designation, "the everlasting gospel". The word "gospel" simply means glad tidings or good news. While in each dispensation or period of human history the terms of God's good news to men may be different, yet essentially it is the same gospel. In this church age, it is the gospel of God, for God is its source, and the gospel of the grace of God, for grace is its basis and content. It is founded on the work of Christ on the cross, His burial and bodily resurrection on the third day (1 Cor 15:1-3).

At Thessalonica the Gospel was boldly preached "with much contention" or conflict. The original word for "conflict" is *agōn*. It is an athletic term taken from the Olympic games. A related word *agōnia* is transliterated into English in the word "agony". In 1 Tim 6:12 and 2 Tim 4:7 the word is translated "fight" and applied to soldiers and warfare. In Col 2:1 it is applied to agonising prayer.

2. *Paul's Motivation in his Preaching*
2:3-6

v.3 "For our exhortation was not of deceit, nor of uncleanness, nor in guile:

v.4 But as we were allowed of God to be put in trust with the gospel, even so we speak; not as pleasing men, but God, which trieth our hearts.

v.5 For neither at any time used we flattering words, as ye know, nor a cloak of covetousness; God is witness:

v.6 Nor of men sought we glory, neither of you, nor yet of others, when we might have been burdensome, as the apostles of Christ."

The enemies who chased Paul and his fellow-workers out of the city of Thessalonica are now engaged in a whispering campaign to undermine his character. This is the background to ch.2. Paul is no stranger to this kind of treatment. He reminds us of the cruel and brutal treatment he and Silas had received at Philippi. But slander and untrue insinuations against his character fall into a different category. Unfortunately many of God's honoured servants have suffered in this way. Paul wrote 1 Thessalonians from Corinth. In Thessalonica the slander came from his unconverted enemies, but in Corinth it came from his children in the faith. They questioned his apostolic authority, "Where is your letter of commendation and credentials as a servant of Christ?" They criticised his preaching and his personal appearance. "He writes weighty letters", they said, "but his bodily appearance is weak and his speech contemptible" (2 Cor 10:10). Then there was the insinuation that when he asked them to minister help to the poor saints in Jerusalem, there was some crooked financial motive behind it (2 Cor 12:17-18). Practically all of 2 Corinthians is a defence and vindication of Paul's character, ministry and motives. In ch.2 of 1 Thessalonians we have the same defence in concise form. Hogg and Vine in their commentary on the passage list seven charges made against Paul and his companions by their enemies at Thessalonica: "of deception, of sensuality, of fraud, of sycophancy, of flattery, of coveteousness, of seeking material advantage".

Paul was keenly sensitive about charges against the correctness of his message and the purity of his life.

3 "Not of deceit" is *ouk ek planēs*, "not out of error as a source". *Planaō* means "to lead astray" (2 Tim 3:13). Paul's preaching had its source in the pure, unadulterated Word of God and was clothed in the power of the Holy Spirit. All heretical cults, of the present day and throughout church history, have and had their source and origin in doctrinal error.

"Nor of uncleanness" shows the association that is usually to be found between error and sensuality (2 Pet 2:18). Paul and indeed all the NT writers insist on holiness and personal purity. This is in contrast to the pagan religions of ancient times where worship was mixed with prostitution and the basest sensual rituals. Lightfoot comments: "Startling but not unneeded (i.e. Paul's mention of uncleanness) amid the impurities consecrated by the religions of his day".

In "nor of guile", guile (*dolos*) means "bait". The cognate verb (*doloō*) signifies to catch fish with a bait and later came to mean crafty design to entrap or catch. Cf. Matt 26:4 (the noun's first occurrence) and 2 Cor 4:2 (verb).

4 "Approved by God to be entrusted with the gospel" (RSV) shows Paul was a chosen vessel (Acts 9:15). God put him through a series of tests in Damascus, Arabia, Jerusalem, in his home city of Tarsus, and at Antioch. This involved experience with his brethren, in the world, in his home and in the assembly. It covered a period of approximately fourteen years. When he was called by God and commended by his brethren in the assembly at Antioch to the work of the Gospel, he was not a novice. He had passed the test and was approved by God to be entrusted with the Gospel. His fellow-workers, Silas and Timothy, were also tested and tried men. It is a serious thing to be entrusted with the Gospel. Heaven and hell, human destiny, the Person of Christ and the Cross are all solemn realities. Peter says: "If any man speak, let him speak as the oracles of God" (1 Pet 4:11). It is a solemn responsibility to be God's mouthpiece to the people. "Not as pleasing men, but God, which trieth our hearts" deals with his attitude to three of the pitfalls facing the preacher in his preaching: will it please the people? ; will it pay me? ; will it raise my reputation? It is a great temptation to gear one's message to certain people in the audience, to tickle their ears, to tell them what they want to hear, never to say anything that will reach their consciences, to speak to the gallery! But one of Paul's great ambitions in life was to be well-pleasing to God in view of the judgment-seat of Christ (2 Cor 5:9). The final test of one's preaching is: what does God think of it? It is God who tries or tests our hearts.

5   In the words "neither at any time used we flattering words, as ye know, nor a cloak of covetousness; God is witness", the apostle is outlining the negatives of his ministry, the things he did not do, relative to his manner of speaking and his attitude to money. Flattery is the use of inflated adjectives to boost a person's ego, such as: "You are wonderful!" or "That was marvellous". The term "flattering words" is found only here in the NT but the use of such is a very common practice in our modern society. "Covetousness" is derived from a verb meaning "to have more". It is the craze for material things, especially money, and is called idolatry in Col 3:5. A cloak of covetousness is a cover-up or a disguise for a hidden motive. The word for "cloak" is *prophasis*, meaning a pretext, a disguise, something used for appearance to conceal what lies behind it.

A man's attitude to money is an acid test of his character. Modern methods of raising funds resorted to by some organisations and individuals bring the Lord's work down to a low level. Fervent long-drawn-out appeals and begging letters for financial support provoke criticism even from the world. Paul never stooped to these methods for his own needs. Later on, in v.9, he tells the Thessalonians how he laboured night and day, so that he would not be chargeable to any of them in preaching the gospel of God. Regarding flattery, he appeals to their witness, and concerning covetousness, he looks to God as his witness.

6   A third temptation of the preacher is self-promotion. The word "glory" in this context could mean dignity, pre-eminence, to be put on a pedestal. This was the craving of Diotrephes (3 John 9). The Lord taught His servants humility, both by example and precept (John 13:3-17; Phil 2:3-8). The preacher must speak with authority, realising the source and importance of his message (Matt 7:29; 1 Pet 4:11), but never adopting a domineering or patronising attitude to his hearers. Paul gloried in the Cross, not in himself. The preachers were careful not to be burdensome as the apostles of Christ. The servant of God engaged in an itinerant pioneer ministry, often away from his home environment for months and even years, must be prepared to face a different climate, different food and sleeping accommodation. If he is a faddist about diet and demands special treatment from his host, he could be a nuisance or, using Paul's word, "burdensome". His departure would be greeted with relief and his return would not be welcome. At all times the servant of God must be courteous, appreciative, and gentlemanly in the best senses of the word.

3. *Paul's Attitude to his Converts*
   ## 2:7-12

v.7	"But we were gentle among you, even as a nurse cherisheth her children:
v.8	So being affectionately desirous of you, we were willing to have imparted unto you, not the gospel of God only, but also our own souls, because you were dear unto us.
v.9	For ye remember, brethren, our labour and travail: for labouring night and day, because we would not be chargeable unto any of you, we preached unto you the gospel of God.
v.10	Ye are witnesses, and God also, how holily and justly and unblameably we behaved ourselves among you that believe:
v.11	As ye know how we exhorted and comforted and charged every one of you, as a father doth his children,
v.12	That ye would walk worthy of God who hath called you unto his kingdom and glory."

7   In this verse we have the positive side of the apostle's behaviour in contrast to his negative attitudes mentioned in vv.5-6. Instead of being burdensome, "a dead weight" as the RV translates v.6, "we were gentle in the midst of you, even as a nurse cherisheth her own children". The word translated "gentle" occurs only here and in 2 Tim 2:24 in the NT, "The servant of the Lord must not strive, but be gentle unto all men". It is the kindness of parents towards their children. David said: "Thy gentleness hath made me great" (2 Sam 22:36; Ps 18:35). The good Shepherd gently leads the young of the flock (Isa 40:ll). Here it is not the professional nurse who performs her task out of duty but the nursing mother who cherishes her own children. "Cherisheth" (*thalpō*) means to keep warm like birds in a nest (Deut 22:6). Cf. Christ and the Church (Eph 5:29).

8   "Being affectionately desirous" means to yearn, to long for. It is derived from the language of the nursery. The verb is a rare one and occurs only here in the NT.
   The pioneer missionary, who has spent the major part of his life in a new field where the Gospel never has been preached, and after much toil and heartache has seen souls saved, local assemblies established and taught the great principles of the Word, can in some measure enter into the feelings of the apostle Paul in his attitude to his children in the faith. He was like a nursing mother to her child. Each one is precious to him. Some have cost him sleepless nights and many tears. Some have given great joy in their growth and development, while others have been trapped and fallen by the wayside. In modern times some have literally laid down their lives for Christ and have won the crown of life (Rev 2:10). The days of nursing them in the faith has resulted in maturity and stability. The time of Smyrna-suffering still continues and the anticipatory joy of the pioneer preacher is to meet those that have been faithful unto death in the presence of our Lord Jesus Christ (v.19). In "we were willing to have imparted unto you", "to have

imparted" translates *metadounai*, "to share a thing with anyone". The prefix *meta* has reference to fellowship, participation. Instead of being greedy and self-seeking (v.5), they were willing as a matter of considered and deliberate choice to share with them, not only the good news of salvation but also their own innermost being. The word "souls" (*psuchas* from *psuchē*) has various meanings. It could mean in this context "our own lives". They would have been willing to die, to lay down their lives for them. Cf. 1 John 3:16. To impart the Gospel is the work of the evangelist, to lay down their lives for them is the work of the shepherd (John 10:11). The soul also is the seat of emotion, love, affection etc. The underlying motive behind this bond of affection between the missionaries and the Thessalonian believers was "because ye had become very dear unto us". It was a feeling that had grown as a result of seeing and knowing them. It is evident that the feeling was reciprocated by the converts (ch.3:6).

9 The words "labour" and "travail" are not synonyms. Labour emphasises the kind of work; travail its intensity. Paul, though he was a highly educated man, had learned the trade of making tents of goats' hair cloth. In those days in orthodox Jewish families, it was the responsibility of a father to teach his son the law, to circumcise him, and to teach him a trade so that, if necessary, he could earn his living in an honourable way. At Corinth and likely at Thessalonica Paul and his companions engaged in this hard toil. Later at Ephesus, Paul, when bidding goodbye to the elders, could say: "These hands have ministered to my necessities and to them that were with me". Those hands were undoubtedly lined and calloused by hard work. William Carey, the missionary pioneer in India, who became one of the world's greatest linguists, could say in early life: "My business is to preach the Gospel, but I cobble shoes to pay the expenses". Our Lord Himself spent more than half of His earthly life as a carpenter in Nazareth (Mark 6:3). Paul laboured night and day, i.e. from before daylight to after dark; in the daytime, visiting, preaching and praying, and long into the night working with his hands. It was not a 40-hour week and then relaxation. The reason that Paul gives for working with his hands is that he "would not be chargeable unto any of you". He must have been a man of an independent temperament and shunned giving the impression that he wanted remuneration for his services. He goes into some detail about his feelings in the matter in 1 Cor 9:1-18. As an apostle and a servant of God he had certain rights which were divinely ordained. He uses the illustrations of the soldier, the farmer and the shepherd; also of the priest and the Levite. All were compensated for their work. But he, Paul, preferred not to exercise or insist on his legitimate rights. His motive was to make the gospel of Christ without charge. He came to Thessalonica to give and to share, not to be a burden or to enrich himself. His daily toil at tent-making helped to pay expenses, but at the same time he had much joy in receiving on at least two occasions the sacrificial gifts of the saints in the church at Philippi which he had founded (Phil 4:15-19). There is an important principle here concerning the financial support of the work of the spread of the Gospel both at home and abroad. The preacher, called and fitted by God for the work and commended by a local assembly, goes forth in simple faith, looking to God alone for material supplies. He is dependent on the Holy Spirit for guidance in his movements and for blessing on his work. On the other hand it is the responsibility of the people of God intelligently to follow such with their prayers and sacrificial giving. There are many hundreds of God's devoted servants in every part of the world today who follow this pattern and who can testify to God's faithfulness and to the devotedness of the saints who minister to them.

10   This is the second time he calls God and the Thessalonian believers as witnesses to the sound character of the preaching and the blameless life of the preachers (vv.5,10). Four times he uses the expression "as ye know" (vv.1,2,5,11). In spite of the insinuations and calumnies of their enemies, their manner of life was open and known to all. "Holy" describes one's relationship to God; "righteous" one's straightforward dealing with men; "blameless" means that no charge could be made and proved against self. The preacher is an easy target of Satan and the world; how necessary it is that both his private and public life should be above reproach and be able to survive the closest scrutiny.

11-12   "As ye know how we dealt with each one of you, as a father with his own children, exhorting you, and encouraging you, and testifying, to the end that ye should walk worthily of God, who calleth you into his own kingdom and glory" is the RV rendering.

The emphasis is on the words "each one of you". The converts were not dealt with *en masse* but individually. It points up the importance of follow-up work in each separate person. People are different, one may need encouragement and another comfort, while another needs enlightenment and teaching. Paul acted as a father to each one of his children in the faith. "The simile of the mother nursing her babes shows the tenderness of the missionaries' love; the simile of the father dealing with his children is the complement of this, showing the sterner aspects of the same love" (Hogg and Vine). Cf. 1 Cor 4:14-21; 2 Cor 6:13; Gal 4:19.

These parental relationships are found only in Paul's epistles. It is remarkable that in this epistle he uses the term "brethren" 18 times; at the beginning of the epistle there is the appellation "brethren beloved" (1:4) and at the end "holy brethren" (5:27). This too is a family relationship.

In "that ye should walk worthily of God", "walk" is *peripateō*, from *peri* "around" and *pateō*, "to walk", hence "to walk around". Here it is used in a figurative sense, signifying the whole round of an individual's life. The word is used frequently in Eph 4-6 and is applied to practically every aspect of a person's behaviour and witness.

The adverb "worthily" (*axios*) in "worthily of God" has a verb stem meaning of equal weight, indicating a walk that is in conformity with the holiness and character of the God in whom they had put their trust. This is the highest standard of behaviour of which we can conceive. The original word is used in five other passages of the NT of:

1. receiving a fellow believer in such a manner as befits
   those that bear the name of saints   (Rom 16:2, RV);
2. a manner of life in accordance with the Gospel   (Phil 1:27);
3. a course of life chosen with a view to pleasing Him   (Col 1:10);
4. the calling of believers reflected in their manner of life   (Eph 4:1);
5. assisting servants of God in a way which reflects
   God's character and thoughts   (3 John 6, RV)

A careful consideration of these passages emphasises the important truth that the believer's walk and behaviour should be consistent with his profession of being a Christian. It is illustrated by an incident recorded of a soldier in the army of Alexander the Great, who was brought before the commander on account of a misdemeanour which he had committed. When asked his name the soldier replied, "My name is Alexander". Before sentencing him the general advised him, "Either change your conduct or change your name!"

"Who hath called you unto his kingdom and glory" is better "who calleth you", present continuous tense. The plural pronoun *humas* indicates that the Thessalonian believers had received the initial effective call in the Gospel (Acts 2:39; 1 Cor 1:26), but God continues to call to higher ground. It is a calling to God's purpose (Rom 8:28), and is named a high calling (Phil 3:14); a holy calling (2 Tim 1:9); a heavenly calling (Heb 3:1). In Eph 1:18; 4:4 it is a calling of hope; here it is a calling to God's kingdom and glory. This is the only mention of the kingdom in 1 Thessalonians, but it is evident that Paul must have included teaching concerning the kingdom of God in his preaching in the city. This is implied in the accusation against Jason and his friends before the magistrates, that Paul had said that there was another king, one Jesus (Acts 17:7). The Kingdom of God is a major theme both in the Old and New Testaments. It is prophesied in majestic and beautiful language by Daniel (7:13-14) and by Isaiah (ch.32). It was announced by John the Baptist and by our Lord (Matt 3:2; 10:7). Owing to the rejection and crucifixion of the King, it is now in its hidden mystery-form (Matt 13). The only way into the Kingdom of God today is by new birth (John 3:3). While in a very real sense the believer can enjoy the spiritual benefits of the kingdom of God in this present life (righteousness, and peace, and joy in the Holy Ghost, Rom 14:17), he looks forward to its full consummation in the manifested kingdom during the millennium, when righteousness shall reign and the manifested glory of Christ will fill the whole earth (Zech 14:9). In the meantime we can pray the disciples' prayer: "Thy kingdom come. Thy will be done in earth, as it is in heaven".

4. Results in the Believers
    2:13-14a

> v.13   "For this cause also thank we God without ceasing, because, when ye received the word of God which ye heard of us, ye received it not as the word of men but, as it is in truth, the word of God, which effectually worketh also in you that believe.
> v.14a   For ye, brethren, became followers of the churches of God which in Judaea are in Christ Jesus."

13   Here Paul resumes the thanksgiving of ch.1. He is continually thankful that when the Thessalonians heard the message of the Gospel, they received it not as the word of men but accepted it (RV) as it is in truth the Word of God. The two words "received" and "accepted" have different meanings, as the RV and Alford point out. "Received" refers to the ear, but "accepted" to the heart. Alford's comment is: "The former verb denotes only the hearing, an objective matter of fact; the latter, the receiving into their minds as subjective matter of belief". It is not only hearing the word, but accepting it as the Word of God in a definite act of saving faith. The Word of God applied in power by the Spirit of God is the twofold agency in the great miracle of regeneration. This is the cause for Paul's thanksgiving. It had worked effectively at Thessalonica. It was not only an acceptance of the message as the inspired Word of God but an acceptance of Christ Himself as Saviour and Lord.

14a   Then they became followers (imitators, RV) of the churches of God which in Judaea are in Christ Jesus (cf. 1:9). "This term (Churches of God) is used in the NT by Paul only, and only of local companies of Christians, as those at Ephesus (Acts 20:28); at Corinth (1 Cor 1:2); at Jerusalem (Gal 1:13)" (Hogg and Vine). While each local church was autonomous, responsible to the Lord alone for its government, discipline and procedure, yet there was a happy bond of fellowship with other local churches. There was fellowship but not an ecclesiastical federation. The principles mentioned in Acts 2: 41-42 concerning procedure would naturally be imitated and observed by them all: "They continued steadfastly in the apostles' doctrine and fellowship, and in the breaking of bread, and in prayers". Cf. 1 Cor 11:1-2,16. Sad to say, later developments in Christendom resulted in divisions, sectarianism, and ecclesiastical circles of fellowship, mutually antagonistic to each other. But the pattern is clear; warm happy fellowship among autonomous local churches following the divine ideal so clearly outlined in Holy Scripture.

5. Fierce Jewish Persecution
    2:14b-16

> v.14b   "For ye also have suffered like things of your own countrymen, even as they have of the Jews;

v.15   Who both killed the Lord Jesus, and their own prophets, and have persecuted us: and they please not God, and are contrary to all men;

v.16   Forbidding us to speak to the Gentiles that they might be saved, to fill up their sins alway; for the wrath is come upon them to the uttermost."

14b The reference to the churches of God in Judaea forms a link in the apostle's thinking between Thessalonica and far-off Jerusalem. Just as Jerusalem had been the focal centre of persecution against the early church, so the Thessalonians were receiving the same kind of treatment from their neighbours and fellow townsmen (Acts 17: 5-9). They were in the apostolic succession of persecution for their faith. Paul is speaking from experience. He himself had been one of the leaders and prime movers in that persecution. He now makes one of the strongest statements concerning the guilt of the Jewish nation in their long history of persecution of their own prophets, culminating in the judicial murder of their Messiah, the Lord Jesus.

15 "And have persecuted us" is literally "and drave us out" (RV). "And they please not God", the very thing Paul thought he *was* doing when he was breathing out threatening and slaughter against the disciples of Christ. Persecution can come from various sources, but the most cruel and sadistic is that of religious bigotry. During the Inquisition of the Middle Ages, when thousands of God's choicest saints were tortured on the rack and burnt to ashes at the stake, the prelates who perpetrated it called it an "auto-da-fé " (an act of faith). The day of persecution is not over. During the past 50 years more people have died for their faith in Christ than at any time in human history.

16 "To fill up their sins alway" is language taken from the LXX of Gen 15:16, "The iniquity of the Amorites is not yet full". God is long-suffering and often allows sin in an individual or a nation to go apparently unpunished, but when it comes to a head, then judgment surely falls (Dan 8:23; Matt 23:32). It is compared to a cup that is being filled gradually drop by drop to the brim. When that takes place, God's patience is exhausted and His wrath comes into action; so Paul adds, "For the wrath is come upon them to the uttermost" (*eis telos*). To get the full force of the expression "to the uttermost" we should compare it with John 13:1, "Having loved his own which were in the world, he loved them unto the end" (*eis telos*). Love to the uttermost; wrath to the uttermost. What a contrast! The reference to "the wrath" is no doubt prophetical. It looks back to 1:10, "the coming wrath". As the nation suffered judicially under God's hand of discipline for seventy years in Babylon on account of past sins, so they will suffer again in the future in that period called "the great day of his wrath" (Rev 6:17), also called "the time of Jacob's trouble" (Jer 30:7).

With Paul, his suffering and persecution stemmed mostly from the fact that like his Master he had been rejected by his own countrymen, the Jews, and had taken the Gospel to the Gentiles (Acts 22:21-22; 28:23-28).

6. *Paul's Desire to see them again*
2:17-20

v.17   "But we, brethren, being taken from you for a short time in presence, not in heart, endeavoured the more abundantly to see your face with great desire.

v.18   Wherefore we would have come unto you, even I Paul, once and again, but Satan hindered us.

v.19   For what is our hope, or joy, or crown of rejoicing? Are not even ye in the presence of our Lord Jesus Christ at his coming?

v.20   For ye are our glory and joy."

17-18   The words, "But we, brethren, being bereaved (lit. orphaned) of you for a short season" (RV) are in line with the mother-father-children relationship of Paul with the believers at Thessalonica. "A short season" is literally "an hour of time". "In presence, not in heart" is *prosōpō ou kardia*, "in face, not in heart. His heart was with them, though they no longer saw his face. All of this shows the deep longing and love of the apostle for his children in the faith. It revealed the true heart of the shepherd. He had made two attempts to visit them but had been frustrated. The first might have been from Berea and the second from Athens (3:1) but in each case the way was blocked by Satan. At the beginning of this missionary journey (Acts 16) it was the Holy Spirit who stood in the way of the missionaries' going to Asia and Bithynia (vv.6,7). God had other plans for them. But here it is Satan, the Adversary. The enemy of God and His work has many aliases. As the devil (*diabolos*) he is the accuser or slanderer; as the Old Serpent he is the tempter; and as the Great Dragon he is the persecutor. We do not know the nature of the hindrance that Satan used; but it has been suggested that it was the bail or bond taken of Jason by the magistrates in Thessalonica concerning the riot that had taken place there (Acts 17:9). In any case, "apparently about five years elapsed before the apostle visited Thessalonica again, but neither of that nor of any subsequent visit, are any particulars preserved" (Hogg and Vine).

19-20   This great chapter concerning the preacher, his character, conflict and concern for his children in the faith, ends with his hope of a crown of rejoicing and the coming of the Lord Jesus Christ. The crown reminds us of the judgment seat of Christ (Rom 14:10; 1 Cor 3:13-14; 2 Cor 5:10). The crown (*stephanos*) is the victor's crown awarded to the overcomer. There are five crowns mentioned in Scripture to be awarded on that day:

The crown of life for the martyr (Rev 2:10; Jas 1:12);
A crown of rejoicing for the soul-winner (1 Thess 2:19);
A crown of glory for the faithful shepherd (1 Pet 5:4);

An incorruptible crown for the winner in life's race (1 Cor 9:24-27);
A crown of righteousness for those that love His appearing (2 Tim
4:8).

Another great word, used here for the first time in Paul's writings, is that
translated "coming" (*parousia*). It is used 18 times in the NT of the second
coming of Christ. It occurs seven times in the two Thessalonian letters: 1 Thess
2:19; 3:13; 4:15; 5:23; 2 Thess 2:1,8,9. The word merits careful study and
interpretation. (See Appendix.)

20   In "for ye are our glory and joy" the words "ye are" are emphatic. They were
his pride and joy. He gloried in speaking about them to others and at the same
time his heart was filled with joy as he thought of the great reunion in the
presence of the Lord Jesus when life's toils and anxieties were forever past. The
passage suggests that there will be mutual recognition between the soul-winner
and those he has led to the Saviour in his work for Christ here on earth. There
will be both prizes and surprises at the Bema. There is a temptation to speculate
about details, but there are some things about which we can be certain; we shall
be with Christ; He shall be the centre of attraction and worship; the complete
body of Christ will be present at the great harvest-home when the sower and the
reaper will rejoice together (John 4:35-38).

Note

"If I were in the position to influence the life of a sincere young man today, I would say to him,
rather choose to be an Evangelist than a Cabinet minister or a millionaire. When I was a
young man I pitied my father for being a poor man and a humble preacher of the Word. Now
that I am older I envy him his life and his career. This is life's real satisfaction. There is nothing
I admire quite so much as the Evangelist. The supreme source of satisfaction" (Lord
Beaverbrook, Max Aiken).

1V. Timothy's Mission and his Report   (3:1-13)

1. *Timothy's commendation and mission*
     3:1-5

v.1   "Wherefore when we could no longer forbear, we thought it good to
        be left at Athens alone;

v.2   And sent Timotheus, our brother, and minister of God, and our fellow-
        labourer in the gospel of Christ, to establish you, and to comfort you
        concerning your faith;

v.3   That no man should be moved by these afflictions; for yourselves
        know that we are appointed thereunto.

> v.4   For verily, when we were with you, we told you before that we should
> suffer tribulation; even as it came to pass, and ye know.
>
> v.5   For this cause, when I could no longer forbear, I sent to know your
> faith, lest by some means the tempter have tempted you, and our
> labour be in vain."

1   There is a strong link between the last section of ch.2, beginning at v.27 and the first section of ch.3. Paul is again stating his concern for the saints at Thessalonica. He had been banned from returning to the city. All three missionaries had gone to Berea, but when persecution broke out there, Paul was conducted by the Berean brethren to Athens, leaving Silas and Timothy behind at Berea. But on arrival at Athens, Paul sent a message to Berea for his fellow-workers to join him as soon as possible, which apparently they did (Acts 17:15). At this point, owing to the considerable strain and his deep anxiety about the persecuted saints at Thessalonica, he asked Timothy to go back there with a specific task to perform. At the same time Silas went back to Macedonia (Philippi) on a similar errand. In the meantime, Paul was left alone at Athens to face the sophisticated and sceptical philosophers there. The term "left alone" is a strong one. It indicates the feeling of desolation and loneliness which overwhelmed him when his dear friends left on their various missions. But the need was so great and his mind so distraught that he was willing to go through with it.

At critical points in Paul's relations with the churches which he founded, if for some reason he was not able to visit them himself, he did three things: firstly he wrote them a letter; secondly, he sent them a deputy or envoy in whom he had complete confidence, and thirdly he prayed. This was his method at Thessalonica and later at Corinth. In each case there were satisfactory results.

2   Timothy must have been quite young, but Paul gives him the highest commendation: "Our brother, minister of God, and fellow-labourer in the gospel of Christ". As the years passed by, Paul's appreciation of Timothy did not decrease. Writing to the Corinthians (AD 59) he says: "Now if Timotheus come, see that he be with you without fear; for he worketh the work of the Lord, as I also do" (1 Cor 16:10). Later to the Philippians (AD 60) he writes: " But I trust in the Lord Jesus to send Timotheus shortly unto you, that I also may be of good comfort, when I know your state. For I have no man likeminded, who will naturally care for your state. For all seek their own, not the things which are Jesus Christ's. But ye know the proof of him, that as a son with a father, he hath served with me in the gospel" (Phil 2:19-22). Then in his last writings he calls him "my dearly loved son" (2 Tim 1:2), and "a man of God" (1 Tim 6:11). Here we have an important principle in the work of the Lord: an older man, with ripe experience learned in the school of suffering, helping and advising a younger man and he willing to learn. This was a happy relationship between Paul and Timothy which lasted for 20 years.

In this, Timothy's first responsible mission which he had to undertake single-handed, he was given a twofold task, to establish (*sterizo*, to strengthen, make firm) and comfort (*parakaleo*, to call to one's side, to console and encourage) the Thessalonian believers. This was a congenial task, for which Timothy was spiritually and temperamentally fitted. The strengthening and encouraging was "concerning their faith". The word "faith" occurs five times in the chapter, vv.2,5,6,7,10. Considering the context in each occurrence, it has at least three meanings: first, saving faith exercised at conversion; then faith in God and His Word in the daily life; then "the faith", the whole body of Christian doctrine, called in the pastoral epistles "the good deposit" (2 Tim 1:13-14) and in Jude 3 "the faith once (for all) delivered unto the saints". It is very likely that all three meanings of the word would be involved in Timothy's work of establishing the saints at Thessalonica.

3   The aim is specific and definite: "That no man should be moved by these afflictions; for yourselves know that we are appointed thereunto". "Moved" is the present infinitive passive of *saino*, to wag the tail, to fawn upon, beguile, cajole with smooth talk. In this sense it is found only here in the NT and is in sharp contrast to Timothy's work of establishing. It is not "by" but "in" these afflictions; they were actually going through them. Both our Lord Himself and all the apostles indicate this appointment, warning us that affliction and tribulation will be the common lot of the believer in the day of His rejection: "These things have I spoken unto you, that in me ye might have peace. In the world ye shall have *tribulation*; but be of good cheer; I have overcome the world" (John 16:33). Peter writes: "Beloved, think it not strange concerning the fiery trial which *is to try* you, as though some strange thing happened unto you. But rejoice, inasmuch as ye are partakers of Christ's sufferings; that when his glory shall be revealed, ye may be glad also with exceeding joy" (1 Pet 4:12-13).

4   Paul reminds them that when he was with them he repeatedly told them (imperfect tense) that they should expect persecution, and that was what actually happened as well they knew. Not only the missionaries, but also the individual members of the church had suffered in the same way.

5   Here he comes back to his original thought expressed in vv.1-2. He repeats the reason why he had sent Timothy back to them. It was on account of his troubled mind and the anxiety that perhaps the tempter had tempted them and his work in reaching them with the Gospel had been in vain. The arch-enemy, that old serpent, the devil and Satan (Rev 12:9), who had successfully tempted our first parents in the garden of Eden, and had tried the same tactics on the Last Adam, our Lord Jesus Christ in the Judaean desert, was still doing his nefarious work. Was he successful at Thessalonica too? As our Lord gloriously overcame him by the use of the Word of God, so too Timothy's work of strengthening and comforting had a happy outcome.

2. *Timothy's Encouraging Report*
    3:6-9

v.6   "But now when Timotheus came from you unto us, and brought us
       good tidings of your faith and charity, and that ye have good
       remembrance of us always, desiring greatly to see us, as we also to
       see you;

v.7   Therefore, brethren, we were comforted over you, in all our affliction
       and distress, by your faith;

v.8   For now we live, if ye stand fast in the Lord.

v.9   For what thanks can we render to God again for you, for all the joy
       wherewith we joy for your sakes before our God."

6-7   When Timothy returned to Paul and made his report of what he had found
in the young church at Thessalonica, it was to the overwrought apostle like water
to a thirsty soul. The word he uses for bringing "glad tidings" is *euangelizomai*.
This is the only place in the NT where the word is used in this sense. It is the usual
word for preaching the Gospel. It was certainly an evangel to the mind and heart
of God's dear servant. Their faith and love and attitude to the missionaries were
intact. But one word is noticeably missing. In chapter 1 there was faith and love
and hope (v.3). Had anything happened to the hope? Apparently there was a
problem in their minds, stemming from the fact that some of their loved ones had
fallen asleep (died) and they were anxious to know what would be their position
when the Lord returned at the Rapture. Paul deals with this in chapters 4-5 and
also in his second letter. But as far as faith and love were concerned there was no
need for anxiety. He had sent Timothy to comfort the saints, but now as a result
of Timothy's report, he is comforted himself (vv.2,7).

8   Paul's whole life seems to have been centred in the welfare and spiritual
condition of the churches which he founded. If there was any moral or doctrinal
trouble, he tells the Corinthians, "I die daily" (1 Cor 15:31). In the list of his
many trials in the service of Christ, one of his greatest burdens was "the care of all
the churches" (2 Cor 11:28). His "red hot" letter to the Galatians shows that he
was a sensitive, highly-strung person, liable to periods of depression on the one
hand and flights of ecstacy on the other. Any servant of God who has toiled and
laboured for souls, resulting in a newly-born church, and has seen it under attack
which could dismember it, can appreciate and sympathise with the apostle's
feelings. " 'Stand fast' is not the usual word for standing, but *stēkō* meaning 'to
stand firm' with an emphasis on firmness. It is in the continuous tense. The word
'if' is not to question their stability, but to suggest that the apostle's peace of mind
depended on their steadfastness; that is, while ye are standing fast, we are happy"
(Hogg and Vine).

9   Paul returns for the third time to thanksgiving for his dear friends at
Thessalonica. In ch.1:2-3 it is for the visible results and evidence of their

conversion; in ch.2:13 it is for their attitude to the Word of God. Here it is for the overflowing joy that all his anxiety had been laid to rest as a result of the glad tidings that Timothy had brought to him. They were going on well and he was content!

3. *Paul's Prayer*
3:10-13

> v.10   "Night and day praying exceedingly that we might see your face, and might perfect that which is lacking in your faith?
> v.11   Now God himself and our Father, and our Lord Jesus Christ, direct our way unto you.
> v.12   And the Lord make you to increase and abound in love one toward another, and toward all men, even as we do toward you;
> v.13   To the end he may establish your hearts unblameable in holiness before God, even our Father, at the coming of our Lord Jesus Christ with all his saints."

There are three petitions in the prayer:
1.   That God will overcome the hinderer of ch.2:18, and allow the writer to visit his friends.
2.   That they may be knit together, enlarging and excelling in love to the church within, and to the world without.
3.   That at the coming of Christ with His saints, they may stand before the Father in blameless sanctification (Outline from H. St.John).

10   In ch.2:9, referring to his manual toil in tent making, Paul speaks of "labouring night and day", but here he is praying exceedingly night and day. Twenty-four verses, more than one fifth of the 136 verses in the two epistles to the Thessalonians, are occupied with prayer or teaching about prayer. Paul's life and ministry were steeped in prayer. The word "exceedingly" (*huperekperissou*) is a double compound adverb, the full meaning of which is: "exceedingly overflowing all bounds". The word is found also in Eph 3:20 and 1 Thess 5:13. One forms the impression of a man struggling to find words to express a feeling too deep for words. His object in this intense longing to see them was "to perfect that which is lacking in your faith". "Perfect" (*katartizō*) means "to mend, restore, set in order, equip". Paul had been only a comparatively short time at Thessalonica, and naturally there were some points of doctrine which were not clear to the believers. "The things lacking in their faith" would be in the area of the apostles' teaching (Acts 2:42) and moral behaviour. (Cf.comment v.2).

11   "This verse is of much importance because of the doctrine of the deity of Christ therein implied. The epistle, it will be remembered, is one of the earliest Christian documents, and as such supplies most valuable testimony to primitive apostolic teaching . . . From this verse then it is evident the Thessalonians had been taught to think of the Lord Jesus as One with God for:

(a)   Prayer is addressed to the Lord Jesus conjointly with the Father. It is equally important to notice that while the Lord Jesus is united with the Father in respect of his Godhead, He is distinguished from the Father in respect of His personality.

(b)   The Lord Jesus is associated with God the Father as controller of the ways of men.

(c)   The Greek verb translated 'direct' is in the singular number notwithstanding that two names form its subject. Thus the simple grammatical law, that a verb must agree with its subject in number, is set aside in order that the unique relationship between the Persons may be indicated.

(d)   The sentence may be translated thus: 'But God Himself, even our Father and our Lord Jesus, direct our way unto you'. Cf.John 5:19" (Hogg and Vine).

This prayer for direction was probably granted. Later on, several times we find Paul in Macedonia, which would likely take in Thessalonica (Acts 20:1,3; 1 Tim 1:3).

12   The second petition in Paul's prayer was "that they might increase and abound in love one towards another and to all men". Love (*agape*) is the characteristic word of Christianity. It has been called "the greatest thing in the world". It is a command. Among our Lord's last instructions to His disciples are the words: "A new commandment I give unto you, That ye love one another; as I have loved you, that ye also love one another. By this shall all men know that ye are my disciples, if ye have love one to another" (John 13:34-35). In the Thessalonian context it is declared to be the means God uses to develop likeness to Christ in His children.

13   The third petition is: "that he may establish your hearts unblameable in holiness before God, even our Father, at the coming (*parousia*) of our Lord Jesus Christ with all his saints". Holiness is an important subject in Holy Scripture. God is a holy God and He expects His children to be holy people. Fundamentally the word means "to set apart". Our words, holiness and sanctification, are the same in the original, they mean the same thing. The original word *hagios* and its derivatives are applied in a fourfold way in relation to the believer.

1.   It is God's *Purpose* for his children that they be holy (Rom 8:29; 1 Cor 1:2; 1 Pet 1:2; Jude 1).

2.   It is a *Position*, a standing before God, granted immediately on conversion. This is not a gradual change, a progressive work or a moral attribute, but a once-for-all act like justification (1 Cor 1:30; 6:11).

3.   It is *Practical and Progressive* throughout the earthly life of the believer (2 Cor 7:1). This is the work of the Holy Spirit, using the cleansing agency of

the Word of God (Eph 5:26-27; John 17:17).

4.   Finally the work of sanctification is *Perfected* at the coming (*parousia*) of our Lord Jesus Christ with all His saints (1 Thess 3:13; 5:23; Jude 24).

The question may be asked, when will this great work of perfection in holiness for the believer take place? Will it be at the Rapture (4:13-18) or at the public appearing and revelation of Christ described in 2 Thess 1:7-10? The fact that the word *parousia* (presence) is used and not *apokalupsis* (revelation) surely points to the Rapture. It is then that the believer receives his glorified resurrection body and is raptured to be for ever in the presence of the Lord.

Another debatable point is the meaning of the words: "with all his saints". Some would translate the words, "with all His Holy Ones" and apply them to angelic hosts that will be present at the coming. It is true that angels will accompany Christ at His appearing in glory, but that is not the teaching here. Paul uses the word *hagios* (saints) many times in his epistles, but always with reference to believers and never once to angels. Why make an exception here?

One further question: Does "with all his saints" include the patriarchs and men of faith in the OT? Will they be raptured along with the church at the coming? (1 Thess 4:13-18). This is discussed in the appendix to chapter 4; here we simply express our view that OT saints form a different group or body from the church, but that they surely are included in the term "they that are Christ's". Hogg and Vine comment: "All his saints — i.e. all who are Christ's, cf. 1 Cor 15:23, whether of this age or of the last, and of this age alike those who have fallen asleep, and those that are alive, that are left".

Notes

The Epistles indicate four missions which Timothy undertook at the suggestion of Paul:

1. Comfort and encouragement at
   Thessalonica   1 Thess 3   AD 54.
2. Correction at Corinth   1 Cor 4:17   AD 59.
3. Construction at Ephesus 1 Tim 1:3-4   AD 65.
4. Companionship at Rome   2 Tim 4:9,11,13,21   AD 66-67.

V. Exhortation to Holy Living   (4:1-12)

1.   *Personal Purity*
     4:1-8

v.1   "Furthermore then we beseech you, brethren, and exhort you by the Lord Jesus, that as ye have received of us how ye ought to walk and to please God, so ye would abound more and more.

v.2   For ye know what commandments we gave you by the Lord Jesus.
v.3   For this is the will of God, even your sanctification, that ye should
        abstain from fornication;
v.4   That every one of you should know how to possess his vessel in
        sanctification and honour;
v.5   Not in the lust of concupiscence, even as the Gentiles which know
        not God;
v.6   That no man go beyond and defraud his brother in any matter;
        because that the Lord is the avenger of all such, as we also have
        forewarned you and testified.
v.7   For God hath not called us unto uncleanness, but unto holiness.
v.8   He therefore that despiseth, despiseth not man, but God, who hath
        also given unto us his holy Spirit."

1 "Furthermore then" may be translated "For the rest" (JND) or "Finally" (RV). This is not meant to conclude the epistle but to introduce the final major section of the letter. As is usual in Paul's epistles, he deals with doctrine first and then goes on to the practical application of it: first precept then practice. But there is a vital link between the end of ch.3 and the commencement of ch.4. "The three prominent words at the close of chapter 3 are holiness, love, and coming. These are the three principal subjects of chapter 4: holiness vv.1-8; love vv.9-10; coming vv.13-18" (Wm. MacDonald, *Letters to the Thessalonians*, p.49).

The subject of sanctification is continued from 3:13. There it is seen as perfected at the coming of the Lord Jesus, but here the saints are exhorted to practise it in their daily lives.

To "beseech" is to ask or "beg" (JND). "The Gk. word *erōtaō* is generally used between those who are equal in rank, and again shows Paul's esteem for these people. It is the only word used by the Lord Jesus in His prayers to God. (Cf. John 14:16; 16:26; 17:9,15,20.) This occurrence and those in 1 Thess 5:12; 2 Thess 2:1 and Phil 4:3 are the only ones in Paul's letters; it is interesting to notice that they all occur in letters to the Macedonian churches, as if to indicate that he held them in special esteem" (Chas. Ryrie, *First and Second Thessalonians*, pp.52-53).

"Brethren" (*adelphoi*, from *adelphos*) signifies from the same womb and refers to believers only, members of the family of God. The word occupies an emphatic position in the sentence. "Exhort" is the present tense of *parakaleō*, made up of *para* "alongside of" and *kaleō*, "to call". The word means "to admonish", "to comfort and encourage". In the present context, it means to exhort in the sense of urging or encouraging. His use of the modifying phrase "by the Lord Jesus" (lit. in the Lord Jesus) shows that Paul does not urge a line of conduct upon them because of his own personal desire or will; the authority originates with the Lord Jesus and he is simply His mouthpiece. The verb "walk" is again *peripateō* (see on 2:12). The word came to mean "to regulate one's life", "to conduct oneself", the present tense speaking of continuous action, steady progress in the Christian walk. " 'Walk' is the common Hebrew and OT figure for the conduct of life" (*The Epistles to the Thessalonians*, Cambridge Bible for Schools and Colleges, p.70). To "please" (*aresko*) carries the added emphasis of striving to please. Among its usages the following may be noted: Acts 6:5; Rom 8:8; 15:2; 1 Cor 7:32-34; Gal 1:10; 1 Thess 2:15; 4:1; 2 Tim 2:4. Most people aim to please somebody, whether himself, his wife, his parents, his employer or some other person. Paul's supreme motive in life was to please God (2 Cor 5:9 RV). It is impossible to please everybody, but the over-riding principle of the believer's life should be to please God. The important clause "Even as ye also do walk" is omitted by the AV but included in the RSV and by JND. "The AV omits this grave clause, so encouraging to those addressed. The authority for it is overwhelming" (W. Kelly, *The Epistles of Paul the Apostle to the Thessalonians*, p.39 footnote). "This he adds lest they should be grieved by an apparent assumption on his part that they had failed to heed his former councils" (Hogg and Vine).

"Abound" is *perisseuō* as in 3:12. "Their life is to be an abounding or overflowing one. Thessalonica was a famous centre of hot springs, and had once been called after them, Thermae. So their life — and ours — is to be a hot spring, always bubbling over with love. Paul's fondness for the word 'overflow' is seen in his epistles to Corinth, Thessalonica and Rome. He mentions several degrees of development in this high level of life; an extra overflow (*perisseuein mallon*, 1 Thess 4:1); an extraordinary overflow (*huper-perisseuesthai*, 2 Cor 7:4); and a very extraordinary overflow (*huper-ek-perissou*, Eph 3:20; 1 Thess 3:10; 5:13)" (Harrington Lees, *Thessalonians*, p.50).

The life of Enoch is pictured in this chapter. He walked with God (Gen 5:24); he pleased God, and he was translated that he should not see death (Heb 11:5). Enoch in his day lived in an environment characterised by violence, corruption and immorality (Gen 5-6), yet he walked with God and pleased God; he also witnessed for God (Jude 14-15). Whether or not Paul had the antediluvians in mind we cannot be sure, but we know from history that conditions in Greece and the Roman empire in Paul's day parallelled those that obtained in the days of Noah and later in those of Lot. The sins that brought down God's judgment on the antediluvian world and on the cities of the plain were common in Thessalonica and in Corinth. (They are common in our day too. Heinous crimes of sex and violence no longer shock mankind.) In view of this Paul outlines the principles of holy living that were to govern the personal conduct of the believers at Thessalonica.

2   "Commandments" is *parangelia*, from *parangellō* "to give a message to", "to give a charge, a command". The word is military language, carrying with it connotations of weight and authority. Cf. Acts 5:28; 16:24; 1 Tim 1:5. The word is variously translated: "charges", JND; "instructions", RSV; "orders", NEB; "charge", Hogg and Vine; "instruction", NIV. Again they are issued "through (*dia*) the Lord Jesus". Paul is not giving orders on his own responsibility. They are following a chain of command, from the supreme commander, the Lord Jesus,

through Paul, His servant, to the embattled Christian soldier, fighting the battle of purity against the wiles of the wicked one.

3   Here Paul goes into detail about the subject of practical holiness, mentioned in the last verse of ch.3. The teaching is not just Paul's own personal ideas about living an ascetic life, but he puts it on the highest plane, it is the will of God. The word "fornication" (*porneia*) means "illicit sexual intercourse" (Vine's *Expository Dictionary*). "Pagan religion did not demand sexual purity of its devotees, the gods and goddesses being grossly immoral. Priestesses were in the temples for the service of the men who came" (A. T. Robertson). The temple at Corinth housed 3 000 religious harlots. The circular letter sent to the Gentile churches from the council at Jerusalem (Acts 15:23-29) mentioned among other things, fornication. Sexual impurity was so common in Greek and Roman life, that apparently no one thought of it as a heinous sin against God and their fellow man. It was a part of their ritual religion as it still is in many parts of the pagan world today. For this reason it is condemned in every part of the Bible. Above all, it is a part of the revealed will of God that the Christian should abstain from it, both in his thinking and in his daily life.

4   There is debate over the meaning of "vessel". Some think it means "body" and that Paul is saying that the believer is to gain mastery over his body in order to keep himself pure in matters of sex. If this be the meaning, the idea is similar to 1 Cor 9:27, "But I keep under my body, and bring it into subjection; lest that by any means, when I have preached to others, I myself should be a castaway (disapproved)". In this case the use of the word "vessel" is parallel to 2 Cor 4:7, "But we have this treasure in earthen vessels" etc.

Others think that the word "vessel" means "wife" as in 1 Pet 3:7, "Likewise ye husbands dwell with them according to knowledge, giving honour unto the wife, as unto the weaker vessel" and that the verb "possess" indicates courtship and the contracting of marriage. In this case Paul is expressing an idea similar to that in 1 Cor 7:2, "Nevertheless to avoid fornication, let every man have his own wife, and let every woman have her own husband". But the context and the fact that Paul is emphasising the necessity for sexual purity, seem to show that in using the word "vessel" he means the human body of the believer (cf. 1 Cor 6:15-20).

5   "Lust" (*pathos*) means passion, excited emotion, used here in a bad sense (Col 3:5; Rom 1:26), an ungovernable desire. It is the passive side of vice. "Concupiscence" (*epithumia*), desire, craving, again used in a bad sense, is the positive side; a man with his basest passions completely out of control. "The Gentiles which know not God" are described in graphic language in Rom 1:18ff. There are 21 items of departure from God, outlining the downward trend from a primitive knowledge of God in creation, a divine revelation upon which they deliberately turned their backs and went into the dark night of pagan idolatry.

Immorality followed idolatry. The word "lust" is used twice; women with women and men with men doing that which is against nature, defying God's revealed will. Three times we are told that God gave them up, or gave them over. These are the Gentiles which know not God of Paul's day and of our day too. The description was written in Corinth where Paul had these sordid conditions daily before his eyes.

6-7 Apparently Paul is speaking here of the sin of adultery, "That no man transgress and wrong or take advantage of his brother in the matter". "Paul is using delicate language but the context makes it clear what he means" (A. T. Robertson, *Word Studies*). It could refer to a man seducing and running off with his neighbour's wife. Both the Bible and modern life give many examples of this. One outstanding case in the OT is David and the wife of Uriah (2 Sam 11-12); in the NT there is Herod Antipas and the wife of his half-brother Philip (Mark 6:14-29). In David's case there was true repentance and forgiveness, but the prophet added the sentence from God: "The sword shall never depart from thy house, because thou hast despised me". Sins of this character bring repercussions. David later had the agonising experience of seeing his own sons commit the same sins in his own home. The tragic results of his sin followed him to the end of his life. God is the Avenger of all such. When there is genuine repentance, there can be forgiveness and a measure of restoration, but God's Word declares: "Be not deceived, God is not mocked; for whatsoever a man soweth, that shall he also reap". This inexorable principle is true, both of the believer and the unbeliever. God hath not called us unto uncleanness but unto holiness. All of this had been a part of Paul's original teaching at Thessalonica. He had forewarned and testified to them concerning the importance of holy living and blameless behaviour. God's call was not only to liberty (Gal 5:13) but also to good works (Eph 2:10).

8 The word "therefore" (*toigaroun*) introduces a conclusion to the subject with which he has been dealing, that is, holiness, sanctification and purity in the life of the believer. Then comes the warning about despising (*atheteo*, to nullify, to make void, to frustrate). Again he goes to the highest authority. The person who despises the teaching about holiness, despises not man but God. Anyone who regards sexual sin as of no importance is in effect treating God and His Word as of no account. Therein lies its seriousness. The prohibition against the abuse of the human body is of divine and not human origin. In addition to the teaching and exhortation to practical sanctification, God has graciously given us the power to carry it out in His blessed Holy Spirit. At the moment of conversion, He comes to dwell permanently in the body of every believer (1 Cor 6:18-19). He is a member of the Holy Trinity with infinite power and, when ungrieved by sin or indifference, He can help us to overcome the sins of which Paul is speaking and enable us to live a life well-pleasing to God.

2. *Brotherly Love*
4:9-10

> v.9　　"But as touching brotherly love, ye need not that I write unto you; for ye yourselves are taught of God to love one another.
> v.10　　And indeed ye do it toward all the brethren which are in all Macedonia: but we beseech you, brethren, that ye increase more and more."

9-10　"Two things in particular marked off the Christian Church of NT days from contemporary society; the purity of the lives of its members, and the love that they so freely practised. Here we find Paul passing from the one (vv.7-8) to the other (vv.9-10)" (Leon Morris). Apart from the name of the church in Rev 3, *philadelphia* ("brotherly love") occurs five times in the NT. It is used twice in the ministry of Peter and twice in the ministry of Paul and is the introduction to Hebrews 13, "Let *philadelphia* continue!" It is variously translated in the AV "brotherly love", "love of the brethren" or "brotherly kindness", but the RV uniformly renders it "love of the brethren". It is interesting to notice the contexts where Peter and Paul use it.

1. 1 Pet 1:22,　linked with conversion, a product of the new birth.
2. 2 Pet 1:7,　a part of the "adding in" process to initial saving faith.
3. Rom 12:10,　included in Paul's list of gifts in the body.
4. 1 Thess 4:9,　Paul's exhortation that *philadelphia* increase more and more.

The word *philadelphia* is composed of *philia* ("love, affection, fondness") compounded with *adelphos* ("one from the same womb"). It is the family love that is begotten in the soul of the believer when he becomes a child of God. His whole heart and affections go out to every saint that loves the Saviour. Paul had seen this manifested in the Thessalonians and he had no need to write to them about it, but he begs them that it may increase and abound. They were in their first love and it was seen not only in their own little circle but had reached out to all the saints in Macedonia. Those in Philippi and Berea and probably other places had felt its warmth. It was displayed practically by gracious, kindly hospitality being shown to visitors from these places. They had been "taught of God" to love one another. "Love" here is *agapan*, present infinitive of *agapaō*, the highest form of self-sacrificing divine love. Affection (*philia*) had developed into this divine sacrificial love (*agapē*) and the Teacher had been God Himself. (Cf. the use of the two words for love in John 21:15-17.)

3. *Attitude to the World*
4:11-12

> v.11　　"And that ye study to be quiet, and to do your own business, and to work with your own hands, as we commanded you;

v.12   That ye may walk honestly toward them that are without, and that ye
         may have lack of nothing."

11   Earlier in the epistle (3:10) Paul mentioned some things that were lacking in their faith and his desire to correct them. In his second letter (3:10-12) he refers to some who were disorderly, working not at all, but were busybodies, and he commands that if any would not work, neither should they eat. He had taught them the great truth of the Lord's coming and some of them probably had reasoned, if His coming is imminent, then why bother with daily toil? As far as brotherly love was concerned, the majority in the assembly excelled in this, but there were those among them who took advantage of the situation. They piously folded their hands and counted on their brethren to support them. It was not a good testimony to the world. He exhorts them to study to be quiet and do their own business and to work with their hands. This is a command. Moulton and Milligan in their *Vocabulary of the Greek New Testament* state that the word "study" means "to strive eagerly". It has the sense of being ambitious. The word is used elsewhere only in Rom 15:20 and in 2 Cor 5:9. "Quiet" (*hēsuchazō*) is the opposite of restlessness and means "tranquility of mind". The word was employed to describe those who do not run hither and thither, but who stay at home and mind their own affairs. The Thessalonian believers are told to practise the quiet, unobtrusive, relaxed kind of life in the midst of persecution and their daily occupation.

12   Paul himself set the example by working with his hands when he was in Thessalonica (2:9). Our Lord spent the major part of His earthly life working with His hands as a carpenter. This verse dignifies manual labour. The Greeks despised manual work and had slaves to do it for them. But the Jews held it in esteem; every Jewish boy was taught a trade regardless of his family's wealth. There is nothing more honourable and commendable than a man doing a full day's work to provide for himself and his family, and dedicating any surplus of his earnings to God for His work and for helping the poor and needy. It is summed up concisely in v.12, "that ye may walk honestly toward them that are without, and that ye may have lack of nothing". The world recognises and respects an honest man.

VI. Revelation of the Rapture   (4:13-18)

v.13   "But I would not have you to be ignorant, brethren, concerning them
         which are asleep, that ye sorrow not, even as others which have no
         hope.
v.14   For if we believe that Jesus died and rose again, even so them also
         which sleep in Jesus will God bring with him.
v.15   For this we say unto you by the word of the Lord, that we which are
         alive, and remain unto the coming of the Lord, shall not prevent them
         which are asleep.
         For the Lord himself shall descend from heaven with a shout, with the
         voice of the archangel, and with the trump of God; and the dead in
         Christ shall rise first;

> v.17   Then we which are alive and remain, shall be caught up together with
>   them in the clouds, to meet the Lord in the air; and so shall we ever be
>   with the Lord.
> v.18   Wherefore comfort one another with these words."

There are three crucial passages in the NT dealing with the Rapture, the first stage of the second advent of Christ.

1. John 14:1-3. This is the basic passage. All previous references to the Lord's second coming, both in the OT and in the synoptic Gospels have to do primarily with His coming in glory to take up His kingdom and reign on the earth. But here it is different. Before going to Gethsemane and the Cross, He told His disciples that if He went away He would not leave them orphans. He would come again and receive them unto Himself to the Father's house where there were many abiding places. This was a definite promise. In the meantime the Holy Spirit would take His place as their Comforter (Paraclete) and Guide. It is evident that the Lord is not referring to a spiritual coming at the believer's death to take them to heaven as some would interpret the passage. Twice He used the term "a place" indicating a location, not just a state. Later references in the NT, under the inspiration of the Holy Spirit, give us the details.

2. 1 Cor 15:20-58. The literal resurrection of the body was being denied by some at Corinth (v.12). Paul bases his teaching relative to the resurrection body of the believer which he will receive at the Rapture on the nature of the resurrection body of Christ. This is the great proof and test. Did our Lord rise from the dead with the same body in which He had died on the Cross? The historical record (Luke 24:36-43; John 20:19-20) shows that it was the same body with the wounds of His suffering upon it, but yet it was different. It was a glorious body and a spiritual body. The apostle uses three illustrations concerning the nature of the resurrection body of the believer: first, from botany, the dry wrinkled seed and the glorious harvest; second, from zoology, four creatures with four different kinds of flesh, that of man, beasts, fish and birds; each of these creatures is perfectly adapted to the environment where God has placed it, so the terrestrial body is adapted to the environment of earth and the celestial body will be adapted to the environment of heaven; third, from astronomy, the variable glory of the sun, moon and stars; the supreme glory of the sun is Christ; the reflecting glory of the moon — the church; and the varied glory of the stars, the individual glorified believers. Vv.51-58 tell us how it will take place: "Behold, I show you a mystery; We shall not all sleep, but we shall all be changed, in a moment, in the twinkling of an eye, at the last trump; for the trumpet shall sound, and the dead shall be raised incorruptible, and we shall be changed". This reference to the second coming of Christ is called "a mystery", that is, something that has not been revealed until this point.

3. 1 Thess 4:13-18. In this parallel passage there was also a problem. At Corinth it was the resurrection of the body, but at Thessalonica it was doubt about what had happened to the spirits of the believers who had died. Had they missed any blessing reserved for the believers who were alive when the Lord returns? This great passage was written to relieve their minds and comfort their hearts.

1. *Certainty instead of Ignorance*

13   Each of the major passages relating to the second coming of Christ arose in answer to a problem: Matt 24-25 is addressed to deception; John 14:1-3 to distress; 1 Cor 15:1-28 to denial; 1 Thess 4:13-18 to doubt, "I would not have you to be ignorant, brethren". This is a formula quite frequently used by Paul, often accompanied by the affectionate appellation "brethren", to inform his friends of some important point which was new to them (Rom 1:13; 11:25; 1 Cor 10:1; 12:1; 2 Cor 1:8). "Ignorant" (*agnoein*, cf. English agnostic) means "not knowing". They had had teaching from the apostle concerning the *parousia* and future events but apparently there was still some confusion in their minds as to their deceased loved ones who had died in the Lord, "concerning them which are asleep". *Koimōmenōn* (from *koimaō*, "to cause to sleep") is present and continuous in tense denoting them who are falling asleep rather than them which are asleep. The participle gives the idea of repetition, of what is presently going on; from time to time a believer falls asleep. In the NT the word is used of natural sleep (John 11:12) and of the death of the body, but only of believers, but never of Christ (John 11:11; 1 Thess 4:14,15; Acts 7:60; 1 Cor 7:39; 11:30; 15:6,18,51; 2 Pet 3:4). When it speaks of the Lord Jesus, Scripture says He died, but of the believer it says they sleep. Christ entered into all that was involved in death and judgment for us on the Cross; we who trust in Him will never see death but will sleep. Death has been changed to sleep by the work of Christ. It is an apt metaphor in which the whole concept of death is transformed (Acts 7:60). "Christ made it the name for death in the dialect of the church" (Findlay). Early Christians adapted the word *koimētērion* (used by the Greeks of a rest-house for strangers) for the place of interment. Hence comes the English word cemetery, a sleeping place (cf. dormitory). But sleep has its waking and death its resurrection. In the NT resurrection is used of the body alone. For the body of the believer there will be a glorious awakening.

A number of modern heretical cults teach soul-sleep. This is completely unscriptural. Sleep applies only to the body which goes to the grave, and not to the spirit of the believer which at death goes to be with Christ which Paul says is very far better (Phil 1:23). The subject is dealt with in some detail in 2 Cor 5:1-9. Paul says "For we know that if our earthly house of this tabernacle were dissolved (that is, the death of the body), we have a building of God, an house not made with hands, eternal in the heavens. For in this we groan, earnestly desiring to be clothed upon with our house which is from heaven. If so be that being clothed we shall not be found naked. For we that are in this tabernacle do groan, being burdened; not for that we would be unclothed, but clothed upon, that mortality might be swallowed up of life". That unclothed state (the spirit without the body) he describes as being absent from the body, but being at home with the Lord (v.8). While the body is asleep in the grave, the spirit is consciously in the presence of the Lord in heaven. The spirit does not sleep.

Christians do grieve over the loss of loved ones. This is a normal human experience in which even Jesus shared, "Jesus wept" (John 11:35), but it differs from the grief of unbelievers. They have no hope. The Greek and Roman world of Paul's day was a hopeless world as far as the future was concerned (Eph 2:12). There was no hope for the body. It was the soul's prison-house. The hopelessness of the pagan world is amply illustrated in ancient writings and especially in the inscriptions on their tombs. Apart from Christianity there was no solid hope in the after-life. But pagan sorrow does not characterise the Christian. This can be seen even today in places like Central Africa, where the weeping, heart-rending wailing and hysterical tearing of the hair at a pagan funeral is in sharp contrast to the quiet submission and singing of hymns of praise when a Christian goes home to be with the Lord. The believer has that "blessed hope and appearing of the glory of our great God and Saviour Jesus Christ" (Titus 2:13, JND)

2. *The Basis of the Hope*

14   Note the human name "Jesus" occurs twice in the verse. In Paul's epistles where the titles "Lord" and "Christ" are omitted, the purpose of the writer is apparently to call attention to His humanity and His work as Saviour (cf. Matt 1:21). The resurrection of Christ is the best attested fact of history. It is the foundation truth of Christianity and the ground and certainty of the hope. It is the basis of the faith of a Christian in its briefest and simplest form. Everything else is involved in it. It is the essence of the Gospel (1 Cor 15:1-3). The "if" does not mean that there was any doubt; it means that Paul was appealing to foundational truth in the minds and hearts of the believers. The fact that Jesus died and rose again was the guarantee that they too would be participants in the resurrection of life.

"Even so" is the vital link between what happened at Calvary and the resurrection of Christ in the past and what will take place at the Coming. The resurrection of the believer is vitally linked with the resurrection of Christ. As God raised Him from the dead (Heb 13:20), even so will He bring from the dead those that sleep. There are at least two different interpretations of the passage advocated by competent orthodox scholars. There are no punctuation marks in the original manuscripts and the meaning depends on how we phrase the verse, i.e. where we pause or put a comma. If we put a comma after the word "Jesus" then it means that it is Jesus who puts the believer to sleep, "Even so those also put to sleep through Jesus" as it is here beautifully described, "will God bring with him". This is the interpretation of Wm. Kelly: "They were laid to sleep by

Jesus; and far from forgetting or even postponing their joy and blessedness, God will bring them with Jesus in that day" (*The Epistles of Paul the Apostle to the Thessalonians*, p.49). On the other hand if the comma be inserted after "sleep", it could read, "Them also which sleep, through Jesus will God bring with him". In this case it means that at the Rapture, through God's almighty power, the spirits of the redeemed will accompany the Lord Jesus and will be reunited with their bodies which are resurrected. "As a matter of grammar the words 'through Jesus' may be taken either with what precedes or with what follows" (Hogg and Vine). If the question be asked, From whence will God bring the dead along with Christ? it must be answered, From heaven. The persons brought must be the disembodied spirits of believers now with Christ, for in v.16 this coming of the Lord is the signal for the dead, that is for their bodies, to be resurrected.

Some interpreters apply the words "bring with him" to the appearing of Christ in glory at His apocalypse. That Christ will bring His saints with Him in that day is of course true, but the context here is the Rapture. The simplest exegesis of the passage seems to be: not only will the spirits of the dead return with Him but also their bodies will be resurrected at His coming.

3. *Participants in the Rapture*

15 This formula "by the word of the Lord" marks a new revelation, not just a quotation from some unrecorded saying of our Lord. "It is a most direct claim to plenary inspiration" (Ellicott). Here is the third great basic truth on which the resurrection and rapture of the believer are based; first on the atoning work of Christ on the Cross, then on His bodily resurrection and here on the inspiration of the word through the apostle Paul. It is called a mystery (1 Cor 15:51), that is, something revealed for the first time. It is not found in the OT or in the synoptic Gospels. The truth of the Rapture has a firm foundation. From this he goes on to explain the order of events, "We which are alive and remain unto the coming (*parousia*) of the Lord shall not prevent them which are asleep". "Prevent" is used in its old English sense and means "go before" (*phthasōmen*, from *phthanō*, "to come before", "to precede", "to anticipate"). The dead in Christ shall have precedence. There are two distinct groups, those that are alive when the Lord comes and those that have died. The living will be changed (1 Cor 15:51-52) and the dead shall be raised. The raising and changing will all take place in a moment of time, but the order is that the dead will have priority, they will be raised first.

4. *Three Sounds at the Rapture*

16a "For the Lord himself shall descend from heaven" envisages the literal fulfilment of the promise of John 14:3, "I will come again and receive you unto myself". Not just an archangel or a deputy but He Himself comes. He is coming to claim His bride!

a. With a shout

Keleusma (a word of command, authority and urgency) is a military word, "Attention!" J. N. Darby interprets: "that which follows 'stand at ease' "; suddenly called back to the ranks. Luther translates the word "Feldgeschrei", a war-cry, a shout of command from a general. It is not the battle cry of combatants but a rallying shout calling the church militant. Cf. 1 Cor 15:23, "But every man in his own order" where "order" (*tagma*, a company, troop, division) denotes a corps or body of troops in proper position. We have heard the voice of the Shepherd (John 10:27); at the tomb of Lazarus Jesus cried with a loud voice, "Lazarus come forth! and he that was dead came forth" (John 11:43). We remember Calvary's loud cry, "It is finished" (John 19:30). He went out with a shout of triumph in death. In Psalm 47:5, a great millennial psalm, we read: "God is gone up with a shout, the Lord with the sound of a trumpet". But here He is coming down; the shout intimates the pent up emotion in the voice of the Bridegroom: "Rise up my love, my fair one, and come away" (Song 2:10). It is also the bugle blast of reveille to the sleeping dead to arise and march.

b. With the voice of the archangel

In the OT, among the angelic hierarchy of heaven, we read of cherubim and seraphim and princes. In the NT they are called principalities and powers in the heavenlies (Eph 3:10). We know the names of only two of them; Gabriel, who appeared to Zechariah the priest and announced to him the birth of his son, John the Baptist (Luke 1:19); and Michael, called "the archangel" in Jude 9. He is mentioned six times in Scripture: Dan 10:13,21; 12:1-2; Jude 9; Rev 12:7 and 1 Thess 4:16. In Daniel 10 he is engaged against satanic powers in clearing a passage between heaven and earth for Daniel's prayers. In ch.12 he is Israel's defender during the Great Tribulation at a time when many saints will be martyred (Rev 20:4). Jude alludes to his disputing with Satan about the body of Moses. He seems to be very much interested too in the resurrection bodies of the saints. Satan claims to have the power of death and the grave, but there is a Stronger than he (Heb 2:14). The Lord Jesus by His death on the tree annulled him who had the power of death. In Rev 12 Michael is the leader of the angelic forces that fight and defeat the satanic hordes that have access to heaven. It is not surprising therefore to find Michael the archangel at the rapture of the church. Satan is the prince of the power of the air (Eph 2:2), a realm in which Michael has had considerable experience. We shall be quite safe passing through enemy territory to the peace and joy of the Father's house.

In our Lord's earthly life here below, He enjoyed angelic ministry at His birth, at His temptation in the wilderness, and at His agony in Gethsemane, but not at the Cross. All four Gospels tell of angelic manifestations at the tomb where His body had been laid. In Matt 28:1-7 it was the angel of the Lord that rolled away the stone from the sepulchre and sat upon it. His countenance was like lightning and his raiment white as snow. The women who came to anoint Him, entered the sepulchre and saw a young man sitting on the right side clothed in a long white garment. He said "He is risen; he is not here; behold the place where they laid him" (Mark 16:1-7). Luke 24:4-6 relates that they saw two men in shining garments which said: "Why seek ye the living among the dead? He is not here, but is risen". In John 20:11-12. we read: "But Mary stood without at the sepulchre weeping; and as she wept, she stooped down, and looked into the sepulchre, and seeth two angels in white sitting, the one at the head, and the other at the feet, where the body of Jesus had lain". Again at the Ascension (Acts 1:9-11) there was angelic ministry. Two men in white apparel assured the disciples: "This same Jesus which is taken up from you into heaven, shall so come in like manner as ye have seen him go into heaven". While the greatest manifestation of angelic power will be at the revelation of Christ at His apocalypse (Matt 25:31; 2 Thess 1:7) we can be reasonably certain that they will be in full attendance at the Rapture.

c. And with the Trump of God

There are two trumpets in 1 Thessalonians. In 1:8 they "sounded out" the word of the Lord is literally they trumpeted it. By the trumpet of the Gospel we were gathered to the Lord and at the trump of God we shall be caught up to be forever with the Lord. Our Christian life began with a trumpet, and it will be consummated with a trumpet. This is the last trump of 1 Cor 15:52, but obviously it has no connection with the last trumpet of Rev 11:15 or with the trump mentioned in Matt 24:31 that calls the elect of Israel. Paul was not referring to the book of Revelation for it had not yet been written. The seven trumpets of Rev 8-11 are trumpets of the wrath of God poured out in the 3½ years of the Great Tribulation. "Every one of them is a judgment of God upon a Christ-rejecting world. They assemble no one; they are not symbols of salvation; they are not symbols of deliverance; there are no resurrections; they are symbols of judgment upon men living in the world who have rejected the Lord Jesus Christ" (J. F. Walvoord).

It is more likely that Paul has in mind the silver trumpets of redemption described in Num 10:2-10. They were made of the silver half-shekels of redemption (Exod 30:12-13). There were six occasions on which they were used: for gathering the people, for guidance in their journeys, in war, in worship (over their offerings), at the jubilee, and at their set feasts. In their journeys through the wilderness, the last trump was the signal to pack up and march. They were on their way to the promised land. The last trump is a beautiful symbol of the Rapture.

5. Resurrection, Rapture and Reunion

16b   Resurrection of the dead was a fundamental truth among the Jews (Heb 6:2). The OT teaches the resurrection of the body: Job 19:23-27; Ps 16:9-11; Dan 12:2-3; Isa 53:10-12. Abraham believed in resurrection (Heb 11:19); the Pharisees believed in resurrection, but not the Sadducees (Matt 22:23; Acts

23:6-9); Mary and Martha believed in the resurrection of the body (John 11:24). But the supreme authority is the Lord Himself; He taught it. In John 2:18-21, when asked by the Jews for a sign of His authority to cleanse the temple, He said: "Destroy this temple and in three days I will raise it up". V.21 gives us the explanation of this strange statement: He spake of the temple of His body. In John 5:28-29 He mentioned two distinct resurrections, the resurrection of life and the resurrection of damnation. In Matt 17:9 as He and His disciples came down from the Mount of Transfiguration, He spoke of His rising "from (lit. from among) the dead". The newness of the expression (see Mark 9:9-10) caused them to wonder, and raised among them questioning as to what it could mean. This selective resurrection from among the dead, first of the Lord Himself (Acts 26:23) as Firstborn (Col 1:18) and Firstfruits (1 Cor 15:20) and afterwards of all His people (1 Cor 15:23) was then for the first time made known, but now fully revealed in this great passage. It is "the dead in Christ", those who belong to Him through saving faith, who will be resurrected at the Rapture. This is the resurrection of life. The resurrection of damnation, that of the Christ-rejector, will take place more than a thousand years later at the end of the millennium (Rev 20:12-13). The question may be asked, How will God raise up the bodies of those who were buried hundreds of years ago? What about those who were eaten by lions in the arena at the Colosseum or burned at the stake at the Inquisition? Many have been buried at sea and others blown to pieces in a nuclear blast. This may pose a problem to the faith of some. The answer surely is that the same omnipotent God who raised Christ from the dead through the working of His mighty power (Eph 1:19-20) and who spoke the universe into existence with a word, will be able to reassemble the bodies of the saints in a moment of time (1 Cor 15:35-58).

17   Having dealt with the first group, "the dead in Christ" who are to be resurrected, he turns now to the second group, "we which are alive and remain", who shall be changed. These represent a whole generation of born-again believers, of which Enoch and Elijah who were translated without dying, are typical. These are the "mortal" of 1 Cor 15:54 who put on immortality while "the dead in Christ" are the "corruptible" who put on incorruption. The word translated "shall be caught up" (*harpagēsometha*, from *harpazō*, "to snatch") conveys the idea of "force suddenly exercised". In Matt 11:12 it is rendered the violent "take it by force". Note its occurrence in John 10:12 where it is translated "catcheth", and in vv.28,29 where it is rendered "pluck out". Cf. 2 Cor 12:2,4 where Paul was "caught up" and Acts 8:39 where Philip was "caught away". In Latin the word for "catch away, carry off" is *rapio*, from which comes the term "Rapture". It means "to seize and carry off by force". It is an apt word to describe what will happen when Christ returns for His own. Its suddenness is in keeping with 1 Cor 15:52, "In a moment, in the twinkling of an eye". Both the dead and the living will be snatched from Satan's grasp and will be delivered from the woes and the wrath of the day of the Lord described in 2 Thess 1-2. The divine

deliverance of Lot from the judgment poured out on Sodom and Gomorrah is a graphic illustration of what will come to pass at the Rapture (Gen 19:12-25).

Fellowship (koinōnia) is one of the warmest words in Holy Scripture; fellowship with the Father and the Son; fellowship at the Lord's supper; fellowship in the Gospel; fellowship in His sufferings, and fellowship with loved ones in the family circle. Here it reaches its climax "caught up together with them". It is our "gathering together unto him" (2 Thess 2:1). Some interpret the words "in the clouds" (en nephelais, lit. in clouds, plural) as meaning clouds of saints; others apply it to the Shekinah cloud of glory as appeared at the Transfiguration (Matt 17:5) but it more likely refers to literal clouds in the lower atmosphere.

"To meet the Lord in the air" anticipates the moment of meeting. What a meeting that will be! For the living the first glimpse of the Saviour. It is beautifully illustrated in Gen 24. At the end of Rebekah's long wearisome journey across the desert, she meets her bridegroom Isaac in the field at eventide. He takes her to his mother Sarah's tent and he loves her; this is only the second time the word "love" is found in the Bible. The first expresses the feelings of a father for his son (22:2) and here those of a bridegroom for his bride.

"So shall we ever be with the Lord" assures us that we shall never again be separated from Him. We shall assemble in the atmospheric heaven and ascend through the stellar heavens to the third heaven, the immediate presence of the Father. This is indicated by the last part of the preceding chapter where Paul speaks of our being in the presence of God the Father blameless in holiness. From that time on wherever Christ is, whether in heaven, or reigning on (or over) the earth, or in the new earth, or in the new heaven in eternity future, there shall the church also be, with the Lord forever.

6. Comfort and Consolation

18 "Wherefore comfort one another with these words." Paul's revelation is the complete answer to the anxiety of the Thessalonian believers about the position of their deceased loved ones. Instead of having missed something, they will have the precedence in resurrection and will share in all the future glories and privileges that are reserved for the people of God.

VII. The Day of the Lord (5:1-11)

1. The Character of the Period
5:1-3

v.1   "But of the times and the seasons, brethren, ye have no need that I write unto you.

v.2   For yourselves know perfectly that the day of the Lord so cometh as a thief in the night.

v.3   For when they shall say, Peace and safety; then sudden destruction cometh upon them, as travail upon a woman with child; and they shall not escape."

It is very important to notice that chapter 5 introduces an entirely new subject. The Greek expression *peri de*, translated "but of", which opens the chapter is Paul's usual method of introducing a new line of thought (1 Thess 4:9,13; 5:1; 1 Cor 2:1; 8:1; 12:1; 16:1). The last part of chapter 4 is totally different from the first half of chapter 5. Ch.4:13-18 intimates the Rapture and relates to the Church; ch.5:1-11 is about the Day of the Lord, relating solely to Israel and the Gentiles. The Rapture is a NT mystery (1 Cor 15:51) intimated by the Lord Jesus in John 14:1-3, but revealed for the first time in detail in 4:13-18. On the other hand "the Day of the Lord" is mentioned between 30 and 40 times in the OT. There it is described as a time of judgment, ending in millennial blessing with Christ upon the throne of universal dominion. This is the vital distinction between the last paragraph of ch.4 and the first paragraph of ch.5. The joy of Rapture for the church is followed after the church has been raptured up to heaven by the period of unparallelled judgment on the world that has rejected Christ.

1   "The times and the seasons" (*chronoi kai kairoi*) remind us of the words of the Lord Jesus in Acts 1:7. When asked by the disciples whether at that time He would restore the kingdom to Israel, He replied, "It is not for you to know the times or the seasons, which the Father hath put in his own power, but ye shall receive power after that the Holy Ghost is come upon you and ye shall be witnesses unto me". "Times" refers to the periods, dispensations or ages (Heb 1:3 RV marg.) while "seasons" denotes the characteristics of those periods. The chronology of the Bible clearly outlines these periods in human history, especially in the Book of Daniel. They have a close relation to the nation of Israel. The church occupies a dateless, sign-less period sometimes called by prophetic students "the gap". For that reason we have been warned by the Lord of the futility of setting fixed dates for either the Rapture or the Appearing in glory. Our attitude should be that of waiting, watching, working and warning, in daily expectation of His return.

Apparently when Paul was at Thessalonica, he had taught the believers about God's prophetic programme and there was no need to write about it (v.1). They had received careful teaching from the apostle and they were perfectly aware of it. "Perfectly" is *akribōs*, meaning "exactly", "accurately". It is the word used by Luke to describe his gathering of material for the writing of his Gospel (Luke 1:3), and the manner in which Aquila and Priscilla instructed Apollos (Acts 18:26). The word emphasises the need for accuracy, both in the study and in the teaching of the Scriptures.

2   The word "day" (*hēmera*) is used in both the OT and the NT with a variety of meanings:

1.   A period of 24 hours of alternate light and darkness (Gen 5:1)
2.   A period marked by certain characteristics: e.g. day of salvation (2 Cor 6:2), day of judgment (Rom 2:5)
3.   A period with dispensational connotations. The following should be distinguished
(a)   Man's Day (1 Cor 4:3 RV marg.)
This covers the present period of man's rebellion against God.
(b)   The Day of Christ (Phil 1:10; 2:16)
The Day of Jesus Christ (Philem 16)
The Day of the Lord Jesus (1 Cor 5:5; 2 Cor 1:14)
The Day of our Lord Jesus Christ (1 Cor 1:8)
The context of each of these designations shows that the same day is in view, that of His joy and satisfaction when His church is complete at the Bema.
(c)   The Day of the Lord
In the OT, the expression occurs in the prophets Isaiah, Jeremiah, Ezekiel, Obadiah, Amos, Zephaniah, Zechariah and Malachi. While in some cases it is applied to local conditions in Israel's wars with her enemies, in many cases it points forward to a "a great and terrible Day of the Lord" in the future (Joel 2:31; Mal 4:5). "That day will see Jehovah's final triumph in the complete overthrow of gentile world power (Isa 13:9-11; 34:8; Dan 2:34,44; Obad 15) and the consequent deliverance of His ancient people and the establishment of 'His King upon His holy hill of Zion' (Ps 2:6; cf.Ps 110)" (Hogg and Vine). Zech 9-14 in describing the events of the Day of the Lord, uses the term "that day" 18 times. In the NT the phrase the Day of the Lord occurs only in Acts 2:20; 1 Thess 5:2, 2 Thess 2:2 (RV); 2 Pet 3:10 (cf.Rev 6:17). A careful study of all these passages indicates that the Day of the Lord describes conditions on the earth after the Rapture of the church. It is a time of judgment on Israel and the nations. It includes the Great Tribulation, the battle of Armageddon, the Appearing of the Lord in glory and His millennial kingdom, with the final revolt at its close.
(d)   The Day of God (2 Pet 3:12-13)
This term occurs just once in the Scriptures. It describes the dissolution of the heavens and the earth and the commencement of the eternal state in which righteousness dwells.

While the Day of the Lord lasts for a very long time including many earth-shaking events, Paul is dealing here with its commencement. He compares it to a thief working in the dark. When a thief breaks into a house, he does not announce his arrival. His object is to steal and do it as silently as possible. The simile is used by our Lord in Matt 24:43 and by Peter in 2 Pet 3:10, both referring to the Day of the Lord. The Lord does not come as a thief at the Rapture (v.4) but as a Bridegroom. The thief comes silently in the dark, often carrying a weapon of destruction. His visit results in loss and fear. The Bridegroom returns with a conquering shout, and transports His own to a scene of indescribable light and joy (2:19-20; Jude 24). The figure of the pillaging thief speaks of the suddenness of the inception of the Day of the Lord and of the character of the period; it is a dark night.

3   The RV translates, "When they are saying, Peace and safety" (the verb is in the present continuous tense). The word for "safety" (*asphaleia*) means security. It is a rare word occurring elsewhere in the NT only in Luke 1:4 and Acts 5:23. They are repeating the delusion of the false prophets in Ezek 13:10, "Peace, peace, when there is no peace". Paul here describes conditions among the earth-dwellers after the church has been raptured to heaven. Organisations like the United Nations and movements calling for a nuclear freeze and "one world" will proliferate. The first half of Daniel's seventieth week will be a time of comparative peace (Dan 9:27). The rider of the white horse of Rev 6:2 will ride forth conquering and to conquer and a treaty will be signed that will seem to bring peace to the Middle East. It will look as if a new day has dawned and the promises of the politicians are about to be fulfilled. Peace, safety and security will be the peoples' slogan. Men will settle down with a sigh of relief hoping that utopia has come at last. But suddenly, like a thief in the night, the red horse of war, the black horse of famine, and the pale horse whose rider is Death linked with Hell ride forth. "And power was given unto them over the fourth part of the earth to kill with sword, with hunger, and with death, and with the beasts of the field" (Rev 6:1-8). This dramatic change will be sudden and devastating. It will be similar to the judgment that overwhelmed Belshazzar and the great world empire of Babylon recorded in Daniel 5. The writing is on the wall today as it was in his day. It will be unexpected and fear-inspiring like the birth pangs of a woman in childbirth. "Sudden destruction" does not mean annihilation. "Destruction" (*olethros*) means ruin, the loss of all that gives worth to existence, not the destruction of being but of well-being, not putting an end to the existence of a person or thing, but bringing about its ruin as far as the purpose of its existence is concerned. It involves death, but the whole social fabric is involved as well. The word "sudden" is emphatic. "In the vivid order of Paul's Greek, then suddenly over them stands destruction. Without a moment's warning ruin comes, not seen approaching, but first visible hanging over the doomed transgressors" (Findlay). The certainty of the judgment is again emphasised by the last clause in the section, "they shall not escape".

2.   *Sons of the Day and Sons of the Night Contrasted*
   5:4-8

v.4   "But ye brethren, are not in darkness that they should overtake you as a thief.

v.5   Ye are all the children of light, and the children of the day: we are not of the night, nor of darkness.

v.6   Therefore let us not sleep, as do others; but let us watch and be sober.

v.7   For they that sleep sleep in the night; and they that be drunken are drunken in the night.

v.8   But let us, who are of the day, be sober, putting on the breastplate of faith and love; and for an helmet, the hope of salvation."

4   In this section of the chapter there is a series of sharp contrasts. It has been called "the great divide". It highlights the differences between the true believers who will be glorified as a result of the Rapture, and the unbelievers on earth who will suffer the woes and judgments of the Great Tribulation. There are at least six points of contrast:

1.   Persons: the Thessalonian believers and Paul, the ye, we, us (vv.1,4,5,6,8,9,10); the they, them, the world of unbelievers (vv.3,7).
2.   Sons of light and of darkness (v.5).
3.   Day and night (v.5).
4.   Asleep and awake (v.6).
5.   Sober and drunken (vv.6-7).
6.   Day of destruction and the day of deliverance (vv.2,9).

All of these show the cleavage between those who will be raptured and those who will be left behind for judgment.

5   "Sons (*huioi*) of light" is a common Hebrew idiom. A man is said to be a son of any influence which dominates or determines his character. In the OT we read of "sons of Belial" (Jud 19:22), and in the NT of "sons of thunder" (Mark 3:17); Barnabas is called "the son of consolation" (Acts 4:36). Both our Lord and the apostles have a lot to say about light. The Lord said, "I am the light of the world". He was the embodiment of light both in His Person and His doctrine. Peter tells us that through the Gospel we have been called "out of darkness into His marvellous light" (1 Pet 2:10). John speaks of "walking in the light" (1 John 1:7). Paul tells us, "Now are ye light in the Lord" (Eph 5:8). The Thessalonian believers were "sons of light" both in their new nature and their testimony. Light was their native element and abode. They were also "sons of the day" (v.5); they were not of the night nor of darkness.

By contrast the worldling is characterised by night and darkness. We are not in darkness but in the sphere of glory. We belong to a different dispensation, a different day. As sons of light, the believers are additionally sons of the day. This is not the day of the Lord as some mistakenly interpret it. Those that have been illuminated by the Spirit of God (Heb 10:32) live and walk in the light and move forward to the day when they become partakers of the inheritance of the saints in light (Col 1:12). Lightfoot remarks, " 'sons of the day' is an advance on 'sons of light' ". Doubling of the idiom produces emphasis. Not only have they an illumination of their own, but they are living and moving in an enlightened sphere. Day is the realm. By a change to first person plural the apostle tactfully identifies himself with his readers. The use of "we" extends through v.10. It is the basis for the exhortation to live as sons of the day.

6-7   These verses are the practical application of the truth. "Therefore let us not sleep as do others; but let us watch and be sober. For they that sleep, sleep in the night; and they that be drunken are drunken in the night." Here is the twofold contrast between sleep and watchfulness and between being sober and being drunken.

The word for "sleep" in vv.6-7 (*katheudō*) is different from the one used three times in 4:13-15 (*koimaomai*) referring to physical death. Here indifference to spiritual realities is in view. The non-Christian may be wide awake and shrewd in the things of this life, but fast asleep and overcome with stupor in regard to eternal realities. "Watch" (*grēgoreō*) implies mental alertness, the condition of the mind opposite to that which characterises it in sleep. The word reflects the teaching of Christ in relation to His coming (Matt 24:43-44; Mark 13:33-36; Luke 12:37). Waiting is linked with watchfulness in 1 Cor 1:7; Titus 2:13; Heb 9:28; 2 Pet 3:12.

"Sober" (*nēphō*) denotes "freedom from the influence of intoxicants, but in the NT is used only in the metaphorical sense of freedom from credulity, excitability. Watch denotes alertness, sober stability" (Hogg and Vine).

To watch and to sleep, to be sober and to be drunken are all used figuratively here, with every positive having its negative counterpart. "The others" of v.6 are the dissolute worldlings of darkness and night. Like the foolish virgins of Matt 25 they sleep on, oblivious to the danger that lies ahead. "To watch" on the other hand is to be mentally alert to the portents on the horizon of the coming of the Lord.

8   Note the strong military atmosphere of the chapter: the sentry on the alert (v.6); the soldier's equipment (v.8); the guides (v.12); those out of step (v.14); then, in a series of short staccato commands, the marching orders (vv.16-22).

Paul as a Roman citizen was very familiar with the appearance and uniform of the Roman soldier. Later in life, in his imprisonment in Rome he was chained to a soldier, likely one of the Praetorian guards (2 Tim 1:16), and had plenty of time to observe every part of his equipment. Throughout his written ministry he uses the figure of the Christian soldier and his war against infernal enemies. The metaphor is no doubt taken from Isa 59:17 where it is said of Messiah in His ministry of conflict, "For he put on righteousness as a breastplate, and an helmet of salvation upon his head, and he put on the garments of vengeance for clothing, and was clad with zeal as a cloak". The Christian is regarded as a soldier, not on the parade ground, but on active service in wartime (2 Tim 2:3-4). He is equipped and supplied by the government that has enlisted him (1 Cor 9:7). He is sent on missions that may jeopardise his life (Phil 2:25-27). There are three passages that mention his equipment: it is called "the armour of light" in Rom 13:12; its fullest detail is described in Eph 6:13-18 where it is called "the whole armour of God". In our present passage it is the armour of faith and love and hope. Just two articles of the panoply are mentioned, the breastplate and the helmet. The one takes care of the heart and vital organs and the other of the head, the seat of the mind and intelligence. "The soldiers of salvation are defended by faith, love and hope. Their armour is not unproved, for their Lord has worn it already (Isa 59:17). The outer surface of their breastplate gleams with faith; its inner lining glows with love, and thus the heart is guarded and warmed. The helmet of salvation protects the thoughts, for our strength and safeguard is the Advent hope" (Harold St. John).

The passage opens with an exhortation to be sober, emphasising the need to be well-balanced, characterised by spiritual poise. Sobriety is the steady attitude of those who keep their presence of mind when under attack. In Eph 6 he wrestles not against flesh and blood, but against principalities, against powers, against the rulers of the darkness of this world, against spiritual wickedness in high places. In this case the Christian soldier is on the offensive, needing every item of the panoply at his disposal. In 1 Thessalonians he is on the defensive. His enemy is the infiltrating power of the moral conditions of the last days. His heart and his head need protection. The Greek tenses are revealing. "Sober" is the present tense, denoting a continual attitude. Paul uses an aorist participle for "putting on" suggesting a once-for-all act. If "putting on" were in the present tense it might imply that at some time it could be put off, which would be disastrous. The aorist enjoins that it be put on and kept on. In no passage is a covering for the back mentioned. The true soldier does not retreat but, continuously on the alert, faces the enemy and is able to anticipate and counter every blow.

3. Promise of deliverance from the Wrath of that Day 5:9-11

v.9   "For God hath not appointed us to wrath, but to obtain salvation by our Lord Jesus Christ,

v.10   Who died for us, that, whether we wake or sleep, we should live together with him.

v.11   Wherefore comfort yourselves together, and edify one another, even as also ye do."

9   This is one of the great key verses of the epistle. It brings to a head and a climax the teaching of the first part of the chapter in which the difference between the Rapture of the church and the Day of the Lord is demonstrated. In one sense it is a summary of the whole epistle.

In 1:10 we are assured that Jesus is our Deliverer from the wrath to come. There it is linked with His resurrection. Here it is based on His vicarious death on the cross (v.10). God has not appointed us to wrath but to obtain salvation through our Lord Jesus Christ. "Appointed" is *tithemi*, meaning "to put, to place". God, according to His own good will and pleasure has decreed that we shall escape the outpouring of His wrath during that part of the day of the Lord, called the Great Tribulation. The context makes this clear. It is the sudden destruction of v.3. (Cf. 2 Thess 1:7-9). The salvation mentioned here is our full and completed salvation when the Lord comes. Salvation as revealed in Scripture has been described as threefold. First, the believer is delivered from the guilt of sin by the death of Christ on the cross; secondly, he is enabled to overcome sin by the indwelling Spirit of God; then finally he will be delivered from the presence of sin at the Rapture. This is salvation in its completeness, the consummation of salvation in deliverance of the believer from the coming wrath. The redemption of the body is a part of our salvation. Instead of the terrestrial body, we shall be clothed with a celestial, immortal, glorious body (1 Cor 15:40-44).

10   The preposition in "Who died for us" is *huper*, on behalf of. "This is probably the oldest written statement of the fundamental doctrine of the Christian faith, that the Lord Jesus died on behalf of men" (Hogg and Vine). Some have stated that this is the only mention of the death of Christ in the epistle. But it is referred to again in 4:14 as the basic doctrine, along with His resurrection, on which the truth of the Rapture is assured. The fact that the death of Christ is only mentioned twice in the epistle does not mean that it was not important in Paul's teaching and preaching. It was no doubt a fundamental part of the Gospel which he preached when he came to Thessalonica (Acts 17:3). Nor does it mean that he was still developing his theology. He had been saved for nearly 20 years and had been active in the Lord's work for almost a decade. This letter to the Thessalonians was written from Corinth where he preached the cross and the death of Christ in all its fulness and power (1 Cor 1:17-24; 15:1-3). This major doctrine was firmly fixed in his mind and theology. Hogg and Vine mention four prepositions that are used in connection with the death of Christ for men.

1. *dia* with accusative: "on account of"   (1 Cor 8:11; cf. 1 John 2:12)
2. *peri*: "concerning"   (Matt 26:28)
3. *huper*: "in the interest of" "on behalf of"   (2 Cor 5.14; 1 Thess 5:10)
4. *anti*: "instead of"   (Matt 20:28; cf. 1 Tim 2:6)

The preposition used here is *huper* indicating the vicarious nature of the death of Christ on the Cross. Paul wrote that Christ died, not "was killed". He laid down His life voluntarily, no man took it from Him (John 10:18). Christ died for us. This simple statement of the substitutionary nature of the death of Christ is foundational. He had taught it when he first came to Thessalonica. Scholars and commentators are divided in their interpretation of the words "wake" and "sleep". Hogg and Vine in their commentary on the passage state: "It is obviously impossible to understand the words of natural wakefulness and natural sleep.

And inasmuch as *grēgoreō* is not used elsewhere in the metaphorical sense of 'to be alive', and as *katheudō* means 'to be dead' in only one place out of two and twenty occurrences in NT and never elsewhere in Paul's epistles, there does not seem to be any justification for departing from the usual meaning of the words, i.e. vigilance and expectancy as contrasted with laxity and indifference. . . . That the lax and indifferent will suffer loss is elsewhere plainly taught by Paul (1 Cor 3:15; 9:27; 2 Cor 5:10 etc), but in this place he does not deal with that aspect of the subject. He does however, put beyond question that the rapture of believers at the Parousia will not depend on their condition or attainment but solely on the death of the Lord Jesus for them" (*The Epistles to the Thessalonians*, pp.172-173).

On the other hand many commentators apply the words "wake or sleep" to the two groups of believers referred to in 4:13-17 who will be raptured at the coming, those who are alive and remain and those who have fallen asleep. "Whether we wake or sleep, i.e., whether we survive to the coming or have died. Paul does not mean that it will not matter in the end whether we have been watchful and sober or not. He means that no difference will be made between living and dead saints at the Parousia; both groups will live together" (F.F. Bruce). "The words whether we live or die are a further reassurance for the Thessalonians in their difficulty treated in 4:13-18" (Morris).

Both lines of thought are of course true, whichever one we adopt as paramount. The important point is that at the Rapture there will be no difference. Based on the death and resurrection of Christ every true believer will live together with Him.

11 The chief words are "comfort" and "edify". Binding up and building up were the objectives of Timothy's mission to Thessalonica, "to establish you and comfort you concerning your faith" (3:2). Here the same incentive beautifully concludes this section of ch.5.

VIII. Final Instructions in View of the Coming (5:12:24)

1. *Attitude to Church Leaders*
5:12-13

> v.12   "And we beseech you, brethren, to know them which labour among you, and are over you in the Lord, and admonish you;
>
> v.13   And to esteem them very highly in love for their work's sake. And be at peace among yourselves."

This is the first mention in Paul's written ministry of church government. We know from the historical record in the Acts that in all of his missionary labours, as soon as possible after a local church had been planted, he was anxious to see godly and competent leadership raised up and recognised. At least four terms are used for church leaders in the NT:

1.   Elder, *presbuteros*, characterised by spiritual maturity (Acts 11:30; 14:23; 15:2,4,6,22,23; 20:17; 1 Tim 5:17,19; Titus 1:5; Jas 5:14; 1 Pet 5:1)
2.   Overseer or bishop, *episkopos*, characterised by spiritual delegated authority (Acts 20:28; Phil 1:1; 1 Tim 3:1,2; Titus 1:7)
3.   Shepherds, *poimēn*, characterised by spiritual capacity and sympathy (Eph 4:11 and cf. 1 Pet 5:2)
4.   Guides, *hēgoumenos*, characterised by spiritual wisdom and discernment (Heb 13: 7,17,24)

Only the Holy Spirit can raise up spiritual leadership in a local assembly. The elders were not self-appointed nor were they elected or voted in by a show of hands. There was always a plurality of leaders in each local church. In their first missionary journey in Southern Galatia, chronicled in Acts 14, churches were established by Paul and Barnabas in Antioch, Iconium, Derbe and Lystra. About a year later the apostles returned confirming the souls of the disciples, "and when they had ordained them elders in every church, and had prayed with fasting, they commended them to the Lord, on whom they believed" (v.23). The word "ordained" is misleading in the language of today. The original word is *cheirotoneō* meaning to stretch forth the hand (*cheir*, the hand, *teinō*, to stretch). The apostolic missionaries, divinely-directed, pointed out those who had been manifesting themselves as gifted of God to discharge the functions of elders. There is no record that Paul did this at Thessalonica but the passage seems to show that there was an incipient group functioning as elders in the church. The saints were exhorted to know them and to esteem them very highly in love for their work's sake. As for the leaders, they laboured among the saints; they were over them in the Lord and admonished them.

12   "To know" (*oida*) means to recognise and acknowledge, to appreciate and value. This requires spiritual insight and discernment. The sheep know the hand that feeds them. The elder is known and recognised by his work. "Labour" is *kopiaō*, "to labour with wearisome effort, to toil". Pastoral work is hard work, often a night and day occupation, weighed down with anxiety and tears. It is exercised "among" the saints. "And are over you" (*proistēmi*) means lit. "to stand before" used here in the sense "to lead, to care for". It is translated "rule" in reference to the church in Rom 12:8; 1 Tim 5:17. But "rule" here is qualified by the phrase "in the Lord". It is not the domineering, autocratic rule of Diotrephes (3 John 9) but the kindly gracious guidance and love of leaders with shepherds' hearts. "Admonish" (*noutheteō*, lit. "to put into the mind, to train by word"; from *nous*, "mind" and *tithēmi*, "to put") is used of instruction and of warning. "The difference between 'admonish' and 'teach' seems to be that whereas the former has mainly in view the things that are wrong and call for warning, the latter has to do chiefly with the impartation of positive truth" (Hogg and Vine). The presence of the word "warn" in v.14 and the lengthy rebuke of the disorderly in 2 Thess 3:6-12 show that there were certain elements in the church at Thessalonica that needed this ministry of admonishing.

13 "To esteem" is from *hēgeomai*, "to think, to consider". Here it means to honour and respect a person. "Very highly" translates the compound superlative *huperekperissōs*, (made up of *huper*, "over", *ek*, "out of" and *perissos*, "abundant") which means "exceedingly overflowing all bounds". Note the increasing intensity of the prefixes in this word, until like a mighty river, it finally overflows its banks. Cf. ch.3:10; Eph.3:20. It is motivated by love (*agapē*). This should be the attitude of the saints towards the spiritual God-appointed elders in the assembly. It is "for their work's sake". As the years went by, Paul seemed to realise more and more the importance and the necessity for a competent and recognised oversight in each local church. Note his address to the Ephesian elders in Acts 20:17-38 and his instructions to Timothy and Titus in the pastoral epistles. How much more are they needed in our lax Laodicean days of church history!

Here in a few pregnant words, the apostle mentions a thorny and delicate subject, that of harmony, fellowship and peace in the local church. The wedge is one of Satan's most potent weapons. When God is working in manifest blessing, Satan will try in a subtle way to introduce some root of bitterness and by all means seek to divide and destroy. Paul said "we are not ignorant of his devices" (2 Cor 2:11). In his public ministry among the churches, Paul was faced with three great controversies. In Galatia it was legality; in Corinth it was partyism and pride, they were puffed up; at Colosse it was empty philosophical speculation about the Person of Christ. Any one of these could have wrecked the united testimony of the church. But the devil has many other weapons in his arsenal. The history of the church through the ages is a sad record of how successful he has been in introducing strife and division. Yet the Bible provides a remedy, both for the collective company and for the relationship between individuals. First of all, genuine sincere humility is needed. Of this humility Christ Himself is the supreme example. He girded Himself with the slave-apron and washed the feet of His unworthy disciples. That attitude and the practical application of the new commandment to love one another (John 13:34-35) would solve most of our difficulties and promote peace in any local church.

2. *Attitude to problems among themselves*
5:14-15

v.14   "Now we exhort you, brethren, warn them that are unruly, comfort the feebleminded, support the weak, be patient toward all men.

v.15   See that none render evil for evil unto any man; but ever follow that which is good, both among yourselves, and to all men."

This section gives counsel and instruction to the leaders concerning six situations which could arise among the saints.

14 "Warn" is the same word as "admonish" in v.12, where see comment. "Unruly" is translated "disorderly" by the RV; *ataktos* is a military term meaning not to keep rank, to be out of step. It occurs only here in the NT. The cognate verb occurs only in 2 Thess 3:7 and the adverb only in 3:6,11. There it refers to lazy busybodies who would not work and who expected other people to support them. But it could also mean insubordination to legitimate commands and regulations. There always seem to be difficult individuals who love to take an opposite view from that of their brethren, resulting in friction and tension. He may contend that he is "standing for the truth" but in reality it may be no more than the manifestation of an inflated ego and stubborn self-will. He is out of step with the elders and with his brethren. This spirit of contention could be exhibited in various ways. It could have doctrinal bias, emphasising one side of truth to such an extreme that the balance of scriptural teaching is lost, e.g. hyper-calvinism vs. arminianism. Such a faction-maker is mentioned in Titus 3:10. He is to be admonished twice; if this is ignored it becomes a matter of church discipline. The difficulty at Thessalonica seems to have been of a more practical nature. In ch.1 Paul commends them for their work of faith, and labour of love and patience of hope in our Lord Jesus Christ. Each chapter mentions the blessed hope of the Coming of Christ. It is obvious that the majority of the believers continued their labour of love but there were some who argued that if the coming of Christ was imminent, why work for a living? They were the idlers, drones and burdens on the workers in the assembly. Their disorderly conduct was a blot on the local testimony and for this reason it was necessary that they be warned by those responsible for maintaining discipline in the church. "Comfort" is *paramutheomai*, "to encourage, to console". The word is used in John 11:19,31, where it speaks of comforting the bereaved. "Feebleminded" is not a good rendering of *oligopsuchos* (composed of *oligos*, "little or small" and *psuchē*, "soul") which means "little-souled" or "faint-hearted". Perhaps the reference here is to those at Thessalonica who were discouraged because they had been recently bereaved of loved ones and needed comfort and encouragement. They were the opposite of the disorderly who were bold and aggressive and needed rebuke. But these sensitive souls required sympathy and understanding. The word does not mean that they were senile or mentally-retarded but despondent and depressed on account of trouble and trial. Weakness (*asthenēs*, "without strength") can be either physical or spiritual. Both need tender care and compassion. The person with the shepherd heart will come alongside, put his arms around them (*antechomai*, "to hold on by" or "keep close to") and minister the spiritual support which they so very much need. Paul uses the same expression in Acts 20:35 while in 1 Cor 8 there is a lengthy passage concerning the danger of stumbling the "weak brother". Some believers with a Jewish background might have had sensitive feelings about dietary laws while others had scruples about eating meat at all and preferred to be vegetarian. Such were to be received, but they were not to force their scruples on other people (Rom 14:1-3). Some who were spiritually immature through lack of knowledge of the Word could easily be side-tracked by a clever teacher of heretical doctrine. Spiritual weakness can take many forms but all need the care and counsel of the under-shepherd in the flock of God.

"Be patient towards all men" enjoins long-suffering towards all (RV). "Long-suffering" (*makrothumeō*, lit. "long-tempered", compare "short-tempered") means to keep one's self-control, whether dealing with the rude and self-assertive or the overly timid and sensitive. It is one of the outstanding Christian graces: "love suffers long, and is kind" (1 Cor 13:4), and is one of the attributes of God (Exod 34:6; Rom 2:4; 1 Pet 3:20). Patience is that kind of temperament which does not break down under provocation or trying circumstances. It maintains a steady course in the storms of life and is closely allied with hope.

15 Paul now includes all the believers in his exhortation. "See" calls attention to a common failure in human nature, the tendency to repay in kind a real or supposed wrong. In the law it was eye for eye and tooth for tooth (Exod 21:24; Lev 24:20). But under grace the Lord taught His disciples: "But I say unto you, That ye resist not evil; but whosoever shall smite thee on the right cheek, turn to him the other also" (Matt 5:39). "Render" is *apodidōmi* ("to give back, to recompense") and "evil" (*kakos*) that which causes injury or works any kind of mischief. The preposition *anti*, translated "for", is "the preposition of equivalence, denoting a price paid, or a balance made, as on the scales" (Hogg and Vine). The Thessalonian believers were suffering persecution and receiving much wrong from their enemies but there must be no vengeful reaction or retaliation. Cf. Rom 12:19-21; 1 Pet 3:9. Fallen human nature acts on the principle of "tit for tat" but for the Christian it is not rendering evil for evil, or railing for railing, but contrariwise blessing, and that towards all men, whether believer or unbeliever.

With the words "But ever follow that which is good, both among yourselves, and to all men" the injuctions concerning problems among the believers come to a climax; every word is weighty: "ever" is *pantote*, "at all times"; "follow" is *diōkō*, "to pursue earnestly" (follow after, RV); "that which is good" translates *to agathon*, "the good". Robertson aptly remarks: "keep up the chase after the good". There is a contrast between evil in the previous verse and "the good" here. It should be the way of life for the believer, to be intensely interested in the well-being not only of all those in the intimate fellowship of the assembly but also in the wider circle of a needy world. All around us there are those that desperately need the love and sympathy of the dedicated Christian. In one of the earliest books of the NT James the Lord's brother writes: "Pure religion and undefiled before God and the Father is this, To visit the fatherless and the widows in their affliction, and to keep himself unspotted from the world" (1:27).

And again: "If a brother or sister be naked, and destitute of daily food, and one of you say unto them, Depart in peace, be ye warmed and filled; notwithstanding ye give them not those things which are needful to the body, what doth it profit? Even so faith, if it hath not works, is dead, being alone" (2:15-17). Paul, the theologian and the great apostle to the gentile world, who in his 13 epistles has expounded the deep mysteries of the Christian faith, at the end of his life in writing to Titus emphasises the practical side of Christianity. He mentions good men, good things and five times uses the term "good works" as the badge of the Christian. His final message to Titus as he laboured in Crete was: "And let ours also learn to maintain good works for necessary uses, that they be not unfruitful" (Titus 3:14).

3. *Seven Rules of Conduct*
5:16-22

v.16   "Rejoice evermore.
v.17   Pray without ceasing.
v.18   In everything give thanks: for this is the will of God in Christ Jesus concerning you.
v.19   Quench not the Spirit.
v.20   Despise not prophesyings.
v.21   Prove all things; hold fast that which is good.
v.22   Abstain from all appearance of evil."

While vv.12-13 deal with the attitude of the saints to their leaders who have the responsibility of guiding and admonishing, and vv.14-15 deal with problems among themselves, this section gives a series of imperative commands relating to their inner devotional life and their relationship to God. The first three are closely linked and have been called "diamond-drops".

16 "Rejoice evermore" is *pantote chairete*. "Rejoice" is an imperative in the present continuous tense. *Pantote* translated "evermore" means "at all times." Apparently the word "rejoice" was a watchword among the early saints. It was used by our Lord as a greeting to His disciples on the resurrection morning, translated in our version: "All hail!" (Matt 28:9), and occurs again in Acts 15:23 (greeting), while in 2 Cor 13:11 it is translated "farewell". Joy is one of the fruits of the Spirit (Gal 5:22). The angel of the Lord announced "good tidings of great joy" to the shepherds of Bethlehem at the incarnation, and in His final ministry to His own recorded in John 13-17, our Lord mentions "joy" and "full joy" eight times. Along with His peace, it was the legacy which He left them (John 14:27-28; 15:11). The theme of "joy" and "rejoicing" is prominent in the Epistle to the Philippians where the word and its derivatives occur about 16 times. God's redeemed people have every reason to be a joyful people considering their multiplied blessings, not only in this life but in that which is to come.

17   There are four different words used in the NT for addressing God in prayer: the one used here, *proseuchomai*, is the most common and comprehensive. It simply means, "to pray, to offer prayers". Paul uses four words in 1 Tim 2:1 to describe different forms of prayer, "I exhort therefore, that, first of all, supplications, prayers, intercessions, and giving of thanks, be made for all men". These might be likened to the four ingredients of the sweet incense offered on the golden altar of incense described in Exod 30:34-38. Supplication emphasises the intensity of the prayer, while intercession, pleading with God on behalf of others, draws attention to the beneficiaries of the prayer. Giving of thanks is closely allied with worship, our hearts overflowing with gratitude to God for His mercy and blessings. Each one of these forms of prayer is exemplified in the life of the Lord Jesus; He spent whole nights in prayer. Paul, too, mentions praying night and day for the Thessalonians (3:10). "Without ceasing" is *adialeiptōs*, "without intermission, incessantly". This does not mean praying in relays all day and all night as is practised by certain religious orders. But it does mean that a child of God should be in the spirit of prayer, in conscious communion with God at all times wherever he happens to be, whether at home, at work, or in the gatherings of the saints.

18   This is the third member in this list of the believer's responsibilities in relation to God: first his inward joy and rejoicing in God; then his devotional prayer life in communion with God, and here his daily thanksgiving going up to God for everything he receives from God. Thanksgiving is a rare commodity in modern life. The worldling considers that society owes him a living. Anything he has, he has earned by his own efforts and he has no need to thank anybody. He is selfish and self-centred. Rom 1:20-32 describes the apostacy of the dark pagan world. The list of 21 items of departure from God is headed by the words: "when they knew God, they glorified him not as God, neither were thankful". Paul, in 2 Tim 3:1-5, gives a list of 19 items describing the conditions of society in the last days; in the centre is the indictment "unthankful". There is a chilling similarity between the paganism of ancient days and the conditions of society in our day!

Israel's great sin in the wilderness was murmuring and unbelief. But for the believer in this day of God's grace and mercy attitudes should be different. Four times in the earthly life of our Lord we find Him giving thanks: Matt 11:25-30; 15:32-39; John 11:41; Luke 22:19-20. As always, He is our great Example. There are 43 references in Paul's epistles to thanksgiving. They could be summarised by his statement in Eph 5:20, "Giving thanks always for all things unto God and the Father in the name of our Lord Jesus Christ" and in our present passage, "In everything give thanks, for this is the will of God in Christ Jesus concerning you".

The "will of God" is *thelēma Theou*, a thing willed and designed by God. There are a number of other things in Scripture that God has designed for us to do, but these three injunctions mentioned in vv.16-18 are specifically His will for us. The dynamic to carry them out is "in Christ Jesus". He works in us "both to will and to work of his good pleasure" (Phil 2:13; Heb 13:21). "Concerning you" (*eis humas*) is literally, "into you". "The preposition expresses not merely the fact that God desires these things in His children, but also that what is thus taught may be made effectual in them by His power" (Hogg and Vine). The plural form *humas* "you" has reference to all the Thessalonian believers.

It may not be easy to give thanks "for" everything. Trials, persecution, sickness and bereavement are the common lot of most Christians. But we can give thanks "in" them, and when the complete pattern of our lives is revealed, we will be able to see the divine plan for each of us.

19   "Quench not" is the translation of *me sbennute*, the present imperative of *sbennumi*, "to extinguish, to stifle, to quench". In its other occurrences in the NT *sbennumi* refers to fire, either literal (Matt 12:20) or metaphorical (Eph 6:16). The strong negative *me* (not) with the present continuous tense means, stop continually stifling the Spirit! Desist from attempting to extinguish the fire. In the exercise of spiritual gifts in the church there can be two extremes; on the one hand a cold formal intellectualism, and on the other hand, wild excess. Both were manifest in the church at Corinth. But when the Holy Spirit is working in power among His people, the gifts of the Spirit are characterised by light and warmth and power. Paul exhorts Timothy "to stir up the gift that is in thee", literally, blow into a flame! All too often, a young Christian who has an emerging gift has been turned aside by a caustic criticism or an unkind remark. The fire has been extinguished. There are four words in relation to the Holy Spirit which we must distinguish.

1.   Quenching the Holy Spirit (v.19). This can be done in others.
2.   Grieving the Holy Spirit (Eph 4:30). The Holy Spirit permanently indwells the believer as a seal and earnest of redemption (1 Cor 6:19; Eph 1:13-14). When a believer sins the Spirit is grieved and communion is interrupted.
3.   Resisting the Spirit (Acts 7:51). The unbeliever may refuse His work of conviction.
4.   Blaspheming against the Holy Spirit (Matt 12:24-32). This is the sin of the apostate, attributing the Person and the work of Christ to Satan.

20   It is a serious thing to stifle or to smother the working of the Holy Spirit in the local church, but it is much worse to despise it. We must remember that the Thessalonian believers did not have the written NT. The canon of Holy Scripture was not complete. As in the OT "the prophecy came not in old time by the will of man; but holy men of God spake as they were moved by the Holy Spirit" (2 Pet 1:21). Prophecy was both foretelling the future and forthtelling the oracles of God. The true prophet had a message from God, inspired by the Holy Spirit for the people of God. In the early days of Christianity there were apostles and prophets. The apostle had seen the Lord and had been commissioned by Him

(Acts 1:21-22). In a primary sense, the prophet in apostolic days was inspired by God to complete the writing of the NT. It is obvious that this ceased with the death of the Apostle John towards the end of the first century AD. We do not have apostles and prophets in that sense today. They were in the foundation of the church. But in a secondary sense the prophet speaks to men for edification and exhortation and comfort, building up, stirring up and binding up. His message is addressed to the conscience and heart of the believer and is based on the divinely-inspired Word of God. The teacher has taken the place of the prophet. At all times his mind and his tongue must be kept in control (1 Cor 14:32). His hearers and not he himself are the judges of whether he is speaking the truth of God or not (v.29). Spiritual people will be able to recognise a message that is delivered in the power and unction of the Holy Spirit. This kind of prophetic ministry must not be despised or ignored but acted upon.

21 "Prove" is *dokimazete*, present imperative of *dokimazō*, "to try, to examine, to test in order to approve". (Cf. 2:4; 3:5.) It means "to put to the test for the purpose of approving". There seems to be an obvious reference to the prophesyings of the previous verse. The margin inserts "but" on good authority, "But prove all things". The believer is not to be credulous or gullible. In every age there have been deceivers and false prophets. While it is true that certain members of the body of Christ have the special gift of discernment (1 Cor 12:10) yet all those indwelt by the Spirit of God have an unction from the Holy One (1 John 2:20,27) which enables them to distinguish in any teaching what is genuine and what is false. John tells us to try the spirits whether they are of God; because many false prophets are gone out into the world. His touchstone is the Person of Christ, "Every spirit that confesseth that Jesus Christ is come in the flesh is of God". His true Deity and sinless Humanity must be owned. A standard test of all teaching is: "To the law and to the testimony; if they speak not according to this word, it is because there is no light in them" (Isa 8:20). Since we have the completed revelation of God, verbally inspired and authoritative, we must reject any teaching or practice which is contrary to the Word of God. After the testing, that which is discovered to be good and in harmony with the revealed Word, must be tenaciously retained. "The good" (*to kalon*) is the genuine in contrast to the counterfeit. "The chaff must be separated from the wheat" (Findlay).

22 "Abstain" is from *apechō*, "to hold back from, to keep off". When used in the middle voice, as here, it means, "to hold oneself off". The Thessalonian believers were to keep away as far as possible from any visible outward form in which evil showed itself. "Evil" is *ponēros*, which word refers to "evil in active opposition to the good, that which is pernicious". It is used of Satan (Matt 5:37) and of demons (Luke 7:21). "Verse 22 states the negative of verse 21 and broadens the principle to include all areas of life. Every appearance or visible form of evil is to be avoided by the Christian" (Ryrie, p.82). Evil can manifest itself in many varied and often subtle forms. One of the worst is erroneous doctrine presented in an attractive way. The believer should never compromise his testimony by listening to or lending his presence to any religious association that endorses teachings that have been proven to be detrimental to the Person of Christ or contrary to the revealed Word.

4. Prayer for Complete Sanctification
5:23-24

> v.23   "And the very God of peace sanctify you wholly; and I pray God your whole spirit and soul and body be preserved blameless unto the coming of our Lord Jesus Christ.
> v.24   Faithful is he that calleth you, who also will do it."

23   In the OT God graciously associated His name with the names of seven outstanding men. He is the God of Abraham, Isaac, Jacob, Shem, Jesurun, Elijah, Elisha and Daniel. In the NT the name of God is associated with one pre-eminent Name, He is the God and Father of our Lord Jesus Christ (Eph 1:3). Of course, as members of His body we are forever linked with Him. In the NT the Name of God is linked with seven lovely virtues; He is the God of love, hope, patience, glory, peace, all comfort and all grace. The title "the God of peace" occurs in the following passages: Rom 15:33; 16:20; Phil 4:9; Heb 13:20. After the warfare in the early part of the chapter, this noble title, "the God of peace", is introduced. The RV and JND insert the word "Himself" in the passage. "And the God of peace himself sanctify you wholly". The pronoun "himself" occupies the position of emphasis in the sentence. The spiritual power to carry out the fifteen imperative injunctions of vv.14-22, and to perfect that work of sanctification for which the apostle prays in v.23, lies in that blessed pronoun, "Himself". Paul has already referred to sanctification in 3:13 and 4:3. In the first passage and in ch.5 he refers to its consummation at the coming (*parousia*) of our Lord Jesus Christ. He asks that their whole spirit and soul and body be preserved blameless until, or "in" that time. This indicates the tripartite nature of the human being and that each part could be subject to the attacks of the enemy. Spirit (*pneuma*) has been defined as God-consciousness, soul (*psuchē*) as self-consciousness, and body (*sōma*) as earth-consciousness. This definition may be an over-simplification. (For a lengthy and detailed exposition of the three terms, see *The Epistles to the Thessalonians*, Hogg and Vine, pp.204-210). All three words are used of the humanity of our blessed Lord in His sojourn here below. On the Cross He cried: "Father, into my hands I commend my spirit (*pneuma*)" (Luke 23:46); in Gethsemane, "My soul (*psuchē*) is exceeding sorrowful unto death" (Mark 14:34); prophetically, "A body (*sōma*) hast thou prepared me" (Heb 10:5). While He was perfect sinless Man, body, soul, and spirit, at the same time He was true God manifest in the flesh (1 Tim 3:16).

   "Preserved" (*tēreō*) occurs frequently in the NT and is usually translated "keep" e.g. John 17:12; Jude 1,21; Rev 3:10. The eternal security of the believer has been guaranteed by Christ Himself (John 10:28-29), by the promise and oath of God (Heb 6:17-20) and by the seal of the Holy Spirit (Eph 1:1,13). But in his daily life he needs divine power to overcome the attacks of the evil one. The attack could be in the realm of the spirit, his worship and prayer life; or in the sphere of his soul, his desires and emotions; or in some form of the abuse of the body. These were the three elements of man which Satan attacked in Eden at the beginning (Gen 3:6), and his methods are the same today.

"Blameless" (*amemptōs*, with no legitimate ground for accusation, cf. 2:10) is not sinless; sinlessness is not possible while still in the mortal body (Rom 7:18-25). But by the power of the indwelling Spirit and God's preserving, keeping care, it is possible to live a life at which the world cannot point an accusing finger. It is for this that Paul prays.

The use of the preposition *en* in the phrase "In (*en*) the coming (*parousia*) of our Lord Jesus Christ" is significant. It is not "at" or "until" but "in" the coming, and points to the consummation of the work of sanctification in the believer when Christ returns at the Rapture, and his subsequent manifestation at the judgment-seat of Christ (2 Cor 5:10) when his works and life of service will be examined and evaluated. The prayer ends with the full title, "our Lord Jesus Christ" which is used so often in the epistle.

24   What a delightful conclusion to the prayer, "Faithful is he that calleth you, who also will do it". "This prayer seems like a staggering request, but over against the feebleness of man Paul puts the faithfulness of God: God is faithful! He is not false in making His promises or fickle in failing to keep them. God is the Caller and the Doer, the Promiser and the Performer! He cannot but impart to the believer and perfect in him the holiness to which He has divinely summoned him" (H. C. Woodring).

IX.   Four farewell requests (5:25-28)

v.25	"Brethren, pray for us.
v.26	Greet all the brethren with an holy kiss.
v.27	I charge you by the Lord that this epistle be read unto all the holy brethren.
v.28	The grace of our Lord Jesus Christ be with you. Amen "

25   Paul was a man of prayer. Most of his correspondence with the churches commences with a prayer and is suffused with intercession and thanksgiving. He was a man of exceptional gift and ability and yet he recognised his need and that of his fellow-workers for the prayers of the saints. Very seldom does Paul put the word "brethren" first, so that it becomes the more effective when he does so. Those dear converts at Thessalonica were first and foremost his brethren, linked to him by ties of love and affection. He needed and appreciated their prayers.

26   Culture and customs among peoples vary from country to country, and from age to age. People display their friendliness and brotherly love in various ways. That which would be quite normal in one country would be abnormal in another. The main objective is to show affection for those of like-precious faith without partiality or undue familiarity, particularly between the sexes. Christian love can be shown by kindly words and a hearty handshake or a sincere "God bless you."

27   The request that the epistle be read to the whole assembly is given in the strongest possible language. The word "charge" means "to adjure, to bind with a solemn oath". The words are unique in the NT. The fact that Paul uses the personal pronoun "I", here and previously only in 2:18 and 3:5, shows the importance which he puts on his request. He realises that the epistle is the inspired Word of God for His people. The doctrines, exhortations, admonitions and warnings came from God Himself through His servant, and he is anxious that all should hear, understand and obey. The word "read" means "to read aloud". It reminds us of Ezra reading the book of the law to the whole congregation of Israel. "So they read in the book in the law of God distinctly, and gave the sense, and caused them to understand the reading" (Neh 8:8). Paul had likely been informed by Timothy of certain elements in the church which gave cause for concern, and he is anxious that all be present when the epistle is publicly read. It was not just the advice of an itinerant preacher, but the voice of God Himself to their hearts and consciences. He was concerned that all should heed the warnings, but also that they might know that his love and affection for them was intact.

28   Paul concludes this his first epistle with his autograph, the sign of every genuine letter which he writes. All of them conclude with the words "Grace be with you" (see 2 Thess 3:17-18). "Grace" (*charis*) is the dominant theme in all his writings. Like a golden thread it is woven into every letter from Romans to 2 Timothy, and each is signed with the same words. God's "unmerited favour" had captivated his heart. Here it is linked with the full title "our Lord Jesus Christ". Grace is not only a divine attribute, but it is also an attitude. We speak of a graceful figure and of a gracious person. There should be something about every Christian that displays the divine grace that has been bestowed upon him. Paul's wish for the Thessalonians is that it be with them all, and hopefully with us too. Amen!

Appendix

Some Questions Concerning the Rapture of the Church

1. *Will the Rapture be Pre-tribulational*

The Church and the Great Tribulation

Names:		
The time of Jacob's trouble	Jer 30:7; Dan 12:1	
The Great Tribulation	Matt 23:21	
The Hour of Temptation	Rev 3:10	
The Great Day of His Wrath	Rev 6:17	

The following reasons are adduced for the Church being raptured before the commencement of the Great Tribulation.

1. Promises of the Church's deliverance from wrath
    1 Thess 1:10; 5:9; 2 Thess 2:13; Rev 3:10.
2. The penal nature of the Great Tribulation judgments.
    The church's tribulation is disciplinary and instructive.
    The church is eternally exempt from penal judgment (Rom 8:1).
3. It is impossible for two divinely-appointed testimonies, that of the church and that of Israel, to be functioning on earth at the same time.
4. The consistent interpretation of the Book of Revelation requires this view.
    Rev 1-3: An outline of church history from God's viewpoint;
    Rev 4-5: The church in heaven, represented by 24 elders, seated, clothed, crowned with victor's crowns (*stephanos*);
    Rev 6-20: The Day of the Lord. Events associated with the Great Tribulation, a remnant of Israel forming God's testimony on earth.
5. Analogies of the OT: Enoch and Lot were removed before judgment fell.
6. The church going through the Great Tribulation is a mistaken term. The greater part of the church is in heaven; only a remnant of the church is on the earth at any given time.
7. Chronologically the millennium comes after the Great Tribulation; therefore the Rapture of the church will be both pre-Tribulational and pre-millennial.

2. *Will there be a Partial Rapture*

The idea that only the faithful and those that have attained a certain degree of spirituality will be raptured at the parousia is based on a mistaken interpretation of Scriptures including the following
(a) 1 Cor 9:24-27: Danger of being a *castaway*, disapproved, rejected.
(b) Phil 3:11: *Attaining* unto the resurrection of the dead.
(c) Heb 9:28: To *those that look for him* shall he appear.

(d) Rev 3:21: *The overcomer,* sit with me on my throne.
(e) 2 Tim 2:11,12: *If we suffer* we shall also reign.
The false interpretation of these passages:

1.   Confuses the Rapture with rewards for faithful service.
2.   Undermines the work of Christ on the Cross. The believer's salvation
        depends entirely on the sovereign grace of God, not on works of merit
        or on spiritual attainment of any kind. The redemption of the body at
        the Rapture rests on the same ground. It is possible for a believer to lose
        a reward or miss receiving a crown at the Bema, but every member of
        the body of Christ will be caught up at the Rapture. Otherwise it would
        be a ruptured body instead of a complete raptured body.
3.   Fails to take into account the context of Scripture. Consider the
        Corinthian church. They were "saints", they were washed, sanctified
        and justified (1 Cor 6:11). But they were carnal (3:3), indifferent to
        gross evil in their midst (5:2), some had been disciplined by God for
        serious abuses at the Lord's supper (11:30). And yet they were Christ's
        (3:23). In 1 Cor 15 Paul speaks thus of the Coming of Christ: "Christ
        the firstfruits; afterward they that are Christ's at his coming" (v.23).
        Speaking of those who will be alive at His coming, he uses the inclusive
        word "all", "we shall all be changed" (v.51). The vital test is not
        whether the professing believer has arrived at a specific degree of
        spiritual maturity, but whether or not he belongs to Christ.

3. *Will OT Saints Participate in the Rapture*

This is a question about which competent, godly, orthodox scholars differ. Some
emphasise the words "the dead in Christ" (1 Thess 4:16) as referring only to the
church. The OT saints, being an entirely different company, will not be raised
until after the Great Tribulation and immediately prior to the Millennium, in the
resurrection mentioned in Rev 20:5. They quote Dan 12:1-2 to substantiate this,
"And there shall be a time of trouble, such as never was since there was a nation
even to that same time; and at that time thy people shall be delivered, every one
that shall be found written in the book. And many of them that sleep in the dust
of the earth shall awake, some to everlasting life, and some to shame and
everlasting contempt". This was the view held by the late William Hoste, a
former esteemed editor of the Believer's Magazine. He wrote:
"In 1 Cor 15:23 we have the general truth that Christ is 'the firstfruits' of the
resurrection, 'afterward, they that are Christ's at His coming'. This expression
seems to include here the whole completed Second Coming, when the first
resurrection will be finished. This will have taken place in different stages and
categories. Thus supposing the resurrection in 1 Thess 4 is of the saints of this
dispensation alone since Pentecost (to such only applying the expression —'dead
in Christ'), that will be the beginning of the first resurrection, which will not
reach its final stage until Rev 20:4, where the resurrection of more than one
category of saints is indicated, of which we read in v.5, 'this is (i.e. completes) the

first resurrection'. This will no doubt include the OT saints. To conceive of OT saints however, being included in the first resurrection, at the same time as the Church, is very difficult and indeed impossible. How could such be caught away to meet the Lord in the air along with the Church? In that case there would be two distinct companies, each in a distinct relationship with the Lord."
(*Bible Problems and Answers*, W.Hoste & W.Rodgers, pp.64-65)

The late Mr. William Rodgers, who was also a distinguished Bible scholar, after quoting Mr Hoste's statement, made the following comment about its final paragraph: "Personally I cannot see that this last point presents any difficulty; but on the other hand I do find it difficult to think of the twenty-four elders of Rev 4, clothed in white raiment, and wearing victor's crowns (see Newberry) as representing saints of the Church period only; and indeed to even conceive of the Lord leaving any of His saints still in their graves, when the glorious event described in 1 Cor 15:51-53 and 1 Thess 4:15-17 takes place. I therefore, with the late Mr. J. Ritchie and many others, believe that when our Lord comes to the air, all the saints who up till then have died will be raised again."
(*Bible Problems and Answers*, p.65)

Without being dogmatic, the present writer is inclined to agree with Mr Rodgers' viewpoint. While the OT saints are a different body from the Church, 1 Cor 15:23 states: "But every man in his own order (company, group); Christ the firstfruits, afterward they that are Christ's in his parousia" (Gk.) Surely the OT saints are included in the words "they that are Christ's".

The Difference between the Rapture and the Revelation

The Rapture	*The Revelation*
A. Christ comes to the air. 1 Thess 4:17	Christ comes to the earth. Zech 14:4
B. Christ comes for His saints. 1 Thess 4:16,17	Christ comes with His saints. Jude 14
C. Chiefly for the church. 1 Thess 4:16,17	Chiefly for the Jews. Jer 30:7; Matt 24:29,30
D. Is before the Day of the Lord. 2 Thess 2:1-12	Is during the Day of the Lord. Matt 24:29,30
E. A time of joy. 1 Thess 2:19	A time of judgment. 2 Thess 1:8-9
F. A mystery (not previously revealed). 1 Cor 15:51	Not a mystery, revealed in the OT. Dan 2:44
G. Is not dated. Acts 1:7	Is dated, time marks clearly given. 7 years, 3½ years, 1260 days, Rev 12:6

2 THESSALONIANS

T.W. Smith

2 THESSALONIANS

Introduction

1. Authorship

There has been but little sustained challenge to the Pauline authorship of the epistle and there is written evidence that it was so accepted by the early Church. The style is unquestionably that of Paul. Some have suggested that Silas or Timothy may have written one or both letters or that possibly they were co-authors, but have raised little support. Indeed the "signature" at the close of the second epistle and its internal comments upon forgeries seem to be conclusive evidence of genuine Pauline authorship.

2. The City of Thessalonica

See Introduction to 1 Thessalonians.

3. The Foundation of the Assembly

See Introduction to 1 Thessalonians.

4. The Recipients of the Letter

Attempt has been made to establish that there were in fact two assemblies in Thessalonica, one Jewish and one Gentile, and it is suggested that the first letter was written to the Gentile company, the second to the Jewish. The arguments are based upon matters in the text, and are too complex to be entered into here, but they are largely self-defeating. For example, the statement in 1 Thess 1:9, "ye turned to God from idols", is used to demonstrate that the epistle was intended for the Gentile group, whilst it is pointed out that many quotations from the OT (LXX) in the second epistle indicate a Jewish readership. However competent authority has demonstrated that there are in fact more OT quotations in the first epistle than in the second. The proposition must founder on the basic point that the author of Galatians and Ephesians would never have countenanced such a division, so contrary to all he taught; besides there is not one jot in Scripture, or indeed in other writings, to support the idea.

Accepting then that the epistles were written to one assembly, composed of Jews and Gentiles as one, we must turn to another difficulty posed by the critics. Some argue that the first epistle is in fact the second, and the second the first. There are many points upon which this hypothesis must fail. Not the least is the note of recency in the section 2:17 to 3:6 of the first epistle. Then there is the relatively mild tone of the rebuke to the disorderly in the first letter (5:14) as compared with the final chapter of the second epistle. Furthermore the second epistle undoubtedly refers to the contents of the new revelation unfolded in the first; cf. 2 Thess 2:1 with 1 Thess 4:17. Whilst the first epistle is concerned much with the joyous detail of conversion recently experienced, the second speaks more of progress in the faith. Finally, the reference in 2 Thess 2:15 to another epistle is adequate proof in itself that this epistle cannot be the first. To attempt to nullify this by suggesting that there could be another, a missing epistle, is to relegate the canon of Scripture to a maelstrom of confusion. The suggestion must be dismissed as totally unfounded.

5. Date and Place of Writing

It is certain that with the possible exception of the letter to the Galatians (which cannot be dated with any degree of accuracy), 1 and 2 Thessalonians were the first of the Pauline epistles.

The salutation proves that Silas and Timothy were with Paul at the time of writing; for proof that it was written from Corinth see Introduction to 1 Thessalonians. The last scriptural reference to their being together is in Acts 18:18. The internal evidence of the epistle shows that it was written after Paul had suffered at the hands of the Jews (3:2), hence after the matter in Acts 18:14-17, so late in his stay at Corinth. This is confirmed by the comment in 1:4 as to other assemblies having been planted, probably in Achaia. Now as indicated in the Introduction to 1 Thessalonians, it is not possible to identify the date of Gallio's period of office as proconsul to within one year, because although we know that the proconsular year was from early summer, it is not certain whether Gallio was granted a second year of office. Most worthy scholars are satisfied that the date of writing was, on this basis, somewhere between the winter of AD 52 and spring of AD 54, and certainly prior to Paul's second visit to the area of Macedonia recorded in Acts 20.

6. The Purpose of the Letter

Soon after sending the first epistle, the main purpose of which was to teach the saints more excellently upon the subject of the Lord's return, and especially with reference to those of the assembly who had died, reports reached Paul at Corinth of further difficulties at Thessalonica. Word may have been brought back by the messenger who conveyed the first letter, but we are not told. The difficulties in the young assembly (now seemingly satisfied with the points clarified in the first epistle) appear to have been under two headings:

1. There was confusion as to the various aspects of the Lord's return, and seemingly a failure to regard the clear distinction between the new revelation of the Rapture in 1 Thess 4 and the day of the Lord in the following chapter. It also appears that the Jewish element in the city, and possibly in the assembly, was demonstrating from the OT Scriptures that the Lord's coming involved God's outpouring of wrath against men on the earth, and equating the awful and growing afflictions, which the saints were suffering, with the prophesied events of the day of the Lord.

2. The disorder mentioned in the first epistle (5:14) and referred to in 2 Thess 3:10 had not ceased, but rather intensified. Despite much conjecture, we are not told the exact cause of this disorder, but we are shown that it involved some in irresponsible behaviour; they did not seek to work for their subsistence, but relied on those who did to provide for them, and spent their own time "walking around" and, no doubt by gossip, adding to the distress in the assembly. The conjectured reasons for this disorderliness fall into four categories:

    a. euphoria over their new-found faith,
    b. eager expectation of the Lord's immediate return,
    c. taking advantage of the supposed reign of Christ,
    d. distress and depression over the idea that the Tribulation had already started.

    It is certainly true that there was some disorder at the time of the first letter, but this does not appear to have been so specific nor as severe as that indicated by the second epistle. To attribute the reason to any particular cause would be unwise, though to regard the trouble as stemming from error as to the Day of the Lord is not an unreasonable deduction in view of Paul's remarks in 2:2. It may well have been that some felt there was no good purpose in pursuing the things of this world if, as they thought, "the day" had arrived. However as the epistle does not give the definite cause, our best deductions have no greater validity than the speculations of others.

What then are the objects of the letter? A comparison of 1 Thess 1:3 with 2 Thess 1:3 will show that whereas the former speaks of their faith, love and hope, the latter mentions only faith and love; they had lost their blessed hope as a living and active force in their daily lives. The letter was to restore this hope by dispersing the dark clouds of error which had blotted it out. Based on the contents of the letter itself, we can see that its first aim was to demonstrate that the sufferings they were enduring had no relationship whatsoever to the Day of the Lord; that to suffer was indeed the portion of those who belonged to the Kingdom in its present form, and that there was to be a day not only of reward for such endurance, but also of retribution upon the persecutors. That day was truly the Day of the Lord, but such was not a day for the saints to fear, much the contrary; it would be for them a day of rest and infinite glory. However, that day could not begin until certain events had come to pass, all of which were under the control of "our God". The greatest of these, for their anticipation, was the Rapture, when they would be "gathered up" from earth to be for ever with the Lord. They should have known from the first letter that the day of God's wrath referred to men upon the earth, hence that their own presence here was an impediment to that day. In a wonderful pronouncement of the basic truth of the Rapture as the hope of the saints (2:1) the apostle certifies their security from the terrors of the Day of the Lord, before proceeding to explain the other features which held back that day of the Lord's vengeance.

Paul demonstrates the vital truth that the events of the great and terrible Day of the Lord hold no fear for His own; the church has no part in the awful period, the Great Tribulation, which these afflicted saints were being deceived into believing was now upon them. Wrath was not their portion, but rest; earth was not their place, but heaven; not for them Tribulation, but glory. Fear, mental and emotional distress (2:2) could be banished; they were the elect of God; they were not appointed to wrath but to salvation. They had been called to inexpressible glory, the glory of our Lord Jesus Christ.

Yet, such abounding privilege involved responsibility. They were to show the flag of the Kingdom by a life which glorified the Name of our Lord Jesus Christ. The imminence of the dawn of the new world did not justify indolence and carelessness in this world. We are to be here in practice what grace has made us there; the Kingdom involves government as well as grace. Let us behave ourselves.

The waiting seemed long — Paul and his companions knew that, for they too were suffering — but let them pray for each other, that they might know the abiding love of God as a real experience. As they waited for the Lord, let them remember that He too was waiting. Let us wait like Him. His grace is sufficient for all, always.

It has been well said that second epistles are for the last days, and for correction; hence for our day, and our correction.

7. Outline

8. Bibliography

Alford, H. *New Testament for English Readers*. Deighton and Bell. Cambridge. 1869.

Bengel, M.E. *Gnomon of New Testament*. T & T Clarke. Edinburgh. 1873.

Bellett, J.G. *Brief Notes on Ephesians and Thessalonians*. Bible Truth Publishers. Oak Park Ill. U.S.A.

Bloomfield, S.T. *Greek Testament*. Longman, Brown, Green & Longman. London, 1843.

Darby, J.N. *New Translation, Collected Writings, Synopsis,* Etc. Stow Hill Bible & Tract Co. Kingston on Thames.

Denney, J. *Expositor's Bible. The Epistles to the Thessalonians.* Hodder & Stoughton. London.

Ellicott, C.J. *Epistles to the Thessalonians.* Longman, Green, Roberts & Green, London. 1866.

Grant, F.W. *The Numerical Bible.* Loizeaux Bros. Neptune, N.J. U.S.A. 1902.

Hendrikson, W. *1 and 2 Thessalonians.* Banner of Truth, Edinburgh.

Hogg and Vine. *The Epistles to the Thessalonians.* Pickering and Inglis. Edinburgh.

Kelly, W. *Epistles to the Thessalonians.* Bible Truth Publishers, Oak Park. Ill, U.S.A.

Kelly, W. *Gospel of John,* Hammond Trust, London.

Lincoln, W. *Lectures on the Thessalonians.* J. Ritchie. Kilmarnock.

Lunemann, G. *Meyer's Commentary on the New Testament.* T & T Clarke, Edinburgh. 1880.

Morris, L. *The Tyndale Commentaries.* 1 & 2 Thessalonians. Inter Varsity Press, Leicester.

Nestle. *Interlinear Greek New Testament.* Bagster, London.

Nicholl, W.R. *The Expositor's Greek New Testament.* Eerdmans. Grand Rapids. U.S.A. (Reprint).

Robertson, A.J. *Word Pictures in the New Testament.* Broadman Press. Nashville. Tenn. U.S.A. 1931.

Vincent, M.R. *Word Studies in the New Testament.* Eerdmans. Grand Rapids, U.S.A.

Wigram, G.V. *Englishman's Greek Concordance of New Testament Words.* Bagster, London.

Winer, G.B. *Grammar of Greek New Testament Words.* T & T Clarke. Edinburgh. 1877.

Text and Exposition

I. The Salutation (1:1-2)

v.1   "Paul, and Silvanus, and Timotheus, unto the church of the Thessalonians in God our Father and the Lord Jesus Christ;

v.2   Grace unto you, and peace, from God our Father and the Lord Jesus Christ."

1 Paul includes his companions Silvanus (Silas) and Timothy in the greeting, for not only were they now with him as he writes from Corinth, but they were also involved with Paul when the assembly was founded: see Acts 16 and 17. This accords with the first epistle which was written only a few months before. Silas is mentioned first after Paul as he was senior to the youthful Timothy, and one of the "chief men among the brethren" (Acts 15:22) and "a prophet" (Acts 15:32). He was a Jew (Acts 16:20) and, like Paul, a Roman citizen (Acts 16:37). Paul's companions are not referred to in Scripture as apostles, and the comment in 1 Thess 2:6 should not be regarded as an inference that they were such.

Paul does not seek to establish or vindicate his apostleship in the course of his greeting, as in most other epistles, because, as in the case of a similar omission in the letter to Philippi, such was not called for in a letter where loving intimacy rather than authority was the key-note.

"Church" is *ekklēsia*, from *ek*, "out" and *kaleō*, "to call". The word is found in secular Greek writings for an assembly of people regularly called together for any reason, hence in such an early church letter it was necessary for Paul to distinguish his meaning by the phrase which follows. That the letter is addressed to the constituents of the company, rather than to a geographical location as in other epistles, is worthy of note. That the people, a complex mixture of many races, are indicated would first of all appeal as marking the fact that the assembly was no mere continuation of Judaistic influence which was evidently at the root of the trouble in the infant assembly, and was the cause of the letter being written. This personal aspect of the letter is consistent with the attitude taken up by Paul in the first epistle, and seen in his comment in 1 Thess 2:11, where he speaks of "every one of you", in terms of fatherly affection.

The name Thessalonica has historical association with a victory gained. Beautifully, both epistles, addressed as they are to a suffering people under mounting pressure though so young in the faith, are pregnant with the stirring message of assured and glorious victory when the Conqueror shall come for whom their hearts had waited, though this glad anticipation may now be dulled by circumstances about which the letter has been penned.

Their standing is "in God our Father and (the) Lord Jesus Christ". How appropriate to an infant church is this expression of intimacy unique as it is in the epistles (for "of God", indicating origin and responsibility, is used elsewhere). It breathes the warm and tender love expressed for the "little children" in 1 John 2:13-14. These Thessalonians were no longer heathen (cf. 1 Thess 1:9), the God to whom they had turned was their Father; they "knew the Father". Their relationship was not only to Him, but also "in Him", and in that double security, equally and gloriously in the Lord Jesus Christ who had so revealed God as Father. It is a lovely reflection of John 10:20-29. Here is the true Christian position, knowing the Father and owning the Lord Jesus Christ. "God" would indicate worship, "our Father" the exquisite joy of communion, "Lord" the sober matter of responsibility in His claim upon us; "Jesus" speaks of His humility, suffering and shame, "Christ" of His exaltation, honour and glory. What a change, from idols to this.

The beauty of the address being to the individual saint is extended in this thought of the glory of the relationship, for it emphasises that each should receive the full blessing of it personally: "our Father" shows each as the subject of His love, "and the Lord Jesus Christ", each under the Saviour-Shepherd's care. Yet the touching note must not be missed, that in using "our", Paul includes himself, and indeed all saints.

God is known to men intuitively, and manifested by creation (Rom 1) but the relationship as Father is the subject of revelation by the Son (John 17:6), based upon the work at the cross and completed in resurrection (John 20:17); it refers to those who are born again and thus in the family of God (1 John 3:1; Gal 3:26).

2   The expression "grace unto you, and peace", is common in the epistles, and because of this the glorious impact of it is often lost, the term being considered as little more than a courteous formula. Such should never be. Grace and peace are really cause and effect as to the love of God. Grace is love first reaching out to the sinner, and peace the result of that love being received and realised. Some have remarked that "grace" (charis) is like the Greek form of greeting, and "peace" the Hebrew form, and whilst this is true, there are depths in the words far beyond that. The Holy Spirit would remind us by repeated usage that grace (which is not only God's unmerited favour, but such when we deserved eternal punishment) is that which brought salvation, and peace that which salvation brought. Here is the believer's abundant supply; in grace the divine Persons are seen entering into that which concerns us, and in peace we are privileged to enter into that which concerns the Father and Son. We must ever be occupied with the wonder of this. Yet it is the mind of God that we should progress in our experience of grace and

peace (2 Pet 1:2). We are to grow in grace, tutored far beyond the blessedness of security from wrath, as indicated in Titus 2:11-13, and to know the tranquil joy which issues from the assurance that righteousness and peace have kissed each other, as the heart receives ever-growing impressions of what was achieved by that figured in the blood upon the Mercy Seat, the blood of Him who is our peace (Col 1:20).

"From God (the) Father, and (the) Lord Jesus Christ" has no articles in the text. Again the equality of the Persons and their identity is noted. That "Jesus", the name of His self-humbling, and referring strictly to the period of His despised sojourn among men, should be identified as "Christ" (the Messiah, the Anointed One) would have an obvious impact upon those who were Jews in origin, but the title "Lord" (*kurios*) would strike a deep note in all of the assembly. Whilst to the Jew this was the title of Jehovah, to the former pagan citizens of this important Roman centre it is used for, and indeed claimed by, Claudius Caesar. There was, indeed, "another king, one Jesus" (Acts 17:7), the charge made against Paul by the Jews of Thessalonica, although it was to them that he had preached Him as the Christ.

II. The Apostle Praying, Caring, Teaching (1:3-12)

1. *Thanksgiving for Answered Prayer*
1:3-4
v.3   "We are bound to thank God always for you, brethren, as it is meet, because that your faith groweth exceedingly, and the charity of every one of you all toward each other aboundeth;

v.4   "So that we ourselves glory in you in the churches of God for your patience and faith in all your persecutions and tribulations that ye endure:"

3 The word "bound" (*opheilō*) expresses a deep sense of obligation like our Anglo-Saxon word "ought"; it means to owe as a debt (here to God). This was not a matter of continuing duty only, but here specifically because the subject involved a definite answer to the apostle's fervent and constant prayer for them. (See 1 Thess 3:10-13.) Such an attitude of thanksgiving was "meet" (*axion*), "fitting" involving the thought of doing no more than was due, and translated "worthy" in 1 Thess 2:12. The two similar expressions occurring together, "bound" and "meet", represent no mere repetition, for one is subjective and the other objective. The thanks to God was due because, in answer to prayer, the behaviour of the saints merited it. How beautifully we see the heart of the nursing mother with her own children (1 Thess 2:7) in the apostle's joy over the progress of the infant assembly.

Thanksgiving was due "because that your faith (*pistis*) groweth exceedingly". This term as to growth is expressed by *huperauxanō*, meaning "beyond measure", in the sense that no matter what might be the appreciation of the potential development latent in a seed, the result surpasses the anticipation (cf. Matt 13:31). Here is a lovely note of contrast in respect of the concern Paul seems to express in 1 Thess 3:2,10 as to their faith. This description of rapid growth upward is followed by his commendation of their love flowing outward, for "abounding" is *pleonazō*, meaning to overflow or disperse widely – the very word Paul had used in his prayer, now so richly answered (see 1 Thess 3:12).

Note how he says in respect of this love "of every one of you all toward each other", showing that it is individual, corporate, and mutual. Happy is such an assembly. Such love can come only from the divine source (2 Pet 1:7); superficial cordiality, often accompanied by backbiting and criticism, is no substitute for it. Suffering alone cannot promote it, and the apostle shows that fervent prayer is the only channel.

The gentle care of the apostle for the flock of God is demonstrated in this early section of the letter, as he follows the divine standard of commendation before correction. This does not involve any exaggeration of their true state, for it must have gone home to these suffering and perplexed saints, that there was missing from the note of thanks for them, one vital link in the often repeated triad of Christian virtues. In the first epistle Paul could speak of their faith, love and hope (1:3) demonstrated by their state (1:9-10), but where is the mention of hope now? Paul's omission speaks volumes. Here in embryo he introduces the whole basis of the epistle; they had lost the characteristic upon which he had laid stress in the first letter, their hope; the glow of the future certainty of the Lord's return as a moment-by-moment anticipation. They were still running well, and indeed faith and love were flourishing in the soil of adversity and persecution, but they had lost sight of the glorious objective which formerly marked them, "waiting for his Son from heaven". This glad anticipation had been dimmed, if not blotted out, by the evil cloud of false doctrine being superimposed upon their suffering, as will be dealt with in chapter 2. The tragedy of this should be a sobering lesson to those who propagate the altogether false teaching that the Church must endure the terrors of the Tribulation. To cause the Lord's people to anticipate their being included in such a time of God's wrath against men upon the earth, instead of waiting on tip-toe of glad expectancy for His Son from heaven, is to rob them of that most blessed hope of the Church, with which they can comfort one another (1 Thess 4:13-18). By God's grace in giving us this epistle, the sad experience of the Thessalonians has resulted in a warning beacon being established to mark the dark rocks of error, and yet to illumine the path to future glory.

Whilst the apostle introduces the stern fact of reality by the omission of hope, nevertheless he continues affectionately to commend those graces in the saints which made his thanksgiving "meet", albeit turning this to illustrate vital lessons and to feed their faith as to the future, for without hope, faith and love must flag under the pall of fear.

4   Here Paul turns from thanksgiving to God to praise before men. "We ourselves" is in the place of emphasis in the verse. This is to encourage and stimulate, and not, as some would contend, to mark a declension from the state of their testimony as in 1 Thess 1:8 where Paul had 'no need to speak of them'. The contexts are quite different; the reference in the first epistle is to their conversion, and here to their continuance. This whole section is one of commendation, of praising what can be praised, and with a view to encouragement. It might mean, as some suggest, that it was not the apostle's practice to boast of his dear children, but rather, as in the first epistle, to let others speak of them, but in these present circumstances he could not refrain. Of course, such boasting was not of their own work, but of God's. "Boast" is a better rendering of *enkauchaonai* than "glory". Paul was ever ready to detect what was of God, no matter how faintly the light may glimmer. Such is the pursuit of the spiritual man, in contrast to the Pharisaical attitude, born of pride, which seeks only fault in others.

It is of note that "endurance" (or patience) and "faith" share the one article and so stand as linked, but as William Kelly points out, "They need the power of hope to sustain in freshness". Being so joined to "endurance", "faith" here has the sense of "fidelity". It is the same word *(pistis)* as in v.3, and although all faith has its object in Christ and its end in assured salvation, the believer must always be mindful of all the promises of God as matter for belief, and in particular have the eye firmly fixed upon the key to all His purposes being fulfilled in the Lord's coming for His own. "Endurance" is not a matter of merely putting up with the circumstances which prevail, but of stout-hearted fortitude born of trust in the righteousness of God.

"Churches of God" should be seen in contrast with the address of the epistle to the "church of the Thessalonians". In the latter case, the individual saint is in mind, but in the former it refers to the local assembly in respect of its origin, maintenance and responsibility. The local assembly is "God's ploughed field, His treasured possession": let none forget this.

In the phrase "all your persecutions", the word *diōgmos* (persecutions) has the sense of being pursued, and is used of, or by, Paul in Acts 9:4; 22:4; 2 Cor 12:10 and Phil 3:12,14. Although "afflictions" (this is a better translation of *thlipsesin* than "tribulations", AV) can refer to all the troubles of life, its association with "pursue" would indicate action against them physically consequent upon the pursuing, like being hounded and caught. "That ye endure" is from a root meaning to hold up, or hold out against pressure, not to give in, as of Paul in 1 Cor 4:12 ("we suffer it"). In the verse under consideration it is in the present tense, indicating the need was to hold out against a continuing state of affliction.

2. God's Righteous Judgment Explained
1:5-6

v.5   "Which is a manifest token of the righteous judgment of God, that ye may be counted worthy of the kingdom of God, for which ye also suffer:

v.6   "Seeing it is a righteous thing with God to recompense tribulation to them that trouble you;"

5 "A manifest token" (*endeigma*) is an unique word in Scripture, but there is a related word (*endeixis*) in a parallel passage in Phil 1:28. It means an open evidence or proof "of the righteous judgment of God". Though not in the text, "which is" is necessary to connect the statements of verses 4 and 5, though in the process it raises a query as to what in the earlier verse displays (as open evidence or proof) the righteous judgment of God. Two factors have been mentioned, "the enduring faith" of the Thessalonians on the one hand, and the "persecutions and afflictions" on the other. It is a question of whether the statement is to be viewed in the nominative case (and so referring to all the preceding words) or in the accusative (when, as in Rom 12:1 and 1 Tim 2:6, the reference would be restricted to the immediately preceding clause and verb). Scholars generally come down on the side of the latter, viewing the endurance of the saints alone as being referred to; but such would ignore the whole contextual argument that God recompenses both good and evil (see Rom 2:4-10). Thus it is concluded that the opening statement of v.5 introduces a declaration of principle, that both the afflictions upon the saints, and the faithful endurance of those afflictions by the saints, each in its own case, demonstrate the righteous judgment of God. As to the persecutors, God's unhurried, patient longsuffering as He moves with majestic leisureliness, is of itself a token of His righteous attributes in judgment. Indeed the salvation of some of the persecutors, and not the least of Paul himself, is a testimony to this. But for the unrepentant, judgment is as certain as it is righteous, and the circumstances of such judgment are recorded in the parenthetical section (vv. 6-10) which follows.

What can be said then of the application of God's righteous judgment to the suffering yet enduring saints? Firstly there is the actual experience of being able to endure, for the term "counted worthy" (*kataxioō*) does not indicate personal merit or even being made worthy, but rather being "accounted worthy", as in Acts 5:41, "deemed worthy" in a sense similar to our being "reckoned righteous". With the inclusion of *eis* (unto) in the verse the idea expressed is "with that end in view".

Thus the Thessalonian saints were to regard (it does not say they were already doing so) their enduring faith in their afflictions as a display of God's righteous judgment, inasmuch as the power to endure was not of their own merit but of Himself, and was granted to the end that through suffering (for so is the kingdom attained, 1 Thess 3:3) they might be declared worthy of the kingdom. Note, it does not say "worthy of heaven".

This does not mean that they were to be accepted because they endured the afflictions; all acceptance is of grace not of works. Grace gave them to suffer, grace bore them up in it (Phil 1:29) and grace alone would account them worthy; but, as Matt 5:10-12 explains, there is a difference between being of the kingdom and receiving the reward, even as it is one thing to be made a partaker of the inheritance (Col 1:12), which is the portion of every believer, and another altogether to receive the reward of the inheritance because of service to the Lord Christ (Col 3:24). To have died with Him involves living with Him, but there is the further thought held out to these saints, that if they suffered (endured) they should also reign with Him. See 2 Tim 2:11-12. The kingdom was not yet manifest, but those who suffered for it must know that not only was it a present thing in respect of its trials, but that it also operated now as to its grace, its power and its principles of justice, that it functioned with a view to future vindication and reward, and that in manifestation.

It is better to translate *huper* as "on behalf of" in the clause "for which ye also suffer". They were to see their suffering in the context of the kingdom, for as Ellicott remarks, "The connection between holy suffering and future blessedness was mystically close and indissoluble" (see Acts 14:22). Thus, by divinely-inspired wisdom, Paul has turned what must have been the very basis of their doubting God's benevolent attitude to them into an assurance of it.

6   The apostle now embarks upon a somewhat parenthetical section in verses 6 to 10, where he deals with matters in respect of the righteous judgment of God which the natural mind might regard as more palatable to the sufferers. First he turns to the other side of the case, to the matter of the afflictors, for it is an elementary and accepted principle that justice must bring punishment upon such. We often see the results of evil received in life, for it has been well said that retribution is the other half of sin, but whether this be so or not, the issue of just recompense is inevitable.

As well as using affliction to the ultimate good of the afflicted (v.5) God's righteousness is balanced, in that the persecutors will receive their recompense also, and they know it (Phil 1:28). We cannot tell what impact Stephen's endurance of suffering and affliction had on Saul of Tarsus, nor the resultant state of mind of a Nero or a Pilate in respect of their deeds, but we have this testimony, that suffering does make its mark; of this there is ample proof in Scripture and in our own experience.

"Seeing" *(eiper)* is better rendered as "since" or "if it be such", for Paul puts his point powerfully in rhetorical fashion by posing it as a question to which there is but an affirmative answer. None could cavil on the issue that judgment must fall on the persecutors. Some have argued that such a readily acceptable hypothesis is unworthy and hardly Christian, even suggesting an interpolation in the text but it is part of a balanced case in which the less palatable aspect has been put first (in v.5). Now, by a designed understatement to gain the hearer, after the Jewish manner of argument, the apostle makes a point which will be readily acceptable to the former Jews now in the assembly, and a counter to any adverse Judaistic influence. Yet he does not score at the expense of truth as men do in seeking to make a point, much the contrary; he poses a righteous basis for reasoned acceptance of the matter which follows in the verses below. His statement might be framed as, "Is it acceptable that it is a righteous thing with God to afflict those who afflict others?"

"Tribulation" is "affliction" as in v.4: "with God" *(para Theo)* has the idea of close location, and gives the sense of the afflictor being arraigned before God.

"Recompense" (*antapodidmi*) is to render back again, to repay; see 1 Thess 3:9 where it is used in a good sense. The reading in the original, "to the ones afflicting you, affliction", gives the solemn idea of "measure for measure" in God's righteous dealings (see Rom 2:5).

3. *Righteous Judgment Executed*
1:7-9

v.7   "And to you who are troubled, rest with us, when the Lord Jesus shall be revealed from heaven with his mighty angels,

v.8   In flaming fire taking vengeance on them that know not God, and that obey not the gospel of our Lord Jesus Christ:

v.9   Who shall be punished with everlasting destruction from the presence of the Lord, and from the glory of his power;"

7   Paul again turns to the case of the afflicted. The word he employs for "rest" (*anesis*) is one he uses elsewhere as the opposite to tribulation. It describes a ploughed field rested after years of toil, the slackening of tension in a bow string, and relief from strain (see its use in 2 Cor 2:13; 7:5; 8:13). Here it speaks of relief from affliction. Note, the rest is "with us", the writers, for all do not suffer affliction. This lovely note would encourage the saints, as Paul indicates that he and his companions were under pressure too, and that they endured under the certainty of future rest, the prize he now holds out to them even as he commences (their minds now the more receptive) to adjust their erroneous view of the day of judgment.

The event referred to, "when the Lord Jesus shall be revealed (*apokalupsei*) from heaven" is the Appearing in power and great glory not the Rapture, the Lord's return to the earth, not His coming to the air. (See Appendix on Rapture, Parousia, Appearing, Apokalupsis.) This Appearing is spoken of in Dan 2:34-35; Zech 14; Matt 24:27; 26:64; Mark 13:26; Luke 21:27; Rev 19:11-16 among other Scriptures.

The point here is not that the Appearing (*apokalupsis*) of the Lord Jesus was to be regarded solely as the occasion of their rest or relief, for the mention of it in that connection is somewhat incidental and parenthetical as the apostle pursues the subject of the righteous judgment of God. Indeed it could be pointed out that the rest for the Church saints commences at the Rapture; however, the Holy Spirit is careful to avoid marking that glorious occasion as one of relief for the saints, but rather keeps before them one central object, the Lord Himself. The mention of rest at the Appearing is to illustrate that this event, with such awful consequences for their persecutors, has no terror for their victims whose portion then is rest.

Having said this however, it must be borne in mind that, in common with all second epistles, this letter embraces the position of saints of the very end of time after the Church has been raptured, those who suffer awful persecution in the Tribulation. For them, even as they cry "How long", the Appearing will be their glad relief. What a blessed comfort and encouragement this epistle will be in those terrible days of affliction and martyrdom.

However, the main thought which will proceed will be of retribution against the persecutors, and in this connection the literal sense of the words "in (en) the revelation of the Lord Jesus Christ" indicates that the retribution will be effected in the process of His being revealed, as indeed the following verse will show.

"With his mighty angels" may be translated literally, and the more awe-inspiringly, "with the angels of his might", i.e. by whom He exercises His power. The "power" is His, the angels are instruments of it in the same way that in v.10 the saints are instruments of His glory.

8   The phrase "in flaming fire" should be compared with Exod 3:2; 19:18; Dan 7:9; Isa 29:6; 30:30; 66:15; Mal 4:1. Scholars are divided as to whether these words should be construed with the preceding or the following statement. As is usual in such cases of doubt, it is wise to consider them with both; first as to the awesome glory of His appearing (in v.7) and then as to the terrible punishment to be inflicted upon the wicked, described in the rest of this verse. These words should cause us to wonder at the glory and magnificence of His appearing before every eye, yet to tremble at the awful and eternal consequences of evil.

The last time this world saw Him was as a humble, despised Nazarene, rejected of men, hanging in agony and shame upon a cross; now they shall see Heaven's response to earth's verdict. He comes as the dispenser of judgment. Here, as a by-product of the narrative, is an illustration of the divine principle noted in the earlier section, for there could be no greater manifestation of the righteous judgment of God, nor stronger encouragement for the troubled saints, than this supreme instance of suffering being answered in ultimate glory, as the apostle continues with the vivid account of the day of retribution.

"Taking (better rendered as giving or awarding) vengeance" (*ekdikēsis*) is from *ekdikeō*, to revenge: some express it as full vengeance. See Ezek 25:14. There has been a tendency to play down the strength of this word, but such is not warranted. It is the fiery indignation of a holy God against evil, not in the sense of a sudden upsurge of emotion, as of a human spirit, for how could such be envisaged in One so marked by long-suffering, mercy and grace. It is the ultimate balancing of the scales by righteous justice; men will reap what they have sown as Deut 32:35 asserts, "To me belongeth vengeance, and recompense". See also Rom 3:5; Ps 149:7; and the words of the Lord Jesus in Luke 21:22; 18:7.

"On them that know not God", or better, as a perfect participle, "not knowing God", shows the wilful neglect of intuitive knowledge and of the evidences of observation, so that they know not God as God.

It is to be noted that in the original text of "and them obeying not the gospel of our Lord Jesus Christ" (some mss omit Christ), the article is repeated, hence the duplication of the demonstrative pronoun "them" in the translation above. This indicates that two distinctive classes are involved. These have generally, and readily, been identified as Gentiles who knew not God (see 1 Thess 4:5) and Jews who obey not the gospel (cf. Rom 10:3,16,21), for Paul never envisages the nation without the gospel. This division is dismissed by others as contradicting the evidence of the past 2 000 years in respect of the gospel, and supporting evidence is produced from Scripture that Jews as well as Gentiles know not God (e.g. John 8:55, although a different word is used for "know"). However our verse is not dealing with history but with eschatology; it is describing conditions when the Lord is revealed from heaven. Whilst it can be fairly argued that God is not dealing with Jew and Gentile as separate entities in this present Church age, He will be after the Church has been raptured, and through the period of the Tribulation which precedes the Lord's Appearing in power and glory. However, this also is not conclusive that the division is between Gentile and Jew, for we have Scriptural evidence that many Gentiles as well as Jews will be saved under the gospel of the kingdom during the Tribulation (Rev 7:14). Thus, it is safer to conclude that the verse is dealing with the ultimate general classification of humanity at His Appearing, and how each class responds to the awareness of God's claim upon them. One thing is evident — their condition is final and irreversible. However the distinctive classes may be viewed, there is a difference to be noted between those who refuse the gospel, and those who seemingly have not heard it, but nevertheless disregard their intuitive knowledge and the evidence of creation (Rom 1:19-22). Whilst the immediate result is the same for both classes at the Lord's return in fiery indignation, there is a difference as to responsibility consistent with the difference in privilege. This will be reflected in the ultimate judgment (see on v.9).

It is a matter to be noted solemnly in connection with the proclamation of the gospel, that its message, its full message, has to be not only received, but moreover, obeyed. God commands; we must not fail to proclaim this. Reconciliation and repentance are part of the same gospel, and continuance is involved as well as conversion.

9 "Who" includes both classes of v.8, for *hoitines* is a relative pronoun which indicates those who are of that kind or quality, showing that they are a class of persons who have been so fitted for what follows.

"Shall be punished" is literally "who shall pay (or repay) the right (or justice)", a word from the same root as "righteous". This is the only use of this formula in the NT. The whole thought illustrates the basis of "vengeance", the inflicting of that which has been justly deserved, by exacting the consequences. In "with everlasting destruction", the Greek for "everlasting" is *aiōnios*. Some commentators and Greek scholars (e.g. Vincent) argue that *aiōnios* is never to be interpreted as everlasting or endlessness, and suggest it indicates "for a period" only. Let the Scriptures speak for themselves. It is used:

of God's eternal Being	:	Rom 16:26
of eternal life	:	John 3:16
of eternal fire	:	Jude 7
of eternal salvation	:	Heb 5:9
of eternal redemption	:	Heb 9:12

and in over seventy other Scriptures the thought is distinctly of endlessness. Ellicott adds the note of scholastic authority to the even firmer foundation of scriptural usage when he comments, "All sounder commentators recognise in *aiōnios* a testimony to the eternity of future punishment that cannot easily be explained away".

To attempt to dilute the endlessness of the judgment recorded here savours of the early words of the enemy, "Hath God said?" An essential attribute of the gospel is its finality, and to seek to modify the meaning of everlasting or eternal in respect of punishment is to infer the opportunity of another and future chance to get right with God. Such has no place in Scripture; "there is no ulterior prospect, all is final. Indeed the gospel has no meaning at all if it is not true that those who refuse to obey it, incur by their decision the infinite and irreversible condition of being lost. Theirs is the final night of judgment which has no prospect of dawn, of unrelieved and irreparable damnation" (Denney). Let no spirit of fleshly sentimentality seek to modify the eternal word of an eternal and offended God. To "see his face" is the sublime consummation of the believer's hope, for it is "to be satisfied" (Ps 17:15). Here the eternal bliss of the believer is contrasted with the eternal loss of the damned. See also Matt 18:10; Rev 22:4.

"Destruction" (*olethros*) has no thought of annihilation or cessation of being, indeed its meaning is clearly set out in what follows. It is exactly the opposite in every sense to eternal life; see Matt 25:46. The only other use of the word in Greek Scriptures (4 Macc 10:15) illustrates this as the lot of the tyrant Antiochus Epiphanes in contrast with the joyous state of a martyred victim.

In "from the glory of his power (or strength)", the word for "power" is not *dunamis* as in v.7, but *ischus*, and the thought in the genitive of origin is of might issuing forth from the majestic glory of the Person of the Lord, giving a similar sense as in such Scriptures as 1 Tim 6:16 ("light unapproachable") and Isa 2:10, 19,21.

From such display of the excellence of His Person the wicked shall be eternally separated. Here is the visible manifestation of the Lord Jesus as He comes in power and great glory at the Appearing (*apokalupsis*), not to the air for His saints, but to the earth with His saints.

The verse makes a division in the purpose of this visible manifestation of the glory and might of God, the earlier portion ("who shall be punished"), pointing back to v.8, shows that He comes in judgment, the latter ("glory of His power") leading on to v.10, that its purpose is glory. Description must fail to give any notion of the awe and issuing glory of this sight which will dawn, yea rather flash, upon this sinful world. It does not however mean that the two ungodly classes will, upon the moment of His Appearing, be "cast into the lake of fire"; it does not speak of the Great White Throne, nor of the events of Matt 25:31-46 when He shall judge the living nations from the throne of His glory, for how they treated His brethren Israel. What is here described is the effect of the revelation itself upon the classes mentioned; it is not the ultimate judgment (at the Great White Throne), but the immediate and awful finality of their being eternally separated from the glory of His presence, to await the eternal verdict which will be according to their works (Rev 20:12-13). Then their degrees of wilfulness will be weighed in judgment and issue in degrees of eternal punishment in the lake of fire, the end of all sinners. See Luke 12:47-48; Heb 10:29; Rev 20:13. This has a distinctive bearing on the immediate context as to God's righteous judgment of the persecutors, for the Word of God indicates that the persecutor is conscious of what he is doing (Phil 1:28; Rom 1:32). What then the awful fate of such wilful action against God's own, inherent in the term "who shall pay the penalty", for *tinō* with *dikē* at the beginning of the verse has, as has been indicated, the meaning of "repaying what is right or just", as in Philem 19.

4. *God's Righteous Judgment Exhibited*
   ## 1:10

> v.10 "When he shall come to be glorified in his saints and to be admired in
>   all them that believe (because our testimony among you was
>   believed) in that day."

10   "When he shall come" *(hotan elthe)* is the masterly stroke of inspiration; the apostle is called upon to choose a word *(hotan)* which heralds the indefinite timing of this future and certain event, for literally as an aorist subjunctive it reads, "whenever he shall have come". What wonder in every word of Scripture.

"To be glorified in his saints" is an aorist infinitive of purpose. The use of *endoxasthēnai* for "glorified" is arresting in its import; only in this chapter is it used in the NT, but it appears in the LXX (Exod 14:4,17; Ezek 28:22) where it signifies God receiving glory either from the punishment of the evildoer or in the salvation of the righteous. How appropriate in the context, where both aspects apply. Whenever He comes its character is glorious; His glory.

Note, He is glorified "in his saints" not by His saints, because in this manifestation, when they appear with Him, they shall be like Him, as a result of the Rapture (see Phil 3:21; Rom 8:29; 1 Cor 15:49; 1 John 3:2). The glory they reflect is His glory, "as of the sun in a mirror" (Alford). This is the day when the world shall know to their eternal loss the value and worth of being His. God's blessed Son will be glorified in grace and vindicated in judgment.

"And to be admired (wondered at) in all them that believed" expresses the wonder and surprise, as an amazed world looks upon the product of God's grace, and sees the glory of His eternal counsels for men — many sons made like unto His glorious Son; they shall come with Him having been perfected at the Bema, His glory shining forth in them.

The aorist expression "that believed" refers back to the time when the redeemed "turned to God" in the sense of 1 Thess 1:9. Some interpret this as looking back from the moment of the Appearing, and the idea of "faith giving place to sight", but the parenthetical portion at the end of the verse, in bringing the Thessalonians' acceptance of the gospel into view, makes it clear that conversion is in mind. In other words, the first step of salvation secures its ultimate.

The question is posed by some commentators as to whether or not there are two classes involved in this verse as there are in v.8, suggesting two distinctive groups being involved in His glory as in His judgment. They see "them that know not God" in contradistinction to "the saints", and the ones "believing not the gospel" contra "them that believe"; they even suggest that "the saints" refers to those of the OT, and "them that believe" to the NT. The grammar here is not specific as in v.8, to support the idea of there being two classes, although Bengel's point that "all" appears before the second group but not before the first is at least interesting in pursuing the matter. That the Lord will return with both OT and NT saints is accepted by many on the grounds that there are but two classes of men, those in Adam and those in Christ, and as the OT saints are therefore "in Christ" they will be raised at the Rapture, and so return with the Lord at His Appearing. Others make a distinction, saying that "in Christ" is a dispensational term, and distinguish between those "in Christ" and "those that are Christ's" (1 Cor 15:23). To pronounce on these issues would complicate what is judged to be a simple issue, for in no other instance does Paul even appear to state that the use of the term "saint" is restricted to the OT as distinct from the NT; indeed 1 Thess 3:13 could be construed as suggesting the contrary. One thing is certain, verses 8 and 10 present the contrasting effect of His Appearing; infinite and indescribable glory for those of v.10, and utter desolation beyond description for those of v.8.

"Because our testimony among you was believed" is better rendered "to you". This peculiar parenthesis, as it has been called, must have been a great encouragement and assurance to the Thessalonian saints. They well knew that they had believed the gospel testimony of Paul and his companions, that they "had turned to God from idols", and here Paul was emphasising that their belief was the sure basis of their being included in this great display of the Lord's glory. Yet the statement was intended to be even more than that, for it is part of the specific case the apostle is going to develop — that, in consequence of their being in heaven during the Tribulation period (2:1) and in view of their having such a glorious part in the Appearing, they had no cause to fear the Day of the Lord of which the Appearing was a part. Construe "in that day" with "when he shall come", referring to the glorious Appearing (*apokalupsis*).

5. *Prayer for Present Power*
1:11-12

> v.11 "Wherefore also we pray always for you, that our God would count you worthy of this calling, and fulfil all the good pleasure of his goodness, and the work of faith with power:
> v.12 That the name of our Lord Jesus Christ may be glorified in you, and ye in him, according to the grace of our God and the Lord Jesus Christ."

11 "Wherefore also" does not give the true sense of *eis ho* in the text; it should rather be, "Unto which", like our "To which end", for, as Ellicott, it is definitive of direction taken (cf. Col 1:29). It is important to the understanding of the verse, that the question be decided as to what end Paul had in mind. It has already been pointed out that verses 6 to 10 form something of a parenthesis, in explanation of the "righteous judgment of God" in connection with the afflictions of His people (v.5). The present verse takes us back over that parenthesis (yet not excluding the explanation in it) to continue the subject of v.5, namely their being "counted worthy" (not being made so, but reckoned so) of the kingdom of God (on behalf of which they were suffering) in that future day when His judgments are manifested. Paul now continues with this matter, stating that it was the subject of his constant prayer for them, not now in respect of that future day, but for the present time, that God may "account them worthy (*axiōsē*) of their calling" (aorist active subjunctive) by their testimony in life. That is, to show forth in their manner of life daily the purpose of their calling, by displaying in this world the characteristics and the power of a world to come. It will be seen that this is consistent with what has been stated in the latter portion of the parenthesis. The saints shall display to the world the glory of Christ in that future day of His Appearing in power and great glory; let them show it to the world now.

It is necessary to emphasise that in this verse, as in v.5, Paul is not speaking of personal merit, but of the action of grace in bestowal. It is God, "our God", acting in grace and power on behalf of, and in, His own suffering children, enabling them so to evidence their calling. All here is in the present and in testimony, as v.5 is of the future and reward.

It would be remiss if in pursuit of the main subject, there was failure to note the solemn example the apostle gives of constant and fervent prayer, "We pray always for you". Note his "always" (at all times) and the presence of the vital little word *hina* (in order that), indicating the object of the prayer. It is not enough to preach only, there should be the "giving of thanks" (v.3) and continuing intercession.

As Paul warmly reminds the saints, the God mentioned earlier in reign and judgment is "our God"; so a lovely note of sympathy is introduced. Paul and his companions were also suffering for the kingdom, but the affection in which he speaks of God must have given assurance to the Thessalonians, that they need fear no wrath from Him to whom they mutually belonged as dear children. For "counted worthy" (or "fitted"), see 1 Tim 5:17, of the elders; Heb 3:3, of Christ and Heb 10:29, of apostates; in each case we note it is a recognition of a state (of worthiness) currently existing. Here the prayer is that God would bestow such grace and power, accomplishing in them all that was in His heart to do, a thought similar to Phil 1:12-13.

"Calling" is used in its widest sense (see 1 Cor 1:26; Eph 1:18; 4:4). Though the whole realm of the calling is in view (as in 1 Cor 7:20) from its first working in the heart and through what Alford calls "its enduring state", the object is its glorious consummation. (By a figure of speech called metonymy, an attribute of a thing is named instead of the thing itself, such as "crown" instead of "king", and "becoming higher than the heavens" (Heb 7:26) where "heavens" stands for everything in the heavens. Here the "calling" stands for its total and ultimate purpose and the life here displaying that.)

In "and fulfil every good pleasure of goodness", the word *eudokia* (good pleasure) is stronger than a desire for goodness. The AV rendering is most unfortunate in inserting the italicised "his" before "goodness", for the goodness intended is not God's but theirs. *Agathōsune* (goodness), a word used four times by Paul, is never attributed to God in the NT. When it is directed towards others it indicates "benevolence", and with reference to self, "a contented outlook or attitude". The sense of the phrase here is God fulfilling in the Thessalonian saints the work of grace which will result in their "having a delight in goodness". This is seen clearly by reference to Rom 15:14, and Gal 5:22 where the same word is used for the work of the Holy Spirit in the believer.

The thought of all this being God's working, as the saint manifests in his life the attributes and purpose of the calling, is underlined in the next phrase "and every work of faith". This is carried over from the preceding thought, so giving a wider concept than 1 Thess 1:3, for there must be growth. Paul, like James, does not regard faith as a passive quality, but as active. As the plant takes in every drop it receives and produces it in its life, so the believer, receiving every blessing, will and word of God, with the power inherent therein, should produce in a life of obedient service and testimony, the fragrance and power received. Such analogy settles the question commentators raise as to whether "with power" should be construed with "God fulfilling" or with "work of faith", for it is both. In fact the tenor of the whole verse is of the child of God reproducing "in the willing and the doing" what God is "working in" (Phil 2:13).

12   The foregoing definition of the prayer, as referring to God's working in the life of the believer now, has a distinctive bearing on the interpretation of this verse.

"So as" *(hopōs)* expresses the issue of his prayer, namely, that as a present thing and in consequence of the operation of God, "the name of our Lord Jesus Christ may be glorified in you". It is still their present position he urges upon them, looking back to the call of God, and on to its goal in glory, that they may, by the operative power of God within them (cf. Col 1:29), have a delight in goodness, and realise faith in action. This could not be so if they allowed the false teachers to delude them into an attitude of gloom and despondency. It is a prayer for the life of kingdom victory to be experienced now. The King is not yet reigning here, but they were to show in their lives by the power of God the future certainty of it, presenting to this world the earnest of the coming day by showing Him forth in a Spirit-filled life of love, joy, peace, longsuffering, gentleness, goodness, faith, meekness and temperance.

"The name" is used in the LXX to describe the character of Jehovah in its revelation to men. See this in Exod 34:6 and further in John 17:6. It denotes what the Person is in Himself. Commenting on this verse, Bloomfield, quoting Schott and Bengel, says, "It cannot but note the dignity and majesty of Jesus Christ, cf. Phil 2:9-10; Heb 1:4. That the word has such a sense in classical Greek writers is indisputable". A profane illustration lies in our practice of describing a product as having "a good name", not referring, of course, to its title but to its qualities. Hence here the saints are to manifest in their lives, by the outworking of divine grace and power, for there is no other way, just what "our Lord Jesus Christ" (lovely expression) is in Himself, so as "He may be glorified in you".

Not the least of their "pleasure in goodness" and "work of faith" would be, having rejected the hidden things of shame, not walking in deceit or craftiness, nor using guile or adulterating the Word of God, by manifestation of the truth commending themselves to every man's conscience before God, as epistles of Christ to let the gospel of the glory of Christ shine forth. For what better receptacle is there for the light of such glory than an earthenware vessel, broken in afflictions. See 2 Cor 3-5 which is a help in understanding this section. "Glorified" is the same word as in v.10; here it has the thought of Him receiving glory in salvation. It is the life of the saint glorifying "our Lord Jesus Christ". Notice how the apostle by the Holy Spirit continually uses such lovely expressions to instil into the Thessalonians the thought that affliction from such a source was unthinkable.

The very mention of "glory" excites Paul's spirit, for he who first met the Lord in His glory is truly the apostle of the glory of Christ. By the Spirit his thoughts race away from the present to be fixed upon the ultimate object of "the calling", as he writes "and ye in him"; that is "ye glorified in him". This expression demands careful and prayerful thought, for its interpretation has a decisive bearing upon the understanding, not only of the immediate words, but also of the verse which follows in ch.2. Most commentators refer it to John 17:22-23, some stating that when the Lord Jesus said "the glory which thou gavest me, I have given them", he was referring to the glory of union with Himself, as a present thing. Now whilst this matter of present union with the exalted Christ is certainly part of the subject of that glorious prayer, such is not the meaning of vv. 22-23. That the Lord has given to His own the specific glory which the Father had given Him, cannot be disputed, but the verses make it clear that its manifestation is not a present, but a future, thing. Notice the important little Greek word *hina*. It is "in order that the world may know that thou didst send me and didst love them as thou didst love me" (note the timeless aorists). It must be confessed that the world does not "know and keep on knowing" this blessed truth now, and shall not know until the future glorious manifestation of the Lord, and of the sons in glory, when He comes in power and great glory at the *apokalupsis* (see Rom 8:17; 1 John 3:1,2). Thus it is established that the glorifying of John 17:22-23 is yet future and beyond the time when "the world may believe" (John 17:21).

However, this leads to the consideration of what glory is spoken of in John

17:22-23. Palpably it is not the glory of John 17:5, for that is the glory of deity, but the glory that is to be seen in the manifestation. This is the glory of incorruptible, immortal, spiritual, celestial manhood (1 Cor 15:40-50) when we appear with bodies like unto His body of glory, that we might share eternal union with the Lord, where He is.

This raises a further vital question. When do we obtain this glory? Scripture leaves us in no doubt: it is at the Rapture, when we see Him and are made like Him, for we must have glory before we display it at the Appearing (*apokalupsis*). How beautifully John describes this in 1 John 3:1-2, "Behold, what manner of love the Father hath bestowed upon us, that we should be called the children of God; therefore, the world knoweth us not, because it knew him not. Beloved, now are we the children of God, and it doth not yet appear what we shall be: but we know that when he shall appear, we shall be like him; for we shall see him as he is". This is when "he shall change the body of our humiliation, that it may be fashioned like unto his body of glory" (Phil 3:21), when we shall be changed to "bear the image of the heavenly"(1 Cor 15). This is our being glorified in Him, and if anything is "according to the grace of God and the Lord Jesus Christ", it surely is this: the saints, morally and physically, like Christ. What glory!

Of course, the thoughts of John 17:22-23 and our chapter coalesce, in that all is with a view to the Lord's Appearing in power and great glory (v.10), and let it not be forgotten that this great event, the world seeing such display in order "to know", has His glory in view; we show forth His glory. Luke 9:26 makes this clear in an engaging way, for there He is seen coming in His own glory, and that of His Father and of the holy angels. The Church saints are not mentioned, because it is their function to reflect His glory ("glorified in his saints"), and it is He that is "to be admired"; blessedly we shall share in the display, but the glory essentially is His.

Thus it is seen that the saints being glorified in Him, whilst with a view to the Appearing (*apokalupsis*), refers to the Rapture (*parousia*). This, for a very good reason, is the thought in the verse, for the apostle is inspired to turn their eyes upon the future glorious prize, as he crowns the chapter with the ultimate object of their calling. He is now holding out to them the blessed hope which had grown dim, setting their hearts on the glory of the day of Christ (see Appendix) before he deals with the events of the day of the Lord (see Appendix). Let them rejoice that this former day refers to His grace to them in salvation, as indeed the word "glorified" (*endoxaēnai*) in v.10 indicates, whilst the latter refers to His judgment of the world (see Isa 66:5).

Thus their testimony in life now, and their hope of future glory, (the latter affecting the former, as 1 John 3:3) is to the end that His Name may be glorified in them now, by showing forth the things of Himself. Their being glorified in Him will be the ultimate aspect of their calling, when He comes and receives them to Himself at the Rapture, to be like Him and with Him for evermore. That the Rapture will come before the day of wrath and of His Appearing to the world is a truth they have already been taught; see 1 Thess 4:14-18 and compare with 5:4-9; 5:23.

The prayer and its granting could only be "according to the grace of our God and Lord Jesus Christ". There is but one article, and so it appears that one Person is indicated, although *kurios* (Lord) does occasionally appear without the article, yet in such a case it would be expected that "God the Father" would be mentioned. It is concluded that what is involved here is not the truth of the unity of the divine Persons, but, as in 2 Pet 1:1 (Greek) and other places, the Lord Jesus Christ as a divine Person; the aim and object of grace are in and through Him.

The calling, the fulfilling, the power and the glory mentioned are all of grace and apart from any cause or merit. We are entirely undeserving of the least of His benefits, bringing nothing but empty hands to receive.

Thus we see in this final section of the chapter that it is fundamental to the manifested glory of the Lord Jesus Christ in His Appearing (*apokalupsis*) that the saints be with Him in the display of His glory. Hence this last verse concerning the Rapture is poised between the mention of the manifestation of the saints with Him in glory (v.10) and the fulcrum of Paul's case, based upon the Rapture in 2:1, before He launches upon further details concerning the day of the Lord. The whole letter is centred upon the blessed truth in these two vital verses (1:12 and 2:1), that the Church must first be raptured to glory, before the awful day of the Lord's vengeance is ushered in.

III. Concerning the Day of the Lord (2:1-12)

1. *The Basis of Truth: The Fulcrum of the Epistle*
   2:1

   v.1   "Now we beseech you, brethren, by the coming of our Lord Jesus Christ, and (by) our gathering together unto Him,"

1   The section we now approach has been confused by mistranslation of the first verse, where men, no doubt with good intent, have introduced words which completely alter the sense of the original text, because they did not, or could not, distinguish the difference between the coming of the Lord for His saints (the Rapture) and His Appearing with His saints (the *apokalupsis*). It is necessary, therefore, to follow closely the wording of the Greek text in order to avoid error, and indeed to note the apostle's example of first establishing truth, before dealing with what is false.

The apostle, by the guidance of the Holy Spirit, has skilfully led the Thessalonian saints through the meaning of their suffering and its reward, and the path of earthly testimony, to the pinnacle hope of the Christian church, the Lord's coming for His saints, when He shall summon every believer to meet Him in the air, and as their eyes behold the object of their hearts' affection, to experience the longed-for change, when the bodies of their humiliation shall be fashioned like unto His body of glory. This is the moment of their being glorified in Him (1:12), the Rapture. The Thessalonians had been truly established in the matter of the Lord's coming; it was formerly their blessed hope; they had been noted for it, as the apostle had reminded them in 1 Thess 1:10. Indeed such had been their occupation with the thought, that they had become concerned lest their brethren who had died would miss out on the glory of it. To deal with this concern was the purpose of the first epistle. They knew that the Lord's coming at the Rapture was a source of comfort (1 Thess 4:18). They should have known also that the Appearing of the Lord in power and great glory was another event altogether, for apart from any oral teaching, Paul had written of it in 1 Thess 3:13, and they should have known from 1 Thess 5:9 that they were not to endure wrath. Evidently, since receipt of the first epistle, they had become confused as to the sequence of events by the Judaistic element among them campaigning, and that without scruple, to prove that the coming of the Lord was, as they could demonstrate from OT Scriptures, a day of darkness and judgment, a day to be feared. In their awful sufferings, and with the subtle propaganda of the false teachers, these young converts would be a ready prey, and they had become convinced that the fearful day of the Lord's wrath had already come. The present letter was to correct this false teaching, to re-establish them in their hope, dispelling the fear that gripped them.

We must not be too hard on these young converts for any doubt or confusion that had arisen consequent upon the dual impact of afflictions and false teaching, for what of our day, and the ignorance of these things, not least among those who write upon them with display of scholarship. It is necessary to remember the shortness of Paul's stay with the Thessalonians; they had a need to be perfected (1 Thess 3:10) as to some teaching. The epistle reminds them of what they had been taught orally and by letter, and gives further revelation of truth. Remembering that the epistle was not written in chapters, as we have it, and regarding this first verse of ch.2 as continuing the pinnacle thought of the last verse of ch.1, it will be seen that Paul is using the blessed certainty of the Rapture as the solid basis for removing their fears. He beseeches them by this event, for if their hearts could but grip the fact that their "gathering together unto him", their being taken to heaven, and thus being "for ever with the Lord" (1 Thess 4:17), meant they would be delivered from the coming wrath on earth, then all fear must vanish. Paul's purpose is to show that grace will operate before judgment, the Rapture before the "dreaded day". He does this by affectionate entreaty, beseeching them as brethren "by the coming of our Lord Jesus Christ and our gathering together (*episunagōgē*) unto him". Paul is, of course, referring to the event of 1 Thess 4:16, the Rapture. Every syllable breathes affection and assurance; could they fear aught from "our Lord Jesus"? The word *episunagōgē* is most touching and instructive. Twice only is it used in the NT and on each occasion it speaks of Christ as the centre of the gathering of saints; here, of the gathering to Him in the air at the Rapture, and in Heb 10:25, of our present privilege in gathering to His Name in the assembly, whilst we await that glorious event.

It is most regrettable that this lovely verse of assurance should have been marred by mistranslation in the AV in one point, and in the RV in another. It is felt necessary to deal with this matter as it has become the basis of false teaching. The AV repeats the word "by" in the verse; there is no basis whatsoever for this, and its insertion before "our gathering" should be disregarded. Not only is this second "by" not in the original text, but its insertion completely and falsely changes the true sense by making one event, the Rapture, appear as two

1.   "His coming", and
2.   "our gathering together unto him".

Such is completely contrary to NT teaching on this blessed subject, and is at variance with what the Thessalonian saints already knew (1 Thess 4:15-17). In this portion of the verse, where the AV has wrongly introduced a word, and so a wrong idea, the RV has got it right, by following the Greek text. What is unfortunate however, is that in the case of the first "by" where the AV is undoubtedly right, the RV has introduced a different word altogether, and with it an entirely wrong notion. Instead of retaining this first, and correct, "by" the RV has rendered it "touching", and in the margin suggests "on behalf of". Whilst it is accepted that *huper* has a wide scope, and that its meaning is dependent upon the context for its value, it must be patent that to render it as the RV does outrages both the text and good sense, for it would then appear that the apostle was, by tender and affectionate entreaty, beseeching these troubled saints on the very ground that caused their fears and anxieties. Such a suggestion is preposterous for it makes the dreaded day of the Lord the subject of the verse, by ignoring the clear wording that speaks of the Rapture. The conclusion cannot be escaped that such a rendering is consequent upon the doctrinal presupposition of the RV translators, that the Lord's coming to the air (1 Thess 4) and His coming to the earth (1 Thess 5) are all one event. Thus we have the confusion that the AV makes one event (the Rapture) appear as two, and the RV makes two events (the Rapture and the Appearing) to be but one. Such would have the effect of reducing the whole tone of Paul's effort, as "a nursing mother with her own children", to comfort and encourage; for it must be peculiar comfort to detract from the ministry which had formerly given them such blessed hope, and to create further confusion. The true purpose of the verse is clear, it is to remove anxiety about the dreaded "day of the Lord" by establishing the troubled saints upon the firm rock of the Rapture, and then later, to show that this, their blessed hope, must precede the day they feared.

It must be fitting here to counsel those who would dampen the hope of the Lord's people, by attempting to rob them of the glorious anticipation of His coming at any moment to Rapture the Church. We see the effects of false teaching upon this little flock in Thessalonica, and it can only be the same today. It is sobering to note that in the verse which follows, this involved fraudulent means, and experience has taught that where such things are propagated, there is invariably the accompanying evidence that "an enemy hath done this". We urge all to defer from such paths; it is wiser to seek prayerfully the basis of truth, than to toy with error. The perverse theories which deny the imminence of the Lord's return for His own, and substitute unfounded ideas of the Church having to endure the awful period of the Great Tribulation, never, no never, produced any Christian virtues. Contrast this with the joy, and noble effect upon the Christian walk, in the heart which breathes with anticipation and fervour, "It may be today".

If the matter of mistranslations, and the erroneous teaching associated with it, is carefully and sincerely considered, it will be apparent that it imposes upon the chapter the very fears Paul was seeking to dispel, and the confusion of the Thessalonian saints is thus perpetuated, instead of Paul's inspired correction.

2. The Methods of Error
2:2

> v.2   "That ye be not soon shaken in mind, or be troubled, neither by spirit, nor by word, nor by letter as from us, as that the day of Christ is at hand."

2   The AV misses the vital connecting words (eis to), which commence this verse, and joins it with the establishing and preserving thought of the Rapture in v.1; translate: "To the end that (eis to) ye be not soon shaken in mind". "Shaken" is *saleuthēnai*, to move from, in the sense of restlessness, as of the sea troubling a ship, even to the point of causing it to break from its mooring. "Soon" is better rendered as "quickly"; it indicates, "by a hasty or rash decision, without much thought", as 1 Tim 5:22. "In mind" refers to the controlling element of judgment, the understanding, and it is literally "from the (or your) mind", and the verb being in the aorist tense would give the whole phrase the sense of, "Do not let any sudden impact knock you off your mental balance and true assessment of this vital subject" (i.e. of the dreaded day); cf. Gal 1:6. In the next phrase "troubled" (throeō) is confused, excited, perturbed; it comes from a root "to cry out", as in an emotional outburst (see Matt 24:6). The previous verb, "shaken", being the aorist, pointed to a specific event, but "troubled" is the present infinitive denoting a continuous state; of course, the one may cause the other. It is thus speaking of mental and emotional disturbance, and it is interesting to see that in 1 Thess 5:8 where the apostle mentions the protecting helmet and breastplate, the former guards the head and the other the seat of the emotions.

"Neither by spirit" supposes a prophetic utterance. This could, by metonymy (the process of identifying the action with the person), refer to persons claiming to have the gift of spiritual utterance (see 1 Thess 5:20). It is necessary to "try the spirits" (1 John 4:1), and to regard that there is danger from "another spirit" (2 Cor 11:4). The purpose of the spiritual forces against us is to turn the believer from God.

"Or by word" (logos) either means by a word as allegedly issuing from Paul, or possibly, as *logos* allows, by process of mental deduction, reasoning, or logical inference. Mental processes are not only dangerous in matters of faith, they are often disastrous. We are not left to human devices, we have the Word of God, and even in this we are not to consider any passage in isolation, but as 2 Pet 1:20, to view all in the full context of Scripture as a whole. (Cf. 2:15 which supports the idea of the spoken word.) "Or by letter as through (*dia*) us" (plural) i.e. purporting to come from us, obviously refers to a forgery (see 3:17). Some relate the term "from us" to all three aspects, spirit, word and letter, and it is true that "word" and "letter" could bear this sense, but the following verse (cf. Col 2:4) would seem to preclude such a notion, as it refers to "any man, by any means". Whichever view is taken, the theme is clear, that even in apostolic times the Enemy was seeking by trickery and artful device, to divert the child of God from the sure and certain prospect of the Lord's personal return to the air to gather them to Himself. How important the blessed hope must be to warrant such action. We must always be on our guard against the subtle wiles of the devil, who will seek by any means to pervert truth and sow seeds of error.

There is no hesitation in condemning the rendering "as that the day of Christ is at hand" as contrary to all the oldest authorities, so states Alford. The correct reading is "the day of the Lord", and "is at hand" should read "is already come" (or "is now present"). The importance of these amendments to the AV, happily correct in the RV, will readily emerge when it is understood that whilst the day of Christ and the day of the Lord run parallel for almost the same period of time, the former concerns believers and heaven, the latter (contextually) speaks of unbelievers and earth. (See Appendix for the Day of Christ, and the Day of the Lord.) We are dealing then with the Day of the Lord, spoken of widely in the OT because it refers to men on the earth, whilst the term the Day of Christ, being about the Church, is a NT truth having no mention in the OT. It is now necessary to establish that the words in the text are that "the day of the Lord is already come", (or "is now present") and not as AV ("is at hand"). To deny the Day of the Lord as being at hand would contradict the whole tenor of Scripture from the prophecies of Isaiah and the cry of John Baptist, to the warning of 2 Pet 3:10. Hence the importance of establishing the correct translation. The verb concerned is *enistemi*, used in Rom 8:38; 1 Cor 3:22; 7:26; Gal 1:4; and Heb 9:9. In none of these is a future sense indicated, rather a reference to these Scriptures will show that present, as against future, things are in view in each case. Thus from the whole range of scriptural usage, and that from Paul (if we assume he wrote Hebrews), it can be confirmed that the closing words of v.2 do not refer to the imminence of the day of the Lord, but deny that the day of the Lord has already come (or is now present). It will be seen how this fits the context exactly, for the Thessalonian believers had been made fearful by false report that the sufferings which had befallen them were those of the awful day of the Lord. It was for this reason Paul was now writing, and why he had recalled for them in ch.1 the difference between the Lord's coming for His saints (v.12) and His coming with them (vv. 8-10).

Here Paul, like Peter (2 Pet 1:12), demonstrates the importance of repeating known truths, especially when the saints are under pressure. This is no less necessary today, when men, both evil and deluded, would still, as at Thessalonica, take Scripture to support false teaching. Now, they will point to such Scriptures as John 16, and particularly v.33, which speaks of the Christian norm as to suffering in this world, in order to unhinge the blessed hope of the child of God, and convince him or her that these passages indicate that the Church must pass through that awful period of God's wrath against sinful men on earth known as the Tribulation, even the Great Tribulation, passages that speak of no such event. Care must be taken to distinguish things that differ: "tribulation" and "the Tribulation" are by no means the same thing.

3. The Events Preceding the Day of the Lord
2:3-5

> v.3   "Let no man deceive you by any means; for that day shall not come, except there come a falling away first, and that man of sin be revealed, the son of perdition;
>
> v.4   Who opposeth and exalteth himself above all that is called God, or that is worshipped; so that he, as God, sitteth in the temple of God, shewing himself that he is God.
>
> v.5   Remember ye not, that, when I was yet with you, I told you these things?"

3   They were to let none deceive (or beguile) them, no way. Note the double negative for emphasis. The Lord Jesus made a comment in similar words on this general subject in Matt 24:4-6. Deceive (or beguile), as of Eve in 1 Tim 2:14, is often associated with Satan. "In any manner" extends the thought as to the methods used in v.2. Paul was ever aware of the prospect of deceitful workers (2 Cor 4:2) and of those "deceiving many" (2 Tim 3:13). 2 John 7 fittingly associates deceit with antichrist, according with v.10 below. "For that day shall not (have) come" has been correctly inserted in the AV to maintain the sense of the passage. "Except there come a falling away first" is literally "because unless the apostasy comes first". The majesty of this statement should be noted; all the events detailed here are the subject of God's timing.

The word "because" (hoti) has import in identifying the reason for Paul's declaration that "the day" was not, indeed could not, come upon them; there were events which must take place first. Note the article vitally before "apostasy", showing it was not only an event known by the Thessalonians, but that it was more than some person deserting the faith as in 1 Tim 4:1, more indeed than the partial apostasy of the Church age. It was that which Paul had told out when among them of the awful final act of defiance of man against God; the rebellion against every word, work, and notion of God. It was an event as marked, specific and unique as that other great event yet to come and bearing the article to distinguish it, the Tribulation. It figures an event without precedent of any kind.

In Greek, the word apostasy is used in the military sense for a soldier deserting from the army; in the political sphere, for rebellion against authority; in Scripture it speaks of abandoning, or turning away from, known truth concerning God, a total renunciation of truth. Such is the consummating act of "man's day" (1 Cor 4:3, Greek) which had its germ in the temptation in Eden, evidenced itself in Babel (where Nimrod is the great type of the antichrist) and expressed itself in "No God for me" (Ps 14:1) of which the course is plotted in Rom 1.

Some have stated that the Greek *prōton* ("first" or "firstly") indicates the first of two successive events, quoting Acts 1:1 as an instance. Whilst this is its general indication, it is not correct to assume from this as some have done, that "the apostasy" and "the revealing of the man of sin" are the two events indicated, for these are "the apostasy" and "the day of the Lord".

The apostle will now identify the ultimate and awful result of the abandonment of God, in the heading up of it in a single figure. Man must have an object of worship. Rom 1 makes that clear, for when he failed to worship God, he changed the glory of his Creator for an idol made like the creature, albeit in some sense associating God with the idol (Exod 32:5); such must have frightful immoral results. But some must go further; man expressed his "dislike for God" by "exchanging" the truth of God for "the lie" (Rom 1:25). God had been displaced in degree, sin deepened, yet still the heart of man must worship, and Satan filled the void, ever providing man with an alternative for his heart, until this time of ultimate declension when man reaches his final depth of shame, the fruit of his turning from God, and the goal of all idolatry, the emergence of the man of sin.

The term "the man of sin" is better rendered "man of lawlessness" for the word is *anomia*, the normal word for law, with the privative (to denote "absence of").

Who is this "man of lawlessness"? As the question is approached it is necessary to have regard to the many fanciful interpretations which have been forthcoming throughout Church history, particularly when saints have tended to do exactly as the Thessalonians did, and interpret prophecy in the light of their own experience of events. Such is fraught with danger; Scripture alone must be its own interpreter. Yet, even on this premise, godly scholars have differed, although it is generally agreed that the apostle affords in the following verses adequate data upon which this awful personage may be identified, even though the answer does not lie on the surface. It is widely accepted that the passage refers to the "beast" spoken of in the Revelation, yet such cannot be a complete answer for there are two beasts identified in the book, and it has to be conceded that the features of both largely fit the description in the chapter. This has caused some confusion, but there are distinctive factors which reasonably decide the issue. By comparing scripture with scripture it appears to be clear that the "man of lawlessness" is the second beast of Rev 13, the beast out of the earth. It is recognised that many regard the other beast as answering to this vile person, but whichever view is held, it must be in the consciousness that in matters of interpretation of prophecy none has peculiar right, hence there is no room for a partisan approach. As in all things in the Christian walk, grace and forbearance have their place here. (See Appendix on the man of lawlessness.)

This man of lawlessness, and let it be stated that he is a man, and not a system, is the incarnation of evil, even as Christ is of all that is holy, and good, and true. The title 'lawlessness" denotes his character. *Anomia* means without law altogether, and this comes out in Daniel's description of him as "wilful", indicating deliberate, arrogant perversity and self-will. Man at his nadir in waywardness, sin having no limit, the flesh without bounds, vileness like a raging torrent without banks, no restraint, man given up to his own devices, God totally abandoned, and Satan filling the vacuum with himself.

"Revealed" (*apokalupto*) is in the emphatic position in the phrase and, as of Christ in 1:7, it indicates a sudden manifestation of one hitherto hidden; the term having all the sense of the action of superhuman power. As God's Son will be revealed, so Satan will reveal his vile counterpart (see v.9). "The son of perdition" (*apoleia*) is used of Judas Iscariot in John 17:12; "son" is an Hebraism denoting character and destiny, here of perdition (perishing); he will be characterised by activity which marks him out as fitted for destruction (see v.8).

The question has been raised as to whether the "man of lawlessness" is in fact "the apostasy". Whilst the answer is in the negative, for each bears the article, it is necessary to regard the event and the person as very closely inter-related. Apostasy has been evident since early Church times (1 John 2:18), even as it was in Israel, but at the end time it will accelerate, reaching its awful peak after the Church has gone home to glory. The utter vileness of this God-rejecting state will then so ripen (if such a word can be used in these dreadful circumstances) as to require the emergence of the man who personifies it. So "the apostasy" is the event itself, the "man of lawlessness" the end which its instigator, Satan, had in view in pursuit of his aim to dethrone God and to have himself worshipped universally (Isa 14:12-15). The spirit of antichrist denies the Father and the Son in any age, but at this time it will reach such a pitch as to be centred in a person who does this by edict. Then on the one hand Israel will deny Jehovah God and His Messiah, on the other the harlot church denies the Christ and the Father He revealed. Thus will the way be open for the Beast to make his claim to be God, and for Jew and Gentile unitedly to acclaim one false christ.

4   This is surely the darkest description of man in the whole of Scripture; man under the power of Satan, acting defiantly against God. In his personal efforts at exaltation he claims place over every religious observance, even to affect to supplant God Himself. How contrary is this one, who arrogantly comes "in his own name", to Him who came in His Father's Name, who humbled Himself, only to be highly exalted by God (Phil 2). Yet, consistent with the principles of God's righteous judgment, this proud, ambitious man will be brought low (Rev 19:20), to depths commensurate with his vile pretence and sin. In "who opposeth and exalteth himself", the literal rendering of the participle gives a stronger sense of the character of the man of lawlessness, namely, "the opposer (withstander, or adversary) who greatly exalts himself". All the defiance, arrogance and wilful pride of this opposer of God come out in this short description. "Opposeth (or opposer)" from *antikeimai*, to be set against, is used in Luke 13:17 of the adversaries of the Lord Jesus; in Gal 5:17 and 1 Tim 1:10 it is given as "contrary to". It figures the Beast in his role as the Antichrist, meaning, "set over against Christ". "Exalteth" (*huperairō*) as 2 Cor 12:7, "exalted above measure", and Phil 2:9, "highly exalted", is defined by Bloomfield, in respect of the man of sin, as "the very extreme of pride", whilst Alford points to the note of hostility in the word, which note, concerning the idea of opposition, is echoed by Darby.

He claims precedence "over everything being called God" (so it is literally), that is, above every sense of deity, true or false, for he openly vaunts himself in opposition to all such (Dan 11:37). Awful thought! "Or object of worship" (*sebasma*, given as "devotions" in Acts 17:23) widens his claims to honour above all else that claims the heart of man, and certainly applies to every form of religion. Whilst in "so that he himself (as God) sitteth down in the inner shrine of the temple of God, showing himself that he is God" there is no authority for the words "as God", shown in brackets, the sense is not weakened by their inclusion. "Temple", in the AV, is *naos*, the inner shrine, the place defiled in time past by heathen idols, and once profaned by another son of perdition with thirty pieces of silver, the price of his vile treachery. The very words must bring a sense of the awful dark and dreadful reality of this scene, for this is the rejection of Calvary, ratified in the heart of man.

There is no case for considering the *naos* as figurative of the Church. Not only has the Church been caught up as a pre-requisite of this event, but the whole background of the emergence of the Beast is the joining together of apostate Jew and Gentile, and what more fitting place for Christendom to have the end product of its association with obsolescent Judaistic practices than in the temple at Jerusalem. The path we see being trodden today must lead there.

"Showing himself that he is God" does not mean that he is Jehovah, but that Jehovah is not God, for He has been dismissed in the apostasy. The point is, that here in Jerusalem where God had placed His Name, a man, a Jew, declares that he, and not Jehovah, is God. Note the absence of the article before "God", which implies this. "Showing", present active participle of *apodeiknumi* (and related to "himself"), marks it as a settled state and not an isolated demonstration. It is generally accepted that this term is used for the installation of a dignitary into office, or for the ceremonial proclamation of a king upon his accession; it has the underlying tone of "as by right", and indeed it is translated "approved" (and that by declaration) in Acts 2:22. A cognate word appears as "prove" in Acts 25:7. However, its main use refers to proclamation or demonstration as in 1 Cor 2:4. See also 1 Cor 4:9 ("spectacle"). The idea of "proclamation" is strong in this verse, and note the incidence of "speak" in the related passages, Dan 11 and Rev 13.

5 Literally, "do ye not remember that when I was with you, I used to tell you these things"; some grammarians take it in the sense of "I kept on telling you these things". This verse is of considerable importance in the understanding of

1. the charge made against Paul at Thessalonica consequent upon inaccurate reports of what he had said (Acts 17:7), i.e. that he had "spoken of another king, one Jesus" and
2. the true meaning of the next verse upon which scholars have wrangled as to the correct sense of the very small word "now".

Most commentators detect a note of gentle impatience or rebuke in this verse, and this would be understandable (even for a nursing mother with her own children), for if this teaching had been grasped, then the current difficulty which prompted the epistle would not have arisen. However it would appear that the real cause of the apostle's comment in this style is that he has now come to the summum bonum of the case he has been developing to counter the anxieties of the Thessalonians. One thing is clearly demonstrated — the depth of teaching which Paul imparted to such young converts in the short time he was with them. A comment might be made here as to the charge by some critics, of the "relative obscurity" of some of the comments in this portion of the letter. Whilst this can largely be answered by the fact that a letter to the family does not necessitate long and detailed references to well-known family matters, there is another point worthy of notice. The epistle was to be conveyed by hand, and then read publicly, circulated and preserved (for us); this would endanger the persons involved if discovered and misinterpreted, (even as Paul's oral message was in Acts 17:7). Consequently, it is submitted that some reserve in comment is understandable. Having said this however, it must be balanced with the statement that such difficulties as expressed by some are those of "the wise and prudent", and it has pleased God to reveal them unto babes, both then and now (Matt 11:25; 1 Cor 1).

To be profitable, ministry should be of such a nature as can be remembered, and again we say, there is an importance about repeating truths already communicated; cf. 2 Pet 1:12-15.

4. *The Restraining Factors*
2:6-7

> v.6   "And now ye know what withholdeth, that he might be revealed in his time.
> v.7   For the mystery of iniquity doth already work; only he who now letteth will let, until he be taken out of the way."

6 There has been much controversy as to the meaning of these two verses, but there are two outstanding factors, which, if borne in mind, help in seeking to establish the true interpretation. The first concerns the matter of the restraining or hindering forces in each verse, for whilst in v.6 the word is translated "withholdeth", and in v.7 "let", in the original they are both the same word. There is, however, a vital difference; in the former verse *katechon* is neuter gender, but in the latter *katechōn* is masculine gender. Thus in v.6 it speaks of something restraining or hindering (from a root "to hold back", see the relative use of the word in Luke 4:42) and in v.7 of a person, a restrainer or hinderer. The second factor refers to the interpretation, for whatever restrained (or held back) the emergence of the man of lawlessness, and the full force of the mystery of lawlessness at the time Paul was writing, must also have restrained in the interim, is restraining now, and shall do so until removal. These matters are fundamental, and upon them much speculation founders.

The word "now" (*nun*) right at the beginning of the verse has caused some difficulty in interpretation. The question arises as to whether it refers to time, or to logical sequence. Some, contrasting the word with "in his time", interpret it as "you know what at the present time" etc, but such can hardly be maintained by the general context in the light of the criteria mentioned above. This point is often used to argue the case that the restraining element was the Roman imperial power. Now whilst it is patently true that Paul himself experienced the restraining hand of Rome against the rabble (Acts 18:12; 21:32; 22:25; 23:17), it could hardly be maintained that in consequence the Thessalonians would regard the Roman power as restraining the revelation of the man of lawlessness. Yet some would say that the "knowledge" as to the restraining power of Rome went beyond the immediate to the ultimate application, in the revival of Roman imperial power in the manifestation of the first Beast of Rev 13. Well, in view of the close alliance, even interdependency, of the two Beasts, surely if the first (imperial Rome) was to hold back the activities, and even the advent, of the second (Rome's religious ally) this would constitute a house divided against itself. Furthermore, if Rome was the restraining influence in Paul's time, and is to be such again in the future, what is restraining now? What too of the awful history of Rome in early Church times?

Another suggestion which has received wide support is that the restraint is "the powers that be", because they are ordained of God (Rom 13:1-7). Now it may well be that God uses such powers, but in view of comments under v.7 it is suggested that this would not constitute these power as other than instrumental, and not the restraint as such. Even so such powers have not always acted to the end indicated, and have often promoted evil, and in respect of man's responsibility to God, have facilitated lawlessness.

Yet another suggestion is that law itself is the restraining element. This however would seem to give lawlessness the sense of being against law as such, but its true meaning is that of no law at all. Lawlessness is the operation of self-will, and the very principle of divine law demonstrates the reaction of the human heart against restraint. If the verse is taken as a logical continuation of the previous statement ("When I was yet with you, I told you these things"), and "now" (nun) is accepted* as "well" or "well now", or "now then", the flow is easy, and the reference to all the information which had already been given, logical. This information would include not only the oral teaching, but also the content of Paul's previous epistle, and even the earlier portion of this one insofar as it emphasised what was already known. They must know (oida) by these things what was preventing the revealing of the man of lawlessness. It was simply that, as Paul had been emphasising, they were still here. The Lord had obviously not come to take them; the fulcrum of it all was "the coming of our Lord Jesus, and our gathering together unto him". This event stood in the way of the resumption of prophetic things as to the earth; such could not happen whilst the saints were still here. They must first be raptured, caught up to heaven. Thus the restraining element was, and still is, the body of believers on earth. The term "Church" has been deliberately avoided in this explanation, for not only is it the case that the Scriptures do not speak of the Church on earth, but by use of the word some have provided occasion to those who oppose this view, for "Church" is feminine (ekklesia) whilst the word for the restraint in this verse is neuter.

It is to underestimate the power in the Church, to suggest as some do, that it could not hold back the devil's plans, for not only shall the gates of hell not prevail against it, but it is joined to Him who has "all power", and the indwelling Holy Spirit determines its strength (1 John 4:4). The Church has a function, as salt, to hold back the advance of corruption and to stem the march of unrighteousness, and it is no argument to speak of salt losing its savour, any more than to point to the often flickering light of testimony in a dark world. This is the "season" of the Church, and whilst she is here God will not permit the man of lawlessness to have "his season" (see below).

"To the end that" (eis to) indicates ultimate purpose, the purpose for the restraint. It is that "he (the man of lawlessness) might be revealed in his time", or more correctly "in his own (autou) season". Contrary to the statement of some commentators, there is adequate authority for rendering autou in this way. Kairos (season) draws attention to the characteristics of the time, not the moment; see 1 Tim 6:15 and cf. Acts 1:7. As there was an exact season for Christ to appear, so also is there for Satan's false christ. He is but a man; God will determine his permitted season.

7   We now come to the matter of the "restrainer" or "hinderer", as distinct from the "restraint" or "hindrance" of v.6. "For" introduces the explanation of the latter part of the previous verse "that he might be revealed in his season". Although the two aspects of hindering are distinctive as to what each hinders, there is the vital connection that both must be withdrawn before the man of lawlessness be revealed (see beginning of v.8).

In the mystery of "lawlessness" the word is anomia, as in v.6. It is unfortunate

---

*This use of nun appears often in Scripture, and that it is so used here is, strangely, supported from unusual scholastic quarters, as well as by Alford, Bloomfield, Bengel and Moffat.

that the AV, by introducing another word ("iniquity") in the translation, obscures the continuation of the thought of lawlessness. (See also as to "Wicked" in v.8). A mystery in Scripture is clearly explained in Rom 16:25 as that which has been kept secret and is now made known only by revelation. Examples are: the union of Christ and the Church (Eph 5:32); the mystery of godliness (1 Tim 3:16); the mystery of the faith (1 Tim 3:9); the change at the Rapture (1 Cor 15:51). Here it is the mystery, the hidden working, of lawlessness, made known by God through His servant Paul; later its purpose and instigator are unveiled (vv.8-10). It is sobering to observe that even so early as the apostle's days, this hidden working of the scheme of lawlessness was operating. The mystery, its covert working, is set against the fulness of it in the final revelation of the man of lawlessness. What is this hidden working? The parable of the leaven in Matt 13:33 shows the secret and ongoing operation of evil in the sphere of profession, with a view to the corrupting of the whole, and the apostle Paul had spoken of such insidious activity in Acts 20:28-30 ("of your own selves shall men arise speaking perverse things, to draw away disciples after themselves"). This beginning of the activities of leaven shows features which are identical to that which is so apparent in its full flood, the actions of the man of lawlessness. He is typified by wilful desire for self-exaltation, and this is what we see in the perverse activities of the false teachers in Acts 20; they desired place and followers. It came in at Ephesus by stealth, developed as we see in Nicolaitanism in Rev 2:6 and widened into a doctrine in Rev 2:15. Such is the spirit of a Diotrephes in 3 John, the aim of the gnostics at Colosse, and of the seducing element of which Paul warns Timothy, "having a form of godliness, but denying the power thereof". It is man exalted in the sphere of religion, be it in Christendom generally or in the cults of the east. One aim is involved, (the trickery, deceit, human reasonings, signs, wonders are but a means to an end) the exaltation of a man. Yet even this is a falsehood; the real aim is to achieve universal worship of Satan himself, for Satan is behind it all, and for his own ends. Man is but the deceived tool in the aspiration which arose in the heart of Satan before time began, "I will be like the Most High". This is the mystery now revealed in all its naked vileness.

Under the sovereign hand of God, the gathering flood and tempo are held back, hindered, (or in the old English rendering "let", meaning to prevent) not as in v.6 by the thing restraining, but here by a person. This personage not only hindered when the letter was written, but has continued to do so, and will so continue, "until he be taken out of the way", or perhaps more accurately, "until he become out of the way". There are some objections to this translation of *heōs ek mesou genētai*, mainly on the grounds that *genētai* cannot be construed as "to be taken", but as William Kelly points out, in a case well supported by such scholars as Alford and Bloomfield, the opposition is ill-founded. Although Kelly gives ample evidence of the correctness of the translation, it being in line with Greek usage, we are not left to the grammar alone for interpretation, for we have the testimony of NT usage, where *ek mesou* with its various verbs, invariably involves "removal out of the way" (or midst) e.g. Col 2:14, *ērken ek tou mesou,* where *erkēn*, the perfect indicative of *airō* (to bear or lift up) is associated with *ek tou mesou* to give the sense (as AV) "took it out of the way". Yet weightier still we have the contextual sense of the phrase. The use of "now" (*arti*) better rendered as "just now", would indicate that there was an interim impediment which could be removed, and "until" (*heōs*) makes the possibility a future certainty. That there was someone in the way who would be taken out of the way, is palpably the point. Before the matter of the grammar is left, it might also be well to point out that the little word "only" (*monon*) is used here to arrest attention; see its use in Gal 2:10; 6:12.

Who then is this restraining person? None other than the Holy Spirit of God. The revealing of the man of lawlessness is hindered by the continued presence on earth of believers of the Church period, and the secret working of lawlessness is held back by the presence on earth, and in the believer, of the Holy Spirit; both must be taken out of the way before the man of lawlessness is revealed. The event which will effect this is the Rapture, for then the saints of the Church age will be taken to glory, and the Holy Spirit, the purpose for which He came completed, will be withdrawn, to operate among men as He did in OT times. It is not a little significant that whilst we see the Holy Spirit as prominent in the churches in Rev 2 and 3, once we read of the figure of the Rapture in Rev 4 (a door opened in heaven) there is little further mention of Him in the book until the end.

When the restraint (v.6) and the Restrainer (v.7) have gone from earth, lawlessness will no longer be a secret thing operating under divine restraint, but the floodgates of evil will be released to display the heart of man given up by God to his own devices, and he who is Satan's choice will be revealed in his awful role.

It is recognised that many other restraining forces have been postulated over the years to explain verses 6 and 7, but almost all fall by the criteria mentioned earlier. No other two forces fulfil the requirements stated. What we have is God, in His own power, operating in His own dear children, until His own chosen time.

5. *The Workings of Satan*
2:8-10

v.8   "And then shall that Wicked be revealed, whom the Lord shall consume with the spirit of his mouth, and shall destroy with the brightness of his coming:

v.9   Even him, whose coming is after the working of Satan with all power and signs and lying wonders,

v.10   And with all deceiveableness of unrighteousness in them that perish; because they received not the love of the truth, that they might be saved."

8 "And then" denotes an emphatic point in time, and is in relationship to "now" (*arti*, just now) in v.7 and not to the "now" of v.6. It would seem to

indicate that immediately the hindrance and the Hinderer are taken out of the way, the revealing of "the Wicked" will take place. It is a matter for wonder how each of these future events is in the calendar of God's timing; God is sovereign. "Wicked" is a further example of how the AV has confused the original wording of the section by not adhering to the word "lawless", for here the related word *anomos* is involved, and correctly the title should be "the lawless one" referring, of course, to the man of lawlessness. It is of interest that this is the only occasion in the NT where the word appears in the singular *(anomos)*, indicating that this man, in himself, is the embodiment of lawlessness. The hidden thing is now revealed in a man. The repetition of the word "revealed" would seem to emphasise the powerful, supernatural activity involved in this awful event.

The swift transition from the revealing of this person to his utter destruction is a matter to be noted, for it is a reminder of the basic purpose of Paul's letter. He is not dealing with a prophetic account of the vile history of this man: indeed mention of him is somewhat incidental to the case; the aim is to encourage the saints by showing them the purposes of God against which no power could prevail. Victory was their assured portion. In demonstrating that the Rapture (by which he had lovingly entreated them, 2:1) was their "day", he sought to rekindle their blessed hope, that amidst all their suffering, they might be seized with the certainty that the "day of the Lord" could not come whilst they remained here. Not only so, but when, after their departure to be for ever with the Lord, that dreaded day did come upon men, it held no terror for them. Much the contrary. Awful consequences indeed there would be for their persecutors, but for them not only rest from persecution, but vindication, public vindication, and indescribable glory.

All this rested upon the Thessalonians grasping clearly that the day of the Lord, the subject of many prophecies (as the Jewish false teachers would not be slow to point out), was quite distinct as to time and purpose from the Rapture *(parousia)* which was not the subject of prophecy but of revelation. The Rapture, and indeed the Church, have no place in OT writings. The Rapture would take them out of this world scene, delivered from "the coming wrath" (1 Thess 1:10) but that wrath would most certainly fall upon the earth even before these dear saints returned with the Lord at His Appearing in power and great glory (2 Thess 1:10). How gladdening then to their poor hearts, to read of the majestic power of the Lord when He so appears to deal with the one who embodied every evil force against them, "whom the Lord Jesus will slay with the spirit of his mouth" (so the original runs). The whole passage is pregnant with the idea of the unhurried majesty of divine control and infinite power; indeed what is man against "our God"?

The word "consume" is *analōsei*, and "slay" which has been given above, is *anelei*; the reading is uncertain. "Slay" has the best support from reliable editors, although Dan 7:26 gives "consume", and that is the stronger expression. "By the spirit (or breath) of his mouth" is a quotation from Isa 11:4; see also Isa 30:33 and Ps 33:6.

The words display the ease with which the Lord Jesus deals with the one who vaunted himself so. The expression illustrates the decisive utterance of the Judge out of the glory and power of His holy indignation. It is not the same thought as the sword proceeding out of His mouth in Rev 19:15, which is characteristic of Him as the Mighty Warrior. Rather would it speak of His power in executing swift judgment.

There is some doubt about the textual authority for including "Jesus", but not only do most scholars favour its inclusion, but its force is most appropriate. God's Man, "come of a woman, come under the law", and fulfilling its every word, the One who came in His Father's Name, humbling Himself in obedient service at the Father's will, and distaining every offer of power from Satan, with the spirit of His mouth, with consummate ease, deals with him who vainly sought to counterfeit Him.

"Destroy" (*katargeō*) is better translated to render useless or inoperative, to make inactive or ineffective; cf. Rom 3:3; 4:14; 1 Cor 1:28; Gal 3:17; Eph 2:15. It would seem to speak not only of this vile man being brought to nought, but also of everything associated with him. "With the brightness of his coming", the *epiphaneia* of His *parousia*, the outshining of His presence, is an instance of *parousia* being used in connection with other than the Rapture, for, of course, this is the Lord's Appearing in power and great glory. *Epiphaneia* is shining forth, and is used of the appearing of a monarch, of a god, of a military force, and of the Lord; see 1 Tim 6:14; 2 Tim 1:10; 2 Tim 4:1,8; Titus 2:13. It indicates the splendour of the display in His coming, although the use of the word always seems to bear the idea of the suddenness of the event. When used with *parousia*, as here, it speaks of the glorious manifestation of His presence, and the use of these two words, each used elsewhere for His coming, is to contrast the event with the Rapture. The Rapture is unseen by the world, but when He comes in judgment it will be manifest. "Epiphany", says Bloomfield, "is used both in Scripture and classical writings, to express divine majesty", and Bengel presses the weighty thought that the word indicates the "first dawn" of His appearing, the point just before His actual presence on earth, cognate with the first light of dawn showing the day has appeared although it would be regarded as still coming. This thought intensifies the solemn majesty of the event described, for even the first process of His appearing destroys the lawless one.

9   Having established the saints in the security of their position in these matters, and described the ease with which the man of lawlessness will be dealt with, Paul now continues with detail about him. "Even him" is supplied in the AV for connection; it is not in the text. "Whose" refers to the "whom" of v.8 and so to the lawless one; "coming" (*parousia*) is the presence rather than the process of arrival. How terrible is the thought in the use of this word, as also of "revealed", in respect of the man of lawlessness, for it shows that Satan will bring in "his man" in mimicry of the coming of Christ. This would mark the event as being in the

matter of evil and unrighteousness what the Lord's coming is in the holy purposes of God. "Is", here, does not indicate an event which has already been effected, as the context above shows, rather is it a statement of the moral principle which applies in this prophecy. As Alford points out, it is not a matter of the apostle projecting his thoughts on the prophetical time when the event will occur, but of the essential attribute involved, the working of Satanic power. "The working" (*energeia*, from which we derive our word energy) is used in Scripture for power in action, and particularly for divine power; see Eph 1:19-20; 3:7; 4:16; Phil 3:21; Col 1:21. Here the working is "of Satan". Thus the idea is that the "presence" of this man is that which might be expected of the operation of Satan's power. The following expression "with (*en*, in or by) all (every kind of) power and signs and wonders of a lie" (*pseudos*, lie or falsehood) describes the nature of his working. Although "power" is singular and "signs" and "wonders" plural, there is no reason grammatically why "lie" (or falsehood) should not be construed as being at the root of all three, but it is better to consider the power as Satan's, being real, and deceit as referring to signs and wonders.

Thus it is revealed that Satan is not only behind this lawless one, but is the source of all his power to deceive. It is noticeable that he employs means which are designated in Heb 2:4 as of Christ and in Rom 15:19 as of the disciples. In Acts 2:22 miracles, wonders and signs are mentioned in connection with God's approval of Christ. See also Matt 24:24 where the Lord Jesus designates these things as applying to false christs. "Power" (*dunamis*) would indicate the superhuman source, "signs" the meaning involved in their display, and "wonders" the resultant effect on the admiring beholder, convincing him that he had witnessed the unexplainable.

Satan is a mimic, he seeks to counterfeit the counsels of God, for as a liar, he cannot introduce truth: hence he seeks to copy it, corrupting it in lies. God's purposes are in a man, albeit in an unique Man, hence Satan seeks to do the same. In his desire to displace God and have himself worshipped universally he operates through a man, the man of lawlessness, the Antichrist, the second Beast of Rev 13. There is no better sphere in which to operate than corrupt religion in which the mystery of lawlessness has now come to its full.

10 The thought of verses 8 and 9 is continued; "with all deceit of unrighteousness" is the better translation. Every kind of deceit, having its source in, and therefore taking its character from, unrighteousness (i.e. from the deceiver who has sought to captivate men with falsehood even from the Garden of Eden), all the craftiness, subtlety and clever trickery of the arch-deceiver, is employed without scruple. Although the expression "all deceit of unrighteousness" is totally extensive, it is peculiarly suggestive of the activities of the second Beast in Rev 13:14-18 with reference to the speaking, breathing image, and the mark 666. The keynote of all these activities is, as always in the working of Satan, falsehood and deceit. Note how these fraudulent Satanic devices operate "in (or for) the ones perishing", present continuous tense as 1 Cor 1:18-20 (which see); they are already on the set course to perdition, "because they received not the love of the truth", the past tense pointing to the time of His Appearing, "that they might be saved" (cf. 1 Cor 16:22). To appreciate the awful meaning of this full statement, the "ones perishing" as a class, must be seen as the object of the working of Satan (v.9) and the lawless one as the instrument of this. The perishing ones are not poor dupes, for they have made a deliberate choice to reject truth (with a view to salvation). Contrast this with 1 Thess 2:13, for the sense is that they did not receive the truth in the way that a host would welcome a desired guest; for this is the force of *dechomai* (to receive kindly, graciously, approvingly, to choose to have such). They "received gladly" something else; they made another choice, and that willingly and finally, yielding to the pretences of the seducer. They are apostates like the one perishing (en route to perdition) with them, rejectors of the truth; theirs is the sentence of John 8:44. Truth came, was offered to them, and they rejected it, desiring to do the lusts of their father the devil. Such are those of Matt 13:15 where "converted", or as the RV "turn again", is indicative of their having turned from known truth. They refused truth, even Truth personified, they received with welcome, the lie personified. Rejecting light, they preferred darkness; refusing God they chose Satan; spurning Christ, they bow to Antichrist. These are of them "which know not God, and obey not the gospel" (1:8) and as such will be the objects of divine "full vengeance". Attitude to truth declares what we are, and so determines our ultimate classification, as saved or lost. We cannot love both truth and falsehood, and because truth often wounds, disciplines, humbles, the flesh inclines to that which is the easier path, but such is the way menaced by the fall-trap of the devil.

The word "because" (*anth' hōn*), meaning "in return for which action", is instructive, for it points not only to the reason for their state, but, by scriptural ysage, to the matter of due recompense. See a cognate use of the term in Acts 12:23, where God smote Herod because (*anth' hōn*) he gave not the glory to God. As we sow, so we reap.

"Love of the truth" is an unique term in the NT, and marks the difference between full acceptance of the gospel and mere assent. Those "perishing" did neither.

6. *The Results Currently and Ultimately*
2:11-12

> v.11   "And for this cause God shall send them strong delusion, that they should believe a lie:
> v.12   That all might be dammed who believe not the truth, but had pleasure in unrighteousness."

11   The apostle now proceeds with the narrative as to the recompense of those willingly deceived. "And for this cause" (or reason), i.e. because they did not receive the love of the truth unto salvation, because they refused God, refused

Christ, ignored the cross, were deaf to the gospel of God's grace, and, like the nation of Israel, would not have "this man", but chose, welcomed, preferred another, "God sendeth them" (note again the present tense with "perishing") "a working (same word as v.9) of error". The verb, though present tense, does not indicate a current action, but, like "is" in v.9 speaks of a moral consequence which God operates, as a principle, at all times. It is not a case of God permitting, but of acting morally in view of their refusal of grace. "Them" refers to the "ones perishing", and it is important to see that this is their ultimate classification. They have refused the love of the truth, and it is in consequence of this that God acts. "God sending" is determined by their "not receiving" (John 12:36-50 is a solemn comment on this). God does not delude them into a state, but acts because of their state, giving them as their portion what they preferred, allowing them to delight in it for a season. This divine principle is seen in the history of Israel; it is the theme of Romans 1. Sin itself brings of itself its own judgment, and its ultimate in death. God is not mocked; it is sin that is the mocker of sinners. This is not the final judicial act of God, but is with a view to it; as sinners they are "condemned already", but there is yet judgment according to works (Rev 20:12). Thus God imposes upon them the moral consequence of their state, with a view to that awful final condemnation.

The AV misses the point in speaking of "strong delusion", for as Alford states, the original is not in such a passive sense, but speaks of the active cause, "the working (same root as v.9) of delusion" (or error). The position of man is that sin has separated him from God; he is at enmity with God, under judgment, condemned to a lost eternity. Only grace, grace from the loving heart of God, grace and love expressed in the sacrificial death of God's beloved Son, can bridge the gulf that man in his awful state might be reconciled to God, and not only reconciled, but justified and, totally beyond our wit to comprehend, glorified, declared to be sons, accepted in the Beloved. This "the perishing ones" refused. This is more than presuming on God's grace; it is the active refusing of it, and preference for something else. In this set condition, man brings upon himself the ultimate judicial consequences of his chosen course of action, sealing him in the result of his own devices. He refuses light and chooses darkness; darkness he shall have. He hardens his heart; hardened it shall be. He refuses love of the truth; he shall receive the lying spirit and embrace the ultimate lie of idolatry and worship the man of lawlessness. He spurned eternal life; he shall have eternal death.

The apostate, the one wilfully turning from God, has no way back; his doom has been sealed, first by himself, and then, as a consequence by God. Thought too awful to contemplate, but the sin of man, and moreover, the righteousness of God demand it. God's holiness cannot be outraged with impunity, nor His love and grace presumed upon, much less outrightly rejected, without the piercing sentence which follows.

"Unto the believing", for so it is literally, gives the sense of believing unto such a result, "the lie" (note the article). The lie here is not just falsehood in its generic sense, but, as in the cognate passage in Rom 1:25, it speaks of idolatry. Here, however, it is in the ultimate sense of the idol to which all idolatry pointed, man having totally rejected God (note the declension in Rom 1 from "change" in v.23 to "exchange" in v.25 Greek) worshipping man as God. It is not unreasonable to see in the expression "the lie" the thought of antichrist being the embodiment of it, in contrast with the Lord Jesus as "the Truth".

Such is the awful meaning of "for this cause" in v.10. These men, in their set class as the perishing ones, in receiving not (as a welcome guest) the love of truth, are given judicially the result of the working of their own error, to the end that they believe the supreme lie; they refused God's Christ, they are given to receive the devil's antichrist.

Note "the working", "operation" or "energies" of lawlessness (v.7), of Satan (v.8), of God (v.11). All are from the same word *energeia*, power in action; cf. "working of truth" in 1 Thess 2:13.

12 Correctly, "in order that" (*hina*) indicates the moral consequence, "they might be judged" (*krinō*, from the same root as judgment in v.5). The result would be the same as the word used in the AV, "damned"; these who were the perishing in life, must be judged in death. It is solemn to see in this action of God how He makes the very working of Satan (vv. 9,10) to bear its own awful fruit in judgment. Satan's working in men causes them to go on headlong to the ultimate of their sin, as is seen in the case of Judas Iscariot.

In "who believed not the truth", the structure Paul uses is an unusual one for him; it is not *eis* with the accusative, indicating "to put faith in", but the negative followed by the dative. This gives a sense much stronger than a mere "not trusting", and indictes a refusal to accept the truth in its entirety. They positively rejected the truth of God. Yet there was even more, for they "had pleasure in unrighteousness". In 1 Thess 2:8 the verb is translated "we were willing"; it might even be given in a stronger sense, "we were well pleased" or "delighted". Once again we have a word used singularly in this passage, for elsewhere "pleasure" is always used in a good sense; here alone of unrighteousness (cf. 2 Tim 3:4). These "perishing ones" not only positively refused truth of God, as true, but as a deliberate choice, delighted in unrighteousness. Compare with Rom 1:28-32, and contrast with 1 Cor 13:6. Scripture sets truth against unrighteousness; see Rom 2:8; 1 Cor 13:6; Titus 3:3-5. We might regard in this antithesis the dependency of righteous behaviour upon reception of the truth, there being no neutral ground.

These men, apostates, turning their backs upon light, delight in the realms of darkness; righteousness derided, they find their pleasure in all that is opposed to God; having actively, and willingly rejected God, they enjoy the fellowship of the devil. This is their willing state, the choice of those classified, and that finally, as "the perishing", and this state not the result of the action of God against them, but the cause of it. The heart of man revealed man apart from the truth, but under the judicial beam of it.

IV. Thanksgiving and Encouragement (2:13-17)

1. *Election and Calling*
   ### 2:13-14

> v.13   "But we are bound to give thanks alway to God for you, brethren
>   beloved of the Lord, because God hath from the beginning chosen
>   you to salvation through sanctification of the Spirit and belief of the
>   truth:
> v.14   Whereunto he called you by our gospel, to the obtaining of the glory
>   of our Lord Jesus Christ."

13   With these solemn thoughts upon his heart, how happily must the apostle have turned to this final section of the chapter, which involves a complete contrast with what has gone before, and deals now with believers in respect of their responsibilities and privileges. Notice the contrast between "the elect", who obtain His glory, and "the perishing" (v.10), who are blotted out from the presence of it: between those who believe the truth, and those who receive not the love of the truth; between the final end of both classes. Mark too the operation of the Holy Spirit, and the operation of Satan.

"But" is in contrast with the foregoing verses, "we are bound" (*opheilō*) as 1:3, is well expressed by our Anglo-Saxon word "ought", meaning to owe a debt. The debt was "to give thanks always" (some would translate *pantote* as "perpetually"), the account, "concerning (*peri*) you, brethren beloved of the Lord", cf. 1 Thess 1:4. Here the apostle expresses his indebtedness to God for His grace in the Thessalonian saints; their position was all of God, never let them forget that. They were the chosen of God; could God fail His own? Notice the mention of God, the Lord, and the Holy Spirit in the verse. "Lord" refers to the Lord Jesus as it does invariably in the two epistles. This points to the basis of their security: His sacrifice had made them His own; they were loved with an eternal love by Himself. The day of the Lord was His day; had they, as His own, beloved of Himself, anything to fear when He came to deal with those that know not God, and those who obey not His gospel? "Because" reveals the reason for the debt Paul owed, "God chose you". "Chose", here is *heilato* (from *haireomai*, "to choose") and in the only three instances this word is used in the NT the thought is of personal choice (see Phil 1:22; Heb 11:25). It is in the aorist, but though the choosing was at a point it was outside of time, for it was "from the beginning", and in the widest sense of that past of eternity. It is also in the middle indicative, God making the choice for Himself, indicating the purpose of the choice and not the realm of selection. The usual words for election are: *exaireomai* (as of the choice of Israel in the OT), *proörizō* (predestinated, marked out beforehand), and *eklegomai* (to choose, as in 1 Thess 1:4; Eph 1:4; Luke 10:42; Acts 6:5).

It is not the intention to launch out on an excursion into the blessed subject of election, for it is not an area for our poor minds to tangle in, rather is it a truth to be believed. However, the apostle gives the true balance of the subject in these two epistles, for whilst in 1 Thess 2:13 he "thanks God unceasingly that they received the word" (man's responsibility), here he gives thanks to God for His sovereign choice.

The choice was "from the beginning" (*ap'archēs*), a term which Paul does not use elsewhere but which like John 1:1 (*en archē*), and 2 Tim 1:9 takes us back into the era "from everlasting"; see also Matt 19:4; 1 John 2:13. It is obviously wrong to limit God's sovereign choice to any point in time, or to attribute it to any merit in the object of His love; cf. Eph 1:4; Rev 13:8; 17:8. The alternative reading, "firstfruit" (*aparchēn*), though supported by a few is hardly consistent with the immediate or general context, for as Kelly asks, "Of what could the Thessalonians be firstfruit; not even of Macedonia, the Philippians being earlier". Furthermore, the verse is expressive of a general principle of God's operation, not one specific to this early assembly. This is emphasised in the purpose of the choice, for it was "unto (*eis*) salvation", see 1 Thess 1:4,5; this is God's goal for those He chose in His sovereignty.

There is a difference to be noted between the first and second epistles as to the purpose of salvation; in the former it is "from" (wrath), and in the latter "unto" (glory). Nevertheless there are some who would still regard salvation here as limited to salvation from wrath in the day of the Lord, as in 1 Thess 1:10; 5:9, and such assurance would have been enough for the troubled Thessalonians. However, the immediate context goes further, setting salvation against "perishing" (v.10) and "judgment" (v.12), the awful state of men in their ultimate classification as lost. Here we have salvation purposed from the beginning (i.e. from everlasting) and in v.14 Paul will speak first of it being effected in time by the call, then of its future consummation in "obtainment of the glory of our Lord Jesus Christ". Thus we have salvation in its full scope, past, present and future; conceived in the heart of God before time, the call in time, and its future unspeakable glory.

The operation of God's choice being effected in time is "in (or, by) sanctification of (the) Spirit (subjective genitive, and therefore, wrought by the Spirit) and belief of (the) truth". The absence of the article suggests the moral force of truth and not truth as such, and being an objective genitive indicates "belief, or faith, in truth". In no sense can "*en*" here, in respect of sanctification, be translated by "through" (as the AV) nor by "unto" or "to" as some suggest. Despite the absence of the article before "Spirit", as in Rom 8:9; 1 Cor 2:4 and 1 Pet 1:2 (where in each case it is evident that the Holy Spirit is intended), the words here speak clearly of the present work of the Holy Spirit in setting apart for God the objects of His love, bringing to them the word of truth for their belief and continuance in the faith. This is the divine side of the work of salvation just as the belief of truth, its reception by faith, looks in the ultimate to the human side. It is positional not practical sanctification, although the practical results must always be envisaged (1 Thess 4:3; 4:7). It is the energy of the Holy Spirit in bringing the grace of God to men, dead in trespasses and sins (see 1 Thess 1:5) and is the essential preliminary to faith in the truth.

The relative verse in 1 Pet 1:2 (see also 1 Cor 6:11) helps in the understanding of this, and particularly shows that the operation of the Holy Spirit is the divine initiative in setting the individual apart for God, by which that person receives the gospel. Well did Luther say, "I cannot by my own reason or strength believe in Jesus Christ, or come to Him"; the Spirit must first set apart for God, awaken those initial faint desires after God, convict of sin, lead to Christ, bring faith to the heart. Being under the influences of the world, the flesh and the devil, the natural man needs as an essential pre-requisite in new birth, this action of the Holy Spirit; without it there would be no salvation. Although the "belief (or faith) in (or of) truth" (no article) is, in the ultimate, man's side of salvation, the Holy Spirit must first introduce to the heart the moral attitude to will it so, that they may be made free by truth (John 8:32). Note the contrast in v.12.

14   The continuation of the process of the Holy Spirit in salvation is now explained. With a view to the initial work being effectuated, God calls by the gospel: "unto which (salvation) He (God) called". In the same way as "chose", this is in the aorist tense but here indicating a point in time. It is interesting to notice that this reference is to a single action in contrast with the present tense of "calling" in 1 Thess 2:12; 5:24, indicating, as indeed the word implies, a call to which there has been a response. This is the effective call, not as we have in Matt 20:16; 22:14, the general call of the gospel.

Paul writes, "by our gospel", for whilst it is essentially "the gospel of God . . . concerning his Son, Jesus Christ", God in His grace uses men and not angels to proclaim it. It was deposited with Paul as a sacred trust, and he, and indeed his fellow-workers, were identified with it not only as to its proclamation, but also as evidence of its effect. It was theirs as the message they preached and which the Thessalonians had heard from them and received, but moreover they shared in its power. The gospel is not merely a theme, but God's power to save. Paul proclaimed that in which he stood as the chief beneficiary (1 Tim 1:11-16; 2 Tim 1:6-14) and he preached Christ as he had experienced Him, a Man in resurrection glory.

Compare "unto the obtainment of (the) glory of our Lord Jesus Christ" with 1 Thess 2:12. There is no article before "glory" in the Greek text, and this points to the gospel call being with a view to the obtaining of such glory as is essentially the possession of Christ. Some, including Bengel, give to *peripoiēsis* ("obtainment") the sense of possession or preservation, as in Eph 1:14, but the weight of support is for "obtainment". This makes the verse parallel to 1 Thess 5:9 where the subject is the obtaining of salvation. The glory referred to is obviously the glory of Christ as the last Adam, the One God has glorified (Acts 3:13) in view of what He achieved at the cross to the glory of God. In the gospel He is set forth as a Man in the glory, and it is in view of His glory as Man, that glory for men can be announced. Again we refer to John 17:22-23, and identify our being glorified in Him (1:12) as the glory spoken of here, the display of which is so beautifully recorded in Romans 8:18-30, where the words are so closely parallel to this verse.

Of course, there is a present glory (the inshining of the gospel of the glory) whereby we see the rich knowledge of the glory of God in that blessed Man, and are given anticipation of a far more exceeding weight of glory eternal, not yet seen but true to faith; but we judge that the thought in the verse is of what is future, indicated by the preposition *eis* (unto). This includes the further aspect of the future glory to be obtained in our Lord Jesus Christ beyond being eternally like Him, of being eternally with Him where He is (John 14:3). Like Rom 5:2 ("the glory of God") this is the glory of heaven itself, the Father's house. Here we shall witness even greater glories, glories which we cannot share, the wonder of the display of John 17:24 (the showing forth to His own of all His glory).

These aspects of the future sharing of the display of excellency of the Lord Jesus Christ are the glorious consummation of the gospel call, for which we were set apart by the Holy Spirit, in accordance with the eternal counsels of God in Christ. Of such unspeakable glory the believer's present graces of union and communion with Him are the earnest.

2. *Stand Fast: Hold On*
   ### 2:15

> v.15   "Therefore, brethren, stand fast, and hold the traditions which ye have been taught, whether by word, or our epistle."

15   The apostle now enjoins them to stand fast in God's work, and to hold on to God's Word: "so then (referring back to verses 13 and 14) brethren, stand fast". The word *stēkete* means only to stand, but being in the imperative, stand fast gives a good sense of the meaning, as also in 1 Thess 3:8. Thus the apostle is commenting upon what he has just written above concerning the glory of their position present and future, secure in the Lord Jesus Christ, the elect of God and the object of God's counsels from the beginning. As a consequence they can look upon the worst that men can do in the light of such divine certainty. In v.2 Paul had used the opposite expression "be not quickly shaken", but in view of what he had revealed, perhaps repeated, they should now stand fast, for "if God be for us, who can be against us". No need to fear "that day" nor that wrath was to be their portion; theirs was the future glory of, and with, Christ; fear could be banished, they could "continue to stand, and withal to stand". They stood upon the impregnable rock of God's eternal purposes in the Lord Jesus Christ.

In "hold the traditions", "hold" is the present imperative of *krateō*, and speaks of maintaining a firm grip on, by the exertion of full strength; see the use of the word in Mark 1:31; 9:10; Col 2:19; Heb 4:14; 6:18; Rev 2:13; 2:25 all of which are instructive as to its meaning. "Traditions" is *paradosis*; although this word is more often used in a bad sense in the NT, in respect of the thoughts of men being passed on from one generation to another, either orally or in writing, when the apostle uses it of traditions in respect of the faith the sense is quite different. It envisages that the thing being conveyed issues not merely from an authority to be accepted, but from God Himself. See 1 Thess 2:13: "Ye received it not as the word of men, but as it is in truth, the word of God". See also 1 Cor 11:23 (where "received" and "delivered" are related to the thought here); 14:37; 15:3. The contrast of the traditions of men with those from the divine source is seen by comparing Gal 1:12 with Gal 1:14. See also Matt 15:2; Mark 7:8; Col 2:6-8 in respect of the traditions of men. God Himself is the source of that which the apostles passed on, and though the church is the custodian, she is in no way empowered to supplement or supplant what God has given; nor is she the interpreter of its meaning: such is the work of the Holy Spirit. We see the wisdom of the mind of the Spirit, in that, even before the apostolic period has ended, the vital truths were established in written form. This is illustrated in 2 Pet 1:1-12, where the apostle states his determination that what he had passed on orally should be recorded in writing as a permanent remembrance of the truth imparted, and which was even then "present with them". Peter knew his end to be near, hence he left not the oral word (with all the dangers in its passing from one to another in a time of grievous wolves) but was diligent to record it as Scripture for our learning and obedience.

"Our" refers to both the oral and the written word of the apostle, for the literal rendering is "either through speech or through letter of us", the conjunction "either" joining the two, not separating them. As the oral traditions passed in favour of the written Word of God, as we have it today, there emerged in the full canon of Scripture the mind of God for His people, and there is no other authority for our obedience in the faith "once for all delivered to the saints". See also 3:6. It is significant that no later writings have value in this respect, for all either duplicate or deny what God has said through His chosen servants in His Word. From God, through these chosen vessels, we have instruction for His people of the Church age; there are no oral traditions today. Ministry does not bring to us what God says, it can only bring what God's Word says God says.

For "word" and "epistle" see 2:2. There is no doubt that "word" (*logos*) here is the spoken word, as may well be the case in 2:2.

3. *Grace and Comfort*
2:16-17

> v.16   "Now our Lord Jesus Christ himself, and God, even our Father, which hath loved us, and hath given us everlasting consolation and good hope through grace,
>
> v.17   Comfort your hearts, and stablish you in every good word and work."

16   The thanksgiving of vv. 13-15 is now followed by intercession; cf. 1 Thess 3:11. But Paul first speaks of what the believer has already received from the Son and the Father.

"But" (de), not "now" as the AV, speaks of contrast or condition. The thought behind this is consequent upon the feelings the Thessalonians may have as to their frailty in respect of keeping the "traditions" mentioned in v.15, and indeed because of their inadequate appreciation as to the source of such traditions. They may well be limited in their view that such was "of Paul", hence the apostle now lifts their thoughts beyond their own ability to stand and hold fast, above any lowly comprehension that the origin of "our word or epistle" was in himself, to the unfailing care and steadfast assurance in the Lord Jesus Christ and God the Father. Again he does so with the touching note of affection and security enshrined in that reassuring word "our" (of us).

Each of the divine Persons in "our Lord Jesus Christ and God our Father", is indicated by the article (although a few MSS omit the first) thus their equality is demonstrated, but it will be noticed that here the Son is mentioned first. This would seem to be because the Lord Jesus has been the main subject of the preceding verses, contra the antichrist. It cannot be accepted that it is because it was the Lord Jesus who brought to His own the knowledge of God as Father, else this form would be used regularly, and this is not so (e.g. 1 Thess 3:11). See also Gal 1:1. "Himself" has the position of emphasis in the verse as in 1 Thess 3:11; 5:23 (Greek), possibly in contrast with "our" of v.15, as something of a concession to their state and knowledge (as mentioned above) and in order to lift them to the highest plane of assurance.

The participle, "the one having loved us", is in the singular, and some have questioned whether it refers to the Father only, as the immediate antecedent, or to the Father and Son in total unity. Alford argues for the former, stating that it refers to a single act, the love of the Father in sending the Son, although he does concede the possibility of it referring to the love of Father and Son in accomplished redemption. Others point to the singular verbs in v.17 to establish the statement as indicating absolute unity, but it must be borne in mind that Paul never uses a plural verb when speaking of Persons of the Godhead together. Thus it is better to conclude that the reference is to the inter-related actions of Father and Son based upon the mystery of divine unity of function: the Father's counsels of grace, the Son's executive actions to accomplish those counsels. "Which hath loved us" and "hath given us" are both aorists, thus, "the One having loved us and having given us". Here, in establishing the Thessalonian saints in the things that God (Father and Son) has wrought in them, he takes them back to the first principles of the gospel of grace, exactly as we have it in John 3:16 (God loving and God giving). How this must have arrested their hearts in acknowledging the essential goodness of God in His attitude towards them, even when they were idolators. The verse is set in the same sense as Rom 5:10: if God did these things when we were yet enemies, what will such love dispense now we are His own children?

"Everlasting (consolation)" would be better as "eternal (consolation)" as what is in view is not its duration, but its quality, its unshakeableness in time or eternity. "Consolation" is *paraklesis*, a calling to the side, containing the thought of comfort and given as such in v.17. It suggests the whispered encouragement of a fellow, exhorting, "quieting the mind when troubled by anxious fears as to salvation, or when tempted to let go confidence in God under affliction or persecutions" (so Bloomfield). It is the consolation arising from a well-founded hope of eternal life and salvation, from the God of all comfort (2 Cor 1:3).

If "comfort" is for our present condition, then "good hope" is the certainty we have of future and eternal blessing; cf. Titus 2:13, "Looking for that blessed hope", and 1 Thess 1:10, "to wait for his Son from heaven". See also 1 Pet 1:3, "lively hope". Paul reminds them of the hope they had been given, and which (1 Thess 1:3) they once enjoyed. The adjective "good" refers to the quality and result.

It is not correct to limit the expression "by (or in) grace" to "good hope", it belongs to the verb "gave" (having given). The glory of the blessed things the divine Persons have given is that they are by grace, and grace alone. Election, and the gifts which are associated with it, are not upon the ground of any merit but out of grace, and without any cause save the love of God. Because the believer's total position is dependent upon grace alone, it is all of God, and whilst on the one hand it can never be earned, on the other it can never, no never, be taken from him. Yet there must be the heart's receiving of it in every circumstance; this is by the firm grasp of faith in the Father, our Father, and the Son, our Lord Jesus Christ. All is revealed to, and secured by, faith, but betimes, like Peter, saints are prone to look at the waves, instead of the eye being firmly fixed upon Him. Hence the lovely concession to such weakness in the prayer for strengthening which follows.

17 "(May He) comfort" is the verbal form of *paraklēsis,* which is translated "consolation" in v.16. The word is sometimes given as "strengthen" or "encourage" (JND). Here it is in the singular, conforming to the unity of the divine Persons in the previous verse. Furthermore the verb is in the optative mood, denoting a strong wish or desire, which is expressed in prayer. This is a request for present encouragement (or comfort) in the afflictions mentioned in 1:4. Paul could so pray with conviction because he had sought to give such encouragement himself. See 1 Thess 2:11; 4:18; 5:11. It is interesting that the word *paraklēsis* is used in Scripture with reference to God (2 Cor 1:3), to Christ (Phil 2:1) and to the Holy Spirit (John 14:16; Acts 9:31). "Confirm" (*stērizō,* to establish) is used in 1 Thess 3:2; 3:13. In Exod 17:13 (LXX) it appears as "supported, stayed up"; in Luke 9:51 as "steadfastly set" (His face), in Luke 16:26 as "fixed" (great gulf); in Rev 3:2 as "strengthen". It can be contrasted with "shaken" in 2 Thess 2:2.

Paul adds "in every good work and word" (JND) (*logos*). "Word" speaks of the ministry they had received from the apostle, and which they should now pass on to others, but what they in turn preached must be backed up by a life consistent with what they said, for "work" is the testimony of actions before men. Paul will illustrate this in the very practical teaching of ch.3. This matter of the relationship between the oral presentation of truth and the practical outliving of it, is particularly apposite in the matter of prophecy; there is no greater stimulus to holy living than a sincere anticipation of the Lord's return. See this in the culminating verse which follows the apostle's great discourse on the subject in 1 Cor 15:58 and exemplified by the Lord in the parable of Matt 24:48 ("My Lord delayeth His coming"). The scriptural principle is action before words, and this in fact is borne out by the text, for the order of the words should be as given above and not as in the AV; see JND. This matter of practice before precept is beautifully borne out in the record of the life of the Lord: Luke 24:19, deed and word; Acts 1:1, do and teach. See also Phil 2:15: seen as lights, holding forth the word. There are some who prefer to translate *logos* as "doctrine", although where it is so translated in the AV (Heb 6:1), it is an idea derived from the context and not the literal sense. The use of *logos* in the following verse (3:1) would support the usual sense. Hence the prayer is that, based upon the experience of God's past goodness by grace (v.16) and out of His present comforting and strengthening, these dear saints, in their full testimony (what they do, as read of all men, and what they say), may bear a good confession with a sense of conviction like the Psalmist who could say, "My heart is fixed, ... my heart is fixed (Ps 57:7)". The steadfast testimony of saints under trial has spoken to opposing hearts over the centuries, as Paul himself no doubt often recalled, when he remembered how Stephen was faithful and unmoveable, even unto death.

V. The Lord's Faithfulness (3:1-5)

1. *Paul's Need*
   3:1-2

   v.1   "Finally, brethren, pray for us, that the word of the Lord may have free
           course, and be glorified, even as it is with you:
   v.2   And that we may be delivered from unreasonable and wicked men; for
           all men have not faith."

1   From the outpouring of his own heart on behalf of the Thessalonian saints, with the strong individual note of "every one of you", Paul now turns to ask for their prayers for himself and his companions. Even in this they would have the encouragement of one who could express sincere sympathy with them, for Paul also was troubled by wicked men. Here the spiritual giant, a man used of God possibly above all others, shows the true, unfeigned marks of meekness by asking the petitions of even the weakest among the saints. This is true greatness indeed, a man walking in the power of God, yet deeply conscious of personal inadequacy, dependent upon the prevailing power of prayer. The preciousness of it must have touched the hearts of his own dear children, and emboldened them in the realisation of the effectiveness of prayer. His gracious entreaty, in which he addresses them all as brethren, even though some must be rebuked as to their walk, is most instructive, for it shows the necessity of marking the essential

difference between what the saints do, and whose they are. Despite every action, even in the need for discipline, they must in heart remain as brethren.

"Finally", literally "for the rest", is not always used to preface Paul's closing thoughts (e.g. 1 Cor 1:16; 4:2; 7:29; Phil 3:1) but here, as in 1 Thess 4:1, it is so used after the main points of encouragement and strengthening have been expressed. Any note of admonition is introduced gently and in kindly fashion, with further expressions of affection, for such is the scriptural pattern where saints are under affliction.

"Brethren, keep on praying for us" has the verb in the present tense. It was the apostle's practice to seek the prayers of the saints (1 Thess 5:17,25). If any man had grounds for confidence as being a chosen vessel it was Paul, but it was the keynote of his life to have no confidence in the flesh; pray without ceasing was the call of one who did just that. See his request in Rom 15:30-32: "Strive together with me in (your) prayers . . .that I may be delivered from them that do not believe in Judaea, and that my service (ministry) which I have for Jerusalem may be accepted of the saints"; 2 Cor 1:11: "Helping together by prayer"; Phil 1:19: "Shall turn to my salvation through your prayer, and the supply of the Spirit of Jesus Christ"; Eph 6:18,19: "Praying for me that utterance may be given .... to make known the . . . gospel"; Col 4:3: "Praying also for us that God would open unto us a door of utterance"; Philem 22: "I trust that through your prayers I shall be given unto you". Some of these petitions are even from prison. Note how Paul's requests for prayer are not for self, but for service. His deep sense of need, which all heralds of the gospel should share, was because he was always aware of the root of the opposition; see 1 Thess 2:18: "Satan hindered us".

One of the healthiest spiritual activities is praying for others, and especially for those in the forefront of the battle, for it is the acknowledgement not only of absolute dependence, but, in affection, of our interdependency. Such exercise ennobles, purifies, strengthens. If one is moved to pray for the Lord's servants, it is a good thing to tell them; how we are encouraged that the righteous pray for us. Prayer is also an excellent antidote to bad feeling against others; if we are disturbed at the relationship, it is good to pray fervently for the one who is causing the distress. Intercession does things for the intercessor also; to be concerned for others is to be elevated above thoughts of one's own lot.

It is noteworthy that in 1 Corinthians, where moral evil was to be judged, and in Galatians, where doctrinal error was involved, there is no request for prayer. Whilst this is also true of 2 Corinthians there is mention of prayer for Paul in 1:11.

In the clause "in order that (hina) the word of the Lord may run and be glorified", the present tenses, as earlier, give the sense of continuous action, "keep on running" and "go on being glorified". The connection of these two verbs is attributed to the parlance of the games, as Rom 9:16; 1 Cor 9:24. The "word of the Lord" is that which He "delivered", which is preached in His power, to His glory, unto salvation. *Trechō* is the normal word for "run", as in Gal 2:2; 5:7; Heb 12:1; see Ps 148:15 (LXX); cf. Acts 12:24 (another metaphor).

Expositors are agreed that the sense is of determination and success, indicating the apostle's ever-present consciousness of the urgency of proclaiming the gospel; no servant was more aware of the call to harvest. Paul envisages the Word of the Lord under the figure of a strong and determined athlete running over a free and unobstructed course, making rapid progress towards the mark. From this we can see conversely, and soberingly that the Word, which is not bound (2 Tim 2:9), can be baulked or hindered by human agencies; see on v.2. The Word is "glorified" or "crowned" (with a crown of glory, the crown of salvation) when it has run unhindered to its perfect result in being received by faith, even as it was with the Thessalonian saints, hence "as indeed with you" (literally). The "crowning" is its effect on the receiver. For the Word to have its end result in the glory of salvation is no less important than its free course in the spread of the gospel; the glory of the one is the race, of the other the prize. See 1 Thess 1:5-10; Acts 13:48-49 (where the word "glorified" is less strong).

It is significant that in these related Scriptures, the thought seems to be that the Word having been received is then passed on; the race is a relay race. As we, by grace, have received the relay baton (of the gospel message) is it being "glorified" in running further, or is it discredited (Titus 2:10)? the message is as attractive as our lives.

Paul's heart longed to see the results in Thessalonica (Acts 17:4; 1 Thess 1:9-10) repeated in Corinth from whence he was writing. Things were initially difficult at Corinth (Acts 18:6) and the later reception of the gospel there may well have been a testimony to the prayers of the Thessalonians here requested; cf. Acts 18:6, 9-10.

2 "And" (so continuing the subject of the prayer) "in order that (hina) we may be delivered (rhuomai, to rescue)" changes from the earlier present tense to the aorist of effective conclusion. This does not mean that Paul is now asking that they shall be kept for their own sakes, but to use the metaphor of v.1, that they as runners in the race (identified with the Word itself) may not be hindered in pressing to the mark. As in Rom 15:30-31, his personal preservation always has his service in view. It must be noted that this request for prayer was almost certainly in the light of God's assurance of Paul being kept from harm in Acts 18:9-10, judging as we do from the context that this was well before the events of Acts 18:12 onwards. Both God's promise and the prayers resulted in the desired deliverance. God's faithfulness does not discharge His people from responsibility; indeed it is the more precious to pray in accord with the known purposes of God.

"Unreasonable" (atopos, better translated as out of place, or odd, perverse, truculent) here alone in the NT refers to persons, as opposed to its normal reference to things; "wicked" (poneros) originally meant men who do not like working, but later evil, bad, vile, mischievous (some would say in the active sense); it is a common word in the NT. The idea of being unreasonable or out of place, is however quite strong, and points to the irrationality of the opposition.

One has said "such men are morally insane". This would remind us that we cannot "reason" the gospel with such opposition, or seek to persuade by logical argument; the love of God to men cannot be explained. In the light of such a task only the power of God avails, and it is most noteworthy that in this the apostle does not seek to state how the Lord should do His work of delivering from such men. Both classes have the article, hence it is "the unreasonable and the evil men": the former have their behaviour marked by the adjective, and the latter their character. The use of the articles, especially with the aorist, points to a definite occurrence, and the events of Acts 18:6 (and the ensuing action from v.12 onwards) appeal as the immediate case in mind. The whole record of Acts 16-18 together with the reference in 1 Thess 2:14-16 support the notion that these men were the Jews. "For not all men have the faith", so the next clause runs, literally. Some have expressed doubt as to whether *pistis*, as abstract with the article, indicates the faith, the body of Christian truth; "faith" as belief or trust; or even "faithfulness". The latter may be discounted concerning men, the fact being obvious. As to the remaining alternatives, although some commentators say there is but little difference in the two, it is hard to accept that Paul was stating the obvious fact that all do not have the Christian faith. Thus we take "faith" (as belief or trust) to be the meaning; it is also consistent with the immediate context (v.3) and the play on *pistis* and *pistos*. See a similar idea in Rom 3:3. The simple sense would then be that faith, as such, was not the characteristic of all men, hence, by the typical Hebrew mode of marking emphasis by understatement, "only few have faith"; cf. Rom 10:16. Accepted in this sense, the term is marking the difficulty in the way of the "running of the gospel"; it is an obstacle race.

Bengel makes the interesting point that the readiness with which the Thessalonians received the word gladly might have led them to assume that all men would be equally ready to accept it, so Paul is illustrating that such is not the case. One thing is certain, men in the main do not receive the love of the truth (2:10) as did the Thessalonians (1 Thess 1:6). There were few in whom the Word was glorified (reached its perfect end) but many the opponents of the gospel, hence adversaries of its heralds.

2. *Paul's Resource*
3:3

> v.3   "But the Lord is faithful, who shall stablish you, and keep you from evil."

3 The relationship of the two expressions is marked in the literal translation, "For not of all men the faith, faithful yet is the Lord"; cf. 2 Tim 2:13. Lest he should discourage by pointing too strongly to the formidable opposition, Paul turns the thought to the mighty fortress of his own unfailing, unchanging, sure resource. No matter the state of the restless sea of humanity, be it the muted ebb and flow of indifference, or the violent swell of fierce opposition, the Lord controls the waves, and he is faithful in every circumstance. He is as faithful as when he called (1 Cor 1:9); being faithful, He will not allow unbearable temptation, but will ensure we can endure (1 Cor 10:13); being faithful, He will preserve (1 Thess 5:23-24), for He is always faithful (2 Tim 2:13); being faithful, He is as good as His promise (Heb 10:23). Why, His very name is Faithful (Rev 19:11).

"Who shall stablish you" is the same word as in 2:17 (*stērizō*, to confirm, strengthen, support) and shows Paul had confidence that God would answer that prayer. Notice how, in typical fashion, the apostle has switched from a passing consideration of his own need to theirs, and that within the infectious confidence of his own experience of the Lord's faithfulness.

From the positive aspect, he now turns to the negative: "and guard" (*phulassō*, a word the Lord uses for guarding His little flock in John 17:12) "(you) from the evil" (or the evil one). "Evil" (*tou ponērou*) could be either neuter or masculine, and this has thrown consideration open to;

1.   the evil men of v.2
2.   the evil one, Satan, as in Eph 6:16, as behind all evil (see 1 Thess 2:18)
3.   evil generally, as in Rom 12:9.

As so frequently in such cases of doubt, it is suggested that it refers to evil of any kind and from any source, for the Shepherd does not guard selectively, and His capability is as great as His care; in His hands, we are safe from every foe, whether they be the agencies, or the evil one himself. See a similar thought in 2 Tim 4:18 and cf. "deliver us from evil" in the prayer of Matt 6:13.

3.   *Paul's Confidence*
   3:4

> v.4   "And we have confidence in the Lord touching you, that ye both do and will do the things which we command you."

4   Paul continues, "And we are in a state (or condition) of trust (such is the sense of the perfect intransitive of *peithō*) in (*en*, in the sphere of) the Lord towards (*epi*, with the accusative) you". It is generally accepted that *epi* with the accusative indicates the thought of movement towards, and of proximity, e.g. Luke 6:35, "He is kind (in moving) towards those who are unthankful". The

basis of the trust or confidence is essentially in the Lord (a similar thought to Gal 5:10 and Philem 20,21), because of His faithfulness; there can be no confidence in the flesh, in man apart from God. If Paul's confidence as to them was in the Lord, that is where theirs as to self must be. All the good worked into the believer is of Him; cf. Phil 2:13; Eph 2:10; and see 2 Cor 3:5. We might have expected the apostle to go on "concerning (or touching) ourselves", as the logical sequence to what has gone before, but his shepherd heart turns to the troubled flock, and he says, "concerning (or as better rendered, towards) you".

In the clause "that what things we command ye both do, and will do", note the exclusion of "you", which the AV inserts after "command". Although this is generally regarded as an interpolation, v.6 suggests it. What God works in must be worked out; there is the side of responsibility. Grace and responsibility are concomitant. "Command" is *parangellō*, to charge, or call upon to do. Here, from a request for prayer, and after an expression of confidence based on the Lord's faithfulness working in them for which he had earlier (in both epistles) given thanks, Paul now turns their carefully-prepared minds to his entitlement to command; his apostolic authority. This is not harshly introduced, for he relates his confidence for the future to their faithful behaviour in the past: "Ye are already doing (present tense) and will continue to do" (future tense). William Kelly, thinking back to 1:7 and the future promised rest from affliction at the Appearing, relates that to grace, and sees in the command the side of government producing present rest for the soul. The apostle's command was indeed a command of the Lord, and by simple-hearted subjection and confidence in Him, the believer may day by day find rest to his soul.

The question arises as to what these commands are. As to the past, it was those things laid upon them whilst Paul was present with them (1 Thess 4:2) as well as the instructions contained in the first epistle: see 1 Thess 4:11; as to the future, the connection is taken up again in v.6, but first the apostle will give the basis of their own faithful response to the faithfulness of the Lord.

4. *Paul's Prayer*
   ### 3:5

> v.5   "And the Lord direct your hearts into the love of God, and into the patient waiting for Christ."

5   The verse opens with a prayerful wish for, like 2:17, the verb "direct" is in the optative, expressing a desire as to the future. "But" (better than "and" and with the sense of "not only, but also") "may the Lord direct your hearts". "Direct" is *kateuthunō*, to make a straight, smooth, and direct way, by removing all impediments; it is used in 1 Thess 3:11. Here it expresses the desire that the Lord might remove anything which would interfere with their hearts' affections being centred "into the love of (the) God, and into the patience of (the) Christ" (not as the AV, "waiting for Christ", for which there is no textual basis). There has been much controversy as to whether the love is God's love for the saints, or the saints' love for God. We hold that the meaning of *agapē* is subjective love (i.e. having the lover in view) and here, therefore, that it is God's love for His own, which is indeed Paul's normal usage. It could be no other, for the wish is that they should be directed into it. Kelly says it is that we may know the reality of divine love experientially, (John 17:23,26; 1 John 4:16,17). Such love generates response in us (1 John 4:19), a thought so adequately expressed by the poet:

> "I love Thee, Lord, yet 'tis no love of mine
> That goeth forth to that great heart of Thine.
> 'Tis Thine own love which Thou hast given me
> Returning back, O loving Lord to Thee.
> Oh! help me Lord, to take by grace divine,
> Yet more and more of that great love of Thine:
> That day by day my heart may give to Thee
> A deeper love, and growing constantly."

We take the same view (the subjective genitive) of "the patience of (the) Christ". Patience is *hupomonē*, and it does not refer to the patience He showed here as the perfect Servant, humbling as that perfect pattern is to the heart, but rather that which makes the inner man leap in response — His patient waiting now for the full fruit of His "labour for the Bride". As she waits, so does He; He has waited these nigh 2 000 years in infinite patience and love, hence the cry "How long?" is stayed in affectionate response.

Thus the verse envisages for these suffering saints a circle of love and patience born of communion with the Father and the Son, divine communications flowing back in responsive love; the prayer of John 17 sealed in grateful hearts.

For the Lord (the Lord Jesus Christ) to grant this prayerful wish will give that resource from the heart of the Father and the Son which will make the command which follows a labour of love, and give the patience of hope a quality which the Thessalonians had never hitherto known; their patience a sweet savour of Christ to God and their love for Christ such as their hearts yearned to have. Such is our resource too.

VI. Godly Discipline (3:6-15)

1. The Disorderly: The Lord's Command
3:6

> v.6   "Now we command you, brethren, in the name of our Lord Jesus Christ, that ye withdraw yourselves from every brother that walketh disorderly, and not after the tradition which he received of us."

6   From v.6 to v.15 is a connected section on the subject of the conduct of the saints, perhaps particularly in the crisis of affliction and the related speculation as to the matter of the Lord's return. It might seem that after the tremendously solemn yet magnificent passage on the main subject of the epistle that thoughts on personal conduct are relatively unimportant and merely something of an adjunct in moving towards the closing of the letter. This is far from the truth. The space given to the subject by the Holy Spirit is full testimony to this, for it almost equals that given to the main theme. Furthermore, as in the first epistle, the matter of the relationship between inner reality and outward testimony is present in almost every section. The first epistle commences with such a note: 1:3; 1:7; 1:8; 1:9-10, and ends in the same way. In the second epistle, the theme of the practical outliving of the glory of the saint's position in Christ is integral with the highest note of the Lord's future manifestations; see this for example in 1:10, and the consequent responsibility as to conduct in 1:11,12. This is the case also with 2:1,2. Personal behaviour in outward testimony is vital; what we are before God must reflect in what we are before men. This section is not, therefore, to be passed over as of lesser import, for its message strikes at the reality of the Christian position. Of this the apostle was keenly aware as to his own manner of life, and if ever there was a man who could rightly command others as to the Christian walk, it was Paul.

His charge was not merely to do as I say, but to do as I do, for the command issued from the highest authority: "Now we command you, brethren, in the name of our Lord Jesus". "Command", is again *parangellō*, as in v.4, and we have retained "our" in respect of the Lord Jesus, as having better support in the MSS than "the". By issuing the command or charge in the name of the Lord Jesus (cf. 1 Cor 5:4), Paul gives the statement the authority of that Name. This makes the verse stronger than 1 Thess 4:2 ("through the Lord Jesus"), and the "exhortation" of 5:14. This leads to the conclusion that there is no case for assuming, as some do on the grounds of "excitement" being derived from *throeisthai* in 2:2, that the disorder was solely of a kind of euphoria based upon wrong deductions as to the Lord's coming. That wrong deductions may have been made is not denied, but the patent fact here is that the unruly behaviour dealt with in 1 Thess 5:14, which seemingly was of a more general sort, is now more specific and serious in that it strikes at the hope of the saints. It is not a matter of excitement, but of conduct having an effect not dissimilar to that of the mixed multitude in Israel. Not that the offenders were not true believers, but they were a source of discouragement, and of havoc to the testimony. Their behaviour had not hitherto constituted outright and wilful disobedience to a specific command; it seems to have been more a matter of ignorance, and that in very trying circumstances, but the issue of disobedience will arise if they persist. The firmness of the command is not however lacking in affection: all, including the disorderly, are addressed as brethren.

How were the disorderly to be treated? Certainly not by excommunication, as for serious immorality or false doctrine, but by "drawing back" from them, for that is the sense of *stellesthai*, present tense, middle voice. The aim is to make them realise that they were "out of step" with the company in its desire to walk in accordance with the delivered traditions. This is less strong than totally avoiding as in Rom 16:17, where conduct contrary to the doctrine was involved. The "shrinking back" was to be consistent with the term "brethren", and it is judged that at this stage the withdrawing refers to having no part in the offending conduct, rather than the total isolation mentioned later. This withdrawal would be accomplished by the bulk of the assembly following Paul's example, and then not affording the offenders any material support, nor engaging in their idle chatter. The attitude to fellowship within the gathering is not dealt with; the issue is one of walk. No public rebuke is mentioned, and certainly no withdrawal of privilege within house of God. We must go no further than the Word of God in such matters. Externally, because testimony is involved, there would be obvious dissociation from their behaviour, yet no demonstration of attitude which would cause the Name of the Lord to be dishonoured in any way.

The disorderly walk is indicated in the rest of the section; cf. 1 Thess 5:14-15. "Disorderly" is *ataktos*, only found in Thessalonians, meaning (to march) out of rank in a military sense, a term consistent with "command". It appears in the next verse in its verbal form, in v.11 adverbially as here, and in the earlier epistle as an adjective. Some render the word as "idly", others as "unruly", but the military sense indicated is better, and in the context disorderliness may be regarded as not marching in line with the delivered traditions we now have as Scripture, there being no other rule of life, instinctive or otherwise. Obedience, and not discretion, is the requirement for the Christian walk, and as in 1:12, everything to His glory, born of love for Himself, and in anticipation of His soon return. It is evident that these traditions had been received previous to this epistle, and indeed the root of the word would suggest "which you received by ear" (see this sense in 1 Thess 2:13-14). This, of course, was in addition to Paul's personal example.

The idea of idleness is not absent from the passage, but the true sense of the word *ataktos* is gained from its relationship to keeping the traditions, and not from local failure to do so in any particular direction.

There is some doubt as to whether the end phrase should read "he received", "they received" or "ye received". "They" is the best supported of five varying readings and accepted by Westcott and Hort, Kelly, RV, Alford, and Ellicott. The error seems to have crept in because copyists have inserted their own ideas, relating the verb to "every brother" individually, rather than the general sense of those who walk disorderly ("they"); the plural referring to all rather than each one.

"Walking" (*peripatountos*) refers, of course, as elsewhere in the NT to manner of life. To behave in any unseemly way is to dishonour the Lord, mar the testimony and negate the value of the spoken word.

2. *Orderly Example*
3:7-9

> v.7   "For yourselves know how ye ought to follow us: for we behaved not ourselves disorderly among you:
>
> v.8   Neither did we eat any man's bread for nought; but wrought with labour and travail night and day, that we might not be chargeable to any of you:
>
> v.9   Not because we have not power, but to make ourselves an ensample unto you to follow us."

7   Paul continues, "For yourselves know" *(oida)*, that is by process of observing our manner of life. The next verb, *dei* ("how ye ought"), is really stronger than our casual use of "ought", which strictly means to owe a debt, but the sense is correct if it is looked upon as something really due, a vital and compelling duty, a necessity. "Imitate" *(mimeomai)* is from a root from which we get "mimic", to act the same, to copy. It is used twice in this chapter, in Heb 13:7, and in 3 John 11; see a similar word in Phil 3:17; 1 Thess 1:6. It would be a bold man who would use such an expression, bold to the point of foolishness, unless his life bore the stamp of a Paul. The Thessalonians needed no lengthy set of rules for they had seen the pattern lived out before their eyes. To follow Paul was to follow an imitator of Christ (1 Cor 11:1). Originally they had followed the model of Paul as to the gospel (1 Thess 1:6), and throughout the first epistle there are marks of his walk: in suffering (2:2), in gentleness (2:3), in honesty (2:5), in humility (2:6), in tender care (2:7), in affection and self-sacrifice (2:8), in hard work (2:9), in holiness, righteousness and unblameableness (2:10), in comforting (2:11), as worthy of God (2:12), because he sought to please not men but God (2:4), in constant prayer for others (3:10), in holy living (4:1), in a peaceable and busy life (4:11), in testimony (4:12), in watching and sobriety (5:6), in succour (5:14). Such a man could indeed say, "be ye imitators of me", for we see in Paul the pattern of unselfish, devoted, sacrificial service which so marked the One he imitated.

"For we behaved not ourselves disorderly among you" is more accurately "we were not disorderly", for Paul uses the aorist indicative active of the verb *atakteō* which he has used in its adverbial form in v.6. Hence he is stating that they never saw him "marching out of line", that is, contrary to the traditions he taught. His life honoured God, projected the Master; he practised what he preached.

8   The apostle lays down the lines for approaching the particular disorder he has in mind, though, of course, the lesson applies in the widest field of Christian conduct.

"Nor as a gift (or gratis) did we eat bread from anyone" can be expressed as in 2 Cor 11:7, "I preached the gospel freely" (free of charge, as a gift). Paul employs a Hebraism, "eating bread" standing for having a meal (cf. v.10) or being maintained. He supported himself by "labour and travail"; the latter (*mochthos,* struggle or hardship) indicates a more difficult task than toil *(kopos)*, and both stand in apposition to "for nought". It involved "working night and day (that is, reading *nukta kai hēmeran* and not *nuktos kai hēmeras*, which is probably a carry over from 1 Thess 2:9 and 3:10), a course which he chose "so as *(pros,* expressing determination or purpose) not to lay a burden upon *(baros,*with *epi)* any one of you". The cost, the burden, of Paul's devoted service was his alone; he determined that there would be no smear of financial motive in respect of all his labours. He worked diligently, hard and long for the kingdom, whilst in another realm (whose claim he also met). He did not seek their goods, but their good; he did not covet theirs, but them, and that for Christ. His life of constant labour was not only an example to those who sought to follow, but an open rebuke to the slothful, if they could see it. See Acts 18:3; 20:34; 1 Cor 9:12-19; 4:12. Paul uses similar language in 1 Thess 2:9; the difference in the two statements is that in the first epistle he is showing clean hands as to his motive, and in the second, worn and labouring hands in example.

9   Paul uses the same Greek words *ouch hoti* ("not that") in Phil 4:17; 2 Cor 1:24 for the same purpose as here, to explain, and so avoid misunderstanding of his position or action; to limit what has been said before. In "we have not authority", *exousia* indicates a legal, and often a delegated power to act. (This sense of "a power given by another" is not always present, as some suggest; see Rom 9:21, and cf. Matt 10:1. It is perhaps better to consider its relationship to *dunamis* in this way: *dunamis* is the power itself, *exousia* is power brought into use executively). Paul insists on this right in his powerful case in 1 Cor 9:3-14, where he follows with an explanation as to why he did not exercise it. He would take nothing where his motive could in any sense be misconstrued, and even more so where, as here, he desired to be an example to others: "But in order that *(hina)* we might give *(dōmen,* from *didōmi,* a telling word as opposed to AV "make") ourselves an example *(tupos,* type) to imitate" (same word as v.7). "Ourselves", as the gift, is emphatic by position; the sense from this is: we have the authority (from the Lord, 1 Cor 9:14) to receive from you of what you have, but in reality we give, not only of what we have, but our very selves. What power in such example; how high the standard for us to imitate.

In this verse we have very sober admonition as to the motives for service, and the pressing necessity for the Lord's servant to have clean hands that no slur should be cast upon the testimony. It does not demand that the labourer in the Word should forego the divinely-given right to live by it, but the fact that it calls for much exercise of heart makes it apparent that for such not to maintain themselves by their own labour, must be the exception rather than the rule; it is an exception we gladly honour. In these intimate spiritual matters every man must judge the issues in the presence of the Lord, and elsewhere we must keep our own counsel lest we speak ill of the Lord's anointed. How grateful we are that we have known some true imitators of Paul; whose faith follow.

A point which must not be lost in this connection is the place of the giver, for if it is a command of the Lord that His servants have the right to be maintained, it follows that we have a duty so to act. Kelly gives sound advice, "an eye single to Christ preserves from any snare".

3. The Divine Equation
3:10

> v.10   "For even when we were with you, this we commanded you, that if any would not work, neither should he eat."

10 "For" throws the thought back to the continued consideration of the subject of the "traditions" in v.6, and with "even" (or also) which follows, gives the equivalent of our English expression "and I went even further". "Even when we were with you (and so whilst behaving as in vv.7,8) we commanded you", or better, being the imperfect tense, "we used to command you". He is claiming that in respect of the traditions they had not only his example but also his instruction — the sense of "do and teach" again. The teacher who practises what he preaches commands respect for his message.

The little word *hoti* ("that") has a use similar to our use of quotation marks or the prefix "quote". Known as the *hoti recitative*, it is generally used to mark the quotation of the actual words employed. Hence it would appear that Paul had found it necessary to use the expression so frequently that they would recall (as he did) the actual words he used. It may have been, as some suggest, a Jewish proverb based on Gen 3:19, though there is no concrete evidence of this, or a well known Greek saying; but whatever its origin, we have the command now as an expression of the divine mind. "If anyone does not wish (*thelo*, to have the will) to work" involves an attitude of mind (like "the world owes me a living") of careless indifference to moral responsibility, issuing in a notion that it is by no means outrageous to depend upon those who do labour, in order to live. In "neither let him eat" there is emphasis on the two negatives, not (*ou*) and neither (*mēde*), a fair moral equation: no work, no food. This, coming from the apostle whose heart was ever with the needy, to wit his collections for the poor saints, ("which I also was forward to do", Gal 2:10; see also Rom 15:26-28; 2 Cor 8:1-15; 9:1-15), has the greater force, illustrating as it does that the workshy lack the same compassionate consideration for others.

Kelly makes an important point about this verse when he says, "It is a striking characteristic of Christianity that as . . . not one thing is too great or high for the saint, so neither is aught too little or low for God", for how blessed it is that even our working day is under His eye. Paul could say out of his own example, "Whatsoever ye do, do it heartily, as to the Lord" (Col 3:23). All service is to Him, and life is not in two separate compartments, secular and Christian.

Many have been the conjectures as to why the Thessalonians needed such firm instruction: some have suggested it was because of their overwhelming occupation with the Lord's return, others that it was due to the initial excitement and buoyancy of their conversion (hardly a tenable suggestion in the context of the letter). Whatever the truth of the matter, the Scripture gives no diagnosis, but observation would teach us that the malady has not been eliminated by the years. Sadly, not all Christians are good workmen. Whilst it is right that we should not be occupied with the material for its own sake, we should have a deep sense of responsibility above men of the world, for we serve the Lord Christ. None looked more fervently for the Lord's coming than Paul himself, none worked harder, longer, better; indeed for him to live, Christ.

4. The Disorderly Identified and Exhorted
3:11-12

v.11 "For we hear that there are some which walk among you disorderly, working not at all, but are busybodies.

v.12 Now them that are such we command and exhort by our Lord Jesus Christ, that with quietness they work, and eat their own bread."

11 The cause for Paul's concern was not consequent upon their early failure during his presence with them, for the present tense seems to convey the meaning "For we keep on hearing", more than "we hear". In any case it indicates a current state of affairs (cf. 1 Cor 1:11; 11:18); Ellicott suggests it is an idiom to mark a state or action (known to be) now in existence. Even in those days news travelled, but compared with our present easy communications affording facility for detail, the fact of an item being transmitted then would tend to indicate its importance. "Of some walking among you disorderly, doing no work, but walking around" is the literal sense. Now whilst Paul often uses "among you" when meaning "of you", this is not always the case as v.7 shows, and we note a difference between "some walking among you" and "some among you walking". Paul has called them all "brethren" and will yet refer to the workshy as such in v.15, but we wonder if the note here is to make the offenders become keenly aware that they were seen as walking among the saints, instead of being, by their testimony, of the saints. Are we not oft-times convicted in this way? The offenders were "disorderly", a word used in verses 6 and 7, and it is of interest, as some commentators point out, that it was "loungers about the market-place" which the Jews used against Paul in Acts 17:5, indicating that a lazy do-nothing type was known in Thessalonica of that day. The Romans called such *subrostrani* (hanging around the rostrum) and as we see in the account of Mars' Hill, such were always ready to listen to a philosophical or religious debate. Nothing of that sort must be allowed to mar the Christian testimony.

Periergazomai (going, or walking, around) occurs only here in the NT, but a similar adjective is found in 1 Tim 5:13, "wanderers around houses"; it is used here for "busybodies" but it is not the same word as is similarily translated in 1 Pet 4:15. There is an interesting play on words here (called paronomasia); "working" is *ergazomai*, and "busybodies" is *peri-ergazomai*, to walk around. Ellicott says of them "doing no business but being busy bodies". Such cause others, even those who wish to work, to lose time in idle chatter, and as for themselves, if they do not use their hands the devil will find full employment for their tongues. "Idleness is a stimulant to curiosity", says Bengel, "for nature abhors a vacuum".

12 Paul now addresses the offenders personally, "Now them that are such we command (or charge, same as v.6) and exhort", (*parakaleō*, as in 1 Thess 3:2, to call to the side of, as of the Holy Spirit; it was used of a lawyer or counsellor). He exhorts them as a counsellor or helper, to obey the command and "fall into line" with the traditions (see v.6), but the vital factor is the nature of the command now. It is not, as earlier, "in the name of the Lord Jesus", and so giving the command His authority, but "in (the) Lord Jesus", which is positional. This introduces a lovely touch, for the command and exhortation being "in" (not "by" as the AV) means they are not on the grounds of delegated authority, but in loving intimacy, based upon union; the truth of the one body, as Paul will teach later. Thus the pressing note of "getting into line" is because of the relationship of each to all, and above that, of all to the Lord Himself. So the bond of affection is involved, as well as the honour of the Lord and of the local testimony. In the obligation being placed upon the erring saint by way of gracious appeal, we see it having more force upon the unruly than an authoritative command. Paul uses the full divine authority to the assembly in v.6 because he could count upon general obedience, but such is not appropriate in the case of the undisciplined; a command has force only where it is enforceable. Here is the ultimate persuasion of love as the cohesive force in the one body; to refuse such is to be oblivious of membership of that body, and that isolation must be felt. In stating this we are conscious that the explanation of the basis of this truth was yet to be revealed to the Church, but the principle is clear, a principle of marked importance as to our behaviour; we must at all times be governed in the ultimate by consideration of the effect of our actions upon the one body.

The appeal is "in order that (*hina*, denoting purpose) working with quietness, they keep on eating their own bread". Note the present tense not brought out in the AV. "Bread" is an idiom for sustenance, and what is implied is that they provide for themselves instead of living off others. "Their own" is in the emphatic position in the sentence. Thus it is an appeal to act in a manner reversing the conduct condemned in v.10 and to conform to the example mentioned in vv. 7-9 in line with the traditions spoken in v.6. "Quietness" is the same word as in 1 Thess 4:11 and, as generally in Scripture, refers to moral attitude (see 1 Pet 3:4; 1 Tim 2:2); it stands in contrast to disorderliness with which they have been charged. It speaks of the ordered life of quiet consistency, as opposed to the meddlesome activities of a busybody which may well have been the process by which the false doctrine as to the day of the Lord was disseminated, causing alarm and disquiet. "With quietness" modifies "working", giving the latter its character.

5. *Instruction as to Continued Disorder*
3:13-15

v.13   "But ye, brethren, be not weary in well doing.
v.14   And if any man obey not our word by this epistle, note that man, and
         have no company with him, that he may be ashamed.
v.15   Yet count him not as an enemy, but admonish him as a brother."

13   As Paul now turns to address the whole assembly again, he draws attention to an important weakness. When we see others pinpointed for failure this can result in us feeling highminded, superior, even to the point of disgust, and so applying fleshly attitudes of judgment and condemnation. This in turn dampens our spirit, and tends to promote like failures even to the point of giving up doing anything. Paul, by the Holy Spirit, faces and deals with this. We must not cease from doing the right thing because some take advantage of it. The Christian aim is not solely that of providing for self; we must ever be mindful of the needs of others, as Paul's own manner of life so clearly testified (Acts 11:27-30; 20:33-35; Rom 15:26; Gal 6:10).

"But ye, brethren", as stated above, means the whole assembly, yet particularly with the orderly in mind; "but" *(de)* denotes strong contrast; it is not to be read as "and" as in some versions. The verb *enkakeō*, from which *mē enkakēsetē* (be not weary") is derived, has a wide range of meaning, from behaving poorly to being faint hearted, but here the sense is clearly in the range of fainting, flagging, becoming weary, losing heart. Paul uses the verb in 2 Cor 4:1; 4:16 ("faint not"), Gal 6:9 ("weary"), Eph 3:13 ("faint not"); apart from Paul, only Luke uses it in the NT, 18:1 ("not to faint"). The general grammatical structure, the verb in the aorist with *me*, gives the sense of "do not begin to become faint, or weary", which incidentally indicates that in general they had not become so. "Well doing" *(kalopoieo*, to do the right and proper thing) is not in any sense "bestowing benefits", as Chrysostom suggests, nor any sort of "do-gooding", for such runs counter to Paul's thought here. It is an appeal for what is right, correct, proper, not just for being good or kind. The meanings of *kalos* and *poieō* from which this word, unique in the NT, is derived, may be gained from their use in Scripture: Rom 7:21 ("good" as opposed to evil); Gal 6:9 ("well doing"); 2 Cor 13:7 ("honest"); see also Lev 5:4 (LXX). In each case it is an urging to do the will of God contrary to fleshly indications. Milligan hits the right note when he urges that the sense of *kalos* is stronger than doing what is right, but relates to what is perceived to be right.

Thus, in toto, the meaning is "Do not begin to become faint, or weary, in what you know to be right". Let the Word of God be the guide in such matters and not the behaviour of others.

14   "And if anyone obey not our word by this epistle" changes from the foregoing plurals to the singular. Well such a rare possibility might be noted, for apart from placing the responsibility on each individual, this phrase involves the only instance in the NT where possible disobedience of an apostolic command could be envisaged on the part of a believer. "Obey" is *hupakouei,* having its root in the idea of a doorkeeper listening intently, and then acting upon what he hears; a thought most apposite here. "Our word through *(dia)* this (the) epistle" is a more sensible association of the words than attempts to interpret them as "mark this man by letter", which does despite to grammatical usage. Bishop Middleton points out that such a sense would not require the article, and the scholarly Bloomfield shows that "mark" does not permit of such a sense. The article before "epistle", as here, at the end of a letter, is common in Greek, and is used in order to refer to what has been written. (See example in Rom 16:22, and indeed at the close of the first epistle.) "This" is therefore fully justified, and the suggested alternative reading to be discounted.

The gravity of the offence of continued disobedience is increased because "this letter" is now part of the Word of God, an inspired command, thus the essential discipline announced will bear this weight in being more severe than previously indicated, and involving concerted assembly action.

"Keep on noting that man" is in the continuous tense. "Noting" is *semeioo,* from a verb meaning "sign" or "mark"; it is used in secular writings for a signature or mark of personal identification. Only later was it employed to identify persons as good or bad. It is stronger than "keep an eye on", but it does not suggest that the offender was publicly "pointed out", for it is in the middle voice; hence "mark that man for yourselves", a personal notation, but here referring to the assembly as a whole. Lightfoot translates "not to have company with him" as "do not get yoursleves mixed up with him", which is a good rendering of the compound word *sunanamignumi,* mingling together with, or having close contact with. Bloomfield counts it as very similar to "no dealings with" in John 4:9. The question raised by some whether this expression is in the imperative, as the preceding verb, or the infinitive, has no impact upon the true sense which results.

The instruction, whilst short of excommunication, is now more grave; it is not only a matter of drawing back from, as in v.6, but of total social withdrawal. (We say "social" because there is no note here of a person being put away from the company.) This because wilful and continued disobedience of a specific command would now be involved.

Thus we see the progress of the case; first the initial drawing back from those who walk in disorder, then the warning to the disorderly, and now, if any so continue, complete isolation because of disobedience to the Word. (Note "by this epistle".) This constitutes a solemn comment as to our attitude in the matter of obedience to the Word of God. In the clause, "in order that he may be ashamed", the verb *entrepō,* to turn upon (here in the middle voice), has the sense of, "that he may turn upon himself", but it can also convey the idea of giving heed to what has been said, and is sometimes translated "reverence". In all, it indicates a change of heart, and as such, is what the Lord through Paul looked for.

15   The gentle and tender object of recovery, not perhaps very pronounced hitherto, is amplified in this verse, lest there be any all-too-ready attempt to deal harshly with the offender. (We use the singular as Paul does.) There is first an affectionate note, ensuring a balance in the matter contained in the previous verse. This gracious principle of discipline being tempered with mercy is illustrated in an extreme case in Num 25:6, where the execution of God's judgment was accompanied by weeping; the two should go together. Failure is the sad portion of us all, and we must deal with others in the full consciousness of this, and where the Lord's honour is at issue, and severe action is indicated by the Word of God (and nothing else), then it must be taken in sorrow, even with tears, and always in full hope of recovery.

We see neither grammatical nor doctrinal reason for the insertion of "yet" instead of "and", for the verse is introducing balance, not a qualifying plea. Alford points to the effect of the word "as" in "not as an enemy count him", for it softens the thought by making the aspect of "enemy" more remote. The word "enemy" calls for some comment in view of the fact that some have related this statement to Christ, as in Phil 3:18. The word has its root in *echthos*, hate; it will be appreciated therefore that it is necessary to stand in awe before applying it other than as Scripture indicates. There appears to be no other sense in the context, than that it stands in contrast with "brother", and so is a warning to members of the assembly not to count the disorderly person as their enemy, which fleshly frailty is often too ready to do. There is no justification for any wider or more serious application.

"Count" (*hēgeomai*, to consider or deem) is rendered "esteem" in 1 Thess 5:13. We do well to regard the word "admonish" (*noutheteō*) in the light of its use in Scripture. It does not mean to remonstrate with, or to give such "a piece of one's mind", and most certainly not to denounce. The basic thought is of instruction in the best sense of teaching or training, and as these would never be regarded as abrasive things in the positive matter of imparting truth, the word calls for no other attitude in the negative side of seeking to indicate what is not right. Col 3:16 would seem to give the qualifications for such " instructors", that the word of Christ dwell in them richly, in order that the admonition be of the tone of 1 Cor 10:11, and in the light of the leadership mentioned in 1 Thess 5:12 (see 5:14 as to the assembly). Sadly, it is often found that the relatively unspiritual, and those with other than a shepherd heart, take it upon themselves to "discipline", but that is another word, and another meaning entirely. See Acts 20:31; 1 Cor 4:14; Eph 6:4 and Titus 3:10, for the use of "admonish".

The aim is that the admonition, or instruction, be in the spirit of Christ, and if any wounds result they will be the faithful inflictions of a friend (Prov 27:6). Indeed this is indicated in the term "admonish as a brother"; feeling you are his brother, and he yours, but feeling more how precious he is to Christ who died for him as well as you, and that as such he is part of the same body. If there be any weight here in "as", then such holy thing must be left to the righteous Judge.

Admonition is with a view to building up, not breaking down, nor cutting off; it is love in the light of holiness.

Some commentators raise the question, "But what if the erring person persists in his conduct?", and indeed one of them has remarked that "Christian tolerance has its limits". These limits are not defined by our capacity for patience, but by the Word of God, which gives both letter and spirit in matters of assembly discipline.

It is good to look back on the two verses 14 and 15 and see the order of the words, words given "in our Lord Jesus Christ" (v.12), now for us the written Word of God. We see in them the very attitude of the Lord Jesus Himself, righteousness and love acting in holy consistency. What sorrow, what sadness, what division, what loss, could be avoided if holiness in the house of God was administered in this spirit.

VII. Conclusion (3:16-18)

Benediction and Salutation
3:16-18

v.16   "Now the Lord of peace himself give you peace always by all means. The Lord be with you all.

v.17   The salutation of Paul with mine own hand, which is the token in every epistle: so I write.

v.18   The grace of our Lord Jesus Christ be with you all. Amen."

16   Only a heart tutored by like circumstances could appreciate the task which the apostle has placed upon these hard-pressed saints; to deal righteously and yet in love is beyond the strength of men. Well might their hands hang down at this further daunting prospect; how could they do this? Indeed how could they go on? Conflict raged all around, persecution pressed ever more heavily upon these young converts, and added to all this there was distress from within the company. The enemy, as always, would bring in the age-old counsel to give it all up. It is in these circumstances, by the inspiration of the Holy Spirit of God, the apostle introduces a description of the Lord Jesus as lovely as it is unique. Such is the contrast that well may Ellicott prefer "but" to "now" for the opening word, which is emphasised in the original text; "But the Lord of peace Himself give you peace". Amidst the clamour, pain, tears, suffering, anguish, and the hunger for spiritual strength, there was resource, infinite resource. The apostle (man indeed himself, flesh and blood like themselves, and who had suffered all such more than they all) could direct their heavy hearts to the calm serenity of peace within, the Lord's own peace, the peace of Him who is our peace (John 14:27). As we read the lovely words, we can hear the voice of the Saviour on that most awful night, the night in which He was betrayed, in the midst of the onslaught such as demons and men had never mounted before. As hell itself had already prepared for the conflict, as the vile heart of man was now exposed in unspeakable treachery, and even as the sword of God's holy justice lay bare, in absolute calmness of soul, and looking upon that little band of perplexed and anxious men, with eyes full of tender compassion, the Lord of peace Himself had breathed those words of comfort which have come with undiminished sweetness down the centuries, "My peace I give unto you". Upon such resource, Paul fastens their souls.

In 1 Thess 5:23, Paul had commended them to the God of peace, because God's action over death was the subject, but here it is the Lord Jesus in High Priestly sympathy bringing, in conditions He, also Man, knew by experience, the peace He Himself both felt and displayed. There is also another, though perhaps less obvious, connection between the two passages apart from that of the unity of the divine Persons; for as the prayer in the first epistle relates to the full man, "spirit, soul, and body", so here too, for the Hebrew word for peace (*shalom*) is a wish for the welfare of the complete man.

The apostle does not pray for their deliverance out of the trials, but for peace, as the sufferings continue, for he goes on, "always" (with the sense of "at all times", or "continually") "and in every way". The reading *tropos* (way) is to be preferred to *topos* (place), not only on the grounds of the MSS, but because "place" could not impose any limit on such peace. "At all times" would give them a sense of proportion as to their expectations of the Lord's coming, without imposing any suggestion of its remoteness, whilst "in every way" would exclude any circumstance for alarm. His peace is unbroken as to time, and unbreakable as to conditions. The world may inflict tribulations, but did He not say, "I have overcome the world"?

Compare "the Lord (be) with you all" with Rom 15:33; Phil 4:9. Not only His wonderful peace, but Himself is involved in what is no mere empty consoling wish. Again it brings before us the scene of the Lord Jesus; here in Mark 6 it is the darkest hour, the winds of satanic forces which opposed Him in Mark 4 now storm against them, and who is sufficient for these things? Darkness, demons, the raging sea, fear, helplessness appal and He is so far away, on the mountain praying. It is often like that: we feel the need for the Shepherd more than the Intercessor, but the Intercessor is still the Shepherd and the Conqueror. First the sight, and then the voice "Be of good cheer; it is I; be not afraid". It is the Lord of peace Hinself, and walking on the sea; the world overcome. "And he went up unto them into the ship; and the wind ceased"; all is calm and peaceful when He, the Lord of peace, is "with you".

We must not miss the "all" of the prayer, for it includes the disorderly brother; none more than he needed the Lord of peace in the "ship". Hogg and Vine bring out a lovely point in this verse when they remind us that Paul had known for himself the "I am with thee", according to Acts 18:10, and at Corinth too, from whence he wrote this letter, hence he could comfort wherewith he had himself been comforted (2 Cor 1:4).

17   By using the genitive of his name (*Paulou*) together with the possessive pronoun (*emē*) the apostle gives the rendering, "The salutation by the hand of me, Paul", not "my salutation" as the AV, but "my own hand"; cf. 1 Cor 16:21; Col 4:18. Generally Paul dictated his letters to an amanuensis, but at the end took the pen himself to authenticate the epistle as genuine. The exception to this is Galatians, which was at least partly, if not wholly, written by Paul; See Gal 6:11, (where "letter" means the writing itself) and Philem 19. In this early epistle to the Thessalonians we see why such a personal verification was necessary to prevent forgeries; see 2:2. The salutation would include v.17, "which thing (referring to the salutation, not the sign) is a sign (same as mark in v.14) in every epistle". This refers to all future epistles, and is itself a strong counter to the spurious suggestion that 2 Thessalonians was written before 1 Thessalonians, not that there is not also ample internal evidence to dismiss such a notion. Most of the epistles written later do not contain, as 1 Corinthians and Colossians, actual evidence that Paul so autographed them, but that is not to say he did not do so, and in any case each either bears evidence of a similar nature (e.g. note 2 Cor 13:10 onwards, and Eph 6:21), or was delivered by a trusted emissary: Romans by Phebe, 2 Corinthians by Titus, Philippians by Epaphroditus.

"So I write" may be interpreted, "after this fashion is my writing and signature" (or "sign"), and was included that the handwriting and signature might become known for future recognition.

18   "The grace of our Lord Jesus Christ (be) with you all" concludes Paul. With grace he commences to write (1:2), and with grace he ends. We must note how this varies from the customary Greek form of ending a letter with *errosthe* (be strong), for in ourselves we have no strength; everything we are, have, shall have, and shall be, is all, all, of grace. Yet there is strength, infinite strength; for the free unmerited favour is "of our Lord Jesus Christ", in whom dwelleth all the fulness of the Godhead bodily, and in Him we are filled full. By this divine power (the very *dunamis* of God) He has given us all things for life and godliness (2 Pet 1:3) through the full knowledge of Him that called us by His own glory and virtue. That call issued from the cross at Golgotha, there He displayed the excellency of God, there the demonstration of His infinite ability to accomplish all the purposes of God for God, for us. What glory, what virtue, what power, what grace. May we know in grace, and (even) in the knowledge of our Lord and Saviour Jesus Christ.

The final greeting is identical with that of the first epistle, but for one word; the apostle here adds "all". For with typical love and grace, Paul excludes none, rather very deliberately he indicates that his heart embraces the disorderly brother.

The word "Amen", and the footnote ("written from Athens etc") do not appear in either epistle in the better MSS. We echo the suggestion that the superscription is a gloss, added by some scribe, but if it be that Paul did not in fact end his letter by writing, "Amen", having fed our souls upon the glories of it, we add ours. Amen, and Amen!

Appendix

The Appearing

This event, usually described by the Greek word *apokalupsis* (which see), refers to the occasion often mentioned in both the OT and the NT when the Lord Jesus returns to earth in power and great glory. He does not come alone but with His saints (who will have been caught up at the Rapture about seven years before) and with the angels of His power. This event will not be unwitnessed by the world, like the Rapture, but though it will flash upon mankind with great and unexpected suddenness, it will be an occasion of awesome but majestic display. Every eye shall see Him. Unlike the Rapture, which has grace and salvation as its purpose, the Appearing is connected with government and judgment.

The Appearing of the Lord in power and great glory is not of itself the day of the Lord, nor does it usher in that day, but it is an event within that day, although in the Thessalonian epistles this distinction is not made. (See "The Day of the Lord".) The Appearing takes place at the end of the Great Tribulation; it finalises Daniel's prophecy of the seventy weeks of years and is described in 1 Thess 5:1-12; 2 Thess 1:7-10; 2:8; Isa 66:15; Zech 14:4; Mal 3:1-6; Matt 24 (note the signs in vv. 3, 5, 6, 7, 10, 11, 12, 14, 15, 21, 22, 23, 24, 26, 27 and the visible manifestation in vv. 29, 30); Matt 25:31; Luke 21:28. There are many other Scriptures relating to the subject, some of which do not specifically mention the Appearing but in which the reference to it is clear (e.g. Dan 2:44; 9:27; 11:36).

The Appearing relates to Israel, the nations, and the earth, whilst the Rapture is about the saints and heaven. See also *epiphaneia*.

The Day of Christ

The Day of Christ commences with the Rapture, and its course is almost synchronal with the Day of the Lord, although its application is very different. The Day of Christ relates to events in heaven and concerns the saints raptured there, whilst the Day of the Lord refers to earth and concerns Israel and the nations. As the two relate to the Thessalonian epistles, it could be said that whilst the Day of Christ involves reward, the Day of the Lord is marked by retribution, but in the general application of the terms this is not entirely the case, for the Day of the Lord is more extensive than indicated in Thessalonians (see "The Day of the Lord").

The Day of Christ includes the Judgment Seat of Christ (the Bema), the Marriage of the Lamb and, we judge, also the Marriage Supper of the Lamb (though all may not agree), and the heavenly reign of Christ. See 1 Cor 1:7-8; 5:5; 2 Cor 1:14; Phil 1:6; 2:16. 2 Cor 1:14 is included as being the Day of the Lord Jesus, but not 2 Thess 2:2, which should read "day of the Lord".

The Day of the Lord

In the context of Thessalonians, the Day of the Lord is largely identified with one event within that day, namely the Appearing, although it will be observed that even there, as indicated in 2 Thess 2:2-12, matters which occur before the Appearing are clearly identified. These include the full emergence of the apostasy and the revelation of the man of lawlessness, which relate to the Tribulation period which precedes the Appearing.

The Day of the Lord does not involve the Church period and is widely mentioned in the OT in respect of God's dealings with Israel and the nations. It commences after the Church has been caught up at the Rapture, and indeed cannot begin until then. It includes the following major events (and many less notable ones):

> The two periods, each of three and a half years, known as the Tribulation and the Great Tribulation: they are the two halves of the seventieth week of years of Daniel's prophecy (Dan 9);
>
> The Appearing which brings to an end the Tribulation period (including the Great Tribulation);
>
> The taking of the two beasts of Rev 13, and the casting of them into the lake of fire;
>
> The binding of Satan for a thousand years (Rev 20 1-2);
>
> The judgment of the living nations (Matt 25:31-46);
>
> The establishment of Christ's thousand years reign of righteousness, (the Millennial reign, Rev 20);
>
> The loosing of Satan at the end of the Millennial reign (Rev 20:3);
>
> The last great rebellion (Rev 20:7-9);
>
> Satan's final doom (Rev 20:10);
>
> The judgment of the Great White Throne (Rev 20:11-15).

It issues in the new heavens, and the new earth in which dwelleth righteousness, and so bears us on to the great Day of God (1 Cor 15:24-28). The Day of the Lord should be regarded as in contrast with Man's day, which term is the correct translation of "man's judgment" in 1 Cor 4:3 (AV). The Scripture references to the Day of the Lord are numerous, and the various portions which mention it stress particular aspects of this lengthy "day".

The Man of Lawlessness

The matter of identifying the man of lawlessness has occupied the Lord's people over centuries, but in general two candidates have emerged; these are the two beasts of Rev 13. In pursuit of the solution as to which of these is referred to in 2 Thess 2, two vital points from that chapter are quoted below, together with verses from other Scriptures which, it is judged, relate.

1. "He exalts himself above all that is called God, or that is worshipped ....
   showing that he is God" (v.4).
   Related Scripture: "He shall exalt himself, and magnify himself above every
   god, and shall speak marvellous things against God". "Neither shall he regard
   the God of his fathers .... nor regard any god, for he shall magnify himself
   above all" (Dan 11:36, 37).

2. "Whose coming is after the working of Satan, with all power and signs and
   lying wonders, and with all deceivableness of unrighteousness ..." (vv. 9-
   10).
   Related Scripture: "And he doeth great wonders .... and deceiveth them that
   dwell on the earth by means of those miracles which he had power to do ....
   and he had power to give breath (not life) unto the image ...." (Rev 13:13-
   15).

The second quotation is of the second beast, but there is some controversy as
to which of the beasts is indicated in the first quotation. It is submitted that the
reference in Dan 11:36-37 is also to the second beast of Rev 13. The expression
"the God of his fathers" is one often used in the history of Israel in the OT; see 2
Kings 21:22; 2 Chron 21:10; 28:25; 30:19; 33:12. It identifies the "wilful king" as
an apostate Jew. Hence the verse cannot refer to the first beast of Rev 13, because
he is a Roman. This conclusion is based upon the statement in Dan 9:26, which
describes the future head of revived imperial Rome, as being the prince "of the
people that shall destroy the city and the sanctuary". Now it is widely accepted
that this is a reference to the sacking of Jerusalem in AD 70, and the people
concerned were the Romans.

On this basis alone, it is considered that the man of lawlessness is the second
beast of Rev 13, and whilst in the context of the Thessalonian epistle it is not
possible to elaborate further, it might be remarked that what we have in other
Scriptures about this coming religious leader accords with that indicated in 2
Thess 2. His being the false prophet (Rev 16:13; 19:20) with lamb-like features
fits one who is revealed as Satan's false christ (anti, instead of), and Matt 24:5
shows that deceit is a mark of antichrist. Here is the one coming in his own name
(John 5:43) showing himself in all his vaunted self-sufficiency, "the liar"
personified (1 John 2:22), the wilful king (Dan 11:36), the "worthless shepherd"
(Zech 11:17, RV). Like Saul, he will be the people's choice for the throne of
Israel, before God reveals the Man after His own heart. The apostasy will
certainly pave the way for this apostate Jew; and his great satanic powers of deceit
will suit him for his role in welding decadent godless Judaism and Christless
Christendom into one vast theatre for the true purpose of his emergence, the
worship of Satan. He is like a lamb but has a dragon's voice. His two horns show
that Satan, having been cast out from his anti-priestly role of accusing the
brethren in heaven, now seeks on earth Christ's offices of prophet and king. The
assembly gone to heaven, the apostasy fills the void; the Holy Spirit withdrawn,

Satan is now active on earth; God disowned, a man, a Jew, in the temple of God, poses as God. Here is man, at the end of days, aspiring to that with which he was tempted in Eden, "Ye shall be as gods". Satan, having failed to wrest the throne from God in heaven, seeks to do so on earth. Did Christ show the power of God by miracles and wonders and signs? The devil will by his power have his man to do the same. Did Elijah, Jehovah's prophet, bring down fire from heaven to prove Jehovah is God? Then Satan's false prophet will do likewise, but in deceit.

Satan gives to the first beast the political and military might which causes men to cower before this fierce figure, but to the second beast he grants the greater tool of religious influence, with all his own subtlety, craft, deceit and guile, that he, disarming as a lamb, might corrupt men. The aim of Satan is the same in both beasts, that men should do what God's blessed Man refused to do — fall down and worship him. "And they worshipped the dragon" (Rev 13:4).

The Rapture

This is the event for which the Church waits. The English word Rapture does not appear in Scripture; it means to be caught up and transported from one place to another and is thus a convenient term for describing the event recorded in 1 Thess 4:13-18 where, incidentally, the Greek word for "caught up" (*harpazō*) is found in v.17. The Rapture refers to the coming of the Lord Jesus to the air to gather His own and take them to heaven, to be for ever with Himself. The verses cited above make it clear that it matters not whether these saved persons have died or are alive at the time; all those who are in Christ will be included in this glorious event.

The word used in Scripture to describe this event is *parousia* but such is not the exclusive meaning of that word. (See Parousia in the Appendix.) It is important to distinguish the Rapture, the Lord's coming to the air, from the Appearing, His coming back to the earth. These events are distinct as to time and purpose; the Rapture is unseen by the world and is distinguished by sounds (see 1 Thess 4:16; 1 Cor 15:52), whilst the Appearing is marked by signs (see under Appearing).

The precise timing of the Rapture is not revealed, but it could occur at any moment, and will immediately take place when, according to divine purpose, the last living stone has been built in to the glorious edifice, the Church. Then the Church age will be complete, and two distinctive but concurrent "days" commence; these are the Day of Christ and the Day of the Lord (which see).

There is no mention of the Rapture in the OT because the Church is not the subject of prophecy but of revelation. Nevertheless, the type of it is seen in the catching away of Enoch and Elijah. When in 1 Cor 15:51 Paul refers to a "mystery", he is not speaking of the *fact* of the Lord's coming, but of the *change* involved in our bodies (see also Phil 3:21).

Parousia

The word *parousia* is widely used in the NT to express "presence". Literally, it means "being with", from *para*, with, and *ousia*, being. It may refer to the process of arriving, but it is used more commonly of the extent of the stay, of any time during the stay up to the moment of the conclusion of the visit, or all three. Like other words connected with the Lord's coming, its sense must be judged from the context. Its use does not always refer to the Rapture, but when it does it has reference either to the moment of the Lord's arrival in the air, as in 1 Cor 15:23; 1 Thess 4:15; 2 Thess 2:1, or to the period of His presence with the saints in heaven, and until His Appearing (see below) as in 1 Thess 3:13. But *parousia* is sometimes used in conjunction with *epiphaneia* (which see below) in connection with the Lord's Appearing, as in 2 Thess 2:8, meaning "the outshining of His presence".

It is interesting to note that in the next verse (2:9) *parousia* is used of the man of lawlessness, demonstrating its varied use. See 1 Cor 16:17; 2 Cor 7:6; Phil 1:26 and 2:12 for its use in connection with Paul and others. Hence, whilst in general *parousia* is used of the Lord's coming to the air at the Rapture, this is not always the case, and the context must decide.

Apokalupsis

The word means "an unveiling", "revealing", or "uncovering"; it is derived from *apo* and *kalupto*, to uncover, or reveal from hiding. In the NT it is used for the action of bringing into sight, or understanding, what had hitherto been obscured. In connection with the Lord's coming, it refers to His coming to the earth, as distinct from His coming to the air, and speaks of His open manifestation, in contrast with the Rapture which will be secret, in the sense of its being unseen by the world. In the exposition it is referred to as the Appearing, or His Appearing in power and great glory: it is defined as the event when, accompanied by His saints and the angels of His power, He returns to earth in the manner described in 2 Thess 1:7,8. The event of the Lord's Appearing is sometimes referred to as the Manifestation, or the Revelation.

As in the case of *parousia*, *apokalupsis* must be judged by its context for it does not always have a reference to the Lord's Appearing; it is used to indicate revelation of any kind. See Luke 2:32; Rom 16:25; Eph 3:3; Rev 1:1 for examples of its wider use.

Peter uses *apokalupsis* in his epistle (1 Pet 1:7,13; 4:13) because in its Jewish context he does not hold out the Rapture as the hope of the saints, but the Lord's Appearing on earth as a time of relief.

Epiphaneia

This is the word from which our English equivalent, epiphany, is derived. It means a "shining forth". Although it is used with *parousia* in 2 Thess 2:8, "the outshining of His presence", the context of that verse, and indeed the Scriptural parallels, show that it refers to His arriving on earth at His coming in power and great glory (His Appearing) to bring in judgment, and, in the very process of His coming, to deal with the Beast, the man of lawlessness, and his wicked system. The use of *epiphaneia* in the NT always has reference to His coming to earth: 2 Tim 1:10 refers to His incarnation; 1 Tim 6:14, as the following verse shows, to His coming to earth as King of kings and Lord of lords; 2 Tim 4:1 to His coming to earth to judge the quick and the dead, a term always used in respect of responsibility; 2 Tim 4:8 to the time when Paul on earth shall display the decision of the righteous Judge, no matter what Nero may decide, and Titus 2:13* where Paul looks with joyous anticipation for the day of complete vindication, when He who was so shamefully treated on earth, shall appear here in all the majesty and glory which this world is yet to see. Thus, the shining forth, though linked with *parousia*, never speaks of the Rapture, but of His Appearing, His glorious manifestation, His shining forth on earth. The Rapture has no relationship to the visible display which *epiphaneia* involves.

The word is sometimes translated "brightness", or "manifestation" (RV).

*There is also the aspect of the blessed hope in this verse.

1 TIMOTHY

J. Allen

1 TIMOTHY

Introduction

1. The Author

This letter to a young fellow-worker bears the name of the apostle Paul (1:1), as do 2 Timothy (1:1) and Titus (1:1). For those who accept the genuineness of this claim the matter of authorship is thus settled.

From the letter itself considerable information concerning the movements and plans of the writer can be gathered. It is clear that Paul must have been at liberty when he wrote the epistle. It is a fair inference from the language of 1:3 that he had recently been at Ephesus and left Timothy there to complete the task of dealing with the false teaching that had arisen. While there are other possible interpretations of the language used, Paul's obvious personal acquaintance with the situation in Ephesus coupled with his action against Hymenaeus and Alexander (1:20) all support this view. Paul also raises in the letter the possibility of rejoining Timothy at Ephesus (3:14); any problem in the fulfilling of the promise would seem to arise from the demands of the Lord's work rather than any physical imprisonment.

Further information can be gleaned from 2 Timothy and Titus, letters which it is commonly agreed all come from the same writer and at approximately the same period of time. It is generally accepted, while impossible to prove with absolute certainty, that 1 Timothy preceded Titus by a short interval. The facts that we possess are most readily explicable on this basis. It is clear from the letter itself that 2 Timothy was written from a Roman prison, subsequent to the other two letters, when Paul was facing imminent death.

It is pertinent to our study to point out that there is considerable external witness, from a very early date, to the acceptance of 1 Timothy as a perfectly genuine writing of the apostle Paul. References to and quotations from the epistle are found in the writings of the early Fathers, men who represent the voice of history from the opening centuries of the christian era. These were men who were in a good position to know the facts since they lived in the years closest to the time of writing of the epistle. In the First Epistle to the Corinthians by Clement of Rome, dated about AD 95 there are several indisputable references to this epistle which show his intimate acquaintance with it. In the Epistle to the Philippians by Polycarp, written c. AD 110, he quotes without apology or explanation from both the epistles to Timothy and never hints at any possibility of fraud or forgery. Several other writers could be quoted in similar fashion including Ignatius (writing c. AD 110), Justin Martyr (writing c. AD 140) and Athenagoras (writing c. AD 176). These writers all bear testimony to the fact that from within a generation of Paul's death eminent teachers and writers had accepted this letter as a genuine writing of the apostle Paul.

It would be true to say that in the early centuries of the history of the church the only writers who rejected all or some of the Pastoral Epistles were certain gnostic heretics. Their quibbles arose, not so much from any real intellectual doubt as to the genuineness of the epistles but from an intense dislike of their teaching. Having taken up their doctrinal position it was typical of the heretics to discount the portions of Scripture that did not support their particular views. Marcion (c. AD 140) is typical of this school of thought and he produced a canon of Scripture that omitted all three Pastoral Epistles. Since he preached the strictest asceticism, denied the lawfulness of marriage, and issued rules for fasting, he could scarcely do otherwise, if he was to maintain the credibility of his heretical system. However, this very heretical attack, focused scholarly attention on the Pastoral Epistles in order to defend them. It would thus be a fair summary of the historical evidence to say that orthodox opinion was absolutely unanimous in accepting the Pauline authorship of these epistles. As far as the record goes there does not seem to be a dissentient voice. This testimony of the early Fathers has remained unshaken to the present day; it has never been seriously challenged.

From early in the 19th century, however, modern critical scholarship has raised new problems with regard to the authorship of the Pastoral Epistles. These problems have not arisen as a result of any new historical evidence but are based on internal considerations. These problems could be summarised under four headings:

1.   The Chronological Problem. Attention is drawn to the impossibility of fitting these epistles into the chronological framework of the Acts of the Apostles.

2.   The Ecclesiastical Problem. It is suggested that 1 Timothy reflects a state of ecclesiastical organisation far too developed for the days of Paul.

3. The Doctrinal Problem. Critics point out that many of the major themes of Pauline theology as reflected in his other ten epistles are missing in the pastorals. Paul, they infer, could not have written in the subdued tones of these letters.

4. The Linguistic Problem. The most serious argument against the genuineness of the Pastorals is their difference in style and vocabulary from Paul's other epistles. This would be the main point emphasised today by negative critics.

Based on arguments arising out of these supposed problems, some critical scholars have proposed that a follower of Paul composed these letters in the second century. Some suggest they are based on Pauline teaching applied to second century situations; others suggest they are composite productions made up of fragments of Pauline correspondence. Most negative critics subscribe to one or other of these views.

However, as in the case of the gnostic attack of the second century, this more modern attack on Pauline authorship has led to increased scholarly investigation which has but afforded increased evidence of the genuineness of the epistles. Competent and satisfying answers have been provided by conservative scholars to these problems to leave the student thoroughly satisfied as to the correctness of the traditional view that Paul wrote these letters. While a complete examination of each problem is beyond the scope of this work some guidelines are provided in Appendix A and the reader is referred for further detailed information to *Introduction to the Pastoral Epistles* in *The Expositors (Greek) Testament* or *The Pastoral Epistles* by H.A. Kent Jr.

J.N.D. Kelly of Oxford in *A Commentary on the Pastoral Epistles* in Black's *New Testament Commentaries* after having answered all the problems posed carries the attack to the liberal critics to show the falsity of their position and summarises the case thus: "The cumulative effect of these arguments is impressive. Taken in conjunction with the early external testimony to the letters, the relatively primitive situation they presuppose, the mass of convincingly Pauline material they embody, it tips the scales perceptibly, in the judgment of the present editor, in favour of the traditional theory of authorship".

2. The Addressee

i. Conversion: Timothy first appears on the Scripture record in Acts 16:1 when Paul on his second missionary journey came to Derbe and Lystra. That Timothy belonged to Lystra is supported by

1. the statement "a certain disciple was there" linking most readily with the last city named,

2.   the mention of the high esteem in which Timothy was held by his brethren (v. 2). Lystra and Iconium are mentioned and not Derbe,
3.   Acts 20:4 where Paul's companions are identified with their home cities. Timothy is mentioned separately and not linked with Gaius of Derbe.

Timothy's mother was a Jewess (Acts 16:1) and both his mother (Eunice) and his grandmother (Lois) were believers (2 Tim 1:5). The only mention of his father states that he was "a Greek"; from the absence of any further references it could be inferred he was not a believer, and, since Timothy had not been circumcised, it is unlikely he was a proselyte.

Since Paul calls Timothy "my child" (1 Cor 4:17; 2 Tim 2:1) and "my genuine child" (1 Tim 1:2) it is clear that Paul was the one to whom Timothy owed his spiritual life in Christ. It is a fair inference that Timothy had been saved on the first missionary journey when Paul had first preached at Lystra and suffered so much for his testimony to Christ (Acts 14:1-20). Timothy's conversion would thus date from about AD 47.

ii. Commendation: On the second missionary journey the Holy Spirit identified Timothy as equipped and gifted for full-time service in the company of the apostle (1 Tim 1:18). Timothy had already a good testimony in the local assemblies at Lystra and Iconium (Acts 16:2), so the elders of the local assembly (1 Tim 4:14), and the apostle (2 Tim 1:6), acknowledged the guidance of the Holy Spirit in the symbolic identification with Timothy in his call by the laying on of hands.

Timothy submitted to circumcision at the hands of Paul (Acts 16:3). This, of course, had nothing whatever to do with Timothy's salvation, since he was already saved, but it was done to avoid unnecessarily antagonising the Jews who knew of his Greek father. As uncircumcised, Jews would treat him as a Gentile; while Gentiles would regard him, on account of his mother and his preaching, as a Jew. This simple surgical operation would regularise the position so that he could accompany Paul into the synagogues to preach Christ. Timothy's case was very different from that of Titus who was a Gentile (Gal 2:3). To have circumcised Titus would have been a concession to the Judaistic teachers who sought to impose legalism on believers. The circumcision of Timothy was not to make him acceptable to believers but to make him acceptable to unbelieving Jewish audiences who, otherwise, would have refused to listen to him. The circumcision of Timothy would be an example of the principle stated by Paul in 1 Cor 9:20. This would be about the year AD 51.

iii. Career: Timothy joined Paul on his second missionary journey (Acts 16:2-4) and accompanied Paul into Macedonia, to Philippi and Thessalonica. When Paul and Silas were driven out of Thessalonica, it would appear (Acts 16:10) that Timothy stayed behind to help the infant church, and then rejoined Paul and Silas at Berea. Silas and Timothy remained at Berea (Acts 16:14) while Paul, instead of travelling by sea (note the expression "as it were" in Acts 16:14), was conducted through the mountains to Athens. Instructions were sent to Silas and Timothy to join Paul there but it would seem they were only able to link up with him again in Corinth (Acts 18:5), bearing reports from Philippi and Thessalonica.

Timothy was with Paul on the third missionary journey (Acts 19:22; 20:4). From Ephesus Timothy and Erastus were entrusted with a special mission into Macedonia (Acts 19:23) and with instructions to return to Ephesus via Corinth (1 Cor 4:17; 16:10). He obeyed these instructions and accompanied Paul back to Corinth, for he salutes the Roman saints in that epistle written from Corinth (Rom 16:21).

Timothy was one of Paul's companions on the trip to Jerusalem to deliver the bounty of the Macedonian and Achaian believers to the saints there. During Paul's imprisonment at Rome Timothy was his close companion and he is mentioned as associated with the apostle in three of the four Prison Epistles (see Phil 1:1; Col 1:1; Philem 1).

After Paul's release from imprisonment at Rome (see Appendix A), if he kept to his expressed intention (Phil 2:19-24), he sent Timothy to Philippi, possibly with instructions to rejoin him at Ephesus. It would seem that Timothy did just this and the winter of AD 63 was spent in Ephesus. In the spring of AD 64 Paul leaves Timothy at Ephesus and moves into Macedonia (1 Tim 1:3). Paul writes to Timothy from Macedonia the first epistle, possibly in the summer of AD 64. In the study of Paul's movements in Appendix A it will be shown that it is likely that the apostle and Timothy only met on one further occasion, at either Ephesus or Miletus. The parting on this occasion was a sad one (2 Tim 1:4) as the Neronian persecution had already begun and both preachers of the gospel knew that testimony for Christ had become very dangerous.

Whether Paul was rearrested at Troas, Corinth, or Rome, is not known. His second imprisonment seems to have been a short one, and, after the first hearing (2 Tim 4:14) Paul is satisfied that he is to die shortly. Under this threat he writes his last letter to Timothy and urges him to join him in Rome before the winter (2 Tim 4:21). This would be the winter of AD 67. Whether Timothy arrived in Rome before Paul's martyrdom is not known.

Sometime in his career Timothy was imprisoned and subsequently released (Heb 13:23) but no further details of time and place are on record.

iv. Character: No other companion, or fellow-worker, held such a place in the heart of the apostle Paul as did Timothy. No other person earned such commendation from the apostle for devoted service to the Lord (1 Cor 16:10-11) and his selfless interest in the welfare of the saints (Phil 2:20-22).

It is certainly true that Timothy received words of encouragement and words of warning from the apostle. Both encouragement and warning sprang from that concern of the apostle that Timothy should, in practice, evidence the qualities that Paul could see in him. An affectionate and self-effacing personality (2 Tim 1:4) could take refuge in timidity (2 Tim 1:7); warmth for saints could become weakness for truth (1 Tim 4:12); physical disability (1 Tim 5:23) could put him at a spiritual disadvantage in facing the problems of his work. Paul's love and care for the younger man necessitate the encouragements and warnings.

This relationship between the older man and the younger man, with personalities and background so obviously different, is surely a triumph of grace. That Paul should display such selfless love in the helping and instruction of Timothy, without a trace of jealousy or resentment is surely admirable. That Timothy should respond with confidence and respect without a trace of youthful impatience is certainly commendable. That this relationship should persist over at least a twenty year period is indeed remarkable evidence of grace at work in human hearts. In this they present a challenging picture of christian fellow-workers.

v. Commission in Ephesus: The status of Timothy at Ephesus was, in many respects, unique. The church there seems to have been very dear to the heart of the apostle. He stayed longer at Ephesus than at any other centre on his various journeys (Acts 20:31). On his release from the first imprisonment Ephesus would seem to have been the city he had in mind as he moved towards the east. It must, therefore, have been with considerable dismay that he discovered that his fears of some years before (Acts 20:29-30) had been realised in the emergence of false teaching. Paul took steps to deal with the most prominent false teachers (1 Tim 1:20) but realised that to complete the task and deal with the effects of the teaching would take more time than was at his disposal. Feeling compelled to depart into Macedonia he left Timothy at Ephesus to complete this particular task. For this responsibility Timothy had special and unimpeachable qualifications; qualifications that no other possessed. He had been with Paul as a fellow-worker in the early preaching at Ephesus and was associated with the foundation of the church. Paul could, therefore, feel perfectly justified in the special circumstances in leaving Timothy to act and teach as Paul himself would have done, had he remained in Ephesus.

It should be clear from this examination of Timothy's status at Ephesus that it would be wrong to use the term "apostolic delegate" to describe it, as if in some way apostolic powers could be passed on to another. There is no suggestion of this anywhere in the NT. Timothy exercised a special authority since he had been with Paul, as a fellow-worker, when the church was established at Ephesus and he enjoyed the confidence of the apostle and of the saints. "Apostolic delegate" and "apostolic succession" are terms that represent ideas foreign to the NT and came into vogue in centuries subsequent to NT times when the original simplicity of church order had been abandoned. It should also be equally clear that the function that Timothy fulfilled in Ephesus should not be confused with the present-day "pastor". The official and technical use of this word used in christian circles is unknown in the NT. Pastoral work as carried out by a plurality of men within a local assembly is perfectly scriptural (Eph 4:11-12; Acts 20:28) but the designation of one man as "pastor" has no NT support. To make Timothy the pattern for such is a serious anachronism.

3. The Date and Place of Writing

A consideration of the evidence available makes it clear that this letter was written by Paul from Macedonia (possibly Philippi) in the summer of AD 64.

This date rests on the premise that Paul was imprisoned in Rome, not once, but twice. The evidence for this seems unanswerable. The main considerations are as follows:

The major problem with the Pastoral Epistles has been the difficulty of fitting them into the movements of Paul and Timothy as recorded in the Acts. It is clear from 1 Tim 1:3 that Paul left Timothy at Ephesus while he went into Macedonia. On the first missionary journey Paul was neither in Ephesus nor Europe and, of course, Timothy did not accompany him as he had not yet joined the apostolic team. On the second missionary journey he did call at Ephesus on the return trip (Acts 18:18-23), but it was only a brief visit, and leaving Priscilla and Aquila there, he moved south-eastwards to Caesarea and Antioch. The Ephesian church was established only on the third missionary journey (Acts 19). After three years in Ephesus he passed into Macedonia (Acts 20:1) but Timothy, far from being left behind at Ephesus, had already been sent with Erastus to Macedonia (Acts 19:21-22) and on to Corinth with instructions to rejoin Paul in Macedonia (2 Cor 1:1; 1 Cor 4:17; 16:10). With Paul, Timothy goes back to Corinth, returns to Macedonia, is with him at Troas, and accompanies him to Jerusalem. The arrest and journey to Rome close the story of the Acts. Thus the three missionary journeys recorded in the Acts, ending in Paul's arrest and imprisonment in Rome, leave no place for such a movement as envisaged in 1 Tim 1:3.

With respect to Titus the situation is similar. According to that epistle Paul has left Titus in Crete with responsibility for certain tasks (Titus 1:5). He now instructs him to meet him at Nicopolis (on the west coast of Greece), where he expects to spend the winter (Titus 3:12). As a prisoner, Paul passed "under the lee of Crete" (Acts 27:4), but no mention is made of gospel activity or the establishment of churches. It seems therefore conclusive that Titus was left in Crete and Timothy in Ephesus at some point after Paul's release from the first imprisonment.

Further, the second letter to Timothy presents an imprisonment, the issue from which Paul is satisfied will mean death under Nero. He knows that he is writing his final letter. This stands in clear contrast with the predominant note in the Acts and especially in the Philippian epistle (Phil 1:25-26; 2:24) where Paul confidently expects his release. Either a dramatic change had taken place in the circumstances (about which Scripture is silent) or there are different imprisonments involved.

A study of the final statements of the Book of the Acts is significant in this connection: "And Paul dwelt two whole years in his own hired house, and received all that came unto him, preaching the kingdom of God, and teaching those things which concern the Lord Jesus Christ, with all confidence, no man forbidding him" (Acts 28:30-31).

We have two alternative conclusions to face: either that Paul was executed immediately following the two years mentioned, or, that he was released. As far as the record of the Acts is concerned both conclusions are hypothetical. However a consideration of the following points would indicate that his release would seem to be, by far, the more likely alternative.

1.   The Acts contains no charge against Paul that would cause his continued imprisonment and eventual execution when his case came up for judgment in a Roman court. This is the conclusion of Festus (Acts 25:26-27) and the conclusion of Agrippa (Acts 26:31-32).
2.   The Acts takes us to the end of the two year period. If Paul had been executed at this point we might reasonably ask why Luke did not tell us of this fact. This would have closed the story of Paul. The fact that Luke does not tell us of Paul's death would, at the very least, suggest that execution did not take place at this point.
3.   The phrase "two whole years" may be drawing attention to the legal limit under Roman Law during which charges could be pressed against the accused. When no one appeared to do this against Paul the case would fail by default, and Paul would be released.

Very early tradition confirms this. Clement of Rome, writing c. AD 90 from Rome, wrote of Paul as "having gone to the limits of the west", which, on the simplest interpretation, could be seen as the fulfilment of the apostle's desire to go to Spain (Rom 15:24-28). Eusebius (Ecc Hist II xxiii 1-2) gives a full statement of Paul's movements which includes his release from imprisonment, his subsequent journeys, his reimprisonment and death.

If we accept that Paul was released from prison and visited Ephesus again then there is a problem in the language that Paul uses in his address to the elders of Ephesus in the spring of AD 57. The problem arises if we interpret his words "I know that ye all . . . shall see my face no more" as a prophetic recognition that this would be the last time he would ever be in Ephesus. However, the simple solution is to see in the words, not a prophetic statement, but a reflection of his feelings at that time concerning the individual men listening to his voice. For several years he had been living amongst them, now the gospel would take him to other regions, and this farewell message reflected his feelings as he closed a period in his ministry.

Accepting the argument, therefore, of a release from Roman imprisonment early in AD 63, it is possible to suggest a possible reconstruction of Paul's movements. (See Appendix A for more detailed suggestions.) If Paul did as he intended (Phil 2:19-24) he sent Timothy to Philippi. He himself, with a party including Titus, moved eastwards to Crete and enjoyed a period of evangelism there. Leaving Titus behind in Crete, the apostle continued to Colossae and finally arrived in Ephesus to spend the winter there. Timothy rejoined him from Philippi. Early in AD 64 Paul, feeling compelled to visit Macedonia (1 Tim 1:3), leaves Timothy at Ephesus, with instructions to complete the task of dealing with the false teaching already in evidence there. Out of his burden of heart for Timothy and the saints, Paul writes this first letter from Macedonia (possibly from Philippi) in the summer of AD 64.

For a more detailed investigation of the movements of Paul subsequent to his release from prison see Appendix A(1).

4. The Background to the Letter

Timothy, in Ephesus, found himself in one of the chief cities within the Roman Empire. The proud capital of Ionia, it had a beautiful location on the Bay of Ephesus near the mouth of the Cayster river.

Commercially it was a prosperous city. It was the centre of communications for Asia where three great trade routes met. Roman officials landed here en route to their posts. All kinds of commodities passed through Ephesus; its warehouses were stored with the wealth of Europe and the East; its streets were thronged with merchants and travellers. One of the earliest banking systems known to us was established at the Temple of Artemis. One of its most lucrative industries was the manufacture of small silver images of Artemis and her world-famous temple. The impact of the gospel on this trade gave rise to the riot of Acts 19:24-41.

Politically Ephesus was not the capital of the Roman province of Asia, but an assize city where court sittings were held periodically. It had its own assembly administered by a town clerk (or recorder) (Acts 19:35). The great Artemisian Games were held here annually in May. The Asiarchs (Acts 19:31) were presidents of those games; they were wealthy men chosen by the chief cities of the province to arrange and supervise this national spectacle.

Architecturally Ephesus was the most famous city in Asia. Its theatre (mentioned Acts 19:29) was 495 feet in diameter and held 25 000 people. The temple of Artemis (Diana was her Roman name), the Marble Way, the Arcadian Way, the gymnasium, the stadium, the baths and the library were known for their stately grandeur.

Religiously the centre of worship was the Great Temple of Artemis. Built on a platform 425 feet by 220 feet, the building, itself 340 feet by 165 feet, had 120 Ionic columns each 60 feet high. The roof was covered with large white marble tiles. Brilliant colours, as well as gold, were used to decorate the stonework of the temple. The sacred object within the Temple was an image of Artemis. Mythology describes Artemis as the daughter of Zeus and the twin sister of Apollo. This virgin huntress had become identified with an Asiatic cult whose centre of worship was a crude meteoric stone which, according to legend, "fell down from Jupiter" (Acts 19:35). The top part of the image was a representation of a woman, carved grotesquely to emphasise the fertility of nature. Fertility rites were associated with this goddess and prostitution was an essential element in the worship.

Ephesus had also gained a world-wide name for itself in the study of magic. Its magical art, in the shape of talismans, amulets, incantations, charms, was world-acclaimed and the books associated with black art and spiritism were highly valued far and wide. The effect of the gospel in this realm is clearly seen in that costly bonfire mentioned in Acts 19:19.

Spiritually the history of Ephesus as far as the gospel is concerned begins with Paul's brief visit there, probably in the early spring of AD 52. Following this visit, Aquila and Priscilla resided there (Acts 18:19-28) and doubtless would bear witness to Christ. The effective gospel activity, however, was carried out by Paul and those associated with him in the period from the summer of AD 52 to the spring of AD 55, as recorded in Acts 19:1-20:1. Paul preached the gospel, and with others, took the message to the whole of the province. A strong assembly was established in Ephesus. Thus when Paul wrote to Timothy the assembly there had been established about ten years.

While on his way to Jerusalem in the spring of AD 57, the apostle summoned the elders of Ephesus to Miletus (a distance of 30 miles) as recorded in Acts 20:17-38. In a moving address to these elders he reviews the years he spent there, reminds them of the tears he shed on their behalf and reveals the fears that filled his heart for them. He foresaw the "grievous wolves", which from without would destroy, and the men of sectarian spirit, who from within would divide the saints.

As suggested in Appendix A, it seems probable that within a reasonably short time after his release from imprisonment in Rome Paul arrived at Ephesus and was joined by Timothy from Macedonia. Paul finds his fears for Ephesus have been fully justified and recognises that teaching is urgently required.

Urgent and compelling reasons caused him to leave Ephesus for Macedonia before he felt all matters had been satisfactorily adjusted. Thus he left Timothy at Ephesus to complete the task of putting things right. Out of the burden of heart for his young fellow-worker left at Ephesus comes the writing of this first letter, likely in the summer of AD 64 from Macedonia. For the reasons behind the writing of the letter see next section, The Purpose of the Letter.

5. The Purpose of the Letter

i. A Clarification of the Use of the Word "Pastoral": We have been accustomed to group the two epistles to Timothy and the epistle to Titus together and label them Pastoral Epistles. The term would seem to have been first used, in writing, early in the 18th century; it appears in the writing of D.N. Berdot in 1703 and was popularised by the writings of P. Anton in 1726. If the term is used simply to describe a particular group of letters from the pen of Paul, there is no quarrel with it. This is done for The Evangelical Epistles, comprising Galatians, 1 and 2 Thessalonians, 1 and 2 Corinthians, Romans; and The Captivity Epistles, comprising Colossians, Philemon, Ephesians and Philippians. Thus, there can be no objection to the final three epistles from the apostle's hand being linked together as The Pastoral Epistles.

If, however, we permit present-day ecclesiastical terminology to limit the word "pastoral" to the work of a minister or clergyman, we shall be in danger of thinking these epistles were written for the guidance of younger "pastors" faced with their first congregation. This would place a serious limitation on the value and usefulness of the epistle.

We have already noted that Timothy and Titus were not "pastors" in the modern ecclesiastical sense of the term. They were fellow-workers of Paul, who had been associated with him in the founding of the different assemblies and now left in specified locations for a limited period to carry out or complete a specific task. This task constitutes the basis of the "charge" contained in 1 Timothy and is examined in detail in the following section. The charge has in view the preservation of the local assembly from false teaching that would destroy its essential nature. To use the term "pastoral" as describing the work of a "pastor" is thus misleading and tends to obscure the vital nature of the ministry in the epistles.

With this reservation, however, we may permit the term "pastoral" as a convenient grouping. Two matters do distinguish these three letters and set them in a group apart from the other Pauline epistles.

1. They are written to individuals and not to local assemblies (Philemon is the only other Pauline exception, and that was written on a personal matter). Although this is so, it is clear that the letters were meant for a wider audience. Each letter carries, in the salutation, specific references to apostolic authority, which are inexplicable if meant only for the eyes of Timothy and Titus. That Paul anticipated that his first letter to Timothy would be read in Ephesus is shown by the plural "ye" in 1 Tim 6:21 (the best MSS read thus). The plural "ye" occurs again in 2 Tim 4:22 and Titus 3:15.

2. The language and style show similarities within the group and differences from other Pauline epistles. Many modern commentators proffer the argument that the experiences of recent years had left Paul

not only "old" in the chronological sense, but "aged" in mind and spirit. They suggest that these last writings from Paul reflect a subdued apostle not now capable of the doctrinal heights of an earlier day. Such notions, without any solid evidence, tell more of the commentators than they do of Paul. This argument limits, in no small way, the value of inspiration and fails to grasp what a vital part subject matter plays in the determination of language and style.

The chronological gap between the Prison Epistles and 1 Timothy can only be, at the very most, three years; a period inadequate to explain differences of vocabulary and style on the basis of the ageing of Paul. Yet the language and style differences are there. For a fuller discussion, see Appendix A. Suffice to note here, in explanation, that the subject matter determines the style and vocabulary used. A real concern for the preservation of assembly testimony under satanic attack weighs on the heart of the apostle in these epistles; he writes soberly and skilfully under the control of the Holy Spirit to show the nature of local congregational testimony for God. Language and style reflect, as they always must do, the nature of the subject treated. To expect identity in such cases of diverse subjects is to impose unjustifiable limitations on the apostle and the Spirit of God.

ii. The Purpose of the Letter: It is clear that Paul has three aims before him:
1.   To Set Forth Teaching Related to the Assembly: "that thou mightest know how men ought to behave themselves in the house of God" (3:15 RV).
2.   To Sound Forth a Warning Related to False Teaching: "that thou mightest charge certain men not to teach a different doctrine" (1:3 RV).
3.   To Encourage Timothy in his Responsibility: "that by them thou mightest war a good warfare" (1:18 RV). As Paul fulfils his aim in the epistles it would be made plain to all that as Timothy carried out his responsibilities he was acting with the full support of the apostle.

1. To Set Forth Teaching Related to The Assembly
We are left in no doubt as to the positive purpose of this letter. This is expressed in chapter 3:14-16: "These things write I unto thee . . . that thou mayest know how thou oughtest to behave thyself in the house of God".
While the AV text would give the impression of personal instruction for Timothy, the meaning of the sentence is better expressed by the RV, "These things write I unto thee . . . that thou mayest know how men ought to behave themselves in the house of God", or by JND: "These things write I unto thee . . . that thou mayest know how one ought to conduct oneself in God's house".
A certain standard of conduct is expected of those associated with the House of God. Thus the letter is not a series of loosely-connected personal instructions but a closely-integrated whole centred around a basic purpose.

This purpose is to unfold to Timothy in a systematic way, and through him to the believers in the Ephesian assembly, the conduct expected of those who form part of a scripturally-gathered company seen here under the figure "House of God". We shall see in the exposition that "House of God" does not refer to a building but has the thought of a "household belonging to God". Thus there will be a certain standard of conduct expected of those associated with this local assembly.

2. To Sound Forth a Warning Related to False Teaching

Alongside this clear statement of the positive purpose of the writing there is discernible another purpose. Paul, from his own observation and experience, recognises that there has emerged in Ephesus teaching, which, if not checked, will destroy the distinctive character of the testimony for God. The letter is designed to show up such false teaching.

If, as suggested in the previous section, Paul came to Ephesus in the late summer of AD 63 and, joined by Timothy, spent the winter there before leaving for Macedonia in the spring of AD 64, he would have had ample time to evaluate the state of the assembly. He finds the fears expressed some years before (Acts 20:28-31, spring AD 57) have been fully justified:

i.   Men of Jewish background were introducing some of the most speculative lines of rabbinical lore into their teaching. Paul calls them "fables and endless genealogies" (1:4). Allegorical and legendary interpretations of OT genealogies were the stock in trade of these proud "Law Teachers" (1:3-5).

ii.   Men, wearing the mask of spirituality, assuming matter was evil, would prohibit marriage, and use only certain kinds of food (4:1-3); some taking this to its logical conclusion denied even the physical resurrection (2 Tim 2:18).

iii. Men, of philosophic turn of mind, puffed up in pride were building up a "knowledge" (a misnomer, Paul says) that was against all that the gospel revealed (6:20). The motive of these men was simply to make a profit out of religion (6:5).

Paul could see, that while these things were present the testimony for God was at risk. With Spirit-given perception he could see that they were the very features that would develop and affect testimony for God in the latter times. Behind these doctrinal aberrations there was, undoubtedly, satanic agency (4:1) which already had had terrible success in lowering the moral and ethical standards of conduct. This lowered spiritual tone was evident to the apostolic eye in the gatherings of the saints. Hence the false teaching identified in the epistle had a very real existence at Ephesus. But, in prophetic anticipation, Paul recognised that this was but the beginning of that apostasy that would be fully manifest in "the latter times".

3. To Encourage Timothy in his Responsibility

The letter breathes the affection and concern of Paul for Timothy in such a situation. The personal reminiscences (1:18; 4:14) would serve to encourage him, the personal charges (5:21; 6:13) to strengthen him in this responsible task for God. The apostolic "charge" (1:18) and the recognition of "the deposit" (6:20), when read publicly in the assembly, would lend authority to his youth (4:12) and make his ministry more effective. No one could be in any doubt, when this epistle was read in the assembly, that Timothy had the confidence of Paul and that he was expected to act for God for the preservation of the saints (4:16).

6. The Plan of The Letter

7. Bibliography

Text

The Greek New Testament, K. Aland, M. Black, B.M. Metzger, 1st Edition 1966. Wurttemberg Bible Society, Stuttgart, West Germany.
A *Textual Commentary on the Greek New Testament*, Bruce M. Metzger. Corrected Edition 1975. United Bible Societies.

General

Alford, Henry. *The Greek Testament*. Moody Press 1968 Edition, Vol III, Galatians-Philemon.
Berry, G. Ricker. *A Dictionary of New Testament Synonyms*. 1979 Zondervan.
Coneybeare, W.J. and Howson, J.B. *The Life and Epistles of St. Paul*. 1949 Reprint Erdmans 1951.
Custer, Stewart. *A Treasury of New Testament Synonyms*. 1975 Bob Jones University Press.
Earle, Ralph. *First Timothy* in The Expositor's Bible Commentary. Ed. F.E. Gabelein. Zondervan 1978.
Ellicott, C.J. *Bible Commentary*. 1971 Zondervan.
Eusebius. *The Ecclesiastical History and the Martyrs of Palestine*. (Trans, Lawlor and Oulton) London SDCK 1927.
Gromachi, R.G. *Stand True to the Charge*. 1982 Baker Book House.

Guthrie, D. *The Pastoral Epistles*. Tyndale New Testament Commentaries. Tyndale Press 1st Edition 1957.

Hanson, A.T. *The Pastoral Epistles*. 1982 The New Century Bible Commentary. Eerdmans Pub. Co. Michigan U.S.A.

Harrison, P.N. *The Problem of the Pastoral Epistles*. London U.P. 1921.

Hendricksen, W. *A Commentary on Epistles to Timothy and Titus*. 1964 Ed. The Banner of Truth Trust.

Hiebert, D. Edmond. *First Timothy*. 1957. Moody Press Chicago.

Hiebert, D. Edmond. *Behind the Word Deacon: A NT Study*. Bibliotheca Sacra Vol 140 1983 No. 558.

Hoste, W. *Bishops, Priests and Deacons*. John Ritchie Ltd., Kilmarnock.

Hole, F.B. *Paul's Epistles* Vol II. Central Bible Hammond Trust Ltd.

Han, Nathan E. *A Parsing Guide to the Greek New Testament*. 1971 Scottdale Herald Press.

Kelly, W. *An Exposition of Timothy*. Third Edition 1948. C.A. Hammond.

Kelly, J.N.D. *A Commentary on the Pastoral Epistles*. Black's New Testament Commentaries. A and C Black. London Reprint 1978.

King, Guy H. *A Leader Led*. 1951. Marshall Morgan and Scott.

Kent, Homer A. Jr. *The Pastoral Epistles*. Revised Edition 1982. Moody Press.

Kubo. *A Reader's Greek English Lexicon of the New Testament* 1975. Zondervan.

Knight, G.W. III. *The Faithful Sayings in the Pastoral Letters*. Reprint 1979. Baker Biblical Monograph. Baker Book House.

Lindsay, Thomas M. *The Church and its Ministry in the Early Centuries*. Reprint 1977. James Family Publisher, Minneapolis USA.

Rackham, R.B. *The Acts of the Apostles*. Third Edition 1906. Methuen, London.

Rodgers, W. *Notes on the Pastoral Epistles*, Lurgan N.I.

Saucy, R.L. *The Husband of One Wife*. Bibliotheca Sacra Vol 131 1974 No. 523.

Simpson, E.K. *The Pastoral Epistles*. First Edition 1954. Tyndale Press.

Thiessen, H.C. *Introduction to the New Testament*. 1943. Eerdmans Pub. Co. Michigan USA.

Tenney, Merrill C. *The New Testament, A Historical and Analytical Survey*. First British Edition 1954. I.V.F.

Vine, W.E. *Expository Dictionary of New Testament Words*. Oliphants Ltd. 1940.

Vine, W.E. *The Epistles of Timothy and Titus*. Oliphants Ltd. 1965.

Walvoord J.F. and Zuck, R.B. *The Bible Knowledge Commentary* 1983. Victor Books Wheaton USA.

White, N.J.D. *The Expositor's Greek New Testament* Vol IV Eerdmans Pub. Co. Michigan USA.

Wuest, Kenneth S. *The Pastoral Epistles*. Word Studies 1952. Eerdmans Pub. Co. Michigan USA.

Wilson, T.E. *The Church in the Pastoral Epistles.* John Ritchie Ltd., Kilmarnock.

Zahx, T. *Introduction to the New Testament* Vol 2. Reprint 1953. Klock & Klock USA.

Text and Exposition

I. Salutation and Greeting (1:1-2)

> v.1 "Paul, an apostle of Jesus Christ by the commandment of God our Saviour, and Lord Jesus Christ, which is our hope;
>
> v.2 Unto Timothy, my own son in the faith: Grace, mercy, and peace, from God our Father and Jesus Christ our Lord."

1 In the manner of the day Paul opens his letter with his own name. Thus introducing the writer, he proceeds to identify the recipient and impart the greeting. As in all his epistles Paul uses his Greek-Roman name and not his Hebrew name, Saul. The second word, apostle, indicates that the letter is more than a personal communication to a friend and fellow-worker; it carries apostolic authority. The word "apostle" signifies simply "one sent forth" (*apostolos* from *apo*, "from", and *stellō*, "to send"). It is used in a technical way of one sent, with proper credentials, to represent another. It is used in this way and translated "messenger" in Phil 2:25 and 2 Cor 8:23 (plural). Paul, however, is not the mere ambassador of any local church; the subjective genitive "of Christ Jesus" (RV) defines his apostleship. He not only belongs to Christ but he is commissioned from Christ to speak for Christ in His interests and for His honour. The word order, "Christ Jesus" (RV), is correct and indicates that his apostleship came from the risen Christ, whose glory had burst upon him on the Damascus road. In contrast Peter speaks of himself as an "apostle of Jesus Christ" (1 Pet 1:1; 2 Pet 1:1).

The twelve disciples (Matt 10:12) were designated apostles by the Lord Himself; a specially qualified and commissioned company. By divine grace (1:14) and divine intervention (Gal 1:16) Paul was added to this distinct body. The unique appointment and ministry of the twelve apostles and of Paul precludes any notion of apostolic successors (Judas, with scriptural authority was replaced by Matthias, Acts 1:26). The clear statement of 1 Cor 15:8 "last of all" with reference to Paul and his testimony to the risen Christ lends support to this truth. No provision is made in Scripture for additions to, or successors of, this company. Apostolic succession is a figment of religious imagination first heard of in the third century, in the writings of Tertullian and Cyprian, when men were beginning to add their own ideas to the word of God.

This apostolic authority is emphasised by the use of the expression "by the commandment of" (kat'epitagēn), a recognised expression in the Graeco-Roman world and used in official notices where it could be translated "by order of". We could translate "commissioned" in the sense of a royal command. Paul recognised that he was a man under divine orders, stressing not the privilege but the responsibility of his apostleship. As in Rom 16:26 and Titus 1:3 it is the authority of a divine commission that is in view.

The source of his authority is "God our Saviour and Christ Jesus our hope" (RV). Usually Paul traces his apostleship to the will of God (1 Cor 1:1; 2 Cor 1:1; Eph 1:1; Col 1:1; 2 Tim 1:1) but this present language is stronger. His commission had come from God and Christ whose action he does not distinguish. See note on "God our Saviour" (Appendix B) which recognises that salvation in its planning and provision finds its origin in God while its execution and embodiment is in Christ Jesus, (most MSS omit "Lord", see RV). The "and" not only links divine Persons in this action but introduces a time element with salvation linking both the past and the future. What had been in the heart of God, belonging to His very nature, is manifest, in time, in Christ Jesus: thus the whole concept of salvation is in the statements. The word "hope" is not to be confined to the end-time coming of Christ (the eschatological coming) but here it embraces all that God has purposed; all that has been worked out and will be worked out in Christ; all that God has designed for the blessing of mankind. Notice the use of the word hope in Acts 23:6; 24:15; 26:6-7; 28:20; Col 1:27. The "our" is a tender way of embracing Timothy in the common apostolic apprehension of faith.

2 The addressee is Timothy (see Section 2 of Introduction), that young man of Lystra who had responded to the gospel on Paul's first missionary journey; who, born of a Greek father in the natural sense, owed his spiritual life to the preaching of the apostle. The intimate endearing term "my true child" (RV) but underlines the affection Paul had for Timothy. The adjective gnēsios (used of one born in lawful wedlock) carries the idea of legitimacy, in contrast to nothos, illegitimate, (see Heb 12:8); translated "own" (RV "true") it indicates the reality and legitimacy of that spiritual life. The expression "in faith" should not be translated "in the faith" which gives too limited a sense. The absence of the article may point to the instrumental use of "in" and we could translate "through faith" emphasising that it is through believing God that Timothy became Paul's spiritual child, (compare the language of 1 Cor 4:15). On the other hand "in faith" may define the sphere of the father-child relationship (compare the expression "in the Lord" in 1 Cor 4:17). The instrumental use seems the better suited to the context. There is little substance to the grammatical argument that the omission of the possessive adjective before "child" makes this a reference to Timothy being "God's genuine child". The omission of possessive adjectives is commonplace in NT Greek and 2 Tim 2:1, where the possessive adjective is present, is drawing attention to the same truth as presented here.

The tenderness and affection implicit in the word "child" draws out the heart of a spiritual parent in affectionate longing for one so dear. Only in 1 and 2 Timothy does Paul add "mercy" (omitted by RV in Titus 1:4) to the more usual greeting.

To grace (*charis*), the wealth of unmerited favour superseding any pagan good wishes (which would be *chairein*), is added mercy (*eleos*), the withholding of that which failure would deserve, and this is crowned with peace (*eirēnē*). The outcome of grace experienced and mercy enjoyed would be a soul in harmony with God: enjoying this harmony the believer would know peace.

The source of such blessing must be divine and Paul traces it thus to God our Father and Christ Jesus (RV) our Lord. Divine Persons have acted through the gospel to bring men into a new relationship to God as Father in conscious submission to One manifestly declared Lord in resurrection (Acts 2:36; Phil 2:11). It is in this sphere from these divine Persons that grace, mercy and peace are experienced.

II. The Reason For The Charge (1:3-20)

An Explanation: The Danger in Ephesus

1. *The False Teachers*
1:3-11

> v.3   "As I besought thee to abide still at Ephesus, when I went into Macedonia, that thou mightest charge some that they teach no other doctrine,
>
> v.4   Neither give heed to fables and endless genealogies, which minister questions, rather than godly edifying which is in faith: so do.
>
> v.5   Now the end of the commandment is charity out of a pure heart, and of a good conscience, and of faith unfeigned:
>
> v.6   From which some having swerved have turned aside unto vain jangling;
>
> v.7   Desiring to be teachers of the law; understanding neither what they say, nor whereof they affirm.
>
> v.8   But we know that the law is good, if a man use it lawfully;
>
> v.9   Knowing this, that the law is not made for a righteous man, but for the lawless and disobedient, for the ungodly and for sinners, for unholy and profane, for murderers of fathers and murderers of mothers, for manslayers,
>
> v.10 For whoremongers, for them that defile themselves with mankind, for menstealers, for liars, for perjured persons, and if there be any other thing that is contrary to sound doctrine;
>
> v.11 According to the glorious gospel of the blessed God, which was committed to my trust."

a. Identification of the False Teachers (vv. 3-7)

3 Paul reminds Timothy of his urgent entreaty ("I besought thee"; the aorist tense would suggest a specific occasion) to remain at Ephesus while he himself moved into Macedonia. It would not be an unreasonable assumption that Paul had already given explicit verbal instructions to Timothy before he left him at Ephesus. Thus this letter would not only serve to refresh Timothy's memory and to re-emphasise the danger, but also to strengthen his hand as he dealt with the false teachers and their teaching. This last point would be further served if the letter was intended to be read publicly in the assembly. The specific identification of the doctrinal danger indicates Paul's first hand acquaintance with the situation.

Vv.3-4 form one long sentence: "As I besought thee . . . which is in faith", and a sentence which is incomplete. The thought, through rapid development, loses touch with the initial clause and is unfinished. This anacoluthon is characteristically Pauline (other examples are Rom 2:17; 5:12; 8:12; 9:22; Gal 2:4 etc). To supply the missing correlative the RV puts in "so do I now", but the AV is much better and stronger, getting close to the thought with the words "so do". In other words, as well as spelling out the charge, Paul encourages Timothy, "act now!" "To abide still" (RV "to tarry") may hint at a reluctance on the part of Timothy to be parted from the apostle who was en route for Macedonia. The participle (RV "when I was going") provides a graphic picture of a traveller already on the way.

Timothy's responsibility is to take a firm stand against erroneous teaching and this will involve acting decisively (note the aorist tense of the verb "thou mightest charge") against those who would thus teach. The verb "charge" *parangellō*) usually denotes "to command" (Vine). It is a military word and could be translated "give strict orders to". The use of this same verb in connection with apostolic authority in 1 Cor 7:10; 11:17 RV; 1 Thess 4:11 emphasises the unique function of Timothy in Ephesus as speaking with delegated authority.

The forebodings of Paul concerning the church at Ephesus, of which he spoke in Acts 20:29-30, sadly, had been only too fully justified. Truly had he warned: "also of your own selves shall men arise, speaking perverse things to draw away disciples after them" (Acts 20:30). Since, it would appear, the letter was to be read in public, the apostle simply designates the false teachers as "some" and thus, under the guidance of the Holy Spirit leaves the identification open down the ages. No names were needed; what they were doing was sufficient identification. In the pronoun "some" there is no indication of numbers, whether few or many, but in its use there is an opprobrious, somewhat slighting, reference that sets this group apart from others. (See on "some" in Appendix B).

"That they teach no other doctrine" is the translation of two words, the negative before the verb "to teach differently" (*heterodidaskaleō*, comprising the prefix *heteros* "different" and the verb "to teach"). It is the same verb as in 1 Tim 6:3. The use of this word clearly implies that a distinct body of teaching, consistent with, and of the same kind as, the gospel that carried apostolic authority, was already clearly recognised. Teaching of a different kind, whatever its origin, would be dangerous and detrimental to spiritual health. Timothy's responsibility was to stop this other kind of teaching at source.

4 The verb "to give heed to" (*prosechō*, repeated in 3:8; 4:1; 4:13) literally means "to turn towards" and is often used to describe the bringing of a ship to land. Figuratively, it is used of "giving one's mind to" as in Acts 8:6; 16:14 but, in the middle voice with the dative case, meant "to attach oneself to", or "to cleave to", a person or a thing. Timothy is charged to act decisively for God against the false teachers. Likewise he is to ensure that the saints would neither give an ear to such teaching nor attach themselves to the propagators of such teaching.

Having spelt out the character of such teaching the apostle now deals with its content ("fables and endless genealogies") and its consequence ("which minister questions"). See under Background to the Letter, Section 4. "Fables" (*muthos*, "a myth") is used in 4:17; 2 Tim 4:4 and Titus 1:14 where the adjective "Jewish" links it with rabbinic Judaism. "Genealogies" (*genealogia*), used again in Titus 3:9, is the normal word for "family trees". W.E. Vine writes: "*Genealogia* is used in 1 Tim 1:4 and Titus 3:9 with reference to such genealogies as are found in Philo, Josephus, and the Book of Jubilee, by which Jews traced their descent from the patriarchs and their families".

There is some evidence, but mostly from a later period, that the word "genealogies" was used with reference to the orders of aeons and spiritual manifestations postulated in gnosticism as linking God and man. Irenaeus and Tertullian taught this (and have been followed by Bengel and Alford), but those second century teachers stood face to face with the full development of gnostic heresy. Here, it is not so much the falsity of such things that is stressed but their utter puerility. In the three references mentioned the word is best taken to describe a line of teaching that combined gnostic-like speculation with the legendary kind of interpretation of the OT built particularly on the pedigrees of the patriarchs.

The word "endless", which signifies "interminable", qualifies both nouns and serves to link them together as the one heresy. Since these were both outside the bounds of Scripture, there never could be any end to such speculative fantasies. They could be developed endlessly.

The consequence of this false teaching is self-evident. The plural "which" finds its antecedent in both "fables" and "genealogies" and these provide (AV "minister", JND "bring") questions. The word is rather "questionings" as in the RV. It translates *ekzētēsis* from the verb *zēteō*, "to seek"; the prefix *ek* (out) making the compound mean "an investigation, a laborious seeking out".

This, in no way, denies the right of believers to ask questions concerning the faith, but it is a condemnation of the many pseudo problems which false and non-scriptural teaching engenders. Fanciful interpretation and imaginative speculation, off the solid ground of Scripture, always end in such a wilderness.

In contrast to such a quagmire produced by this kind of teaching, "sound doctrine" (v.10) will produce different results. The RV follows a better attested reading when it translates the next phrase "a dispensation of God". This word "dispensation" is often used as if it meant an age or period, characterised by certain features. This is a derived meaning in English which the original word does not bear. Its primary meaning is the idea of stewardship, the management of a household. In Paul's writings it refers either to God's redemptive purpose in history (Eph 1:10; 3:19) or to the responsibility entrusted to others to bring this about (1 Cor 9:17; Col 1:25; Eph 3:3). In the context of this letter it is clear that heretical teachings were inimical to the practical outworking of the stewardship, the household management, of divine things in the local assembly. This is the letter wherein the assembly will be seen as the house of God (3:15). This spiritual stewardship is defined by the phrase "which is in faith" — thus it is in the realm of christian believing; this faith is based squarely and solidly on the word of God; to step off this firm foundation is to be lost in the "questionings". Speculative nonsense, however authoritatively taught, does not help the believer to live for God.

5 The use of the word "commandment" in the AV could mislead the casual reader. It is not a reference to Mosaic Law, referred to in the following verses but is the cognate noun (*parangelia*) of the verb used in v.3 (*parangellō*) and the connection is inescapable. Further, this noun is never used in Scripture of the Law. Again, while love is the fulfilling of the law (Rom 13:10), it never could produce it, nor was it meant to do so. The RV translates "the end of the charge". The word "end" (*telos*) has a primary meaning of terminus but a secondary meaning of purpose or aim which is clearly the idea here. The charge that Paul gives to Timothy is not an end in itself, neither is it to preserve doctrinal purity, nor to enable Timothy to win some theological battle, but it has a positive and spiritual objective: to enable believers to live as God expects them to do in the discharge of their spiritual stewardship.

The aim or purpose is love (*agapē*), which doubtless stands in clear contrast to the contentiousness (v.4; 6:4), the product of false teaching. Scripture recognises this love to be the product of divine action (Rom 5:5) which necessarily involves adherence to the "sound doctrine" (v.10). Different teaching, which Timothy is charged to combat, allows the springs of life (the heart) to be polluted and the moral standards to be lowered, so that the conscience is affected and the whole manner of life becomes a sham as if the person were only wearing a mask. Thus it is vital that Timothy act decisively so that love in action may be manifest to be divine, unpolluted, unsullied and unfeigned.

The elements that characterise such love are three:

1. A Pure Heart (*katharas kardias*). In Scripture the heart is the centre and thus the source of a person's moral and mental activity. It is the seat of the will and decisions taken here will control the actions. The adjective "pure" (see 2 Tim 2:22) indicates that there can be no admixture of false or tainted motives at the source of this love. It will spring from fellowship with God who is Love.

2. A Good Conscience (*suneidēseōs agathēs*). The word "conscience" (from *sun*, "with" and *oida*, "to know", literally means "joint knowledge" with others. That the conscience requires a divine standard to be a safe guide is shown in Acts 23:1 by Paul's reference to his pre-conversion days in the statement "I lived in all good conscience before God until this day". The believer, in the light of gospel truth with God's standard therein revealed (Rom 1:17), with the conscience once purged (Heb 9:14), is expected to live with a "good conscience" (3:9; 2 Tim 1:13) and a conscience "void of offence" (Acts 24:16). When the believer walks in simple obedience to Scripture under the power of the Holy Spirit there can be no "self-reproach" — his conscience is good. The word has the same root as consciousness which means "awareness of" and, in general, relates to the physical realm. Conscience is an "awareness" but restricted to the moral sphere: it is a moral awareness. In the OT the word "heart" serves this function as in 2 Sam 24:10: "And David's heart smote him" (see also Job 27:6). Conscience, according to Rom 2:14-15, is innate and universal. It is not the product of environment, training, habit, race, or education; it is one of those essential features that distinguishes man and beast. In man it distinguishes between what is morally right and morally wrong; it urges man to do the first and resist the latter. It passes judgment upon his acts and executes that judgment within the soul.

3. Faith Unfeigned (*pisteōs anupokritou*). The word "unfeigned" is *anupokritos*, a word used to describe the acting of a stage player. This divine love cannot be the outcome of a life lived in insincerity, as if the believer were just acting a part on a stage. It is not just intellectual assent to theological propositions and a sense of duty that produces love, but it springs from a simple genuine trust in God, that needs no pretence. This can only be produced by the sound teaching the false teachers would deny to the saints. It is Timothy's responsibility to make sure the situation is corrected.

6 The antecedents of the plural pronoun "which" are the three elements just mentioned — a pure heart, a good conscience, faith unfeigned. These terms identify the sources that produce this kind of love; they themselves are the product of healthy teaching. From these (which are, after all, the object of the charge) some have swerved. The verb from which the aorist active participle is derived is *astocheō* which means "to miss the mark", "to err", "to fail". This could suggest inadvertent failure due to circumstances or just carelessness rooted in weakness. A more culpable element arises in the context. Alford translates "some having failed" but proceeds to add, "but this seems hardly precise enough; it is not so much to miss a thing at which a man is aiming, as to leave unregarded one at which he ought to be aiming". In other words these false teachers have not set the right object before them in their teaching. The result of such failure follows in the next verb translated "have turned aside". The verb is *ektrepō*, for which Thayer gives as its first meaning "to turn or twist out", and is used of dislocated limbs (note the figurative use of this in Heb 12:13), but his second meaning of "to turn off or aside" better fits the context in this passage. The metaphor in the words shows that these false teachers are like marksmen who will never reach the target (they were not aiming at it) and like travellers who will never reach their destination (they have turned off into another path). The by-path meadow they have reached is described by the phrase "vain jangling". An onomatopoeic expression translating *mataiologia* (from *mataios*, "devoid of force, truth, results", "to no purpose"; *logia*, "talk") — which simply means "idle chatter" or "useless talk"; nothing of spiritual value can come from this "vain talking" (RV). Simpson writes cogently: "These fumblers were on a false trail. The quest of recondite subtleties and tortuous rigmaroles had greater charms in their eyes than the sublime themes of vital christianity. Their lenses were out of focus, their perspective false and erratic."

7 The explanation of that which motivates the false teachers is now revealed. The participle "desiring" (from *thelō*) indicates a settled aim arising from an inclination within (cf. 5:11); a purpose to which everything else has to be necessarily subjected. Their aim is nothing less than "to be teachers of the law", or as JND, "law teachers". Within the context and in view of the explanatory nature of the following verses (vv. 8-11) this can only be the Law of Moses. Within Judaism "law-teacher" was an honourable title and is used of Gamaliel (Acts 22:3) by Paul. These false teachers aspired to this kind of status. Paul is clearly using the title "law-teachers" ironically in light of his exposure and condemnation of their exegetical methods and the content of their expositions. It is not that they were of the same ilk as the Judaisers of Galatia who wished to impose the full ceremonial law upon believers. Rather while reading out of the law of Moses they based on it, and deduced from it, myths and ascetical impositions which clearly indicated that they had missed the point both of the OT revelation and of the gospel itself. What had been of God in the Law of Moses, through human additions and impositions, had become morally powerless in Judaism. Paul through this charge to Timothy desired to preserve the saints from a similar error. Plenty of talk ("what (things) they say"), bolstered by confident assertions ("what they strenuously affirm", JND) simply concealed a complete lack of basic understanding of what they are doing. The same verb "they affirm" (in Hellenistic Greek it means "to dogmatise") is used in a good sense in Titus 3:8. Thus the confident teaching of divine truth based on the word of God becomes in the hands of false teachers a sententious pomposity which displays a basic ignorance. Those who speak most authoritatively, when the teaching is not based on Scripture, show the hallmark of the false. Vincent notes, "false teachers announce their errors with assurance".

b. The Ignorance of the False Teachers (vv.8-11)

The ignorance of these would-be law teachers is not only evidenced by the introduction of philosophic speculations but it is manifested in their misunderstanding of the very function of the law. That this is the Mosaic Law is not only demanded by the Jewish background of the heresy as previously discussed, but the article with "law" in v.8 would identify it thus. We have, in addition, the fact that in the subsequent verses the order of sins mentioned adheres closely to the ten commandments. (The absence of the article with "law" in v.9 carries little weight and it is not necessary to widen the thought to law in general; to do this introduces an idea not relevant in the context).

8 The somewhat ironic reference to "teachers of the law" might suggest that Paul was casting a reflection on the law itself. Paul would hasten to dispel any notion that he would speak lightly or disparagingly of the Law of Moses. The "we", of course, are well instructed believers in contrast to the false teachers. The verb "know" (oida) signifies "primarily, to have seen or perceived; hence to have knowledge" (Vine). This implies a fulness or completeness of knowledge. Thus Paul is saying that a true appreciation of divine revelation by believers places the law in its correct relationship to man. The word "good" (kalos) could be translated "excellent" as implying that which is well adapted to its purpose. There is nothing wrong with the Law of Moses (Rom 7:12).

The word "man" is the translation of "anyone" and widens the idea beyond the teacher, anyone with this true understanding. The adverb "lawfully" (nomimōs) echoes the word law (nomos) and is not to be taken vaguely as if to mean "in a lawful manner", but rather in the sense of "treating it as law". The subsequent verses will show its proper place in the history of salvation.

9-10 The participle, opening the verse, echoes the same verb "know" as in v.8 as the apostle states the true function of the law. It is still the Mosaic Law that is in view. In the context there is little to suggest that Paul moves in thought to law in general. Paul is not discussing a philosophic question in the abstract but a particular problem arising from a particular kind of false teaching.

Of the verb "made" (*keimai*) Vine writes: "To lie" is sometimes used as the passive voice of *tithēmi*, to put; it is translated 'is (not) made' in 1 Tim 1:9 of the law, where a suitable rendering would be 'is (not) enacted'. The absence of the article before the Mosaic Law has numerous examples (Rom 2:25,27; 3:28,31; 5:20; 7:1; 10:4; Gal 2:19; 6:13 etc). It weakens also the force of the argument if Mosaic Law is embraced merely in the wider principle of law in general.

The correct appreciation of the law in question leads to the correct understanding of the word "righteous". This cannot bear the everyday meaning of "honest, decent, respectable" — as if the law was inapplicable to this kind of person. Rather it must be used in the scriptural, forensic sense of a man declared "righteous" before the Law of God. Thus, the false teachers were totally in error in attempting to bind the obligations of law upon a person already declared "righteous" before the claims of this law. Thus "righteous" carries the same sense as in Rom 1:17 ("the just shall live by faith") and Rom 5:19; Gal 3:11; Heb 12:23. In this connection the comment of W. Kelly is pertinent: "If Christ died and bore its curse, and we too died with Him, and we are now no longer under the law but under grace, the truth is kept intact. The authority of the law is maintained and yet we who believe have full deliverance. If we were really under law for walk, we ought to be cursed or to destroy its authority".

Thus for a "just" man, a believer, the application of law is superfluous; he has been cleared of every charge and the re-imposition of it in any form is, to use Paul's word in the negative, "unlawful". See note.

Paul drives home his point by enumerating the types of persons against whom the Mosaic Law stands in absolute condemnation. This list should be compared with those of Rom 1:28-32; 1 Cor 5:10-12; 2 Cor 12:20-21; Gal 5:19-23. That this particular list is based on the decalogue is shown by the table below.

The first six categories are in three pairs. The offences are Godward and answer to the first table of the Law:

1 Timothy 1:9-11		Exodus 20:1-7
(a) **Lawless and Disobedient** (Attitude and Action)	1.	"Thou shalt have no other gods before me".
	2.	"Thou shalt not make unto thee any graven image".
(b) **Ungodly and Sinners** (Conduct and Condition)	3.	"Thou shalt not take the name of the Lord thy God in vain".

(c) **Unholy and Profane**
   (Character and
   Condemnation)

4. "Thou shalt remember
   the sabbath day to keep
   it holy".

"Lawless" used in Acts 2:23 (AV renders "wicked" where it likely means Gentile hands) and 2 Thess 2:8 (AV "that wicked one"), implies flagrant defiance of the revealed will of God.

"Disobedient" (*anupotaktos*) means one not subject to rule or order hence "unruly" (Titus 1:6,10), with the basic idea of insubordinate.

"Ungodly" (*asebēs*) — "without reverence for God" underlies the impiety that has no respect for His demands. See Rom 4:5; 5:6; 1 Pet 4:18; 2 Pet 2:5; 3:7; Jude 4,15.

"Sinners" (*hamartōlos*) are those who miss the mark. The word describes all individuals subsequent to the fall (Rom 5:8-9).

"Unholy" (*anosios*) describes those who are the opposite to what God is — holy. The word "holy" is used of God (Rev 15:4; 16:5) who is opposed to all that is unrighteous or polluted; it is used again in 2:8 and Titus 1:8 of the character and conduct of believers.

"Profane" (*bebēlos*) was used to describe the area outside a temple where the common folk could walk. It came to be used figuratively of all that was outside the "hallowed sphere". In the NT it could be rendered "unhallowed", that which had nothing sacred about it, no affinity to God (see Vine).

The next part of the list corresponds even more closely to the second table of the Law down to the ninth commandment.

(d) **Murderers of Fathers**
    Murders of Mothers

5. "Honour thy father and
   mother".

(e) **Manslayers**

6. "Thou shalt not kill".

(f) **Whoremongers. Them**
    that defile them-
    selves with mankind

7. "Thou shalt not commit
   adultery".

(g) **Menstealers**

8. "Thou shalt not steal".

(h) **Liars**
    Perjured Persons

9. "Thou shalt not bear false
   witness".

Instead of patricides and matricides (d), JND and many others give a wider sense to the words and translate "smiters of fathers" and "smiters of mothers", while "manslayers" (e) embraces all categories of homicide.

The next two words (f) cover all sins of a sexual nature whether of a heterosexual or a homosexual nature. That "menstealers" (g) was a specific violation of the eighth commandment is clear from Exod 21:16 and Deut 24:7. The word for "perjured persons" (h) is *epiorkos* (*epi*, "against"; *horkos*, "an oath") and expresses the idea "to swear falsely", "to forswear oneself". The cognate verb is used in Matt 5:33: "Thou shalt not forswear thyself".

In the final phrase of v.10, the apostle passes from the sinners to the sin — "if there be any other thing". We might have anticipated a reference to the tenth commandment but he closes the list in such a way as to show that there is now an infinitely higher standard available to us in the "sound doctrine" that is in keeping with the gospel.

"Sound doctrine", literally "healthgiving teaching", embodies the apostolic teaching. The excellence of the Law is seen in the glorious revelation of the character of God which unsparingly illuminates, and thus condemns, all that is inimical to Him. Now this is embraced in the fuller revelation in Christ, enshrined in apostolic teaching. That which was ever a violation of Mosaic Law, is still a violation of the full revelation of the glory of God manifest in Christ and the gospel. What was contrary to that law (contrary is *antikeimai* from *anti*, "against"; *keimai*, "to lie", that is "all which lies against" or "opposes" — a good translation would be antagonistic) is still contrary in the light of the gospel.

This health-giving teaching is as free from causistical quibbles and speculative nonsense as it is from legalistic impositions.

11 Law, when applied lawfully, does not feed philosophical speculation and produce the overweening pride of the false teachers, but exposes and condemns sin and sinners. The words "according to" (*kata* with the accusative) indicate that this function of sin-exposure is now embraced in the gospel. The "sound doctrine" unfolds "the gospel of the glory of the blessed God" (RV). This translation (supported by JND) is to be preferred as giving proper weight to the word "glory" as a noun, not as an adjective. The glory ("manifest excellence") revealed in the law, that of the holiness of God, could but condemn the sinner; the glory now revealed in the gospel includes this but allows the full radiance of His righteousness and grace to shine forth so that this same sinner can be cleansed, cleared and changed, and thus fitted for the very presence of God. This is the revelation of the manifest excellence of the blessed God. "Blessed" (*makarios*, used of God only here and in 6:15) signifies what God is in Himself, essentially and inimitably. The thought is not that God is the object of blessing, but that in Him all blessedness is enshrined and He imparts this to men. The law but brings to light the sinfulness of men, but in Christ is revealed through the gospel, divine majesty, power, and infinite love. The same idea is seen in 2 Cor 4:4 where Christ is spoken of as "the image of God". The more usual word for "blessed" is *eulogētos* (Rom 1:25; 9:5) and signifies the ascription of praise to God by redeemed souls.

As the apostle contemplates such a revelation in the gospel superseding the

Mosaic Law, a sense of wonder seems to overwhelm him as he recognises that he has a responsibility in the matter. "I" is in the emphatic position as the final word in the sentence. "Committed to my trust" is the aorist passive of the verb "believe" (*pisteuō*) thus signifying that someone placed confidence in him. This would point back to a past event that began a divine stewardship; most likely to the happening on the Damascus road (Acts 9:3-9; 26:12-19). See the same verb in the following passages: Luke 16:11; 1 Cor 9:17; Gal 2:7; 1 Thess 2:4 where the idea of "trust" is present.

Notes

9 Two matters need explanation with regard to the law. Some rightly point out:
(a) that each of the commandments (except the fourth, with regard to the Sabbath) has a NT Scripture to emphasise its truth, such Scriptures as 1 John 5:21 (second); Heb 13:4 (seventh); Heb 13:5 (tenth) come to mind, and
(b) that the OT law is used to emphasise NT truth as in Eph 6:2, 1 Cor 14:34 and 1 Cor 9:9.
This is correct and reflects the fact that the OT law revealed the divine standard of righteousness which can never change. The revelation of law but highlighted man's weakness and failure.
   The law was not designed to produce righteousness but to reveal it. With the material upon which it had to work (fallen man) it could not produce righteousness and hence became an instrument of condemnation and death. The believer now, because of what Christ has done (Gal 3:13),is placed beyond its condemnation and has the Holy Spirit within to produce what the law could not produce, practical righteousness in the reproduction of Christ-likeness (Col 3:10). This is set forth clearly in Rom 8:3: "For what the law could not do in that it was weak through the flesh, God sending his own Son in the likeness of sinful flesh, and for sin, condemned sin in the flesh; that the righteousness of the law might be fulfilled in us, who walk not after the flesh, but after the Spirit".
   Any legalistic imposition of law upon the believer, no matter how well-meaning the motive, comes under the condemnation of this verse.
10 Some see a problem with regard to the Sabbath (the fourth commandment), and many would wish to impose a legalistic sabbath-keeping on believers today in spite of the clear teaching of Col 2:16-17 and Gal 4:10. It would appear that the Pharisaic misunderstanding of the place and purpose of the Sabbath (Matt 12:1-14; Luke 6:1-11) is still with us today. That which was ceremonial and typical pointed to a reality which the believer now enjoys in Christ. We have this reality expressed in Heb 4:9: "There remaineth therefore a rest (keeping-of-sabbath, Newberry) to the people of God". To work to achieve salvation (see Titus 3:5; Gal 2:16) is to deny the Sabbath rest presented to human hearts in the gospel. The typical is no longer needed when the antitype, the reality of which the former was the picture, is now experimentally enjoyed.
11 Gospel preaching is concerned not with preaching the law but with presenting Christ (Rom 1:16) and in this full-orbed message there is that which the Holy Spirit uses to the conviction and conversion of the sinner. While the law pointed to sin (Rom 3:19) and awakened fear, the gospel message goes further and points out, not only sin, but a sin-bearer, (1 Pet 2:21-25) to awaken faith.

2. The Apostolic Authority
1:12-20

v.12 "And I thank Christ Jesus our Lord, who hath enabled me, for that he counted me faithful, putting me into the ministry;

v.13 Who was before a blasphemer, and a persecutor, and injurious: but I obtained mercy, because I did it ignorantly in unbelief.

v.14 And the grace of our Lord was exceeding abundant with faith and love which is in Christ Jesus.

v.15 This is a faithful saying, and worthy of all acceptation, that Christ Jesus came into the world to save sinners; of whom I am chief.

v.16 Howbeit for this cause I obtained mercy, that in me first Jesus Christ might shew forth all longsuffering, for a pattern to them which should hereafter believe on him to life everlasting.

v.17 Now unto the King eternal, immortal, invisible, the only wise God, be honour and glory for ever and ever. Amen.

v.18 This charge I commit unto thee, son Timothy, according to the prophecies which went before on thee, that thou by them mightest war a good warfare;

v.19 Holding faith, and a good conscience; which some having put away concerning faith have made shipwreck:

v.20 Of whom is Hymenaeus and Alexander; whom I have delivered unto Satan, that they may learn not to blaspheme."

This divine action that entrusted to Paul "the gospel of the glory of the blessed God", especially in light of his former bitter antagonism to Christ, leads him to burst out in thanksgiving. It is clear he means all to see that no law teaching could produce what grace has done in one who, previously, had been a fanatical exponent of law. Thus while he traces the twin streams of mercy and grace, ministered through Christ, up to God Himself (note doxology in v.17) he is keeping before him the reality of the divine action that has placed himself (vv. 12-17) and Timothy (vv. 18-20) in positions where they have responsibility for the preservation of the truth entrusted to them.

a. Paul — A Pattern Conversion (vv. 12-17)

12 The word "and" in the AV lacks manuscript authority and weakens the outburst of praise. The first word in the text is therefore "thanks". He renders praise to "Christ Jesus our Lord" since all is attributable to Him as the source of enablement. The aorist participle translated "who hath enabled me", has, as its cognate noun, "power" (*dunamis*) as in Rom 1:16. This is the One who arrested Saul of Tarsus, the law exponent, on the Damascus road; it is this same One, who as the Judge Advocate of the work of grace in his soul ("counted me faithful") placed him into service. "Putting me" of the AV is preferable to the RV "appointing me" as contextually this is the result of Christ's judgment. The verb *tithēmi* simply means "to put" and ecclesiastical

ordination is as foreign to this context as it is in 2:7 and in 2 Tim 1:11, where the same verb is used. The aorist tense of "judged me faithful" with the aorist participles ("enabled", "putting") would suggest the completeness of what Christ has done with Paul. His life work is summed up in the action of Christ. The word "faithful" has the same root and echoes "committed to my trust" of v.11. See the similar expression with regard to Sarah in Heb 11:11, "she judged him faithful". The AV translation "the ministry" is misleading as *diakonia* is anarthrous (no article) and simply indicates "service" as appointed by the Lord. In Paul's case it was apostolic service that Christ entrusted to him.

13 In language, neither of false humility nor of exaggeration, but which surpasses any he has previously used to describe this period of his life (1 Cor 15:9; Gal 1:13-14), Paul describes how a fanatical exponent of law appears in the light of the gospel.

"Blasphemer" (*blasphēmos*, probably from *blaptō*, "to injure"; *phēmi*, "to say"), denotes injurious speech, usually directed against God (see v.20; 6:1; and Acts 6:11-13). When directed against men the translation is generally "railers" (2 Tim 3:2 RV). Saul in Acts 26:11 describes how he treated the saints: "I . . . compelled them to blaspheme". Persecutor (*diōktēs* from *diōkō*, "to pursue") describes activities against the saints and thus against Christ (see cognate verb in Acts 9:5). The cognate noun is translated "persecution" in Acts 8:1. Whether under the first table of the law (against God) or under the second table (against men) Saul stood condemned.

"Injurious" (*hubristes*) describes an insolent or outrageous man. The cognate verb describes the treatment Christ received in Luke 18:32 ("spitefully entreated") and Paul received the same at Philippi (1 Thess 2:2 "shamefully entreated"); thus in identification with Christ he had become by that time the recipient of that which he once meted out to others.

The conjunction "but" (*alla*) is adversative and marks the contrast between what he deserved and what he received. The verb "I obtained mercy" to mark the aorist passive could be rendered literally "I was mercied". The explanation of why it was mercy and not wrath on the Damascus road lies in the word "ignorantly" which has in view the OT distinction between sin arising out of ignorance and that committed presumptuously (with a high hand). For this distinction see Lev 22:14 and Num 15:22-31. The realm, in which he acted his whole life lived up to that point, was "in unbelief". (The words that he used of Timothy in v.4, "in faith", show the realm in which he now lives). Thus Paul had belonged to the same class as those for whom the Lord prayed in Luke 23:34: "Father, forgive them; for they know not what they do".

There is something staggering in the fact that Saul of Tarsus trained in the highest school of rabbinical knowledge, even at the feet of a "law teacher" like Gamaliel, should have to confess "I did it ignorantly". There is a realm of knowledge closed to the keenest natural intellect unenlightened by the Spirit of God (1 Cor 2:14).

14 "Grace" (*charis*) echoing the word "thanks" (*charin*) of v.12 is the subject of one of those compound verbs that Paul loved to coin. The verb stands first in the sentence (*huperplenonazō* from *huper*, "over"; *pleonazo* "to abound" — thus JND "surpassingly overabounded"). It shows how Paul viewed that grace, that undeserved favour, bestowed on him. The new realm "in Christ Jesus" stands opposed to the previous one "in unbelief". Acceptance of His Lordship (Acts 9:6) brought a sense of unmerited favour ("grace") with the inseparable accompaniments ("with") of "faith and love". These latter are the visible effects produced by grace that manifest a new relationship within a new realm. "In Christ Jesus" is that characteristically-Pauline expression that with him has become almost a technical description of the position saints of this dispensation occupy before God. The presence of the singular article after "faith and love" qualifies both substantives and in its position, after "love", allows it to act as a relative pronoun to identify the result of being "in Christ Jesus". The AV gives the correct sense "with faith and love which is in Christ Jesus".

15 "This is a faithful saying" occurs five times in the Pastorals (1:15; 3:1; 4:9; 2 Tim 2:11; Titus 3:8). On two occasions the additional phrase "worthy of all acceptation" is added (1:15 and 4:9). It would appear that certain expressions were well known in christian circles and accepted as expressing vital and valued truths. Paul cites five of these and thus not only emphasises their truth, but, in so doing, places them within the scriptural record as bearing the stamp of inspiration. For further reference to this expression, see Appendix B.

The saying that is so trustworthy, and to the truth of which Paul can personally testify, is "Christ Jesus came into the world to save sinners". "To come into the world" would define how the saints viewed the advent of Christ. John will give emphasis to this in his gospel at a later date (note the six occasions of its use in John's gospel: 1:9; 3:19; 11:27; 12:46; 16:28; 18:37). The expression testifies in unequivocal fashion to the pre-existence of Christ. The words echo Christ's own statement to Zacchaeus (Luke 19:10). The order of the names (Christ Jesus) indicates that the anticipated one, the expected One, stepped into historical time. The word "world" (*kosmos*) depends on the context for its meaning. For example in John 1:10 "He was in the world (the physical realm) and the world (physical and the world of mankind) was made by him, and the world (mankind alienated from God) knew him not". What is emphasised here is not merely a change of location, of physical descent from heaven to earth, but of situation. The moral and spiritual environment was different and, yet, it is within this very realm that salvation's action is completed. Where men were held in bondage and death Christ acted to bring liberty and life. The aorist tenses of "came" and "save" indicate the completeness of the redemptive action. In these two verbs the whole action of Christ in history is summed up decisively. From the incarnation, through the crucifixion to the ascension in glory, divine purpose is revealed in Him. He fulfilled and completed this purpose and the evidence is seen in the salvation made available to men belonging to this realm.

Those for whom this salvation has been accomplished are denizens of this realm — appropriately called "sinners" (the usual word descriptive of the condition of fallen men, Rom 5:8,19). That this is no mere theological concept is shown by the fact that the mention of the word awakens within the apostle a fresh evaluation of himself. The emphatic position of "I" (last word in the statement), the use of the word "first" (*prōtos*, AV "chief", JND "first"), and the present tense "I am" (not "I was"), indicate neither mere rhetoric or hyperbole but a deeply felt sense of unworthiness. (Compare 1 Cor 15:19 "least of the apostles" and Eph 3:18 "the least of the saints"). While the word "first" (*prōtos*) can be used with reference to time, the more usual reference is to status or degree; hence "first in rank" is the idea. Paul may through grace carry apostolic authority from the Lord, but he is just a sinner redeemed through the saving action of Christ Jesus.

16 The expression (*alla dia touto*), translated "howbeit for this cause", invariably looks to what follows (see examples in Rom 4:16; 2 Cor 13:10; Eph 6:13; 2 Thess 2:11; Philem 15). Thus it was not his status as chief of sinners that caused God to act but this saving action lay within the divine purpose to be explained in the next statement.

While the RV "as chief" echoes the word of v.15, the AV "first" may more accurately combine the two thoughts previously mentioned as in the word *prōtos*. Not only would one who headed the line of sinners become a pattern of salvation but he would be the representative of a great host of "the ones coming to believe" (literal). There would be many throughout the subsequent centuries who would experience what he had experienced. "Pattern" is the word *hupotupōsis*, originally a sketch or outline, and could properly be translated "illustration"; as if God had given in Saul of Tarsus an illustration of superlative grace that would be an encouragement to others.

"Longsuffering" (*makrothumia*, from *makros*, "long"; *thumos*, "temper") is how God responds to the recalcitrance and rebellion of men (Rom 2:4; 9:22; 1 Pet 3:20; 2 Pet 2:15), a quality that ought to be reflected in believers (2 Tim 3:10; 4:2). Here it is used of Christ's attitude to a stubborn Pharisee. The "all" emphasises the degree: there was no limitation upon it. Vincent points out that the article with "all longsuffering" will have possessive force and should be translated "all His longsuffering".

The more usual statement of faith is "believe in Him" (*eis auton*, John 3:16 etc.), or "believe on" (*epi ton kurios Iēsoun*) where "on" (*epi*) with the dative case (*ep'autoi*) as also in Rom 9:33; 10:11, suggests a resting, a reliance upon Him. This reliance upon Christ brings us "unto (*eis*) eternal life" (RV). This is what the believer enjoys resting upon Christ. The adjective "eternal" (*aiōnion*) is a better translation than "everlasting" as it is not simply duration that is described but the quality of that life that inherently is of God. The same adjective qualifies God (Rom 16:26), His power (6:16), His glory (1 Pet 5:10) and the Holy Spirit (Heb 9:14).

17 The personal thanksgiving of v.12 swells to praise as Paul appreciates the saving action of Christ made good in his experience. He sees in his own case an illustrative outline of how God acts towards sinners in long-suffering; He shows mercy and He bestows grace.

This is the first of three doxologies in these epistles (others are 6:16; 2 Tim 4:18). The one worshipped is God; there is no need to distinguish persons. The title "King" has a Hebraistic background as reference to "King of saints" as the "Song of Moses and of the Lamb" (Rev 15:3) will show; it is used again in 6:15 and draws attention to the absolute sovereignty inherent in deity. "King eternal", (JND "King of the ages") echoes the last word of the previous verse and shows that there is one who stands apart from time who will in absolute sovereignty work out His purpose.

Three words are linked with absolute deity revealed in eternal sovereignty.

1. "Incorruptible" (*aphthartos*, from *a*, negativing particle; *phtheirō*, "to decay", "to corrupt"); not immortal (as in AV) but incorruptible (as in RV). This quality belongs inherently to deity (Rom 1:23). God is not subject to decay. The same word is used of the bodies of saints in resurrection (1 Cor 15:52), of the inheritance that saints enjoy (1 Pet 1:4) and of that spiritual adornment produced here on earth (1 Pet 3:4). In these instances the quality is, of course, dependent on, and derived from, Him to whom it belongs essentially.

2. "Invisible" (*aoratos* from *a*, negative; *horaō*, "to see") used of God in Col 1:15; Heb 11:27. Distinct from His creation God cannot be encompassed within human vision (which belongs to this creation); yet in Christ He has revealed Himself to His creatures (John 1:18; Col 1:15).

3. "Only" (*monos*, "alone, solitary") an attribute of deity, John 5:44; 17:3; Rom 16:27; 6:15-16 which stresses the uniqueness of deity. He is alone in solitary dignity. MSS support is weak for "wise" and RV and JND omit it.

One use of the word "honour" (*timē*) has the thought of valuing. This idea underlies its translation "price" as for example in Matt 27:6,9; Acts 4:34. However in appreciation of deity it indicates the soul overwhelmed with holy reverence and awe in the presence of One who is beyond human evaluation. It is used in ascriptions of praise to God in 6:16; Rev 4:9, 11; 5:13; 7:12.

"Glory" is the word *doxa* (from which we get the word doxology) which comes for *dokeō*, to seem, and thus primarily signifies an opinion, an estimate, and hence the appreciation resulting from a good opinion. In the heart of the believer a contemplation of God revealed in the gospel brings forth this ascription of praise. It is used in this way in Luke 2:14; Rom 11:36; 16:27; Gal 1:5; Rev 1:6.

Believers as represented by the chief of sinners, reached by sovereign grace, have begun an appreciation of God now that produces praise which shall never end. The phrase "forever and ever", translated by JND "to the ages of ages", both in Greek thought and in Scripture means "interminably", or "unendingly". It is used in ascription of glory to God (Phil 4:20; Heb 13:21; 1 Pet 4:11; 5:11) and to the Lord Jesus (2 Tim 4:18). The same expression describes in Revelation the felicity of the redeemed (Rev 22:5), the punishment of the harlot (Rev 19:3), of the beast and false prophet (Rev 20:10), and of the worshippers of the beast (Rev 14:11). Is it any wonder the heart of the apostle responds with "Amen"?

b. Timothy — A Personal Charge (vv. 18-20)

Timothy's natural inclination would have been to be with Paul (see comment on v.3), so Paul draws attention to the fact that prophetic direction had placed him at Ephesus. This consciousness would strengthen Timothy's hands in the difficulties with which he was faced there.

18 In the word "charge" the apostle repeats the noun of v.5 and the cognate verb of v.3. In the verb, "I commit", Paul as he often does, uses another metaphorical word that changes the picture and adds a new thought. When the word "commit" is used in the middle voice as here, this verb often refers to a bank deposit. It describes something given into the care of another to be recovered when demanded. It shows the trust Paul placed in "child Timothy" (the term of affection of v.2) to put into his care such a deposit for the well-being of the saints at Ephesus.

Paul did not choose Timothy for this task out of partiality or sentimentality but in keeping with divine direction through prophetic ministry. This is the force of the expression "according to", i.e. "in keeping with", (kata with the accusative). The participle describing the prophecies (proagousas from pro "before"; agō "to go") in the present active means "to lead the way" and could be interpreted to mean "pointed you out to me". This would then refer to the prophetic ministry associated with the call of Timothy when he accompanied the apostle as he moved into full-time service (Acts 16:1-31). This is what is in view in 4:14, and is the kind of prophetic ministry illustrated in the case of Barnabas and Saul in Acts 13:2. The laying on of hands of the elders acknowledged this divine guidance and Timothy's fitness for the task.

However, the participle could refer to a subsequent occasion, when the prophecies given of the Holy Spirit directed that Timothy should remain at Ephesus. In Acts 21:8-11 there is just such an illustration of this kind of guidance. This latter view is to be preferred and finds support in the expression "by them", (this is to accept the instrumental use of the preposition "in"). J.N.D. Kelly translates "braced by them"; thus in the conflict in Ephesus Timothy would have the inward assurance not only of a general fitness for the Lord's service (4:14) but a specific direction that he was there by divine arrangement and direction. This would strengthen him immeasurably for the task.

Paul is very fond of military metaphors and likes to picture the christian as a warrior (1 Cor 9:7; 2 Cor 10:3; Phil 2:25; 2 Tim 2:3). The phrase "mightest war a good warfare" graphically depicts not an isolated battle but a life-time campaign. The noun at the close echoes the verb. The article before "warfare" indicates that while there is special relevance for Timothy at this juncture as he engages in the conflict in Ephesus, this is but an episode in a lifetime experience of conflict for truth, in which all saints share. "Good" (*kalos*) may be translated "noble".

19 "Holding" is contextually a good translation for the participle of the verb "to have" (JND "maintaining") as it continues the metaphor of conflict. See 1 Thess 5:8 and Eph 6:11-16 for other items, defensive and offensive, required in the battle. Faith and conscience are linked on three occasions in the epistle (v.5 and 3:9 are the other occasions) thus showing the link between the spiritual and the moral. Believing God through His word (faith subjectively) produces a corresponding agreement in conduct. Conscious of a divine standard through believing the word of God, the christian so acts in conformity with this that no accusing voice is raised within his moral being to point to fault or default. His conscience is good (see 1 Pet 3:21 for the same expression). Any inward doubt arising from a particular action or known disobedience would undermine the confidence of the believer in the battle and leave him at the mercy of the enemy.

The antecedent of the relative pronoun "which" is the nearest noun "conscience". Thus some folk at Ephesus, in refusing to bring their conduct into line with the word of God, instead of pursuing a straight course had ended up on the rocks of spiritual disaster. The aorist participle (*apotheō*, from *apo*, "away from"; *ōtheō*, "to shove", thus push away from one) is from a strong word and would suggest a deliberate, wilful, even violent act. It implies a positive spurning of conscience rather than mere carelessness. The same verb in Acts 7:29, 39 is translated "thrust him away", in Acts 13:46 "put it away", and in Rom 11:1,2 "cast off". The aorist tense (not the perfect as in the AV) of "made shipwreck" graphically sums up the disaster that had befallen those who refused the appeal of conscience. The RV "concerning the faith" draws attention to the article and suggests that it is faith objectively, that is the body of truth which comprises the christian faith. This would find support in 6:21 and 2 Tim 2:18 as indicating how some now stand regarding the great historical and doctrinal truths of the gospel. However, it is submitted that it agrees much better with the immediate context (both the anarthrous use of faith in the previous verse, v.18, and the disciplinary action in the following verse) as well as with the wider context of the use of "faith" in the chapter (see vv.2,5,14) to understand it in the subjective sense. The translation "concerning their faith" is fully justifiable. This would emphasise that a moral failure, rather than a doctrinal aberration, is described by the word "shipwreck" wherein their testimony has failed.

20 Two tragic examples, doubtless well-known in Ephesus, are named whose moral failure has manifested the shipwreck of their faith. The not-so-common name, Hymenaeus, would identify him with the man in 2 Tim 2:17, where details are given of the false teaching. Alexander, a much more common name, is difficult to link satisfactorily with any of the other four Alexanders in Scripture. It would be arbitrary to say he is the Alexander of the riot (Acts 19:33) of many years before; more tempting would be identification with the Alexander of 2 Tim 4:14, assuming this man belonged to Ephesus, but the addition of "the coppersmith" may be to distinguish this one from any other.

Towards these men Paul had acted decisively with apostolic authority. "Delivered unto Satan" recalls the sentence to be put into effect on the immoral Corinthian (1 Cor 5:5), a sentence which could well be derived, in principle, from Job 2:6. Paul acted apostolically, the Corinthians were expected to act congregationally. The expression describes the excommunication of an individual, or individuals, from the local assembly. However, it must go further, and imply the expulsion from a sphere where divine care and protection is experienced, to another where he, or they, will be, or can be, subject to actual physical harm brought about by Satan. Physical consequences could be anticipated (see Matt 18:34). It is clear that while Satan is ever subject to divine limitations, he is permitted, on occasions, to damage the well-being of those under scriptural discipline. This serves two purposes. In the first place, it is not judicial but remedial. The word "learn" (*paideuō*) is translated in the RV "that they might be taught"; it is the disciplinary process in child education, but with the emphasis here on the discipline rather than the education. Note the use of the word *paideuō*, in 1 Cor 11:32; 2 Cor 6:9; Heb 12:6; and Rev 3:19. Secondly it is admonitory; others, recognising how painful the lesson, will seek to avoid the necessity for it. The treatment would be seen to be effective when these two men would "cease to blaspheme". The present active infinitive with the negative could thus be translated. The cognate noun is in v.13 ("a blasphemer"); these men were doing what Saul had once done prior to conversion; they were speaking contemptuously of God, His word, His people; possibly they were ridiculing the simple presentation of gospel truth. In doing this they reviled the Author of truth. The aim of scriptural discipline would be to cause this to cease.

Notes

17 The word "eternal" (*aiōnes*) is translated "worlds" in Heb 1:2; 11:3, and shows that the physical universe within a time frame is in view. It is within this universe (time-space-matter) that God will work out His purpose (Eph 3:11) which is centred in Christ. This is evident in Heb 9:26 where we have "the consummation of the ages" (JND), and in 1 Cor 10:11 where we have "the ends of the ages" (JND); this latter reference showing that the issues and lessons of previous ages find their culmination in the church age and the full display of this will be in the "ages to come" (Eph 2:7). Absolute sovereignty will work out the purpose of the unoriginated and eternally-abiding One within the time framed universe created and ordered by Himself.

In the mouth of men the word "Amen" indicates solemn assent; in the mouth of deity, emphatic confirmation — "It is and shall be so" (Isa 65:16 RV; Rev 3:14). Vine pertinently points out that "In Rev 3:14 it is used as a title of Christ through whom the divine purposes are established".

18　It should be noted that prophecy was the divinely-given method of communicating the mind of God in NT times before the revelation of Scripture was complete. This is seen in the Acts (11:27-28; 13:1-2; 21:8-11). References to prophecy in the epistles go back to this particular period. However, 1 Cor 13:10 speaks in anticipation of the cessation of the gift; while 2 Pet 2:1 suggests its supersession by teaching from the completed revelation of Scripture. It is clear that any claim to prophetic ministry of this kind today has no scriptural support and is, therefore, false.

III. The Unfolding Of The Charge — An Exhortation (2:1-4:5)

1. *The Atmosphere Enjoyed Within the Assembly — Public Prayer* 2:1-15

The exposure, in ch.1, of the main tenets of the false teaching already in operation in Ephesus has provided the background for the necessity of such a solemn charge laid upon Timothy (1:3, 5, 18). In light of this, certain vital and specific matters must be emphasised; this explains the "therefore" (*oun*) of v.1, and introduces the most important matter ("first of all"). In the public gatherings of the saints there must be prayer. In this will be evident how much of the will of God in this age has been apprehended by the saints. This will be seen, not only in the character and content of the actual prayers, but in the corresponding conduct (v.8) and consistency (v.9) of the saints when the men, audibly, and the women, silently, pray together in public witness. Both male and female, together, must reflect an atmosphere consistent with the House of God (3:15).

a. Men — Audible Prayers (vv. 1-8)

v.1   "I exhort therefore, that, first of all, supplications, prayers,
       intercessions, and giving of thanks, be made for all men;
v.2   For kings, and for all that are in authority; that we may lead a quiet
       and peaceable life in all godliness and honesty.
v.3   For this is good and acceptable in the sight of God our Saviour;
v.4   Who will have all men to be saved, and to come unto the knowledge
       of the truth.
v.5   For there is one God, and one mediator between God and men, the
       man Christ Jesus;
v.6   Who gave himself a ransom for all, to be testified in due time.
v.7   Whereunto I am ordained a preacher, and an apostle, (I speak the
       truth in Christ, and lie not;) a teacher of the Gentiles in faith and
       verity.
v.8   I will therefore that men pray every where, lifting up holy hands,
       without wrath and doubting."

Six matters are summarised in these verses:

1. The Exhortation to Prayer	v.1 (a)
2. The Elements of Prayer	v.1 (b)
3. The Embrace of Prayer	v.1 (c)-2
4. The Encouragement to Prayer	vv.3-4
5. The Explanation of the Basis of Prayer	vv.5-7
6. The Engagement in Public Prayer	v.8

1 The first requirement ("first of all") in the apprehension of the charge is
the right appreciation of the value of public prayer. The verb "exhort" is the
same verb as in 1:3 (*parakaleō*) but here without an object, it is more general in
import and should be translated "urge". It is the same verb as in Rom 12:1
(translated "I beseech") and is an appeal to their conscience. The "therefore"
stresses the consequence of the charge just given (1:3,5,18) and modifying the
verb "exhort", introduces the first element of the charge; the request that
must have priority. There is nothing more important than public prayer.

We need not press the distinctions in the next four words as if there were
four different types of prayer, rather they are four elements that will be found,
in varying proportions, in any one prayer.

1.   Supplications (*deēsis*, from the verb *deomai*, "to want, to need, or to
      beg") generally refer to specific needs so they become "petitions" (Eph
      6:18; Phil 4:6; 1 Tim 5:6).
2.   Prayers (*proseuchē*) is the sacred word for drawing near to God with our
      requests. In our dependent state there are needs always present that God
      alone can meet. Generally linked with supplications as in 5:5; Eph 6:18;
      Phil 4:6, these requests are directed to the only One who can meet such

needs, so, in the immediate presence of God, any irreverence in manner or word is inexcusable. According to Calvin this is the genus of which supplications is the species.

3. Intercessions (*enteuxis*) is found only here and in 4:5 (AV "prayer"); the basic idea is "a meeting with", hence "an intimate conversation with" and the "presentation of a case". The word itself does not, as in English, demand a pleading on behalf of others, though this is implied in the cognate verb in its usage in Rom 8:27,34; 11:2; Heb 7:25. Thus it indicates an exercise to seek the presence of God, to hold converse with Him in the intimacy of communion, and present our petitions, sometimes, but not necessarily, on behalf of others.

4. Thanksgivings (RV) (*eucharistia* from *eu*, "well", and *charis*, "thanks") are an essential element of all true prayer as shown in Phil 4:6; Col 4:2. The opposite ("unthankful" of 2 Tim 3:2) is characteristic of the latter day atmosphere in the world. The saints in collective testimony are different and recognise how much they owe to God (1 Thess 5:18).

Embraced within this exercise of supplications, prayers, intercessions, and thanksgivings, are "all men". The present tense of the word "be made" shows this is to be habitual and repeated practice. The assembly intercedes on behalf of (*huper*) all men.

Clearly, different persons, different problems, and different periods will govern which element is prominent in the prayers, but the scope is universal. Thanksgivings, of course, could only be rendered for a cruel, despotic ruler, after his conversion; but he would previously have been the object of supplication. The phrase "all men" is a standard one that embraces all humanity (the word used is *anthrōpos*, used generally of a human being, male or female, without reference to sex or race). The repetition of the phrase "all men" with regard to the purpose of God (v.4) and in connection with the provision of Christ (v.6 where the word "men" is understood), will underline the full scope of the design of God for mankind. Saints in their praying are expected to evidence a grasp of these matters. Any gnostic-Judaistic exclusivism imposing any limitation upon divine purpose or provision is implicitly denied. The publicly expressed petitions of the saints should bear testimony to their apprehension of these truths that embrace "all men".

2 One particular group that must specifically be publicly included in the prayers are "kings and all that are in authority". While Josephus applies the title "king" to Nero it cannot be limited to the reigning emperor. Any attempt to see in the plural a date subsequent to AD 136,when the emperor associated others with him under this title is totally without justification. The absence of the article makes the word general and descriptive of supreme rulers. "All that are in authority" is translated by the RV "all that are in high places"; we would say "all holding high office".

The result would be "that we may lead a quiet and peaceable life in all godliness and honesty". The public prayer for such dignitaries would remove any suspicion of disloyalty or rebellion and the believers would be able to live for God without disturbance. There is a mistaken notion that this is to be the subject of prayer. Far from it, the subject of prayer is the men (v.2) and their salvation (v.4). As a consequence of this public intercession for the dignitaries of the state the believers could expect to be above suspicion of subversive activities.

"We may lead" translates the same verb as used in Titus 3:3 ("living in malice and envy") where it describes a contrasting way of life. But this "living" is "quiet", free from outward disturbance, and "peaceable", a synonym for "tranquil" which, all embracive, envisages a calm within and without. The only other NT usage of the word is in 1 Pet 3:4 where it is translated "quiet". "Godliness" and "honesty" (RV "gravity") are words used only in these epistles. "Godliness" (*eusebeia*) describes the true reverence for God which comes through the knowledge of Him; and this is necessarily reflected in character and conduct. "Gravity" describes the dignity of a life springing from a moral earnestness governing inward thought and outward act. It is the balance between the extremes of churlish moroseness and frivolous levity; an inherent dignity attached to true christian character. The "all" is to be construed with both "godliness" and "gravity" as indicating that both reach their fulness in the believer. Alford suggests "all possible" or "all requisite"; no area of life is untouched.

3 The second, and more profound, reason for this public prayer ("this" refers back to the exhortation of v.1) is that it is intrinsically good (*kalos*), excellent in itself and fitted for divine purpose. Further, it is "acceptable in the sight of God our Saviour". The adjective "acceptable" is related to the verb "to welcome" or "to receive" and its cognate noun is "acceptation" in 1:15. The adjective is used only here and in 5:4, and stresses that which God can receive as being in keeping with His own nature. "In the sight of" translates *enōpion* (from *en* "in" and *ops*, "the eye") and primarily means "face to face" and shows the consciousness of the praying saints of their fellowship with the activity of God, described as God our Saviour (see Appendix B). This public prayer of the saints collectively has a special dimension, a special welcome from God Himself, that would seem to go beyond private and family prayer.

4 Having known God as "Saviour" the praying saint consciously shares in a divine intention that embraces "all men". The RV is more accurate here as it reads "who willeth that all men should be saved". The verb *thelō* (Newberry and JND translate "desireth") expresses intention and purpose arising from inclination. The other verb related to the will of God is *boulomai* and expresses intention and purpose arising out of deliberation. Thus this latter verb stresses the determinative will of God expressed in sovereign action. It is used in 2 Pet 3:9 "God is longsuffering . . . not willing (the verb is *boulomai*) that any should perish": if souls perish the reason is found not in sovereign determinative will but in other factors, indeed in their rejection of His purpose and grace. If men through the exercise of divinely-given free will reject the declared purpose and inclination of God, and the provision made in Christ, this inevitably has its consequence in their perishing. This appreciation of the role of man's free will in individual salvation finds support in the passive voice of the verb "to be saved". God wishes men to experience salvation through Christ; it is available for them, the onus now rests with them. If the active voice had been used, i.e. "to save them", the problem of the frustration of divine will would arise. As this Scripture makes plain, the inclination and purpose of God is that all men should experience salvation. That some will not be saved cannot be blamed on the divine will but on human obstinacy and obduracy.

The expression "all men" (all within the genus "men") covers the same group as those for whom prayer (v.1) is offered, and for whom provision will be shown to be made in Christ (v.6). It indicates the embrace of the divine inclination and purpose. It is false exegesis to limit the "all" to "all men without distinction" as if the sub-group of v.2 was meant to list men ethnically, nationally, or socially and make the statement mean that God can save from each of these groups.

The verb "to be saved" sums up in one word the spiritual and eternal deliverance effected for men and made available to them in Christ. Salvation is viewed comprehensively in this passage — it is salvation in its entirety. Other Scriptures in the tenses used define the time element; the perfect tense of Eph 2:8 indicates a past act with present results, "ye have been saved" relates to the spirit; the present tense of 1 Cor 1:18 "which are being saved" relates to the soul; and the future aspect is envisaged in Heb 9:28 "unto salvation" when the final element of salvation as relating to the body will be experienced. All this lies within the purpose of God for men.

The passive "to be saved" is parallelled by the active aorist infinitive "to come", which highlights the responsibility of men to embrace what God has provided. In doing this, they find themselves experiencing "the knowledge of the truth". The two statements are synchronous, i.e. they take place at the same time and are descriptive of the one act viewed from two different angles. One is not the consequence of the other; you cannot have one without the other. This latter sentence draws particular attention to one vital aspect of salvation. Salvation delivers men from all that is "untrue" (false) and brings believers into the realm of "truth".

The word for knowledge is *epignōsis* — a strengthened form of *gnōsis* and thus "full knowledge"; there is nothing beyond this completeness of knowledge. To show that it goes beyond the intellectual to the experiential we may quote W.E. Vine on 1 Cor 13:12 on the difference between *gnōsis*, and *epignōsis*: "Now I know (*ginōskō*) in part; but then shall I know (*epignōskō*), (i.e. fully know) even as also I am known (*epignōskō* — fully known).

When the sinner comes to Christ he is not only saved (Acts 16:31); he has come to the One who said "I am . . . the truth" (John 14:6) and he finds in Christ truth absolute. The fact that there is no article before either "knowledge" or "truth" shows that it is the quality or essence of each that is in view and not specific items. Thus truth here is not to be limited to evangelical truth (as 3:15 is not to be limited to ecclesiastical truth) but it is truth in its fulness and absoluteness as found in Christ (John 14:6), the Spirit of truth (John 14:17) and the Word of truth (John 17:17). For the same phrase see 2 Tim 2:25; 2 Tim 3:7; Titus 1:1, and compare Heb 10:26 (where each word has the article).

The public prayers of saints gathered in testimony (vv.1-2), not only express divine purpose for all men (vv.3-4), but have a solid foundation in the provision (vv.5-6) made in Christ for all. The proclamation (v.7) based on this may now transcend all national boundaries, and with apostolic authority goes out to all nations (AV Gentiles). Any Jewish, gnostic or modern exclusiveness is out of keeping with this message.

5-6 There are four rhythmical balanced clauses in these verses that explain why such prayer in line with the purpose of God can be effective.

1. The Uniqueness of Deity — "For there is one God". The emphatic position of the word "one" as the first word in the sentence echoes the LXX in the passage recited daily in the synagogue (Deut 6:4-9). One God stands over against one humanity (all men) and thus no conflicting purposes are possible. In Rom 3:29 Paul uses the same argument to show that oneness of deity is the basis of the universality of the gospel. The "for" introduces supportive argument for the divine purpose reaching out to all humanity.

2. The Uniqueness of the Mediator — "One mediator between God and men". In one concise statement all Jewish ideas regarding Moses (Gal 3:19) or angels (Heb 2:6) are set aside; all gnostic speculations regarding intermediaries, as aeons or emanations, are swept away; all unscriptural claims in Roman Catholicism of an intermediary function for the Virgin Mary, saints or priests, are ruled out. Only one person can fill this role "mediator between God and men", described as "Man — Christ Jesus". The RV brings out the force of the word order and absence of the article by translating "Himself man". He is unique, in that absolute deity and full humanity are in Him alone. He can thus have complete understanding of the claims of God and of the need of men and thus is fitted to bring to men the full benefit of the purpose of God. Monotheism and the solidarity of humanity demand One who can share deity and humanity to be the sole channel of divine blessing to men. Job's pathetic cry for a "daysman" (Job 9:33, where the LXX has "mediator", or "middleman") has been answered in Christ. Moses (Gal

3:19) is the only other to bear this title but it is clear he acted in the administration of the Law and for national Israel. Christ acts in grace and for all mankind. The oneness of humanity, the oneness of deity, and the oneness of the mediator form an inescapable progression of thought.

3.   The Uniqueness of the Ransom — "Who gave himself a ransom for all". Nothing was withheld by the "Man Christ Jesus". According to His own statements He gave His life (Matt 20:26); He gave His flesh (John 6:51); He gave His body (Luke 22:19); here, all are summed up in the expression "He gave himself". The same verb (*didōmi*) is used in Titus 2:4 and Gal 1:14 while a strengthened form (*paradidōmi*) is used in Gal 2:20; Eph 5:2,25. Notice that it says that Christ gave Himself not that He was given. This shows that He is God and man. A participant in divine counsel, He willingly gave what no other could give for the salvation of men.

The word "ransom" (*antilutron*, from *anti*, "instead of", and *lutron*, "corresponding price for release of a slave") stresses the cost of salvation envisaged as the freeing of a slave from bondage. The prefix *anti* attached to the word stresses the substitutionary nature of an equivalent price to what was to be set free. In its very nature the death of Christ was vicarious and substitutionary. This is emphasised by the ensuing clause, "for all" (*huper pantōn*), where the preposition *huper* indicates the scope of the work "on behalf of all men"; the glorious truth is that there is no one of all humanity excluded from the scope of that work, its value is universal. Bernard rightly remarks: "Both the elements represented by *anti*, instead of, and *huper*, on behalf of, must enter into any scriptural theory of the atonement".

The universality is asserted in the "all". This ransom was not made for a limited number but for "all men". In Matt 20:28, and Mark 10:45, the preposition is *anti*, (translated "for") but it governs "many". Thus the price paid, in the sacrifice of Christ, was paid "on behalf of" (*huper*) all, and it is effective in the case of those believing who appropriate its value; it is thus "instead of (*anti*) the many". The "many" is limited to those availing themselves of the provision. This incalculable price, substitutionary in character, has been paid for the same company — "all men" — who have been the subject of the prayers of saints (v.1) and the object of the divine purpose (v.4).

4.   The Uniqueness of the Historical Period — "To be testified in due time". The great act of sacrifice, when Christ gave Himself a ransom for all, took place in time at the moment fixed by God as suitable. The word for "time" (*kairos*) draws attention to the suitability and fitness of the time in the calendar of God. The attitude governing the act is timeless (Heb 9:14; 1 Pet 1:20; Rev 13:8) and its benefits are timeless but at a particular date in history set by God, Christ gave Himself, to display the saving purpose of God (Rom 5:6; Gal 4:4). The words "to be testified" translate

an appositional noun (*marturion*), the witness or the testimony. As a consequence of that sacrificial act in time there is a witness borne to it in the uniqueness of this gospel age. Consequent upon the cross this age has been established in the descent of the Holy Spirit at Pentecost and the despatch of apostolic messengers bearing witness to His person and work. The preaching of Christ crucified and risen bears testimony, in the power of the Holy Spirit, to the saving purpose of God towards men.

7 The final argument in support of the exhortation (v.1) to public prayer is a personal one from the experience of the apostle himself. "Whereunto" is the AV translation of the words "for which" and the antecedent is the noun "testimony" of v.6. In this witness Paul had a place. The RV translates "I was appointed" in place of the AV "I am ordained". "Ordained" suggests some ecclesiastical ceremony, foreign to the original word, and without scriptural support. The verb used is *tithēmi* ("to put") and has been shown to mean "putting into service" in 1:12 and 2 Tim 1:11; it is translated "I have set thee" in Acts 13:47 and "hath made you" in Acts 20:28. Any claim for scriptural sanction for clerical ordination ceremonies from this verse is patently false.

The service into which Paul has been placed is described by two words. "Preacher" is *kērux* (generally a herald, and used here and in 2 Tim 1:11 of Paul, and in 2 Pet 2:5 of Noah) which is akin to *kērugma*, "the thing preached" (1 Cor 1:21) and to the verb *kērussō*, "to preach" (Acts 10:37 etc.). The emphasis in "preacher" falls on the act of announcing, the activity. The second word (*apostolos*, see 1:1) stresses the authority for the activity in which he is engaged.

The parenthetic and vigorous assertion, "I speak the truth in Christ and lie not", which, in keeping with the present tenses, could be rendered "I am speaking the truth and not lying", may be taken with the foregoing statement. This, indeed, is certainly characteristic of Paul who was sensitive to insinuations with regard to his apostolic authority (see similar vehement statements in 2 Cor 11:31; Rom 9:1; Gal 1:20). While this defence would of course, be unnecessary in the case of Timothy, it would be useful when the letter was read in public (see introduction) to silence possible counter-attacks by the false teachers.

However, there is more weight in the view that this statement is linked, not with the previous statement, but with the assertion he is about to make. In spite of Paul's background of Judaistic exclusivism and elitist chauvinism God had acted to make this converted bigot not only an herald and apostle, but also, most startling manifestation of grace, a "teacher of Gentiles", the emphasis falling upon "Gentiles". None of the substantives (herald, apostle, teacher) has an article; it is thus the character of the work that is in view. In keeping with the whole programme of divine purpose and divine provision for all and in this divinely-appointed period of grace, the message is going out to all nations. There is no lie about the intention of God and this is seen in the task He has given to Paul.

The anarthrous "Gentiles"(*ethnos*, from which we derive the word "heathen" describing all nations outside the Jew) emphasises, from a different angle, the all-embracing nature of the divine purpose. No national or elitist boundaries could limit the scope of the commission of the apostle. Further his preaching and teaching would not be in the sphere of political or national emancipation, social amelioration or theological disputation but in a realm where "faith and truth" (RV) would be in evidence. Men of all nations would be blest in "believing God" and "realising truth" (v.4). While the terms may be taken subjectively, as suggested, and this makes excellent sense, there is difficulty in distinguishing between the "believing" and "what is believed" and between "truth realised" by the saints and "truth embodied" in revelation. The single preposition "in" governing both abstract nouns suggests that, despite the absence of any article, they had best be taken objectively as in the paraphrase "in the realm of the faith delivered and the truth unfolded in the gospel". It is in this sphere that Paul finds his role in divine purpose.

8 The emphatic position of the verb "I will" (RV "I desire") as the first word in the sentence stresses, as does the verb itself (*boulomai*), the authoritative nature of the apostolic command. The verb (contrast *thelō* in v.4) indicates a desire arising from conscious and deliberate thought. The implication of all that he has set forth in the previous section (vv.1-7) is emphasised in the "therefore". Action must be taken. The action is in the third word of the sentence translated "to pray", the present infinitive of the verb *proseuchesthai* whose cognate noun is in v.1 (translated "prayers"). The present tense of the verb shows what is to be habitual practice.

Up to this point the word translated "men" in vv. 1, 2 and 5 has been *anthrōpos*. Men are viewed generically as distinct from any other genus; it is mankind in view, without distinguishing male or female. Now Paul uses the word for "males" (*anēr*) and the inclusion of the article marks a class; in other words — "the males". This bears out the truth emphasised previously that we have in view the collective public praying of the saints in the assembly.

This verse therefore will solve some further questions respecting public prayer within gatherings of saints who would desire to act in conformity to the Scriptures. The questions the verse settles are as follows:

1. Who are to pray audibly in public? The answer is "males" as distinct from "females". No sophistry that seeks to distinguish certain classes of meetings or certain situations may negate such a plain Scripture as this. To say that 1 Cor 11:15 permits a sister, with covered head, to lead the saints in public prayer is to misunderstand that Scripture and, of course, to cancel this passage. Scripture must not be treated like this.

2. Where are the believers to pray? "Everywhere" (AV) is better translated
    in RV by "in every place". A study of the occurrences of the phrase in 1
    Cor 1:2; 2 Cor 2:14; 1 Thess 1:8 suggests that it has become, in apostolic
    writing, almost a technical phrase to describe the meeting place of the
    saints. He is simply saying "wherever it is you are meeting", (see
    examples of meetings in a hired hall, Acts 19:9, and believers' homes,
    Rom 16:5; 1 Cor 16:19; Col 4:15; Philem 2). Neither "place of worship"
    in common speech, nor "consecrated building" is either authorised by,
    or contemplated in, the NT (see the solemn words of Acts 17:24). The
    first mention historically of any special building being used for church
    gatherings does not come until the close of the third century when NT
    simplicity had been widely abandoned.

3. How are believers to pray? "Lifting up holy hands". While in the OT this
    expression is literal (see 1 Kings 8:22; Ps 28:2; 141:2; 143:6) as
    ceremonially evidencing a godly sanctification, in the NT it has a
    metaphorical implication (see Heb 12:12) and denotes not simply bodily
    posture but the corresponding reality. All actions and activities are to be
    described by the word "holy" (*hosios*). While all believers are saints
    (*hagioi*), i.e. "sanctified" or "holy ones", by the action of God (1 Cor 1:2)
    through the Holy Spirit, the consequence of this action ought to be that
    all their actions, activities and associations are "holy" (*hosios*). In other
    words, those who pray publicly must not be engaged in anything that is
    at variance with their profession of faith and the character of the One to
    whom they pray. "Hands" is the common symbolic representation of a
    daily life, open to divine scrutiny and thus unpolluted by the evil of a
    corrupt society around. Two particular evils are now specified, and while
    endemic in human society, must not be associated with saints engaged in
    the holy exercise of public prayer. First mentioned as being absent from
    public prayers is wrath (*orgē*). When used of men the word describes the
    inward passion that flares up in outbursts of uncontrolled temper (Eph
    4:31; Col 3:8; Jas 1:19). No element of this may enter into the holy realm
    of prayer, even against persecutors or those who have sorely wronged
    the saints. Stephen's prayer for his murderers (Acts 7:60) reflects the
    spirit of his Saviour (Luke 23:24). The second matter mentioned is
    doubting. The word used is *dialogismos* (from *dia*, "through", *logismos*, "a
    reasoning") which is translated by Newberry and JND "reasoning", but
    by the RV "disputing". These varying translations reflect the two ways
    of understanding the word. If the argument is viewed as "within the
    saint" then the translation should be "reasoning" — "an argument with
    yourself"; this idea underlies the AV translation. If the argument is
    viewed as "without", the translation should be "disputing" — "an
    argument with others" — which is the view taken in the RV. The latter
    meaning fits the context more appropriately (J.N.D. Kelly gives
    "quarrelsomeness"). For a man in praying to display temper arising from

ill-will or resentment, or to use the opportunity of public prayer to
further an argument verges upon the blasphemous. Those who lead the
saints in such a holy exercise must evidence purity in motive and in
conduct.

Notes

2   The NT provides clear instructions for believers in their attitude to imperial
     and civil authorities in Rom 13:1-6; 1 Pet 2:13-17; Titus 3:1. This passage takes
     the matter further. The men who comprise such authorities often are the object
     of hatred. In the NT period these men were frequently the originators, and the
     administrators, of edicts against the believers. In the days immediately
     subsequent to this epistle the believers were living in mortal fear of the
     magisterial powers of local administrators. The answer did not lie in rebellion
     or civil rights protests but in prayer for the salvation of the men. The words of
     the Lord Jesus were certainly applicable: "Pray for them which despitefully use
     you, and persecute you" (Matt 5:44). For the names of such men to be publicly
     mentioned in prayer would be a testimony to supernatural grace in the hearts
     of the believers.
         It is an interesting fact that the records of history show that Jewish believers
     took no part in the rebellion that led to the destruction of Jerusalem in AD 70,
     and in general, down the ages, NT truth in respect of the civil administration
     has preserved the saints from anti-state activities. It is only when the state
     begins to interfere with obedience to the word of God that conflict arises and
     the principle enunciated by Peter in Acts 5:29 has to be faced, "We ought to
     obey God rather than men". "State churches" and "anti-state" churches are
     both totally foreign to Scripture; believers as individuals are expected to obey
     the civil authorities as far as their obedience to the word of God will allow.
         Saints may not like a communist regime but they have no mandate to take up
     arms against it; they may not approve of apartheid, but they are not
     scripturally justified in formenting rebellion against it. The believers pray for
     communists and capitalists, for black and white, as individuals who need
     salvation. God changes man and institutions change. The non-carnal weapons
     of the believers have just been listed, i.e. supplications, prayers, intercessions
     and giving of thanks, and these, exercised before the throne of God, carry
     power beyond that of either ballot box or gun.

3   Comment on v.2 has shown that the special mention of this group of eminent men
     had a specific purpose and to limit the "all men" of this verse to these savours of
     special pleading to escape the clear teaching of a salvation that in divine
     inclination reaches out to every individual.
         Subtle restrictions upon the plain meaning of this text are not new. Tertullian
     (3rd century AD) defined the "all" as "all whom He adopted"; Augustine (4th
     century AD) defined the "all" as "all the predestinated". Recent proponents of this
     line of teaching are Calvin and, in modern times, Hendricksen, who expresses it

thus: "All men without distinction of race, nationality, or social position, not all men individually, one by one".

Such teaching is more intent on preserving a preconceived theological position than seeing the contextual force of the passage. Alford cogently states in reply, "As if kings and all men in eminence were not in each case individual men".

Paul here takes issue with the Pharisaic notion that only the righteous could be the subject of divine interest (see Luke 15:1) and also with incipient gnosticism that insisted that salvation belonged to a spiritual elite. His teaching here still challenges any exclusivism that limits the purpose of God.

5   The title "God-man" is not used in Scripture and, in rationalistic minds being capable of misinterpretation, should not be used.

6   Any attempt to place a limit upon the provision made by Christ in His death must necessarily place a limit on the value of His Person. This is unscriptural. The truth has been very cogently expressed by William Blane in *The Atonement*

The Atonement was no business act
In which the Saviour did contract,
To undergo so many pains,
That He might cleanse so many's stains.
He gave ***His All*** — His life's blood flowed
To reconcile ***the World*** to God.
'Twixt God and man, to close the rent,
The spotless Lamb of God was sent,
If all the sins of Adam's race,
With perfect justice to each case,
In Heaven's balances were laid,
They would be utterly outweigh'd
By Jesus' death. The value lies
All in th'infinite sacrifice:
When Christ for man was crucified,
Th' Creator for the creature died.

*Emphasis by Blane

8   The vitality and vision that set the atmosphere in an assembly are publicly manifest in the prayer meeting. The rambling, stereotyped, lengthy praying so often displayed in many assemblies manifests the condition of those taking part. Short, specific prayers rising out of a heart burdened on behalf of saints and sinners would draw forth a hearty "amen" (1 Cor 14:16) to break the cold silence of many prayer meetings.

b. *Women — Visible Presentation (vv.9-15)*

v.9   "In like manner also, that women adorn themselves in modest apparel, with shamefacedness and sobriety; not with broided hair, or gold, or pearls, or costly array;

v.10 But (which becometh women professing godliness) with good works.

> v.11   Let the woman learn in silence with all subjection.
> v.12   But I suffer not a woman to teach, nor to usurp authority over the
>   man, but to be in silence.
> v.13   For Adam was first formed, then Eve.
> v.14   And Adam was not deceived, but the woman being deceived was in
>   the transgression.
> v.15   Notwithstanding she shall be saved in childbearing, if they continue
>   in faith and charity and holiness with sobriety."

While the men speak audibly to God the question will arise as to the contribution of the women. While they will, by implication (v.8) and instruction (v.11), remain silent, they have nonetheless, a vital part to play in the public gathering. This will be seen in their attitude and appearance, both of which will be in contrast to those manifest in the society around them.

Three matters concerning godly women are mentioned:

1. Women: Their Sobriety vv.9-10
2. Women: Their Silence vv.11-12
3. Women: Their Salvation vv.13-15

9 The word *hōsautōs* ("similarly"), translated "in like manner", is to be construed adverbially with "I will" of v.8; so the ensuing instructions are part of the same directive. A vital part of the atmosphere in the public gatherings of the saints will be established by the dress of the women present. Generally dress expresses taste and interests and, in fact, displays character; thus how a woman dresses shows what kind of a woman she is. While the apostle has still in mind the gatherings of the saints, inevitably the subject has wider implications, for the habitual and daily apparel of the sister reflects what she is. The key word is "apparel" (*katastolē*), of which Elliott says, "It conveys the idea of external appearance as principally exhibited in dress". It is deportment, as viewed externally in appearance, manner, dress. The verb "to adorn" (*kosmeō*) and the adjective "modest" (*kosmios*) are cognate words from the root "to arrange" or "to order". Thus women are to "arrange themselves" in "well-arranged" dress. We would say "in good taste" — but, it must be emphasised, the "arrangement" or the "orderliness" is not to be that of the chic fashion model of the world. It extends beyond the blending colour scheme or matching fabrics to the relationship of that apparel to her christian character and testimony. Only then will it be in the scriptural sense "well-arranged" or "well-ordered".

Two things must positively be in evidence; to retain the clothing metaphor two "accessories" (the conjunction is "with" *meta*), must go along with the outward appearance. "Shamefacedness" is the word *aidōs*, used only here in the NT, and describes a moral revulsion from all that is unseemly, a rejection of even the appearance of the overstepping of the limits of womanly reserve.

"Sobriety" (*sōphrosunē* — from *sōs*, "sound", and *phrēn*, "the mind", thus "sound judgment") used in 2:15 and Acts 26:25, stands for that inner judgment, produced in the believer by the Scripture and the Spirit of God, that provides a restraint on every merely physical or human appetite. Thus the word indicates the judgment that lies behind the moral revulsion of the previous word. Outside Scripture the word generally had a sexual nuance that implied chaste behaviour. The well-ordered dress (in the scriptural sense) reflects a well-balanced mind.

There are four "accessories" that are not in keeping with the "well-arranged" apparel of godly women. These belong to a different society, a worldly one, whether Roman, Hellenistic or modern. "Broidered hair" refers to the elaborate hair styles, costly and time consuming to arrange, produced by plaiting and braiding the hair; possibly entwined within this were golden clips, and pearls, causing the hair to scintillate in the light, thus emphasising the wealth reflected in the "costly array" (RV "costly raiment").

10 The adversative conjunction "but" (*alla*) turns from the negative (what is not to be seen) and introduces the positive (what is to be seen). The preposition "with" (*dia*) before "good works" stands in contrast to the "in" before "modest apparel" (v.9). The idea is not that she wears the good works as a garment, but through this channel (*dia*) is shown an exhibition of christian character, an attractiveness that far surpasses the merely external appearance adorned with the empty baubles of earth. To a Phoebe (Rom 16:1-2), a Lydia (Acts 16:14-15), a Dorcas (Acts 9:36-38) there is an adornment that is independent of mere dress. The word "becometh" draws attention to the fact that in godly women what they profess by lip will be fittingly reflected in their activities. The present participle "professing" (used again in 6:21) is from the verb "to promise" (see Titus 1:2) and allows us to see lip and life corresponding in an attitude Godward of respect and reverence worked out manward in works described as good (*agathos*). This latter word stresses the benefit these works bring to others; they are beneficent in character. The word for godliness is *theosebeia* which emphasises that the vital controlling element behind the dress and the deeds is an attitude to God Himself. When the fear of God fills the heart with respect and reverence for Him the dress and the deeds harmonise with the profession.

11-12 The first word in the text is "woman" (*gunē*) which in the singular number and without the article stands as the subject of the sentence, as representative of the female sex. "In silence" (*en hēsuchia*) opens the sentence and the same expression "in silence" closes it. Within these two expressions there is a positive injunction and a negative injunction. The positive instruction is "let . . . learn" where the verb is *manthanō* (akin to *mathētēs*, "a disciple") which indicates the attentive listening and observation of the woman to take in that which is for her spiritual growth and blessing. The present tense with the imperative stresses the command and its continuity: "let them go on learning". The negative instruction comes under apostolic direction "I suffer not (*epitrepō*), better translated in the RV "I permit not". The same verb reflecting the same authority is used in Acts 26:1; 1 Cor 14:34; 16:7 where the RV translates "permit" in each case. The prohibition is on a woman with regard to teaching, the present infinitive of the normal verb *didaskō* (used again in these epistles 4:11; 6:2; 2 Tim 2:2; Titus 1:11). Grammatical evidence is presented in Dana and Mantley (*Manual Grammar of the Greek New Testament*, p.199) to show that the present infinitive should here be translated "to be a teacher". That place is denied to a woman.

The word "silence" (translated "quietness" in 2 Thess 3:12), is a more comprehensive word than that used in 1 Cor 14:34 where the instruction is similar; the greater scope of the word is explained here by the added phrase that follows the conjunction "nor". To break this apostolic instruction would be a specific example of a woman stepping out of the place given her in Scripture and thus "to usurp authority over the man". Man is *anēr*, anarthrous and singular and thus generic, one of the male sex.

The silence evidences neither resentment nor bondage but stems from a willing acceptance of the sphere that Scripture gives to women. This is the force of the expression "in all subjection" (JND) where the subjection is not to man but to the truth of Scripture. The "all" has similar force to its use in v.2, a subjection manifest in every possible way, not looking for an escape from the truth enjoined. No surrender of conscience is implied but simply the acknowledgment by the woman that in the public testimony her role precludes teaching. To suggest that praying is not teaching and that therefore a woman may take part in public prayer is to do violence to the word "silence". This, of course, does not preclude the teaching of children (implied in 2 Tim 3:15 with 2 Tim 1:15) or of her own sex privately and informally (Titus 2:4). It is clear from this verse that for a woman to take the place of a teacher in public gatherings of the saints is to step out of her God-given place and to act in disobedience to Scripture.

The phrase "to usurp authority" (*authentein* from *autos*, "self" and a lost noun *hentēs*, "working", see Vine) means "to exercise authority on one's own account", "to domineer over". In light of the subsequent verses the RV translation "to have dominion" is most suggestive. This dominion is that God gave to Adam in Gen 1:26.

13 The explanation of the prohibition of v.12 is not based on any local or temporary situation arising out of Ephesian conditions, but finds its full and sufficient justification in Scripture. The authentic historicity, absolute reliability and full authority of this final court of appeal is assumed as Paul goes back to Genesis for the record of creation and the Fall.

The word "for" explains why women should not teach publicly in the assembly. The word "formed" is the word used in the LXX in Gen 2:7 and means "to mould", or "to fashion" (the same word is used in Rom 9:20). "First" (*prōtos* as in 1:15-16) not only suggests chronological priority but also includes the secondary meaning of rank and should thus be translated "as chief" (Kent), (cf. 1 Tim 1:15). The argument (as in 1 Cor 11:8-9) would thus hinge on the fact that Adam was head of the race and as a result of this he had not only priority in time but also primacy in dominion. In Gen 1:26 "God said, Let us make man in our image, after our likeness; and let them have dominion over the fish of the sea . . ." The subsequent chronological development in the formation of Eve thus showed that the sphere of her blessedness lay in this recognition of divine order. The female was dependent on the male (as in 1 Cor 11:9). When she acted independently in denying this divine order, disaster followed.

14 The record of the Fall, not some allegorical tale, but presented in Scripture and accepted by Paul as historical fact, stresses that the woman moved out of her sphere and, acting independently of Adam brought spiritual disaster upon herself and the race. The RV "hath fallen into transgression" draws attention to the perfect tense which indicates that the past action has results that still continue.

The word "transgression" is in Rom 5:14 linked with Adam, but here linked with Eve. It is used literally of "over-stepping a boundary" but metaphorically indicates "a breach of law" (see 1 John 3:4). The contrast between the man and the woman is stressed: Adam was not deceived (*apataō*) but the woman was "being deceived" (*exapataō*), the strengthened form of the verb used of Eve, shows how completely she was beguiled (Vine suggests "thoroughly deceived"). Both verbs in the aorist tense illuminate the contrasting state of mind of Adam and Eve at the moment of the Fall. In the final analysis, it is clear that the guilt of Adam was greater. He acted deliberately, conscious of what he was doing. The argument, as often presented, is not the chauvinistic one that women-kind, as represented by Eve, are more gullible than men and thus more susceptible to error than men, with the corollary that, therefore women should not be teachers. Rather, Eve stepped out of her place; in so doing she overturned a divine order and Adam, with eyes open, accepted her leadership with disastrous results. Both thus violated their God given status; Eve by an assumption of authority or dominion she did not rightly possess, and Adam, in a renunciation of authority he had no right to make. Disaster must ever follow in the wake of such failure. Paul will show that the preservation of male and female in testimony for God lies in the acceptance of this scriptural creatorial order.

15 The fact that God has not given women a teaching role in divine testimony is thus not a chauvinistic invention of Paul arising out of his background but a fact of divine order revealed in Scripture. Notwithstanding (RV "but") there is a place for women in the testimony wherein lies salvation.

The key words are "in childbearing" which are more literally rendered in the RV "through the childbearing", where the article, grammatically, may have the function of a possessive adjective "through her childbearing".

This difficult statement has been variously interpreted. See note for two other interpretations. However, within the context, the best interpretation is to see that salvation is experienced and enjoyed by believing women, when they accept, in the subjection of faith, their God-given place in a divine order. This statement needs clarification, however, on two points:

1.   We know that salvation is "not of works" (Eph 2:8) so the word "salvation" must include "spiritual preservation". Support for this more embracive meaning of the word is found in 4:16 and Phil 1:19; 2:12. The penalty upon Adam's transgression in Gen 3:17 is "in sorrow shalt thou eat of it" (the ground); the penalty upon Eve is in Gen 3:16: "in sorrow thou shalt bring forth children". In the case of the man, because of the Fall, the toil and the sweat express the necessity, privilege and dignity of man under these fallen conditions. Paul might have said "he shall be saved through toil" — the very acceptance of the conditions bringing faith to light. In the case of the woman, with whom Paul is here dealing, all the sorrow brought by sin, associated with her place in the divine plan, should thus become the very means of her salvation. "She shall be saved through childbearing" where *dia* has its weaker meaning to describe the accompanying circumstances through which the salvation is manifest. *Dia* has this meaning in 1 Cor 3:15, "saved through fire"; the fire is not the agent of salvation but the accompanying circumstance that makes the salvation manifest. So the "childbirth" is not the agent of salvation but the circumstances that make the salvation manifest.

2.   The second matter that requires clarification is dealt with in the next phrase "if they continue in faith, and charity and holiness, with sobriety". The verb "continue" (*menō*, "to remain, to abide") thus limits the promise; it is not to women in general but to believing women. They had entered the realm, so different from that in which they once lived, where the dominant features are faith (believing God) and charity (*agapē*, "love") and holiness (sanctification, same word as 1 Thess 4:3,7), accompanied by (*meta*) the manifestly chaste behaviour reflecting a well-balanced mind (AV sobriety, see v.9). This, in keeping with their acceptance of divine order, is the evidence of subjection that speaks of salvation. The plural "they" in the verb "continue" may be interpreted as "husband and wife" but is more likely to embrace simply the whole genus of believing women.

So the salvation of the saved woman is not manifest in her assumption of a teaching role in the assembly, but in her acceptance, by faith, of a divine order revealed in creation, but now conditioned by the Fall to that vital realm of the home. Under the literary figure of metonymy, using the word "childbirth", the apostle defines the circumstances wherein salvation is evidenced and experienced.

Some see a problem in that all believing women do not marry and even those who do, do not all bear children. This verse does not demand that they do, but indicates simply that any women grasping by faith, as Eve did, her place in divine order, finds in this the special preservation from the spiritual, social and satanic evils of society. (Contrast the false teaching in 4:3 designed to destroy the home).

Notes

9   1. In the modern age the dignity of womanhood has been sadly impaired by the flamboyant fashions and unisex trend of commercially orientated fashion-houses. While godly sisters with sound judgment quite rightly reject such insults to womanhood, the point of this passage is that all such displays of wealth and worldliness ill-become the sister professing godliness (v.10).
2. Some have attempted to link the word *hōsautōs* (in like manner) with the verb "to pray" of v.8, and, thus suggest that the public praying is to be done also by women with certain dress qualifications. Such is grammatically untenable and does violence to the text of scripture. The predicates of the verb *boulomai* ("I will") are the infinites "to pray" and "to adorn"(coupled by the adverb *hōsautōs*).These two verbs are parallel directives for men and women respectively; no other interpretation is possible.

14   This teaching does not stem from Paul's Jewish background or any supposed anti-feminist views. It is squarely based on Scripture and directly derived therefrom. It is in the interests of womanhood to ignore the clamant dictates of our godless society and accept the God-given role. To permit otherwise, and allow women to step out of their place in the assembly is to destroy the very testimony this charge to Timothy was given to preserve.
It is certainly true that women down the centuries have been the agents of many false cults: Mary Baker Eddy in Christian Science, Ellen White in Theosophy, Amy Semple McPherson in Pentecostalism, and a host of others in present-day movements including the "charismatics". These evidence the gullibility and susceptibility of women to error but as shown in the exposition this is not the point of the passage. A host of names could be marshalled on the male side to show how gullible men have been! But if Eve was gullible the emphasis here shows that Adam was culpable. Is this not true where we have such disobedience to divine order manifest in assembly circles today?

15   Two other views of this difficult verse are worth consideration:
1. That women may be assured of physical deliverance through the act of childbirth. Two major objections can be presented to this suggestion — (a) Paul never uses the verb "to save" (*sōzō* merely of physical deliverance; this would be the exception.

(b) Many a godly and faithful woman has died in childbirth. This would imply that they were deficient in faith, love or holiness; an unwarranted and unscriptural suggestion. Physical preservation through childbirth is no more promised to a godly woman than good health is promised to a godly man.

2. That "the childbearing" relates to the unique event in the birth of Christ through whom salvation comes. This view suggests that "Eve" of v.13 is "the woman" of v.14 and the subject of the verb "shall be saved" in v.15. This explains (a) the definite article before childbearing, (b) the use of the word "childbearing" instead of the better known word "child rearing" (see 5:10), (c) gives the verb "to save" its usual Pauline meaning interpreting the future tense in light of Eve's act of faith in the promise of the "seed", and (d) gives the preposition *dia* (with the genitive — by means of) its proper weight as the channel by which salvation comes. Thus the channel of disaster in the transgression (the women) becomes by grace, the channel of redemption through the function of motherhood in bringing in the Christ.

faith as she becomes the prototype of godly womanhood accepting her place in God's order and fulfilling it. Since salvation is not a theological abstraction but is demonstrated in the life, godly women will continue (in the line of Eve) with the evidence of faith and love and holiness under the control of a well-balanced mind (AV "sobriety").

Attractive as this interpretation is, the main weakness lies in the use of the vague term "the childbearing" as a reference to the birth of Christ without further explanation. The interpretation given in the text agrees better with the context.

2. The Authority Exercised within the Assembly
3:1-13

a. Overseers — The Qualifications Stated (vv.1-7)

v.1   "This is a true saying, If a man desire the office of a bishop, he desireth a good work.

v.2   A bishop then must be blameless, the husband of one wife, vigilant, sober, of good behaviour, given to hospitality, apt to teach;

v.3   Not given to wine, no striker, not greedy of filthy lucre; but patient, not a brawler, not covetous;

v.4   One that ruleth well his own house, having his children in subjection with all gravity;

v.5   (For if a man know not how to rule his own house, how shall he take care of the church of God?)

v.6   Not a novice, lest being lifted up with pride he fall into the condemnation of the devil.

v.7   Moreover he must have a good report of them which are without; lest he fall into reproach and the snare of the devil."

The second element of the charge given to Timothy for the preservation of the testimony deals with the qualifications that must be evident in those who will exercise authority within the assembly. Certain moral and spiritual qualities will be evidenced in men fitted for this task. Such men by their work and character play a vital part in testimony for God.

1 The work is described as "the office of a bishop" (*episkopē*) which is better rendered "oversight" (JND). This stresses not an office but the work involved. Thayer points out that the noun means "inspection, visitation, and the cognate verb has a range of meaning, to look upon, to inspect, to oversee, to look after, to care for". All these meanings have, as the underlying thought, the idea of watchfulness and vigilance.

Within the immediate context the following points should be noted:

1. This work involved will be defined in two words. The first word is "take care" (v.5) and the second is the participle translated "that rule well" of 5:17. The words bring out the nature of the responsibilities in the work of an overseer.

2. That males only are contemplated as undertaking these responsibilities follows from the teaching of 2:13-14 (see "usurp authority", v.12) and, in keeping with this, all the adjectives that follow are masculine.

3. When seen in operation, overseers are mentioned in the plural number (Acts 20:17,28; 5:17). There are always a number of overseers within the one assembly.

4. Timothy is not called upon to appoint such men; Titus was instructed to do this (Titus 5:5) amongst the new converts in Crete. Already in Ephesus overseers were acknowledged within the assembly (Acts 20:28; 1 Tim 5:17). This list of qualifications enjoined for the overseer, is thus not given only, or mainly, for the benefit of Timothy, but that the saints should recognise divine fitness in such men. There is no scriptural justification for the idea that only apostles or apostolic delegates could appoint overseers. Each assembly, divinely gathered, should expect to have such men divinely-fitted, raised up amongst them for their recognition (1 Thess 5:12).

These requirements do not present an ideal standard to which approximation is permitted, but the essential qualifications in one undertaking this work. No selection and/or election by the assembly can secure such fitness. Neither is it achieved by co-option to a board, but the Holy Spirit fits a man for the task, provides the opportunity of its execution and the saints recognise (1 Thess 5:12) the person who is actually doing the work.

For the implication of the phrase "this is a true saying", see Appendix B. This wording is exactly the same as the other four occasions of its use and there is no justification for the AV replacing the word "faithful" by "true". It is the only one of the three occasions of its use in this epistle that does not carry the additional phrase "and worthy of all acceptation". Some have tried to link the saying with the statement at the end of the previous chapter, but there is nothing to support this. No "reliable saying" is apparent in 2:15. Once again Paul uses a current christian expression familiar to the believers and by the supervision of the Holy Spirit in placing it within the scriptural record puts the stamp of divine authority upon it. It could well be that, in light of the onerous task of the overseer and the propensity of the civil authorities to persecute such leaders, there was a certain reluctance on the part of some whom God had fitted for the task, to accept responsibility in the assembly. Paul would show the excellence of such work. The word "good" is *kalos* and Vine translates the phrase "a noble work". The word "work" is *ergon* (in physics we get the word *erg*, a unit of work); the task demands an expenditure of energy, both physical and spiritual.

Two strong verbs are used to describe the yearning for this work. The first (*oregō*) means "to stretch one's self out", in order to touch or grasp something; it means more than "to desire" as it includes the reaching out after an object. The second word (*epithumeō*) means "to passionately long after" and it stresses the impulse that moves towards the object. This is the motive behind the movement envisaged in the first verb.

Three scriptural words are used for men exercising authority in the assembly:

1. Elders translates *presbuteroi*, an adjective, the comparative degree of *presbus*, "an old man", thus an older man, an elder. Used in Acts 14:23; 20:27; Phil 1:1; 1 Tim 5:17; Titus 1:5, this term has a Jewish background from the OT and emphasises the *spiritual maturity* of those fitted for the work.

2. Overseers (*episkopoi*, from *epi*, "over", and *skopeō*, "to look or watch") is found in Acts 20:28; Phil 1:1; 1 Tim 3:1; Titus 1:7; 1 Pet 2:5. From its Greek background, Thayer defines the word in a secular context as "an overseer, a man charged with the duty of seeing that things to be done by others are done rightly, any curator, guardian or superintendent". In the assembly the word describes those who "look over" or "watch over" the believers. This word lays emphasis upon the nature of the actual *spiritual work* that is done in supervision for God.

3. Shepherds (*poimen*) used in Eph 4:11 (AV "pastors" and the cognate verb in Acts 20:28 (AV "feed") and 1 Pet 5:1-2 (AV "tend"). This lays stress on the *spiritual capacity* of those who will necessarily take character from Christ who is described as the Chief Shepherd (1 Pet 5:4), the One, who gave Himself unsparingly in the interests of the flock (John 10:11).

That these terms are used interchangeably of the same persons is clear from a comparison of Acts 20:17 (the elders) and Acts 20:28 (the overseers) where the men are clearly the same group. In v.28 this group of men is instructed "to feed" (*poimainō*, "to act as a shepherd", cognate verb of the noun *poimēn*) the church of God. Peter uses the same interchange in 1 Pet 5:1-2 between "feed" (*poimainō*) and "oversight" (from *episkopos*). A reference to "elder" (*presbuteros*) and "bishop" (*episkopos*) in Titus 1:5 and 1:7 indicates the same truth. All official ecclesiastical connotations of these terms or hierarchial distinctions between them, elevating one above another, are of post-apostolic origin and find no support in scriptural usage.

Spiritual maturity (elders) and spiritual capacity (shepherds) will be manifest in men equipped of God to do the spiritual work of overseers. That work will demand an unimpeachable character and irreproachable conduct for it involves caring for (3:5) and ruling (5:17) in the church of God.

If we accept that the all-embracing qualification is given in the first statement, "blameless", then there are fourteen qualifications (the RV on good MSS evidence omits "not greedy of filthy lucre", v.3), and a convenient division is to see, generally, four broad areas in which an overseer must stand out amongst the saints.

1. In Conduct	Personal Morality	4 Statements
2. In Company	Patent Maturity	4 Statements
3. In Character	Patient Personality	3 Statements
4. In the Community	Public Integrity	3 Statements

2 The use of "bishop" (overseer, JND) in the singular with the article is generic; it describes one of a class, as in Titus 1:7; when viewed in the assembly the plural is always used (e.g. in 5:17). "Must" (*dei*) stresses the necessity of such a qualification (Reinecker translates "it is necessary") and "then" (AV), or "therefore" (RV), links with the previous verse to show that such a good work will require a good man. The all-embracing qualification is *blameless*. The word is *anepilēptos* which the RV translates "without reproach", indicating that the overseer must present no defect of character or conduct upon which ill-disposed persons, within or without the assembly, could seize and use as a weapon against him. The word is used only in this epistle. The other two occasions are 5:7 and 6:14 (AV "unrebukeable") where, as here, it signifies one not justly open to censure or criticism.

"The husband of one wife" (*mias gunaikos andra*) literally translated is "one woman man". Various views have been taken of this phrase as it describes the marital qualification of the overseer:

1. That the overseer must be married. This would be in keeping with the high value placed on marriage in this epistle, as in 4:3; 5:14; and it is certainly true that Scripture generally assumes that the overseer will be

married. However such an interpretation is most unlikely in this passage, as it leaves the emphatic "one" meaningless. Thus the insistence on the married state for an elder cannot be based on this statements.

2. That the elder must not remarry if his first wife dies; in other words the elder is permitted one wife only in his lifetime. While many have taken this view, this again is a most unlikely interpretation. It suggests some kind of suspicion about second marriages as if, while assowable, they are not to be encouraged, as if the spirituality of such remarried believers was slightly suspect. This is contrary to Rom 7:23 and the clear instruction with regard to younger widows in ch. 5:14. To assume that the claims of overseership require priority after the first wife dies is to attach a merit to the unmarried state that is never suggested in Scripture. It is difficult to see how Paul could insist, even by implication, on celibacy for a widower aspirant to overseership, and denounce the enforced celibacy of the false teachers (4:3). See also Heb 13:4 and note the "all" in that verse.

3. That the elder must have only one wife at a time. Thus on this view the statement forbids bigamy and polygamy; the elder being faithful to one woman. This again, is a most improbable interpretation. The NT never envisages that a bigamist or polygamist would ever be received into a NT assembly much less aspire to overseership. No historical evidence exists that polygamy was ever accepted in church testimony. It is not so well known that polygamy was forbidden in the Roman Empire in the days of Nero.

4. The simple interpretation is to see this statement as laying emphasis on the absolute fidelity of the overseer to one woman. Against the pagan background, locally Ephesus, with its moral degradation centred on the cult of Artemis, with prostitution, concubinage, fornication, adultery, and divorce prevalent, the elder must have an evident marital fidelity from which nothing could arise, even from unsaved days, that could lead to a sustainable charge against him. To take the place of overseership places a man in such a position that personal morality and marital fidelity must be unassailable. If, for example, even from the unsaved past a divorced wife or illegitimate children came to light, would it not furnish a charge against him, so that he would be no longer "without reproach"? That this personal morality embraced pre-conversion days arises from the fact that God's standards of morality are for all men, not only for the saved ones.

"Vigilant" (*nēphalios*, JND "sober") — used in v.11 (of wives) and Titus 2:2 (of aged men) originally meant total abstinence from alcohol (RV "temperate"), but here is used metaphorically (since drunkenness is specifically mentioned in v.3) to describe a temper that is not easily excited. J.N.D. Kelly aptly translates "clear-headed". This metaphoric use is also in the cognate verb "be sober" of 1 Thess 5:6,8..

"Sober" (*sōphrōn*) is the adjective of the noun in 2:9 (sobriety) and is used three times in Titus (1:8; 2:2,5). It indicates the quality of self-control arising out of a well-balanced mind (RV "soberminded").

The adjective *kosmios* ("of good behaviour") is translated "modest" in 2:9, and in the RV "orderly". It suggests that orderliness of mind reflected in a well-arranged life; disciplined thought leading to disciplined, dignified behaviour. Too many christian lives are lived in a whirl of chaotic activity, that manifests lack of order and discipline in the thought life.

"Given to hospitality" (*philoxenos*, from *phileō*, "to love" and *xenos*, "a stranger") denotes a man who is no misanthrope withdrawing behind a closed door, but expresses a willingness to receive into his home and care for the stranger. Vital in the days of Paul, when suitable accommodation for christian travellers was almost non-existent, it is still vital to offer the warmth and love of a christian home to those in need. The word is used again only in Titus 1:8 and 1 Pet 4:19. Here the overseer is in the *company of strangers*.

"Apt to teach" (*didaktikos*) is used again only in 2 Tim 2:24 of the "servant of the Lord". It stresses not only the knowledge itself but the ability to impart that knowldge. Readiness and skill in this respect make the elder one who formally or informally can present the truth. A skilled and ready teacher, in company, never misses an opportunity to instruct. Here the elder is in the *company of saints*.

3 "Not given to wine" (*mē paroinos*, RV "no brawler") expresses not merely the absence of drunkenness which is necessarily basic to the word, but the absence of that rudeness, self-assertiveness that flows from a diminution of control caused by wine. It is out of this that brawling comes. No believer is excused drunkenness (see 1 Cor 6:10), but the overseer is expected to be apart from all the noisy scenes springing from indulgence in wine. Here he is seen in the *company of sinners* and is markedly different.

In this word "no striker" (*mē plēktēs*) the temper of the man is evident *whatever his company*. Whatever the provocation whether from saint or sinner, he remains in control of himself and never resorts to violence. The adjective comes from the verb "to smite" found in Rev 8:12. An elder who responds to provocation with physical violence disqualifies himself.

"But" turns our thoughts from the two previous negatives to the positive in this statement, "patient" (*epieikēs*, RV "gentle"). In Titus 3:2 the same word is linked with meekness, and in 2 Cor 10:1 the related noun is used of Christ, the model of considerate patience. Consideration and feeling for others underlies the word which Matthew Arnold translates "sweet reasonableness" and J.N.D. Kelly "magnanimous".

For "not a brawler" (*amachos*, RV "not contentious") Vine gives "non-combatant". In character, neither quarrelsome nor pugnacious, he will be ever ready to forego his personal rights. It does not mean he does not "contend for the faith" (Jude 3) but he does not do this in a harsh, contentious spirit.

"Not covetous" (*aphilarguros* from *a*, negative particle, *phileō*, "to love", *argurion*, "silver" — thus "not a lover of silver") is used elsewhere only in Heb 13:5. To love money displays a serious defect of the christian character. The overseer must manifestly be free from avarice; the desire for money must not rule his life. If it does, he becomes mercenary and stingy.

Three matters are introduced to complete the qualifications of the elder that fasten upon how he is viewed objectively, by others:

1. His moral authority   vv.4-5
2. His evident maturity   v.6
3. His good testimony   v.7

4 A man's character is clearly evident within the framework of his own family. His qualification for leadership will be revealed in a well-ordered household. The word "ruleth" is *proistēmi* (meaning "to stand before", thus "to lead" or "to preside") and is the word used in 5:17 and in Rom 12:8; 1 Thess 5:12 (AV "are over you") to describe the work of the overseer. Thus the home displays his fitness for the wider sphere of responsibility in the assembly. While this verse does not demand of itself that an elder be married and have children, it reflects a normal pattern of maturity, and assesses a vital aspect of character.

The adverb "well" (*kalos*) shows that it is not simply autocratic authority that is in view in the thought of rule. Rather it is rule exercised in such a way that the outcome is admirable. The admiration, of course, is based not on educational attainment or social graces of the children but in spiritual blessing seen in the family. It is with the children, particularly, that this will be observable, in that he secures their obedience in a dignified way ("with all gravity"). While some see this as descriptive of the modesty and deportment of the children, it seems more in context to see it as descriptive of the way the man handles the family. He does this with a firmness that makes it advisable to obey, with a wisdom that makes it natural to obey, and with a love that makes it a delight to obey.

5 Paul supports the value of this requirement by a very typical Pauline parallel; an argument from the lesser to the greater. If a man displays incompetence in the home, in the management of his own children, then, the problem must be faced, how will he be able to take care of the assembly? "His own house" (*oikos*, "household" as in v.4) stands in contrast to the "church of God". The absence of the article before "church" stresses the character of the local assembly (see v.15). The term "church of God" in the NT is used only of the local assembly (Acts 20:28; 1 Cor 1:2,10,33; 11:16,22; 15:9; Gal 1:3; 2 Thess 1:4). It describes the company of saints who have been gathered in a locality to the name of the Lord Jesus Christ (Matt 18:20).

The second contrast is between the verbs used. In connection with the household it is "ruleth", in connection with the assembly it is "take care", a verb used only in the NT in Luke 10:34,35 in the parable of the good Samaritan. It expresses the loving interest that will be shown by the overseer in the welfare of the members of the assembly; just what a father would display towards the members of his own household. In this connection see the interesting use of the cognate noun in the statement of Acts 27:3 translated "to go into the house of his friends to refresh himself" (literally to have their care); this is a lovely illustration of such care!

6 The word "novice" (*neophutos*) found only here in the NT literally means "newly planted" and describes a recent convert. (In the LXX it is used of newly planted trees, Ps 144:12; 128:3 and, thus metaphorically of children in the family.) This is not meant to set any arbitrary limit on the chronological age of an overseer, for experience is not confined to men in the older age group, but it shows that experience in the things of God, the truths of Scripture and amongst the people of God is essential. No recent convert can have this. Lack of this experience carries an inherent danger for an overseer. That danger will arise out of a possibility that is defined in the participle translated "lifted up with pride" (RV "being puffed up"). The verb "puffed up" (*tuphoō*) originally meant "to wrap in smoke" and, used metaphorically, indicates either a mental "puffing up" (as in the RV; compare also its use in 6:4, "proud" and 2 Tim 3:4, "highminded"), or that, as smoke blinds physically so pride blinds spiritually and inevitably leads to a fall. In either case this overseer will be in danger of the same fate as befell the great exponent of pride, the devil. The article with the devil, shows that no human slanderer is in view but the personal devil. The expression "condemnation of the devil" should be taken objectively as the condemnation (JND "fault") the devil incurred because of his over-weening pride (Is 14:12-15; John 8:44). The aorist participle (translated "being lifted up with pride") and the aorist tense of the verb "fall" indicate how quickly, suddenly, and disastrously lack of experience can be evidenced.

7 In the community, as distinct from the church of God (v.5), the overseer must have "a good report". The word "report" is *marturia* (RV "testimony") and this must be "good" (*kalos*). An excellent testimony will help to fit the man for the excellent work (v.1). Those outside the local assembly must be able to speak highly of his honesty, integrity and purity. "Them that are without" are those not in the fellowship of the local assembly. This incidental reference provides clear demarcation between those gathered to the name of the Lord Jesus Christ and all others. The Scripture expects each believer to obey the word of Scripture in this matter and if they do they will gather to the "name of the Lord Jesus Christ" (Matt 18:20). Within the fellowship of the assembly, the principles of Scripture, power of the Spirit and presence of the

Saviour are experientially known. However, those "without" (*exōthen*) the fellowship, of course, will be critically observing the lives of the saints. For a man with an unsavoury reputation for temper, language, dishonesty or impurity to take the place of an elder would be to "fall into reproach", i.e. to invite scorn and the sneer of those who know him. Even the unsaved, with the law of God written in their hearts (Rom 1:15) have an instinctive appreciation of right and wrong and can form an accurate estimate of the worth of a profession. White has an interesting note: "There is something blame-worthy in a man's character if the consensus of outside opinion be unfavourable to him, no matter how much he may be admired and respected by his own party". To rule within requires respect from without and to defy outside opinion is to invite disaster. This suspicion and censure (reproach) arrayed against such an elder might readily discourage him. In this condition he would be an easy prey for the devil who would be sure to set a trap (AV "snare") for him. The word "snare" (*pagida*) refers to the pitfalls Satan provides for unwary feet. The image in the word depicts the devil as a hunter of souls. This would cause great harm to the man and great damage to the assembly. For recovery from the snare of the devil (same expression as here) see 2 Tim 2:26. The aim of the devil is ever to destroy the leaders and failure to meet this qualification would provide him with the opportunity. It is clear that "snare of the devil" must be taken as a subjective genitive, i.e. the snare that the devil sets for the saint.

b. Deacons — The Qualifications Stated (vv.8-13)

> v.8 "Likewise *must* the deacons *be* grave, not doubletongued, not given to much wine, not greedy of filthy lucre;
> v.9 Holding the mystery of the faith in a pure conscience.
> v.10 And let these also first be proved; then let them use the office of a deacon, being *found* blameless.
> v.11 Even so *must* their wives be grave, not slanderers, sober, faithful in all things.
> v.12 Let the deacons be the husbands of one wife, ruling their children and their own houses well.
> v.13 For they that have used the office of a deacon well purchase to themselves a good degree and great boldness in the faith which is in Christ Jesus."

The deacons here are those men (see note) gifted by the Lord for ministry and teaching within the assembly. If that ministry is going to be of spiritual value certain qualities must mark the men. These are set out again under four headings:

1. Their Personal Dignity   v.8
2. Their Spiritual Vitality   vv.9-10
3. Their Conjugal Integrity   v.11
4. Their Family Fidelity   vv.12-13

8 "Likewise" (*hōsautōs*) has the same function as it had in 2:9 to mark a parallel of the same character. Thus deacons in their qualifications must meet the same standards as overseers. The same verb (*dei*) translated "must" in v.2 has to be understood to complete the grammar of the verse. "Grave" (*semnos*) combines the thought of dignity with gravity; dignified comes close to the thought. Thus there is evidenced in the outward bearing that which corresponds to the seriousness of purpose filling the mind of the deacon. The cognate noun is in 2:2 (AV "honesty") and in v.4 ("gravity"). The display of this dignified behaviour would stand in manifest contrast with the behaviour prohibited in the next three negatives:

"Not double-tongued" (*mē dilogous*) refers to *words*; literally it would be "not double-talkers"; used only here in NT it conveys the thought of inconsistency in speech. Bengel put it, "Saying some things to some men and other things to others". We would say "suiting the message to the audience". There is no seriousness of purpose shown in this.

"Not given to much wine" (*mē oinō pollō prosechontas*) draws attention to *wine*. Compare what has been said of the overseer in v.3. The cognate verb, used in 1:4 (neither giving heed to) and in 4:1 (giving heed to), means not only not paying attention to, but "not giving assent to" or "adhering to" in any way. Nothing causes a believer to lose dignity as quickly as indulgence in wine; control is lost and disaster follows. The social drink has destroyed many a testimony.

"Not greedy of filthy lucre" (*mē aischrokerdeis*) fastens attention on *wealth*. This is a very strong word from *kerdos*, "gain", and *aischros*, "filthy", and is used again only in Titus 1:7. The gain becomes contaminated by the motive that inspires it. The deacon must be free from any suspicion that his motive in service is personal profit. The gain becomes "disgraceful" (Wuest's translation) when a man makes the acquisition of it, instead of the glory of God, his prime object. There is nothing less dignified than handling divine things hoping, through this, to get rich. Such money deserves the transferred epithet "filthy!".

9 The deacons must have a vital spiritual life if they are to validate their ministry. The emphasis falls on the concluding words "in pure conscience", showing the intimate relation between sound belief ("the faith") and a conscience free from stain and self-reproach. Mystery in the NT does not mean something secret, mysterious or incomprehensible, but that which, formerly unknown, has now been revealed (see Appendix B and on v.16). So when Paul uses the word (as in Rom 16:25; Col 1:26) he is referring to that which, outside the realm of human apprehension naturally, has now been revealed in Christ to His people by the Spirit (1 Cor 2:7-10). This revelation is embodied in "the faith", which, taken as a descriptive genitive, i.e. explaining what the mystery is, speaks of the objective body of teaching and is equivalent to the totality of truth, inaccessible to unenlightened human reasoning but made known by divine revelation. To use a metaphor — this valuable "jewel" must be preserved in a suitable "casket". That "casket" is the central core of the deacon's moral nature — the conscience (see on 1:5). This faculty, which distinguishes between good and evil, is now enlightened by revelation and purged by the blood of Christ (Heb 9:22) to bear witness to the correspondence between what is believed ("the faith") and what is practised in the life. The deacon can only have such a conscience when he practises in the life what he preaches with the lip. Theological abstractions must be reflected in purity of life.

10 Alford suggests that the first word of this verse in the English translation should be "moreover" to indicate that the deacons require not only testimonials to their charcter but a period when their work is put to the test. The use of the word "also" is probably linked to this additional requirement. The word "proved" (*dokimazō*) was the word used of the literal testing of metals (Prov 8:10; 17:10 LXX), generally by passing them through the fire, with a view to putting the stamp of genuineness upon them. Metaphorically it is used by the apostle of himself in 1 Thess 2:4 "approved of God to be entrusted with the gospel" (RV). This is not the achievement of permission to preach, but divine approval after testing. Here it is not a period of probation or a formal examination, as established now in ecclesiastical circles, but a constant observation and scrutiny of the man and the work he is already doing. This on-going examination leads to approval. The present imperative carries the thought of "keep on putting to the test". The idea is not constant critical condemnation but an appreciation of those character traits in a man whom God is fitting for service, as well as an evaluation of the effectiveness of his ministry. "Blameless" (*anenklētos*) is a synonym of the word used of the elder (v.2) and means there is nothing for which the man may be called to account. No accusation stands against him. "Let them use the office of a deacon" is the AV translation of one word, which is better given in the RV "let them serve". The man and his work having been tested and approved, the deacon is encouraged to fulfil his ministry.

11 Many commentators have questioned the translation "their wives" pointing out that there is no article that could be translated as a possessive "their". Rejecting, quite rightly, the RV translation "women" as if it were women in general who are in view, such expositors (Elliott, Alford, Vine, *The Expositor's Greek Testament*) have suggested that here we have an order of deaconesses, whose qualifications are outlined. In support of this view Phebe (Rom 16:1) is quoted as the representative of this class of women recognised within the assembly as undertaking special duties within their sphere. Grammatical support is sought in pointing out that "even so" (*hōsautōs*) marks off classes. It does this in v.8, so now in v.11, it is claimed, a third class is introduced.

The case is very weak. Paul could have used the word "deacon" in the feminine singular, (the plural would have been the same as the word in v.8) if he had wished to identify another class. At least we would have expected something more specific than *gunaikas*, (women or wives) without the article. A study of the four occurrences of *hōsautōs* in the epistle (2:9; 3:8,11; 5:25) or the other thirteen NT occurrences, does not support the view that it necessarily introduces a new class, but rather it serves to compare a new statement with what has gone before. The blameless overseer (v.2) corresponds to the blameless deacon (v.8) and, in keeping with this, their wives (both that of elder and deacon) must have a certain character. It would be very strange to introduce a new class here, and resume the qualifications of the deacon in v.12. It is clear that the AV translation of "their" wives is to be sustained. The reason for the inclusion of the statement here may be that since deacons will necessarily be much in the public eye, even more so than elders, their partners must be at one with them in character and conduct.

The qualifications of the wives reflect closely the qualifications of the deacons. The word "grave" is the same as in v.8 and points to the seriousness of purpose underlying dignified conduct. In Phil 4:8 it is translated "honest" and in the RV "honourable".

"Not slanderers" (*mē diabolous*) echoes the word used 34 times in the NT of Satan as the accuser (the devil); in 2 Tim 3:3, and Titus 2:3 translated "false accusers", it highlights the danger of malignant and malicious gossip which does the devil's work. Compare the word in v.8 "not double-tongued". *The Expositor's Greek Testament* cogently remarks "while men are more prone than women to be double-tongued, women are more prone than men to be slanderers".

"Sober" (RV "temperate"), the same word as in v.2, has the idea of the self-control arising from a well-balanced mind (see on the cognate noun 2:9). Compare the parallel instruction in v.8 "not given to much wine".

Paul now adds "faithful in all things". We have had in the epistle a "faithful" apostle (1:12), a "faithful" word (1:15; 3:1) now a "faithful" woman, where the idea is "trustworthy". She can be depended upon in every sphere. Like the virtuous woman of Prov 30:10-11, "the heart of her husband doth safely trust in her". One of the "all things" would doubtless be the handling of family finance (cf. v.8 "filthy lucre").

12 The moral standard required of deacons is the same as that required of the elder. The expression "the husband of one wife" is the same expression as in v.2 (except, of course, in the plural). See the discussion on that passage. In those taking a prominent and responsible part in testimony there must be no record of marital misconduct, from which, even from unconverted days, any charge may arise against them.

Like the elder, the character of the deacon will be manifest within the home. See v.5 for the comments on "rule" and "well" (*kalos*). The management of the children and the household provides visible evidence of the calibre and character of the deacon.

13 The "for" in this verse and the participle of the verb *diakoneō* limit this encouragement to the deacons under discussion. The aorist active participle translated "they that have used the office of a deacon" is better expressed by the RV "served as deacons" and more simply "have ministered" (JND). This is an incentive to faithful service in deacon ministry and forms a suitable conclusion to the passage.

Two promises are held out:

1. "A good degree" (RV "a good standing"). The word "degree" (*bathmos*) literally means a "base", "foundation", or "step". Based on the mistaken idea that deacons were subordinate church officials some have seen here the promise of promotion to overseer. Though the word later came to acquire this meaning in ecclesiastical writings, it is totally foreign to its usage in NT times. Others have seen the word as referring to the revelation of service at the Judgment Seat. They point to the aorist tense in the participle ("they that have served well as deacons", RV) as indicative of a completed service. But Paul is referring neither to ecclesiastical promotion (not a scriptural notion) nor to future reward. The reference is to the excellent standing in the assembly that the deacon acquires through his excellent ministry. The aorist tense draws attention to completed acts of service. The verb "purchase" (used of God, Acts 20:28) is the verb "gain" and in the middle voice, as here, means to "gain for himself"; the present tense indicates that the good standing is the present result of his faithful service.

2. "Great boldness". The word "boldness" (*parrhēsia*, from *pas*, "all", and *rhēsis*, "speech") literally interpreted means freedom of speech. See its use in Acts 2:29 (AV "freely") and in Acts 4:13,29,31. The word however, came, in general usage, to be understood as that confidence or courage that lay behind the freedom of speech and it is better represented by the word "assurance".

   This assurance can be before God (Eph 3:12) or before men (2 Cor 7:4; Phil 1:20; 1 Thess 2:2). Here it speaks of that inward assurance, born of the consciousness of personal integrity and assembly acceptance that enables the deacons to speak with authority and conviction.

   Some regard the "faith" as the subjective believing in Christ of the deacon personally that is strengthened. Thus he gains in confidence as his ministry is faithfully discharged. Weight is lent to this by the absence of the article before "faith" and the final phrase "which is in Christ Jesus" where Christ is the Person in whom faith rests. However, this is difficult to support from the context. The idea is rather to stress developing confidence in the teachings of the faith which he clearly expounds. These teachings all find their embodiment in Christ Jesus. A majestic summary of this faith follows immediately in v.14. It would be expected that "holding the mystery of the faith" (v.9) would issue in the confident exposition of it as the ministry of the deacon is accepted in the assembly. While there is no article before "faith" there is one immediately after, where grammatically it acts as a pronoun "in faith, the (one), in Christ Jesus".

Notes

8   The word "deacon" (*diakonos*) occurs 29 times in the NT and is always translated "servant" or "minister" in the AV except on three occasions, where deacon is the translation (Phil 1:1; 1 Tim 3:8,12). It is very clear that ecclesiastical tradition coloured this translation. The primary idea is "servant", but with particular reference to the work that he does. Another word generally translated "servant" is *doulos* but this views him as a slave in relation to his master. The word "deacon" is used of Christ in relation to His people (Rom 13:15) and of the magistrate in respect of the function he exercises for God (Rom 13:4).

   The two aspects of deacon work that become clear in the NT, with regard to assembly service, are traceable back to Acts 6, where although the word itself is not used the cognate words are instructive. In Acts 6:1 we have the noun: "their widows were neglected in the daily administration (*diakonia*)". In v.2 we have the verb "it is not reason that we should leave the word of God and serve (*diakonein*) tables". These two verses link the deacon ministry with the handling of material things. But in v.4 we have the apostolic statement "but we will give ourselves continually to prayer and to the ministry (*diakonia*) of the word". This indicates that deacon ministry had another aspect to it, a spiritual side exemplified in the apostolic work. W. Hoste points out (*Bishops, Priests and Deacons*, p.115) "Both the seven and the twelve fulfilled their respective deaconships. As a result of one, we no longer hear of murmuring among the widows; and as the outcome of the other, 'the word of God increased, and the number of the disciples multiplied in Jerusalem greatly', Acts 6:7."

   Thus it is clear that the deacon has to be viewed in two separate spheres of service:

(a) A physical, material, administrative level for the benefit of the company, by men chosen by, and responsible to, the company (Acts 6:5). In support of this the cognate noun is used in this way in Acts 12:25; Rom 15:31; 2 Cor 8:4,9,12. Within this same sphere would fall all the administrative duties to be carried out for the benefit of the assembly: the care of the meeting place, the distribution of hymn books, the duties of treasurer, etc., all of which contribute to the well-being of the assembly in a material way.

(b) A spiritual work of ministry to saint and sinner which, though exercised within and through the assembly, is ministered by men fitted and appointed by the Lord for that responsible task. Paul used it of himself and others in 2 Cor 3:6; 6:4; Eph 3:7; 6:21; Col 1:7,23,25; 4:7; 1 Thess 3:2, in the preaching of the gospel and in ministry to the saints. It is in this context that the three occurrences of the word in this epistle must be viewed, twice in this chapter, v.8 and v.12, and of Timothy in 4:6, "a good minister (*diakonos*) of Jesus Christ". Gifted by the Lord and responsible to Him, they exercised a ministry within the local assembly to the edification of the saints.

It is the qualifications of such deacons that are set out in 3:11-13 and explains why these qualities are of the same standard as that required for elders. In some respects, indeed, especially with regard to "the faith" (vv.9 and 13) they are even more demanding. The use of the plural term will serve to suggest that there could be more deacons than elders in an assembly.

11 With reference to women: Phebe is called "a servant (deacon) of the church" (Rom 16:1), and would be acknowledged as one to whom definite acts of service, consistent with her sex, could be entrusted by the church. Within this sphere her service would encompass both the material and the spiritual. Within the material, physical, administrative sphere would be the works of mercy, the care of the sick, the hospitality within the home, etc; within the spiritual realm would be the teaching of the younger women, the teaching and care of children,etc. Those who would undertake such work must, just as surely as the male deacon, have the qualifications from the Lord and the confidence of the saints to whom they minister.

3. *The Divine Concept Governing The Testimony*
3:14-16

a. Divine Purpose In The Assembly — The House of God (vv.14-15)

> v.14   "These things write I unto thee, hoping to come unto thee shortly:
> v.15   But if I tarry long, that thou mayest know how thou oughtest to behave thyself in the house of God, which is the church of the living God the pillar and ground of the truth."

These verses are the key to the epistle. Paul explains why he is writing, and in this, indicates the importance and urgency of the charge he is giving to Timothy.

The issue at stake is the maintenance of a testimony for God, locally, that would reflect honour upon God Himself. Terms are used to indicate that this testimony is divine, in character and constitution, and this demands corresponding conduct in those associated with it.

14 The reason for the writing of the epistle is given in this verse. Uncertainty of his future movements, within the will of God, led Paul by the Spirit to put on record "these things". This expression would, primarily, refer back to matters already set forth but the graphic picture in the present tense of the verb "write" (I am writing), necessarily includes matters in the succeeding verses that will complete the charge. The word "shortly" does not adequately present the comparative degree in the adverb *tachion* ("more quickly" JND); which is aptly caught by Alford in the translation "come unto thee sooner (than may seem possible)". This simply means that, despite the unfavourable looking circumstances the apostle was hoping to arrive at Ephesus sooner than expected.

15 Out of the possibility of delay in his coming we have this epistle vital to local assembly testimony. The verb "know" (*oida*) indicates that which is "come within the scope of the knower's perception" (Vine), hence divine revelation is frequently involved. This epistle will bring within the scope of the readers' perception matters affecting the conduct required in those associated with the local assembly. Timothy in the exercise of his authority as a good minister (deacon) of Jesus Christ (4:6) would be responsible to bring these matters to the notice of the believers. With the impersonal verb (*dei*) the subject would normally be the neuter "it". The person upon whom the duty falls would be put in the accusative case. Here there is no accusative pronoun so it is possible to insert the "thou" as in the AV or "man" as in the RV, or "one" as in JND.

Any suggestion that the conduct of Timothy was at fault is without foundation and it would be best to keep it impersonal "how it is necessary to behave". (Note the use of the verb *dei* in the epistle: v.3 (must), v.7 (must) and 5:13 (ought).) This impersonal translation is supported by the comprehensive verb "to behave" (*anastrepho*) which, in the middle voice, means to "conduct oneself" and describes, not isolated actions, but a whole manner of life. In whichever group one may fall, whether male or female, elder or deacon, younger or older, there is a fitting manner of life implied in being associated with this testimony. That the verb has this scope is seen in Eph 2:3 "we had our conversation" (RV "we lived"), in 2 Cor 1:12 "we had our conversation (RV "behaved ourselves"); it covers a whole life style.

The behaviour (manner of life) must be in keeping with the dignity of the testimony which is described under the term "the house of God". The word house (*oikos*) has already been used three times in this chapter, of the elder twice (v.4,5), and of the deacon (v.12), so the concept is already established as that of a household. All the references to "house" in the Pastorals imply the thought of "household" (see 5:4; 2 Tim 1:16; 4:19; Titus 1:11). So Paul uses the analogy of a human household to define a responsibility: as belonging to an earthly household makes certain demands upon men so, in a far greater way, to belong to the house of God does likewise. A different figure is used in 1 Cor 3:9 "ye are God's building", where the word is *oikodomē*. Another figure is found in 1 Cor 3:16, "Ye are the temple of God" where the word is *naos*, a shrine or sanctuary.

The expression "household of God" in Eph 2:19 has individuals in view, as emphasising their place in the purpose of God when linked to Christ. "Christ as Son over His own house" has the church of the dispensation, the aggregate of believers in the "church which is his body" (Eph 1:22-23) in view. Here, it is the local company of saints gathered in the name of the Lord Jesus Christ in obedience to Scripture and viewed as a unit of testimony. The absence of any article stresses the character of such a gathering.

The appositional description in the next phrase adds further dignity to the local testimony. For the expression "church of God" see on v.5. The adjective "living" sets the activity of a God who has thus acted in the formation of such a company through His Son, the Scriptures and the Spirit, in contrast to the dead idols of paganism. In 4:10 and 6:17 (although the RV omits the adjective, see comment there) the same adjective will indicate the constant care and unfailing supplies saints may expect from this God who has thus called them out in testimony. The absence of the article again stresses the character of the gathering.

The final appositional clause further enhances the value of divine testimony. Two architectural figures are employed. The pillar (*stulos*) denotes a column supporting the weight of a building. Metaphorically it is used of men in Gal 2:9 and of the overcomer in Rev 3:12. In the temple of Diana of the Ephesians there were 127 pillars each bearing testimony to a man. In divine testimony the assembly bears testimony to a risen Man in whom is embodied truth, the absence of the article again testifying to the character of each local company. The word "ground" (*hedraiōma*) denotes a support, bulwark or stay (RV margin). This latter would be the preferred reading, as fitting the context, where the idea is the positive witness to the truth (pillar) and the maintenance of it (stay) in the face of all opposition.

The expression "the truth", as in 2:4 is not to be limited to any one aspect of truth. It is that which, revealed in Christ who is the truth (John 14:6), is maintained in a witness to Him. All aspects of absolute truth will thus be maintained as to His Person and work (evangelically), as to His purpose and witness in this age (ecclesiastically), and to His promised return and kingdom (eschatologically).

b. The Divine Person In Testimony — The Son of God (v.16)

> v.16 "And without controversy great is the mystery of godliness: God was manifest in the flesh, justified in the Spirit, seen of angels, preached unto the Gentiles, believed on in the world, received up into glory."

That which is embraced in "the truth" to which each local assembly bears witness is here set forth. This has been embodied, historically, in a Person, and it is in witness to Him as God that divine testimony reaches its apex.

16 "Without controversy" translates an adverb *homologoumenōs* from the verb *homologeō*, "to confess" (*homos*, "same", *legō*, "to speak") and thus indicates all speaking the same thing, by common consent; no dissentient voice is heard. This is the great public confession to the truth in Christ, borne witness to, by every believer in the assembly. It is to be construed with "great" and Vine translates "confessedly great". All who bear witness to the truth will acknowledge how great is the Mystery of godliness. The "mystery" (see on v.9) has its normal NT meaning of that which, formerly hidden, is now revealed. In this case the revelation is that of godliness (see Appendix B). One could see here the christian answer to the cult cry of Ephesus "Great is Diana of the Ephesians" (Acts 19:28). (The only other NT mystery to be called great is in Eph 5:32.) "Godliness" (*eusebeia*) is not an attribute of God, like holiness or righteousness, but it is an attitude to God that, in those knowing and revering Him, is reflected in a way of life. This has been historically and evidentially manifest in Christ preeminently; the implication in the epsitle is that this witness to godliness be reproduced now in the saints in corporate testimony to Him.

Textual battles have raged over whether the next word in the text is "God" (*Theos*) as in the AV text or "who" (*os*) as in the RV. Vine puts it clearly: "It will be well to point out the reason for this RV rendering. In the ancient manuscripts the relative pronoun 'who' was written thus, *os*. Again the word *theos*, God, was frequently abbreviated to *os*. The most important of the earliest, or uncial, manuscripts and all the versions older than the seventh century are distinctly in favour of the relative pronoun. The latter would readily arise from the former, and confusion of the two would be easy".

In an extensive passage W. Kelly defends the rendering "who" and shows that no infringement of absolute deity can be involved; since for none other than deity could "manifest in flesh" be a possibility.

Nonetheless, the AV reading *theos* had weighty textual support and was the reading known to many of the early fathers. It means also that the problem of the antecedent of the relative pronoun does not arise. This antecedent cannot be mystery grammatically (else the reading would be "which"); so most commentators are driven, as Ellicott, to describe it as "a relative to an omitted though easily recognised antecedent, viz. Christ". Thus it is contextually justifiable and exegetically sound, as well as textually acceptable to retain the AV "God was manifest in flesh".

The mystery of godliness is presented in six rhythmical, balanced statements. The careful parallelism of the lines, the marked assonance of the syllables and the six third person aorist verbs, have led some to speculate that it may be an excerpt from a primitive hymn, or, perhaps, a deliberately formulated credal statement. This speculation is unnecessary and rather robs the statement of that entrancement of spirit that clearly filled the apostle's heart as he contemplated the full embodiment of truth in the Person of Christ in whom historically there was divine manifestation of purpose.

The six statements have been variously sub-divided, either into two groups of three, or into three groups of two. A simple way of setting forth the balance between the statements is presented in the diagram which, with double chiasmic (X) structure, combines three groups of two units into two groups,

thus:
1. Was manifest in the flesh   2. Justified in the Spirit
3. Seen of angels   4. Preached unto the Gentiles
5. Believed on in the world   6. Received up into glory

the antithetic parallelism is also clear from the above diagram.
1. In flesh .... In Spirit
2. Angels .... Nations (RV)
3. In World .... In Glory.

"Was manifest in the flesh" stresses the Incarnation, where the term includes both His birth and His life upon earth. The RV reading "was manifested" translates the aorist tense as describing the time when Christ was on earth in manhood. The same verb is used of this same event in Heb 9:26; 1 Pet 1:20. "In flesh" (*en sarki*), without the article, covers the period from incarnation to ascension (Rom 8:3) when He was visibly present on earth as a Man. No mystery can be more inscrutable than incarnate deity.

"Justified in the Spirit" is the parallel statement. "In flesh", the judgment of men put Christ on a cross as if unfit to live. But God has declared Him righteous; He has justified, vindicated Him in His resurrection. The resurrection is both the vindication of His Person (Rom 1:4) and His work (Rom 4:23-25). This is not yet seen by men; but in this realm, as yet unseen by men, He has been vindicated. God has in fact reversed the verdict of earth. Thus, in this light, the contrast is not between Christ's flesh and spirit, or between the action of men, and the action of the Holy Spirit in resurrection, but between the realm of the seen, "in flesh", and the realm of the unseen, "in spirit" (see 1 Pet 3:18 for a similar contrast). God has placed a Man on the throne but in the earth realm this is not yet seen.

"Seen of angels" is the first of the next two parallel statements, drawing attention to the denizens of the two realms mentioned above, but in reverse order, based on the chiasmic structure. In that realm, invisible to mortals, angels have observed Him ascended and enthroned (1 Pet 3:23). It is certainly true that they announced His birth (Luke 1:9-14), attended Him in life (Mark 1:13; Luke 2:13; 24:23), and must have been appalled at His death when He went to the cross alone, but this is not the point of the contrast. This statement emphasises the observation and, by implication, the wonder and worship angelic powers offered to Christ as in resurrection they observed His triumphant ascension to the throne (1 Pet 3:22; Heb 1:6).

"Preached unto the Gentiles" emphasises that in the realm of the seen He has been heralded (the verb is *kērussō*, the cognate of "herald" in 2:7) in, or amongst, the nations (RV) (see 2:7 for "Gentiles"). Not now within the national limits of Israel but world-wide the proclamation has been centred on a Person. Ambassadors of this risen Christ (2 Cor 5:20) carried such an announcement to every nation.

The final statements stress the dominant features of the two realms. In the visible realm of mankind, in which the enthroned Christ is not seen, faith is exercised in Him. In the realm invisible as yet to mortal eyes, He is enthroned in glory, a fact yet to be demonstrated universally (Phil 2:9-11).

"Believed on in the world" is clearly linked chiasmically with the preceding statement. It is on earth the message is proclaimed and faith exercised (John 20:31; 2 Thess 1:10). What has not been seen is accepted by faith based on the word of God.

"Received up into glory" as in Mark 16:19; Acts 1:2,11,22, emphasises the welcome offered to One rejected on earth. Other words for the ascension are "received up" (Luke 24:51), "taken up" (Acts 1:10), "ascended up" (Eph 4:10). The term "in glory" (RV), in a technical sense, goes beyond the act of ascension and exaltation to show the dazzling brightness of the very presence of God: there a Man is enthroned.

The antithetic parallelism and chiasmic structure of the six statements thus declare in a chronological way the mystery of godliness revealed in Christ from incarnation to enthronement in glory. God and glory are manifest in a Man.

This majestic summary of truth embodied in Christ and now to be maintained in assembly witness forms a fitting conclusion to the first section of the epistle. The maintenance of the testimony as evidenced in the atmosphere and authority within the house of God takes on new significance when viewed against the historical background of truth revealed in Christ. It also forms an appropriate starting point for dealing with the danger of satanic attack which opens the next section of the letter.

4. *The Deadly Challenge To The Testimony*
4:1-5

v.1 "Now the Spirit speaketh expressly, that in the latter times some shall depart from the faith, giving heed to seducing spirits, and doctrines of devils;

v.2 Speaking lies in hypocrisy; having their conscience seared with a hot iron;

v.3 Forbidding to marry, *and commanding* to abstain from meats, which God hath created to be received with thanksgiving of them which believe and know the truth.

v.4 For every creature of God *is* good, and nothing to be refused, if it be received with thanksgiving:

v.5 For it is sanctified by the word of God and prayer."

In contrast to the sublime mystery of godliness revealed in Christ, and now manifest in His redeemed and gathered saints in local church testimony, the apostle warns of a coming apostasy, i.e. a departure from the faith, the signs of which are already observable in his day. This warning serves as the background for the completion of the charge in the following sections of the epistle.

In connection with this apostasy this section will identify:

1. The Times and
   Their Revelation   v.1
2. The False Teachers and
   Their Recognition   v.2
3. The False Teaching and
   its Refutation   vv.3-5

1 The RV "but" correctly evaluates the adversative conjunction *de* and sets the passage in contrast to what has preceded. In the grim knowledge of coming apostasy Timothy must carry on the witness to truth. The revelation does not stem from Paul but from the Holy Spirit. It is true that such warnings came in the OT (for example Dan 7:25). These warnings have been repeated in the words of the Lord (Matt 24:4-12) and in apostolic writings (see especially 2 Thess 2:3-12 which has close links with this passage); the Spirit of God has borne such witness. However, the present tense of the verb "speaketh" and the use of the adverb "expressly" (*rhētōs*, in stated terms), suggests the ministry of NT prophets. Either at an earlier stage to Paul, or now, through Paul, this is the authentic voice of warning lest saints should be taken by surprise. The adverb indicates that the time for symbolic language has passed and explicit terms are to be used to describe the danger.

The phrase "in the latter times" includes the word *kairos* (seasons) which draws attention to the character of the period. This period would be identifiable by certain spiritual and moral features prominent in it. When we speak of the winter "season" we imply in that word certain climatic conditions belonging to that period, which thought is absent if we talk merely of winter "time" — the actual time span of months. While in Hebrews 1:2 "in these last days" covers the whole dispensation of grace, here the phrase "latter days" would indicate a period, at least beyond the time of writing (note the future tense of the verb "will depart"), while in 2 Tim 3:1 "in the last days" emphasises the closing stages of this period.

The verb rendered "shall depart from" (RV "shall fall away", JND "apostatise") can be used, literally, of departing from a place (Luke 2:37) but, used metaphorically, it means "a standing away from" an original position. What these stood away from is not only the assembly, but "the faith" (note the presence of the article). They had deliberately abandoned what they had formerly professed to believe. That they were but nominal and not true believers, this departure makes clear.

The cause of this departure is traced beyond the human agents to its source, the activity of demons. The participle, "giving heed to", has been used in 1:4 (where see comment) and the cognate verb is used positively in v.13, "give attendance to"; it means, not merely "to assent to" but, more strongly, "to attach one's self to" or "to cling to" a person or a thing. In departing from truth men place themselves under the influence of "seducing spirits". In contrast to the Holy Spirit, of whom the Lord Jesus said "He will guide you into all truth" (John 16:13), these spirits are "seducing" (*planos*) which in other occurrences is translated in the AV "deceiving", and implies a wandering, a leading astray. This is the source of the teaching and it is further defined as "doctrines of devils" (*didaskaliais daimoniōn*). "Doctrines of demons" is the better rendering since Scripture knows only one devil, but there are many demons, his evil agents controlled by him as the "prince of the power of the air" in relentless opposition to all that is for God in this age (Eph 2:2; 2 Cor 2:11). "Doctrines of demons" is a subjective genitive and does not mean doctrines about demons, but the doctrines which demons teach.

2 Having identified the victims ("some") and the source of the false teaching that will give rise to departure, Paul, by the Spirit, now marks out the agents. The RV is correct in treating the word *pseudologōn* not as a participle (as the AV which translates "speaking lies") but as a substantive, translating "men that speak lies". The whole phrase reads "through the hypocrisy of men that speak lies". These are human agents, moved by evil spirits, marked by hypocrisy. Hypocrisy, with its background of play-acting, the wearing of a mask to conceal the real identity, fits such human agents. Their acts of devotion and hyper-spirituality are only a specious mask. They wore a mask of holiness derived from false asceticism and abstinence from things legitimate.

They can act thus because their own conscience has been "seared". The perfect passive participle of the strong verb *kaustēriazō*, used only here in the NT, (JND "cauterised") demands a radical action more drastic than that in our English work "seared" which implies repeated actions. The word was used in medical circles of the application of a hot iron to a body member to render it inactive. This suggests that there was a time in the past when these false teachers deliberately turned away from the word of God, put on a mask to act a part, and thus became the agents of satanic powers. Their conscience, cauterised, was no longer responsive to right or wrong.

3 Two elements of the false teaching are mentioned. Under the guise of a hyper-spirituality they were "forbidding to marry" and "commanding to abstain from meats". The words "and commanding" are not in the original text but bring out the sense where "to marry" and "to abstain" come under one verb by the literary device of zeugma (yoking of two, even disparate, words), thus both are elements of the false teaching. These teachers regarded abstinence from marriage as an avenue to hyper-spiritual sanctity, and placed the celibate life on a higher plane than the married life. They regarded the abstinence from certain foods, and perhaps all foods for certain periods, as of meritorious and spiritual value. The word for "meats" (*brōmatōn*) really means solid food, but was, generally, applied to animal flesh.

The neuter plural relative pronoun "which" or "which things" is generally referred to the meats alone and reasons are then sought for Paul failing to deal with the marriage issue. The answer to the latter problem, generally suggested, is that Paul has already made his position on this abundantly clear with regard to the elder (3:2) and deacon (3:12) and feels it unnecessary to deal with it specifically. However, there is more substance in seeing the neuter plural as referring to both marriage and meats. The false teaching ran counter on both these points to the creative purpose of God. The words "to be received" translate an unusual expression (*eis metalēmpsin*) that means "for partaking", "for reception" that stands in contrast to v.4, "nothing to be refused". God meant men to participate and share in what He had created for their benefit. False teaching would deny men this privilege and thus inhibit the thanksgiving that should be normal for believers.

God expects all men to believe, and in so doing, to be brought into the knowledge of the truth. Satan acts, through his agents, to deprive God of this thanksgiving. With the one article before "them which believe" and "know the truth", it would seem, according to the Glenville-Sharpe rule of grammar, that one class is in view. Believers have fully known (*epiginōskō*, to discern fully or recognise) the truth. Teaching the truth within the assembly (3:14) would preserve from such lies, and the result would be seen in the conduct of the believers with particular regard here to marriage and meats. The abstract becomes concrete. Unconverted but nominal christians readily fall under the spell of the false teaching and God is robbed of thanksgiving.

4 Paul moves to the second reason for the refusal of such false teaching. While certain philosophic speculations, later to mature into fully-developed gnosticism, would regard material things as inherently evil, Jewish thinking had always in mind the distinction between things clean and unclean. Hence, going back to creation, Paul shows that "every creature of God is good". The word "good" is *kalos*, excellent, nothing detrimental can be said about it; it is perfectly fitted for the purpose envisaged of God. The word is used in Gen 1:31 in the LXX to describe creation. "Creature" (*ktisma*), used in James 1:18; Rev 5:13;8:9, is not Paul's usual word (which is *ktisis*, Rom 1:20; Gal 6:15), but draws attention to the end product of the creative process. It describes what God brought into existence. That marriage was brought in to complete the creation is shown in Gen 2:18 and the same word "good" is used in the passage. Thus God Himself instituted marriage and provided food to sustain life. Both are intrinsically good. The corollary follows inescapably; these are "nothing to be refused". The word "refused" is *apoblētos* from *apo*, "away" and *ballō*, "to throw"; indicating in a graphic way how false teaching would reject these good things. The sole condition for their beneficial use is that they are received with thanksgiving. This is the upward movement of praise from the hearts of men which the false teaching (v.3) would deny to God.

5 The explanation of why the created things, marriage and meats, can be received with thanksgiving is given in the final sentence following the explanatory "for". The believer understands through the word of God the true relationship of the created things to the Creator. Further he enjoys fellowship with God. Prayer is that special word (*enteuxis*), used again in the NT only in 2:1, which describes the freedom of access to, the confidence in, and the holy intimacy with God enjoyed by the believer. Under these circumstances he values these things as created for his benefit; this makes their reception a special blessing to him. The present tense of the verb "sanctified" is thus explained as descriptive of the things being presently set apart for the believers' blessing. In this way they have a special character not appreciated by unbelievers. This applies both to meats (Rom 14:5) and marriage (1 Cor 7:39).

Notes

3 The seeds of such teaching are seen in the Essenes in the days before the church age. In post-apostolic days it came to fruition in the gnostic teachings in the second century. As the church abandoned adherence to Scripture it was increasingly affected by false spirituality, and 'the monastic teachings of the 4th century crystallised within the Roman Catholic system that is with us still. Most cults and heretical systems incorporate some aspects of this false asceticism in their teachings. This scripture identifies the source of such ideas as satanic.

The error springs from a false concept of the physical body as inherently evil, and reasons that to deny the body's normal appetites is praiseworthy. This is to deny God's institution of marriage (Gen 1:28) and the permission regarding meats (Gen 1:29; 9:3). Neither celibacy nor vegetarianism is a means to sanctification, and the practice of either to achieve a spiritual purpose is to be wise above what is written and to disregard the plain word of God.

4 The restrictions within the OT ceremonial law were not given because there was something wrong with the creature. Rather, God would train His people through these restrictions to develop a moral faculty of discernment and to apprehend the truths of separation. The Lord showed in Mark 7:15, as Paul taught in Rom 14:4 and as confirmed in Peter's experience of Acts 10:9-16, that all such national and ceremonial restrictions had a limited purpose and are now no longer applicable. Their whole typical purpose is now absorbed in the real sanctification of which they were only the shadow. To reimpose these abolished regulations is to profess a holiness that goes beyond the word of God and impugns the character of God as having created something evil.

5 Some see in the phrase "word of God" a reference to those portions of Scripture, which in the normal Jewish thanksgiving before a meal formed the content of the prayer. Since "through" (*dia*) governs both substantives there is something to be said for this view. However, on this view it is difficult to explain the present tense of the verb "sanctified" and why some formula, however scriptural, should affect these created things is hard to see. The view given in the exposition is preferred.

The Lord always gave thanks before a meal; see Matt 5:36; Mark 8:6; John

6:11,13. This practice is emphasised in Luke 22:19 and 1 Cor 11:24; Paul in his writings takes it for granted as implied in Rom 14:6; 1 Cor 10:30; and he practised it himself as recorded in Acts 27:35. Here, it is specifically implied in the word "thanksgiving" and believers should make a practice of this in private and in public. What is in view is not a formula of words but a fellowship with God that acknowledges Him as the giver of these beneficial things.

IV. The Continuation of the Charge (4:6-6:12)
Application Envisaged Within the Assembly

1. *A Pattern Ministry*
4:6-16

In the continuation of the charge to Timothy the apostle shows the two sides to an effective ministry for the preservation of the testimony against such an attack as just envisaged in the last paragraph.

a. Proper Exhortation and Teaching by the Servant (vv.6-11)

v.6   "If thou put the brethren in remembrance of these things, thou shalt be a good minister of Jesus Christ, nourished up in the words of faith and of good doctrine, whereunto thou hast attained.

v.7   But refuse profane and old wives' fables, and exercise thyself *rather* unto godliness.

v.8   For bodily exercise profiteth little: but godliness is profitable unto all things, having promise of the life that now is, and of that which is to come.

v.9   This *is* a faithful saying and worthy of all acceptation.

v.10 For therefore we both labour and suffer reproach, because we trust in the living God, who is the Saviour of all men, specially of those that believe.

v.11 These things command and teach."

Timothy in life and lip could contribute to the preservation of the assembly. The advice is wholly constructive and designed to be the positive answer to the negative character of the false teaching. These verses set before us the characteristics of "a good minister of Jesus Christ". Thus:

1.   The Servant's Attributes   v.6
2.   The Servant's Activities   vv.7-9
3.   The Servant's Ambitions   v.10
4.   The Servant's Authority   v.11

6 Two things will mark such a servant:

1.   His care for the saints — he fortifies them; he is "a good minister of Jesus Christ".

2.   His care for his own spiritual well-being — he feeds himself "on the words of faith and of good doctrine".

Tauta ("these things") is the first word of the Greek text, drawing attention to the matters set out in the previous paragraph as the answer to the false teaching. The instruction "put in remembrance" is a participle construction that does not imply any doubt that Timothy was already doing this. It is translated by JND "laying (these things) before" and is a relatively mild word. It indicates the necessity of showing the character and consequence of false teaching without any compromise, but implies as well, that delicacy and tact are required to deliver the saints. The use of intemperate and denunciatory language in such a situation is not necessarily helpful. The positive unfolding of truth carries the much stronger language of v.11 where the instruction is given "command and teach".

The phrase "a good minister" carries no ecclesiastical connotation of clergyman or pastor; it is the word "deacon" of 3:8 (see similar usage in 1 Cor 3:5; 2 Cor 11:2,3) and describes simply "one who serves" Christ Jesus (the RV order of names is correct); no thought of status can be read into the word, it describes service, the activity, what is done in submission to Christ Jesus. "Good" is *kalos*, excellent, well-adapted to the purpose, which J.N.D. Kelly translates "admirable".

The effective ministry of the servant will evidence that he himself has been well fed on a healthy and suitable diet. The former is the result of the latter. This thought is in the second participial construction translated "nourished up" which, with the present tense, and possibly the middle voice, could be translated "nourishing thyself on" and suggests the spiritual diet of scriptural truth that is his daily portion. The metaphor of food is often used in this way, e.g. 1 Cor 3:2; Heb 5:12. There is nothing in error to feed the soul; true nourishment comes from Scripture. This is shown in the expression "the words of faith" where the article present before "faith" indicates that the body of truth objectively is meant. It is these truths revealed in Scripture to faith upon which the servant is sustained spiritually. The expression "the words of faith" (note again the article) suggests that the actual words of Scripture in which the truth is expressed are vitally important. The recognition of this is in keeping with the truth of the verbal inspiration of Scripture (2 Tim 3:16). The good servant will keep this in mind as he puts the brethren in remembrance of "these things". The "words of faith" are the vehicle which convey the "good doctrine". The doctrine here must be the actual body of teaching encompassed in the words of Scripture (1:10; 6:1,3); this, of course, stands in contrast to the "doctrine of demons". While it is the body of truth that is in view the thought of "instruction" (what is taught) cannot, however, be completely discounted, as there is a hint in the next phrase, "whereunto thou has attained", that what Timothy had made his own of the teaching would be evident in his ministry.

The RV more accurately translates this single final word *parēkolouthēkas*, as "which thou hast followed until now". This is the highest commendation for Timothy and the perfect tense shows that, over the past, he has both diligently studied and perseveringly preached, that which has fed his own soul and formed his own character.

7 "But" (*de*), an adversative conjunction, links this verse closely with the previous verse. In fact the first statement can be treated, as in the RV, as the concluding sentence of that verse; this makes admirable sense. However if we take it, as in the AV, it shows that the activity of the servant is twofold containing both a negative and a positive element.

The negative aspect of the activity is seen in the verb "refuse". It is the word *paraiteomai* which means "beg off from" or "decline" (see Luke 14:18); JND renders "avoid". In the present tense and imperative mood it is not advice but a clear command that may be translated "keep on refusing". "Fables" is the word "myths" (same word as in 1:4), and these stand in marked contrast to the "the words of faith" (v.6). The inclusion of the article indicates that there was a particular body of silly stories and myths current at the time, arising from rabbinic moralising that embroidered Scripture and ended by trivialising Scripture. The two adjectives are significant. "Profane" (*bebēlos*) is used in 1:9 of persons but here of things. Used again in 6:20 and 2 Tim 2:16, its consistent meaning is that which is radically separate from God, and so is outside the realm of the holy (contrast the word "sanctified" in v.5). That which lies outside the realm of revealed truth can have no scriptural claim on saints and is to be refused. The second adjective is *graōdes* — only here in the NT and translated "old wives' " — on which J.N.D. Kelly writes "a sarcastic epithet which was frequent in philosophical polemic and conveys the idea of limitless credulity!" These disdainful and dismissive adjectives describe the myths (one article covers the phrase) as neither sacred nor sensible, silly fictions suitable only for senile old crones to chatter about. There is no spiritual nourishment there.

Instead of being coupled with such follies, Timothy has a positive command pressed upon him. The present imperative of the verb *gumnazō* could be translated "go on training thyself" which removes any implied rebuke to Timothy conveyed in our English translation. Paul uses frequently the metaphor of physical training to teach lessons for christian living (e.g. 1 Cor 9:24-27; 2 Tim 2:5; Heb 12:1). The contrast implied here is, of course, between the imposition of heretical asceticism, based on false ideas of physical discipline, and genuine spiritual training. The aim in view is "godliness". See Appendix B, where it is shown that this word describes an attitude towards God of reverence and respect that characterises the life of the believer and issues in a standard of conduct based on the revelation of God in Christ and the Word. This godliness does not come without the continuous exercise of discipline in the life, based on meditation on the Scriptures, and the prayerful application by the Spirit of those Scriptures to each phase of the believer's life. This demands the active and deliberate cooperation of the believer.

8 Developing the athletic metaphor he has introduced in the word "exercise" (*gumnazō* from which we get the word gymnasium), Paul applies to it a "faithful saying" which in v.9 is retrospective and looks back to this verse. Paul recognises that this saying current amongst believers carries the hallmark of truth and by the Spirit of God places it within the scriptural record. The "for" shows that this is explanatory of the exhortation of v.7 and highlights the real contrast between physical and spiritual training.

The functioning of the physical body is dependent upon proper physical exercise. The apostle is neither advocating asceticism (already clearly condemned as anti-scriptural, vv.1-5) nor advocating or excusing participation in worldly games. To use these verses for this purpose is totally inadmissible. The purpose is to show that while physical training for the body has a limited value, spiritual training has values and benefits that are measureless.

Two aspects are dealt with in regard to the benefit of spiritual discipline:

1. "Bodily exercise profiteth little". The RV "for a little" (*pros oligon*) indicates the extent of the gain from that which is merely physical; it is measurable and limited, producing for a time a more efficiently functioning organism. This stands in contrast to *pros tauta* ("for all things" RV) that sees spiritual training as affecting not one part, the body, but all the parts, spirit, soul and body; spiritual training brings all under a divine discipline that yields benefits temporal and eternal. That the body is included in this spiritual exercise is seen in 1 Cor 9:27 where a voluntary subjection is in view and in 2 Cor 11:27 where an involuntary sacrifice is envisaged as demanded in the service of God. This is part of true godliness. Over-indulgence of even legitimate bodily appetites is a contradiction of disciplined godly living. Godliness as the product of spiritual discipline affects spirit, soul and body.

2. "The life that now is". The contrast here is between the "now" life and the "coming" life. The word "life" is *zoe*, the higher principle of life, and in 6:12 the same word has the adjective "eternal". The benefits of physical training are limited to the present life; beyond this is a realm where the physical cannot reach, that "coming" life (AV "that which is to come"). But spiritual training brings benefits even now emanating from communion and fellowship with God, in a conduct and character that is a testimony to divine life enjoyed in time, and envisages the highest blessing and well-being in eternity. This interpretation takes "promise" in the concrete sense of "blessedness" (cf. Luke 24:49; Acts 1:4; 13:32), a clear suggestion that the saint will carry the capacity to enjoy God from this life into the coming ages. How vital that spiritual training should develop that capacity and consciousness in the present life in fellowship with God.

9 The statement "This is a faithful saying" in its five occurrences in the Pastorals is discussed in Appendix B. Some authorities (amongst them

Alford and Guthrie) link this occurrence with the following v.10. While this is in keeping with the usage in this first epistle (1:15; 3:1), it is difficult to see any "saying" in that verse, and the explanatory "for" seems in fact to rule it out. Rather, v.10 explains the impact of the truth of v.8, this trustworthy saying, as it becomes a vital factor in the believer's life. It seems, therefore, that this ninth verse is a parenthetic approval of the statement of v.8. This is the second of the two occasions when the statement has the added clause "worthy of all acceptation". the other is 1:15.

10 "For", as in 2 Tim 2:11, introduces an argument in support of the "saying" of v.8. *Eis touto* ("therefore") is better translated "to this end" (RV) and refers to the promised blessedness (the concrete "promise" of v.8) attached to godly living. This goal provides the motive for dedicated, devoted service. "We" unites Timothy and Paul as sharing the same goal, but must embrace, of course, all who share the same appreciation of the importance of godliness.

The service is described by two verbs. The first is "labour" which means to toil to the point of exhaustion (used again in 5:17); what it meant to the apostle personally we note from 1 Cor 15:10; Gal 4:11; it covers weariness of mind and body as strength is expended in service for God. The second word in the TR is "suffer reproach" (*onedizometha*) where the metaphor of the athlete is abandoned and the picture changes from the internal struggle to the external reproach induced by those who would live godly and serve God in this age. There is, however, much weighty MSS support for the RV reading "strive" (*agōnizometha*) which, developing the athletic metaphor, shows the contestant in the games putting every ounce of energy into the effort to reach the goal. Paul uses this word again in 6:12 and 2 Tim 4:7. While this latter reading is attractive, and the association of the two verbs can be seen in Col 1:29, the succeeding sentence, as giving the explanation for the reproach, fits the TR reading in a far more satisfactory way.

Instead of honour, as one would naturally expect in recognition for such toil and fatigue, reproach and shame are the portion of the godly and the reason for this is simple: "because we trust in the living God". The statement offers the explanation of both matters mentioned. It shows why saints toil so devotedly; it also shows why they suffer reproach on earth. The RV reading is helpful: "we have our hope set on the living God". The perfect tense emphasises the past act, the result of which continues into the present. The preposition "on" (*epi*with the dative case) depicts the hope resting squarely, solidly, on the living God. The living God (see 4:15) and Matt 16:16) is our foundation; living is the participle, used adjectivally, of a verb related to the word "life" (*zōē*) of v.8. It describes the One, self-existent and possessor of unoriginated, self-sustained life in contrast to the dead idols of paganism. To have the hope firmly placed on Him is to shre in the life eternal, despite present oil and reproach.

This God is described as the One "who is the Saviour of all men, specially of those that believe". Universalist views suggesting that, ultimately, all men will be saved, are in conflict with so many Scriptures (John 3:36; Mark 16:16 etc.) and with this statement itself that it is surprising that they still need contradiction. Equally, views that would translate "who is the preserver of all men" (JND) and limit this action to physical preservation, in no way do justice to the statement and are in conflict with both Scripture and fact. This verse cannot mean that God acts to preserve believers in a special way from danger, disease and death itself. He sustains them in such circumstances, and uses the circumstances to their blessing but no other NT Scripture promises such preservation for saints. further, the alternative idea that God, potentially, is the Saviour of all men, if they believe, does not give sufficient weight to the word "specially" (*malista*). This word is the key and demands that all men enjoy to some degree what believers enjoy to an unlimited degree. The true understanding of the statement lies in giving to God the full weight of the redemptive title "Saviour". With regard to "all men" (humanity) at the present time, He is not acting as Judge but as Saviour. Sinners enjoy this relationship in a limited way, for this God does not cut them down in instant wrath but acts patiently towards them. Believers enjoy this in an unlimited way: they possess life in its blessedness and in its eternity now, and will enjoy if forever. They have founded their hope on Him.

11 "These things" are those that have been dealt with in vv.6-10, and embrace the negative (refusing the fables), and the positive (the training unto godliness). The present imperative serves to encourage Timothy to "keep on charging", "keep on teaching". The word "charge" reminds Timothy why he was in Ephesus (the same word as 1:3) and of the authoritative way he must deal with the situation there. In some cases mere suggestion (v.6) or silent example (v.12) will not do, straight words are needed. The word "teach" stresses the positive exposition (note the cognate noun "doctrine" in vv.6,12) of truth required in the refutation of "doctrines of devils" (v.1).

b. Personal Example and Testimony Before the Saints (vv.12-16)

> v.12   "Let no man despise thy youth; but be thou an example of the believers, in word, in conversation, in charity, in spirit, in faith, in purity.
>
> v.13   Till I come, give attendance to reading, to exhortation, to doctrine.
>
> v.14   Neglect not the gift that is in thee, which was given thee by prophecy, with the laying on of the hands of the presbytery.
>
> v.15   Meditate upon these things; give thyself wholly to them; that thy profiting may appear to all.
>
> v.16   Take heed unto thyself, and unto the doctrine; continue in them: for in doing this thou shalt both save thyself, and them that hear thee."

The secret of personal testimony and that which underlies the servant's power with men is touched upon in this paragraph. Three matters are dealt with:

1. Spiritual Grace	— How the Servant Lives!	v.12
2. Spiritual Gift	— How the Servant Serves!	vv.13-14
3. Spiritual Growth	— How the Servant Develops!	vv.15-16

12 Timothy as compared to Paul and, possibly, to some of the elders in Ephesus was a mere youth; despite the fact that he must have been in his late thirties at this time. The word "youth" (*neotēs*) was used in the Roman Empire of a man of military age (below 40); this is noted by Irenaeus (Haer ii.22.5). Paul must have been in his thirties when Luke uses this term of him in Acts 7:58. In view of the responsibility devolving on Timothy in the Ephesian situation, this comparative age difference, aided by a natural diffidence (see 1 Cor 16:11), could have led to a reticence of which some ill-disposed persons in Ephesus might try to take advantage. The word "despise" (*kataphroneō*, from *kata*, "down", *phrēn*, "mind") means literally to "think down upon", "to think slightingly of" (see 6:2), and this attitude will be made plain in the actions of those who think like this. White says it "connotes that the contempt felt in the mind is displayed in injurious action". The NT references all imply the action stemming from the thoughts (Matt 6:24; 18:10; Luke 16:13; 1 Cor 11:22; Heb 12:2; 2 Pet 2:10). The answer to this attitude of others to his youth is not self-assertion, or vocal protest, but a life of such a pattern that every adverse reaction will be silenced. This is a more excellent way. By character and conduct he is to ensure that there is no possibility that he might be "looked down upon". "Be thou" is the present imperative of *ginomai*, and could be translated "keep on becoming". "Example" is, contextually, a good translation of *tupos* (JND "model") as implying a pattern to be imitated. The objective genitive is better translated as in the RV, "to them that believe" — as making clearer the purpose of the example. That the genitive can have this meaning is clear from 1 Pet 5:3 where the same construction must be translated "example to believers". The subjective genitive may be admitted as a secondary thought since Timothy would certainly be an example of believers who imitated him.

Paul now names five things (not six as in the AV, for "in spirit" is without good MSS support and is omitted in the RV and JND).

1. In Word — (*en logō*) in speech. This is *conversation*, whether public or private. Others could use words wrongly; "speaking things which they ought not" (5:13); "whose word will eat as doth a canker" (2 Tim 2:17) but Timothy was to use speech carefully.

2. In Conversation (*en anastrophē*), the old English word for the whole manner of life. This is *conduct*, whether in public or private, covering the whole life style. (See Paul's usage in Gal 3:13; Eph 4:22.)

3. In Love (en *agapē*). This is not merely an emotional impulse but a volitional interest that seeks the welfare of others, whether believers or unbelievers. It is necessarily the product of divine action in the human heart (Rom 5:5); it displays the features of Christ (1 Cor 13) and impels sacrificial living on behalf of others.

4. In Faith (en *pistei*). This is what men owe to God because He is God. This is trust and confidence placed in the Person, and consequently in His Word, which produces evidence in the life. This is where Timothy's confidence and belief of the word of God produces that in the life which becomes a pattern for others to imitate. While the word *pistis* may be taken in its secondary meaning of "faithfulness" or "trustworthiness", the former idea suits the sequence of evidences manifest in the life, i.e. conversation, conduct, compassion and now confidence in God displayed in action and ambition.

    The echo of faith in the chapter is not to be missed:— "them which believe" (v.3), "words of faith" (v.6), "this is a faithful saying" (v.9), "those that believe" (v.10) and now we have a pattern for believers of faith in evidence.

5. In Purity (en *hagneia*). The word *hagnos* is repeated in 5:2 and describes a chastity that is not limited to avoidance of the sins of the flesh but describes the purity of motive that disdains all that is improper or impure. What is rooted in love and faith will be pure.

13 Paul anticipates (as he did in 3:14) his coming to Ephesus, but feels the necessity, before he arrives, of re-emphasising important matters in regard to Timothy's public service in the assembly. The idea is not that Paul would displace Timothy on his arrival, but rather, he anticipated that if Timothy fulfilled his ministry, both could move to further tasks leaving the assembly at Ephesus fortified against the dangers described. Apostolic ministry never anticipates ecclesiastical office as now established in christendom. The verb "give attendance to" (RV "give heed to") is *prosechō* — already used in connection with the dangers in Ephesus, as in 1:4, "give heed to fables" (see note on the verb there), and in participle form in 4:1, "giving heed to seducing spirits". In the countering of such dangers Timothy was to devote himself wholeheartedly to the responsibilities inherent in his ministry. These responsibilities are described in the next three words. There is an interesting use of the word "attendance" in Heb 7:13, "of which no man gave attendance at the altar", which depicts the absolute absorption of the Aaronic priest at the altar, all thought and energy taken up with the object. This picture lies behind the exhortation to Timothy.

The three matters mentioned are important as stressing the features evident in a NT assembly. All three nouns have the article thus indicating a specific and recognised practice. To indicate this the article may be translated.

1. The Reading (*anagnōsis*). In the NT this is the public reading of the

Scriptures. The synagogue practice of reading the OT Scriptures (as in Acts 13:15; 2 Cor 3:14) was carried over into the assembly gatherings where, in addition, the acknowledged NT Scriptures would be read as Paul evidently expected (Col 4:16; 1 Thess 5:27). This public reading would likely be the primary meaning of Rev 1:3. Since the words in the codex were not divided, this called for care as well as technical ability. This public reading was a vital channel in the *dissemination* of truth.

2. The Exhortation (*paraklēsis*). In the synagogue this followed the reading (see Acts 13:15, "a word of exhortation") and was an exposition and application of the Scripture by way of exhortation or encouragement to a certain course of conduct in keeping with that Scripture. Examples of the cognate verb are in 1:3 (besought), 2:1 (exhort), 5:1 (entreat), 6:2 (exhort) where not only the range of meaning but the application is apparent. This implies a vital appeal in the *application* of truth.

3. The Doctrine (RV "teaching", *didaskalia*). In 1:10 and possibly v.6 (see on this verse) doctrine is to be understood as the body of teaching. Here the emphasis falls upon the act of teaching (as also in v.16); this is the exposition of revealed truth. This played a vital part in the *understanding* of truth.

14 This service as envisaged in the previous verse was not the prerogative of every saint but of those whom God by His Spirit had gifted for the task. This point Paul now stresses with regard to Timothy. Timothy, naturally diffident, and as a younger man somewhat unsure of himself as to whether he has the ability, knowledge, and judgment to carry out this ministry in such difficult circumstances, requires a forthright word from the apostle.

The verb "neglect" (*ameleō*), rendered in Matt 22:5 "made light of", means not to take sufficient account of, or to be careless about. Grammatically, the present imperative with the negative could, in this case, be translated "stop neglecting the gift". This, of course, implies failure on the part of Timothy who by inference is seen as hesitant, vacillating and careless in the exercise of his ministry. This does not in any way fit the picture of Timothy presented in the NT. Both A.T. Robertson and J.H. Moulton have shown that while this is generally a fair translation of the grammatical construction, it is not always to be demanded. It is better to see this statement as a litotes in which a positive command is expressed as a double negative. The exercise of the gift is not automatic but requires the attention and application of the servant.

The "gift" (*charisma*) is that which God has given on the ground of grace (*charis*) to believers through the Holy Spirit, to fulfil functions within the assembly (Rom 12:6; 1 Cor 1:7; 12:4,9,28,30,31; 1 Tim 1:6; 1 Pet 4:10). Three prepositions define this gift to Timothy. "In thee" rules out any question of office, it was given to him personally as a divine enablement for the responsibilities he would bear and the ministry he would be called upon to fulfil. It was "by prophecy"; the preposition being *dia* (through). This refers to the prophetic ministry within the assembly whereby a prophet, either the apostle himself or another, had marked out Timothy as one fitted and gifted for a particular service. (For an example of prophetic ministry of this kind, see Acts 13:1-3.) The identification of Timothy was by means of a prophetic utterance from the Holy Spirit of God. The third preposition is "with (*meta*) the laying on of the hands of the presbytery" or as translated in JND "with the imposition of the hands of the elderhood". This action shows identification with one fitted for, and called to, new responsibilities. The OT picture of Num 8:10 and Deut 34:19 illustrate the NT practice. There is no suggestion in the NT references of any conferment or impartation of gift but simply a recognition of what God has already given. In 2 Tim 1:6, in keeping with the personal nature of the appeal, the apostle alone is mentioned, but here it is the "body of elders" (AV "presbytery") who in this act publicly identified themselves with Timothy in the work for which God had equipped him.

The mention of this gift and the confidence placed in him by God, by Paul and by the elders, would be a great encouragement to Timothy and strengthen the spiritual muscle for the conflict.

15 "Meditate" (AV) and "be diligent" (RV) reflect two shades of meaning in the verb *meletaō*, which, originally carrying the thought of "preoccupation with", came to mean "prosecute diligently" (so RV) and thus "to practise". In this sense of "practising" it was used in athletic training. So picking up the metaphor of v.8, the apostle emphasises the mental and spiritual discipline required in spiritual things. "These things" refers back to the injunctions given from v.12; this is the fifth verb in the imperative mood in the section. Timothy would feel the urgency in the letter.

While "these things" are to be "in" Timothy in the sense of filling his thoughts and occupying his mind, the next phrase shows that he is to be "in them". Literally rendered the phrase would read "in these things be thou". This indicates the very sphere in which he is to live, absorbed, all his thoughts, his time, his talent engaged in these holy things. The AV rendering is an excellent translation, "give thyself wholly to them". We would say "be wrapped up in them" (Hiebert).

The result, if "these things" are the subject of his thoughts, the sphere in which he lives, is that spiritual progress will be so evident as to settle every quibble about his youth and every doubt as to his fitness for the responsibility. The word "profiting" (*prokopē*) had a military background and was used to describe an "advance", "a striking forward". It pictures an advance party cutting a way through difficult terrain or jungle by stern effort. Metaphorically, Paul uses it of the spread of the gospel (Phil 1:12) and of the spiritual progress of the Philippian saints (Phil 1:25). Here it shows that spiritual progress results from disciplined concentration of heart and mind on the things of God.

The word "appear" (AV), which is translated in the RV "manifest" (*phaneros*), means "open to sight", "visible".

Paul uses it often with the verb "become" (as in 1 Cor 3:13; 11:19; 14:25; Phil 1:13) as having a future aspect, but here the present subjunctive of the verb "to be" indicates his present desire for Timothy depending, of course, on how closely Timothy obeys these imperatives. All men (the "to all" of the AV) should be able to recognise in his spiritual progress Timothy's fitness for the responsibility placed upon him.

16 The final two imperatives of the section from v.11 are in this verse. The first imperative is "take heed" (*epechō*) which is closely akin to the verb *prosechō* (in 1:4; 4:4,13). Its use in Acts 3:5, "he gave heed unto them", depicts the total absorption of a man who has been commanded by Peter, "Look on us". Thus "to take heed unto thyself" means simply that "the teacher must prepare himself before he prepared his lesson" (*The Expositor's Greek Testament*). Compare the expression of Acts 20:24, "Take heed (*prosechō*) to yourselves", the instruction of Paul to the Ephesian elders. The second part of the predicate is given, correctly, by the RV in the expression "and to thy teaching". The "teaching" (*didaskalia*) here is not so much the body of teaching as implied in 1:10; v.6, but draws attention to the actual exposition of the matters that comprise the body of teaching. The teacher himself must be right with God in his own personal life, and then he will handle the teaching effectively; principle will underlie precept and will be supported by practice. The article has the force of the possessive "thy"; that teaching which falls within "your" responsibility and exercise in the circumstances and conditions that God has fitted "you" to fill.

"Continue" is the second imperative in the verse, the eighth from v.12, and the final one of the passage. "Continue" (*epimenō*) is a strengthened form of the verb *menō*, to remain or abide. Within the sphere of divine things (v.15) Timothy is to remain preoccupied with these important matters and nothing is either to intrude into, or draw him out of, this realm. While "in them" (*autois*) could refer to the matters to which Timothy was to "take heed" in v.16, it is more fitting to refer "them" back to "these things" of v.15. Alford suggests a full stop after doctrine and links the expression with the concluding sentence of the verse. This gives excellent sense, as the final imperative instruction becomes a recapitulation and, in addition, a foundation for the final promise.

The translation "in doing this" is grammatically and contextually correct (rather than "by doing this") as indicating the sphere wherein Timothy and his hearers would be saved. Salvation is not to be procured "by doing" but "in doing". It is not that spiritual activities save, but in the sphere where these spiritual activities are carried out salvation is experienced and enjoyed. Salvation here is not to be limited to salvation from difficulties or to preservation from false teaching, though these are included, but it must have its full soteriological significance. This is in keeping with v.10 and indicates the close connection between eternal salvation and the doctrinal and practical responsibilities of "a good minister of Jesus Christ". Some have found difficulty in the fact that salvation is ascribed to Timothy and have sought the explanation in a limited view of the salvation. However, while we know that salvation is, in its entirety, of God, it pleases Him to use the human agent. Calvin, not given to undervaluing God's part in salvation, has an interesting note: "True it is God alone that saves; and not even the smallest portion of His glory can lawfully be bestowed on men. But God parts with no portion of his glory when He employs the agency of men for bestowing salvation".

Paul sees Timothy as just such an effective agent under God in the salvation of men. The faithful and devoted application of these imperatives in the life of the "good minister of Jesus Christ" would evidence that in this sphere salvation is enjoyed. Effectively demonstrated in the servant it spreads out to embrace all others who would be prepared to listen. The present participle translated "them that hear", while it must first embrace all those who hear physically, cannot be limited to this but demands the further thought of positive volitional response to the message borne by the servant. This would, indeed, be an effective saving ministry for the good servant of Jesus Christ.

Notes

7   Many of the Roman Catholic stories concerning the "saints", and especially those of more recent date, with which they embellish the history of the church, fall under the condemnation of this verse. Lying outside the realm of revealed truth, and in many cases contrary to the explicit teaching of Scripture they can contribute nothing towards the spiritual health of the believer.

8   There is no assurance here of any material benefit acruing to the godly while on earth; no promise of worldly prosperity is attached to godliness (2 Tim 3:12 will show the opposite). In the midst of trouble and tears, the true "well-being" of the saint is developed in spiritual exercise, which develops in his own experience the right relationship with the world and the physical things in it. This relationship develops a consciousness and a capacity for spiritual apprehension that the believer takes into a "coming" life. How important godliness really is.

13 The practices mentioned in this verse must still be in evidence in a scriptural assembly. Public prayer Godward (2:1-8) has for its corollary public reading and preaching saintward. Where this is neglected the dissemination of truth will be restricted, the application of truth to the conduct will be restrained and the understanding of the truth will be limited.

14 1. The grammatical references are: *Grammar of the Greek NT in the Light of Historical*

Research, Broadman, 1934, Page 854. A.T. Robertson; *A Grammar of the Greek NT*, T & T Clark 1908 J.H. Moulton.

2. Prophetic ministry was given of God in the early days of church testimony and may be seen in operation in Acts 11:27-28; 13:1-3; 21:8-11. The principles governing it are set forth in 1 Cor 14. Since the completion of the canon of Scripture as envisaged in 1 Cor 13:9-10 the prophetic gift has ceased (as have all sign gifts) since all that is required for church testimony has been furnished in the sacred Scriptures. The permanent gift to replace prophecy is teaching (as indicated in 2 Pet 2:1 in the change from "prophets" to "teachers") and in keeping with this, all ministry now is based on the Scriptures. Any claim for renewal of this prophetic gift in charismatic teaching is totally without scriptural foundation, manifestly false, and places such claimants in the category of those spoken of by the Saviour in Matt 7:21-23.

3. This verse is often presented as authority to hold "ordination" services for clergy. Since such officials have no scriptural support, since apostles and prophets have long since gone, such a deduction is without scriptural foundation.

15 There is a verbal link between "neglect" of v.14 where the verb *ameleō* can be rendered "to be careless about" and the verb "meditate" in its basic meaning. The verb "to meditate" (*meletaō*) comes from *meletē*, care, and means "to care for". Not being careless about the gift will involve Timothy in an absorbing care.

2.   A Collective Testimony
5:1-6:2

Paul now turns, in continuing the charge, from a consideration of Timothy's personal testimony and responsibility in effective service to consider the responsibilities of individuals within different groupings in the assembly. Each individual has a part to play within his own sphere and thus a contribution to make to the effective testimony of the assembly. Paul will deal with different age groups (5:1-2), instruct Timothy regarding the material circumstances of widows (5:3-16), stress duty with regard to elders (5:17-24) and conclude with a word in the social sphere to slaves (6:1-2).

a. General Instructions — For All Age Groups (vv.1-2)

v.1   "Rebuke not an elder, but intreat *him* as a father; *and* the younger men as brethren;

v.2   The elder women as mothers; the younger as sisters, with all purity."

As in any family, differences of age and sex in the household of God are to be recognised and respected. The servant must set the pattern of courteous and godly behaviour towards the different groups comprising the assembly. The standards required are set out in these verses. While given in the first place by Paul to Timothy, the instructions were doubtless meant for the benefit of all. In the exercise of an effective deacon ministry (4:6) within an assembly these instructions become invaluable as the servant deals with individuals from the different age groups.

1-2 While the word "elder" (*presbuteros*) is the same word used in the plural in v.17, it is clear from its inclusion with the different age groups, that it is not a member of the body of elders (presbytery, 4:14) who is in view, but simply "an older man". The statement implies that there is something wrong in his life; age gives no immunity to folly. However, age, as always, carries respect and the instruction is "rebuke not ... but intreat". The verb "rebuke" (*epiplēssō*), found only here in NT and much stronger than the word used in 2 Tim 4:2, literally means "to strike", "beat with blow", and thus the metaphorical force of the word is to "hammer with words".

The aorist tense shows he is not to start doing this. Rather he is to "intreat" (*parakaleō*) which is a good translation of the verb already used in 1:3; 2:1, embracing comfort and exhortation but also bearing an admonitory note when required. No minimising of the misdemeanour is involved but the matter is to be handled as a dutiful son would handle the failing of a loved father. Courtesy and respect are implied.

Grammatically, all the age groups are governed by the verb "intreat", thus presupposing folly or failure; but there is little doubt that Paul has passed from this particular point to relations in general. Behaviour towards each individual is to manifest family affection and, above all, individual respect. Younger men (the comparative degree is used in all the nouns) are to be treated as brothers (not with superior condescension), older women are to be treated as a dutiful son would treat a mother (not with dismissive disdain), the younger women as sisters (no with unholy familiarity). While strictly "with all purity" can be construed with the verb, and thus governs all the injunctions, it is particularly appropriate when linked with the younger women. Purity (*hagneia*) is the same word as in 4:12 and implies an inward chastity of thought manifest in perfect propriety of behaviour.

b. Special Instructions — For Different Groups (5:3-6:2)

v.3   "Honour widows that are widows indeed.
v.4   But if any widow have children or nephews, let them learn first to shew piety at home, and to requite their parents: for that is good and acceptable before God.
v.5   Now she that is a widow indeed, and desolate, trusteth in God, and continueth in supplications and prayers night and day.
v.6   But she that liveth in pleasure is dead while she liveth.
v.7   And these things give in charge, that they may be blameless.
v.8   But if any provide not for his own, and specially for those of his own house, he hath denied the faith, and is worse than an infidel.

v.9   Let not a widow be taken into the number under threescore years old, having been the wife of one man,

v.10   Well reported of for good works; if she have brought up children, if she have lodged strangers, if she have washed the saints' feet, if she have relieved the afflicted, if she have diligently followed every good work.

v.11   But the younger widows refuse: for when they have begun to wax wanton against Christ, they will marry;

v.12   Having damnation, because they have cast off their first faith.

v.13   And withal they learn *to be* idle, wandering about from house to house; and not only idle, but tattlers also and busybodies, speaking things which they ought not.

v.14   I will therefore that the younger women marry, bear children, guide the house, give none occasion to the adversary to speak reproachfully.

v.15   For some are already turned aside after Satan.

v.16   If any man or woman that believeth have widows, let them relieve them, and let not the church be charged; that it may relieve them that are widows indeed.

v.17   Let the elders that rule well be counted worthy of double honour, especially they who labour in the word and doctrine.

v.18   For the scripture saith, Thou shalt not muzzle the ox that treadeth out the corn. And, The labourer *is* worthy of his reward.

v.19   Against an elder receive not an accusation, but before two or three witnesses.

v.20   Them that sin rebuke before all, that others also may fear.

v.21   I charge *thee* before God, and the Lord Jesus Christ, and the elect angels, that thou observe these things without preferring one before another, doing nothing by partiality.

v.22   Lay hands suddenly on no man, neither be partaker of other men's sins: keep thyself pure.

v.23   Drink no longer water, but use a little wine for thy stomach's sake and thine often infirmities.

v.24   Some men's sins are open beforehand, going before to judgment; and some *men* they follow after.

v.25   Likewise also the good works *of some* are manifest beforehand; and they that are otherwise cannot be hid.

6 v. 1   Let as many servants as are under the yoke count their own masters worthy of all honour, that the name of God and *his* doctrine be not blasphemed.

v.2   And they that have believing masters, let them not despise *them*, because they are brethren; but rather do *them* service, because they are faithful and beloved, partakers of the benefit. These things teach and exhort.''

Mosaic legislation had always been solicitous of widows and special regard was paid to them. Together with the fatherless and strangers they were specifically provided for in the triennial third tithe (Deut 24:29; 26:12), in the harvest gleanings (Deut 24:19-21) and in the religious festivals (Deut 16:11,14).

In NT times when Jews turned to Christ, the immediate consequence was alienation from family and friends and, very specially, from participation in these scriptural beneficent provisions often administered through the local elders in the synagogue (see John 9:22). This situation posed a problem for local churches very early in their history as is evident from Acts 6:1.

In subsequent years when persecution raged and many saints were martyred for their faith in Christ, many wives were prematurely bereft of husbands. Since women could not readily find employment of an honourable kind and with no secular social institutions to care for such, they were truly, in the natural sense, in dire straits. The treatment of such became, thus early in church history, a test for the churches of their spiritual calibre and character. This was one area in a callous world where the love of Christ could be demonstrated in a practical way in the material and financial support of such widows. This is the problem that Paul addresses in this section.

The word "widow" (*chēra*) is the feminine of the adjective *chēros* used as a noun; *chēros* meant "bereft", "robbed", "having suffered loss"; in this case the loss of the husband. It should also be pointed out that where the expression "widows indeed" occurs (v.3,5,16) the bereavement is obviously wider and includes not only the loss of a husband, but with him all family support.

There are two classes of widow in this passage.

1.   Widows Indeed
2.   Widows With Family Connections

3 The word "indeed" (*ontōs*) means "actually", or "really", and stresses the meaning of bereavement implied in the word itself. It distinguishes a class of widows who, having been bereaved, are in indigent circumstances and, in addition, have no relatives to support them. This is the definition that is amplified in v.5 by the addition of the word "desolate", where this adjectival participle is the passive voice of the verb *monoō*, "to be left alone". This same definition is implied and explains the instruction given in v.16 with regard to the real widows or the genuine widows, or widows that are not only such in name or status but are actually widows in the real meaning of the word.

The verb "honour" (*timaō*) uses the imperative of the fifth commandment but, of course, makes it more embracive. In light of the general instructions given in vv.1-2 it would seem natural to give to the word its regular meaning "to show respect". But widows would certainly be included in the women whether elder or younger of v.2 and thus it is a fair deduction that the word must go further. The Lord's use of the word in connection with the fifth commandment in Matt 15:3-6 indicates that it can include the idea of material and financial support. An assembly could hardly "honour" a widow and let her suffer financial need. It seems likely that this word is deliberately chosen to show that material and financial support is not the doling out of meagre and reluctant charity to paupers but to indicate that it arises from a true estimate of the worth of, and the consequent respect due to, christian women. In this way the assembly honours them.

4 This second class of widows are those who have family relatives. These are not truly "alone" in the sense of "desolate" (related to *monos*, "alone"). The widow in this class has children or grandchildren (RV). The word "nephews" (in the AV translation) originally meant "grand children" but is now obsolete. "Grandchildren" is a fair translation of the word *ekgonos* (from *ek*, "from"; *ginomai*, "to become or be born") which in the plural means "descendants".

The children and grandchildren (not the widows) are imperatively commanded to learn, as their primary responsibility, to show piety at home. The command lies in the imperative mood of the verb and the thought of primary spiritual responsibility comes from the adverb "first". They must face this obligation first. The infinitive (*eusebeō*) rendered "to show piety" means to act respectfully and dutifully towards those in their own household (see Acts 17:23 where the respect and duty are Godward). "At home" is better rendered by the RV "towards their own household" indicating that it is not the place but the members of the family who are owed proper respect. The second infinitive is the verb "to requite" (*apodidōmi*) which means to discharge a responsibility. The verb is linked with *amoibē*, which is the cognate noun of a verb meaning to repay, used in the papyri by way of making a return, conferring a benefaction in return for something already given (Moulton and Milligan). Children and grandchildren are indebted to parents for the care bestowed in earlier years; it is only right this obligation should be repaid. In practical terms they are required to assume responsibility for the support of the parents and grandparents.

The word "parents" is too limited a translation for the word *progonos* which means "forebears" (2 Tim 1:3) and the reference would include all living ancestors.

This requital as the repayment of an obligation is "acceptable before God". The word "good" has weak MSS support and is omitted in JND and the RV. "Acceptable" (*apodektos*) is the same word as in 2:3 and lifts this injection from the merely natural or philanthropic level to that which, as the outcome of divine love in men, delights the heart of God.

5 The adversative conjunction (*de*), translated "now", points the contrast between the widow who has a family to whom she may look for support, and the widow who, in the fullest sense of the word "widow" is bereft, not only of husband but of all means of support. The word "desolate" (see v.3) stresses her "aloneness"; she is permanently alone and forsaken. This widow, however, while she cannot look to the family, does not look to the assembly, but the direction of her gaze is Godward. The word "trusteth" (*elpizō*) is better translated as the RV "hath her hope set"; the perfect tense refers to an action in the past with results that continue into the present. The preposition, *epi* with the accusative, indicates her hope is directed towards God. (See the similar construction in 4:10.) Wuest says, "One could translate 'has directed her hope at God', or 'has her hope settled permanently on God' ".

With her hope thus directed towards God the widow continues "in supplication" (deēsis), those petitions for special needs, and "prayers" (proseuchē), a word that embraces the thought of worship and communion as well as requests. What she has known as practised in the assembly (see these same words in 2:1), she continues in private exercise, night and day. This latter expression is characteristically Jewish and does not mean "without interruption" but "without intermission" showing that she enjoys an unbroken fellowship with God; there are no gaps in her spiritual life (cf. Anna in Luke 2:37 where the same expression "night and day" is linked with her dwelling in the temple).

This final statement is in no sense a qualification the widow must strive to meet; rather, it is the identification for the saints of a God-dependent widow whose support is obligatory upon the assembly. In such a case the assembly becomes the channel for God's supplies to such a dependent widow.

6 The repetition of the adversative conjunction (de), in this case translated "but", throws into contrast one who is very different from the widow in v.5. This verse should be treated parenthetically as a side-glance at one who has no claim upon the assembly for material support. The present participle from the verb spatalaō (used again only in James 5:5) indicates a course of life characterised by riotous, luxurious living. There is clearly no material need evident in her case. There is also no necessity to see this widow involved in prostitution (as do some commentators) and the verb does not demand this. It simply describes a life lived sensually for self-gratification without any thought for, or interest in, divine things. In one sense "she liveth" (zōsa), physical life is there, but it is so selfish, sensual and sinful it declares unambiguously that she is, indeed, dead; there is no evidence of any spiritual life whatever. Such a widow has no claim upon the saints for material assistance.

This is not to deny to unsaved widows material support from believers within the assembly. This responsibility in a personal way will come under the more general instructions of 6:18 and will be based upon a different principle. To introduce this wider issue here would be to confuse the point the apostle is making. Paul is making clear that for a certain kind of widow the assembly has a spiritual and moral responsibility to provide for her material and financial support on a permanent basis. In v.5 we have the identification of one to be supported in this way: in v.6 there is no obligation to support one exhibiting these features.

7-8 "These things" will recall the instructions of vv.3-4 regarding the two classes of widows, with the incidental and parenthetic reference to a different class in v.6. The repetition of the word "charge" (parangellō, see on 1:4 and 4:11) reminds Timothy that these matters were not for personal guidance only but for transmission to the whole assembly. The purpose is that "they", not widows only but all the believers in the assembly, should be "blameless". This latter word has been used with regard to the "overseer" (see on 3:2); it will be used again with regard to Timothy himself in 6:14 (AV "unrebukeable"). On this occasion the RV translates "without reproach"; in this particular matter care is to be taken that no opportunity be given for any ill-disposed person to blame the believers in assembly fellowship for callous indifference to the plight of indigent and needy relatives.

One such just cause for blame would be evident if any believer failed to provide materially for "his own"; this phrase embraces his own relatives. "Specially" emphasises that that which is an obligation for relatives generally becomes an even weightier responsibility for those of "his own house" (the RV translation is better, "for his own household"). Clearly a wide circle of relatives is in view in the first expression and the closer circle of the immediate family is in view in the second.

The verb "provide" (*pronoeō*) means to perceive before, foresee, think of beforehand (see the same verb in Rom 12:17; 2 Cor 8:27 where the RV translates "to take thought for") and shows that out of forethought a need is foreseen and provision is made for it. While in the context of children and grandchildren providing for parents and relatives, the general statement "if any one" makes it sufficiently wide to include the forethought required of parents to provide for the children.

Failure in this very practical aspect of christian living is no minor matter; it is, in fact, a denial of faith. "The faith" here embraces the whole body of things believed; such an act abrogates, renounces, denies in practice what may be eloquently professed by lip (the same word "deny" is used in 2 Tim 3:5 with reference to godliness: "denying the power thereof"). Far from relaxing natural obligations in family life, faith in Christ makes them stronger, closer and more demanding. Thus "the faith" is not just a set of theological propositions but it involves practical fulfilment of what these teachings set forth. Lack of such care and forethought is a clear violation of the teaching of Christ given, for example in Mark 9:9-13. Firstly, such behaviour in an evident way denies "the faith", the very body of teaching that in the eyes of the world constitutes the individual a believer. Secondly, it makes that individual worse than "an unbeliever" (RV). The word "infidel" (AV) is too strong a translation for the word *apistos,* which simply means "one who does not believe God" (hence unbeliever). The word "worse" is *cheirōn,* used as the comparative degree of *kakos* ("evil"). A christian who acts like this is worse than an individual who makes no pretence of believing God on two counts. Firstly, to profess adherence to a body of teaching and then flagrantly deny a basic tenet of this teaching is worse than making no such claim: it proclaims the person insincere or dishonest or both. Secondly, many an unbeliever, recognising the duties of family responsibilities, does what the believer, with the full revelation of grace, fails to do.

The sharp tone of this rebuke would suggest that some of this improvident and irresponsible sort were already identifiable in the assembly at Ephesus. One fears that this kind of practical infidelity would still need apostolic censure even today.

9-10 The two main classes of widows have already been identified:

1.   Widows indeed — those without family support.
2.   Widows technically, but not indeed — those with family support.

Now the apostle takes the first class and sub-divides it into two groups. These are distinguishes as follows:—

1.   Those widows to be enrolled (vv.9-10)
      v.9 AV "taken into the number"
2.   Those widows not to be enrolled (vv.11-15)
      v.11 AV "refuse" (JND "decline")

In the final verse of the section (v.16) the subject is concluded with reference back to the responsibility of the assembly towards widows technically and widows indeed.

The distinction between these two groups is drawn by the use of the imperative verb (*katalegō*) in v.9, which literally means "to be enrolled" and was the technical term for being placed on a recognised list or catalogue.

While the teaching of this passage is clear, the purpose of this "enrolment" has presented expositors and commentators with many problems. Many have found in this passage support for an "order" of widows enrolled as "deaconesses". The qualities listed here, on this interpretation, would be required before they would be allowed to serve as such in the assembly. Most of the expositors who support this view insist that there is no suggestion of the woman stepping out of her sphere. Within that sphere much could be done in hospitality, charitable work in the community, the care of orphans, the help of the sick. These widows would, on the grounds of their age and character, take a pledge to abstain from marriage and devote themselves to the welfare of the assembly on the pattern of Phebe (Rom 16:1). Such would require and deserve financial remuneration, hence the purpose of the list. These qualifications would thus, as in the case of elders and deacons (ch.3), enable the saints to identify suitable candidates.

There are weighty considerations that rule out such a view:

1. There is no vestige of scriptural support for any such "order" of widows.

2. There is no historical evidence, whatever, that such an order was ever established; no early historian makes any reference to it.

3. It seems strange, to say the least, that if such an order were in view that it should be restricted to widows at an age (60 plus, v.9) which in the Roman Empire was equated with the loss of physical powers. Further, no hint is

given here, or in any other Scripture, as to the duties of such an order. The tenses in v.10 with regard to the works done by the widow are in the past; they look back to what she had done, not what she should do in the future. Thus stronger scriptural support than this would be required before such an interpretation could be accepted.

On the other hand in the context of this passage, it is clear that within the "widows indeed" grouping already identified, there would be those who would require, not occasional financial assistance, but regular, constant support. Having no relatives to assume responsibility for their material needs; having passed the age when remarriage normally might be expected; and having little possibility, again due to the age factor, of self support, these widows would become the responsibility of the assembly in a special way. It is submitted that it is this list of widows, wholly dependent upon assembly funds, that is in question. For those whose names were placed on this list the assembly would accept full responsibility for their material well-being. Paul recognises that such would be the number of claims, the danger of favouritism, the probability of malpractice, that the criteria for emplacement on such a list should be made abundantly clear. This is his purpose now: to make clear beyond question those entitled to be placed on this list and by implication be able to claim regular financial assistance from the assembly.

This also explains why the younger widows (vv.11-15) are not to be "enrolled". To place their names on this list for regular support would grant them an independence that could be disastrous for their spiritual well-being. For such there was another path open (v.14) that would provide for their material needs and make unnecessary total dependence on the assembly.

The existence of this list did not rule out the occasional support to be given to any widow who through the immediate circumstances found herself in need. Even unsaved widows would come under the general expression "do good" of 6:18. This occasional aid would in the very nature of the case be particularly necessary in the case of younger widows. Many difficult years would likely have to be faced by such widows particularly when the children were young prior to, or failing, a remarriage. These needs would certainly be supplied by the assembly under the provision of v.3. However, for the reasons given, their names were not to be placed on the list of those "totally dependent" on the assembly.

The word "taken into the number" (katalegō) is translated in the RV "enrolled" and was the technical word for placing a name on a list; it was used of soldiers or citizens to distinguish them from others not listed. For the purpose of this list see comments above.

In the Roman Empire sixty years of age was the recognised age when a man or woman became "old" and when sexual passion was deemed to wane. Thus it is most likely that this age qualification was meant to mark out those who now, not able to work and support themselves, would also be very unlikely to remarry.

Two further qualifications are added to the chronological. The first has to do with her character and the second with her conduct. "The wife of one man" is the parallel qualification for the widow as for the elder (3:2) and the deacon (3:12) and would literally read "one-man woman". It does not mean that she must not have remarried again after the death of her first husband; if this were so, then Paul's instruction to younger widows (v.14) would bar them from regular financial support in old age. It cannot mean she had one husband at a time in contrast to many husbands (polyandry). Rather, as seen in the comments on 3:2, it stresses the fidelity she gave to her husband when alive and indicates that she had the scriptural understanding of the nature of the marriage bond. She had not shared with a pagan society its flagrant violation of a divine institution in immorality, in infidelity and unscriptural divorce. This serves as her character reference in submission to the Word of God.

The present passive participle translated "well reported of" has its cognate noun in 3:7, "a good report" (*marturia*), and the sphere in which this witness is borne is "good works". The adjective *kalos* describes the intrinsic excellence of what she has done as a believing wife and mother.

The adjective in the last phrase of v.10 translated "good" is *agathos* which stresses the beneficial effects to others of what she is doing. This verse highlights the difference in the two words both translated into English by the word "good".

Five areas are now specified as bearing testimony to the widow and furnishing her with this good report. Each clause being introduced by "if" (*ei*) makes them indirect questions; in modern terminology this would be a check-list, and mark out areas wherein the conduct of the widow will have been most clearly evidenced.

These five indirect questions provide a worthwhile light on the life of a godly woman.

1. In "if she has brought up children", the verb *teknotropheō*, used only here in NT, means "to rear or nourish children". It is within the home that godliness and moral standards are most readily seen — in the bringing up of children; so this area is examined first. The normal use of the word implies that the children are her own but this is not part of the word itself. If the Lord's path for a believing sister has precluded children of her own, this qualification should not deprive her of regular financial support in her old age. Such sisters, even without children, would be included under qualification number five in this list.

2. "If she hath lodged strangers" translates the one verb *xenodocheō* (from *xenos*, "a stranger" and *dechomai*, "to receive"). The word used in connection with the elder in 3:2 is *philoxenos*, "a lover of strangers"; but of course it falls to the wife to receive, entertain, and care for those strangers and hard work is involved. It is this thought of sacrificial devotion to the

welfare of others that is involved in this expression. Unknown to most saints, yet well-known in heaven, godly sisters, wives and mothers have sacrificed much in this area in the interest of strangers.

3. "If she hath washed the saints feet" is clearly a reference to John 13:5-14 and the command given by the Lord Himself (v.17). This would explain why this is restricted to the feet of saints. This service to guests was usually performed by the host or a slave but here the apostle highlights absolute obedience to Christ, even at personal inconvenience, as betokening a humble and obedient service to the Lord. Outside the social and cultural context, the Lord was not establishing a mechanical and ritualistic ceremony but indicating a ministry of care and refreshment out of love to the saints at personal inconvenience and cost.

4. "If she have relieved the afflicted" in its use of the participle from the verb *thlibō* describes those under pressure, those being pressed. The verb was used literally as in Mark 3:9 concerning the multitude lest they "should throng" him; but its more common use is metaphorical to describe physical, mental and spiritual pressure as in 2 Cor 1:6; 4:8; 7:5; 1 Thess 3:4; 2 Thess 1:6,7. Such pressure can arise from circumstances or from the antagonism of people. The pain can thus be external (physical) or internal (mental). Godly women using the home as a refuge can do much to relieve this pressure. The verb "relieve" is used again in the NT only in v.16 where it has to do with monetary or material aid, but this would only be a specific case of the multitude of ways a gracious wife and mother, even without the possession of large means, can relieve the pressure upon those squeezed by circumstances. An open door to the home, a kind word, a simple meal, a haven for the night, provide the background for spiritual help and guidance. The godly woman has a vital part in this ministry.

5. "If she have diligently followed every good work" in our translation expresses the strengthened form of the verb "to follow" and stresses the dedication put into every good work. The word "good" (*agathos*) fits most beautifully the devotion to the well-being of others here manifest; the work that is done is beneficial in the very best sense; the physical benefits open the way for the spiritual. The statement is embracive enough to cover all the previous four areas of her testimony.

11-12 The widows of these verses, as explained in the introductory comment to this section, are "widows indeed". They therefore qualify for financial help from the assembly when required. However, though equally bereft of a husband there is a particular reason why their names should not be placed on the list of widows that are to be supported on a regular and permanent basis by the assembly. The reason is very simply their youth. To place younger widows amongst those thus entirely supported by the saints would present certain dangers to them and to the testimony. Two dangers that could arise if this prohibition is not obeyed are mentioned. One arises from the fact of youth itself and the other as a consequence of giving younger widows a financial independence they are not equipped to handle (v.13). There is an alternative pathway open to the younger widow as set out in v.14 that would preserve both the widows themselves and the testimony of the saints from spiritual disaster and satanic attack.

Concerning the word "younger" which in the context of v.9 would suggest a widow under sixty years, *The Expositor's Greek Testament* points out "may be rendered positively, young". The word "refuse" is used in 4:7 of "profane and old wives' fables", in 2 Tim 2:23 of "foolish and ignorant questionings" (RV), and in Titus 3:10 of "a man that is an heretic". At first sight this seems a harsh word to be used of young widows. But in the context, the refusal is not of them personally but of their admission to the roll of dependants of the assembly.

The explanation for this refusal is introduced by the word "for" and indicates the danger that could arise to the testimony if the assembly accepted financial responsibility for such younger widows. This danger is described by the verb "wax wanton against" (*katastrēniaō*) and means "to display a restiveness towards"; the usual implication of the word is that it describes the impulse of sexual desire. The subjunctive mood in the verb following "for" is the grammatical way of expressing a contingency; and with the adverb "when" expresses no more than the existence of such a possibility. It certainly does not imply the expectation of such a thing in every case, but describes a possibility that could arise in the case of young widows.

Due to her youth Paul recognises that the time could come when this young widow will set her heart upon remarriage at any cost. The word "will" is not an indication of the future tense but translates the verb *thelō* ("to wish"), which expresses a desire influenced by the emotions. This determination to remarry, arising from the sexual impulse of youth rather than from submission to the Lord, explains the reference to Christ, as the One whose covenantal claims are set aside.

The verb *atheteō* translated "have cast off" (RV "have rejected") is used in Mark 6:26 of Herod's pledge to Salome, in connection with which Vine says, "It almost certainly has the meaning 'to break faith with' ". The same meaning fits the context here. Since there is nothing wrong with remarriage in itself (see v.14) many commentators feel that the rejection of the "first faith" refers to the breaking of a pledge not to remarry which, they assume, the widow accepted when placed on the list of assembly dependants. In this case the condemnation (RV translation is to be preferred over the AV reading of "damnation") would then be the opprobrium incurred because of such a disavowal by the widow of her commitment to the service of Christ. This gives the word "faith" (*pistis*) its classical rather than its scriptural meaning. It is admitted that in classical Greek the word *pistis* can sometimes have the meaning of pledge.

Two vital matters are against such an interpretation. Firstly there is no evidence either in this passage or in any other Scripture that such a pledge, even if required which is more than doubtful, had any scriptural validity. This is to read back into this passage anachronistic notions of a later age when ecclesiastical departure had already set in and extra-scriptural notions had been accepted. Secondly, it is very difficult to see, in light of v.14, why such a remarriage should incur such censure.

The situation is better explained by the recognition that financial independence would relieve a young widow of absolute dependence upon God and thus give opportunity for the impulses and inclinations of nature to dominate a younger woman instead of devotion to Christ. The danger would then arise that so dominated by fleshly impulse the young woman would set her heart on marriage at any cost, and, eventually in defiance of Scripture she would accept an unbeliever as a husband. That financial independence rather than financial need would lead a younger widow to marry an unbeliever may be explained by:

1. her now having time on her hands with no necessity to seek work and Satan using the impulses of nature with the opportunity provided by idleness to suggest to her another path;

2. her having her financial needs met on a regular basis encouraging an independence even of God, so that she no longer feels cast entirely upon the Lord and, perhaps blaming God for her bereavement, seeks in the exercise of her own will to display her independence.

In acting like this, with the determination to marry at any cost even an unbeliever, the widow is repudiating her early commitment to Christ when she came to Him as a sinner and accepted Him as Lord. This action in fact is the "casting off their first faith", an act that sets aside the principle of godly separation implicit in the acceptance of Christ as Lord. This action inevitably incurs the judgment (*krima*, translated by the RV "condemnation") of God. That a particular act is in view is suggested by the aorist tense of the verb "cast off" and the consequence is seen in the present participle "having" judgment — this is their position now. That is, they have placed themselves by deliberate action under the judgment of the word of God for their disobedience and they may expect governmental dealing from God (Rev 3:19). If such had had to earn a living or had married again in the Lord (v.14), this would have preserved them.

13 The second reason for refusing to put younger widows on the list for regular support, is a very practical one: it would leave too much time on their hands. This would expose them to the dangers inherent in such a condition, and develop harmful habits. J.N.D. Kelly translates the AV "they learn to be idle" as "they qualify as idlers" and adds a helpful note: "In the Greek the feminine adjective 'idle' (*argai*) and the verb 'they learn' (*manthanousin*) are simply juxtaposed, which has led commentators to infer that the infinitive 'to become' should be understood. Numerous parallels, however, prove that the verb *manthanein* ('to learn') with a substantive denoting a profession or occupation was an idiomatic construction signifying 'to qualify as such and such" (e.g. a doctor, wrestler, etc.). The translation adopted attempts to reproduce this idiom and at the same time to bring out the touch of sarcasm implied".

With nothing to occupy time the danger would be that these young widows "going about" (this is the RV translation, more accurate if less graphic than the AV "wandering") from house to house (literally "the houses") without sufficient reason or purpose, would become tattlers and busybodies. "Tattlers" is the noun from the verb *phluō*, "to babble" which according to Wuest means "to utter nonsense", "talk idly", "prate", "to bring forward idle accusations", "make empty charges", "to accuse one falsely with malicious words". A good example of its use is in 2 John 10, "prating against us with malicious words". "Busybodies" is the plural of *periergos* which literally means "one who works round", the idea being of one who out of curiosity goes round and round and pries into something that belongs to another. The cognate verb is found in 2 Thess 3:11.

The social intercourse of idlers quickly degenerates into silly chatter which not only affects the persons who indulge in it but soon produces a mischievous interference into the affairs of other people. This evil is further compounded by the communication of matters likely under some pledge of secrecy which had been much better left unspoken. That these sessions of idle gossip have a potential for moral evil is not only clear from this passage but that doctrinal errors may be introduced in them is emphasised in 2 Tim 3:6 and in Titus 1:11 where false teachers take advantage of the opportunity to spread their heresies.

14 Having shown the very real dangers arising out of a misplaced philanthropy that would make younger widows financially independent by placing their names on the list of assembly dependants, the apostle goes on to show that there is an alternative path open to them in keeping with their faith in Christ and in obedience to the word of God. This alternative path of preservation for the young widow is introduced by the positive injunction that she should remarry. The verb "I will" (*boulomai*) expresses a desire based on a rational calculation of intelligent appreciation of the situation. It stands in contrast to "they will" of v.11, which translates the verb *thelō*, which is a desire produced by the emotions. The word "younger" is the same word as in v.11. There is no word "women" in the text, but the following word "therefore" indicates that it is the same group "the younger widows" (see RV) who are the subject of the instruction.

Scripture is perfectly clear that there is nothing whatever wrong with a second marriage of a widow (see Rom 7:1-3; 1 Cor 7:39). In fact, as this

Scripture makes plain, in certain circumstances it is not only allowable but it is advisable. Any suspicion or opprobrium arises from a misunderstanding of the phrase "husband of one wife" (3:2) and attaches an unscriptural value to celibacy after the death of a partner. The sole qualification governing such a remarriage is given in 1 Cor 7:39, "only in the Lord". This Scripture shows that the very preservation of the young widow lies in her remarriage and the acceptance of the responsibilities of such a sphere involving the bearing of children and the responsibilities of managing a home. This is the scriptural answer to the problems that have just been discussed in the previous verses (vv.11-13).

The cognate noun of the verb that is here translated "bear children" has already been used in 2:15 to highlight the importance of a woman's role and the value that God attaches to her willing acceptance of it. "Guide the house" (*oikodespoteō*) describes in one word the direction and management of the household. The ultimate responsibility for rule in the home is that of the man (3:5) but the administration is in the hands of the mother. Liddon has a pertinent remark on the word used here: "The application of such a word to the christian wife implies the new and improved position which was secured to women by the gospel".

The word "occasion" (*aphormē*) was used in a military context to describe "a place from which a movement or attack is made, a base of operations" (see Rom 7:8-11; 2 Cor 5:12; 11:12; Gal 5:13). Failure in respect of the dangers mentioned in vv.11-13 either in the personal testimony of the young widow or in the idle gossip leading to mischievous interference in the affairs of others, provides a good base from which the adversary can launch an attack against either an individual or an assembly. The word for adversary is *antikeimenos*, the noun from the verb *antikeimai* which, when used literally, means to "lie opposite to" or "to be set over against". Paul uses it in the plural to describe human opponents in 1 Cor 16:9 and Phil 1:28, but here in the singular and with the article, it suggests the arch-opponent, Satan himself. Though it is quite possible this satanic adversary could use a human agent to do his work, the evil intent is traced to its evil source. The metaphorical picture in the phrase is that of an attacker, from the bridge-head or beach-head as a base of operations launching an attack upon a fortress. It is a matter of regret that often the indiscreet conduct of saints in these respects (in the case before us it is the young widow but the principle is of wider application), allows Satan a foothold from which to attack the testimony. "To speak reproachfully" (RV translates "for reviling") is translated "railing" in 1 Pet 3:9 and pictures words used as weapons in this satanic attack.

15 Paul's acquaintance with the conditions and individuals in the assembly at Ephesus is clear as, sadly, he notes that for some (see Appendix B) this counsel has already come too late. For some whom the saints had helped materially, unrestrained sexual desires, and much idle time had proved a fatal combination. The verb "turned aside" (*ektrepō*) already used of the false teachers (1:6) describes a "twisting out of the right path", they were off the highroad of christian testimony and had fallen in behind (*opisō* translated "after") Satan. Moral and spiritual disaster are depicted in the aorist tense and passive voice of the verb "turned aside" used to describe a moment when the pressure upon them became too severe; circumstances and unrestrained desires led to a wrong step and they found themselves following not Christ but Satan. This counsel will preserve others from joining the ranks of the arch-enemy of all the purposes of God — Satan himself.

Paul, in a concluding comment, returns to his original two classes of widows. See introduction to section.

For Group 2 (widows technically) family responsibility is restated,

For Group 1 (widows indeed) assembly responsibility is re-emphasised.

16 The restatement of family responsibility is not a mere repetition of v.4; there the responsibility for support is limited to children and grandchildren; here the responsibility to support widows is much wider in its scope. The actual phrase "if any believing" (*ei tis pistē*) is translated in the RV "if any believing woman" since the word *pistē* is feminine. The MSS authority for the inclusion of "man" (AV) is very weak. Paul would seem to have in mind a comfortably-off woman, either unmarried or with an unconverted husband or a widow herself, who has within her extended family circle or household (there would be slaves and many dependants of such a household) a widow or widows whom she could easily assist materially. Such could easily overlook the moral responsibility involved in this position and Paul sees the need of clear instruction. The word "relieve" has been used in a very wide sense in v.10 but, here, would refer principally to the provision of material aid.

"Be charged" is from the verb *bareō*, translated "heavy" (Matt 26:43), "were pressed" (2 Cor 1:8), "being burdened" (2 Cor 5:4) and metaphorically is used of a mental or spiritual burden seen as a load. Its cognates all carry a financial implication as can be seen in the use of the word in 2 Cor 11:9; 12:16; 1 Thess 2:9 and 2 Thess 3:8. The principle is very clear: the "burden" for the support of these widows falls first, naturally, on the children and grandchildren, v.4; then scripturally, upon the wider circle of believers within the extended family unit who are in a position to help. When needs cannot be met from these private resources, it is then that the assembly assumes responsibility. The assembly does have a moral and scriptural responsibility to "relieve them that are widows indeed". These are widows in the real meaning of the word, totally bereft of resources and relatives able to help as well as husband.

On the word "church" see the previous two references in this epistle at 3:5 and 3:15 where, as here, the local company of saints is in view.

Three sub-divisions may be noted in this section:

1. Respect for Elders   vv.17-18
2. Rebuking of Elders   vv.19-21
3. Recognition of Elders   vv.22-25

17 The elders here are to be distinguished from the older men of v.1. The same word (*presbuteroi*) is used in Acts 20:17 of the men from this very assembly; the same men are called "overseers" in Acts 20:28 (see comment on 3:1). There is therefore no basis for regarding these men as different and forming a different class from the overseers already mentioned. The word "rule", (*proistēmi* literally "to stand before", "to lead") is used of leadership in the local assembly in Rom 12:8 and in 1 Thess 5:12. In 3:4-5, it was made clear that leadership within the home is the preparation for and the pattern of leadership within the assembly. With rule in the home as the analogy and the picture of rule within the assembly, it is easy for the believers in an assembly to recognise those with qualifications for leadership. The adverb "well" (*kalos*) describes how the elders are expected to fulfil their responsibilities: there is to be nothing perfunctory or mechanical about their work; it is to be done "excellently" or "commendably". The verb "be counted worthy" (*axioō*) describes "an estimate reached in the thinking"; it is used of God's estimate of the saints in 2 Thess 1:11 and with respect to Christ in Heb 3:3. Here it describes the estimate formed in the minds of the believers with regard to the elders who are discharging their responsibilities commendably. The discharge by the elders of their duties in a commendable way lays an obligation on the believers to recognise this in their estimate of them. The obligation is stressed in the imperative mood of the verb "be counted worthy". The word "honour" (*timē*) describes the respect to be shown to such elders; they are to be valued for the work they do. The word "honour", in itself, does not demand financial remuneration (see its usage in 6:1 where remuneration cannot be involved), but that it can include this is shown by its use in Matt 27:6,9 and in the translation of the same word as "price" in Acts 4:34; 7:16 and 1 Cor 6:20.

The word "honour" in 1:17 (towards God), and in 6:1 (towards masters) demands, in the basic meaning of the word, respect and appreciation arising from a true estimate of worth. That the word may include financial remuneration or support arising from this evaluation has already been noted. This is supported by the use of the cognate verb in v.3 in connection with the widow where the context demands material support. This financial aspect is also implied by the scriptural quotations immediately following in v.18.

Appreciation of the spiritual value of such men, who sacrifically spend themselves for the saints, would scarcely allow them to suffer material need, particularly when this need was brought about by their unremitting attention to the needs of others. Thus the assembly should face an exercise to support materially those who would spend sacrificially on their behalf, if and when such a need arises.

The word "double" has posed many a problem to commentators. Some see it almost as indicating a "pay scale" depending on the worth of the elder; the more diligent the elder in the discharge of his spiritual responsibilities the higher his pay! There is nothing in the passage that would in any way support such a materialistic view. There is much more to be said for the view that recognises the respect due to the position he takes as an elder is supplemented by the respect earned due to the faithful discharge of his responsibilities. In this way he has "double honour". The word "especially" (*malista*, see also 4:10; 5:8) does not distinguish two classes of elder, one "ruling", the other "teaching"; both functions are to be carried out by the one person (see on 3:2, 4); but the word rather emphasises how the responsibilities are discharged. The word "labour" (*kopiaō*) means to toil to the point of exhaustion, and Paul uses it frequently to describe spiritual activity (4:10; Rom 16:12; 1 Cor 15:10; Gal 4:11; Phil 2:16; Col 1:29; 1 Thess 5:12) with all the consequent demands upon the constitution of the servant, both physically and mentally. Simpson translates it "painstaking" which lays emphasis upon the careful thought behind the toil. The absence of any article and the one preposition governing the two words identify the expression "word and doctrine" as describing the oral ministry within the assembly. It indicates the careful and sometimes exhausting preparation required if the instruction given is to be of spiritual profit to the saints.

18 In support of the instruction of v.7 Paul uses his usual formula, "For the scripture saith" (cf. Rom 4:3; 9:17; 11:2; Gal 4:30 etc.), which here covers two quotations, one from Deut 25:14 and the other from Luke 10:7.

In the quotation from Deut 25:14 the major point is simply that God expected the humane spirit of His people to be manifest even in their treatment of oxen. While the ox toiled for the good of others, it had a legitimate claim to have its needs met from this source. The present participle presents a graphic picture of the ox in the process of threshing. But God had more in mind than kindness to an animal. The basic teaching was designed to awaken thoughtfulness and kindness towards those from whose labours we benefit. In 1 Cor 9:9 where Paul uses the same quotation, it is abundantly clear that the meeting of the need is the material support by the saints of those through whom spiritual blessing had been experienced. The inference from the quotation in v.9 is spelled out very clearly in the words of v.11: "If we have sown unto you spiritual things, is it a great thing if we shall reap your carnal things?"

The same principle applied, and the same inference drawn, in this passage would support the view that "honour" includes an element of financial acknowledgement to the elder who, sacrificially, spends himself and his time in the interests of the saints. The principle is the same in both cases.

If, as suggested in the introduction, this letter was written about the summer of AD 64, then Luke's gospel would have been in circulation some two or three years; modern conservative scholarship would place the date of Luke's gospel around AD 60. Thus this quotation from Luke 10:7 indicates that from the time of writing the gospel was acknowledged as Scripture and of equal authority with the OT. The word "labourer" (*ergatēs*) is translated "workman" (2 Tim 2:15), and while it originally meant a "field worker", it came to be used more generally of any workman. The word "worthy" is the cognate adjective of the verb in v.17, "be counted worthy". "Reward" (*misthos*) is translated "hire" (Matt 20:8) or "wages" (John 4:36). There is to be equivalence between work and wages; but ever remembering that spiritual matters are not to be measured by materialistic concepts, the warning words of the Lord Jesus to hypocrites are relevant in this connection from Matt 6:2,5,16: "Verily I say unto you, They have their reward (*misthos*)."

19 The mention of elders who carry out their responsibilities in a commendable fashion leads Paul, logically, to consider the possibility of an elder failing. Care must be exercised in the case of a man who occupies such a prominent position. Due to misunderstanding, party faction or personal animosity, charges could so easily be laid against an elder of personal sin or of doctrinal error. Vine points out that the word *katēgoria* (accusation) has a background of legal action; he writes: "It is derived from *agora*, a place of public speaking, prefixed by *kata*, against; hence it signifies a speaking against a person before a public tribunal".

When such accusations are made, they must not be entertained unless supported by "two or three witnesses". This standard principle of scriptural justice taken from such OT Scriptures as Deut 17:6; 19:15, must be rigorously applied, else the door is open for slander and innuendo sufficient to destroy the moral authority of an elder. The word "before" is *epi* which does not mean "in the presence of" but, with the genitive is more accurately translated as in the RV, "at the mouth of" or, as J.N.D. Kelly, "on the evidence of". The principle of "two or three witnesses" established in the OT still permeates the NT as may be seen in such Scriptures as Matt 18:16; John 8:17; 2 Cor 13:1. This principle is doubtless emphasised with regard to elders because the preservation of their moral authority is absolutely vital for the well-being of the assembly. If there is sin or failure, evidence is to be examined and evaluated in a scriptural way but innuendo and slander based on gossip are not to be entertained.

20 The plural participle opening this verse, translated "them that sin" is generally understood to be the elders who sin, and thus, because of their public responsibilities they merit this public rebuke. That such elders who, as the present participle would suggest, were actually in the process of sinning should merit only a rebuke, albeit "in the sight of all" (RV) seems strangely weak. That a number of them should merit this censure poses further problems.

The situation here described may be viewed in another way. This is to understand the participle "those that are sinning" as descriptive of those, who out of malice and ill-will persist in laying charges that cannot be substantiated against the elders. They continue to do this even when it is pointed out they have not the two or three witnesses required. What these detractors are doing is destructive of the authority of an elder, and this must be publicly rebuked. The word "rebuke" (*elenchō*) can be generally translated "convict"; so that words of rebuke are supported by proof sufficient to reach the conscience; cf. John 3:20; 1 Cor 14:24; Eph 5:11,13; 2 Tim 4:2; Titus 1:9,13; 2:15. The idea is aptly reflected by J.N.D. Kelly in the translation "publicly expose them". Dealing with this matter publicly will cause "others to fear". On this view "the others" or "the rest" (RV and JND) are the others within that same group who are seeking to destroy the personal credibility of the elder by laying unsubstantiable charges against him.

21 The serious nature of the matter just dealt with (vv.17-20) is reflected in this solemn entreaty that Paul now makes to Timothy. The word "I charge" is not the one formerly used in 1:3 or 4:11, but the word "earnestly testify" (*diamarturomai*) that Paul uses as a solemn asseveration as in 1 Thess 4:6; 2 Tim 2:14; 4:1. One can hardly miss the echo of the word "witness" (*martur*) from v.19 in this verb. However, this witness is not borne before (*enōpion*, in the presence of) any earthly tribunal but in the presence of God, Christ Jesus (the RV order of names is correct and "Lord" is not in most MSS.) and the "elect angels". These angels are described as "elect" (*eklektos: ek*, "from", *legō*, "to gather, to pick out") in contrast to the fallen angels who, under Satan, rebelled against the authority of God. Other Scriptures show that such angels are interested spectators of the character, condition and circumstances of testimony for God on earth: 1 Cor 4:9; 11:10; Eph 3:10; 1 Pet 1:12. One article before "God and Christ Jesus" links them together as deity while a second article before "elect angels" sets them apart from deity as mere creatures. God, Christ Jesus and the elect angels can be the only witnesses in the realm where decisions demanding moral courage are taken. These are vital decisions that affect the testimony for God, and Timothy is here reminded that he makes them under the direct gaze of the spiritual world. Ths solemn adjuration would arise from Paul's apprehension that Timothy, whether out of physical disability or personal timidity, might hesitate to act with sufficient vigour against forceful personalities in the assembly.

The word "observe" is *phulassō* (in 6:20 translated "keep") and has the same idea as "keeping the law" in Pauline usage; see for example its use in Gal 6:13, "keep the law", or Rom 2:26, "keep the righteousness of the law".

For the younger man faced with problems in the assembly there could arise difficulty in two ways. The first could arise from inexperience: "preferring one before another" translates the word *prokrimatos* (RV "prejudice") and simply means to reach a judgment before the case is heard. We would say "prejudge the issue". This would lead of course to a faulty judgment which would be a source of trouble. The second way in which trouble could come is from "partiality" (*prosklisis* from *pros*, "towards", *klinō*, "to lean") which could be translated "favouritism", a leaning or inclination towards a person or a party. Within an assembly this can lead to a mistake in judgment that can become a real source of trouble. Too hasty a judgment before the whole case is known or a judgment "bent" in favour of one party can still destroy an assembly; is it any wonder that Paul begins his warning to Timothy with such a solemn adjuration?

It is difficult to escape the impression that some influential saints were attacking the authority established within the assembly represented by the elders. Paul is encouraging Timothy, without fear or favour, without prejudice and without partiality, but in keeping with the judicial principle established in Scripture, to deal with this attack firmly and openly.

22 The expression "lay hands on" (4:14; 2 Tim 1:6) implies the recognition of and identification with a person. This is clear in the OT passages that established the practice on divine instruction (Num 8:10; 27:18,23). The call and fitness were divinely given and this was publicly recognised by the act of laying hands on the particular person. In this passage the subject of elders is still the matter under consideration and Paul warns that too hasty recognition of an elder could lead to problems later. Favouritism (v.21) could lead to the hasty recognition of a man as an elder without adequate time for his character to be fully displayed. Thus, if in subsequent days doctrinal error or moral obliquity came to light, Timothy, in the eyes of others, would be a partaker of (*koinōneō*) these sins. The RV "hastily" is a better translation of the word *tacheōs* than the AV "suddenly" as it is not the manner of the act but the rashness of the act that is in view. Perhaps there is an additional point that the too-hasty recognition of a man, who proved eventually to be unfitted as an elder, had provided opportunity or occasion for him to sin. Thus, those who placed him in that responsible position would bear the blame as, in this sense, they share his failure. The sins in this verse (contrast v.24), following this line of interpretation, could be future. It is in this context that the instruction becomes pointed "keep thyself pure", where "keep" (*tēreō*) means to "exercise watchful care" and "pure" (*hagnos*) bears its secondary meaning of "upright" or "honourable" or "unstained". A good illustration of this meaning of *hagnos* is in 2 Cor 7:11 where it is translated "clear" (see also Phil 4:8 and 1 Pet 3:2). Timothy could be held, in some degree, responsible if a man, recognised too hastily as an elder, became the subject of a scandal. With this warning before him Timothy would exercise very watchful care over those with whom he, or the assembly, would identify themselves in the recognition of them as elders.

23 Because of the abruptness with which what appears to be a new subject is

introduced some commentators suggest that this verse has been displaced in
the text or is an interpolation. Neither suggestion has the slightest MSS
evidence. Further, the verse is not so irrelevant to the context as, at first sight,
it would seem. The injunction to "keep thyself pure" has obviously reminded
Paul of a personal rule that Timothy would seem to have adopted out of
personal exercise as a guideline in the midst of sensual Ephesian conditions
(see 3:3,8) so that he refused to drink wine even for medicinal purposes.
Vincent gives the true force of the injunction as he translates "Be no longer a
drinker of water", and goes on to comment that "Timothy was not enjoined
to abstain from water but is bidden not to be a water-drinker, entirely
abstaining from wine". Water in the Roman world was often unsafe and the
carrier of disease. Timothy was therefore putting himself at risk, particularly
in view of his physical weakness, by insisting on drinking water only. Wine
(*oinos*) was the most important medicine, in the Roman world, suited for use
internally. For dyspeptic conditions ("thy stomach's sake") and frequent
indispositions ("thine often infirmities") it was, in fact, the only remedy
medical care had to offer. It may be relevant to point out the normal word for
wine (*oinos*) is used here and refers to the fermented juice of the grape.

The reason for the adoption of this personal rule by Timothy can, of
course, be only a matter of speculation but there is no suggestion in it of any
ascetic practice (such as has been condemned in 4:3); it could well be that he
desired to set before the saints an example of abstention from that which was
productive of so much human misery and social evil. Paul is clearly concerned
lest his commitment to this personal rule should cause him to reject a
legitimate medicinal use of the wine. This could be detrimental to his health
especially in view of his physical disabilities. In the use of wine as a medicine
the two stipulations mentioned here would still preserve from any misuse

1. "a little" (the quantity).
2. "for thy stomach's sake and thine often infirmities" (the purpose).

No licence for social drinking is included. It is the necessary use (the verb is
chraomai, from *chre*, "it is necessary") of wine that is permitted, not its abuse.

24 After the parenthetic personal advice of v.23, the subject of the
recognition of elders is resumed and closed. There is a possible antithesis
between the "infirmities" of v.23 and "sins" mentioned in this verse (see also
v.22). In considering fitness for responsibility, Timothy is to remember that
sins can be of two kinds, open or hidden. Open sins are immediately evident
(*prodēlos*, means "evident beforehand") and graphically depicted as running
ahead (*proagō*, see on the same verb used in 1:18) to judgment. The judgment
in this case would be the assessment and evaluation of a man's actions and
activities by his contemporaries. It is clearly manifest in these actions what
kind of a person he is. In other men their sins are not so clearly seen, "they
follow after", or retaining the metaphor, "they trail behind them" (J.N.D.

Kelly), i.e. they are not immediately evident. Thus judgment is reached in this case without all the evidence being available. Paul is advising that the mere absence of adverse evidence is not always enough upon which to approve a man; caution is necessary if positive evidence is not available. The judgment (*krisis*) here, as is evident from the context, is not the judgment of God, though that stands in the background, but the evaluation by Timothy and the assembly of men who would aspire to leadership. Such language could scarcely apply to the Judgment Seat of Christ, nor would that assessment aid now in the recognition of elders.

25 The antithesis presented in this verse is between the "sins" of v.24 and the "good works" here. This is the force of the first word "likewise" (*hōsautōs*) which Alford renders "on the other side of men's conduct". Some good works are clearly evident (*prodēlos*, the same word as in v.24), they stand out conspicuously. "They" (the works) that are "otherwise" (*allos*, others of the same kind) refers to those good works which are not conspicuous. The contrast is not between good and bad works but between good works that are clearly seen and those that are not immediately observable. However it is impossible for this latter class of good works to be permanently hidden (passive voice of the verb *kruptō*, "to hide", "to conceal", from which is derived the English word crypt), they will most assuredly come to light (see Matt 5:14-16). This final verse of the section is clearly meant as an encouragement to Timothy who might fear that, through delay in their recognition, some worthy aspirants to oversight could be undervalued or overlooked. Paul assures Timothy that there is no danger of this; we would say "time will tell"; delay in recognition can only serve to bring out the true calibre of worthy men as their good works come to light.

Since slaves formed a large proportion of the population of the Roman Empire it was but to be expected that this would be reflected in the composition of the early assemblies. Thus it was essential to give special spiritual instruction to such lest the dignity and freedom they enjoyed in Christ should blind them to the obligations they owed to their masters even if those masters were unsaved masters. Their standing in Christ did not change their status in society, but it did lend a new dignity to their service.

In Eph 6:9 and Col 4:1, following directions given to slaves, instructions are given to slave owners. The fact that Paul says nothing to the masters in this passage may be an indication of the numbers of such in the assembly. However it is likely that the insidious false teaching inculcating a spirit of independence of scriptural authority was having an effect socially amongst the slaves and breeding a spirit of rebellion. This would call for the clear teaching of these verses.

1 The word "slave" is *doulos*; the word for "master" is *despotēs*. These are the correct terms in current use in the Roman Empire where the slave was only a chattel; in the thinking of aristocratic Romans slaves differed in degree, not in kind from cattle. The master had total, unrestricted control of the person even to death itself. Only in the Pastoral Epistles does Paul use the term "master" (Titus 2:9). It is interesting to compare his use of the same word with reference to Christ in 2 Tim 2:21, where the christian is viewed as "a vessel unto honour ... and meet for the master's use". His normal word for master is "lord" (*kurios*). "Under the yoke" (*hupo zugon*) is tautologous and describes the oppressive nature of the servitude; hard, restricting, disagreeable conditions are depicted.

The phrase "under the yoke", as appositional, does not apply to service under heathen masters only but is descriptive of all slavery. Alford translates "as many as are slaves under the yoke".

Vine makes an interesting comment on the words "their own" (*tous idious*) in the phrase "their own masters". He writes: "There is no stress on the word 'their own' as if in counter-distinction to other masters; the word *idios* here practically has the meaning of 'several'; the word had a tendency to be weakened in force (cf. Eph 5:22)".

"Count" (*hēgeomai*), used previously in 1:12, means an estimate based on external considerations as opposed to internal sentiments or feelings. The obligation of the slave, emphasised in the imperative mood of this verb, is that whatever he thought of his master personally, he was to respect his standing and authority. "All honour" suggests the greatest respect in every area. The middle voice in the verb "count" suggests that the slave's own best interests lay in willing obedience to his master.

If, however, christian slaves treated their heathen masters with insolence or disobedience, they, of course, would be subject to and have to bear the normal penalties imposed in such cases. What, however, was a matter of deeper concern to the apostle was that this kind of behaviour would bring scandal (the word *blasphēmeō* means "to speak ill of") upon the "name of God and his doctrine". The "name of God" is a Hebraism for God Himself. This passage echoes Isa 52:5 and Rom 2:24. Disobedient and rebellious slaves were a poor advertisement for God and for the teaching they professed. Such attitudes would brand the gospel as subversive of the social order. While in this passage it is the disastrous results of insolence that are in view, it is interesting to compare the beneficial results of true christian behaviour in the same situation in Titus 2:10.

2 Freedom from class distinction in assembly relationships (because they are brethren, i.e. brothers in the same family) likely tempted many a slave to carry the idea of equality into social life. In certain circumstances a christian slave might easily come to "despise" his master. The word "despise" is *kataphroneō* to "think down upon", thus to under-value in thought so that due consideration is not given to the other person's status (see the use of the same verb in connection with age and youth in 4:12). This despising of a master by a slave could arise for a variety of reasons: the slave might have expected his freedom; his master may not have had a very prominent spiritual gift, or perhaps he was not making the same spiritual progress as his slave.

Equality in the family of God, far from affording a pretext for laziness or insubordination, demands, rather, a more dedicated service. The emphatic position of "rather" (*mallon*) is caught by Alford in the translation "all the more serve them". The word "serve" is from *douleuō*, to serve as a slave. Thus believing masters should get the better service. This better service is defined by the phrase "partakers of the benefit" (AV). This is better given by JND, "who profit by the good and ready service". The word "benefit" (*euergesia*) means the higher quality of service given by the christian slave to the christian master. The quality of the service is better because its motivation is not fear, as in normal slave/master relations, but now the motivation is love. The love for a master who is in the class described as "believing and beloved", produces a higher quality in the service of the slave.

As Paul concludes his instructions concerning widows, elders and slaves, all touching on relevant, practical matters vital for true testimony in the world, he adds a final imperative that could be rendered: "these things keep on teaching and exhorting". This positive teaching with regard to the relationships within the assembly would likely not be very popular with progressive elements at Ephesus, hence the need for Paul to encourage Timothy to keep at it. A very natural tendency, particularly for the more timid personality, is to avoid the unpleasant subjects; often these are the ones that are vital in the circumstances.

Notes

1   As pointed out in the comments on this verse the grammar demands that the second verb ("intreat") governs each group. This emphasises that courtesy and respect are to mark all the actions between individual believers even when failure and folly are manifest. To treat any saint in a rough-shod manner is contrary to the teaching here. The present tense indicates that this courteous treatment is to be the habitual practice in dealing with such matters. Proper handling of rebukes is the key to harmonious relationships within the assembly. Each individual is to be treated with the same consideration that we would use within the natural family remembering that each believer is a member of a heavenly family. (There may be in this verse a hint of teaching given by the Lord Himself in Mark 3:31-35).

4   While the welfare state in some lands has undertaken many aspects of the care and support needed by the elderly and destitute, for believers to shelter behind this

secular provision and refuse responsibility for the maintenance and care of relatives
is to deny the spirit of this passage. Divine love in human hearts will continue to be
shown in sacrificial interest in others, very specially with regard to the aged and
needy. Those of this class within the extended family circle still have large claims
upon believers.

13 In light of the Ephesian background the use of the neuter plural of this word
(*periergos* "busybody") in Acts 19:19 (translated "curious arts") is suggestive. Paul, in
careful language, may be warning that these idlers, with time on their hands, out
of curiosity may pry or be led into matters outside divine revelation, and, with
the use of charms, incantations and astrology, become involved in occult
practices forbidden in Scripture. The prying may go beyond the affairs of men
and intrude into the occult world, which in early days the Ephesian believers
had renounced. This is strengthened by the concluding phrase "speaking things
which they ought not". While it certainly covers the idle and positively
mischievous gossip of the "tattlers", it could well include a dabbling by the
"busybodies" in matters concealed from human knowledge.

14 There is no conflict in this passage with 1 Cor 7:8 where the counsel is given that
widows should remain unmarried. There, the matter is individual and related to
personal exercise particularly in view of the "present distress" (1 Cor 7:26), i.e.
prevailing world conditions. Here it is the maintenance and character of assembly
testimony that is in view. The answer to idleness, gossip, and meddling in the affairs
of others, is the remarriage of the younger widows.

17 Scripture offers no support for a salaried ministry either for evangelists, pastors or
teachers. There is no suggestion of a salaried episcopacy, presbytery or diaconate.
These duties are discharged by believers fitted of God for the task, called by God
into full time service and looking to Him alone for material and financial support.
When the demands of the work to which the individual is called preclude
continuation in secular employment, then both the servant and the assembly will be
aware of such circumstances. An example of such a mutual exercise is given in Acts
13:1-3. As a consequence the servant looks to the Lord alone for his needs, and the
saints on their part feel their responsibility to the Lord to support such servants
engaged in the Lord's work. Thus a path of dependent faith is followed.

To base a salaried class of elders on this verse is going beyond Scripture and
subscribing to ecclesiastical ideas without scriptural authority. Even amongst saints
gathered in the Name of the Lord Jesus Christ (Matt 18:20) who, in former years,
professed to see the dangers inherent in clerisy, there is now an increasing tendency
to pay a man, an elder, a full-time worker, or a missionary to undertake the onerous
responsibilities of pastoral care and visitation amongst the saints. Whether arising
from ignorance of scriptural principle, laziness in spiritual exercise, or simply a desire
to copy denominational practice, this should be seen as an abandonment of
principles set forth in this epistle. The scriptural teaching on the subject is clear from
1 Cor 9:3-14 where the servant looks to his Lord, and the saints feel their
responsibility before the Lord to respond to His grace and the spiritual blessing
received, by responsive giving for the work of God. Thus scriptural practice issues in
the spiritual enrichment of both the servant and saint and precludes any
materialistic motive creeping into spiritual exercise.

While the Scriptures never envisage the one-man ministry entrenched in most
ecclesiastical circles today, neither does it condone any-man ministry, as if every

male had either the right or authority to minister to the saints. Scripture is clear as to the fact that men who teach are equipped by God with a gift (Rom 12:7-8) which is to be exercised within the assembly for edification (Eph 4:11). This will require much waiting upon God, study of the Scriptures and preparation of the message. Saints will soon recognise when such preparation has been omitted. The word "labour" rules out any ritualistic, mechanical approach to the handling of divine truth. That which costs nothing generally achieves precisely the same amount. It would be within the province of elders who "rule well" to ensure that saints are not subjected to profitless ministry.

20 If this verse had not been mistakenly applied to sinning elders (can it be there have been a few?) but had been acted upon in the case of unsubstantiable charges whispered against responsible leaders, many an assembly would have been preserved from heart-break and division fed by evil gossip. While the interpretation relates to elders the principle setting forth the method of dealing with gossip and innuendo against any believer needs to be faced when evilly disposed persons whisper charges against him. There is a scriptural approach to a sinning brother as detailed in Matt 18:15-20.

22 Some see in this verse the reception again into the assembly of a brother (or elder) who had been disciplined under v.20. This is very unlikely, to say the least, as there is no scriptural example of laying on of hands in this connection. Such addition to Scripture as laying on of hands in reception is not known historically until the end of the 3rd century. It is found in the writings of Cyprian.

An additional reason against such an interpretation is that there is no explanation or indication of such an abrupt change of subject.

23 Several inferences may be drawn from this verse:

1. It furnishes scriptural grounds in the case of physical illness for the use of the remedies available to the believer. Neglect of such remedies and consequent bodily weakness may impair usefulness in the Lord's service.

2. Contrary to certain lines of charismatic teaching physical healing is not included in salvation. If the gift of healing was still in operation at the date of this writing, the inclusion of this instruction to Timothy is somewhat strange.

6:1 While slavery has gone in most of the world, the principles here established still apply to employees with regard to employers. Nothing does the gospel so much harm as when those professing faith in Christ display a recalcitrant, disobedient attitude to those lawfully placed over them. Unreasonable demands made on believers should bring out their true character and offer testimony to supernatural grace. Only when the demands of men conflict with the directions of the word of God is the believer allowed to stand on his rights — but they are God's rights, as set forth in the words of Peter in Acts 5:21. Recalcitrance and rebellion bring God and His Word into disrepute.

The apostolic ministry in particular, and gospel preaching in general was not designed to denounce and destroy the abhorrent institution of slavery. This was part of the social fabric of Roman life. The gospel was preached to change men. As men were changed, principles became operative that led eventually to the abolition of slavery. Today, the believer is faced with the same problem in apartheid and in communism. It is not the responsibility of the believer to lead or take part in political or socio-economic protest, but to make known the grace of God that changes men. The social changes will inevitably follow. For the scriptural answers to problems arising from slavery, see 1 Cor 7:21-24; Eph 6:5; Col 3:22; Titus 2:9; Philem; 1 Pet 2:18.

2   It seems inexplicable to many in modern times who pride themselves on their progressive and liberal thinking, that Paul did not denounce slavery and demand the abolition of this degrading institution. This would have been in keeping with the spirit of insurrection that, sporadically, was already sweeping through the Roman world. He would doubtless have found many to support him, but he would have done the gospel terrible and irreparable damage. For Paul to accept, as he does, this vile institution is hard for many social reformers to accept. Paul, however, recognises that his commission from the risen Christ had for its primary object neither national emancipation nor social amelioration but the salvation of men. His business, as ours, was to make Christ known, to see men saved and changed. This would inevitably bring social changes in its train. This is, in fact, the testimony of history. The gospel, as it changed hearts and lives, brought changes in society almost immediately, and as a consequence it was not very long until slavery was abolished throughout the Roman Empire. It took longer to abolish slavery in the British Empire, and it is a sad commentary on the perversity of the human heart that this degrading institution still flourishes under different names in many lands up to the present day.

3.   *The Direct Confrontation with The Testimony*
   6:3-12

v.3   "If any man teach otherwise, and consent not to wholesome words, *even* the words of our Lord Jesus Christ, and to the doctrine which is according to godliness;

v.4   He is proud, knowing nothing, but doting about questions and strifes of words, whereof cometh envy, strife, railings, evil surmisings,

v.5   Perverse disputings of men of corrupt minds, and destitute of the truth, supposing that gain is godliness: from such withdraw thyself.

v.6   But godliness with contement is great gain.

v.7   For we brought nothing into *this* world, *and it is* certain we can carry nothing out.

v.8   And having food and raiment let us be therewith content.

v.9   But they that will be rich fall into temptation and a snare, and *into* many foolish and hurtful lusts, which drown men in destruction and perdition.

v.10   For the love of money is the root of all evil: which while some coveted after, they have erred from the faith, and pierced themselves through with many sorrows.

v.11   But thou, O man of God, flee these things; and follow after righteousness, godliness, faith, love, patience, meekness.

v.12   Fight the good fight of faith, lay hold on eternal life, whereunto thou art also called, and hast professed a good profession before many witnesses."

In contrast to the teaching that Paul has enjoined upon Timothy in v.2, "these things teach and exhort", he now has to expose another aspect of the subtle subversive teaching that, emanating from the false teachers, posed a threat to the personal character of the saints as well as undermining the collective testimony of the assembly.

Before completing his charge to Timothy (resumed at v.13) Paul deals with the third and final element present in the false teaching attacking the assembly at Ephesus. Behind the legalism (1:3-11) and the asceticism (4:1-5) of the false teachers, there lay hidden a materialistic motive that imagined that the gospel and faith in Christ were the way to earthly material advantage. There is possibly a link in this passage with the slave of v.2 who might have been tempted to take advantage of his believing master. However, the thought goes back further to the elders and widows, whose material support, in keeping with the obligations of the gospel, would be costly in material terms. The false teachers, in repudiation of such unworldly and costly ideas and in the rejection of such altruism arising out of sound and spiritual teaching, had very different ideas. These charlatans thought only of the material gain they could get from their profession of Christ. Paul identifies these false men and their motive.

1. The Recognition of the False Teaching vv.3-5
2. The Refutation of the False Teaching vv.6-8
3. The Results from the False Teaching vv.9-10
4. The Response to the False Teaching vv.11-12

3 Again the false teacher is left without a name in the general statement, "If any man"; but he will clearly identify himself in his activity. This is described in the verb *heterodidaskaleō* from *heteros*, "other", and *didaskaleo*, "to teach"; it is the same verb as in 1:3, and indicates that which was of a different kind from the teaching enjoined upon Timothy (v.2). The present tenses in the verbs "is teaching differently" and "is not consenting" are graphic portrayals of this insistent teacher; he is keeping at it. Consent means "to accept what is offered", so, used negatively, this teacher deliberately declines what is presented to him. What is presented or offered to him is the "wholesome words" ("sounds words" RV). "Wholesome" is from *hugiainō* (in English the word "hygiene" is derived from it) which is a word depicting sound health; so these words would be the means of developing spiritual health; no wonder that the one who declines them is described as "sick" (JND v.4). This translation is better than the AV "doting". The absence of any article before "wholesome words", in the expression shows that it is the character of the health-giving message of the gospel that is in view. These words are defined, first as to their source, and then as to the result they produce. The source is "the Lord Jesus Christ" (only here and in v.14 in this epistle do we have the Lord's full title in this word order). For similar use of the genitive to describe the message see 1 Thess 1:8, "the word of the Lord". The expression embraces what the Lord Jesus taught on earth, which became the standard of apostolic teaching (see Acts 2:42), "the apostles' doctrine" or "the teaching" passed on from Paul to Timothy and which he was expected to "commit... to faithful men" (2 Tim 2:2). This teaching is now inscripted for us in the NT through the work of the Holy Spirit in the inspiration of the Gospels and Acts of the Apostles (John 14:26), the Epistles (John 15:13b) and the Revelation (John 15:13c). It is here within the word of God that we find that which produces healthy spiritual life. This healthy spiritual life is not some esoteric mystical experience but is a life which evidences in behaviour that it is in conformity with *"kata"*, "according to") the teaching. This behaviour is described as "godliness" (see Appendix B), a manifest respect and reverence for God that affects every aspect of life.

4 - 5 The false teacher is described as "proud", the same word as in 3:6 ("lifted up with pride") and 2 Tim 2:4 ("highminded"): the word is derived from *tuphoō*, which, when used literally, means "to wrap up in smoke"; metaphorically it has the idea of "conceited". The perfect tense indicates that pride has completed the task and this is the permanent condition of the false teacher.

The bubble of pride in which the false teacher has enclosed himself is pricked in two devastating participles. "Knowing nothing" indicates he has insight into not one single matter; C.B Williams links pride with the verb ignorance in a good translation "a conceited ignoramus". The second sobering participle, "doting" ("sick" JND), from *noseō*, "to be ill", describes, when used of the mind, a morbid preoccupation with a single matter; Hiebert gives "word-sick". Conceited yet ignorant, the false teacher displays a morbid preoccupation with "questions and strife of words". "Questions" (AV) or questionings (RV) is *zetesis*, used in 1:4, 2 Tim 2:23; Titus 3:9, and refers to "idle speculations"; "strifes of words" (*logomachia* from *logos*, "a word" and *machē*, "a fight"), used only here in the NT, means "word battles" and may imply "wordy battles" or "battles over words". The latter meaning better suits the context. The morbidity of mind of the false teacher is revealed in the subtle, hair-splitting discussions of pseudo-intellectual theorising, and the angry disputes centring around trifling distinctions between words. Springing from conceited minds, such teaching, based on idle speculation leading to word battles, produces a sad harvest of bitterness and suspicion. This leads, inevitably, to abandonment of truth and, eventually, to a moral degeneracy. This is a solemn contrast to what is produced by "wholesome words". Five sad results from the "questionings" and "battles over words" are outlined:—

1. "Envy" (*phthonos*) is inward discontent with the advantage or superiority of another and an anxiety to take what he has.
2. "Strife" (*eris*), generally the result of the envy, comes out into the open now as these men vie with and contradict each other. The same word in 1 Cor 1:11 is rendered "contentions", in 2 Cor 12:20 "debates", and in Gal 5:20 "variance".
3. "Railings" (*blasphēmai*) (the cognate verb is in 1:20; 6:1 and the noun in 1:13) describes the slander and the contumacious speech they use against their opponents; the vehement denunciations that the word suggests may be couched in the very language of Scripture.
4. "Evil surmisings" (*huponoiai ponērai*), from the verb "to think under", means to have and foster for evil purposes unfounded and malicious suspicions as to the honesty of those who differ from them. They are adept at ascribing evil motives to their opponents.
5. "Perverse disputings" (*diaparatribai*) denotes a constant or incessant wrangling (*dia*, through, *para*, beside, *tribō*, to wear out), suggesting the attrition or wearing effect of contention (Vine). Constant friction marks the men. (JND gives "constant quarrellings".)

These five things proceed from men described by two perfect participles. The RV reading, "corrupted in mind", indicates that the organ of their moral thinking has been affected by what belongs inherently to mere human nature — corruption (see Eph 4:22; 2 Cor 11:3). The cause of this corruption is revealed in the second perfect participle. "Destitute" is better rendered as in the RV "bereft", indicating a loss of what they formerly possessed. "The truth" is all that God has revealed in Christ (see 2:4; 3:15; 4:3 and comments thereon) and which has become accessible in the wholesome words (v.3). These two participles show that these men, having lost what they formerly possessed, a conscience illuminated by divine truth, had reverted to a natural way of thinking, with the inevitable consequence in their lives. These participles say nothing about the salvation of these men but simply describe their present condition. At one time they had been in contact with the truth, now they have lost it; the passive mood of the participles suggests that they had allowed another to corrupt them and rob them of the truth. While he may have used his agents it is not hard to identify behind this activity the one who is spoken of in Scripture as one "who abode not in the truth, because there is no truth in him" (John 8:44).

Having seen the marks of the teaching and the men who teach it, the apostle proceeds to identify the motive that provides the very reason for this kind of teaching. They were capable of thinking "that godliness is a way of gain" (RV). The AV translation fails to take adequate note that the word order and the article before "godliness" makes this word the subject of the sentence. The article should also carry the possessive force and be translated "their godliness". It is extremely doubtful if anyone in the Roman Empire, especially at the time of writing, ever regarded gain as godliness. In the hands of the false teachers, godliness (the product of the healthy teaching of the gospel revelation) became a mere facade, a religion that became a way of getting wealth. Very possibly in this realm of pseudo-christianity the more idle the speculation, the more bombastic the rhetoric, the finer their academic word distinctions, the higher price these false teachers expected in return for their ministry. They would then be able to compliment themselves on how highly their ministry was valued by the hearers.

The final statement in the AV lacks sufficient manuscript authority and is omitted in the RV and JND.

6 To think that godliness, the reverential attitude to God produced by sound teaching working effectively in the life of the believer, is a "way of gain" (RV), evidences corruption of mind (the thought processes are affected by natural reasoning) and an absence of truth (as revealed in Christ who is the Truth). In contrast to this false way of thinking Paul now shows the true relationship between the believer and material things. "But" (*de*) introduces the contrast. "Is" as the first word in the sentence in the Greek text is emphatic. True profit, on a scale not envisaged by materialists, is called "great gain"; the word "gain" (*porismos*) being repeated from v.5. This is the result of godliness (the right attitude to God brought about by the healthy teaching), coupled with (*meta*) "contentment". The word "contentment" is the translation of *autarkia* which in Stoic tradition described a state of being independent of circumstances; the idea behind this philosophy being that a man ought to be self-sufficient. The Holy Spirit has taken up this word and added a new spiritual dimension to it. It is used to describe not dependence upon oneself or a self-sufficiency arising from one's own resources, but dependence upon God that makes the believer independent of all external things. This is the teaching of 2 Cor 3:5: "not that we are sufficient of ourselves... but our sufficiency is of God". There is no area of christian life in which, and for which, the believer may not put trust in God and thus be independent of all around. That this is something that a believer learns in the experience of life is clear from the adjectival use of the same word in Phil 4:11, "I have learned... to be content". Such godliness is markedly different from the mercenary concept of the false teacher who views godliness as a way to get rich.

7 - 8 The explanation (introduced by the conjunction "for") for the spiritual profit ("great gain"), arising from godliness associated with contentment, lies in the appreciation of the real nature of material things. They belong to a temporary order which, for the individual, begins at birth, when he did not bring any of those material things with him into the world system, and ends with death, when he does not carry any of them out with him. Echoes are found here of Job 1:21; Ps 49:17; Eccl 5:15. Thus the acquisition and use of these things, belonging as they do to a temporary phase of existence, must be subservient to a higher purpose that can affect the believer eternally. When the believer grasps this truth then material things fall into their proper place.

The phrase "it is certain" (AV) or "it is manifest" (JND) is an attempt to smooth out a difficult translation which is given accurately by J.N.D Kelly: "For we brought nothing into the world, since we can take nothing out either. If we have food and clothing we shall be content with that".

The difficulty lies in seeing the relationship between the first statement and the second and why one should depend on the other. The solution may lie in putting a full stop after "world" in the translation above and linking the final statement with the next verse. The sense would then be: "For we brought nothing into the world. Since we can take nothing out either, if we have food and clothing we shall be content with that".

The word "raiment" (*skepasma*) is broad enough to include shelter as well as clothing, but, since like food it is plural, may here be limited to dress. The whole phrase was used colloquially to describe the basic requirements of life. The future passive "we shall be therewith content" (RV) is not to be understood as an implied exhortation (as in AV) but an assertion of a contentment that shows confidence in God (Matt 6:25-26). God graciously gives for this life, and we need nothing more than what He gives. This is the true attitude of the believer to things material. This is no excuse for laziness (see especially 2 Thess 2:10) or carelessness (see 5:8 in this connection) but relieves the saint of inordinate preoccupation with the merely material aspect of life.

9 The danger of such false motivation and false appreciation of material things leads Paul into a more general warning. It is not riches nor the rich, of which there were certainly some at Ephesus (this is a fair deduction from the language of v.17), that he castigates so severely. Riches in themselves are not intrinsically wrong, but the inordinate desire to obtain such often leads into perilous paths and opens the way to moral and spiritual disaster. The adjectival participle (translated "they that will be") is from the verb *boulomai* and suggests a resolve based on deliberate choice, a fixed determination to be rich at any price (note the use of the same verb at 2:8; 5:14 and Titus 3:8). Such a resolution to go after riches, taken by the believer in the innermost citadel of the will, the heart, leads inevitably to spiritual disaster. The apostle proceeds to depict the danger in very graphic terms. The danger of setting the heart on riches is dealt with under three simple headings:—

1. Its Reality — v.9
2. Its Root — v.10a
3. Its Results — v.10b

Four stages are marked off in this downward course. First there is the temptation (*peirasmos*). This temptation is, of course, self-presented because the individual has set the heart on getting rich. The prayer of Matt 6:13 would be ignored; this saint need not pray, "Lead us not into temptation" — he is walking into it. The instruction of the Lord in Luke 22:40, "Pray that ye enter not into temptation" would be forgotten. In consequence the promise of 1 Cor 10:13, "but will with the temptation make a way of escape that ye may be able to bear it" could scarcely be invoked in these circumstances. The second stage is the "snare" (*pagis*). Satan uses the circumstances, as in 3:7 and 2 Tim 2:26, so that the believer, obsessed by his own determination, is tempted to stoop to dishonesty or deception to acquire the wealth upon which he has placed his heart. Immediately the moral sense is blurred, the Scriptures are denied and the saint is trapped. The third stage of the fall allows the cravings for more wealth, now unleashed, to beset the soul. These cravings for undesirable things (see Titus 2:12, where they are called "worldly" lusts) are described by three adjectives. They are "many": this is their *variety* and it is infinite (see 2 Tim 3:6; Titus 3:3, "various lusts"); there will be enough to suit every taste. They are "foolish" *anoētos*: this is the *vanity* of such lusts; the word means "senseless" (Titus 3:3, "foolish") and its antonym is *sōphrōn*, "soberminded" (see 2:9; 3:2); it describes the cravings for prestige and display that is the opposite of christian sobriety. "Hurtful", the third adjective, stresses the *vicious* character of the lusts. It includes a physical element (this is seen in the negative use of the word in Mark 16:18, "it shall not hurt them") but the emphasis here is on the damage to character and testimony. It makes men vain, avaricious, unscrupulous; characteristics that deny the operations of grace in the life. The fourth stage completes the sad picture. What began with "falling" (the present tense is quite graphic) ends in "drowning". The word "drown" (*buthizō*) is used literally in Luke 5:7 to describe the overloaded fishing boats: "and so they began to sink". It is used here metaphorically to describe the soul, overwhelmed in the pursuit of riches, now engulfed in a sea of unleashed passionate cravings, various, vain and vicious, and sinking out of sight.

It is the very lusts from which, through the gospel, God designed to deliver men (Titus 3:12, "denying ungodliness and worldly lusts") that actually "drown" them. To continue the metaphor, the actual sea that engulfs them is described as "destruction and perdition". "Destruction" (*olethros*), used in 1 Cor 5:5 and in 1 Thess 5:3, normally is closely linked with the body. (In 2 Thess 1:9 the word "everlasting" is added to define the special character of the destruction in that passage.) "Perdition" (*apōleia*) is a more terrible word to describe total and eternal loss. No cessation of being is implied in the word, but it describes a total loss of well-being as depicted for the beast in Rev 17:8 of whom it is said "(he shall) go into perdition". The combined force of the words is to imply and teach the total loss of well-being, bodily and spiritually, temporally and eternally. Such is the destructive effect of a soul-absorbing craze for material wealth.

The apostle is careful to make the statement general as characteristic of what lusts do to "men"; but it surely serves as a warning to any professing saint harbouring such a covetous spirit.

10 The actual word order in the Greek text places the emphasis on "root". It is the first word in the sentence. "For a root of all evils in the love of money". While "root" in anarthrous, its emphatic position demands the article in our translation (see *The Expositor's Greek Testament* for the grammatical argument). Alford concurs with this view and writes, "a word like *riza*, a recognised part of a plant, does not require an article when placed as here in an emphatic position". The word "all" in the predicate (implying a distributive use) shows that the RV is correct in the translation, "of all kinds of evil". There are roots that produce evil but there is no kind of evil that cannot come from this root. *Philarguria* (from *phileō*, "to love" and *arguros*, "silver") is translated "love of money". One commentator points out that covetousness (*pleonexia*) is the genus of which the love of money (*philarguria*) is the species. Lilley has a pertinent statement: "there is no kind of evil that the craving for wealth may not originate, once its roots become fairly planted in the soil of the heart". History is stained with the evidence of the truth of this statement.

The possession of riches has dangers (v.17), the acquisition of wealth has its temptation (v.9), but the motivation (love of money), which sets the heart on the acquisition of money for its own sake, is the "root" of the matter. The relative pronoun "which" has for its antecedent the word "money". It is the money, not the "love of money", upon which some men have set their heart. "Coveted after" is the present middle participle from the verb *oregō* which verb has been used in a good sense in 3:1 and pictures a person reaching out a hand to grasp after something. Here the sense is evil for the thing they have grasped after is dangerous. While grasping after money two things happened (aorist tense in each verb) simultaneously. The first is translated "have been led astray" in the RV, which represents the passive voice of the verb *apoplanaō* and points to the pressures upon them which caused them to betray that which they formerly believed ("the faith"). The same verb is translated "seduce" in Mark 13:22. This immediately introduces the second verb as a consequence of this seduction from the faith. The verb is *peripeirō* which was used of putting animals on a spit, hence metaphorically it came to mean "pierce". The thought behind the verb is obviously that of pain, self-inflicted in the sense of being brought about by their own actions. It could be either the moral consequence of their actions, or the governmental dealing of God, or the first as a manifestation of the second. In either case the active voice indicates that the blame lies with the individuals themselves. The word "sorrows" (*odunē*) means "consuming griefs" and may have reference either to body or mind. It is used in Rom 9:2 of mind; here it covers both physical and mental distress and is qualified by the adjective "many". There would seem almost to be a note of sympathy in the language as the apostle considers the multitude of pains that a covetous heart invites in its train. The "many" lusts of v.9 are answered by the "many" sorrows of v.10. The saddest note being that it is all so unnecessary; it could have been avoided if the attitude to material things had been scriptural.

11 Over against the cupidity, identified as an inherent element in the false teaching, is set the character and conviction of one called "man of God" who would thus be closely identified as a product of the "house of God" (3:15). "Thou" as the first word in the sentence is thus doubly emphatic. It set Timothy in contrast with the "some" of v.10 and, going further back, with "any man" of v.3; a point emphasised by the adversative "but" which immediately follows the pronoun. The "O" is most impressive as it is seldom used in direct address; it makes a very personal appeal. "Man of God" (used only once again in the NT, in 2 Tim 3:17) is an echo of the OT where it is applied to men, who, responsive to the Spirit of God, walking in fellowship with God carried messages for God (1 Sam 9:6; 12:22; 13:1; 1 Kings 17:8; 2 Kings 4:7; Neh 12:24). *Expositor's Greek Testament* defines it as "a man belonging to the spiritual order of things with which that which is merely temporal, transitory and perishing can have no permanent relationship". The word "man" *anthrōpos*, is generic, i.e. one of the human race without distinction of sex. It should be the character of every believer irrespective of sex; it is in fact a suitable description of those attached to the house of God (3:15).

There are three present imperatives in this appeal to Timothy which stress the durative nature of the action required of Timothy. These are not matters that can be done once for all and then forgotten about; they reflect the continuing and constantly recurring activity of the man of God; he is doing this all the time. The three imperatives are:

1. Keep on fleeing, or better, continually flee, never let them catch you! (The verb *pheugō* is repeated 2 Tim 2:22.)
2. Keep on following, or better, be ever following, never let them out of sight! (The verb *diōkō* is repeated 2 Tim 2:22.)

3. Keep on fighting, or better, be always fighting, never lay down arms in this struggle! (The verb *agōnizomai* is repeated 2 Tim 4:7.)

"These things" refer to the "love of money" and all that issues from it; the matters which have jsut been considered. The idea of flight, of course, demands action but it is negative. The positive action is "to follow"; the verb *diōkō* is a word Paul uses frequently (Rom 9:30; 12:13; 14:19; 1 Cor 14:1; Phil 3:12,14), and it depicts under the athletic figure, a runner who is making a very determined effort to overtake the one in front. The picture is in the language of Prov 15:9: "but He loveth him that followeth after righteousness" (see 2 Tim 2:22 for "flee" and "follow" in a similar construction).

The next six words, that describe positively the virtues that the "man of God" is to pursue, may be divided into three pairs that cover three aspects of his life. This can be seen as follows:

"*Godward*": 1. "Righteousness" (*dikaiosunē*): the word means right action (Eph 5:9); meeting God's standards as a result of a righteous standing (Rom 8:4) already possessed. Practical righteousness seen as the outcome of forensic righteousness.

2. "Godliness"(*eusebeia*): the word describes a right attitude to God, a reverance and respect that goes behind the conduct to the character. See Appendix B. Note the repetition of the word down this passage vv.3, 5, 6. In a godly man this is characteristic.

"*Inward*": 3. "Faith" (*pistis*): the word defines the principle that produces confidence and trust in God; the application of this in the life of the believer makes the promises of God real in experience.

4. "Love" (*agapē*): the word unfolds that which is the result of the work of God in the heart (Rom 5:5); it reaches out in action to others and moves both Godward and manward.

"*Outward*": 5. "Patience" (*hupomonē* from *hupo* "under"; *menō* "to remain"): the word embraces that aspect of the character of the believer that manifests an enduring steadfastness under every circumstance of life (JND translates "endurance"). This is produced in christian character through the trials of life (Rom 5:3-4). Thayer defines it thus: "In the NT, the characteristic of a man who is unswerved from his deliberate purpose and his loyalty to faith and piety by even the greatest trials and sufferings".

6. "Meekness" (*praotēs*). If endurance is the character trait revealed and moulded under circumstances then meekness is the character trait revealed under the persecution and opposition of men. This word entails and points to a disposition that will not strenuously assert its own rights but will sacrifice these rights for the sake of others. The word is used of the character of Christ (2 Cor 10:1) and the same feature will be reproduced in those who accept his yoke (Matt 11:29).

12 The present imperative of "fight" has the same durative force as the verbs in v.11 and may be translated "be always fighting". Our English translation correctly catches the assonance as the cognate noun re-echoes the verb. The noun is the word *agōn* (AV "fight"). The historical background of this word and its normal use was in connection with the athletic contests of the Isthmian or Olympic Games. It describes the concentration and effort allied with discipline and conviction that was required of an athlete taking part in these contests. Paul, by the Spirit of God, gives the word a richer fuller content as, in various passages (see Phil 1:30; Col 2:1; 1 Thess 2:2; 2 Tim 4:7) he uses it to describe the spiritual conflict in which every believer engages from the moment of salvation. We could paraphrase it "play your part in the noble contest of faith". Since faith has the article many judge that the battle is against the arch-opponent (Satan and his agents) of the great doctrines of the faith. In this battle Timothy is encouraged to play his part. This is attractive and finds support in the use of the adjective "good" (*kalos*, equivalent to "noble") in contrast to the "evil" (*kakos*) implicit in the motivation for the false teaching (v.10). However it is difficult to rule out the subjective personal appropriation of the doctrines in living power in the soul and this accords better with the appositional sentence which immediately follows. This interpretation would, as well, keep the exhortation in line with the previous imperatives.

The verb "lay hold" is used literally in Mark 8:23: Luke 9:47; 14:4, but here metaphorically. The aorist tense in the verb has led some to think that the games metaphor is continued and this points onward to the moment of the accepting of the prize at the Judgment Seat of Christ. This cannot be, for the asyndeton (no conjunction) renders the phrase appositional and therefore autochronous, covering the same period as the previous verbs. We are not to think that Timothy did not possess eternal life; he had been called of God and had confessed his faith; but rather, in the fleeing, following and fighting, he would be laying hold in an experimental way on what he already had, and enjoying this eternal life in all it vitality and vigour.

Two matters now mentioned would serve as real encouragement to Timothy in this battle of faith, one originating with God and the other from his own testimony. "Whereunto" (JND translates "to which") acts as a relative pronoun and has, as its antecedent, the eternal life to which God in His grace has called him. While the aorist tense in the verb "called" may point back to the moment of conversion, it may, more appropriately in the context, sum up how God has acted towards him and view this as one action. This may also be the thought in the aorist tense of the verb in the sentence that follows: "hast professed a good profession". The RV translation "didst confess the good confession" better represents the verb *homologeō* and its cognate noun as showing how Timothy responded to the divine call. While the expression may look back to conversion and the scriptural public confession of this in baptism, it is more likely that, while including this initial testimony, it includes also the confession Timothy has made in subsequent days in the face of every foe. It could, perhaps, include even the imprisonment mentioned in Heb 13:23. The repetition of the identical expression "a good confession" in the next verse in regard to Christ would support this view and the summative view of the aorist tense would allow it. "Before many witnesses" could refer either to his baptism or, more likely, to the many who could testify to the good confession he has bourne throughout his christian life. The adjective *kalos* which could be translated "excellent" or "noble" hints at how God had used such a witness for His own purpose.

Notes

3   Paul would not have subscribed to the modern indifference to doctrine. He recognised that wrong behaviour is, inevitably, the outcome of wrong teaching. The godly conduct and character produced is the scriptural evidence of the soundness (the health-giving quality) of the teaching. This point is made in 1 Cor 13:13: "evil communications corrupt good manners".

5   What was incipient in Paul's day has been demonstrated abundantly in the history of the church. From the days of Constantine (Battle of Milvium Bridge AD 312) when to profess christianity became first popular, then profitable, this sordid materialistic motive has plagued the saints. Simon Magus (Acts 8:18-23) has had many who thought like him; popes and prelates, pastors and preachers have sought to capitalise on the things of God for their own selfish gain. This spirit is manifest in all the cults of the present day. The publicity-seeking propagators of healing and charismatic campaigns, by their emphasis and demand for financial return for spiritual benefits, place themselves in the line of these charlatan predators so clearly exposed in this passage.

8   The reason for the imperative of the AV "let us therewith be content" lies in the fact that the translators understood the future passive as an hebraism, with the force of an imperative. This is worth consideration but the interpretation given in the verse fits the grammar as it stands.

V. The Completion of the Charge   (6:13-21)

v.13   "I give thee charge in the sight of God, who quickeneth all things, and *before* Christ Jesus, who before Pontius Pilate witnessed a good confession;

v.14   That thou keep *this* commandment without spot, unrebukeable, until the appearing of our Lord Jesus Christ:

v.15   Which in his times he shall shew, *who is* the blessed and only

Potentate, the King of kings, and Lord of lords;

v.16 Who only hath immortality, dwelling in the light which no man can approach unto; whom no man hath seen, nor can see: to whom be honour and power everlasting. Amen.

v.17 Charge them that are rich in this world, that they be not highminded, nor trust in uncertain riches, but in the living God, who giveth us richly all things to enjoy;

v.18 That they do good, that they be rich in good works, ready to distribute, willing to communicate;

v.19 Laying up in store for themselves a good foundation against the time to come, that they may lay hold on eternal life.

v.20 O Timothy, keep that which is committed to thy trust, avoiding profane *and* vain babblings, and oppositions of science falsely so called:

v.21 Which some professing have erred concerning the faith. Grace *be* with thee. Amen."

Three sub-divisions may be noticed in this paragraph:—
1. The Importance of this Charge
   — Testimony After A Divine Pattern vv.13-16
2. The Intention of this Charge
   — Trust in a Divine Person vv.17-19
3. The Implication of this Charge
   — Triumph of Divine Preservation vv.20-21

1. *Testimony After A Divine Pattern*
   ### 6:13-16

The reality and solemnity of Timothy's confession leads Paul to complete the charge by reminding him of three relevant matters:—

1. The Persons before whom he bears witness v.13
2. The Period in which the witness is borne v.14
3. The Prospect of the glorious consummation that closes the period of witness vv.15-16

13 The AV translation "I give thee charge" is the rather awkward translation of the simple verb *parangellō*. This verb has been used in 1:3; 4:11; 5:7 and carries again that same note of apostolic authority as it has done in these previous passages. The awkwardness in translation has arisen because the direct object of the verb, "thee" in the Greek text, does not come until v.14. The reading would then be "I charge... thee to keep".

The human witnesses (v.12) to Timothy's good confession may now be far away, but there are other observers of his conduct whose unseen presence will be both a check upon him and an encouragement to him. The two witnesses are God and Christ Jesus. God is characterised as the One "who quickeneth all things". The verb (*zōopoieō*, "to cause to live or to make alive") is used generally in connection with resurrection. For confirmation see Rom 4:17; 8:11; 1 Cor 15:22, 36, 45 etc. This note of confidence in the God of resurrection should encourage Timothy, not only in the light of persecution already experienced, but as an assurance amidst the darkening clouds of social and civil unrest that boded ill for christians. Death itself becomes of little consequence as Timothy witnesses in the sight of One who gives life to all things. The RV margin "who preserveth all things alive" (*zōogoneō*) has some good MSS authority but the above reading, on balance, is better attested. While the thought of "preserving alive" has a certain relevance in the context it is surely considerably weaker than "making alive" of the preferred text. The second witness before whom Timothy acts is "Christ Jesus, who before Pontius Pilate witnessed a good confession". The word "before" (*epi*) has been regarded as meaning "in the days of" or "under" as in the Apostles' Creed, so that it would refer to the whole period of Christ's life on earth. Vine, however, has marshalled considerable evidence to show that the preposition can retain its usual meaning and that it here points to the witness borne by Christ in the judgment hall in the presence of Pilate. Simpson has pointed out that *epi* with the genitive is technical for a judicial appearance. The aorist tense in the verb, while not absolutely conclusive, rather supports this view. It also seems more relevant to the context, and a more appropriate encouragement to Timothy, to remember that Christ Jesus, in the presence of the representative of Roman authority, "witnessed a good confession". Timothy would draw strength, as we do, from the example of Christ; He is the prototype of a witness under pressure and persecution.

The witness borne in "the good confession" by Christ (see the identical phrase in v.12) centred on His Person and work. In no way did he seek to conceal who he was (Matt 27:11) and the place He had as King (John 18:36) in the plan of God. Thus Timothy, who in this would be representative of all believers, is expected to bear witness to a present relationship with Christ and an anticipated association with Him in coming glory. This would be in the pattern of Christ.

14 The word order in the Greek text reads "to keep thee the commandment unspotted, without reproach". "Thee" is the direct object of the verb "I charge" of v.13. The verb "to keep" (*tēreō*) is used frequently in the NT, and especially in John's writings, of keeping a word or saying, e.g. John 8:51, "If a man keep my word", and it simply means to obey, or to observe. Here it means rather "to preserve intact". *The Expositor's Greek Testament* says:

"Perhaps the two meanings were present to the apostle's mind; and no doubt in actual experience they merge one into the other; for a tradition is only preserved by obedience to the demand which it makes for observance". The use of this same verb in the expression of 2 Tim 4:7 illustrates this second meaning of the word "I have kept the faith".

It is too narrow a view, in light of the solemn language, to limit the commandment (*entolē*) to the charges of vv.11-12, or even the whole "charge" of the epistle; it would seem to embrace all that is involved in the gospel of Christ, to which Timothy has borne witness already and of which in the midst of Ephesian conditions he is a trustee. (Note the similar embracive use of the word commandment in 2 Pet 2:21; 3:2.) Such is to be the conduct and teaching of Timothy that no spot (*aspilos*, used of the Lamb, 1 Pet 1:19 and of the believer Jas 1:27), or blame (*anepilēptos*, AV "unrebukeable", used of the overseer, 3:2) could be attached to him and consequently to the faith. Grammatically, the two adjectives, "without spot" and "unrebukeable", must belong to the direct object of the verb which in this case is the word "commandment". The same construction is seen with the same verb in 5:22, "keep thyself pure", and in James 1:27, "keep thyself unspotted". However, despite the evidence produced by Alford in support of the view that it is the commandment that is to be kept unspotted and unrebukeable, it is difficult to see how these epithets can be applied to something impersonal. It is clear that if Timothy keeps himself "unspotted" and "without reproach" (RV) the commandment will be preserved intact. The comma after commandment in the RV suggests that the revisers followed the same line of thought.

This period of testimony is limited by the expression "until the appearing of our Lord Jesus Christ". The word "appearing" (*epiphaneia*) means a "shining forth". It is used of Christ's first advent in 2 Tim 1:10 but its usual setting is in connection with His expected eschatological return as in 2 Tim 4:1, 8; Titus 2:13. In this connection it describes that visible and glorious display when, on His return to earth, Christ is vindicated before men. In light of this glorious manifestation, when the verdict of earth that was manifest in the Cross of Christ will be reversed by heaven, any persecution, even death itself, for Christ's sake seems of little consequence. The vindication of the Saviour involves the vindication of His saints (Col 3:4). Paul, it will be noticed, sees no difficulty about this event occurring in Timothy's lifetime. For Timothy, and for saints in this dispensation, this vindication would begin at the rapture (for details of that event see 1 Thess 4:13-18). However the passage goes further than the rapture of the church and embraces the public and visible diaplay of Christ and His saints in manifest glory on earth, the very scene where Christ and His saints have been rejected.

15 The relative pronoun "which" has for its antecedent the word "appearing". "In his times" (see the same expression in 2:6; Titus 1:3) draws attention to the decisive moments in history that God has set for the working out of the redemption plan. In ligl of Matt 24:36; Mark 13:22 and Acts 1:7 the phrase must mean "in God's good time" and emphasises the fact that the time of the appearing was and is wholly in God's hands. This moment of decisive intervention by God in the affairs of earth lies within His own programme. Further it is God who will act to display Christ.

The verb "show" (*deiknumi*) means "to exhibit,", "to display to the visible sight"; Wuest gives "expose to the eyes". The translation by JND makes clear that the subject of the verb is not the "appearing" but God Himself: "the blessed and only Ruler shall shew". God, in His own times, will shew before the eyes of men the One who once walked in obscurity but in whom is now manifestly displayed all the majesty and sovereignty of absolute deity. The word "Potentate" (JND "Ruler") is *dunastēs*, the noun from the verb *dunamai*, "to be able", "to have power". He is the One in whom all power inherently resides. This supreme One is described by two adjectives. "Blessed" is the word *makarios* (used only here and in 1:11) which signifies what God is in Himself, essentially and inimitably. All blessedness belongs to Him. The second adjective "only" (*monos*), an attribute of deity stressed in John 5:44; 17:3; Rom 16:27, shows the uniqueness of deity; there is none other in this class. He is alone in solitary dignity. This is the One who will bring back Christ in manifest glory. In light of this scriptural anticipation Timothy need not fear the power of a mere Roman Emperor. Since all the following phrases are nominative, the verb "shew" must be treated as intransitive. The next two phrases, preceding the relative pronoun "who", should be treated as appositional to define the "appearing". The visible display will be centred in a person who takes absolute precedence as, with inherent deity and yet absolute manhood, He "is shown". This One is described as "King of kings and Lord of lords" ("the King of those that reign, and Lord of those that exercise lordship", JND), words used of deity in the OT (Deut 2:47; 10:7; Ps 136:3; Dan 2:47 LXX) but only of Christ in the NT (Rev 17:14; 19:16). Christ supersedes all earth rulers, even the mightiest of earthly emperors; in Him, in full and glorious display will be seen at that time, humanity crowned with deity.

16 The antecedent of the "who" is "Potentate", the One who has acted, and will act on His timetable, to display before the eyes of all, deity in manifestation in Christ. Three statements are made of this Potentate:

1. "Who only hath immortality". *Athanasia* means more than "deathlessness", it includes the quality of the life in contrast to death (2 Cor 5:4). This belongs inherently and essentially to deity. He is neither

liable to nor capable of dying. He grants this quality to the believer in resurrection (1 Cor 15:53-54) but this, of course, is derived and therefore dependent; His deathlessness is underived and absolute (see 1:17 where the word is "incorruptible").

2. "Dwelling in light unapproachable" (RV). As God Himself is light (1 John 1:5) it thus is His covering (Ps 104:2). "Unapproachable" (*aprositos*) describes that blinding radiance that shows the inaccessibility of deity to human senses. Exod 33:17-23 provides a striking illustration: "For there shall no man see me and live". (In this connection see John 1:18; 6:46.) The two relative clauses emphasise this invisibility to mortal sight. Not one of the race of mankind has seen God in His essence, nor can he do so; this would be bringing the infinite within the compass of the finite, the Creator within the span of the creature. A revelation has already been made in time in the Man Christ Jesus but it will take eternity to display deity (Matt 5:8; Rev 22:14).

3. In the contemplation of deity Paul is moved to praise. No verb is needed in the Greek. To Him is ascribed honour (*time*). This word has run through the epistle from the first doxology (1:7) in its various connections and cognates, its applications and associations, but essentially all respect and reverence belong to God. Where we would have expected "glory" (as in 1:17) Paul puts "power" (*kratos*) as suited to the theme here treated. The word *kratos* is frequently translated "dominion" (1 Pet 4:11; 5:11; Jude 25) and anticipates the full manifestation of that which belongs to Him as "the blessed and only Potentate". The doxology is not the presentation of a wish but the admission of a fact and this draws from the heart of the apostle that triumphant "Amen" (see on 1:17).

2. *Trust in a Divine Person*
6:17-19

From the sublime heights of praise and adoration rising in the soul to God in the doxology of v.16 these next verses bring us back to earth with a shock. They form, however, a vital part of the charge to which Paul returns after a characteristic digression. Having exposed the materialistic motive of the false teachers (v.5) and given sober warning to the "would be" rich (vv.9-10), Paul recognises that in a wealthy city like Ephesus there would be another group of saints who would require positive instruction concerning their use of the wealth with which they had been entrusted. For such believers he gives Timothy some plain instructions.

17 "Charge" is again the translation of the word *parangellō* that has been repeated throughout the epistle in 1:3; 4:11; 5:7; 6:13. Here we have the final note in the charge that Timothy was required to accept and to pass on to the saints in Ephesus. That the word "rich" refers to those who are materially rich is made doubly plain by the adjectival phrase "in the present world" (RV), where the word "present" translates *nun* ("now"). We might render the expression very literally in the "now" age. Notice the same expression in 2 Tim 4:10 and Titus 2:6. The word for world is *aiōn* (JND "age") for which see note on this verse. While no blame is attached to the fact they they have riches, which may well have been acquired through inheritance or honest work, these riches do present very real dangers.

Two dangers are inherent in the possession of riches. the first danger arises in a wrong attitude displayed towards other, possibly materially poor, believers; the second is a wrong attitude to the riches themselves. The instruction given by Paul to deal with the first danger is "be not highminded". The word "highminded" (used again in Rom 11:20) is unique to Paul and possibly coined by him. It is the word *hupsēlophroneō*, a compound of the word "lofty" (*hupsēlos*) and the verb "to think" (*phroneō*). Humility of spirit is not a normal characteristic of the rich, and possession of wealth gives to some such an exalted notion of their own ability, worth, and importance that they display a proud and arrogant spirit toward other believers. There is no justification for such behaviour and it displays a completely unjustifiable confidence in the reality and the reliability of the riches they possess. Such saints perhaps unconsciously have transferred their confidence from God and have put it in the wealth at their disposal. This is the second danger highlighted in the statement "nor trust in uncertain riches". The word "trust" is *elpizō* ("to hope"); with the preposition *epi*, it is rendered in the RV "nor to have their hope set on" (the same construction with *epi* as in 4:10 and 5:5) and presents the idea of resting on a solid foundation. While the RV, "the uncertainty of riches", is a literal translation, the AV more accurately conveys the idea with "in uncertain riches". Where a genitive precedes the noun (here "of riches" precedes "uncertainty") the emphasis falls on the genitive (see Vine's *Dictionary*). The hope is set on the "riches" which are themselves "uncertain". The perfect tense hints that once this is done the results of such a misplaced confidence will continue to be a feature of the lifestyle of such believers. This foundation, however, is unsafe. Material wealth is limited to time, a truth already brought out in v.7; as such it cannot be taken into the coming age. However it has also a further disadvantage; an inherent uncertainty is associated with it, and as circumstances change the riches can readily be lost. This is the truth taught in Prov 23:5: "For riches certainly make themselves wings; they fly away as an eagle towards heaven". The scorn of the psalmist is relevant (Ps 52:7): "Lo this is the man that made not God his strength; but trusted in the abundance of his riches", and anyone putting a confident trust in such transient things is acting most foolishly. The next words expose the foolishness of putting confidence in the riches when one could put that same confidence in the giver of those riches. The giver is God (the word "living" has weak MSS support and is omitted in the RV and in JND); this is the God who provides for men in a bountiful way. "Richly" (*plousiōs*) is an adverb which echoes the noun "riches" (*ploutōs*) to indicate how bountifully God supplies the material things. He does this "for enjoyment" (JND); the same word is used in Heb 11:25 where the enjoyment is sensual. In this passage the enjoyment is no mere luxurious self-gratification, that would be merely fleshly, but saints whose hope is placed on the Supplier will use that which He has given as He intended and thus bring a spiritual delight into material blessings. There is in the statement a side glance at the asceticism that would despise God's blessings and thus run counter to God's purpose in giving them and deny the saint the spiritual enjoyment and enrichment that comes from their proper use.

18 When handled in the wrong way wealth can bring danger. In view of this the apostle has sounded the double warning of the previous verse. On the other hand the possession of wealth can bring a spiritual delight and satisfaction to the soul when wisely used. The right use of wealth is now described in four infinitive phrases — all in the present tense, as if to stress the constant doing of these things:

1. "Do good" (*agathoergeō*) is to be always working beneficially for others. See Note.
2. "be rich in good works" (*plouteō*) shows that this wealth is not the kind locked up in a bank or business but is the kind that is invested in the mulitplicity of the attractive and excellent works their wealth enables the believers to perform. This is the fourth echo of the word "rich" in these verses; a characteristic of Pauline style.
3. The construction, "that they may be ready to distribute" (RV), is based on the verb "to be"along with the word *eumetadotos*, meaning "to give, generously, to others". The picture in this unique compound word is of one acting towards others as God has acted towards him; the believer stands ready to meet any need that is presented.
4. "Willing to communicate" (*koinōnikos*) embraces the fellowship in material things demanded by the claims of Christ and fellowship with Him. No patronising charity is here envisaged but a sharing based on spiritual appreciation of equality amongst saints.

All the verbs describe that interest in others that overrides all claims of self and issues in sacrificial giving of material things to meet the need of others; it makes no difference whether the others are saints or sinners.

19 In the participle "laying up in store", which could be rendered "treasuring away", the apostle through oxymoron (the figure of speech in which contrary things are placed alongside each other) highlights the truth he has been stressing. The ideas are contrary for the truth is spiritual: to save by sharing; to store by giving! This aptly sums up the action of the previous verbs as resulting in a transfer of funds from earth to heaven. Giving here means storing there. This is doubtless based on the Lord's teaching in Matt 6:19-20, where we have the statement, "Lay up for yourselves treasures in heaven". The foundation *themelion*, described as "good" (*kalos*) which in the context means "sound", stands in clear contrast to the danger of putting confidence in "uncertain riches". However, J.N.D Kelly has an interesting note when he states in connection with this passage: "the Greek word for the latter, *themelion*, can also, in a transferred sense, mean 'fund' ". This "fund" is "for" (*eis*, frequently translated "unto") the future (*to mellōn*). This period stands opposed to "the now" (see on v. 17) where material wealth seems important; then (in the time to come) it will not be how much we possessed, but how much was used for God.

The final statement in the verse, "that they may lay hold on eternal life", includes the same verb in the same tense (aorist) as in v.12. However while v.12 has the verb in the imperative mood here it is in the subjunctive mood, as is required after the word *hina* that we may translate "in order that". The condition for the laying hold of eternal life is thus stressed.

As the wealth is properly used for God and His interests, in that mesasure, treasures are transferred above; and in this same measure eternal life is evidenced, enjoyed, and experienced now. In v.12 the adjective with life is "eternal" (*aiōnios*); here the adjective is *ontōs* translated in the RV "which is life indeed". This is the "real" life in contrast to mere biological existence amidst material benefits; this is the life of God and of eternity enjoyed in reality.

Notes

17 1. The word world (JND age) is *aiōn*. Bengel defines this as "the subtle, informing spirit of the *kosmos* or world of men who are living alienated and apart from God". In this atmosphere it is easy for believers to be so affected by it that, almost unknowingly, they adopt its principles, follow its precepts, copy its practices, believe its maxims and become so absorbed in the worship of its god they are almost indistinguishable from the unbeliever. Such professors suggest in their way of life that material wealth is the most important thing to them. This is the very essence of worldliness and from this very concept the whole revelation of God in Christ was designed to deliver saints. This is the import and one aspect of the truth expressed in Gal 1:4: "who gave himself for our sins, that he might deliver us from this present evil world".

2. The misunderstanding and misuse of this verse amongst many believers is a serious matter. We are certainly not entitled to use it as an excuse for vulgar ostentatious display of wealth, or the sensual gratification of luxurious taste in homes, dress, eating or holidays under the plea that God has given it to us "to enjoy!" This is almost a perversion of this Scripture. The enjoyment is obviously spiritual delight in the right use of wealth as defined in the statements of v.18.

18 It is interesting to note within the epistle the widening circle of those who have a claim upon the material resources of the believer. The claim obviously begins with the family (see 5:8); then within the assembly there is the claim of widows (see 5:3) and elders (5:17); in 5:16 the circle of aid is clearly widened to include others within the extended household and dependants linked to them. But while fellow-saints have first claim upon the believer with regard to material and financial help the generosity of grace-touched lives does not stop here. The principles of the Lord's teaching (Matt 6:43-48) and the practices envisaged in this verse show unequivocally that the saints are required to assist unbelievers when the need is there. Wisdom is required when asked to contribute to organised charities run by unsaved people, but this care must not in any way be allowed to inhibit the reflection of grace (2 Cor 8:9) that reached us through Christ when we did not deserve it. If saints were more aware of this responsibility to those in need it would often open the way for the reception of the gospel message.

19 1. There is no hint in any of these verses that either sinners, or saints, obtain merit by the right use of material possessions. This is a pagan notion of payment to deity entrenched in Romanism and not absent from institutional Protestantism. The very motive behind giving of this nature vitiates the act. Rather the right use of material wealth is the evidence of faith. Justification and salvation so alter the appreciation of wealth that the believer holds all in trust for God, and in the right use of wealth but evidences the "life which is life indeed". He does not obtain salvation in this (he has it already) but he enjoys it and enters into the fulness of it.

2. The corollary to this truth is sobering. If the enjoyment of real life is dependent on the right use of material possessions, is it not an honest inference that the depression of spirit so manifest in many saints could be, in some cases, the result of the wrong attitude to these things? Driving ambition, crushing anxiety and miserly acquisition have impoverished many a life spiritually. Scriptural teaching obeyed early in christian life would preserve from this. The believer is expected to give of his substance to God bountifully, not sparingly or grudgingly (2 Cor 9:6-11), regularly not spasmodically (1 Cor 16:2),

proportionately (1 Cor 16:2) and sacrificially (2 Cor 8:3). When a believer sets aside for God a portion of his income on a weekly or monthly basis there is, of necessity, developed an excercise as to its proper use for God. Thus an interest will be developed in the work of God and the workers for God, both at home and abroad. This will not only be for the help and furtherance of testimony for God but it has a vital part to play in the character development of the exercised believer. Thus the saint will be waiting for the need to be presented that he may use what has been set aside for God, and thus he becomes in this exercise God's channel of communication to sinners, saints, or servants. The contribution to assembly funds through bag or box is first a moral responsibility, devolving on the individual who forms a part of that fellowship. That this is also expected to be a spiritual and sacrificial exercise Godward is clear from the way Paul speaks of the gift that had been sent to him from the Philippian assembly — "an odour of a sweet smell, a sacrifice acceptable, wellpleasing to God" (Phil 4:18). While contribution to assembly funds is a vital part of the exercise of the believer, it is only one aspect of the readiness of the believer to hold his material things in trust for God.

3. The truth of the opening statement of this verse was succintly expressed by C.T. Studd when, after a complete disposal of his share of his father's estate to missionary work and workers, he said to his wife: "The Bank of England may fail, the Bank of Heaven never can". He had transferred his assets.

3. *Triumph of Divine Preservation*
   6:20-21

Paul closes the letter with a moving and affectionate appeal to Timothy which, in fact, summarises the entire contents of the letter. It returns to the thought of a spiritual deposit, emphasises human responsibility, warns of perilous conditions, and invokes divine blessing.

20 For the second time in this chapter (v.11) Paul uses the unusual "O" to introduce a direct personal appeal, and, in addition, addresses Timothy by name (otherwise only in the salutation). The Greek is literally "the deposit guard" (see RV marg; also 2 Tim 1:12-14). The deposit, viewed metaphorically as a precious treasure, must be equated with "the commandment" of v.14 and includes all the revelation in the gospel and all that has been implied in the faith, the truth and the doctrine dealt with in the letter. This deposit is viewed as that which is to be guarded, that nothing is lost from it, that nothing is added to it. Involved in this is the spiritual welfare of the teacher and the spiritual blessing of all those who come after; hence the urgency of the command of the apostle. The word "keep" is *phulasso* (RV "guard"). It is the verb normally used in legal documents when some valued treasure is left in the care of another to be surrendered on the request of the owner. The picture behind the word is that of a soldier on sentry-watch standing guard over a vital installation or a valuable treasure. He must always be alert for danger, never sleeping or even dozing. "Avoiding" (*ektrepō*) is used in the good sense of encouraging Timothy to deliberately turn away from everything that would dilute and thus destroy the vital teachings of the gospel entrusted to him. The danger of the purity of the gospel does not always arise from truths lost although this can certainly happen, but the more subtle and the more usual danger is the introduction of that which does not belong to it and is thus spurious. This is the danger that is presented here. Under one article two things are mentioned whose introduction or acceptance would destroy the character of the gospel. The two things are as follows:

1. "Vain babblings" (*kenophōnia*) is another of those onomatopoeic words that are so effectively used by Paul, reminding us of the "vain janglings" of 1:6, and which give a scriptural evaluation of the teaching of the errorists of Ephesus. This word occurs again only in 2 Tim 2:16, and summarises the profitless chatter that, as to its substance, is labelled "profane" (*belēlos*). This word has been used previously in 1:9; 4:7 and, as it once was used to describe in Hellenistic Greek the areas that lay outside the precincts of a temple, is used in Scripture to describe all that lies outside the realm of truth and thus has no link with God. There is nothing sacred about the myths and stories that the false teachers were adding to divine revelation.

2. "Oppositions of the knowledge which is falsely so called" (RV) indicates a contrary position and describes the tenets of the false teachers; these were counter-propositions they advanced in argument which they claimed sprang from a knowledge superior to that presented in the gospel. With one word Paul denies such a claim labelling that knowledge *pseudōnumos* (from *pseudēs*, "false"; *onoma*, "a name") meaning that it masqueraded under a false name. It was not knowledge at all. Boasting in this knowledge the false teachers displayed their ignorance.

The term "knowledge" (*gnōsis*) is that which in the second century was appropriated and applied to a whole philosophic system that boasted such superior knowledge. This was the gnostic heresy but, it is clear, the seeds of it were already present in Ephesus.

21 There are always those who can be deceived by such claims to esoteric knowledge and it is a sad note at the end of the letter that Paul has to point out that this had happened at Ephesus. Some "professing" this superior enlightenment "have erred". The word "professing" is a participle from the same verb that provides the participle in 2:10: "women professing godliness".

This verb is generally translated "to promise". These false teachers made high claims for what they taught, and either explicitly or implicitly disparaged the gospel revelation as fit only for the ignorant and uninitiated. The verb "have erred" is given in the RV margin as "missed the mark". It has been used in 1:6 ("having swerved") and, as suggested there, the failure is not inadvertent as if they could not reach the target; if this were so an excuse might be made for such people. However, it is clear in the use of this particular word that the failure is culpable in the sense that they were not even aiming at the right target. In the picture behind the word one can see the archer shifting his aim! He has a different object before him now rather than the authorised target. "The faith" is objective and denotes the doctrinal body of truth comprising the whole revelation given in the gospel. The faith, the truth, the doctrine, the commandment have but emphasised throughout the epistle different aspects of that revelation given in the gospel.

This is the briefest of Pauline endings and similar to that used in Colossians and 2 Timothy.

The word "grace" has the article and would embrace all that God would grant of His unmerited favour as "the faith" would be held in trust under most adverse conditions. The echo of the word would take us right back to the salutation and we might translate "the well-known grace" of God our Father and Christ Jesus our Lord.

The better attested texts have the plural "you" and with such scriptural accuracy we may note that Paul recognises that while the charge has been personal, Timothy is responsible to pass on the teaching to the saints and expects the letter to be read within the assembly. "Amen" is omitted in RV and JND.

Notes

20 Marcion, a second century heretic, daringly took this very word *antithesis* as a title for a book in which he set out in order what he judged to be the contradictions between OT teaching and the gospel (he claimed there were one hundred and forty such contradictions).

While the gnostic system was to come to full flower only in the middle of the second century, the seeds of it were already present in Ephesus (and in Colossae, see Epistle to the Colossians in this series). Men like Marcion claimed a superiority of knowledge, based on intellectual insights, that they judged distinguished them from simple believers. Through this enlightenment, so they claimed, salvation comes, and Christ is only a means, a very great one they graciously admitted, to this end. Faith was suited only to the ignorant majority who did not make intellectual progress. In intellectual terms they had two major preoccupations: to explain the work of creation (as ultimately but not immediately from God, since matter was evil) and the existence of evil. Since matter was essentially evil the enlightened could either use it (this led, when carried to its ultimate conclusion, to licentiousness of the darkest kind), or dispense with it (this led to aceticism of the severest kind). Out of this satanic system came the "arguments" to be "placed over against" the gospel: in fact it was, and is, the very antithesis of the gospel. But the name of the whole system was wrong; it was not knowledge but ignorance. In this system was displayed ignorance of the word of God, ignorance of the value of the work of Christ and ignorance of the function of the Holy Spirit in the revelation of grace.

Appendix

APPENDIX A	PROBLEMS ABOUT THE LETTER
1. The Chronological Problem:	The Chronology of Paul's Later Years
2. The Ecclesiastical Problem:	The Church Order Revealed in 1 Timothy
3. The Doctrinal Problem:	The Supposed Change in Paul's Doctrinal Emphasis
4. The Linguistic Problem:	The Vocabulary and Style in the Letters

1. The Chronological Problem: The Chronology of Paul's Later Years

In the introduction it has been shown that it is impossible to fit these letters into the period covered by the Acts. It has also been shown that Scripture presents no insuperable difficulty to the possibility that Paul suffered imprisonment in Rome, not once, but on two distinct occasions. While direct historical support for this suggestion is lacking, there are quite a few hints in the writings that have come down to us from reasonably contemporary sources that this was the generally accepted view in the early centuries of church history.

Among early Christian writers outside the NT there are several pertinent statements. Clement of Rome (circa AD 95) in his first epistle to the Corinthians wrote in ch. 5, "After preaching both in the east and west, he gained the illustrious reputation due to his faith, having taught righteousness to the whole world, and came to the extreme limit of the west, and suffered martyrdom under the prefects". (Translation by Homer A. Kent Jr)

The expression "the limit of the west" in this quotation is most naturally interpreted as the western limits of the continental Empire which is Spain. It should be remembered that Clement was writing from Rome, regarded of course in the world of that day as the hub of the Empire.

In the *Muratorian Canon* (AD 170) in describing the Book of Acts there is an incidental reference to this journey of Paul to Spain where it is pointed out that Luke had not recorded it. The translation given by H.D.M. Spence (see Bibliography) reads: "Luke relates to Theophilus events of which he was an eye-witness, as also in a separate place (Luke 22:31-35) he evidently declares the martyrdom of Peter, but omits the journey of Paul to Spain."

Eusebius (AD 265-340) in *The Ecclesiastical History and the Martyrs of Palestine* (Book II, ch. 23) writes: "Having therefore made his defence at that time, it is recorded that the apostle again journeyed in the ministry of preaching, and, having set foot for the second time in the same city, was perfected in his martyrdom".

While a journey to Spain is not essential to the chronological setting of the Pastorals, if such a journey did take place then Paul must have been released from the Roman imprisonment recorded in the Acts.

If the view of two Roman imprisonments is accepted then it is clear that after his release Paul must have had some years of active service before his second imprisonment and martyrdom in AD 67 (if we accept the dating of Eusebius for the death of Paul).

During this period between the two imprisonments it would appear that Paul travelled widely and wrote 1 Timothy and the Epistle to Titus. At some point during the Neronian persecution Paul was re-arrested and imprisoned again in Rome. It is from this imprisonment that he wrote 2 Timothy as his final testament just prior to his martyrdom.

If we put together the facts that we possess and make three reasonable assumptions we can propose a simple outline of Paul's closing years of service. No certainty is possible and other outlines may be constructed from the same data. (See Kent and Hendricksen for alternative suggestions.)

The three assumptions we have to make are:

1.   that Paul did exactly as he proposed to do — the proposals are taken from the statements he makes in the Prison Epistles,
2.   that Paul followed a natural line of travel in his movements — the movements suggested being based on incidental hints in the Pastoral Epistles,
3.   that the historian Eusebius is correct (and there is no evidence to the contrary) in saying that Paul was martyred in AD 67. The testimony of the early church historians is unanimous that Paul was executed by the Emperor Nero. We do know that Nero committed suicide in June AD 68, so this sets a limit to the date of Paul's death.

Accepting these assumptions it is possible to construct an itinerary for the final years of Paul's ministry as follows:

AD 60 Paul arrives in Rome (Acts 28:16) under arrest. He is detained "two full years" (Acts 16:30). During this period he writes the Prison Epistles, Colossians, Philemon, Ephesians and Philippians, and probably in this order. From Philemon (v.22) and from Philippians (1:25; 2:24) we would understand that Paul expects to be released. These epistles would thus date from AD 62-63.

AD 63 No charge is preferred against Paul within the specified legal period (2 years), so his case lapses and he is released from detention. This would possibly be early in AD 63. His release at any point in AD 64 would be unlikely and after the burning of Rome (19-24 July, AD 64), one would judge, humanly speaking, impossible. Immediately after his release, if he kept to his expressed intention, he sent Timothy to Philippi (Phil 2:19-24) possibly with instructions to meet him at Ephesus.

Late   Paul begins another missionary journey. This time he moves
AD 63   eastwards with Ephesus his ultimate goal. It would be a natural stage
        on the journey to make a stop in Crete. Here Paul and those with him
        found a ready ear for the gospel. Souls having been saved and
        churches established as a result of the evangelistic activity, Paul leaves
        Titus here to complete the organisation of the churches by the
        appointment of elders (Titus 1:5) while he himself moves on.

        Paul is still moving towards Ephesus; the usual shipping route would
        be from Crete to Miletus where he could make a short diversion to
        pass through Colossae. Doubtless Paul would be welcomed and
        waited on by a delighted Philemon (v.22) and one could well imagine
        the joy of Onesimus.

        Paul, however, would likely refuse to be detained long in Colossae
        and soon arrives in Ephesus. Immediately Paul is faced with problems.
        Hymanaeus and Alexander have to be dealt with (1 Tim 1:20) and the
        saints have to be delivered from the false teaching that would destroy
        this testimony for God. Timothy, as instructed, joins Paul here at
        Ephesus, bringing good news of the Philippian believers. Possibly the
        winter of AD 63 is spent here in Ephesus.

AD 64   Feeling the demands of the work of God pressing upon him, Paul sets
        out for Macedonia. He requests Timothy to remain at Ephesus to
        complete the task of dealing with all the effects of the false teachers
        and their teaching (1 Tim 1:3). From Macedonia (possibly Philippi) he
        writes his first letter to Timothy. He expects to return shortly (1 Tim
        3:14-15) but is aware that circumstances may delay his return. About
        the same time he writes a letter to Titus in which he requests Titus to
        meet him at Nicopolis before the winter (Titus 3:12). The word
        "there" in Titus 3:12 indicates that Paul had not yet reached this port
        on the western seaboard of Greece. The winter mentioned would be
        the winter of AD 64. Thus Paul writes 1 Timothy and Titus in the
        summer of AD 64 from Macedonia. If Titus obeyed the apostolic
        direction, they would spend this winter of AD 64 in Nicopolis.

AD 65   If Paul journeyed to Spain in keeping with that earlier expressed desire
        in Rom 15:24, it could have been at this time. The references, to the
        writings of Clement of Rome and Eusebius already given, as well as to
        the *Muratorian Canon* do suggest that the early church was satisfied
        that Paul had done this. Where Scripture is silent and history is not
        absolutely conclusive, the suggestion must be treated as merely a
        possibility. Titus may have been with Paul in Spain but Scripture is
        silent about him until the final mention in 2 Tim 4:10, which implies
        a departure from Rome to Dalmatia at the time of Paul's second
        imprisonment.

AD 66   On his return from Spain Paul likely would make for Ephesus. It is
        possibly on this stage of the year-long trip that Trophimus is left at

Miletus sick (2 Tim 4:20 AV reads "Miletum"). Miletus is 30 miles from Ephesus and the major port of the region. Timothy could have met Paul here, or more likely, in Ephesus. It would well be that at this point the tearful parting mentioned in 2 Tim 1:4 takes place. With the Neronian persecution already sweeping over the Empire both men knew that to preach the gospel put life at risk. It is possible that both Paul and Timothy knew that this could be the final farewell.

AD 67 We know that in the final months of liberty Paul had stayed with Carpus in the city of Troas, the seaport north of Ephesus (2 Tim 4:13). As winter gave way to spring, he no longer needed his cloke and left it there. Through Macedonia to Achaia Paul makes a final call upon Corinth where Erastus remained (2 Tim 4:20). This direction of travel would be, in those days, the normal route to Rome. Whether Paul was arrested at Troas, Corinth, or when he reached Rome is not known. This second imprisonment is very different from the former occasion. The Roman Emperor Nero had placed the blame for the burning of Rome on the christians and launched a programme of extermination upon all who professed or preached Christ. Paul knew after the critical hearing before the magistrate (2 Tim 4:16) that death would be the verdict. He gives Timothy various instructions but presses upon him the urgency of coming before the winter (2 Tim 4:21). This would be the winter of AD 67. It is very likely that as a Roman citizen Paul would be beheaded at the third mile on the Ostian Way. We would long to know whether Timothy and Mark reached Rome before the execution of Paul, but Scripture is silent and history has nothing positive to say.

2. The Ecclesiastical Problem: The Church Order Revealed in 1 Timothy

Many commentators have seen difficulty in equating the clear church order that emerges in 1 Timothy with the primitive order that they profess to see exhibited in the Acts of the Apostles and in the earlier Pauline epistles. Many scholars have considered that the order revealed in 1 Timothy reflects a second century pattern with the emergence of an organised ecclesiastical structure based on a ministerial hierarchy. In 1 Timothy we read of bishops, elders (presbyters) and deacons. We read of the "laying on of hands", the "enrolment of widows", the "proving" of deacons, and many scholars have felt these terms show a more advanced church organisation than existed in the lifetime of Paul. On this basis the scholars suggest that the letter was compiled by a second-century follower of Paul, who was anxious to maintain the Pauline tradition, but betrayed his background by the church order he knew.

However, a careful reading through the Acts of the Apostles will show that wherever local churches were established from Jerusalem to Rome certain features marked them and certain principles were in evidence. When Paul in his earlier epistles had occasion to refer to such matters, the same features and principles are implied. Now in these later writings, the Pastorals, he simply deals in a more detailed way with the same features and principles. We have in 1 Timothy the plurality of elders (presbyters) and the use of the interchangeable term overseers (bishops) that is seen in Acts 20:17, 28. Attention is drawn to the qualifications required in the deacons already seen as part of the local church in Phil 1:1. The reference to the "enrolment" of widows is but the scriptural answer to a problem that existed in local testimony from an early date as seen in Acts 6:1-6. No unusual complexity of church order is demanded by any reference in these epistles. No organisational development in assembly government nor any hierarchal structure is implied in any statement. The pattern for local congregational testimony is that seen throughout the Acts of the Apostles but here explained in further detail. The emphasis lies in the restatement of truths in the light of subtle satanic attack through the efforts of the false teachers. To read back into this letter the ecclesiastical offices and the organisational complexity of later centuries, when Scripture had largely ceased to be the sole authority for local churches, is to import a problem of our own making. If we contrast 1 Timothy with the *Epistles of Ignatius* written AD 115 the differences are very evident. In these epistles each local church has one bishop, several presbyters and a number of deacons. This is not the local church order known to Paul or reflected in the relevant NT writings. Any second century date for 1 Timothy does not fit this situation. The church order revealed in the epistle but reflects what Paul had known and preached throughout his years of service for the Lord.

3. The Doctrinal Problem: The Supposed Change in Paul's Doctrinal Emphasis

One liberal critic has written of the Pastoral Epistles: "If they are indeed Paul's composition he has descended from the lofty plane on which he had moved to the level of mere piety and morality".

Moffatt in the same strain writes: "It is not easy to suppose that in three epistles the apostle would ignore such fundamental truths of his gospel as the Fatherhood of God, the union of the believing man with Christ Jesus, and the power of Holy Spirit in christian experience".

In specific answer to such claims we may note in these Pastoral Epistles the Fatherhood of God mentioned in 1:2, the union of the believer with Christ in the expression "in Christ Jesus" in 1:14 and the specific mention of the Holy Spirit on three occasions: 4:1; 2 Tim 1:4; Titus 3:5. If it be claimed that the subjects are not developed the answer to this assertion is that the great doctrinal themes, so prominent in other Pauline epistles, are not the subject of these letters. These letters are executive counsels for younger fellow-workers of the apostle who needed help in particular conditions of local church testimony. We may assume, very reasonably that they were familiar with the great themes of doctrinal truth developed in the earlier epistles. Now the apostle sees his younger workers battling with idle speculative teaching and its results. We need not be surprised that in these circumstances morality takes precedence, a morality not divorced from, but the very expression of, salvation.

What themes could be greater, their value increased by the incidental way they are brought into view, within the declared purpose of the epistle than:

1. the mediatorial work of Christ and His place in the divine purpose of salvation (2:3-6),
2. the mystery of godliness unfolded in a Person (3:16),
3. the ascription of praise to God in the doxologies (1:7; 6:15-16),
4. the themes of grace (1:14-15) and eternal life (6:12,18).

The epistle is primarily practical exhortation rather than theological exposition. It was meant to defend the doctrine rather than expound it. The defence of the "sound doctrine" lies in the godliness reflected in the lives of those who accept it.

W. Robertson Nicholl in *The Expositor's Greek Testament* has a perceptive comment: "It must not be thought strange that the Providence of God, the Holy Spirit who guides the church, should have called the apostle Paul almost wholly away from thoughts of the church's place in history and in the universe to the administration of, and provision for, the daily needs of the church as actually experienced by man".

4. The Linguistic Problem: The Vocabulary and Style in the Letters

The most serious argument against the genuineness of the Pastoral Epistles is their differences in style and vocabulary from Paul's earlier writings. This is the main point stressed by those who would deny Pauline authorship of the epistles.

P.N. Harrison in his book *The Problem of the Pastoral Epistles* (London O.U.P. 1921) points out that there are 175 words in 1 Timothy that do not occur in the ten acknowledged Pauline epistles. The total number of words in the Greek text of 1 Timothy is 1468 based on a vocabulary of 539 words. This means that 30% of the vocabulary is new. Working on the principle of "new words per page" method he has shown that there is an abrupt rise in this figure when the Pastorals are considered.

These statistics have carried great weight with many modern scholars. Some have in fact gone as far as to deny Pauline authorship on this ground alone.

The answer to the statistical argument is simple. When the words and cognates used by Paul in his messages in the Acts, by Luke in his writings, and those used in the Hebrew epistle are all taken into account, the new words in 1 Timothy are reduced from 175 to around 50 words, or about 10%. This must be viewed against the 2177 words that comprise the vocabulary in the ten acknowledged Pauline epistles. Cambridge statistican G.U. Yale in *The Statistical Study of Literary Vocabulary* (Cambridge 1944) has declared that samples of about 10 000 words are necessary as a basis for any valid statistical study. We have only a fraction of this number of words in the Pastorals. To assume that 2177 words was Paul's total vocabulary is an entirely gratuitous insult to this educated scholar. To further use his wider vocabulary in this epistle as an attack on his authorship is capricious denigration and scholastic nonsense.

Bruce M. Metzger asserts that Harrison's use of the statistical method is unsound and Donald Guthrie sums it up in a cogent statement in *New Testament Introduction: The Pauline Epistles*: "But numerical calculations cannot with the limited data available from Paul's letters take into account differences of subject matter, differences of circumstances and differences of addressees, all of which may be responsible for new words".

The simple and sensible answer is that a different subject calls for a different vocabulary. The discussion concerning the qualifications of elders and deacons, the support of widows, the unmasking of particular aspects of false teaching are new subjects to Paul and naturally he employs new words. Of the stylistic differences, of which much has been made by liberal scholars, notably P. M. Harrison in *The Problems of the Pastoral Epistles* (Forden, Oxford U. P. 1921), E.K. Simpson writes trenchantly, as he concludes an exhaustive summary of the characteristics of Pauline style shown in these epistles: "In conclusion we cannot help feeling that it is the rebukes dealt in these epistles to some of the fondest shibboleths of the modern mind that really chafe that mind. The stress laid on soundness of doctrine built on a fixed deposit of inspiration cannot but give offence, and the sinister portraiture of the last days kindle a spark of resentment. Such an epithet applied to seducers as *tetuphōmenos*, which is the Greek equivalent of swollen-headed or consequential, must rankle in circles where this spirit is not unknown".

This is Simpson's conclusion as he has pointed out that Paul has stamped seven stylistic mannerisms inescapably on the epistles:

1. Figures of speech drawn, not from the physical but the human realm. Examples could be cited of language drawn from:
   a. a martial campaign (1:18)
   b. a competitor in the games (2 Tim 2:5)
   c. figure of the seal (2 Tim 2:19)
   d. stewardship (1:4)
   d. gangrene (2 Tim 2:17)
   f. a cauterised conscience (4:2)

2. Employment of meiosis or understatement, for example:
   a. Onesiphorous was not ashamed (2 Tim 1:10)
   b. not given to wine (3:3)
   c. the word of God is not bound (2 Tim 2:9)
stressing a positive by stating the negative.

3. Apposition, words or clauses set against each other, for example:
   a. "to be testified in due time"
   b. "a pillar and stay of the truth".

Simpson remarks, "We could almost stake the authorship of 1 Timothy on the wording of 3:5, 'If one know not how to rule his own house, how shall he care for the church of God?' a compressed form of interrogation exclusively Pauline, of which there are four examples in 1 Cor 14 alone".

4. Compendious compounds. These are shorthand verbal formatives that Paul loves to use, for example:—
   heterodidaskalein (to teach other doctrine,1 Tim 1:3; 6:3)
   eumetadotos (ready to distribute, 1 Tim 6:18)
   katastrēniaō (wax wanton against, 1 Tim 5:11)

5. Enumerations. Paul's proclivity for lists is seen in these epistles especially of moral or immoral qualities, for example:
   a. Those who fall foul of the law (1 Tim 1:8-11)
   b. The graces evident in the man of God (1 Tim 6:11)

6. Play on words. For example:
   "the law is good, if a man use it lawfully" (1 Tim 1:8)
   "war a good warfare" (1 Tim 1:18)
   the fourfold play on the word "riches" (1 Tim 6:17).

7. Latinisms. It would be strange if the reflex influences of a Roman environment, particularly the Roman imprisonment, were not evident in the vocabulary.

These stylistic mannerisms, in fact, form a far more reliable claim to authorship, even than vocabulary. Vocabulary must of necessity be a function of the subject and therefore changes with the subject, but style of writing remains essentially personal. The style is Pauline.

Appendix B
Significant words and phrases

1. "This is a faithful saying" (*pistos ho logos*)
   This phrase occurs five times in the Pastorals as follows: 1 Tim 1:15; 1 Tim 3:1; 1 Tim 4:9; 2 Tim 2:11; Titus 3:8.
   On three occasions the actual statement follows the phrase as in 1 Tim 1:15; 1 Tim 3:1; 2 Tim 2:11; on the other two occasions the statement precedes the phrase as in 1 Tim 1:15; 4:9.
   Literally translated "faithful the word", the phrase suggests a formula used

to introduce a citation; likely one that was well-known which Paul means to emphasise.

The particular emphasis he wishes to make lies in the word "faithful" in the attributive position, i.e. the first word in the statement. "Faithful" is used of God (1 Cor 1:9; 10:13; 2 Cor 1:18) and is equivalent to our English word "trustworthy". This word or statement is "trustworthy" since it comes from a "trustworthy God". By the inclusion in these epistles each statement is given the stamp of divine inspiration.

"The word" (*logos*) is used on 20 occasions in these epistles and different shades of meaning are demanded by the context in each case. In 1 Tim 4:12 it must mean "speech"; in 5:17 it must be "teaching", but frequently, as in 4:6; 6:3, it summarises the content of the message. Thus, for English readers, the word "saying" is a good translation to introduce a statement that crystallises one aspect of the truth.

The additional phrase "worthy of all acceptation" (1:15; 4:9) in an emphatic way stresses its value. "Worthy" has in its root the idea of a beam-balance. So weighty is this statement that no counterpoise you may advance can outweigh it. In that sense all your weight may be placed upon it.

"Acceptation" carries the idea of approval and thus welcome. In Acts 2:4 the cognate verb is translated, "they that gladly received his word", and offers a good example of the welcome we can give to the statement. Some interpret the "all" in the extensive sense of all persons, i.e. a universal welcome. This is possible but the intensive force better suits the context, i.e. "worthy of full acceptance"; without reservations, without hesitation, and without the least doubt.

2. "God our Saviour"

This expression only occurs outside the Pastorals in two NT Scriptures: Luke 1:47 and Jude 25. In this first letter it occurs, slightly altered, in three places:

"God our Saviour" (*Theos sotēr hēmōn*) as in Jude 25   1:1
"God our Saviour" (*Ho sotēr hēmōn Theos*) as in Titus 1:3; 2:10; 3:4   2:3
"Living God, who is The Saviour", where Saviour is in apposition to God, as descriptive.   4:10

"The God of our salvation" is an OT title and this language is used in the LXX text of Deut 32:15. Deissman in his book *Light from the Ancient East* has shown how blasphemous Nero in the establishment of the Emperor cult had claimed this title. Paul would show that the Saviour God of OT revelation is revealed in the Christ who rightly bears this divine title; this title, by implication, denies the blasphemous claims of any Roman Emperor for worship from men.

The whole teaching of the NT traces salvation to God in the planning (1:1); in the purpose and provision of it (2:3); and in the relation He bears now to man (4:10), not simply a Creator God (4:4), not yet "**God the Judge**" in action (Heb 12:23), but now the **Saviour God**. To God are ascribed all the effective actions in salvation; it is His pleasure to save (1 Cor 1:21); His grace that saved (Eph 2:8), so that all believers trace their salvation entirely to God (Phil 1:28). That Christ also bears this title is seen in 2 Tim 1:10; Titus 1:4; 3:5 and serves but to stress His deity and the part He fills in this divine work of salvation.

3. "Godliness"

The word is *eusebeia* from *eu*, "well", and *sebomai*, "to be devout". Of the fifteen times it is used in the NT, five are by Peter, one in Acts 3:12 when he addressed the crowd after the restoration of the lame man, "why look ye so earnestly on us, as though by our own power or holiness (RV godliness) we had made this man to walk", and subsequently four times in 2 Pet 1:3,6,7 and 3:11.

The other ten occasions are in the Pastorals. Eight are in 1 Timothy with the other two references in 2 Tim 3:5 and Titus 1:1. The cognate adverb is used in 2 Tim 3:12 and Titus 2:12 and translated "godly". There is also the closely-related word *theosebeia* (the word *theos*, "God", is prefixed to *sebomai*, "to be devout"); this simply lays stress on the fact that the devotion envisaged in the conduct goes beyond the immediate action to an attitude to God that motivates it. This is the word used in 2:10 with its cognate verb in 5:4, translated in AV "to shew piety".

W. Rodgers has an informative note: "So far as the English word is concerned there can be little difficulty, for 'ly' as a suffix usually signifies 'like'; and just as 'manly' is 'man-like', and 'womanly' is 'woman-like', so 'godly' means 'God-like'. A final '-ness' turns any of these into a noun of quality, giving us 'manliness', 'womanliness, godliness' etc. Godliness is therefore likeness to God, a standard that is surely high enough for any of us".

However, the Greek word goes much further than the English word. It is not a quality or attribute of God, but rather an attitude to God in the heart of the saint that gives to God His proper place in thinking (the intelligence), loving (the emotions), and doing (the will) that thus renders to Him due reverence and respect. This inevitably issues in character formed and conduct manifest. It is in fact the NT equivalent of the OT "fear of the Lord".

Confining the study to the usage in this first Epistle, it is to be noted that the key passage is 3:16 from which all the other occurrences take character.

"Great is the mystery of godliness" directs the attention to the revelation in the *Person of Christ*. The six statements that follow show that in Christ godliness is fully manifested. Exhibited there are a perfect submission, a perfect obedience, and a perfect expression of godliness in all its completeness. To study Him in His movements as incarnate Deity from the manger to the throne is to have every aspect of godliness enfolded. The juxtaposition of this verse placed in relation to v.15 shows that what was manifest in Christ should now be expressed by the conduct ("how men ought to behave themselves",

RV) of those associated with the local testimony, "the house of God", now the witness of godliness upon earth.

The godliness thus envisaged can only be produced by *The Teaching* that is in keeping with it. This is emphasised in 6:3 in the expression "teaching which is according to (*kata*) godliness". Good teaching produces good conduct. The opposite is also true (1 Cor 15:33). Such teaching, if obeyed, will produce a pattern of godliness that will be of the same character for all saints and will touch every sphere of life, as the remaining references show very clearly:

1. The sisters in their sphere (2:10)
   Not showiness in dress but service to others marks godly women.
2. The children and grandchildren in the home (5:4)
   Not selfishness but unselfishness is shown in godly homes.
3. The servant of Jesus Christ in his work (4:6,7,8; 6:11)
   Not silly stories but sensible teaching marks the godly servant.
4. All saints in their:
   (i) social and political life (2:2)
      Not participation in political life but a prayer interest for the salvation of rulers marks the godly.
   (ii) Business life (6:5,6)
      Not a shadiness of business dealing that marks a covetous heart, but a willingness to share with others (6:18) is the inescapable evidence of the right attitude to God.

4. "Some"

Only two persons are named by Paul in this epistle, Hymanaeus and Philetus (1:20), and what a tragedy their names unfold! Clearly he does so because he has had to deal with them using apostolic authority, which involved, in the first instance, assembly excommunication (see 1 Cor 5:5 for the same expression "to deliver unto Satan"). That the expression goes further is suggested in the exposition.

Clearly, however, there are others who have been affected by the false teaching prevalent at Ephesus. Some have reaped already the fruit of their association with the false teaching and these Paul holds up as warnings of what can happen; in other cases he seeks to identify for Timothy and the assembly those who could thus affect them to their spiritual damage. This can be traced in the use that he makes of the pronoun "*some*". The danger was real not imaginary, the teachers were real men within the assembly and had to be identified and their teaching repudiated. This is shown by a study of the following references:

1. "That thou mightest charge *some* that they teach no other doctrine"
    (1:3)   (*Doctrinal*)
    "From which *some* having swerved have turned aside unto vain jangling" (1:6)   (*Intellectual*)

"Which *some* having put away concerning faith have made shipwreck
(1:19)   (*Moral*)

2.   "That in the latter times *some* shall depart from the faith, giving heed to
     seducing spirits, and doctrines of devils" (4:1)   (*Spiritual*)

3.   "If *any* provide not for his own, and specially for those of his own house,
     he hath denied the faith" ("*any*" is the singular of the pronoun "*some*")
                                                               (*Family Life*)

     "For *some* are already turned aside after Satan" (5:15)   (*Social Life*)

     "Which while *some* coveted after, they have erred from the faith" (6:10)
                                                               (*Business Life*)

     "Which *some* professing have erred concerning the faith" (6:21)
                                                               (*Intellectual Life*)

     Thus healthy teaching is required that saints may be preserved in every
sphere of their living. False teaching has disastrous effects and Paul holds up
some as proof of this truth.

Appendix C

Words used in first Timothy for the first time by Paul
(Not in the 10 Pauline Epistles, Luke, Acts or Hebrews)

Chapter 1
1.   teach no other doctrine (*heterodidaskaleō*) 1:3; 6:13
2.   genealogies (*genealogia*) 1:4; Titus 3:9
3.   fables (*muthos*) 1:4; 4:7; 2 Tim 4:14; Titus 1:14; 2 Pet 1:16
4.   swerve (*astocheō*) 1:6; 6:21
5.   manslayers (*androphonos*) 1:9
6.   murderers of mothers (*mētralōas*) 1:9
7.   murderers of fathers (*patralōas*) 1:9
8.   menstealers (*andrapodistēs*) 1:10
9.   perjured persons (*epiorkos*) 1:10 (cognate verb in Matt 5:33)

Chapter 2
1.   lead (*diagō*) 2:2; Titus 3:3
2.   quiet (*erēmos*) 2:2
3.   ransom (*antilutron*) 2:6
4.   broidered (*plegma*) 2:9
5.   pearls (*margaritēs*) 2:9 (used in Matt 7:6; 13:45,46;
     Rev 17:4; 17:12,16; 21:21)
6.   costly (*polutelēs*) 2:9
7.   godliness (*theosebeia*) 2:10 (adj. *theosebes* in John 9:31)
8.   childbearing (*teknogonia*) 2:15
9.   usurp authority (*authenteō*) 2:12

Chapter 3
1. blameless (*anepileptos*) 3:2; 5:7 ("without reproach")
   6:14 ("unrebukeable")
2. brawler (*paroinos*) 3:3; Titus 1:7
3. striker (*plēktēs*) 3:3
4. novice (*neophutos*) 3:6
5. lifted up with pride (*tuphoō*) 3:6
6. double tongued (*dilogos*) 3:8

Chapter 4
1. expressly (*rhētōs*) 4:1
2. seared (*kaustēriazō*) 4:2
3. old wives (*graōdēs*) 4:7
4. exercise (*gumnasia*) 4:9

Chapter 5
1. rebuke (*epiplēssō*) 5:1
2. nephews (*ekgonos*) 5:4
3. requite (*amoibē*) 5:4
4. parents (*progonos*) 5:4
5. liveth in pleasure (*spatalaō*) 5:6
6. taken into the number (*katalegō*) 5:9
7. brought up children (*teknotropheō*) 5:10
8. lodged strangers (*xenodocheō*) 5:10
9. follow (*epakoloutheō*) 5:10; 5:24 (Mark 16:20, 1 Pet 2:21)
10. wax wanton (*katastrēniaō*) 5:11
11. tattler (*phluaros*) 5:13
12. rear children (*teknogoneō*) 5:14
13. relieve (*eparkeō*) 5:16 (twice)
14. doubt (*diplous*) 5:17 (Rev 18:6)
15. preferring one before another (*prokrima*) 5:21
16. drink water (*hudropoteō*) 5:23
17. stomach (*stomachos*) 5:23

Chapter 6
1. raiment (*skepasma*) 6:8
2. pierce (*peripeirō*) 6:10
3. unapproachable (*aprositos*) 6:16
4. highminded (*hupsēlophroneō*) 6:17
5. oppositions (*antithesis*) 6:20

Additions to Bibliography
Spence, H.D.M. *The Epistles to Timothy and Titus*, Vol VIII of Ellicott's

Commentary on the Whole Bible. Ed. C.J. Ellicott, Grand Rapids. Zondervan.

Moffatt, J. *Pastoral Epistles*, Encycl. Britannica 1946 Ed.

Harrison, P.N. *The Problem of the Pastoral Epistles*. London O.U.P. 1921.

Liddon, H.P. *Explanatory Analyses of St Paul's First Epistle to Timothy*. Reprint by Klock and Klock 1978.

2 TIMOTHY

J. R. Baker

2 TIMOTHY

Introduction

1. The Author
2. The Recipient
3. The Background
4. Date of Writing
5. Purpose of Writing
6. Outline
7. Bibliography

1. The Author

No proven doubt exists that the apostle Paul wrote this and the preceding epistle. He is named in the first verse and there are many personal references throughout the letter. As he writes from Rome, he is wearing a chain and waiting to appear before Nero for the second time (1:16-17; 2:9; 4:6,16).

2. The Recipient

Timothy was converted through the gospel ministry of Paul, as is clear both here and in other New Testament letters where he is referred to as the apostle's "son" or "child" (1:2; 2:1).

The meaning of his name is "honoured of God" and there is no doubt that such is true of this young man who was reared in a God-fearing atmosphere where the Word of God had such a prominent place (1:5; 2:15).

The close spiritual relationship between Paul and Timothy and the help given the one to the other are alluded to in this epistle (1:13; 2:2; 3:10; 4:9,13, 21), and are referred to in more detail in the introduction to 1 Timothy.

3. The Background

This letter chronologically concludes the Pauline epistles. Just as in Gen 49 and Deut 33 we have the last words of Jacob and Moses respectively, so here

315

we find recorded the closing ministry of the apostle to the Gentiles. It is probable that during the liberty granted between his first and second imprisonment the apostle had visited Troas, Corinth and Miletus (4:13, 20). He may have left his cloak and books with Carpus at that time intending to take them up again on his return journey. The purpose of God prevented such a return. No record of the actual place of his arrest is given; many feel it was at Nicopolis where he was intending to spend the winter (Titus 3:12).

It is apparent that the last days of this great man of God were spent without material comfort. There seemed to be nothing of immediate earthly reward to crown his long years of untiring service. Various friends had left him (1:5; 4:10, 12, 16). Thus in the midst of the many limitations imposed by imprisonment the apostle had visited Troas, Corinth and Miletus (4:13,20). enable him to read. He also urges Timothy to come quickly, presumably that he may see him before his death (1:4; 4:9,21). Although various views have been expressed concerning the imprisonments of the apostle Paul there is little doubt that there were two. The first was at Rome and is described in the two closing verses of the book of Acts. Paul enjoyed considerable freedom to engage in a spiritual ministry at that time. He was able to "receive" all who came to him, thus there was good fellowship enjoyed and the facility of being able both to preach and to teach. He also was used by God at this time to write the New Testament letters we refer to as the "Prison Epistles": Ephesians, Philippians, Colossians and Philemon. It was therefore a period arranged by the sovereign design of God, to enable these vital aspects of ministry to take place.

In the Prison Epistles alluded to, there is reference to Paul's expected release (Phil 1:23-26; 2:19-24; Philem 2:2); thus he was looking forward to being completely free again and this can be understood from the type of imprisonment mentioned earlier. Tradition states that he was released and whilst this cannot be proved categorically, it best fits the various pieces of evidence which can be accumulated in the NT. The Pastoral Epistles refer to journeys which are not recorded in the book of Acts, yet some of them fit in with the stated intention of the apostle; thus it would appear that when he was released he made some of the journeys he had intended.

On looking at the whole picture with such a framework in mind it can safely be assumed that 1 Timothy and Titus were written during the period between the two imprisonments, and 2 Timothy during the second imprisonment. In 2 Tim 4:13 the apostle requests Timothy to bring with him from Troas the books and parchments and cloak which he had left there. If the visit here referred to is the same as in Acts 20:5-7, the documents would have been at Troas for about seven or eight years. This would be highly unlikely as they appeared to be of great and urgent value to him. A similar point could be made about the cloak. In 4:20 he speaks of having left Trophimus sick at Miletus. Now this could not have been in Acts 20 for subsequent to that visit, Trophimus is seen to be with Paul at Jerusalem (Acts

21:29). It is also significant to note that when Paul wrote to the Ephesians, Philippians, Colossians and Philemon, Demas was with him (Col 4:14; Philem 24), but in this second epistle to Timothy, Demas had forsaken him having loved this present world and had gone to Thessalonica (4:10).

Earlier reference has been made to the fact that during his first imprisonment Paul seems to be anticipating release from prison and a further period of service for God, but in this letter he is looking towards the completion of his earthly service (4:6-8), and towards the reward at the end of it. This second imprisonment was quite evidently far more severe than the first, when, although he would have been linked to a military guard by a chain, he had lived in his own lodging and was able to preach the gospel to many who came to him; now he is not only chained but is treated as an evildoer (2:9), and it is dangerous and difficult to find him in his confinement (1:16-18). It is also risky to stand by him when in court (4:16-18).

In such a circumstance Paul witnessed boldly not only in a private way but publicly at the trial so that all the Gentiles might hear the preaching of the gospel (4:17). Now out from the same travail is written this, his last epistle, to warn and guide and encourage the man of God in light of the last days.

4. The Date of Writing

We have earlier considered the fact that this epistle describes events which took place after the first imprisonment and subsequent release of the apostle Paul. The letter makes clear that he was imprisoned again. All three Pastoral Epistles were written within a short space of time; this is seen by their resemblance to each other in language, matter, style of composition and in the state of the testimony which they describe. They differ from the remainder of Paul's epistles in these points, a fact which strengthens the argument that they stand together.

The date of this epistle can be reasonably placed within the years AD 66 or 67. It was a time of persecution and danger, all men forsook the apostle (4:16), his temporary respite from being condemned to death is spoken of as a deliverance from the lion's mouth (4:17). These facts point to the closing years of the tyrannical reign of Nero (AD 54-68). It has been suggested that perhaps it would be soon after the outburst of cruel warfare upon christians when the emperor set fire to the city and then turned the popular anger of the people against the suspected followers of Christ. W. E. Vine has suggested that the letter was written probably in the year AD 67 and states that "from his desire for Timothy to come to him before the winter (4:21) we may conclude that it was written in the summer of that year".

5. Purpose of Writing

The late William Rodgers of Omagh stated that a suitable subtitle to this epistle could be "Helps and Hindrances to the man of God in difficult times".

There is no doubt that one of the main reasons for the letter is to prepare Timothy for, and to encourage him in, the trying times which were yet to come. The personal nature of the epistle is evident even on a cursory reading, thus there is varied reference to character and behaviour.

As with other second epistles attention is directed to the last days. The Holy Spirit in this letter is thus, through the apostle's message to Timothy, warning all who would live for God in last day conditions. We would therefore learn how to deport ourselves personally in relation to suffering and trial, to opposition from those from whom we would expect support, and to live, as Paul did, in light of the day of reward.

6. Outline

In the first section of the epistle there are some broad foundations, which whilst relating to Timothy personally, also have their application to each believer today. The second section contains a series of figures which are used by the apostle to describe varies aspects of christian life and service. In the third part of the letter attention is drawn to the future with its various problems and responsibilities and the final section teaches the importance of faithfulness being maintained to the end. A short salutation and personal note conclude the epistle.

I.	*Foundations of the Man of God*	1:1-18
	1. Personal Foundations	1:1-8
	2. Doctrinal Foundations	1:9-12
	3. Practical Foundations	1:13-18
II.	*Figures of the Man of God*	2:1-26
	1. A Child	2:1-2
	2. A Soldier	2:3-4
	3. An Athlete	2:5
	4. An Husbandman	2:6-7
	5. Application of the Metaphors	2:8-14
	6. A Workman	2:15-18
	7. A Vessel	2:19-21
	8. A Servant	2:22-26
III.	*Future of the Man of God*	3:1-17
	1. The Future and Its Features	3:1-5
	2. The Future and Its Folly	3:6-9
	3. The Future and Fidelity	3:10-13
	4. The Future and Being Furnished	3:14-17
IV.	*Faithfulness of the Man of God*	4:1-18
	1. Faithfulness Toward the Wayward	4:1-5

7. Bibliography

Bruce, F. F. *An Expanded Paraphrase of the Epistles of Paul*. The Paternoster Press, Exeter, 1965.

Marshall, A. *The Interlinear Greek-English New Testament (Nestles Greek Text)*. London: Samuel Bagster, 1964.

Vine W.E. *An Expository Dictionary of New Testament Words*. London: Oliphants.

Alford, H. *The Greek Testament*. London: Rivington, 1865.

Angus, J. *The Bible Handbook*. London: R.T.S.

Coneybeare and Howson, *The Life and Epistles of St. Paul*. London: Longmans Green and Co. 1880.

Darby, J. N. *Synopsis of the Books of the Bible*. Stow Hill Bible and Tract Depot, 1948.

Gaebelein, F. E. *The Expositor's Bible Commentary*. Zondervan, 1978.

Godet, F. L. *Studies in Paul's Epistles*. Kregel.

Harding, P. *An Exposition of 2 Timothy*. Glasgow: Gospel Tract Publications.

Hendriksen, W. *1 & 2 Timothy and Titus*. The Banner of Truth Trust, 1957.

Kelly, J. N. D. *A Commentary on the Pastoral Epistles*. Michigan: Baker Book House. 1963.

King, G. H. *To My Son* C. L. C. 1944.

Moule, H. C. G. *The Second Epistle to Timothy*. London: R. T. S. 1906.

Robertson, A. T. *Word Pictures in The New Testament*. Broadman, 1930.

Rodgers, W. *Notes on the Pastoral Epistles*. Lurgan: L. M. Press.

Stott, J. R. W. *Guard the Gospel*. I. V. P. 1973.

Vine, W. E. *The Epistles to Timothy and Titus*. Oliphants, 1965.

Wuest, K. S. *Word Studies from The Greek New Testament*. Eerdmans, 1973.

Text and Exposition

I. Foundations of the Man of God (1:1-18)

1. *Personal Foundations*
1:1-8

v.1   ''Paul, an apostle of Jesus Christ by the will of God, according to the promise of life which is in Christ Jesus,

v.2   To Timothy, my dearly beloved son; Grace, mercy and peace, from God the Father and Christ Jesus our Lord.

v.3   I thank God, whom I serve from my forefathers with pure conscience, that without ceasing I have remembrance of thee in my prayers night and day;

v.4   Greatly desiring to see thee, being mindful of thy tears, that I may be filled with joy;

v.5   When I call to remembrance the unfeigned faith that is in thee, which dwelt first in thy grandmother Lois, and thy mother Eunice; and I am persuaded that in thee also.

v.6   Wherefore I put thee in remembrance that thou stir up the gift of God, which is in thee by the putting on of my hands.

v.7   For God hath not given us the spirit of fear; but of power, and of love, and of a sound mind.

v.8   Be not thou therefore ashamed of the testimony of our Lord, nor of me his prisoner: but be thou partaker of the afflictions of the gospel according to the power of God;''

In this opening section the apostle reminds Timothy of basic matters which relate to him personally. He was Paul's child in the faith (v.2), and was the subject of his constant supplication (v.3). There was also the important family influence of his grandmother and mother (v.5), coupled to the memory of the special commendation to the work in which the apostle had played a particular part (v.6).

1 Paul is writing from prison, yet he emphasises that there is a dignity to his apostleship based upon two important facts:

1.   The will of God,
2.   The promise of the life which is in Christ Jesus.

The order of the RV is to be preferred here. Paul's apostleship was different from others; he had seen the exalted One, whilst the other apostles had seen our Lord Jesus when He was here in humility. The prepositions in this verse are important: "by the will of God" indicates that divine purpose not only lay behind this calling but was instrumental in bringing him into the good of it; "according to" shows that the reason for his apostleship was with a view to the life which is in Christ Jesus.

Here allusion is being made not only to the evangelistic aspect of Paul's work, but also to the "promise of the life", i.e. his ministry would confirm, and prepare for, the development of that life which had been given to the saints. Thus we learn that Paul's apostleship derived from the will of God but was directed towards the promise of life. His gospel ministry was used of God to impart that life and his teaching ministry to strengthen and develop it.

2 Reference has been made in the introduction to the meaning of Timothy's name. Here he is spoken of with tender affection as a beloved child. No doubt he had been converted through the gospel ministry of the apostle Paul. Such a relationship forms an important background to both the appealing and instructional aspects of the presentation of the ministry in this letter. There is reference to the fact that Timothy was "saved" (1:9; 3:14-15), and there is clear evidence within the epistle of the warmth of the heart of a father toward his son. This would be appreciated by one who was being exhorted to stand and serve with courage at a time when many would either oppose him (2:25; 3:8), or turn away (1:15; 4:10,16).

The importance of such an opening greeting should never be underestimated in a letter like this. Paul clearly desired that Timothy would have, and be helped by, the grace, mercy and peace he invokes in this verse. Grace emphasises the loving kindness of our God in giving to us what we never deserved. It emphasises that salvation is the gift of God and ever keeps the child of God thankful to, and humble before, the God who bestowed it. It is also taught in Scripture that grace is not just an initial starting-post to be left behind but is rather a constant enabling stream. John 1:16 speaks of "grace for grace", the idea of which really is that of fresh grace meeting each need. Thus the apostle is desiring for Timothy the experience described by the hymn-writer: "And fresh supplies each hour I meet, whilst pressing on to God." Paul himself had known the blessing of grace which was sufficient to meet his need in the time of trial (2 Cor 12:9).

Mercy is not included in greetings which are addressed to an assembly. Here it is used to add a personal note to Timothy as an individual. Mercy emphasises that God has withheld from us what we rightly deserved. Ps 103:10-11 makes this very clear; but it is more than this. The word implies a sense of pity or a feeling of sympathy which could be felt by Timothy in the days of difficulty which would be his. Heb 4:16 gives clear guidance as to how we can obtain mercy in the time of need.

Peace must be the blessed result of such enabling streams of grace and mercy. The peace of God is a garrison against all forms of satanic attack. The blessings which Paul desires for Timothy are not man-made, they are divine in origin: "from God the Father" indicates resource; "and Christ Jesus our Lord" indicates the means by which they come. There may be, of course, an allusion to the deity of Christ in this statement which clearly links the Father and our Lord Jesus Christ as the common source of these blessings.

3 Thanksgiving to God is an important component of prayer which the apostle had taught to Timothy previously (1 Tim 2:1). We should ever approach God like this; as the Psalmist has stated, "It is a good thing to give thanks unto the Lord". Joy and rejoicing feature highly in Philippians which was written during the apostle's first imprisonment, and here at the outset of the last prison letter the same spirit prevails.

This verse helps us to know that Paul knew and served God before he came to know that Jesus of Nazareth is the Christ the only Saviour. Eph 2:12 shows that Gentiles were in time past "without Christ" and "without God in the world". Paul as a devout Jew could (and often did) claim his close relationship to the God of Israel. He makes clear in 1 Tim 1 that when he blasphemed etc., it was in ignorance and unbelief. He is thus teaching here that from the days of his parentage he had served God to the best of his ability and with a pure conscience. This does not mean that such service could claim the approval or blessing of God because clearly it was on occasion contrary to the purpose of God.

Paul here speaks of the conscience. The word *suneidēsis* is literally "a knowing with", i.e. a knowledge with or within oneself. It has been described as that internal monitor or regulator within man, which has the faculty of discernment (Heb 10:2; Rom 2:14-15; 9:1; 2 Cor 1:12). It can be defiled (Titus 1:15-16) and become evil (Heb 10:22), but at conversion it is purged and cleansed (Heb 9:14; 10:22). The manner in which he describes his service reveals the dedication which motivated him towards God as a pious Jew even before his conversion. That God takes note of such is seen not only in Paul, but also in the account of Cornelius (Acts 10:4,22,31); both men were required to, and did, believe the gospel in order to be saved. A careful comparison of the NT epistles reveals that the apostle was given to regular prayer for others. Assemblies and individuals were on his prayer list. Timothy clearly had a special place on his heart. "Without ceasing" indicates the regularity involved; it only occurs elsewhere in Rom 9:2. One of the results of these prayers was the constant stirring of his memory, as he thought of Timothy. "Night and day" is of particular interest here. As the "widow indeed" (1 Tim 5:5) would have opportunity to pray often, so the imprisoned servant of God was making such good use of the time spent in his isolation, not only in the day periods but also during the night seasons.

4 Aspects of the personal joy and fellowship between the writer and the recipient are evident in this verse. Although some link the closing statement with v.5, a rearrangement of the three clauses suggests a better and more accurate sense. F. F. Bruce in his *An Expanded Paraphrase of the Epistles of Paul* does this as follows: "As I recall your tears, I long to see you, so that I may be filled with joy".

Tears should not be construed as a mark of weakness or timidity here. It has been suggested that Paul was reflecting on the occasion of Acts 20:37 when, with the Ephesian elders, they had knelt to pray and weep together. In that same chapter we learn that the apostle had served the Lord, and also warned the saints with tears. It is more probable that Paul had a different occasion in mind because the Miletus incident had taken place several years previously and no doubt he had seen Timothy in the intervening period. Believing that a second imprisonment took place, it is logical to infer that Paul is thinking of the occasion still fresh in his memory when, having been arrested again, he took his last leave of Timothy presumably before being taken away to Rome. The tears of Timothy are a further evidence of his likeness to his spiritual father and indeed to his Lord (the tears of Christ are worthy of our careful consideration). The service of God's servants should ever be accompanied by tears, the evidence of a heart which has been touched by the gentleness and meekness of Christ (2 Cor 10:1).

Paul's earnest longing to see Timothy is further referred to in ch. 4:9. Those who have attempted to depict him as a hard and calculating man with little affection in his heart, have failed to discern the true man who writes this letter. The present active participle *epipothōn* (homesick yearning) makes clear that he valued the fellowship and company of his brethren, and later parts of the epistle show that he felt the loss when they were away from him. Joy would be caused within the apostle's heart by a renewed sight of Timothy. He had been encouraged when he "saw" the brethren on his journey to Rome (Acts 28:15), and had endeavoured, and prayed exceedingly to see the face of the Thessalonian believers (1 Thess 2:17; 3:10).

5 The RV, "having been reminded", is to be preferred at the beginning of this verse. Paul had possibly been reminded of the faith of Timothy by a letter or message from him. *Hupomnēsin labōn* indicates a reminder received from outside of oneself.

Faith is that exercise which in the ways of God with men is used to bring a soul into the good of salvation (Eph 2:8); it is also a continued and potentially developing characteristic in each believer. It is said of the Thessalonian believers that "your faith groweth exceedingly" (2 Thess 1:3); earlier, having been anxious to "know" their faith (1 Thess 5:5), Paul had been greatly reassured when Timothy brought him the good tidings of their faith (1 Thess 3:6-10). Further example of this is seen in Philem 5, 6. The faith of Timothy is shown to be "unfeigned", which literally means to be unhypocritical (*anupokritos*). Greek actors were called *hupokritēs* because they were acting on stage a character which was not their own. They were feigning to be someone else. This is illustrated in the advice of Joab to the woman of Tekoah: "feign thyself to be a mourner" (2 Sam 14:2). It thus appears that falseness did not characterise Timothy. This is consistent with the comment of Paul concerning him as having a "genuine" care for the Philippian saints (Phil 2:21).

His grandmother Lois and mother Eunice had obviously exerted a profound influence on Timothy. No doubt it was they who had taught him the holy Scriptures from his childhood (3:15). There is no reference elsewhere in Scripture to Lois; Eunice, although not named, is mentioned in Acts 16:1. She was a Jewess and her husband a Greek. It is probable that she and her mother had been converted at the time of the preaching recorded in Acts 14:6-7. It is also probable that Timothy's father was not a believer. A careful reading of Acts 16:1 emphasises that his mother had believed but no such comment is made of his father. Unfeigned faith had "dwelt" in both of these women despite the possible problems of a divided home. "Dwelt" is literally "to be at home". Here is an excellent example of the importance of family influence on the children. *Life* often comes before *lip* in Scripture; here we have the former, whilst in ch. 3:15 we find the latter. Some have suggested that Paul's persuasion concerning Timothy himself is a subtle encouragement to him and is in contrast to the past tense at the beginning of the verse ("which has been in thee"). It seems better to take the statement at face value as the apostle's genuine expressed feeling concerning his child in the faith. In an overall way this verse can be seen in contrast to the later parts of the epistle where the marked lack of, or turning away from, faith is described in named individuals.

6 "Wherefore", or "for which cause" (JND), is pointing back to the unfeigned faith in Timothy and becomes the basis of the exhortation in this verse. W. Hendriksen has pointed out that there are four different expressions in this section that have to do with memory. He shows that they should be carefully distinguished. In the first three Paul is being reminded, but in this last one he is putting in mind of an important matter. To "stir up" has been variously rendered to "rekindle" (JND) or to "keep blazing" (A.T. Robertson). The former could infer that there was a negligence in Timothy in respect of the gift which was in him. There does not seem to be clear evidence that such was the case although arguments based on inference have been drawn. It should be noted that the verb is in the present infinitive which would indicate that a continuous action is being encouraged. The exhortation is thus preventative rather than corrective. The late general Booth is reputed to have sent the message to his younger workers: "The tendency of fire is to go out; watch the fire on the altar of your heart". The gift was "in" Timothy and the giving of it is associated with certain problems which must be considered by comparing our present verse with 1 Tim 4:14. The prophecies of 1 Tim 1:18 have been connected with the prophecy of 1 Tim 4:14, and whilst there may be a connection, it cannot be proved. Timothy's gift was certainly given "by means of" (*dia*) prophecy, exactly how or when this took place is not clear. It was a time of both apostolic and prophetic ministry and it seems that by the revelation which accompanied prophecy the fact of Timothy's gift was made known. It was also "along with" (*meta*) the laying on of the hands of the presbytery (elderhood), thus the elder brethren laid their hands on Timothy not to communicate the gift to him, but to identify themselves with him in it. They thus gave affirmation that what was revealed through the prophecy was in their spiritual judgment supported by Timothy's moral and spiritual condition to receive and use such a gift. In 2 Tim 1:6, we learn that the apostle Paul had a particular part to play in this matter. The gift was in Timothy "by the putting (laying) on of my hands". The preposition here is again *dia* thus indicating that this was a special apostolic occasion when God used the apostle to communicate the gift to Timothy. We cannot look for such unique apostolic and prophetic activity today. Gift is still given to the people of God and will be developed as it is exercised and will also be recognised both by the possessor and by the saints. What the gift was is not specifically stated. It appears to have been of both a pastoral and public nature from the following Scriptures: 1 Tim 4:12-16; 2 Tim 1:13; 2:2,14,24; 4:2,5.

7 In a general way this verse is teaching that when God gives a gift, He also gives the necessary enablement to use it. Looking at the overall picture of Timothy as an individual there does appear to have been some reticence in his disposition. These words would be an encouragement to him in considering the use of his gift for the glory of God.

The giving alluded to was a definite act, as is indicated by the aorist tense, and is probably referring to the time when the gift was given as outlined in the preceding verse. The plural pronoun "us" can refer to Timothy and Paul in particular but is probably wider. Fearfulness implies cowardice and timidity and is a feature of the flesh (John 14:27). If Timothy would be in any way reticent to accept the God-given responsibility implicit in the gift, then this would be the result of fearfulness which the apostle is showing is not from God; 1 John 4:18 is helpful on this point.

Some expositors have laid great stress on the absence of the definite article before "Spirit", and have therefore concluded that the Holy Spirit cannot be in view. It should be noted, however, that able Greek scholars stand on either side in the argument and nothing in the actual Greek grammar stands in the way of inserting the definite article to complete the sense in English. This means that the context must determine whether or not the Holy Spirit is in view. Others have argued that the Holy Spirit cannot be in view because "spirit" here is linked to the genitives of power, love, etc. Such a position cannot be maintained when Rom 8:15 is considered. It is a parallel verse and clearly the Holy Spirit is in view there. Most who comment on this verse admit that the Holy Spirit alone produces power, love and a sound mind in the believer; it would therefore be wise in light of the points mentioned to acknowledge that the Holy Spirit and His effects are in view.

The construction of the statements is interesting and there are similar arrangements elsewhere in Scripture, e.g. Rom 14:17. Seen in the context of gift the Holy Spirit enables with power that there may be the ability to exercise moral and spiritual authority in the use of gift; this would be of particular importance to Timothy both as to his own disposition and as to the times in which he was to serve. Love enables the gift to be exercised in a self-sacrificing way in the interests of others. *Agapē* is used here which refers to the objective divine aspect of love. "Sound mind" is better rendered "self-discipline" and refers to the importance of self restraint and control in the use of all gift. These features are produced by the Holy Spirit who also energises the gift itself.

8 The exhortation to be not ashamed in no way implies that Timothy had become a coward in his testimony. The aorist subjunctive with the negative is used which forbids the doing of an act not yet begun (Wuest). Timothy had clearly proved to be a faithful fellow-servant and had been with the apostle at various places when persecution had broken out. He had remained loyal and the apostle is now strengthening such resolve. Paul is thus showing that on occasion ministry should be preventative. The basis of this exhortation is in the previous verse: in light of the gift itself and the facility given by the features of the Holy Spirit which accompany it, Timothy was not to fall a prey to any form of spiritual cowardice.

Scholars are divided as to whether the genitive "of (our Lord)" is subjective or objective. Greek grammar cannot decide alone and the context could allow either. If subjective, then the testimony is that borne by our Lord and includes His teachings as now taught by those who preach. If objective, it refers to the testimony borne by Paul and Timothy etc., concerning the Lord. On balance it appears to be nearer to the immediate context to view the latter as being correct here, particularly in view of the statements which follow. Throughout the whole letter Paul is encouraging the servant of God in his work of testimony to, and for, the Person of Christ.

It is clear that if such shame did appear it would not only be of the testimony but also of the apostle who was in prison for such testimony. Paul did not regard himself as a prisoner of Rome, but rather of the Lord. He had learned to look beyond earthly circumstance and recognise the hand of God in these matters. Such an appreciation of the sovereignty of God removes all shame. This verse is one of three in this chapter which underlines this great truth. "I am not ashamed" (v.12) and "Onesiphorus . . . was not ashamed" (v.16) are the other two.

The exhortation is not only negative but involves a peculiar appeal to Timothy to become a partaker of afflictions. J.N. Darby is helpful here in rendering the compound word used in the original as "but suffer evil along with the glad tidings". Timothy is thus being invited to be a fellow-partaker not only with the gospel, but also of the hardship that goes with the gospel (see also RV). From a literal point of view "with" goes with "the gospel", but most commentators prefer to support the idea that Paul is looking to Timothy to be a fellow-partaker with himself in such afflictions. The use of the compound word is however best understood by viewing the appeal as being to Timothy not only to enjoy the blessing of the gospel, but to appreciate that with it is the reproach and hardship described. The closing phrase of this verse is best understood as being connected with the verb "be thou partaker". "It is the power of God which enables Timothy to endure suffering for the sake of the gospel" (Wuest).

2. Doctrinal Foundations
1:9-12

v.9   "Who hath saved us, and called us with an holy calling, not according to our works, but according to his own purpose and grace, which was given us in Christ Jesus, before the world began;

v.10   But is now made manifest by the appearing of our Saviour Jesus Christ, who hath abolished death, and hath brought life and immortality to light through the gospel:

v.11   Whereunto I am appointed a preacher, and an apostle, and a teacher of the Gentiles.

v.12   For the which cause I also suffer these things: nevertheless I am not ashamed: for I know whom I have believed, and am persuaded that he is able to keep that which I have committed unto him against that day."

Here reference is made to certain basic truths of a doctrinal nature which the apostle states in a context of encouragement.

Although the persecution is at the hands of men, attention is being drawn to the eternal purpose of God (v.9). It is seen in relation to time; thus reference is made to the past, "before the ages of time" (v.9), to the present, "is now made manifest" (v.10) and to the future, "against that day" (v.12).

9 F.F. Bruce in his expanded paraphrase says, "It was God who saved us". That this is correct is clear from the closing reference to God in the previous verse. Here then is emphasised that salvation is the work of God and this is consistent with the six references in the Pastoral Epistles to "God our Saviour" (1 Tim 1:1; 2:3; 4:10; Titus 1:3; 2:10; 3:4). The epistle to the Romans

opens by describing the glad tidings as the "gospel of God" (Rom 1:1). The tense used here refers the act of saving to a definite point in time emphasising that salvation is not a process where light dawns but rather is a definite divine act. Some have restricted the plural pronoun to Paul and Timothy, but the context allows a much wider application.

"With" (probably from the dative) is better "to a holy calling", indicating not the invitation itself, but rather the service to which we have been called. We have been called to holiness. The early Puritans spoke of the effectual call of the gospel when the sinner heard the message and accepted the salvation of God. Such is in view here. Much is made in the NT of our calling and a comparison of the varied terms used is profitable. It is heavenly (Heb 3:1), high (Phil 3:14) and here designated holy. A very similar phrase to that used here is in Rom 8:28.

Salvation is not "according to" (*kata*) our works. This preposition is literally "down" giving the idea of domination or control. The apostle is teaching that salvation is not dominated by our works, or not "in consideration of" our works. Alford gives the same sense by saying it is not "after the measure of" our works. It is highly significant that here in his closing NT epistle Paul is stating the same truth enunciated so clearly in the epistle to the Galatians which was his first NT letter. It should be noted that whilst salvation is not due to works, yet it should have works as a result (see Eph 2:8-10; Titus 3:4-8).

The believer's salvation and effectual call is "according to" God's own purpose and grace, i.e. it is "dominated by" or "after the measure of" what God has planned. Here is introduced the sovereignty of God in the matter of salvation. Eph 1 and many other passages make clear that God works "according to his good pleasure which he hath purposed in himself", that He "worketh all things after the counsel of his own will" (Eph. 1:9,11). This subject should not be confused with, or compared with, the responsibility of His servants to bring about His will which is seen, and will be dealt with, in vv. 11-12. Grace is introduced here because man neither deserves, not has the ability to achieve, the salvation of God.

The grace was given "in", which here probably carries the sense of "through", Christ Jesus. Divine purpose bestowed this grace before the "ages of time". Long before Adam and the fall, literally before time was reckoned by aeons or cycles, the believer was the subject of grace in divine purpose. Similar expressions in differing contexts should be considered (Eph 1:4; 3:11; Titus 1:2; Rom 16:25).

10 The change from the past tense of the previous verse emphasises that what was purposed before "times eternal" has now been manifested in time. A similar structure is found in Rom 16:25-26. "Made manifest" refers back to the purpose and grace. It is interesting to note that it was "given us" in purpose before the world began but is now "made manifest" (*phaneroō*). The word used means more than merely to be seen. A person could appear in false guise and be seen. This is to be revealed in its true character. The following statements in the verse make clear why such an important word is used. The manifestation has taken place by, or though (*dia*), the appearing of Jesus Christ. "By the appearing" (*dia tēs epiphaneias*) is used elsewhere for the second coming of Christ (Titus 2:13), as indeed in this very epistle (2 Tim 4:8). This indicates that the context must determine what sense a particular word has. Some have often attempted to force interpretation based only upon the actual word used. Titus 2:11 and 3:4 further emphasise this point in relation to the use of this word.

The two appearings alluded to (1:10; 4:8) seem to be similar to the two in Titus 2:11,13. In each case the first relates to our Lord's first coming and the second to the day of future manifestation. The term here is probably wider than, but will include, the incarnation. The references to what He has done confirm this. In the previous verse it has been seen that the One who has saved us is God. Here the Lord Jesus Christ is named as our Saviour. This is particularly a NT truth and was promised at the birth of Christ (Luke 2:11). When salvation is viewed as a concept in the realm of purpose it is attributed to God. When it is seen as an act in practice it is seen as the work of the Lord Jesus Christ. The order of His name is of interest here; whilst the RV reverses it, JND retains Jesus Christ. The emphasis is usually on the first name, thus it is fitting to the context to see Jesus, the One who came to do such a work, now exalted as Christ.

Physical death is in view and it should be noted that whilst He has not yet eliminated it, He has robbed it of its authority or broken its power. This is the force of "abolished" (*katargeō*) as used here. W. E. Vine points out that it literally means "to reduce to inactivity", and in his *Expository Dictionary of New Testament Words* gives a lengthy and helpful paragraph containing many references of example. The teaching of John 11:25-26 is significiant on this subject and the language of Rom 8:38-39 illustrates that for Paul death had become of small importance. Such has been further seen down the centuries in the way many martyrs have faced what, for the natural man, is "the king of terrors".

Life and immortality must be viewed here in the context of the annulment of death: the life which comes from God through the gospel is both qualitative and quantitative. It is enjoyed here but goes beyond the grave and leads to the truth of immortality (*aphtharsia*) which is better rendered incorruption. The word is used elsewhere to denote

1.   A moral quality (Eph 6:24; Titus 2:7) and
2.   The physical state of the believer's body at resurrection (1 Cor 15:42,50,53,54).

The latter best fits the context here. The value of, and facts concerning, eternal life and the incorruption of the body at resurrection are only hinted at in the OT revelation, but are now "brought to light". This expression means to turn the light on; it is used in 1 Cor 4:5 and Eph 1:18. The full glare of divine revelation concerning these matters has revealed the perpetuity of the life which God gives at salvation and which will be enjoyed eternally in the incorruptible resurrection body. The gospel is the means through (*dia*) which we get this light.

11 Paul clearly saw that one of the great purposes in life for him was to be a preacher of the gospel. "Appointed" is literally to be placed or set and implies the personal stewardship in this matter which had been committed to the apostle (1 Cor 9:17; 1 Thess 2:4; 1 Tim 1:11; Titus 1:3). The wider aspect of the gospel is in view as is seen in the teaching of the previous verse and now in the breadth of terms used for its proclamation.

A preacher as used here is a public herald; such were messengers often vested with public authority to enable them to convey official messages from kings, magistrates or military commanders. They would with dignity and integrity proclaim the message, not in any way altering its content. This is the work of all who preach the gospel. It is noteworthy that our Lord Jesus Christ was a gospel preacher (Luke 4:18) and Paul was keen to describe himself thus also (1 Cor 1:17).

"Apostle" is described in two ways in the NT, generally and specifically. The meaning is a messenger; thus in the general aspect all who go forth having been sent are worthy of this designation (Acts 14:14). There is also the specific official apostle spoken of in the NT. These required the qualifications of having companied with the Lord (or having seen Him) and of being a witness of His resurrection (Acts 1:21-22).

Paul argues apostleship of the official category in many of the NT epistles (1 Cor 9:1) and no doubt is doing the same here. The apostolic witness was vital at the commencement of the present dispensation, in publicly confirming the message which was being introduced (Heb 2:3-4).

It is significant to note that although he had a strong Jewish background, yet Paul was reared in Tarsus, which was one of three main centres of Greek learning, the others being Athens and Alexandria. He was therefore suited and prepared of God to be the apostle to the Gentiles. He was a Roman citizen and claimed its privilege on occasion to enable him to further the work. At his conversion, the sphere and extent of his ministry was indicated (Acts 9:15; 22:21; 26:17). Gal 2:7-9 makes clear that he had truly become a teacher of the Gentiles and the many NT epistles from his pen to Gentile-based assemblies confirm the point.

12 It has been seen that the varied aspects of Paul's ministry, as outlined in the previous verse, are all with a view to the furtherance of the gospel; "for the which cause" thus refers back to the gospel. Suffering and affliction were closely linked to Paul and his ministry and this was predicted at the time of his conversion (Acts 9:16). Much reference is made in the Pastoral Epistles to the suffering which necessarily must be the portion of those who serve the Lord. "These things" are the afflictions of the gospel (v.8), and include the imprisonment in the dungeon, the chain and the solitude, as referred to in this letter. For a more complete catalogue of some of Paul's earlier sufferings, 2 Cor 11:23-28 should be read. The apostle is here showing that what he had taught to Timothy in v.8 was being practised in his own life. The idea of "not ashamed" is that Paul, in spite of his sufferings, has not been put to shame, has not been defeated, and has not had his hopes disappointed. He speaks similarly in Rom 1:16 of the gospel, knowing that it was the power of God. It has been said that faithfulness to God frees the believer from bondage to human opinion, regard and reward. "For I know" (*oida*) is not the knowledge gained by experience of fellowship with God, but rather the knowledge of what God is in Himself. Paul knew that He was absolutely dependable in any circumstance. Such is absolute intuitive knowledge as this particular word indicates. The emphasis here is not on *what* the apostle believed but rather on *whom*. "For I know *Him* whom I have believed" (RV) expresses what is in view. "I have believed" is in the perfect tense in the Greek text. Wuest states that its full meaning is "I have believed with the present result that my faith is a firmly settled one". Again "persuaded" is in the perfect tense. The apostle had arrived at a settled conviction on this matter, and no person would be able to shake him from it.

"Able" (*dunatos*) is not mere ability to do something but describes the might and power within the One of whom he is speaking; it has been paraphrased as "He has power to". Scholars have taken fairly even sides in interpreting the following statement in this verse, therefore it is unwise to dogmatise. All are agreed that a literal, more accurate sentence would read "He has power to guard my deposit". It can thus be seen that "my deposit" may be either what He has deposited with me or what I have deposited with Him. Many take the view that it is the former because they feel that the deposit is the gospel as in 1 Tim 6:20 and in v.14 of this chapter; they reason that the phrase here is the same. It should however be noted that the contexts of the verses cited are quite different. In them Timothy himself is to be the guard, but here, there is no doubt that it is God who "keeps" the deposit. The immediate setting is in favour of this as the apostle has just referred to life and incorruptibility which are the blessings of the believer. These cannot be fully realised until the day of resurrection. It would thus be fitting to view the deposit in a comprehensive way as encompassing our salvation, and all we, in our service, are putting into account with the God who is presently receiving deposit in light of a future time of reward (Heb 6:10). "To keep" (*phulassō*) is to guard or defend against robbery or loss (see Matt 6:19-20). "That day" as used here, in v.18 and in 4:8 is looking on to the time of recompense and reward which will commence at the judgment seat of Christ and will be known in an evident way at the time of His manifestation in glory. The same expression should be carefully compared contextually with 1 Cor 3:13.

3. Practical Foundations
1:13-18

v.13   "Hold fast the form of sound words, which thou hast heard of me, in faith and love which is in Christ Jesus.

v.14   That good thing which was committed unto thee keep by the Holy Ghost which dwelleth in us.

v.15   This thou knowest, that all they which are in Asia be turned away from me; of whom are Phygellus and Hermogenes.

v.16   The Lord give mercy unto the house of Onesiphorus; for he oft refreshed me, and was not ashamed of my chain:

v.17   But, when he was in Rome, he sought me out very diligently, and found me.

v.18   The Lord grant unto him that he may find mercy of the Lord in that day; and in how many things he ministered unto me at Ephesus, thou knowest very well."

Having outlined the personal and doctrinal basis of Timothy's spiritual experience and progress, the apostle now applies practical exhortation to the younger servant of God. This is so often the established order of teaching where doctrine precedes, and lays the basis for, our practice.

13 The footnote in J.N. Darby's *New Translation* is very helpful on the opening phrase of this verse. The apostle is not exhorting Timothy to hold fast to a credal type of "form" (outline) which Paul had given to him. The apostle had not given such to him, but rather had given sound words or doctrines. Thus the apostle is encouraging Timothy to have "a summary or outline so as to state clearly and definitely what he did hold" (JND). "Form" (*hupotupōsis*) is a sketch or outline pattern; it is used in 1 Tim 1:16. The servants of God must not be constantly vacillating in their teaching, and such an outline would be for Timothy a model of the sound teaching which he had heard from the apostle Paul. Many have used this clause to defend the use of a creed or statement of doctrine, but such cannot be sustained as the whole of scriptural teaching is the basis of belief. "Sound" is an interesting word used in the Pastoral Epistles a number of times. The original word is the basis of our English word "hygiene" and is better translated as "health-giving". Thus the words of teaching given from Paul to Timothy were with a view to producing spiritual health. God's Word will ever produce life for the sinner and spiritual growth for the saint. "Which thou hast heard of me" emphasises to Timothy the reliability of, and apostolic authority behind, what had been said; this is alluded to later in the letter also (2:2; 3:10,14).

The clause "in faith and love" indicates the way in which the outline of sound words should be held; it should, therefore, be linked to "hold fast" or "have"; faith stresses the Godward aspect, and love the manward. The moral order of these two spiritual characteristics is most important. If the servant of the Lord is right in relation to the Lord then his affection for the saints will be right also. Truth can be held academically but Paul is asking Timothy to hold it with a right spiritual attitude. "In Christ Jesus" indicates the source rather than the subject. The fruits of union with Him are the enabling graces of faith and love. In summary, this important practical verse indicates the importance of what the child of God believes and also how that belief is held.

14 The deposit referred to here is different from that in verse 12. There it was that which Paul had committed to the Lord; here it has been put as a deposit to Timothy. It is probable that the totality of truth given to the younger servant is in view, not just his salvation. In context it would include the "sound words" of the previous verse. "Good" here is literally "beautiful" and reveals the divine value by which truth is estimated. Such is to be well guarded (*phulassō*) as in other NT contexts (Jude 3; 1 Tim 6:20; Luke 11:21; Acts 22:20).

The means by which (*dia*) the truth can be guarded is the Holy Spirit. Here is the only direct reference to the Holy Spirit in the epistle. He who commenced the work of salvation is able to keep (give power for) it in the believer. A fundamental truth is stated here concerning the Holy Spirit, "He dwelleth in us"; thus whilst in v. 12 there is assurance that the believer's deposit with God is secure because of divine power, so here the deposit given to the believer has the same potential for being kept secure, because of divine power within.

15 Asia has changed its area over the years and although we know it as a vast continent forming approximately one quarter of our globe, in the NT it is far smaller. It was not even as large as our Asia Minor, it was really Roman proconsular Asia which was a narrow province including only Mysia, Lydia and Caria excluding Phrygia (Acts 2:9; 16:6). Here it might only be describing the country of Lydia, which was the particular region where the seven churches in Asia stood. The capital was Ephesus where Paul had spent three years (Acts 20:31), the result of which caused Luke to record that "all they that were in Asia heard the word of the Lord Jesus, both Jews and Greeks" (Acts 19:10). It was here that Demetrius the silver-smith had complained that "almost throughout all Asia, this Paul hath persuaded and turned much people" (Acts 19:26). He had various friends in Asia who were solicitous of his welfare (Acts 19:31). Thus the apostle had exerted a profound spiritual influence upon the region. The sadness of Paul's comment here should be weighed against such a background. Timothy would know the detail being in Ephesus at the time of writing. "Knowest" (*oida*) is not merely to have mentally learned; Timothy knew by spiritual intuition is the force of the word. "Turned away" is the aorist tense of the verb implying a marked repudiation. It is not clear what actual event took place; some have felt it refers to the time of Paul's arrest and have conjectured that it was then that those alluded to "turned away". There could be a doctrinal basis to the statement, the turning away being not just personal, but rather a turning from the truth (Titus 1:14). In the absence of detail it is not wise to be dogmatic. Phygellus and Hermogenes were obviously known to Timothy, but are not elsewhere spoken of in Scripture; the fact that they are specifically named indicates that their defection had brought particular sorrow to the heart of God's servant.

16 The phrase "grant mercy" is nowhere else in the NT. The mercy would not seem to allude to the need of salvation as the household of Onesiphorus is mentioned in greetings at the end of the epistle (4:19). It has been seen already that mercy implies a sense of pity or a feeling of sympathy needed in days of difficulty. It can be obtained in time of need (Heb 4:16). The majority of scholars feel that the language used in these closing verses indicates that Onesiphorus was dead at the time of writing. If this was so then the desire within the apostle's heart, for the Lord to grant mercy to the household left behind in the time of sorrow, would be most suitable.

If, as some have argued, he was merely absent, then mercy would still be required in the time of parting. In light of the fact that in this letter Paul gives detail of the whereabouts of other servants of God (4:10-13), and that Onesiphorus clearly is not with Paul (v.17), nor in Ephesus, the most reasonable assumption is that he had gone to be with Christ. His name means "profit-bearer" and he had certainly lived to the character of his name in his relation to Paul. "Oft refreshed" is literally to make cool; thus when the aged apostle was in the heat of the fires of persecution he had been refreshed and this on many occasions by the same devoted servant. Such refreshment would include the visitation alluded to in the following verse and attendance to the material needs of the apostle. Refreshment was no doubt also of a spiritual nature as outlined in Philem 5-7.

"Chain" (*halusis*) means a manacle or hand-cuff, and would be a real symbol of shame and reproach. Onesiphorus is a shining example of what is spoken of in vv.8,12. He was not deterred from visiting Paul, even though he was chained to a Roman soldier twenty four hours a day. There could have been an element of danger for him in such visits, but he did it often.

17 The force of the middle participle here is "coming to Rome". Thus Onesiphorus used the occasion of being there to be of help to the servant of God. "Sought" and "found" are effective aorists emphasising the extraordinary diligence which is alluded to. It should be remembered that whilst Paul had become well known in Asia as seen earlier, he was now hidden away in a dungeon in Rome. The language employed emphasises that it was not easy to find him. Although before God he was a chosen vessel, yet in the eyes of Rome he was but a convict in prison.

18 Some have attempted to teach from this verse the unscriptural doctrine of praying for the dead. The language is but expressing the desire within the apostle's heart that there would be a full and adequate reward for Onesiphorus at the Judgment Seat of Christ. Direct approach to God in prayer is not in view. Wuest is helpful on the opening clause as follows: "The Lord grant to him to find mercy in the presence of and from the Lord in that day". Such is the thought of the preposition (*para*) used within the context. Paul's desire is for Onesiphorus to find the mercy of divine reward in the Lord's presence in the future, in addition to the joy of being with the Lord. "That day" has already been noted as describing the time of recognition and reward (see v.12).

It should be noted that "unto me" is omitted by the best manuscripts, the emphasis being placed on the amount of service rendered by Onesiphorus at Ephesus; not just to Paul but also to others and in the interests of the Lord. Timothy was best able to assess this having been with him at Ephesus. This closing statement makes clear that the service alluded to was not just toward Paul; as, if it was, then Paul would have been the best judge. Being wider and over a longer period than Paul's stay at Ephesus, then Timothy would know best.

Notes

1   Attention has often been drawn to the importance of prepositions and their use in the NT. "By" (*dia*) means "through" or "because of" and thus denotes agency. Paul is therefore showing that the will of God was the very means of his apostleship. "According to" (*kata*) as used here means "with a view to", thus teaching that the apostleship had an object in view. "In" (*en*) means "in the power of" and here indicates the source of the life spoken of. Thus in this verse there are in the prepositions used the means, object and source of Paul's apostleship.

At a time when Paul was facing death, he introduces here the first of some significant mentions of life in the epistle. Here it is "the life"; in 1:10 it is linked to immortality and in 2:10 it is viewed prospectively. The last reference is in 3:10 where it is seen practically.

2   It is commonly accepted that Timothy was saved under Paul's preaching. The use of the expressions "dearly beloved child", "my own child in the faith" (1 Tim 1:2) etc., supports this. A further passage of strong confirmation is 1 Cor 4:14-17 where the apostle speaks of the Corinthians as beloved children and in the same context makes clear that they were so because they had been "begotten" by himself through the gospel. He then refers to Timothy as a beloved child and shows that he would help them to appreciate the ways of Paul, i.e. would display the character of their common spiritual father.

3   The unique position of Jews at the commencement of this dispensation should be noted. God is the God of Israel and Paul's devotion was not merely to a righteous code of ethics as in the many religious systems of today. Judaism was God-given. On many occasions in the Acts Paul shows that his zeal from early days was to the true

God. The zeal was not furthering the purpose of God (see Phil 3:6) and the apostle makes clear that it was pursued in ignorance (1 Tim 1:13).

4   The difference between the reference to Timothy's forebears here and the apostle's in v. 3 should be noted. Personal faith is in view because both Lois and Eunice were in the good of personal salvation as distinct from the Jewish religious features referred to earlier.

10 Immortality when used of man always refers to the body and never to the soul. It conveys two main ideas in the NT
1. Deathlessness
2. Incorruption

The former (*athanasia*) denotes complete freedom from being subject to death which is, and always has been, true of God (1 Tim 6:16), and will also be of the resurrection body of the believer (1 Cor 15:53,54). W. E. Vine points out that it has a more qualitative aspect than just deathlessness (2 Cor 5:4), although that is its basic meaning. The latter (*aphtharsia*) means complete freedom from being subject to corruption, not only in relation to death, but also in the eternal resurrection state of the believer's body (1 Cor 14:42,50,53,54).

Some have attempted to teach annihilation theories from 1 Tim 4:16 on the grounds that man cannot ever have immortality because it says "who *only* hath immortality". This Scripture is however teaching that God alone has it intrinsically in an underived way in Himself. It in no way denies that He gives or communicates it to man. As has been seen, it has been brought to light through the gospel.

13 W. Rodgers points out that the Greek word which in the AV is commonly rendered "sound" signifies "to be healthy" or "healthful". He shows that it is found three times in Luke and once in 3 John, in all four cases having reference to bodily health, whereas in the Pastoral Epistles it occurs no less than eight times, in every instance having to do with spiritual and not bodily health. A careful study of these expressions in their context will richly repay the diligent reader.

14 A particular emphasis is laid in the Pastoral Epistles on the idea of matters which have been committed to Timothy and Titus by Paul. This point is extended in some of the passages where the recipients of these letters are encouraged in turn to pass on the thing committed (the charge) to others. The principle is seen in the various "pairs" who are recorded as labouring together in Scripture. Moses gave a charge to Joshua just as Paul is doing to Timothy. The indwelling presence of the Holy Spirit within the believer, alluded to here, is an important NT doctrine. The prepositions in John 14:17 and their associated tenses should be carefully studied. "He dwelleth (present tense) with you" indicates that the Holy Spirit was not at that time within the disciples but they were witnessing His ministry in the Lord Jesus; "he shall be (future tense) in you" implies that at a time future to that conversation (Pentecost onwards) the Holy Spirit would actually indwell them. For the NT believer this commences at conversion (Eph. 1:13) and is until death or the Rapture (Eph 4:13). Many other NT passages clarify this truth (1 Cor 6:19).

II. Figures Of The Man Of God (2:1-20)

1. A Son
2:1-2

v.1   "Thou therefore, my son, be strong in the grace that is in Christ Jesus.

v.2   And the things that thou hast heard of me among many witnesses, the same commit thou to faithful men, who shall be able to teach others also."

Before introducing more detailed figures throughout the chapter, the personal relationship of being Paul's child in the faith is alluded to. These opening verses describe the need to grow "in grace" (v.1) and "in knowledge" (v.2).

1 "Thou therefore" looks back to the concluding section of the previous chapter and the apostle is encouraging Timothy to be different from the defectors of Asia (v.15), and to be like Onesiphorus(vv.16-18).It is the first.of several exhortations which say "you therefore" or "but you" (v.3; 3:10; 3:4; 4:5). Ministry must have its direct application to the saints to provoke response in the lives of those who hear. This opening statement can be rendered "it is for you then to be strong". Of the seven figures used in this chapter the first and last are literal, whilst the intervening ones are metaphorical. The order of son and servant is instructive. Many attempt to serve who are not sons. Spiritual service can only be rendered on the ground of relationship. "Son" is literally "child" here (see 1:2).

The Greek verb "be strong" is in the middle voice meaning "to strengthen thyself". It is in the present tense and the imperative mood is used; thus there is a directive to be obeyed in a continuous way. The same verb is elsewhere used passively (Eph 6:10) and actively (Phil 4:13; 2 Tim 4:17). A.T. Robertson paraphrases these words as "keep on being empowered" or "keep in touch with the power". It can thus be seen that this is not a reference to the need for mere stoicism but rather an exhortation to draw upon a divinely-provided resource.

"In" (en) is probably instrumental here meaning "by means of" or "in the power of". It has been already seen from the previous chapter (v.2) that "grace" is a constant enabling stream for the believer. The resource is "in (en) Christ Jesus". The context again favours this as being instrumental thus indicating the present source from which the help can be obtained. Timothy is being taught that his needs can be met not from his own nature, but from the grace of God which is in Christ Jesus.

2 Timothy is now encouraged not only to guard the deposit which had been given, but to pass it on. The disloyalty described in chapter 1 necessitated it

being guarded but Paul's imprisonment and impending death necessitated passing it on. Four generations are spoken of in this description of the transmission of divine truth.

1. "Thou hast heard of me" (*par 'emou ēkousas*) is also used in 1:13. The preposition used (*para*) makes clear that Timothy had received the truth personally from Paul. The "things" spoken of here are wider than just the gospel (1:13), and include the truth of the first epistle as well as the variety of oral ministry he had heard. "Among" (*dia*) is an unusual preposition in such a context. It has been taken by many to mean "in the presence of" but the actual preposition could demand a more active role on the part of the witnesses. A.T. Robertson includes the idea of "supported by" many witnesses. The sentence can literally read "by the attestation of many witnesses" and may refer to the ministry of Paul supported and confirmed by the oral participation of those teachers who were so often present (Acts 20:4,7,11). Truth is not merely private and can, and should be, communicated publicly.

2. "The same commit thou" notes that the servant who communicates truth should not alter its content in the act of teaching. It should be "the same". "Commit" (*parathou*) is in the imperative mood which implies a command for Timothy to obey. There is ever the inclination for some to add to, or take away from, the truth entrusted to them. Paul himself did not do this (see 2 Cor 2:17; 4:2). Much of the intent of both of these first and second epistles is to encourage Timothy to get to know the truth (1 Tim 1:4,19; 3:15; 4:13,15; 6:20; 2 Tim 1:13-14; 2:15; 3:1,14) and then to teach it (1 Tim 1:3; 4:6,11-13; 5:7; 6:2,17; 2 Tim 2:14,25; 4:2-5).

3. "To *faithful men*" highlights two particular qualities which are essential if the truth of God is to be passed on effectively. Faithfulness and ability to teach. One without the other is insufficient for the function described. "Faithful" (*pistos*) indicates the thought of being trustworthy and reliable which is consistent with holding in good stewardship the deposit of truth which has been handed on. A consideration of 1 Cor 4:1-2 will show that stewardship and faithfulness are closely linked together. The same word is used of God (1 Cor 1:9) who is the guardian of that which we have committed (1:12).

   "Able (*hikanoi*) to teach" implies competency. Timothy was to encourage faithfulness in all the saints, but only those who were competent to teach are in view here. Not all faithful men have this ability. A consideration of Ecclesiastes (the book of the preacher) will give guidance on this matter. The closing verses of the book (Eccl 12:9-11) show the combination of both the faithfulness and ability required. All who teach must prepare and develop the ability which God has given.

4. "*Others also*" (*heteros*) can mean others of a different kind. All must be taught by the teacher and not all teaching is to equip other teachers, but to guide and instruct all the saints. Some have felt that the word used is

simply to speak of others in addition, but the former is to be preferred. preferred.

2. *A Soldier*
2:3-4

v.3   "Thou therefore endure hardness, as a good soldier of Jesus Christ.
v.4   No man that warreth entangleth himself with the affairs of this life; that he may please him who hath chosen him to be a soldier."

The picture of the christian as a soldier is used here and elsewhere in the NT to emphasise the reality and intensity of the service. The rigorous experiences of Paul in his gospel testimony are good examples of this and no doubt the apostle would have watched many a soldier during his imprisonment and thought of the spiritual lessons to be drawn.

3 Some have felt that hardship here is linked to the function of communicating truth (v.2), but "thou therefore" is more probably linked to the same phrase, and its context of being strong in v.1. To "endure hardness" (*sunkakopatheō*) is to "suffer hardship with"; it is the same word construction as 1:8 where Timothy is called upon to be a partaker of the hardship which goes with the gospel. Here the appeal is more personal and is asking Timothy to take his share of hardship along, and in fellowship, with the apostle Paul himself. Chapter 1 has made clear that Paul is suffering, and now he is calling Timothy to his side in experience, to share a common bond of fellowship in suffering. The Lord Jesus commended His disciples for their presence and fellowship with Him in the time of trial (Luke 22:28), and the same feeling is expressed by Peter (1 Pet 5:9). "As a good soldier" (*hōs kalos stratiōtēs*) is another of the apostle's ready usages of the military metaphor, having used it in 1:18 and in other epistles (1 Cor 9:7; 2 Cor 10:3-5).

4 A "man that warreth" is a soldier who is actively engaged in military service as distinct from one who is within the barracks or at home on leave. The warfare of christian service is always viewed as being active in the light of the constant opposition which abounds. "Entangleth" (*emplekō*) literally is to interweave and is only used elsewhere in 2 Pet 2:20. The term "affairs of this life" implies civilian matters as distinct from military ones. Here there is the first of a number of references in this chapter to the importance of separation from the world. Some have taught that what is emphasised here is the encouragement of Paul to Timothy to be only occupied with the work of the Lord, i.e. to be full-time. The preferable view is that it enjoins freedom from the pull of the world in all who serve the Lord. It should be noted that it is not the existence of the affairs of life that is condemned, but rather being entangled with them. Many have become entangled not necessarily by evil things; Demas (4:10) and many OT illustrations emphasise this danger.

Separation is not negative here but has in view to "please him". Elsewhere in this letter Paul four times refers to his desire to have the approval of the Lord (1:18; 2:15,21; 4:8). Continuing the metaphor, "him who hath chosen him to be a soldier" is the commanding officer who has enrolled (or enlisted) him.

3. An Athlete
   ### 2:5

   v.5   "And if a man also strive for masteries, yet is he not crowned,
              except he strive lawfully."

5 "Competes as an athlete" is one word in Greek and is found in the NT only in this verse (twice). A similar verb is used in 1 Tim 6:12, to fight or struggle. Alford renders the phrase "if any man strive in the games"; the figure appears to refer to one who would compete in the Greek national games. Our word "athlete" came into the language from the Greek word used here (athleō). In 1 Cor 9:24-27 similar ideas are presented although a different Greek word is used.

The victor's crown is in view here and the only other occurrences of the verb are Heb 2:7,9. Such a crown was won as the result of effort in the games.

To strive "lawfully" (nomimōs) is literally "according to the rules". It is used only here and in 1 Tim 1:8. Thus the devotedness of service as seen in the figure of the soldier(vv.3-4)is only part of the divine requirement; here it is the importance of acting lawfully in our service for God that is stressed. H.C.G. Moule and others have shown that to compete in the Greek games the individual must be "true born" i.e. a Greek, must be "trained", having sworn before Zeus that he has completed a ten month period of preparatory training, and then must conform to the actual regulations of the race in which he participates. Many parallels have been drawn from these historical facts. To be in the race of service the individual must be born again and must discipline himself (must lay aside every weight, Heb 12:1). The main import of the figure, however, must not be lost sight of: it is keeping the regulations. Each child of God must live and serve according to the revealed will of God. Paul shows in this letter that he has done so and also that he has served in order to gain a crown (4:8). It should be noted that the implication of the figure is that one could have actively won the race but could be disqualified and not receive the prize. The law is not in view here but rather acting lawfully.

4. An Husbandman
   ### 2:6-7

   v.6   "The husbandman that laboureth must be first partaker of the
              fruits.

> **v.7**   Consider what I say; and the Lord give thee understanding in all things.''

6 In the picture of the husbandman attention is diverted from the excitement and glamour of being in the race with its onlookers and crowning ceremony to the patient toiling farmer engaged in strenuous unobserved labour. A.T. Robertson speaks here of the "toiling tiller of the soil". The vast majority of Greek scholars believe that the emphasis is on the labour involved. "Laboureth" (*kopiaō*) is to grow weary and exhausted, to labour with wearisome effort. The husbandman is here literally a worker of the earth, the field, as in 1 Cor 3:9; 9:7.

"Must" (*dei*), "it is necessary in the nature of the case", indicates that the right of participation in the harvest belongs to him who is labouring in the field. Put a different way, the whole statement may be construed as saying: "don't by relaxing the labour lose that right". Viewed in this way the problems raised by the use of "first" (*prōton*) are not in conflict with the remainder of the verse. Deut 20:6; 28:30 should be considered in connection with this verse. The latter passage will be observed to have a background which correlates with the "keeping of the rules" just previously dealt with (v.5).

Various translators rearrange the closing statements of this verse: "must be the first to partake of the fruits" (RV); "must labour before partaking of the fruits" (JND). It is clear that the one who labours will have a share in the fruits of the harvest; it is not clear whether the future is in view, i.e. the Judgment Seat of Christ, or the present. Those who support the former have argued that all three figures of vv.3-6 have the future in view. The soldier is pleasing to the Lord in light of the day of reward; the athlete receives the future crown; therefore they reason that the husbandman will partake of the fruit then also. Against this it can be countered that the metaphor of the soldier could simply be showing the desire to be pleasing to the Lord whether now or then, as Paul does in 2 Cor 5:9. Similarly the emphasis is on the present in the figure of the athlete in v.5; he strives lawfully now and the reference to the future crown is incidental to the main argument of the verse. The principle of Deut 25:4 may well be in view, for there is no doubt that the servant's own faith is strengthened when the blessing of God is seen in his labour (Rom 1:13). Prov 20:4 has similar truth in view.

7 "Consider", to perceive with the mind, is the present active imperative of the verb used. It is thus an exhortation in the form of a command. A similar form appears in 1 Cor 10:15, "Judge ye what I say". The idea is that of pondering or reflecting so as to grasp the true meaning. Every christian should remember that while it is good to read the Scripture, it is necessary to meditate and ponder over the word to fully gain the intended benefit (Matt 13:51; 15:15-17).

"What I say" may refer only to v.6 but is more likely to cover the three preceding figures which have some common threads running through them.

The apostle has not given a full explanation of the pictures used and thus he is exhorting Timothy to muse upon them. The central clause of this verse should more accurately read "for the Lord shall give thee understanding" (RV, JND); thus there is a promise which is conditional upon obeying the opening exhortation. It is only as we meditate upon the truth of God that further understanding is given. "Understanding" is comprehension, or grasp (Col 1:9; 2:2). The principle spoken by the Lord Jesus (John 7:17) is so very true for all believers and is seen here. The comprehension promised will possibly apply not merely to knowing the meaning of the metaphors, but also to the personal application of them. It can be seen that there is in this verse the human side of responsibility — Timothy must consider — but also there is the divine aspect — the Lord would grant true comprehension. "All things" are probably qualified in the immediate context although as has been seen, broad principles are in view.

5. *Application of the Metaphors*
2:8-14

v.8   ''Remember that Jesus Christ of the seed of David was raised from the dead according to my gospel:

v.9   Wherein I suffer trouble, as an evil doer, even unto bonds; but the word of God is not bound.

v.10   Therefore I endure all things for the elect's sakes, that they may also obtain the salvation which is in Christ Jesus with eternal glory.

v.11   It is a faithful saying: For if we be dead with him, we shall also live with him:

v.12   If we suffer, we shall also reign with him: if we deny him, he will also deny us:

v.13   If we believe not, yet he abideth faithful: he cannot deny himself.

v.14   Of these things put them in remembrance, charging them before the Lord that they strive not about words to no profit, but to the subverting of the hearers.''

The figures in the earlier parts of the chapter have emphasised the importance of diligence in the adversity which the servant of God encounters. Encouragement is now given by viewing Christ risen. The apostle Paul was suffering yet looked on to the day of Kingdom rule, knowing that as his Lord had suffered and died but is now exalted so he could anticipate the day of being with Him when He reigns.

8 It is important to note that the conjunction "that" is not in the original text and should be omitted; thus the exhortation is not to recall facts about Christ but rather to remember, or keep in mind, the person Himself. "Remember" is in the present tense and is in the form of command. Having spoken in varied ways of the hardship, discipline and suffering which precedes the time of reward, the apostle now reminds Timothy that the highest example is seen in "Jesus Christ". This is the only place within the epistle where such is the order of His name. The emphasis is on Him who had been down here in the sphere of affliction, but is now exalted as Christ (Acts 2:36).

Two particular matters are here referred to in relation to our Lord: "of the seed of David" and "risen from the dead". The former relates to His humanity and kingship, the latter to His deity and Saviourhood. The Jewish nation in general was expecting their Messiah to be "out of" (*ek*) the seed of David and out of the town of Bethlehem (John 7:42). There does appear to be a connection of thought between the expression here and that used in Rom 1:3. Both passages refer to the truth of resurrection and use the same order in His name. In each the comparison of His humanity and deity is made. Perhaps it is introduced here to show that although our Lord Jesus Christ had a formal right to the throne by birth, yet it was needful for Him first to enter into death with all that was involved. Such a truth stands out in a passage and an epistle which deals with the need of suffering now in light of glory and reward to follow. He thus has a moral and official right to reign. "Risen" is a perfect passive participle which describes an action completed in the past but having present and continuing results. "From" is really "from among" and emphasises the truth of selective resurrection which is expounded more fully in 1 Cor 15. The closing clause of this verse emphasises the love and application Paul personally had towards the gospel. The same expression is used at the beginning and end of the Epistle to the Romans. In the former (Rom 2:16) it is linked to the future and in the latter (Rom 16:25) to the establishing of those who are saints. Here it is linked with the doctrinal statements which underpin the gospel. It is not without significance that the man who is seen to be suffering so much for its proclamation should so affectionately call it his own.

9 In 1:10-12 the apostle speaks of the gospel doctrinally with his responsibility to it as a preacher and immediately shows that such is the cause of his persecution and suffering. A similar structure is seen in this section. "Wherein" is "on account of" and shows that Paul's troubles with civil authorities were in no way connected to personal breaches of the law, but rather were because of his commitment to the glad tidings. In the earlier passage he endured because true values will be assessed in the coming day (1:12), but here other reasons for enduring suffering are adduced (see v.10).

"Evil doer" is "malefactor"; its only other NT uses are in Luke 23:32-33,39, which passage shows how strong the word is that the apostle uses. It should again be noted that this word is used not to denote what he was, but rather to show the extent of the trouble being imposed upon him. The punishment inflicted upon the malefactors of Luke 23 evidenced what society thought of them and Paul the apostle was regarded in the same way because of his gospel zeal. This is the "hardship" or "affliction of the gospel" of 1:8; its extent was unto bonds. The Bible history describes Paul as being bound when in the

presence of king Agrippa (Acts 26:29) and he himself refers to the same
condition during at least part of his first imprisonment (Phil 1:7,13). The
closing statements in Acts 28 have been understood by many as showing that
he was free from bonds, but this is not necessarily so. Certainly the time of
the second and final imprisonment, when this letter was written, was marked
by bonds. Reference has already been made to his chain (1:16). It is good to
note the confidence which the apostle has in the power and spread of the
word of God. He is really making clear that there is no way in which the word
of God can be restricted. This is the spirit of the OT prophet "the grass
withereth, the flower fadeth . . . but the word of our God shall stand forever"
(Isa 40:8). The implication of Paul's statement is that although he was
curtailed others would carry on with the spread of the message. The same idea
is presented in the passage in Philippians cited above (1:12). Paul saw his first
imprisonment as a means in the hand of God for the spread of the gospel.
This concept of the liberty and movement of the word of God is referred to
elsewhere when the apostle asks for prayer that the word of the Lord may
have "free course" (lit. run) and be glorified.

10 The idea of cause and effect is clearly seen in this part of the chapter. It is
not a mere comparison of suffering and endurance with the blessing that may
follow, but rather that God is using the suffering as a cause for the blessing to
result.

"Therefore" (*dia*) carries the meaning "for this cause" and the apostle is
satisfied to endure the chain and deprivation knowing that such are being
used of God to reach and bless the elect. This interpretation of these
statements is strengthened by the fact that the same preposition is again used
in "for (*dia*) the elect's sakes". The matter of election and its relation to the
preaching of the gospel has been a sad battleground down the centuries. This
verse really brings both aspects into perfect harmony. There is no doubt that
in the NT doctrine of election there is the eternal and sovereign choice of
God. Eph 1:4; 1 Pet 1:2 and many other similar verses enable the believer to
sing gladly:

> "Chosen not for good in me,
> Wakened up from wrath to flee,
> Hidden in the Saviour's side,
> By the Spirit sanctified.
> Teach me Lord on earth to show
> By my love how much I owe."

The knowledge of this great truth in no way lessened the zeal of the apostle,
nor did it hinder his many activities in preaching and spreading the message
of salvation. Paul did not know in this verse, or at any other time, who the
elect were; he simply preached and through the preaching the work of

electing grace was being accomplished. It can thus be seen that election does not ever dispense with the preaching of the gospel or with suffering for the preaching to take place. "That" (*hina*) is "in order that", thus showing that the enduring was with the object of the elect obtaining salvation. The sovereignty of God in salvation in harmony with the responsibility of the servant of God can be seen in practice in Acts 18:9-10. The Lord had revealed to Paul that he had much people in that city, i.e. not yet saved, but in the purpose of God to be saved. It was not revealed to Paul who these people were; the instruction to him was "be not afraid, but speak, and hold not thy peace". "Also" implies that the apostle is desirous that others might come into the enjoyment of what Paul already possessed. The mention of salvation here describes it as "in" Christ Jesus but "with" (*meta*) eternal glory. W.E. Vine has suggested that the idea of reward may be in the mind of the aged apostle, not only of being saved, but of receiving "a full reward" hereafter. He points out that whilst all the saved will be glorified, the following verse speaks of special rewards to be given to those who are faithful to Christ. The same expression in 1 Pet 5:10 in a similar context supports this view.

11 Here we have the fourth of five faithful sayings in the Pastoral Epistles. There are three in 1 Timothy and this is the only one in the second epistle. The concluding one is in Titus. Some suggestions have been made with regard to these sayings: some feel they were in the form of early hymns, and one writer' states that this particular hymn carries the simple title "If". Those who hold this view believe that such would be the spiritual songs of NT mention (Eph 5:19; Col 3:16), Psalms being from the OT Psalter, hymns being songs of praise *to* God, and spiritual songs *about* God and spiritual experience. It will be seen that the Book of Psalms which was Israel's hymn book contains each of these types. Others have felt that before the saints had the completed canon of Holy Scripture, these sayings would be communicated by mouth to each other as statements of doctrine and handed on in much the same manner as anticipated in 2 Tim 2:2. Whichever view is correct each saying is "faithful" i.e. trustworthy; this term (*pistos*) is found seventeen times in the Pastorals and is worthy of tracing through for spiritual profit. Bible scholars are divided as to whether the faithful saying precedes this verse or whether it commences here. On balance the latter view is favoured although the subject matter of vv.11-13 is clearly based upon the facts outlined in v.10. If this is a hymn, then it could be seen to be the martyrs' hymn and would have been a watchword of the early believers.

"Dead with him" is an aorist tense, and because of this many have concluded that this must be our judicial death with Christ as in Rom 6:8. The contexts of the two chapters, however, are entirely different. Romans 6 is clearly teaching the judicial aspect of the believer's death with Christ, but the immediate context here is concerned with physical suffering and affliction. It should also be noted that the aorist tense does not always necessarily indicate that an action has taken place in the actual past. It really views an action "as a whole". W. Hendriksen points out that the statement "for if at any time we have (or shall have) died with (Him), we shall also live with Him", is not grammatically impossible; thus, in light of the fact that grammatically it is allowable and contextually preferable, "dead with him" can be viewed as describing either martyrdom or its possibility (see 1 Cor 15:31). Paul can thus state with confidence in the balancing clause "we shall also live with him". This is precisely the truth of 2 Cor 4:10-14, where the apostle shows that he was continuously being "delivered unto death" but he knew that "he which raised up the Lord Jesus" would raise him also. To view death here judicially demands that the life alluded to be judicial also, which does not fit the context.

12 Not all of the people of God are called upon to experience the ultimate of martyrdom as described in the previous verse, but all in varying measure must suffer for the testimony of our Lord. Such is taught in this very epistle (3:12). The early disciples would not be aware of the reward for suffering taught here, yet they rejoiced that they were counted worthy to suffer shame for His name (Acts 5:41). The balancing clause "we shall also reign with him" emphasises the character of reward in the coming kingdom. The whole matter of reward as given at the Judgment Seat of Christ and manifested in the period of kingdom rule is an evidence of the grace of God. It was rich mercy indeed to deliver us from eternal doom, but the grace of God will give reward for suffering and service which could only be rendered in the power and enabling which God gives to His servants. In Rom 8:17 Paul links our present suffering with being glorified and this is in the context of being heirs. Here there is the more specific relationship to the future kingdom as in Acts 14:22 and 2 Thess 1:4-5. In the former the apostle taught young believers at Lystra, Iconium and Antioch that the kingdom is entered through much tribulation, but in the latter the apostle teaches the close link between present suffering and future kingdom glory. A careful reading of the statements in 2 Thess 1 reveals the principles of retribution and recompense; it is the latter which is in view here. A suitable illustration of this in the OT is the case of Ittai, found by comparing 2 Sam 15:21 with 2 Sam 18:2.
"Deny" in the latter part of the verse is "disown" and the sad possibility exists and has been the experience of some; Peter was a case in point. The balancing clause "he also will deny us" indicates that the blessing and reward which would have been ours for not denying Him (Rev 2:13) will be denied to us by our Lord. The words of our Lord Jesus Christ in Matt 10:32-33 whilst not covering the detail of this verse are an excellent example of the principles within it.

13 "Believe not" is better rendered "faithless" (RV) or "are unfaithful" (JND). W.E. Vine favours the former of these, explaining it not as a matter of unbelief, but a lack of fidelity. The balancing clause makes clear that irrespective of our lack of fidelity the character of God cannot change; He cannot unsay His own plighted word.

It is averred by many that the strength of this clause is that if we are faithless, He will carry out His threats, i.e. He cannot deny Himself of the execution of what He has promised.

14 This verse forms a link between the conclusion of this section and the commencement of the following one. Many see it as the opening verse of the new section. "Of these things" refers back to the preceding clauses and demonstrates the importance of the faithful saying as outlined in vv.11-13. The verb "put in remembrance" is found only here and Titus 3:1. In both contexts it emphasises the importance of verbal ministry as a means, not only of giving information, but of literally putting the particular aspects of truth into the mind of the hearer. It is in the present imperative thus indicating that this is to be his regular practice, i.e. he is to "keep on reminding them". To "charge" (testifying earnestly, JND) is to adjure or warn solemnly. Levity should never characterise a ministry which communicates the realities of divine matters to the people of God. "Before the Lord" is literally "in the sight of the Lord" and implies the importance of knowing that although our ministry is directed to men, it is "in the sight of" God, i.e. God hears and knows all that we say. The whole manner and matter of much ministry would be different if we were more conscious of being in the immediate presence of the Lord.

All ministry should be with a view to profit; one of the features of the false teacher is that he is "sick about questions and strifes of words" (1 Tim 6:4). Words are most important in the unfolding of the truth of God. Vv.11-13 have expounded an extremely important saying or word (*logos*). Paul in Gal 3:16 bases an important doctrinal argument upon the accurate use of one word "seed, not seeds" thus confirming the verbal inspiration of Holy Scripture. The striving about mere words can be most unprofitable and this is being warned against. All ministry should have spiritual substance to it, and not be just a definition of Greek words into English. Strife of any sort has a detrimental effect upon the people of God, and the result of word-fighting is here described as an "overthrow"; the word used is the root from which our English word catastrophe comes. It is used in 2 Pet 2:6 where the meaning is self-explanatory.

6. *A Workman*
2:15-18

v.15   "Study to show thyself approved unto God, a workman that needeth not to be ashamed, rightly dividing the word of truth.

v.16   But shun profane and vain babblings; for they will increase unto
        more ungodliness.
v.17   And their word will eat as doth a canker: of whom is Hymenaeus
        and Philetus;
v.18   Who concerning the truth have erred, saying that the resurrection is
        past already; and overthrow the faith of some.''

Having warned of the dangers of false teaching and squabbling over mere
words there is now given advice to Timothy as to how to be fitted to
understand the word of God and to use it to bring the approval of God and
profit to men.

15 The advice given at the commencement of this verse is not merely to
study the word of God; study is better rendered as "give diligence" (RV) or
"strive diligently" (JND). Various expositors of the Greek text have shown
that there are many ideas presented here. The concept of striving, being in
earnest, exerting oneself, may well be in contrast to those described in the
previous verse as "striving about words". The diligence alluded to can be
better understood by noting the use of the allied terms in 1 Thess 2:17
("endeavoured the more abundantly") and Gal 2:10 ("which I also was
forward to do"). See also 4:9 and 4:21. "To show thyself" means literally to
present one's self. The same expression is used in two familiar passages in the
Epistle to the Romans where its use is well known and understood (6:13,19;
12:1). In the former it is translated by our English word "yield", whilst in the
latter by the word "present". It should be noted that the tense of the verb
implies a whole-hearted act, a decision (as in the Roman epistle), yet, as W.E.
Vine has pointed out, it requires the diligence of repetition. This emphasises
the danger of regarding the aorist as always demanding a once-for-all-act
rather than seeing that in certain contexts it describes that which is complete
at a certain time.

K.S. Wuest states that the words "to God" are to be understood with the
verbal form "to present". It is therefore probable that the correct order of the
opening sentence should be: "give diligence to present thyself unto God
approved". Thus the apostle is emphasising the importance of the servant
being eager to present himself unto God as one proved trustworthy by trial.
"Approved" (*dokimos*) carries the idea of being put to the test and then
receiving the approval of the tester. It is used in James 1:12 of the man who
endures temptation and is promised that after he is tried (approved), he shall
receive the crown of life. Although there are NT contexts which teach the
importance of the servants of God being approved by the saints and by their
fellow-teachers, yet it is important to note the highest value is in presenting
one's self before God for divine approval; this is the teaching here. The noun
"workman" is not specific to any category of labourer and, although the main
emphasis is on the diligence of the labourer, it should be noted that such
eager desires demand toil and exertion. Elsewhere the same apostle speaks of

those who "labour" in the word and doctrine (1 Tim 5:17). No servant of God can earn divine approval or be of help to the saints without expending much effort. "That needeth not to be ashamed" implies that such is not put to shame by his work being unworthy. Thus, putting the early parts of the verse together, the idea is of one who has no reason for feeling shame as he is presented to God as a workman. Much has been written and said regarding the term "rightly dividing". There is no doubt that the original term according to literal meaning meant to cut; thus a multiplicity of explanations and applications have been made, the most popular being the cutting of a way or road, i.e. cutting in a straight line. Some have felt that it has agricultural connotations, i.e. ploughing a straight furrow, and therefore links with the labour of the workman. Many of the illustrations are suitable; whichever is adopted the main idea would seem to be of guiding a straight course through the Scripture. The actual word is used only here in the NT, but is found in the OT in Prov 3:6 ("direct thy paths") and 11:5 ("direct his way"). There will be no distortion of truth by such a workman. This is the opposite of those spoken of in the previous verse who engage in word battles. Later papyri have shown that this word was also used in an architectural context when the planning of a building was taking place. Each part would be set out in its right place, with the floor in its right relationship to the walls. Such use of the word shows the importance of giving to each part of the word of God its rightful setting and place, i.e. understanding the dispensational settings which are taught. The word of truth is a description here of the totality of the divinely-given revelation.

16 The positive approach has been set out in the previous verse enabling the believer to be prepared by an understanding of the word of truth. Here the apostle now turns to the negative aspect giving warning against erroneous matters in advance. "But" emphasises such a contrast and "shun" the extent of attitude which must be shown in such circumstances. The advice is to avoid or turn away from. The same word is used in Titus 3:9 in a similar context. Thus it can be seen that a proper handling of the word of God as taught in v.15 implies rejection of whatever is in conflict both with its content and meaning.

"Profane" is that which is unholy, "vain" is empty and "babblings" sounds. Empty sounds can be profitless amongst the people of God, but when they are of an unholy (profane) nature such will be most detrimental. Some have rendered the whole statement as "to irreligious and frivolous hair-splittings give a wide berth" or "avoid Godless chatter". It should be noted that this type of exhortation is made in other parts of the Pastoral Epistles and each should be viewed in its own particular context (1 Tim 4:7; 6:4,20).

The effect of unhallowed and empty babblings is described at the conclusion of this verse. To "increase" is to advance or make progress. It should be noted that this progress is not of what is said, but rather is of those

who say it. Here we are being reminded that what men say will have an effect
upon how they live. If we speak of, and enjoy, holy things then there will be
an increase in holiness, but those who speak of profanity and emptiness, as
here, are described as making progress in ungodliness. They are depicted as
advancing to the worst state of impiety, like the progress of some mortifying
disease.

17 In the previous verse the spread (increase) is seen to relate to persons, but
here the word of those persons is also seen to be spreading.

It has been seen in v.14 that too much importance can be attached to
words; yet here there is presented balancing truth of the importance of what a
man says. "Will eat" is literally "will have pasture", clearly implying the idea
of feeding upon. It is only used here and in John 10:9 where the sheep are
described as going in and out to "find pasture". "Canker" (*gangraina*) is the
word from which our English word gangrene is derived. It has the meaning of
"to gnaw or eat", and was often used by early medical writers in a general way
to describe the spread of disease. It therefore is not necessary to restrict the
idea to gangrene as we know it. The idea is of a sore eating of the flesh. Some
writers use the term cancer and from the medical point of view the description
is both fitting and accurate. In such a condition abnormal cells spread and
infiltrate and replace healthy tissue. W.E. Vine commenting on this verse has
said that they spread corruption and produce spiritual mortification and that
"their word" is not only the teaching of the errorists but their talk. He
further states that "perverse doctrines and even discussions tend to spread
their evil influences through the whole assembly".

"Of whom" must refer back to "they" of v.16 and "their" of v.17. Such a
pronoun reveals that those named are only two of a larger company of such
erroneous teachers. Of the two who are identified Hymenaeus is named in 1
Tim 1:20, but Philetus appears only here in Scripture. It has been suggested
that the former being named first was the ring-leader. Certainly he is
described in the first epistle as being under discipline having made shipwreck
concerning the faith (note the article in 1 Tim 1:19 RV). The suggestion could
be considered that here is a man who is still troubling the saints even after
assembly discipline has been imposed. Such should never be the case.

18 Reliable translators (JND and RV) insert "men" at the commencement of
this verse no doubt indicating the serious charge aimed at the two who are
named. As stated earlier the implication of the language used is that
Hymenaeus and Philetus were only the more conspicuous members of a class
of false teachers. The use of the term "who" would help to support this.

"The truth" is synonymous with "the faith" as used elsewhere (1 Tim 1:19
RV). The former is the doctrine as unadulterated and free from evil teaching
whilst the latter term describes it as a body of truth from the point of view of
what is to be believed. To "err" is to deviate and miss the mark; this is one of

the "ways away from the faith" described in the Pastoral Epistles. It is a serious matter to miss the mark in matters which are doctrinal and even more serious when this happens to those who teach the word of God. Such is in view here. Sadly many who do miss the mark doctrinally, and are teachers, have done this deliberately; it is not in ignorance (1 Tim 1:6-7). The particular error in view here concerns the truth of resurrection. This does not allude to the resurrection of Christ which obviously had taken place. The problem lay in a denial of physical resurrection as a future truth for the believer. Such teachers would attempt to give their proof from Matt 27:52 and would then teach from passages such as Col 2:12 and Rom 6:4-5 that the only aspect of resurrection which can now apply to the believer is that spiritual, mystical aspect taught in such Scriptures. Coneybeare and Howson state the following in a footnote from Tertullian: "The Gnostics taught that the resurrection was to be understood of the rising of the soul from the death of ignorance to the light of knowledge". It should be noted that Paul had written 1 Corinthians some 7-8 years earlier with a detailed treatment of the whole subject of physical resurrection in chapter 15. These teachers then were denying basic doctrine taught by the apostles and reiterated in a divinely-inspired document. The denial of physical resurrection is truly a denial of the resurrection of Christ (1 Cor 15:13) and thus implies the complete overthrow of faith. Many of the false cults of our day have taken a similar doctrinal stance on the subject of resurrection. To confuse the mystical with the tangible has proved a danger even to those who are sound evangelically. "Overthrow" is to upset. The word is used in John 2:15 when our Lord "overthrew" the tables in the temple. Here the word is used metaphorically as also in Titus 1:11 (subvert).

7. A Vessel
2:19-21

v.19   "Nevertheless the foundation of God standeth sure, having this seal, The Lord knoweth them that are his. And, Let everyone that nameth the name of Christ depart from iniquity.

v.20   But in a great house there are not only vessels of gold and of silver, but also of wood and of earth; and some to honour, and some to dishonour.

v.21   If a man therefore purge himself from these, he shall be a vessel unto honour, sanctified, and meet for the master's use, and prepared unto every good work."

In this section the believer is viewed in relation to evil teaching and teachers. To be a vessel unto honour demands separation from evil and sanctification unto the Lord.

19 "Nevertheless" is an emphatic word which connects the defection of some from the truth (vv.16-17) with the fact that the foundation standeth firm. Having described the activities of evil teachers, the apostle is now encouraging Timothy to be associated with that which is real and true. "Firm" is an adjective which is describing the foundation. It is therefore more accurate to restructure the phrase as "the firm foundation of God standeth" or "God's firm foundation standeth".

Many and varied suggestions have been made as to what foundation is in view here. Is it Christ, the apostles, the gospel, the church, the saints or even the great truth of resurrection dealt with in the preceeding context? The very fact that there is so much speculation implies the difficulty in being specific where the Scripture is not. The statement is more probably an objective one, making the point that in contrast to the speculative teachings of evil men in general, God's firm foundation standeth. It is perhaps summarised in the words of the poet "Thy truth unchanged hath ever stood". "Standeth" is a perfect participle meaning "has stood" with the present result that it stands permanently. The stability of such a foundation is demonstrated by the twofold seal alluded to. A seal in Scripture usually carries the thought of security and ownership as the words of this verse emphasise.

The divine aspect is one particular part of the seal alluded to. It gives great confidence to appreciate that the Lord knoweth them that are His (1 Cor 8:3; John 10:15). The human side of responsibility is also seen and this in turn is in two parts. To name the name of Christ is the function of our lips; to depart from iniquity is the foundation of the life. A strong connection between the statements of this verse and the events recorded in Num 16 has been shown. The language of v. 5, "the Lord will show who are his", is set against those who gather themselves against Moses and Aaron. Such is a parallel to the evil teachers of our chapter, and illustrates the one aspect of the seal. V.26 of the same chapter illustrates the other aspect of that seal: "Depart I pray you from the tents of these wicked men and touch nothing of theirs". There is another OT illustration of this verse in Jer 32 where the evidences of a purchased redemption were placed in an earthen vessel; they were two-fold, sealed and open, as we have here.

"Christ" is here more accurately "the Lord". All who name His name must depart from iniquity. Here is a clear injunction to separation not only from evil, but from those who teach it. Such passages as Isa 52:11 and 2 Cor 6:17 should be studied carefully in conjunction with this passage. It should be noted that Hymenaeus and Philetus did the opposite to the exhortation here. They named the name of the Lord but tended toward iniquity. To "depart from" is to apostatise, but here not from the faith but from the iniquity of evil teaching and teachers.

20 Many believe that in the expression "great house" there is a description of religious christendom. It should however be noted that it is "*a* great house", not "*the* great house". Many large houses in Ephesus would contain various types of vessels for many uses, and thus it is more likely that the apostle is simply using this as an illustration. The emphasis of the verse lies more in the vessel than in the house itself. Some who believe that christendom is in view state that the vessels of gold and silver illustrate the real, and the wood and earth the unreal. They further relate the vessels "unto honour" with the former and "to dishonour" with the latter.

It is wiser to view the house merely as illustrative with varying types of vessels within it. It is however important to note the closing clause of the verse. A vessel "unto honour" must refer to its state of cleanliness when viewed in light of v.21. A vessel "unto dishonour" would thus describe an unclean vessel. However great and important the house, and however valuable the material of a given vessel, it must be clean to be of value and this appears to be the main lesson being stressed, in preparation for the following verse.

21 The interpretation of this important verse must take account of the main idea being presented, which is of being clean and acceptable to the Lord under the metaphor of a vessel.

To "purge" is to "cleanse out" thoroughly; "from" is "away from" (*apo*). The same verb is used in relation to the need for moral purity of the assembly at Corinth (1 Cor 5:7). The idea is to avoid defilement and so keep one's self pure. The object of such "out-purging" is to be a vessel unto honour, i.e. clean and therefore suitable for honourable use.

The main interpretative problem in this verse lies in the meaning of "these". Various Greek scholars have pointed out that the word is a genitive plural, which could refer to persons or to what has been taught or to inanimate things. Wuest sees the term as describing men under the term "vessel to honour" and referring back to vv.16-17. He believes it is the obligation of pastors to refuse to fellowship in the work of the ministry with another pastor who is a modernist.

An overall view of the preceding context would support the fact that Paul is calling for separation not only from evil, but from evil teachers. It has been observed that the unholy babblings of v.16 are seen in the individual of v.17 and the withdrawal from iniquity of v.19 must include not only the evil taught, but the bearers of that evil. "These" is therefore a comprehensive plural including both. The perfect tense used here signifies a past action on his part of separating himself from such and his present practice of maintaining that separation.

"A vessel unto honour" is one sanctified, i.e. hallowed, set apart. This is not the positional aspect of sanctification; it is the practical out-working of such a truth. "Meet" is profitable (see 4:11; Philem 11). The evil teachers were overthrowing the faith of some, but the separated, sanctified life can be profitable for the Master's use. "Master" is *despotēs*, emphasising the absolute authority which Christ would have in the life of His servants.

"Prepared" is "equipped" for every good use which the Master would desire. It should be noted that the figure of a vessel implies the emptiness of self in addition to the cleanliness, seen in the teaching of the verse.

8. A Servant
2:22-26

v.22   "Flee also youthful lusts: but follow righteousness, faith, charity, peace, with them that call on the Lord out of a pure heart.

v.23   But foolish and unlearned questions avoid, knowing that they do gender strifes.

v.24   And the servant of the Lord must not strive; but be gentle unto all men, apt to teach, patient,

v.25   In meekness instructing those that oppose themselves; if God peradventure will give them repentance to the acknowledging of the truth;

v.26   And that they may recover themselves out of the snare of the devil, who are taken captive by him at his will."

In light of the benefits gained from a consideration of the previous figures the servant of the Lord is seen in this closing section free from both internal and external impurity, serving the Lord to the benefit of others.

22 Some feel that the intervening verses from v.16 have been a digression from the teaching of the chapter and that the writer now returns to the main stream again. Whilst it is difficult to see a real parenthesis yet there are clear links with the subject matter of v.16.

Timothy would be between 37 and 42 at the time of writing, and it is important to see that, having been warned of the errors of the mind or intellect, now he is reminded of the dangers and weakness of the flesh. It should not be forgotten that all of the servants of God are exposed to these problems and it is the means by which many have fallen. The verb "flee" is imperative, it takes the form of a command. The present tense of continuous action is used; i.e. he must keep on fleeing youthful lusts. There are situations where the believer must stand and fight, but in the matter named here the answer is to flee or fly from. Joseph is a good OT example of this very attitude. He left his garment in the hand of Potiphar's wife and fled when confronted with the temptation to the flesh (Gen 39:12). The command here is consistent with 1 Tim 6:11 and 1 Cor 6:18. "Lust" is a passionate desire, a craving; it can be good or evil depending on the context where it is described. It is used of the Holy Spirit (Gal 5:17). It has been pointed out that the youthful lusts referred to should not be restricted to the sensual aspect. Other strong desires characterise the early part of life, e.g. intolerance, self-assertion, short-temper. All impede the work of God.

The verb "follow" is also imperative and in the continuous present tense.

The apostle is thus saying "but also keep on pursuing". Positive truth is always the best antidote to the need of the believer in matters such as this. Here the apostle is applying the principle of Rom 12:21 showing in both passages that the child of God should, instead of being overcome with evil, overcome evil with good. "Righteousness" is moral rectitude, and "faith" is probably better rendered "faithfulness", the sense being fidelity or trustworthiness. "Charity" is not the word as we use it today. *Agapē* is love not merely affection. These first three are included in a similar passage in the first epistle (6:11). "Peace" is included here possibly in light of the contextual points made concerning strife in the following verses.

The concluding statement of this verse is interesting. The pursuit of these qualities is in fellowship with a particular company. Calling upon the name of the Lord is associated with salvation in Rom 10:12-14, and with assembly fellowship in 1 Cor 1:2. There is here a qualifying aspect; it is those who call upon the name of the Lord out of (*ek*) a pure heart. The false teachers alluded to earlier would call upon the name of the Lord but not out of a pure heart. We cannot decide who is a believer, "the Lord knoweth them that are his" (see v.19), but we are to associate with those who so manifest themselves; such is the teaching of this passage with its emphasis upon separation from evil teaching and teachers.

23 "But" stands in contrast to the previous verse. When we breathe the pure atmosphere of calling on the Lord, all that is corrupt and unprofitable will appear to be what it really is. "Foolish" (*mōros*, "of the nerves") carries the meaning of sluggish and dull. Our English word moron comes from it. "Unlearned" is senseless, untrained and undisciplined. "Questionings" are debates or arguments. The apostle is thus speaking of the ignorant and useless debate or controversies, which many take pleasure in. The advice is to "avoid" this, a strong verb meaning to refuse. A similar statement occurs in 1 Tim 4:7 in a like context. The whole matter of questionings, both profane and empty, is raised in many places in the Pastoral Epistles. It is worthwhile to note them and to heed the consistent advice of the apostle given to enable Timothy to have a right response. The advice of v.14 is being repeated here. The result of such worthless activity is to gender (beget) strifes or contentions. Strife is the result of carnality (1 Cor 3:3) and is one of the works of the flesh (Gal 5:20). Strife is dispute or controversy. Not all controversy is condemned in Scripture. Paul in Gal 2:11-14 is recorded as engaging in dispute but it was in defence of truth.

24 Here is the title of the closing section of the chapter. The order can be changed to "the Lord's servant" (RV). Alford shows that "and" can be rendered "but" and is a word of contrast. "Servant" is *doulos*, a bond-slave (see 2 Cor 4:5). Thus instead of being proud and boastful in attempting to use senseless words, the true child in the faith will be humble, conscious of the fact that he is a bondservant of the Lord. Such a servant must not strive. Here is likeness to our Lord Jesus Christ in servant character. Isa 42:2; 53:7; Zech 9:9; Matt 11:29; 21:5 and 1 Pet 2:21-24, all make it clear that our Lord Jesus showed true meekness and gentleness (2 Cor 10:1). Matt 11:19 uses of the Lord Jesus the very language used here. To "strive" is to fight and wrangle. "Must" conveys the idea "it is a necessity, in the nature of the case".

The positive aspects required in a servant of the Lord are now referred to. "Gentle" is used only here and in 1 Thess 2:7 where the apostle himself is seen to be gentle amongst the new believers at Thessalonica. Thus Paul is not asking Timothy to show features which he himself had not manifested. Many preachers and teachers "traffic in unfelt truth", but not Paul. "Gentle" is kind and affable in demeanour; God's servants should not be unapproachable in demeanour, nor forbidding in manner. "Unto all" emphasises how impartially this attitude should be shown.

"Apt to teach" is used only here and 1 Tim 3:2; the Greek word means skilled in teaching. P. Harding has made the extremely valid point that the teacher of the Word should not be mysterious and hard to follow.

"Patient" is a word which means bearing evil without resentment. It occurs only here in the NT. The teacher must be patient in his handling of the ills and wrongs with which he comes into contact. As there is a moral element in the rejection of truth, so this verse emphasises that there must be right attitude in the servant as he deals with such issues.

25 The way in which truth is taught is most important. Corrective ministry must be accompanied by personal meekness in the teacher. W.E. Vine has commented on meekness as follows: "the meaning of *praütēs* is not readily expressed in English for the terms meekness and mildness, commonly used, suggest weakness and pusillanimity to a greater or less extent, whereas *praütēs* does nothing of the kind . . . It must be clearly understood therefore that the meekness manifested by the Lord and commended to the believer is the fruit of power. The common assumption is that where a man is meek, it is because he cannot help himself, but the Lord was 'meek' because He had the infinite resources of God at His command" (*Expository Dictionary of NT Words*). Paul himself had written a corrective epistle to the Corinthians, but that it was stained with his tears is clear from 2 Cor 2:4. These examples reveal that spiritual forbearance does not in any way require abstention from truly faithful teaching. The following Scriptures will give examples of these matters: 1 Cor 4:21; 2 Cor 10:1; Gal 5:23; 6:1; Eph 4:2; Col 3:12; Jas 3:13; 1 Pet 3:15. "Instructing" is better rendered "correcting". It is helpfully seen contextually in Titus 2:12, where it is rendered "teaching", and is used to show that the reason for the instruction given is to produce a reversal of behaviour. Such is the object of its use here. "Those that oppose themselves" is a phrase found only here in the NT. Literally it means they place themselves in opposition, and can refer both to the false teachers and to those who have been influenced by them.

It is clear that the apostle Paul rested upon the sovereignty of God as much in respect of his teaching ministry as in his gospel preaching. God alone can give repentance and this is the force of the statement used here. The servant of God should be as gentle with the saints in his ministry as he is with sinners in his gospel preaching, and be equally dependent upon God for the result. Repentance is a change of mind which will result in a change of behaviour; it should not be confused with sorrow. A careful consideration of 2 Cor 7:9-10 reveals that the saints at Corinth were not only sorry but their sorrow was unto repentance. The contexts, both there and here, make clear that repentance is not restricted to the unsaved. The teacher of the word of God should be ministering truth with a view to a change in the people of God.

"To" (*eis*) shows what the repentance has in view — the acknowledgment of the truth — thus emphasising the link between what is intellectual and what is moral. "Acknowledging" (*epignōsis*) implies full knowledge; it stresses the need there is for those who are in such opposition to have a fuller knowledge than they presently possess. The expression "acknowledging (full knowledge) of the truth" is peculiar to the Pastoral Epistles.

26 This closing verse of the chapter has difficulties both textual and interpretative. It is therefore important to approach it carefully and without dogmatism.

"They" must refer to "them" of the previous verse, thus the teaching is describing what happens to those in whom God has wrought repentance.

"To recover" is "to awake up"; it has been described as a restoration to soberness or a return to the senses. The picture is of one who has been caught in a trap or snare whilst mentally intoxicated, a fitting metaphor when seen in the context of repentance in the previous verse. A return to awareness enables the mental aspect of repentance to take place. "Out of" (*ek*) implies escape and "the snare of the devil" the means of captivity; "of the devil" is a subjective genitive meaning the snare which the devil had set for them. Putting these expressions together it will be seen that reception of error produces a state of insensibility to the will of God, recovery from which is of God through the instrumentality of the teacher in his corrective ministry.

The closing statement has been a battleground for expositors over the years. Taking the AV at its face value it appears that the captivity imposed is by the devil and is at his will. Some expositors adopt this view, believing that the pronouns him and his both refer to the devil. Others believe that the two pronouns, being different in Greek, refer to different persons. The RV supports this by rendering the clause "having been taken captive by the Lord's servant unto the will of God". W.E. Vine, commenting on the Revised rendering, says: "this rendering is in part an interpretation instead of a translation; there is no mention of the Lord's servant in the original, which reads as follows: 'and that they may recover themselves out of the snare of the devil (having been taken captive by him) unto his will'; the *him* in the parenthetic clause refers to the devil. Recovery from the captivity is recovery to the will of God. The pronoun in the original used for 'his' clearly points back to God. The phrase in the RV 'by the Lord's servant' is inserted to make sense, but it does not represent the meaning". Mr Vine thus elucidates the view that "him" refers to the devil and "his" refers to God. However, H.C.G. Moule and G. King along with other expositors have shown that no rule of Greek grammer is violated if both pronouns in the verse are made to relate to the one person. Taking all into account and in light of the preceding context this appears to be the preferable view. Moule paraphrases the verse as follows: "and that they may wake up and escape out of the devil's trap, held willing captives henceforth by Him who sets them free to do His will, the will of God". Thus the apostle is teaching that the blessed position which follows repentance is the willing captivity of those who now desire to do the will of God.

Notes

2   Two Greek words are used in the NT which mean another. *Heteros* is another of a different kind and *allos* another of the same kind. They are best illustrated from Gal 1:6-7: "another (*heteros*) gospel: which is not another (*allos*)". Such a statement in English appears most confusing, but the difficulty disappears when the true meaning of the words is understood. A fuller treatment of this can be found in *Synonyms of the New Testament* by R.C. Trench.

3-6 The three figures linked in this part of the chapter have been helpfully commented on by W. Rodgers. He suggests that they should be viewed as "one full-length picture" and sees allusion in them to the three-fold enemy of the world, flesh and the devil. They should also be considered in light of the same figures used in 1 Cor 9:7,25.

5   Two particular Greek words are translated in English as "crown": *diadēma* and *stephanos*. The former denotes the kingly crown worn by emperors and kings. The *stephanos* is the victor's crown awarded to those who were successful in the games.

8   The order of the names of our Lord Jesus Christ as used in the NT epistles is significant. The emphasis is usually upon the name used first; thus when it is Jesus Christ, the main thought is of the Man down here who came from the presence of God into the world. When the order is reversed to Christ Jesus, the emphasis is on the One who is now exalted in heaven as Lord and Christ, but was once here amongst men. The latter expression is unique to the writings of the apostle Paul who unlike the other apostles met the Lord Jesus in the period after His ascension. The others met Him and were commissioned by Him whilst He was still on earth.

18   In the NT "faith" is spoken of in two main ways: subjectively in a general way where the act or attitude of believing is in view, i.e. "our faith"; objectively when it signifies what is believed, i.e. "the faith", the latter requiring the definite article. The late

William Rodgers showed that Paul, in the Pastoral Epistles, speaks of "various ways away from the faith". He was speaking of deviations referred to, from the body of doctrine which has been once delivered to the saints (Jude 3). The following Scriptures from 1 Timothy should be noted in this connection:

1:19-20	Shipwreck	affecting private life
4:1	Departing from	affecting assembly life
5:8	Denying	affecting home life
5:11-15	Casting off	affecting social life
6:9-10	Led astray from	affecting business life
6:21	Missed the mark	affecting intellectual life

20 The term religious christendom refers to the large sphere of christian profession. It includes not only the real, but also the false. The parables of Matt 13 unfold stages of this sphere and there are clear references to it in these Pastoral letters. Some of its features will be seen in ch.3.

III. Future of the Man of God (3:1-17)

1. *The Future and Its Features*
3:1-5

v.1   "This know also, that in the last days perilous times shall come.
v.2   For men shall be lovers of their own selves, covetous, boasters, proud, blasphemers, disobedient to parents, unthankful, unholy,
v.3   Without natural affection, trucebreakers, false accusers, incontinent, fierce, despisers of those that are good,
v.4   Traitors, heady, highminded, lovers of pleasures more than lovers of God;
v.5   Having a form of godliness, but denying the power thereof; from such turn away."

In this section reference is made to nineteen particular features which will characterise the last days, the presence of which will cause those days to be difficult in the extreme. A cursory glance at these features will reveal the presence of many of the characteristics which mark our own day. The change in the apostle's tone here should be noted. In the preceding chapter there is to be a patient teaching, but after depicting scenes of advanced evil the advice is to "turn away". Here then is a description of christendom with its form of godliness.

1 "This know" emphasises that opposition is not a passing situation but rather a permanent characteristic which will be most marked in the last days. Although the detailed personal future is not made known to the believer, yet it is good to know that many warnings are given to enable the child of God to be prepared when the days of problem come. The Lord Jesus did this for the disciples (John 16:1) so that when the persecution broke they would not be stumbled. The same expression is used by the apostle elsewhere (1 Cor 11:3; Phil 1:12). "This" is a demonstrative pronoun pointing to the facts in vv.2-5, and "know" (*ginōskō*) implies that Timothy was to learn these important facts. Some have traced the term "last days" through the Scripture beginning with Gen 49:1 and have attempted to prove that each reference refers to the same period. Each must be looked at in its own context and even the OT references will be seen to refer to different periods or times. The expression should be distinguished from "latter times" (1 Tim 4:1) which refers to times later than when Paul was writing. "Last days" are characteristic of the ministry of "second" epistles and point on to the closing part of the present dispensational period.

Some expositors teach that the term "last days" refers to the whole of the present dispensation because of the advice given to Timothy, "from such turn away" (v.5). They further support their view from Heb 1:2 where the same expression clearly refers to the present age from its inception. Against this it should be noted that in our verse "shall come" is clearly future tense. The advice to Timothy in v.5 will be considered in more detail later, but it does not necessarily argue for all the features mentioned in vv.2-5 being present when Paul wrote. The use of the term in Heb 1 is in contrast to "time past" in v.1 and has no real connection with the expression as used here.

"Perilous" is difficult, grievous or hard. The same word is used of the demoniac in Matt 8:28 where it is translated "dangerous"; these are the only two occurrences of it in the NT and there may be significance that satanic control and influence is in evidence in both passages. "Times" (*kairos*) is a word which describes not so much the length of the period alluded to, but rather its characteristics.

2 "Men" is generic here and refers to mankind generally without distinction of sex. "Shall be" in its use of the future tense again shows that, whilst the seeds of such behaviour were present when Paul was writing, the progress of christendom as a system would produce in full bloom the features later outlined. Nineteen characteristic features are now named and an interesting comparison can be made with Rom 1:29-31. There very similar features are seen in Roman heathendom before salvation changed the lives of many of them. Here they are predicted as characterising religious christendom at the end of the age. We thus can see in the one the moral depths to which heathendom had sunk, and in the other a similar condition as the culmination of organised religion without God.

Various attempts have been made to demonstrate a particular order and arrangement of these nineteen features. No real pattern is obvious but it is not without significance that the list begins with "lovers of self" and concludes with "not lovers of God". Four of the words in the list have the

Greek prefix *phil* (love). Where the affections are placed or misplaced is always a reliable index of the state of those concerned.

"Lovers of self" occurs only here in the NT. Trench illustrates this Greek expression from the hedgehog rolling into a ball thus keeping the wool within for itself and the spikes outside for others. Paul had previously taught that "love seeketh not her own" (1 Cor 13:5). "Covetous" is literally "lovers of money"; it is used only here and in Luke 16:14, but the corresponding noun occurs in 1 Tim 6:10, where it is described as being a root of every kind of evil. It is fitting to view the progress of decline here: after "lovers of self" is covetousness, the root or basis of all the evil which is to be described as the list unfolds. There is no doubt that one of the great evils of christendom is materialism.

"Boasters" and "proud" describe a further element in the self-centred attitude of the "last days". The former with its gestures and words is linked to the external whilst the latter is associated with the feelings and the thought life. A "boaster" is a braggart, an empty pretender; the noun occurs again only in Rom 1:30. "Proud" is haughty and disdainful. It is to consider others beneath oneself; this may be socially, materially or in the realm of natural endowment. The apostle is thus speaking of those who have an exaggerated opinion of self and who look down on others.

A "blasphemer" is a railer, one who hurls abuse at others, an evil-speaker or slanderer (see 1 Tim 1:13). "Disobedient to parents" reveals the degeneration in family life which will be seen in the last days. Disobedience is a characteristic of the unregenerate (Titus 1:16; 3:3). Our Lord Jesus Christ was subject to His parents (Luke 2:51), and such is required of those who would please the Lord (Eph 6:1; Col 3:20).

"Unthankful" describes the ingratitude that results from taking everything for granted; it may possibly refer primarily to children within the family, but has a general application to all. Its only NT occurrences are here and in Luke 6:35. The spirit of the last days is evidently: "I have a right to everything I want, and will thank no person for it". "Unholy" embraces irreverence, pollution and irreligion.

3 Natural affection between the mother and her offspring is a basic instinct even in the animal creation; it is cited in the OT (Isa 49:15) as a very high example of affection and relationship.

"Without natural affection", used only here and in Rom 1:31, carries the idea of being heartless and is the opposite to the exhortation given by Paul the apostle to the saints at Rome (Rom 12:10).

"Trucebreaker" is better rendered "implacable"; it denotes one who cannot bring himself to terms with other people and will not consider others. It is only here in the NT. It describes the relentless unyielding character of men in the last days. How different from the exhortation of Paul to the Philippian believers: "Let your moderation (yieldingness) be known unto all men" (Phil

4:5). "False-accusers" are "slanderers"; the word is literally "devils" (*diaboloi*). The devil is the false-accuser and his character is impressed on the perilous times described. The literal meaning of the related verb is to pick holes in others.

"Incontinent" indicates a complete lack of self-control, profligacy; the adjective occurs only here in the NT but the noun is found in Matt 23:25 and 1 Cor 7:5; unrestrained lust is implied. It too is a feature of the closing days of this dispensation. "Fierce" is savage and untamed, again only here in the NT. It describes the merciless nature of unregenerate man and is the opposite of gentle.

"Despisers of those that are good" refers to those who can recognise good but hate it and are strangers to it. This is the opposite to the character of the overseer detailed in Titus 1:8 and to the advice given in Phil 4:8.

4 "Traitors" draws particular attention to the *treachery* involved, the *readiness* to betray. Judas is described as "the traitor" in Luke 6:16 using the same word. In Acts 7:52 Stephen refers to those of his audience as being "betrayers" of the just One. Such a characteristic would no doubt be seen in the betrayal of believers in days of persecution. The prefix *pro* (in preference to) exposes their selfish ends.

"Heady" (lit."falling forward")is found only here and in Acts 19:36(where it is translated "rashly") in the NT but occurs in LXX in Prov 10:14; 13:3, where the calamitous outcome is stressed. It means to be reckless, to stop at nothing, to be thoughtless in word and deed. The exhortation by James is quite different (1:19): "be slow to speak, slow to wrath". This word implies the rash and precipitate action of the ungodly. "Highminded" is puffed up and swollen with conceit. It is also found in 1 Tim 3:6 ("lifted up with pride") and 6:4 ("proud"). These passages should be read carefully to see the use made of this term within the respective contexts. The literal idea behind the original word is to be filled or enveloped with smoke with a consequent clouding of the mind and judgment. Wuest has pointed out that it is a perfect participle, meaning one who in the past has come to a state of such pride and is so puffed up that his mind as a permanent result is beclouded and besotted by it. Our modern description of being "swollen headed" is an apt equivalent of the word used.

The closing statement of this verse is an appropriate climax to the description of the days being predicted which are in fact the days in which we live. The result of being "lovers of self" and "lovers of money" is seen to develop through the evils just described to its culmination in the love of pleasure. "More than" should read "rather than"; thus the emphasis is not that there is *some* love for God, albeit exceeded by love of pleasure, but rather that there is none at all. The expression is exactly as in John 3:19: "Men loved darkness *rather than* light". A similar example is in 1 Tim 1:4. The expression "lovers of pleasure" is unique in Scripture. It depicts a life lived in pursuit of selfish aims with the claims of God ignored.

5 Here we find a scriptural definition of what is often described as christendom: "a form of godliness but denying the power thereof". Such began to be prevalent within a few centuries of apostolic times. A paganised form of christianity or, perhaps rather, a christianised form of paganism, became prominent throughout the sphere in which the christian faith had spread. W.E. Vine states that in medieval times the reformation restored a measure of purity but did not prevent a revival of the evil. There has been the continued presence of a mixture of christian profession with elements of paganism. The spread of christendom was forecast by our Lord Jesus Christ in the illustrative parables of Matt 13. "Having (holding) a form of godliness" expresses the idea of maintaining an outward appearance of religion. The same principle is alluded to in Titus 1:16: "They profess that they know God, but in works they deny Him . . .". "Form" (*morphōsis*) refers to an external outline (see its use in Rom 2:20). The original root related to "shape", thus there is being described the outward shape or form without the reality (see Matt 23:25; Isa 1:14-17).

"Denying" is literally "having denied". The idea is that they have renounced or repudiated "the power thereof" — a reference to the Holy Spirit. The form is empty, devoid of the true power, present within and available to the true believer. There is no doubt that there is a power energising christendom; it is from Satan, but the power alluded to here is that which would be present if there was reality instead of mere form. 1 Cor 4:20 should be compared with this statement. The power of the Holy Spirit has a living and renewing influence over the heart and life, thus enabling the believer to be free from the practices outlined in vv.2-5.

"From such" implies that, although a strong predictive element has permeated this section thus far, the characteristics outlined would be evident in measure even in Timothy's day. It should not be implied from this fact that the exhortation is to Timothy alone; it is also to those who would face the features fully-developed.

"Turn away" is a present imperative in the middle voice meaning "constantly turn thyself away from". This is a command to keep clear of such people, to avoid them. The true people of God should not be in the midst of christendom but must obey the command given here. It should be remembered that denominationalism of any sort is part of religious christendom.

2. The Future and Its Folly
3:6-9

v.6　　"For of this sort are they which creep into houses, and lead captive silly women laden with sins, led away with divers lusts,

v.7　　Ever learning, and never able to come to the knowledge of the truth.

> v.8   Now as Jannes and Jambres withstood Moses, so do these also
>   resist the truth; men of corrupt minds, reprobate concerning the
>   faith.
> v.9   But they shall proceed no further; for their folly shall be manifest
>   unto all men, as theirs also was.''

Having outlined specific evil characteristics which mark "last day" conditions, the apostle now applies specific aspects of such evil seen in men and the methods they use. These evil teachers are illustrated by similar men who withstood Moses in his day, but who, by their folly, were finally manifested as to what they really were.

6 "Of this sort" (*ek toutōn*) is literally "out of these" meaning out from the group of evil-doers spoken of in vv.2-5.

"Are they" means "there are certain". These opening words of the verse are very instructive regarding the matter of religious christendom. It is clear that these teachers who visit homes to ply people with their doctrines are out from those who have only the form of godliness. The methods of such teachers should be noted. "Creep into" is used of a person clothing himself with a garment, i.e. he insinuates himself into it. The idea is "to worm oneself into". "Crept in unawares" (Jude 4) is a good parallel; see also Gal 2:4 ("unawares brought in"). An interesting link has been noted between Gen 3 and this verse: the serpent and his subtle activity can be seen in the verb "creep into", and Eve, tempted and taken as a moral captive, in the "silly women" spoken of here. Certainly these teachers would worm their way into homes to achieve their evil designs. It has become evident that this is precisely the method used by many of the false cults of our day. "Lead captive" is a present active participle (2 Cor 10:5; Rom 7:23). It connotes the influence acquired by those who are described by Alford as "sneaking proselytisers". The term implies "to gain control over".

"Silly women" is a term which could be easily misunderstood: "silly" here does not mean lack of intelligence but rather lack of stability. The verse is not implying that all women are devoid of such stability; a diminutive form is used which some have translated as "little" women, others "weak-minded" women and others as "womanlings", i.e. those who, being without discretion in the moral or doctrinal sphere, lack the qualities which characterise true womanhood. "Laden" is from a verb meaning to heap up, only elsewhere in the NT in Rom 12:20 ("heap coals of fire on his head"). The thought appears to be that such teachers would find,on their visits to houses, some who would have a conscience with the sense of sin and therefore open to the insidious attacks of wrong doctrine. There is no doubt that in our day many false-cult teachers have been more active in visiting homes than christians have been. Many a person has been contacted who would have been ready to receive the gospel message but the false teacher has led them into the captivity referred to. To be "led away" is to be swayed ("away" is superfluous), here by all kinds of lusts, i.e. evil desires. Within the context lust is not so much moral as doctrinal, although so often the one influences the other aspect of life. The evil desires therefore are more likely to be desires of the spirit rather than of the flesh. It can thus be seen that doctrinal seduction is in view in this verse. It has also been stated that here are those who work shadily but the true believer will not "walk in craftiness": his life and manner of service will be open and transparent (John 3:20; 18:20; Acts 26:26).

7 "Ever learning" endorses the interpretation that being led away with various lusts in the preceding verse refers to desires of the spirit and not of the flesh. The thought is of those who are easily captivated by new-fangled notions and as the result have been led into ungodly practices. There are those who are eager to listen sympathetically to anything which is presented to them, and such are being described here. The Athenians and other strangers spent all their time in either telling or hearing of some new thing (Acts 17:21). It is good to learn, but learning should produce a knowledge and understanding of what has been imparted; it is not so in the case spoken of here. "Never able" highlights the cause of this inability: they have not submitted to the truth. A.T. Robertson has described such people as being hypnotised and priding themselves in belonging to the intelligentsia. There is a great danger of being overtly proud of knowledge, and of learning just for the sake of learning. It will be seen from the following verse that the false teachers *resist* the truth, but here we see that their followers have not sufficient discernment to *understand* it. "Knowledge" (*epignōsis*) is full knowledge. The word used refers to precise and correct experiential knowledge, i.e. it has caused the heart and life to submit to it. The evil exposed in the teachers referred to in our passage can be seen in principle amongst the people of God. Instead of the simple acceptance of divine truth, there are those who read *into* Scripture, so that they can elicit views which suit natural opinion. Then, by their persuasive language and presentation, they beguile the minds of those who have read superficially, but have not patiently and reverently studied the word of God.

8 "Now as" can be rendered "in which manner"; thus the apostle now turns to an OT illustration to show that Satan has ever produced counterfeit men in an attempt to emulate that which is of God and to ensnare the hearers of God's Word. Jannes and Jambres are not named in the OT but here are identified as those who withstood Moses. Various scholars have pointed out that their names occur frequently in late Jewish, pagan and early christian literature. They are reputed to have been the two leading magicians of Egypt who took the major part in the events recorded in Exod 7 and 8. The apostle Paul would be well-acquainted with such facts having a strong Jewish background and having been educated in the school of Gamaliel (Acts 22:3). They opposed Moses by counteracting the signs which he had wrought by the

power of God (Exod 7:11,22). "Withstood" is literally "stood against"; it is used of Elymas the sorceror (Acts 13:8) when he opposed Paul and Barnabas in their testimony on the island of Cyprus. W. Hendricksen states that the names Jannes and Jambres probably mean in Aramaic "he who seduces" and "he who makes rebellious". If such be true there is a clear significance to the names given. The fact that they were magicians is of interest to the context of 2 Timothy. The power of Satan and his evil hosts have been referred to in the first epistle (1 Tim 4:1), and Ephesus, where Timothy was living, had a history associated with the powers of evil. The story of the sons of Sceva, and the power behind Diana of the Ephesians are included in the account of Paul's time in Ephesus in Acts 19. It should also be noted that the demonic power of evil has always been evident in times of great crisis in human history. The following periods should be considered in respect of this: before the flood, Israel's coming out of Egypt, the early days in Canaan, Christ's life on earth, and now the "last days". "So do these" emphasises the strong link between the activity of Jannes and Jambres and that of the false teachers of the closing days of the dispensation of grace. "Resist the truth", says Paul, for as Moses found he had satanically-controlled opponents, so Paul found the same and predicted that such would be present to oppose the truth of God. "Men of corrupt minds" is more accurately "men corrupted in mind". W.E. Vine points out that it is not an adjective as in the AV and therefore not merely a condition but rather the effect of yielding the heart to evil powers. See also 2 Cor 11:3 ("lest your minds should be corrupted") and 1 Tim 6:5 ("men of corrupt minds"). Here it should be seen that the apostle is again drawing attention, not only to what these men were teaching and doing, but also to what sort of men they were in themselves. Uncleanness in man's mind will produce uncleanness in his teaching.

"Reprobate", disapproved, carries the idea of being rejected after testing. There is a contrast between the workman of 2:15 who is to present himself unto God approved, and the teachers who are described here as being worthless, having been put to the test. They are therefore not to be trusted to teach. The same word is in 1 Cor 9:27 where again it carries the idea of being rejected. The article before "faith" should be noted here; these men are disapproved concerning the body of teaching, that is they are judged in light of what they teach and are found wanting.

9 The opening statement of this verse appears to be a contradiction of 2:16 and also appears to be in conflict with 3:13. It should, however, be read in light of the preceding verse; although Jannes and Jambres did emulate Moses to a certain extent, there was a limit beyond which there was no evil power available to them to continue to imitate the power of God. When they cast down their rods which became serpents, even as the rod of Aaron had, yet the rod of Aaron swallowed up their rods (Exod 7:12). Then although they were allowed to emulate some of the divine power that followed yet they

could not bring forth lice as the Lord had through Aaron (Exod 8:18), and when the plague of boils was given these very men were themselves afflicted (Exod 9:11). God was thus showing that there is always a limit to satanic power. Now the apostle is teaching that just as there was a limit beyond which those in the OT could not go, so it is in the case of these leaders also. Ch. 2:16 is simply showing that to continue in profitless babblings will only allow an increase unto ungodliness, and 3:13 that the evil teachers continue on through the dispensation in which we presently live. The real attempt and purpose of such teachers is to deceive the very "elect" (Mark 13:22), but this will not be. As 2:17-18 is followed by v.19, so here is taught that "their folly" shall be "manifest". "Folly" is a want of sense and is illustrated in Luke 6:11 ("madness"). Thus whilst men of the world may be captivated by the spell of evil teaching, to the true child of God it will be evident that there is utter folly in what is being propounded. "Manifest" is "evident with exposure"; "unto all" does not refer to the world ("men" in the AV is italicised) but to the people of God. The closing phrase emphasises again that the interpretation of this verse must be made in light of the OT illustration used. The structure should really be "as theirs also came to be", thus showing that the true character eventually was shown as it really was.

3. The Future and Fidelity
3:10-13

v.10   ''But thou hast fully known my doctrine, manner of life, purpose, faith, longsuffering, charity, patience,

v.11   Persecutions, afflictions, which came upon me at Antioch, at Iconium, at Lystra; what persecutions I endured; but out of them all the Lord delivered me.

v.12   Yea, and all that will live godly in Christ Jesus shall suffer persecution.

v.13   But evil men and seducers shall wax worse and worse, deceiving, and being deceived.''

Having dwelt upon the darkest of matters in the early part of this chapter, the apostle now turns to a ministry of encouragement to Timothy by reminding him of the example he had seen when with Paul, and this in spite of the fact that there was a price to be paid for such fidelity.

10 The pronoun "thou" is emphatic thus emphasising a clear contrast to the false teachers of the previous verse. In the AV "hast fully known" implies that Timothy knew of the facts stated by mental comprehension only. Many translators do emphasise, however, that the expression used is "to follow closely". It is found in Luke 1:3 ("having had perfect understanding") and 1 Tim 4:6 ("thou hast attained"), making three mentions in all. The term can bear the meaning of so following as to be always at the side of one who is the pattern, and to conform wholly to his example. The problem with this

model/follower view is that of making it fit consistently with the statements
in the next verse, because some of the experiences spoken of would almost
certainly have taken place before Timothy's conversion. Taking the
expression to mean a simple mental knowledge of all the things described
solves this problem, but leaves the difficulty of the more probable meaning of
the actual expression. It is more likely that the answer lies in a combination of
the two ideas. It is quite possible that Paul's courage in suffering for his
preaching had first spoken to Timothy, just as Stephen's courage must have
been a voice from God to Paul (Acts 7:58; 8:1). Timothy had followed Paul in
the character of his life of service involving suffering and persecution, and
thus "knew" in an experimental way all that is described here. Paul is thus
looking over his whole life of service, beginning with his first missionary
journey, right up to being in a dungeon in Rome, and, in an objective sense,
could see in Timothy a likeness to himself.

Paul was not one of the "boasters" of v.2, but like Samuel he is able to
recount the faithfulness of God in his life of service (1 Sam 12:3-5). It would be
a means of encouragement to Timothy for his future pathway to be reminded
that in all circumstances Christ is true.

The order of the nine features which follow does not appear to have marked
significance, although it can be seen that each one becomes the spring of the
following one. "Doctrine" is really "teaching" and it is clear that what the
apostle had taught was seen in his "manner of life". Often our conduct is not
consistent with what we teach, but Paul, in this respect, was like his Master.
"Purpose" marked the apostle just as Barnabas had exhorted the new
christians at Antioch (Acts 11:23), and "faith" (fidelity) expressed such
purpose. Loyalty should ever be seen in God's people. Faith is not only an
initial spiritual exercise; a study of Paul's interest in the development of faith
in the Thessalonians would illustrate this. "Longsuffering" is the quality of
self-restraint when faced with provocation. It is the opposite of anger.
"Charity" (*agapē*) is that divine love which is produced in the heart of the
yielded believer by the Holy Spirit. How different from the love of self and of
money and of pleasure attributed to the false teachers (vv. 2-5). "Patience" is
more accurately rendered "endurance". It is to endure whilst under pressure
and is that quality which does not surrender to circumstances, or succumb
under trial. It is the opposite of despondency.

11 The word "persecution" comes from the verb "to pursue". There is no
doubt that the man, who had himself at one time pursued those who
belonged to Christ, was often pursued by the enemies of the gospel. An
example of such pursuit with malignity is in Acts 17, where Paul and Silas,
having been troubled by the Jews of Thessalonica because of their gospel
testimony, travelled on to Berea. V.13 records that when these same Jews
heard that Paul was preaching at Berea, "they came thither also", i.e. they
pursued the preachers with the intention of stirring up the people against

them. Here the apostle shows that not only was he persecuted, but that it issued in suffering ("afflictions"). There are many NT passages which give detail of the numerous sufferings Paul experienced as a servant of God. The apostle now singles out circumstances which would be well-known to Timothy, even though he had not necessarily been present in all the incidents which had taken place. "Which came unto me" is literally "what things befell me", i.e. they were actual experiences through which the apostle had passed. It is Pisidian Antioch which is referred to and the record of the visit is in Acts 13:14-50. This was early in Paul's first (so-called) missionary journey. In addition to Timothy being acquainted with such places, another reason why he alludes to Antioch may be that it is the first place, after Paul's commendation to preach among the heathen, where there is a record of opposition to the preachers and the preaching (Acts 13:45,50). It is of interest to note that after such gospel preaching with power as is recorded in Acts 13, the preachers were expelled "out of their coasts". No doubt Timothy would have heard of this.

It is not always appreciated that many of the journeys of Paul and his fellow-servants are passed over with little or no comment. The distance between Antioch and Iconium is approximately 80 miles, which, in the absence of modern transport and with the difficulties of terrain and climate, must have been arduous. The record of the visit to Iconium is brief but most eventful (Acts 13:51-14:5). It was there that the minds of the Gentiles were poisoned against the preachers by the unbelieving Jews and as a result they passed through severe and bitter experiences.

Although Lystra is often linked with Derbe in the NT (Acts 14:6; 16:2), yet it is not so here, probably because there is no record of persecution at Derbe, the reason for naming these places being to remind Timothy of the presecutions to be faced. Lystra is approximately 20 miles from Iconium and was quite possibly Timothy's native city (Acts 16:1-2). Timothy probably first heard Paul preach the gospel there (Acts 14:7), and may also have witnessed the cure of the cripple and the restraint by Paul and Barnabas of the people who wanted to sacrifice to them as to gods (14:18). It was at Lystra that those same people stoned Paul, leaving him for dead (v.19). The endurance of v.10 is now seen effectively in Paul, as "what persecutions I endured" shows.

As the aged apostle reviews these experiences, he can assert the goodness and faithfulness of God. "Out of them all" indicates that however severe each persecution and affliction, it had not been able to hold him. It is also important to note that the deliverance is not "from" (apo) but "out of" (ek). God could keep His servants from difficulties if He so desired, but there is divine purpose in them all. For "the Lord delivered me", see Ps 34:19.

12 The writer of this epistle had learned at the outset of his christian life that he was to suffer for the Lord's name (Acts 9:16). Here he is teaching that this is not peculiar to himself. It should be noted that it is not all christians who are spoken of here, but all who would live godly. "Will" is more accurately "would", thus the apostle is not speaking merely of desire but rather of a determined and constant exercise of the will. The matter of the pious, godly or devout life occurs and recurs in the Pastoral Epistles. This is a piety which is characterised by a Godward attitude and does that which is well-pleasing to Him. Piety is not sanctimoniousness; it cannot be exercised except in communion with Christ. It can thus be seen that the consistency of our life in Christ must necessarily always be opposed by the world. The devil can afford to ignore worldly christians, but faithfulness to the Lord draws the hostility of the foe. Piety is in itself not sufficient, it must be in Christ Jesus.

"Shall suffer persecution" indicates that such is the pathway of the godly. It is preparation in advance (Mark 10:30; Acts 14:22; John 15:20; 16:1-4; 1 Thess 3:4).

13 The opening sentence of this verse emphasises the contrast between the two classes which are in view in vv.12,13. It should be also noted that there is an emphatic objective statement regarding each of the groups (note the future tense "shall" both in the preceding verse and again here).

The expression "evil men and seducers" does not describe two classes of evil men but rather gives a two-fold description of the same men. The evil aspect of their character is described in vv.2-5 whilst the seductive aspect is outlined in vv.6-9. Evil denotes that which causes labour, pain and sorrow, and is malignant. The apostle is showing that such would continue throughout the whole period with an increasing development of wickedness. "Seducers" (impostors) are literally wailers, howlers, jugglers and enchanters. A connection of thought can be understood with the earlier references to the magicians of Egypt. Putting both of the terms together it can be seen that in the "last days" there will be men who characteristically are evil, and who are bent on deceiving the people of God.

"Shall wax worse and worse" or "from bad to worse" is literally "shall advance towards the worse". It is only here in the NT. "Wax" is an old English verb meaning to increase but sadly the increase is in the wrong direction. "Advance" (*prokoptō*) is literally to cut forward, suggestive of the pioneer hacking his way through the undergrowth. It is used beautifully of the increase of the Lord Jesus (Luke 2:52); here and in 2:16; 3:9 its implications are fearful. The reference then, is not to their success as evil teachers but rather to the personal deterioration in them, both intellectually and morally. Thus while the godly suffer throughout the day of grace, the evil deteriorate more and more. The Psalmist pondered the mystery of the godly suffering whilst evil men and their deeds continued to progress (Ps 73). It was only when he went into the sanctuary of God, where he could view it from the divine perspective, that he realised that the end is more important than the course (v.17).

"Deceiving" is "leading astray". Those who deceive others, in so doing, impair their own sense of distinction between truth and falsehood, they thus weaken their power of resistance to self-deceit. The principle of retribution is seen in this description in that those who deceive others are themselves enticed into darker types of evil; they become victims and not leaders. In Titus 3:3 the apostle reminds Titus that one mark of the unregenerate is that they are deceived. When we are saved we have the Spirit of God and are brought into a sphere of enlightenment. How solemn to view this divinely-given picture of the future of christendom and its leaders.

4. *The Future and Being Furnished*
3:14-17

v.14   "But continue thou in the things which thou hast learned and hast been assured of, knowing of whom thou hast learned them;

v.15   And that from a child thou hast known the holy scriptures, which are able to make thee wise unto salvation through faith which is in Christ Jesus.

v.16   All scripture is given by inspiration of God, and is profitable for doctrine, for reproof, for correction, for instruction in righteousness;

v.17   That the man of God may be perfect, throughly furnished unto all good works."

Although this chapter has looked on into the future with many aspects which would bring fears and apprehension to Timothy, there is now the reminder of the importance of remaining true to that which is worthy of our confidence. The unchanging value of the word of God will fit the man of God for every need.

14 As v.10 began with the use of an emphatic pronoun, so it is here. In the original text, "but continue thou" really begins with an emphatic "thou", thus distinguishing Timothy from the people which have been described in the preceding verse. "Continue" is the present imperative of the verb to abide or to remain, thus the exhortation is not for Timothy to hold on to the truth of God, but rather to continue in it, i.e. to let it hold him.

As the evil increases, the man of God can take courage from the fact that the truth remains constant and is unchanging in its character. Although there would be so much knowledge falsely so called, Timothy can cling to the faith which he had been taught, and which he had carried with deep conviction.

The doctrines based upon the holy Scriptures, which are later referred to, are "the things" spoken of here. "Which thou hast learned and hast been assured of" emphasises that Timothy had not just mentally imbibed the statements of the word of God, but there had been a change wrought. "Assured of" implies the idea that Timothy was fully persuaded of the truth of them; he had become convinced. This statement is found only here in the

NT. Two particular reasons are given for the reliability of the doctrinal ground upon which Timothy stood; firstly because of who had taught it; and secondly because of what it consisted of.

"Knowing of whom thou hast learned them" makes clear the importance of the trustworthy character of those who had communicated the truth to Timothy. Just as the character of the evil teachers described earlier in the chapter gave meaning to their teaching, so does the moral worth and weight of those who teach the truth of God. It should also be noted that "whom" is important and not where. Rome makes much of the Church being the interpreter of truth, but such is not supported here. Many of the best manuscripts give "whom" as being plural, although the Received Text, supported by Newberry, presents it as being singular. As scholarship is divided, the contextual arguments should be considered. Those who support the singular do so because they feel that Paul is referring to himself in vv. 10 and 11 ("my", "me", "I") and has used himself as an example to Timothy in earlier parts of the epistle (1:13; 2:2). They also believe that as two reasons are being given for reliability, then v.14 must logically refer to Paul so that Eunice and Lois can be seen separately in v.15.

Against these arguments it should be noted that the apostle is not doubling up from vv. 10, 11 but rather summarising the reasons why what he had learned is reliable: because of who are involved in v.14 (i.e. the persons) and because of what is involved in v.15 (i.e. the holy Scriptures). It is therefore best to view "whom" here as being plural, which would include Lois and Eunice (1:5) and Paul (2:2; 3:10); these, and possibly others, had exerted a moral and spiritual influence in the life of Timothy.

15 Timothy had the great benefit of being taught the truths of holy Scripture from infancy. "Child" here is "new-born babe" or "infant" (*brephos*); the same word is used even of the unborn child (Luke 1:41-44) and of the very young babe (Luke 2:12,16). It was customary for all Jewish children to be taught the Scripture and to commit parts of it to their memory.

The "holy Scriptures" are literally the "sacred writings". Strictly it can refer here only to the OT, because none of the NT documents would have been available to those who had reared Timothy. The term is only here in the NT. The fact that these writings are described as "holy" is most important. It is "holy" as in 1 Cor 9:13, where those who functioned in the OT sanctuary are spoken of as dealing with things which were sacred or holy. The word *hieros* means that which is consecrated, as given and devoted to God. The word of God is set apart from all other writings; it is sacred. "Scripture" is from the Latin word *scriptura* meaning anything written. The Greek word used here (*grammata*) comes from the same root as our English word grammar. The literal meaning is "alphabet letters". Some have made the interesting suggestion that Timothy, as an infant, may even have learned to read by tracing out the actual letters of Scripture. This is speculative, but there are people in our day who were illiterate before salvation, and who learned to read in this way. It should be remembered that the example of those who reared Timothy should be emulated by all, and that children should be taught the sacred writings of the word of God from their earliest days. Lois and Eunice served God within the home which is the God-appointed sphere of service for our sisters (1 Tim 5:14).

This verse declares the sufficiency of the OT to lead a soul to Christ for salvation. When teaching the word of God, we are not attempting merely to impart knowledge, but rather to put within the mind of the hearer that which can bring divine life.

"Are able" is a present participle of the verb which expresses the abiding power and sufficiency of Scripture. The teachings of holy Scripture are able to impart wisdom to the human mind. The psalmist makes reference to this aspect in various Psalms (Ps 19:7; 119:98) but here we learn in "wise unto salvation" that the divinely-imparted wisdom is in preparation for salvation. The Scripture had disciplined Timothy in obedience to God and pointed forward to the coming Messiah. Another NT example of this is seen in the Ethiopian eunuch who was reading the OT in his chariot and became wise unto salvation which he gained when Philip preached to him. "Unto" (eis) should therefore be allowed its full significance and understood as "towards the attainment of". The God-appointed means by which men and women gain possession of salvation is "through (dia) faith". Faith is thus the instrument which brings us to the One who can save. "In Christ Jesus" makes clear who is the object of such faith. We must not underestimate faith, but neither must we overestimate it. It is not faith that saves, but it is faith which links us to the only One who can save. "Christ Jesus" emphasises the glorified Man in heaven in whom salvation is found.

16 Although the chapter and verse numberings of our Bible are not inspired, it is of interest to note that this is one of the references chapter 3 verse 16 of Scripture. Malachi, John, 1 Timothy and here are all outstanding verses worthy of careful attention. This and 2 Pet 1:21 are two of the greatest NT verses on the inspiration of Scripture. The latter indicates something of how the inspiration took place, whilst here the fact of inspiration is stated.

Although there are parts of this verse which have been hotly contested by varying expositors, most are agreed that "all" is more accurately rendered "every". The term "Scripture" has been commented on in the previous verse. Here the word used is *graphē* which means "a writing"; it comes into our language in autograph, paragraph and like words (see also Matt 26:54,56). "Every scripture" is referring not just to the whole, but is a reference to each separate passage of the whole of Scripture. In v.15 the OT is in view but clearly a more expanded description of Scripture is presented here. "Every scripture" would include the NT writings also. 2 Pet 3:2 links together the "words" of the OT prophets with those of the NT apostles, and vv. 15-16 of the same chapter include the writings of Paul with "the other scriptures". The apostle Paul asks that his letters be read publicly in various assemblies (Col 4:16; 1 Thess 5:27) and calls his message "the word of God" (1 Thess 2:13). 1 Tim 5:18 is a very significant verse in this respect, where the apostle links the OT with the words of our Lord using the one expression "Scripture" to bring them both together (see Deut 25:4 and Luke 10:7). The AV has been strongly challenged in the opening sentence of this verse and variant renderings have been given by differing scholars. The RV will suffice to give the main difference proposed as follows: "Every scripture inspired of God is also profitable". In the original the Greek sentence has no main verb; it is therefore allowable from a grammatical point of view to insert the verb "is" after, rather than before, the adjective "God-inspired" and so translate as the RV. The main argument against this, however, is that it does not do justice to the little word "and" (*kai*) which comes between the two adjectives "God-inspired" and "profitable". This "and" would suggest that the apostle is stating two facts about Scripture: 1. it is inspired and 2. it is profitable. It would therefore be preferable to retain the AV rendering. It will be seen that the RV construction could be construed as throwing doubt on the inspiration of parts of Scripture. Those who support the change, and yet believe in the full inspiration of Scripture, argue that there is no evidence in the context that the inspiration of Scripture was being questioned, and emphasise that the whole passage is directed to the usefulness of Scripture in fitting the believer for service (see later note on this discussion).

"Inspired of God" is literally "God-breathed", an expression used only here in the NT although the idea is in many other passages. It does not convey the idea that the authors were breathed into by God, but rather that the actual Scripture was breathed out by God; it was brought into being by the very breath of God. This great truth of inspiration does not destroy the individuality of the different writers. A consideration of 2 Pet 1:21 is helpful in this matter. The divine origin of holy Scripture explains why it is profitable. F.F. Bruce in his *Expanded Paraphrase* says "Every part of those writings is divinely inspired and useful for teaching the truth".

"Doctrine" is a very general word describing both the act and content of teaching. It envisages the impartation of knowledge (1 Tim 5:17) and the subject of all teaching should be the word of God. "Reproof" has its root in a verb meaning to rebuke and bring conviction (Titus 1:9); sections of the Epistle to the Galatians would be a good example of such scriptural teaching. "Correction" literally means the setting right of that which is wrong or restoration to an upright position. "Instruction" conveys the idea of training; the word used originally meant the rearing of a child. All believers need to be trained in righteousness and this must be by the application of the word of God. W.E. Vine states that the righteousness here not only characterises the instruction, but is also the condition of uprightness before God, which is the effect of the instruction.

17 Although Timothy is the only one in the NT who is termed "man of God", yet it can be applied generally to every true follower of Christ. A consideration of those so designated in the OT will show men raised up by God to face particular circumstances; here such are viewed against the backcloth of "last days". To be "perfect" is to be complete and mature; this can only be gained through the effect of the word of God. "Throughly furnished" is a perfect participle meaning "fitted out", envisaging the completion of the fitting out process and the abiding readiness of the vessel thus "furnished". The same verb is in Acts 21:5 where it is rendered "had accomplished". Nothing else is needed if the man of God has been fully equipped in this way; he will be competent to meet all exigencies.

Notes

8 W. Hendricksen makes some interesting suggestions regarding Jannes and Jambres showing that just as they opposed Moses as God's representative, so were the licentious leaders opposing the truth of God as revealed in His Word and as proclaimed by Paul, Timothy etc. He states further possibilities as follows:
"1. Jannes and Jambres were deceivers; so are the purveyors of strange doctrine against whom Paul warns Timothy.
2. If Jewish tradition can be credited in this respect Jannes and Jambres became proselytes, faking conversion, to the Jewish religion. When they saw that they could not prevent Israel's exodus from Egypt, they are said to have joined the departing multitude. Later (according to the Jewish tradition!) they were the ones who induced the people to make a golden calf and to worship it. They were pretenders, therefore; hypocrites, and as such very dangerous. Similarly the false leaders whom Paul describes are all the more dangerous because they pretend to be genuine converts to the christian religion".

15 W. Hendriksen has stated concerning Jewish education that: "The devout Israelite taught his children because Jehovah commanded him to do so. And he instructed them with respect to the *verba et gesta dei* (words and deeds of God), as recorded in the sacred Writings. This is evident throughout the OT (Gen 18:19; Exod 10:2; 12:26,27; 13:14-16; Deut 4:9 and many other passages). In Israel, God-centred education was begun when the child was still very young (1 Sam 1:27,28; 2:11,18, 19); the purpose of beginning early is expressed beautifully in the words of Prov 22:6: 'Train up a child in the way he should go (literally according to his way) and even when he is old he will not depart from it'."

16 W. Hoste comments on the RV "Every scripture inspired of God is also profitable" as follows: "Does it mean 'being inspired of God' "? If so, it is a somewhat feebler edition of the AV, and the passage need not have been meddled with at all; or it may mean, 'if inspired of God' which does question the inspiration of Scripture, and it is in this sense that most readers understand the words. . . . If it be maintained that the antithesis is between human writing and the divine oracles, the reply is that the word translated, 'Scripture' (*graphe*), in its NT usage only refers to the Scriptures in their technical sense as equivalent to our Bible. The word occurs in 50 other places, e.g. Matt 21:42; 22:29; 26:54 etc., and always thus. Only twice is a descriptive adjective attached (Rom 1:2; 16:26), so familiar is the term. Thus the RV is as though it read 'every part of the Bible, if inspired of God, is also profitable'! Dean Alford states that he supports the RV construction 'hesitatingly I confess'."

iv. Faithfulness of the man of God (4:1-22)

1. *Faithfulness Toward the Wayward*
4:1-5

v.1 ''I charge thee therefore before God, and the Lord Jesus Christ, who shall judge the quick and the dead at his appearing and his kingdom;

v.2 Preach the word; be instant in season, out of season; reprove, rebuke, exhort with all long-suffering and doctrine.

v.3 For the time will come when they will not endure sound doctrine; but after their own lusts shall they heap to themselves teachers, having itching ears;

v.4 And they shall turn away their ears from the truth, and shall be turned into fables.

v.5 But watch thou in all things, endure afflictions, do the work of an evangelist, make full proof of thy ministry.''

Although dark days are predicted and although there will be much opposition to the man of God, he must remain faithful. Having been equipped as seen at the close of chapter3, now he can live before the wayward, and preach the word although many will not endure the sound doctrine he will present.

1 Reference has been made to this epistle being the last from the pen of the apostle Paul, and in this section we have the final advice and warnings given. The "charge" spoken of here is the last of three which all have a similar form but with a differing emphasis. Each is stated to be given "before" (in the sight of) God and Christ Jesus. The apostle is conscious of the fact that he is to pass on from the sphere of tesimony, and in view of the impending declension, this emphatic closing charge is given to Timothy.

The verb "I charge" is intensive and carries the meaning of charging with all solemnity. It is similar to 2:14 where the idea is to testify earnestly. In pagan Greek the word was applied to call the gods and men to witness to a certain fact. It carried the weight of a legal affirmation, "I adjure thee". The best manuscripts omit "therefore", although there is no doubt that a clear link exists between the preceding verses at the end of ch. 3 and these statements. The word of God has been spoken of in some detail and now the advice is to "preach" it.

"Before" is "in the sight of" or "in the presence of", and the construction of the Greek sentence demands that "God" and "Christ Jesus" refer to the same person. It should be noted that "Lord" is not in the best manuscripts. The phrase, then, can read "our God, even Christ Jesus"; here then is an indirect testimony to the truth of the deity of Christ.

The Greek word for "shall" can be rendered "about to" or "on the point of doing it" and this is the sense here. The Lord Jesus indicated that all judgment has been committed to the Son (John 5:22) and reference is made here to this. The root from which "judge" comes is the same from which we derive our English words critic and criteria. An entirely different word is used of the Judgment Seat of Christ, when the assessment of the believer's service will take place. The point being made appears to be that the apostle is adjuring Timothy in the sight of the One who is the appointed judge and discerner of all. Both living and dead are to be discerned in judgment, but it must not be taken that such judgment will all take place at the same time. A general objective statement is being made. It is also important to note that "at" is omitted by the best manuscripts; "and" should be inserted instead. Making these adjustments to the verse as it appears in the AV, it will be seen that the judgment is in no way identified with a time or with the events named. The charge then really has two bases:

1.   In the sight of the One who will judge the living and the dead
2.   And his (or by his) appearing and kingdom.

The term "appearing" (*epiphaneia*)must be interpreted within its context. It does not refer to the same event each time it is used (see 1:10). Here it is linked to the coming kingdom and points on to the day when our Lord Jesus returns to earth to be manifested in His glory; the word is used like this in 1 Tim 6:14 The second basis for the appeal is important; the apostle is charging Timothy to behave, in the most difficult of conditions, in light of the fact that Christ, who is now set aside by men, will return in power and great glory. The appearing and kingdom introduce the truths of responsibility and reward; ch. 2 has already made allusion to this (vv. 11-12) and although the reward will be given at the Judgment Seat of Christ which is prior to the appearing, yet the public display of such reward will be in kingdom conditions. The anticipation of this would spur Timothy to respond to the requests of the following verse.

2 One of the NT words translated "preach" refers to conversation, but the term employed here describes public proclamation. It was used of the imperial herald, spokesman of the emperor in Roman times. In our own history the parallel would be the town official or crier making a public announcement.

The message made known by such men would be formal and authoritative and often would contain a summary command to be obeyed. It should be remembered that such public heralds would not themselves have formulated their message; as they were expected simply to communicate the message given to them, so Timothy must preach the Word, not his own opinions but God's authoritative message. "The word" has been taken by some to refer specifically to the message of the gospel, but in light of the earlier references in the epistle it should be seen as describing the whole body of revealed truth: he is to hold it (1:13); he is to rightly divide it (2:15); it is to be the guide and instructor (3:15-16), and now he is to preach it. The use of this term to Timothy regarding "last days" would remind us that preaching is the divinely-given means of communicating the truth of God in this dispensation.

To be "instant" is to stand by, to be at hand, "to seize every opportunity without paying regard to the prejudice or wishes of others, where these would be in conflict to what had been committed by the Lord" (W.E. Vine). The exhortation then is to be in constant readiness to preach the Word. This readiness is further amplified in the following statement which has been freely rendered "in all sorts of seasons". "In season" is only here and in Mark 14:11 where it is given as "conveniently" the idea is of an opportune time.

"Out of season" is only here in the NT; it conveys the thought of times which might be inopportune. The apostle himself had preached when the occasions were easy, but also when they were difficult. He had shown that there was no "closed season" for preaching and had taken every opportunity which was open to him.

Of the five imperatives found in this verse, which are all in the aorist tense, the closing three describe aspects of the preaching alluded to. To "reprove" is to "bring to proof"; the same word is used in John 16:8 of bringing demonstration to the world. It is correction which results in conviction of sin or the confession of the guilt. Here we are reminded that the preacher must deal, in his preaching, with sin in both saved and unsaved. To "rebuke" is to censor and admonish; thus after the reproof has exposed the guilt, the rebuke makes clear how wrong the individual was in doing such things and chides him accordingly. Its use in Luke 17:3 could be studied with profit. Exhortation is always an important aspect of preaching. It means to comfort, and encourage people to put the wrongs right and to be strong in faith. It has been shown that these three are addressed to reason, conscience and the will respectively. The manner in which all preaching should be given is taught here. It must be ever with self-restraint, not in the spirit of irritability or indignation. A comparison with 2:24-25 will help here.

"Doctrine" is "teaching" or "instruction", thus showing that the preacher must be diligent in applying the teaching of Scripture for every need. Without this, reproof can be defeated by controversy (see 2:24-25).

3 By an interesting play on words, attention is drawn to one of the "out of season" times spoken of in the previous verse. The phrase literally is "there shall be a time". It has already been seen that so many parts of this epistle are pointing to the development of religious christendom as it is seen today and "they" refers to the many of the professing christian world.

To "endure" is to hold oneself upright or firm against a thing; the implication of such a term in the present context has been described as a refusal to measure up to the truth of God. Paul in the Pastoral Epistles frequently uses the expression "sound doctrine", which describes the teaching given as being healthful and health-giving. Good basic scriptural teaching will be wholesome and helpful to the people of God. In the original text "sound doctrine" is preceded by the definite article; thus the system of teaching is in view. Many today are rejecting what they describe as parts of the "Pauline theology"; they will not put up with, or listen to, the sound teaching and so they fulfil the prediction in this verse.

"After" (*kata*) is "according to" or "after the course of". "Lusts" are "cravings" or "their own desires"; thus those spoken of have no wish to be subject to the revealed will of God, but only to fulfil what they themselves desire. To this end they "heap", i.e. gather to themselves, the sort of teachers they wish to hear. It can be seen that they refuse what they need and will then receive only what they want. The true child of God has often found that the teacher they least wish to hear has brought to them the message they needed most. The "itching ears" belong to the people described, not to the teachers. The expression refers to the idea of a scratching or tickling of the ear which is desired by the hearer for mere gratification. The Greeks at Athens in Acts 17 were happy to hear "some new thing" and hardly had the latest novelty been toyed with, than it was cast aside and a newer one sought. Much of this is seen in the changing philosophies taught in religious christendom in our day. W.E. Vine makes the important point that many congregations in christendom choose their own minister; such was predicted by Paul to Timothy.

4 To "turn away" is to avert; the strength of the expression used is not merely to turn away from the truth, but to have one's ears always in such a position that they will never come into contact with the truth. "Turn away" is in the active voice; it is thus a conscious and wilful action by the ones who are spoken of. When a person averts his ears from the truth, he denies himself the opportunity of hearing the voice of God, lays himself open to every satanic influence and can therefore be easily turned aside to error. This is illustrated by those spoken of in 2 Thess 2:10-11.

The "truth" spoken of here is the subject matter of the preaching of vv. 1-2 and is synonymous with the "sound doctrine" of v. 3. Although "turn away" is in the active voice, "shall be turned" is in the passive voice, indicating that they are now acted upon by an outside force; thus those who themselves turned their ears from the truth fall under the influence of the myths and fables propounded by evil teacher. Here then are those who prefer fiction to the truth. The root meaning of the verb "shall be turned" is "to turn or twist out" as in the dislocation of a joint. A "fable" is fiction as opposed to fact. Religious christendom has its many fictitious accounts of the activities of those who have been canonised as saints. How accurate was the prediction of the "last days".

5 The opening phrase is literally "but as for you", and is viewing Timothy in contrast to those described in the two previous verses. A very similar construction is found twice previously, in 3:10, 14. To "watch" is literally to be sober; it is in the present active imperative, as in 1 Thess 5:6-8, and can be accurately rendered "but be thou sober in thy head". The word used relates to freedom from the influence of intoxicants; here in context it is describing being free from the credulity and excitability associated with imbibing novel ideas which have no basis in the truth (1 Thess 5:6-8; 1 Pet 1:13; 4:7; 5:8). It is to be wide awake keeping oneself controlled doctrinally. One has put it, "steer clear of the heady wine of heretical teaching".

To endure afflictions is to suffer hardship as in 1:9 and 2:9. It is again imperative, given in the form of a sharp command. The emphasis being not so much on physical hardship only, but the context implies that Timothy would suffer hardship even for his ministry, i.e. for teaching the truth. In times of departure from the truth of God, those who would remain faithful will suffer for it. In the OT, Jeremiah and others experienced the same. The meaning of "evangelist" is one who announces glad tidings; the word occurs only three times in the NT. In Acts 21:8 it is used of Philip who is the only person named as such; then in Eph 4:11 it is enumerated as one of the gifts given to the body by the ascended Head. Here is the other reference; it should be noted that there is no definite article before it, therefore Paul is referring to the character of the work rather than stating that Timothy possessed the like gift as Philip. The import of the statement is, let your work be evangelistic in character. It is quite wrong to assert that God has vested all the gifts in one man; thus there were apostles as distinct from prophets, and teachers as distinct from evangelists. The nature of Timothy's gift is not referred to explicitly, although he was to care for the people of God and to teach them the truth of God. Here then we learn that all of God's servants should remember the importance of evangelism and do the work of such as God enables. Timothy had accompanied Paul both in his gospel preaching and teaching ministries and knew exactly what the apostle implied in such an exhortation.

The closing expression is with a view to Timothy filling up every aspect of his ministry so that nothing was left undone. The verb used is very similar to that written to Archippus (Col 4:17), who was to complete the work God had given him to do. If Timothy would apply all that Paul had taught in the Pastoral Epistles then he would fill his ministry full and perform a complete and effective service to the Lord.

2. Faithfulness Toward the Lord
4:6-8

v.6 "For I am now ready to be offered, and the time of my departure is at hand,

v.7 I have fought a good fight, I have finished my course, I have kept the faith;

v.8 Henceforth there is laid up for me a crown of righteousness, which the Lord, the righteous judge, shall give me at that day; and not to me only, but unto all them also that love his appearing."

Here the apostle opens his heart to reveal his personal feelings concerning the pathway of service he has already traversed. He looks on beyond the impending time of departure and knows that, having been faithful to his Lord, there is the prospect of the coming crown.

6 In the Greek text, "I" is emphatic, meaning "as for myself", in contradistinction to Timothy and others. A literal transliteration could be: "as for myself, I am already being offered". Thus, having given detailed instruction to Timothy who was still in the pathway of active service, he now speaks of himself at the end of such a path. What the apostle was suffering presently in the dungeon at Rome marked the onset of the end in his life of service. Paul's life was a sacrificial offering to God because, having lived in the good of his own ministry, he had presented his body as a living sacrifice (Rom 6:13; 12:1).

In the ceremonies of pagan worship this Greek word for "offered" was used to refer to the libation poured out to the gods. It is clear, however, that the apostle had more than this in mind because of the well-known "drink-offering (libation)" of the OT economy (Exod 29:38-4; Lev. 23:13; Num 15:10; 28:7, 14). In the Scriptures referred to, it will be seen that the drink offering was poured out on the lamb of burnt-offering sacrifice just before it was burnt on the altar. In Phil 2:17 the apostle makes the only other NT reference to the drink-offering where he views himself willing, if necessary, to count his own death as a drink offering poured out upon the greater burnt-offering sacrifice and service of the faith of the Philippian saints. Such was his spiritual desire and humility. Here such is no longer a future possibility but rather a present continuing fact: "I am already being offered (poured out)". The statements which follow support the fact that this figure is used to speak of the impending final outpouring. The difference beween the Philippian passage and this may be that he thought of his life of sacrifice as the burnt-offering, and his final suffering and death as the drink offering.

At the time of writing, the apostle had been before Nero for the preliminary hearing (v. 16) and was now awaiting the final one; he clearly knew that death would follow, thus he speaks of the time of his departure. The English word "analyse" comes from the same Greek root as the word translated "departure". Like the kindred verb in Phil 1:23, it denotes a setting free or the undoing of a connection. It has been variously considered as a military or a nautical term. The former suggests the taking down of tents and striking camp, the latter the raising of the anchor to enable the ship to sail away. Both figures adequately describe the though being conveyed. Peter uses the tent metaphor (2 Pet 1:13) as does Paul elsewhere (2 Cor 5:1). "At hand" can read "has arrived".

7 In the previous verse, the *end* of the pathway of service has been illustrated by the use of metaphors; here the *course* of that same pathway is summed up in three clauses involving further metaphors. Two main views have been expressed regarding the metaphors used:
1.   that the guardian;
2.   that all three clauses
refer to the one figure, the athlete.

The latter view argues that the three clauses within the verse can each be applied to the athlete, and indeed that such use is made of them in other NT Scriptures. If this point of view is adopted, the verse could be read: "I have competed well in the athletic contest (of life), I have finished the race, I have kept the rules".

More general favour is given to the assertion that three distinct figures are intended,and, on balance,this appears to fit best the teaching of the epistle, It should be noted that in the original, the object in each of the three sentences is placed before the verb indicating that the emphasis is not on the pronoun "I" as it appears to be in the AV. The verse should be then: "the good fight I have fought, my course I have finished, the faith I have kept". As the apostle looks over the past he has no regrets to express; he had sought to be faithful to the Lord. The perfect tense is used to describe each of the three activities as complete in the past with present results.

The boxer, or wrestler, is a favourite figure with Paul (1 Cor 9:25; Col 1:29; Phil 1:27-30) and he had encouraged Timothy by using it before (1 Tim 1:18; 6:12). The service of God had required the effort of striving for the apostle. "Good" is not so much moral here but aesthetic. Alford has paraphrased it as "I have strived the good strife", and Coneybeare and Howson as "I have completed the glorious contest". Paul did not speak in terms of "toiling on" but rather of being privileged to engage in such a noble contest. The "course" (*dromos*) refers to the athletic race. It should be remembered that the apostle had spoken in a similar vein to the Ephesian elders some years before (Acts 20:24). There, looking forward, he desired to finish his course with joy. Here he looks back having realised this very high spiritual ambition. The perfect tense emphasises that he really felt that he had crossed the finishing line, i.e. his life-work was complete.

Some feel that the apostle, in closing, is stating that he has kept faith with his master, but it is more likely that reference is being made to his having guarded well the deposit which had been entrusted to him. There has been previous reference to a deposit entrusted (1 Tim 1:19; 6:20; 2 Tim 1:14). "The faith" refers to the body of truth; it is described in various ways in different passages. "Kept" incorporates the idea of guarding; certainly the apostle had defended the faith against the attacks of gnostics, Judaisers, philosophers etc. Thus he could say, "I have been loyal to my trust".

8 There is an interesting parallel between the two deposits in ch. 1 ("committed unto him", v.12; "committed unto thee", v.14) and the deposits now mentioned. In v.7 Paul has kept a deposit, and now he refers to something "laid up" for him.
"Henceforth" is literally "what remains"; thus the apostle is saying, "all that now remains is for me to receive my reward". Wuest views it as the athlete looking up at the judge's stand awaiting the laurel wrath of victory. "Laid up" is reserved (Col 1:5); Luke uses the same verb (19:20) of the money kept in the napkin. The "crown" is the victor's crown worn at the games (*stephanos*); it was usually a garland of oak or ivy leaves. It is referred to in 1 Cor 9:25; part of the thought is that it is unfading. The apostle had kept the rules and now looked on to the crown (see 2:5). The definite article should be inserted before crown, thus "the crown", suggesting the assurance of receiving it. "Of righteousness" can be viewed either as an appositional genitive meaning a crown consisting of righteousness (see Gal 5:5) or the genitive of source meaning a crown justly bestowed upon the righteous. There is good reason for accepting either, although the former is probably more fitting in light of the fact that *stephanos* is the victor's crown, and reward for service is in view. Both ideas really blend in that here we have a crown of righteousness which is the due reward of righteousness. The Lord is "the righteous judge"; the idea of the just umpire who makes no mistakes is no doubt in contrast to the unrighteous judge before whom Paul had already stood (v.16), before whom he would shortly stand again, and by whose sentence he would be condemned. Paul knew that at the Judgment Seat of Christ no partiality would mark the One who would assess his service. "Shall give" is the future tense of a verb meaning render an award.
"That day" looks on to the time of reward and recognition (see 1:12). Even in the time of his greatest stress, the apostle is thinking of others; thus he includes "all them also that love his appearing". Moule renders the phrase as follows: "Aye, and not only to me, but also to all who have set their love on his appearing". "Love" is *agapaō* and is in the perfect tense; it is a love called out of the heart because of the preciousness of the object loved. The sense is those who shall be found to have loved, and are still loving his appearing.

To love it is to look forward to it with earnest joy. Prophetic terms must be interpreted within both the immediate and general epistle context. Here the appearing refers to the public manifestation of Christ when He returns to earth. He will then become visible. The crown will be awarded in "that day", i.e. the Judgment Seat of Christ, and it is given to those who have looked, and are looking, beyond "that day" to the very appearing of Christ in glory.

3. *Faithfulness Toward his Fellow Servants*
4:9-16

v.9   "Do thy diligence to come shortly unto me:

v.10   For Demas hath forsaken me, having loved this present world, and is departed unto Thessalonica, Crescens to Galatia, Titus unto Dalmatia.

v.11   Only Luke is with me. Take Mark, and bring him with thee: for he is profitable to me for the ministry.

v.12   And Tychicus have I sent to Ephesus.

v.13   The cloak that I left at Troas with Carpus, when thou comest, bring with thee, and the books, but especially the parchments.

v.14   Alexander the coppersmith did me much evil: the Lord reward him according to his works:

v.15   Of whom be thou ware also; for he hath greatly withstood our words.

v.16   At my first answer no man stood with me, but all men forsook me: I pray God that it may not be laid to their charge."

In this section many personal references are made to those who have laboured, and some who still are labouring, in fellowship with the apostle. Here is seen the importance that Paul attaches to the fellowship and contribution that others have made.

9 Having looked back at life and then on to the future, the apostle now returns to his present circumstances. He was in a cold Roman dungeon, and it is clear that he craved the comfort and sympathy implicit in human fellowship. "Do thy diligence" means to exert every effort (*spoudazō*). The apostle had used the same term regarding being approved unto God (2:15). A present day similar appeal would be "do your best, or make haste" (see 1:4; Titus 3:12). Thus the apostle is longing to see Timothy again and reveals his unshaken confidence in Timothy as a brother beloved.

"Shortly" (*tacheōs*) implies speed (John 11:31; Luke 14:21; 16:6; 1 Tim 5:22) and this is later emphasised in v.21 where "before winter" is added. Of this request H.C.G. Moule makes the following comment: "we shall never know for certain whether Timothy came, and came in time. And for long ages of bliss now, Paul and he have been together. But the pleading call stands here immortal on the Scripture page, to witness to the place of the human heart in the life of faith".

10 Quite apart from the matters considered in the previous verse, reasons are now given for the apostle's desire for Timothy to come to him; the first relates to Demas who had been one of Paul's dependable and trusted helpers. The name is probably a contraction of Demetrius or possibly of Demarchus but there are no grounds for identifying him with Demetrius in 3 John. Twice during the first imprisonment he had been mentioned as one of the fellow workers (Col 4:14; Philem 24). Some have said that the mention here is in his favour also, in that he had gone to Thessalonica on a missionary errand, but it should be noted that the same verb is used here as in v.16 (*enkataleipō*) meaning to abandon, desert, leave in straits, to let one down (1:15; Matt 27:46; Heb 13:5). This must have been a cruel blow to the aged apostle; Paul was in prison but Demas had his freedom. A further reason for viewing this step as being regressive is the reason given for his departure "having loved this present world". Here "loved" may well be a contrast with "love his appearing" (v.8), the former fixing the affections on the present but the latter on the future. The "world" (*aiōn*) is not spoken of as evil here; rather is represents "a floating mass of thoughts, opinions, maxims, speculations, hopes, impulses, aims, aspirations at any time current" (Trench). Demas was not willing to pay the price of hardship and suffering and left the work in favour of the world. "Having loved" is literally "through love of" and can be rendered "he fell in love with"; such satisfies the aorist tense used here and emphasises the causal nature of the expression. The exhortation of 1 John 2:15 is still needed in our day. For "this present world" see 1 Tim 6:17; Titus 2:12; 1 Cor 1:20. Some have averred that Thessalonica was his birth place, but no evidence for this has been offered. The assembly there had been in a healthy condition but a man actuated by desires for worldly advantage or comfort would not be of help to it.

Crescens is not named elsewhere in the NT; he is traditionally said to have preached the gospel in Galatia, but no evidence of this can be shown.

Titus is named some thirteen times in the NT. He must have completed his work for God at Crete (Titus 1:5) and travelled to Rome (Titus 3:12). The winter referred to in Titus 3 was probably the one previous to this one (v.21). Thus he had met with Paul and been with him, but now had gone to Dalmatia which was on the eastern shore of the Adriatic Sea, north of Macedonia. It was part of the Roman province of Illyricum where Paul had previously preached (Rom 15:19). No reason is given for the journeys of Crescens or Titus and the apostle does not speak in critical terms of their departure. The movements of the servants of God must be under spiritual exercise before God.

11 The use of "only" refers to Paul's fellow-labourers; he had some christian friends in Rome (see v.21) and it would appear that they were still able to visit him and send their greetings to Timothy through him. This in no way takes from the loneliness felt by this great servant of God.

Luke was a Greek doctor of medicine who had obviously left his medical practice to be with Paul in his itinerant preaching. The use of the plural pronoun (we, us) in the book of Acts should be carefully noted. He had shared hardship and privation with Paul. Thus a former Jew and a Gentile worked in happy fellowship together, truly "one in Christ Jesus" (Gal 3:28). Like Demas he had been with the apostle during the first Roman imprisonment (Philem 24, Col 4:14) and was still a faithful companion in those dark hours. No doubt Luke felt the loneliness and privation too; possibly he had been of medical help to the apostle on various occasions. It is clear that these two had much in common, they were both educated men, and men of a large heart with spiritual sympathy and devotion.

To "take" is literally "to pick up", implying that Mark was staying at some place along the journey Timothy would take on his way to Rome and he was to stop at his home on the way to bring him with him.

Mark had a chequered spiritual career; he is first named in Acts 12:12 at the prayer meeting for Peter's deliverance, then later in the same chapter (12:25) in company with Barnabas and Saul returning to Antioch from Jerusalem. When Barnabas and Saul were commended to the work from Antioch in Acts 13:3, he went forth with them (v.5) but turned back to return to Jerusalem (v.13). This was the cause of the division between Paul and Barnabas (Acts 15:36-40). Some have questioned the stand taken by Paul in this matter, but it should be noted that when Barnabas took John Mark and sailed to Cyprus no mention is made of commendation by the assembly; yet when Paul and Silas left at the same time they were clearly commended (Acts 15:39,40). Years later Mark is found with Paul at the time of his first imprisonment at Rome (Col 4:10; Philem 24). Thus there was evidence of recovery and usefulness, and this is strongly confirmed here. The periods of time are worthy of note in the sequence of these events. It was seven years after he went back that the division of opinion occurred (Acts 15:36-40), and nineteen years passed before the time spoken of in Rome (Col 4:10). Now some twenty-two years have elapsed, and he is described as being profitable. It is good to see true recovery in one who is truly exercised. "Profitable" is useful; the word is given as "meet" in 2:21 and again as "profitable" in Philem 11. Mark would be of helpful use to Paul in the work of service.

12 In the Greek text, "and" is adversative; it therefore should be read as "but", which clearly distinguishes between the going of Demas, Crescens and Titus from Paul and that of Tychicus. The former three went of their own will or exercise, but now the apostle makes clear that he himself had specifically sent Tychicus to Ephesus. Tychicus was from the province of Asia and had travelled with Paul on his last journey to Jerusalem (Acts 20:4). He was the bearer of the letters to Colossae (Col 4:7-8) and to Ephesus (Eph 6:21). In both he is described as a beloved brother and faithful servant in the Lord. "I sent" is likely an epistolary aorist meaning "I am sending". If this were so, then he may have been the bearer of this epistle to Timothy in Ephesus. This would answer the objection raised by some of the unlikelihood of using the words "to Ephesus" if Timothy was still there. Such a brother would be potentially of great help to the work at Ephesus having been there before (Eph 6:21-22), especially as Timothy was being encouraged to leave there and journey to Rome. Others believe that he had just been sent on by Paul and would still be on the journey as the letter was bring written. He was certainly a brother in whom the apostle had great confidence to help other saints (see Titus 3:12).

13 Timothy was not to go by ship directly to Rome from Ephesus, but rather to travel via Troas through Macedonia and then across the Adriatic Sea. Here is the only NT mention of Carpus at whose home the apostle had apparently left the cloak and other articles referred to. The apostle had probably paid a visit to Troas following his return from Crete. It is possible that Paul had been rearrested at Troas, thus having to leave in a hurry and not having the time to take these things with him.

Various ideas have been presented concerning the cloak, and some have argued on the basis of the word used that it was a bag (thick bag or case, John 13:29) to carry the books in. It would however be a clumsy statement to use; "the bag of books and parchments which I left" would have been a much simpler form if this had been intended. It is more likely to be a type of travelling cloak with long sleeves which would be needed in the cold environment of the prison and especially in view of the impending winter (v.21). It is thought by many to have been a circular cape of tough Cicilian goats' hair which would be protective. The suggestion that it was an ecclesiastical vestment to be used for ritualistic purposes has been described as a "perverse idea" by Dr. Plummer and Bishop Bernard, thus showing that some who were in ecclesiastical circles knew that such a notion was clutching at straws to justify the garb of clerisy.

"The books" (*biblia*) allude to papyrus rolls or scrolls (Matt 19:7; Mark 10:4). They were in common use in the NT period for bills and written letters or documents. "Parchments" (*membrana*) were dressed skins, first made at Pergamum hence their name. They would be more expensive, being made of sheep, goat or antelope skins or vellum, i.e. young calves' skins. Various suggestions have been made regarding the two words used. Possibly the papyrus scrolls were copies of Paul's own letters and other books which he valued and used, including other of the apostle's notes of Scripture readings and studies. More valuable parchments which are given greater importance by the apostle were possibly actual leather copies of the OT Scriptures and maybe copies of the words of the Lord Jesus which had been recorded (Luke 1:1). It can therefore be seen that the apostle set great importance upon the reading and study of the word of God even in the most desperate of circumstances. Such is a rebuke to us in a day when less attention is sometimes given to serious reading, study and research of the holy Scriptures.

14 Alexander was a common name in NT times, and it is not therefore possible to identify the one of whom Paul speaks with any of the others referred to in Scripture. Some have linked him with the Alexander spoken of in Acts 19, but there is no evidence for this. A reason given for the identification is the occupation "coppersmith" mentioned here. In Ephesus there were the silver shrines of Diana where such metal workers would be profitably employed, but this is in the area of conjecture.

It has been suggested that there is stronger ground for equating him with the Alexander of 1 Tim 1:20, but there are problems even with this more likely view, as it appears inconsistent with him being an Ephesian resident. It has been supposed that he was in Rome and the caution of v.14 refers to Timothy's approaching visit. The whole matter must remain uncertain as Scripture leaves it.

"Coppersmith" refers to any craftsman in metal. The literal reading for "did" is "showed", and this implies that Alexander had not only spoken against him, but had shown him much ill-treatment. What the great harm was is not known; some have conjectured that it related to Paul's arrest and imprisonment. "Did me" can be translated "charged me with", occasioning the thought that he had possibly made some declaration against the apostle, thus accelerating his legal conviction.

Although so badly wronged by Alexander, the apostle leaves him in the hands of the Lord. "The Lord reward him" should not be taken as an imprecatory prayer such as is found in the psalms. The oldest and best Greek texts have the future indicative, meaning "will repay"; thus the reward referred to is not a wish or desire but rather the statement of a future fact. Personal revenge is not in the mind of Paul but rather he knows that since God is a moral governor and that sin is a reality, then the Lord must requite Alexander according to his works. This principle is stated in the Old and New Testaments, quite apart from the imprecatory aspect (Psa 62:12; Prov 24:12; Gal 6:7).

It is of interest to note that "will render" is the future active of the same verb used in v.8, but in a very different atmosphere. That personal revenge is not in view will be seen by comparing this statement with the closing words of v.16.

15 Although the apostle was content to leave the future assessment of Alexander in the hands of the Lord, yet he would warn Timothy of the dangers which would still be possible from him. Paul was really now beyond the reach of such danger; he saw the end of his own pathway as being near, but others were still engaged in the great contest and must be aware of the power of the enemy. The real sense of "be thou ware" is "be on your guard". It is in the present middle imperative, thus meaning "from whom keep thyself away". Here, then, is another exhortation for the servant of God to separate himself from those who would be detrimental to the work of God.

The apostle now makes clear that Alexander had strongly opposed the message (*logois*) or words. This could include not just Paul's preaching but, if the earlier suggestion (v.14) be correct, the defence he had made (v.17). "Greatly" is "exceedingly" and "withstood" is "set himself against". Some feel that this actually took place at the trial (v.16); others that it describes the events of Acts 19:33,34. The latter seems to be unlikely as that had taken place so long before Paul was writing. "Our" (plural) is better then "my" because such "words" are common to all believers in their defence of the faith.

16 The "defence" (*apologia*) referred to has been the subject of differing views by expositors. The word comes from the same root as our English word apology, but there has been a change in its common usage. It now means "I was wrong" but it originally meant a speech in defence, i.e. "I was right" (Acts 22:1). It was a technical word used in the Greek law courts and is used by the apostle regarding his earlier gospel preaching (Phil 1:7,17). The old English use of the word remains in the term apologetics.

Some are of the opinion that the "first defence" referred to is that which took place at the first imprisonment in Acts 28; this is very unlikely; Timothy would not have required such information regarding events which had taken place so long before, and the language used makes it sound recent. Another point to bear in mind regarding the Acts 28 period is that after two years he would have been automatically released without a trial taking place. It is therefore better to regard the "first defence" as the first stage or hearing when he would have stood quite possibly before Nero himself. It has been inferred from the two "answers" that the charge could have been twofold, with the first being an accusation of having taken part in the conflagration of Rome (AD 64). This is unlikely as those who were christians and faced this charge were almost pre-emptorily tortured and put to death.

"Stood" is to be regarded as a technical term denoting the fact that no one was there on his behalf to plead for him and to support him in the time of trial. It carries the idea of an advocate, one who comes alongside to help. Whilst the apostle was a man of great learning with a legal type of mind, and well able to conduct his own defence, yet he felt the loneliness of doing all this alone. It appears that the last great persecution had been so severe that no one had dared to appear for Paul. In "all forsook", the verb and tense are the same used of Demas in v.10, "but all were forsaking me" or, if aorist, "all at once left me" (A.T. Robertson). The apostle clearly felt let down just as he had been by Demas.

The apostle Paul shows the same spirit as his Master (Luke 23:34), and

Stephen (Acts 7:60) at the time of his death. It is interesting to note that Paul had witnessed the death of Stephen and no doubt had heard him say the almost identical words he is now using to Timothy: "May it not be laid to their charge". The significance of the contrast between this closing statement and that in v.14 should be carefully considered.

4. Faithfulness Toward the Unsaved
4:17-18

v.17   "Notwithstanding the Lord stood with me, and strengthened me; that by me the preaching might be fully known, and that all the Gentiles might hear; and I was delivered out of the mouth of the lion.

v.18   And the Lord shall deliver me from every evil work, and will preserve me unto his heavenly kingdom: to whom be glory for ever and ever. Amen."

Here we see that at the very defence of his own life the apostle felt and knew the presence and strength of the Lord and used the opportunity to preach the gospel, possibly publicly for the very last time.

17 Although the apostle stood alone in the trial he did not lack support, for "the Lord stood with me". The promise of Heb 13:5 was made good to him as "stood" (*paristēmi*, to stand alongside) shows. Saul the Benjamite of the OT knew near the end of his life that, because of failure, the Lord had departed from him (1 Sam 28:15-16), but Saul the Benjamite of the NT, in his last and greatest hour of need, was sure of the near presence of the Lord he had loved and served. The Lord Jesus Himself knew abandonment (Matt 27:46), but will never allow His servants such an experience; thus He stood at the side of Paul at the trial. The same word for "stood by" is rendered "to assist" (Rom 16:2). The idea of "strengthened me" is literally "poured strength into me" or "infused me with strength"; thus the apostle was empowered in the time of great need; he was clothed with strength. The identical thought is expressed by Paul at the time of his first imprisonment (Phil 4:13); now he shows that what he had stated objectively there, he had experienced subjectively in Rome.

"That by me" is emphatic. The apostle had encouraged Timothy in v.5 to make full proof of his ministry, and in v.2 to preach the word. The word used here is again the public proclamation of the official herald. What he had asked Timothy to do at Ephesus he had done in Rome, perhaps before Nero the Emperor and certainly before many from the Gentile world. "Fully known" is translated earlier as "make full proof" (v.5), the verb used meaning to carry out fully and completely. Those who opine that the "first defence" refers to Paul's first imprisonment (Acts 28) believe that the time of freedom which followed was to enable the apostle to travel about and preach fully in other parts of the Gentile world. Against this, it should be noted that Paul had also used similar language regarding his earlier preaching (Rom 15:19). The statements are perfectly acceptable when interpreted as referring to a full proclamation of the gospel to the many who were of Caesar's court and present at the trial. The echo of Acts 9:15-16 is clear; in addition to his earlier experiences, it would be a glorious climax to his life of preaching to stand at the very heart of the Roman Empire and preach Christ.

It is not entirely clear what "the lion's mouth" refers to here. Many understand this as a reference to Nero and others see the lion as Satan. If the Acts 28 defence is in view, then the deliverance could be from Nero for a period of freedom ensued at that time. Others have taught that neither of those mentioned is in view, but rather some imminent deadly peril. It should be noted that no definite article is used with "lion", which would support this. Paul is thus seen to be saying that because of the deferment he had at that time been snatched out from the very jaws of death. The preposition "out of" (ek) indicates this.

18 The opening part of this verse must be viewed as closely bound to the preceding context of v.17. Paul is confident that the One who had been at his side in the time of need, and who by His sovereign disposal had delivered him from the very jaws of death, would continue to preserve His servant to the end; the future middle voice "will deliver me" is suggestive. The apostle was not himself afraid of death (Phil 1:21), but he wished to be delivered from "every evil work". "Evil" (ponērous, pernicious) refers to active opposition to that which is good. The term "work" in the Greek text has a subjective force speaking of actions that might be committed by Paul; he is not speaking of external evil but of possible evil deeds of his own doing. Such a desire for deliverance is in perfect harmony with the context. Failure to proclaim publicly the gospel would have been in Paul's opinion "an evil work". Alford expresses "every evil work" as "every danger of faint-heartedness and apostasy". "Deliver" is said to be a very tender word in the Greek text, "draw oneself out of harm's way". Paul was standing alone; yet Christ drew him out of the danger.

"From" (apo) is "away from", being a different preposition from that used in the previous verse. Here the apostle is speaking of possible evils, away from which he would be delivered; in v.17 the circumstance was actual, so "out of" was appropriate.

To "preserve" (sōsei) is to "bring safely"; here, therefore, although in different language, the apostle is voicing again the truth of 1:12. The term "heavenly kingdom" is not found elsewhere in the NT, but is closely parallelled by "the kingdom of heaven". It should however be viewed in the context of this chapter where allusion has already been made both to "the kingdom" and to "the crown of righteousness". It has been seen that these anticipate the time of recognition and reward which follows the hidden life and labours of the pathway of service. This would seem to be again in the mind of the apostle. All the praise must be given to the One who has empowered, protected and accompanied him, but not just because of that. The kingdom will be for the manifestation and glory of Christ, and what will be seen evidentially in the millennium will be implicit in eternal conditions; thus it is for ever and ever. When "Amen" is stated by men it means "so let it be", but when by God, "it shall be".

Notes

1   There are various judgments referred to in relation to the coming of Christ and there are important distinctions which should be observed in considering them. Confusion of thought results if the following distinctions are not understood:
1. *Judgment of the believer's works* This will take place at the Judgment Seat of Christ (Rom 14:10; 1 Cor 3:11-15; 4:5; 2 Cor 5:10). Only believers will be assessed and the location is the Bema-seat, the place of reward.
2   *Judgment of the nation of Israel* This will take place on earth after the period of Great Tribulation and the coming of Christ to earth when the nation shall have been regathered (Ezek 20:37-38; Zech 13:8-9; Matt 25:1-30; Mal 3:2-3, 5; Rom 11:26-27).
3   *Judgment of the living nations (the Gentiles)* This will follow the judgment of the nation of Israel and again will take place on earth (Matt 25:31-46; Joel 3:1-2). It will precede the period of millennial blessing. In this judgment nothing is said of the dead and the term "nations" is never used to designate the dead, thus the term "living nations".
4   *Judgment of fallen angels* The only allusion to time is that this will take place on the "great day" which likely is the Day of the Lord. The judgment of Satan will precede the Great White throne judgment (Rev 20:10); thus this judgment is likely to coincide with that (Jude 6; 2 Pet. 2:4).
5   the Great White Throne judgment (Rev 20:10); thus this judgment is likely to coincide with that (Jude 6; 2 Pet 2:4).
From the above it will be seen that the word of God does not support the concept of a general judgment. The "living and dead" is a general statement in 2 Tim 4:1 referring only to the fact that the One who will preside in all of these judgments is Christ.

V. Closing Salutations (4:19-22)

v.19 ''Salute Prisca and Aquila, and the household of Onesiphorus.
v.20 Erastus abode at Corinth: but Trophimus have I left at Miletum sick.
v.21 Do thy diligence to come before winter. Eubulus greeteth thee, and Pudens, and Linus, and Claudia, and all the brethren.
v.22 The Lord Jesus Christ be with thy spirit. Grace be with you. Amen.''

These closing verses underline the great interest and affection which was in the heart of the apostle Paul towards fellow-saints and in particular towards Timothy, his true child in faith. The apostle has previously alluded to fifteen individuals in the epistle and from this verse onwards he names eight others, the ninth being Onesiphorus who has been mentioned before (1:16).

19 Priscilla and Aquila had played an important part in the life and ministry of Paul. Prosperous Jews did travel a great deal from city to city, and no doubt the purpose of God brought Aquila and his wife from Italy to Corinth at this time (Acts 18:2). Just as Philip was divinely directed to meet the eunuch, so Paul was to meet this couple. He had arrived on his first visit to Corinth, with the mockery of Athens still ringing in his ears (Acts 17:32). He found in the home of this couple a place of lodging and laboured with them at the craft of tent-making (Acts 18:3; 1 Cor 4:12). Perhaps at this time he had become their spiritual father, as no doubt they would have attended the very synagogue where he persuaded the Jews and the Greeks and testified that Jesus was the Christ (Acts 18:4-5). With the blessing at Corinth, the planting of the assembly and the upbuilding ministry to establish them (Acts 18:11), over eighteen months had passed. Then the apostle left Corinth and, in company with Priscilla and Aquila, sailed across the Aegean sea to Ephesus (Acts 18:18, 19). It was at Ephesus that they instructed Apollos expounding to him the way of God more perfectly than he had previously understood (Acts 18:26) and also there that the local assembly at Ephesus met in their home (1 Cor 16:8,19).

Later the apostle refers to them as being in Rome and also to their having risked their own lives for him (Rom 16:3-4). Here they are back again in Ephesus and the NT record makes clear that wherever they were, they brought profit and help to the local assembly; they should be a challenge to us.

Whether the assumptions already suggested are correct or not (see exposition on 1:16), it is evident that the household of Onesiphorus deserved special greetings in light of the place that he occupied in Paul's own heart. It is a similar sentiment to that of David, "for Jonathan's sake" (2 Sam 9:1).

20 Erastus is not a common name in the NT. It is found in three particular passages, the first being Acts 19:22 where Timothy and Erastus travel from Ephesus into Macedonia, having been sent there by Paul. The other reference

is in Rom 16:23, where Erastus is spoken of as the chamberlain of the city of Corinth. Such an office would be the equivalent of the Director of Public Works, or perhaps the City Treasurer. All three passages could refer to the one person although there is no way of knowing for certain. It is more possible that the one described in Rom 16 is the same as described here. He would likely be a native of Corinth.

Trophimus was from Ephesus in the province of Asia. He had helped carry the offering from the Gentile assemblies to the poor saints at Jerusalem (Acts 20:4), and had been at Troas with the apostle when they had stayed to break bread, and when Eutychus had fallen down from the third loft (Acts 20:9). He was also at Jerusalem; there unintentionally he had been the cause of the apostle being put out of the temple and later arrested (Acts 21:29-40). Paul had now left him sick at Miletus. It should be noted that there is no reference here to an attempt at healing him by miraculous means. Such a small point emphasises that, as this dispensation continued, the sign gifts were being withdrawn. It has been suggested that the time referred to was on Paul's return from Crete (Titus 1:5).

21 Again the apostle encourages Timothy to exert every effort (*spoudazō*) to come to him. It seems that he wished to have one last glimpse of his face, and to again enjoy his fellowship before leaving this earthly sphere of service. The wish is expressed as in v.9, but with the more specific appeal requesting him to come before winter. No doubt there would be in this the practical aspect of also having the cloak and the books to preserve warmth and give profitable occupation during the long cold period ahead. There would also be for Timothy the obstacles to travel, if he left the journey much later.

All four persons named as sending greetings are unknown elsewhere in Scripture, but clearly known in heaven and also to Timothy. Three are males, Claudia being the only feminine name. It is clear then that, whilst only Luke was with the apostle as far as fellow-labourers were concerned, yet there were faithful believers in Rome willing to visit the imprisoned apostle and to send their greetings to Timothy. The separate mention of each name in sending greetings should be noted.

22 This closing verse has two parts, the first relating to Timothy personally and the second to all the saints. This is understood by noting the singular pronoun used in the phrase "thy spirit". Here the apostle is desiring that Timothy, in his life and service for God, will know the abiding presence of Christ with him. Just as Paul has been so conscious of this even in the darkest of experiences (4:17), so he longs that Timothy will know it too (see also Gal 6:18; Philem 25). The closing benediction includes all the saints, this is indicated by the plural pronoun "you" in the phrase "with you". Thus the apostle concludes in salutation with the same desire he had commenced with (1:2). As one has said "'Tis grace from first to last".

TITUS
D. West

TITUS

Introduction

1. Authorship

The current of modern criticism is against the Pauline authorship of this letter addressed to Titus, but faith must accept that the apostle Paul ("Paul . . . an apostle of Jesus Christ," 1:1) was the writer. Presumably the letter was carried by Zenas and Apollos (3:13).

A few indications are given in the epistle as to Paul's personal movements. Evidently he had laboured with Titus for some time on the island of Crete (1:5) before the demand for his presence elsewhere compelled him to depart. At the time of writing, Paul intended to send either Artemas or Tychicus to Crete; this would enable Titus to leave the island to meet Paul at Nicopolis where the apostle purposed to spend the following winter (3:12).

2. Locality from which it was Written and Date of Writing

The letter itself gives no suggestion as to where Paul was when he wrote. The "there" (3:12) shows that Paul was not yet at Nicopolis (in spite of the appendix in the AV "written to Titus . . . from Nicopolis of Macedonia").

The statement of Paul's determined plans for the winter ahead reveals that he was at liberty at the time of writing and is an indication that this letter to Titus was written after his release from his first imprisonment at Rome (possibly between AD 63-65).

3. Destination of the Epistle

Crete is one of the largest islands in the Mediterranean Sea. A mainly mountainous island, it lies across the southern end of the Aegean Sea, midway between Syria and Malta. The island is situated almost equidistant from Europe, Asia and Africa; it is about 150 miles in length and its breadth varies from 6 to 35 miles. Crete is not mentioned by name in the OT.

Cretes (*Krētes*), the inhabitants of Crete, were among those present in Jerusalem on the day of Pentecost (Acts 2:11). N.B. The Cretes and the Cretians (Titus 1:12) are now called Cretans.

Later in Luke's second treatise, the island (*Krētē*) is named in the account of Paul's journey to Rome (Acts 27:7-13,21). The ship in which Paul was being carried was driven off her course and sailed round the island; it passed by Salome on the eastern extremity and put into a harbour called Fair Havens, near Lasea, at the centre of the southern shore of the island. Paul himself advised wintering there, but the majority on board ship thought it wiser to leave in order to seek a more suitable place to shelter from the winter storms.

The ship set out to coast round to a better wintering berth to Phenice, on the south western shore, but a tempestuous wind arose and the vessel was again off course under an island called Clauda, off the south of Crete, and at length was wrecked on the island of Melita (Malta).

After his first imprisonment, Paul evidently revisited Crete for a short time, leaving his trusted fellow-labourer, Titus, on the island to carry on the work (Titus 1:5). Titus was evidently in Crete when Paul wrote this letter.

4. Recipient of the Letter

From the historical accounts given to us in the book of the Acts and from the inspired writings of the apostle Paul, it is possible to group together a certain number of men who were fellow-companions and fellow-workers of the apostle. Titus, the recipient of this letter, was one of the most valued and trusted associates of Paul in the work of the Lord; indeed the name Titus means "honourable".

It is by no means an easy matter to bring together information concerning this man. To start with, there is no reference to Titus in the book of the Acts, although it should be mentioned that some have identified him with the Justus of Acts 18:7, to which name, in certain manuscripts, "Titus" is prefixed. We must, however, draw materials for a biography of him from Paul's letter to the Galatians, the second epistle to the Corinthians, the communication to Titus himself and Paul's second letter to Timothy.

As we trace the record of Titus, we find him associated chronologically with certain locations, namely Antioch in Syria, Jerusalem, Corinth, Crete and finally Dalmatia.

It is evident that Titus himself had been converted through the instrumentality of the apostle, since Paul speaks of him as "mine own son after the common faith" (Titus 1:4). Bearing in mind what we are told in the Galatian epistle, it can only be assumed that Titus first came into contact with Paul and the gospel at Antioch in Syria.

The first specific reference to Titus chronologically is at the time of the Gentile controversy. By comparing Gal. 2:1 ("and took Titus with me also") with Acts 15:2 ("certain other of them") we learn that he was evidently one of the saints from Antioch who went up with Paul and Barnabas to the council at Jerusalem meeting to decide whether or not Gentile believers should be made subject to the law of Moses.

The spread of the gospel to the Gentiles had aroused the activity of the enemy. The first pressure came from without (Acts 14:2,19), but when that failed, Satan resorted to more subtle tactics and we learn in Acts 15 of the corruption of the truth from within, "Certain men which came down from Judaea taught (imperfect tense, literally "were teaching) the brethren and said, Except ye be circumcised after the manner of Moses, ye cannot be saved" (Acts 15:1). The truth of the gospel was in this way in danger of being discredited.

The problem had to be dealt with at its source; this is true of all evil, whether moral or doctrinal. Note that the divine side is presented in the epistle to the Galatians, so Paul says "I went up by revelation" (Gal 2:2).

No one was more suited to accompany Paul and Barnabas than Titus, for he was a Greek ("Titus . . . being a Greek", Gal 2:1) and was therefore uncircumcised. By contrast Timothy was of mixed parentage, "the son of a certain woman, which was a Jewess, and believed; but his father was a Greek" (Acts 16:1). Titus was therefore a test case. Must this Gentile believer be circumcised? Must he keep the law of Moses?

The apostles and elders at Jerusalem decided against any such compulsion ("but neither Titus, who was with me . . . was compelled to be circumcised", Gal 2:3). The grace already manifested in the case of Titus was confirmed by apostolic authority, not just among Gentiles at Antioch, but in Jerusalem itself.

The next mention of Titus is in Paul's second epistle to the Corinthians; indeed it is here more than anywhere else that we see something of the character of this servant of God. The work of Titus in Corinth is an example of his devoted service. The nine references to Titus in this letter reveal the maturity of the man as a result of spiritual growth and development. It will be helpful to consider each of the references in turn:

a.   *"I found not Titus my brother"* (2 Cor 2:13)

Evidently Titus had been sent to Corinth in the midst of the critical circumstances of the assembly there. He appears to have been more mature than Timothy and to have had none of the yielding and sensitive spirit of that younger man.

In his first epistle, Paul had blamed the Corinthians for their worldliness and carnality, but had nevertheless written out of much affliction and anguish of heart and with many tears. Paul was deeply burdened in his spirit and concerned about the effect of his letter and so, when he came to Troas to preach the gospel of Christ and when a door was opened to him of the Lord, he had no rest in his spirit because "I found not Titus my brother". There is a warmth about this expression; it brings in the thought of brotherly kindness and brotherly love and points to the dependability and trustworthiness of Titus.

b.   *"God . . . comforted us by the coming of Titus"* (2 Cor 7:6)

Taking leave of the believers at Troas, Paul left for the neighbouring province of Macedonia. It was there that God who comforts (encourages) the lowly, comforted him by the coming of Titus. God so overruled that Titus returned to the apostle just at the right moment. It is not surprising that Paul reminds us at the opening of the epistle that God is "the God of all comfort" (2 Cor 1:3).

Through Titus, Paul learned that his first epistle to the saints at Corinth had produced the desired results. In a very practical way, the encouragement of one can lead to the encouragement of another. Thus Titus' encouragement became Paul's encouragement and the apostle "rejoiced the more" (2 Cor 7:7).

The main reason that Paul gives for being thus encouraged is not simply repentance on the part of the Corinthians, but their readiness to acknowledge his apostolic authority. A spiritual believer is encouraged when he hears of others accepting Paul's apostleship by bowing to the teaching set forth in his epistles ("If any man think himself to be . . . spiritual, let him acknowledge that the things that I write unto you are the commandments of the Lord", 1 Cor 14:37).

c.   *"The joy of Titus . . . his spirit was refreshed"* (2 Cor 7:13)

The emotions of the Lord's servants are often disregarded; at times such are viewed as not having the feelings common to men. Here, however, Paul catches the atmosphere and without hesitation enters into the joy of Titus, "and exceedingly the more joyed we for the joy of Titus, because his spirit was refreshed by you all".

The word "refresh" means "to give rest" and describes the state of a soul released from previous distress. It is interesting to observe that the word "joy" (*chara*), as a noun, is not found in 1 Corinthians but is used five times in 2 Corinthians. Experiences of sorrow prepare for, and enlarge the capacity for, joy; this is well illustrated in this present passage.

d.   *"His inward affection"* (2 Cor 7:15)

The word rendered "affection" is frequently translated "bowels", for the latter were regarded by the Hebrews as the seat of tender affections. Here the apostle shows Titus to be a man of affection; he had a compassionate heart, so needed in the service of God.

The Corinthians had received Titus "with fear and trembling"; he seems to have had a stronger personality and constitution than Timothy, for writing to the same assembly Paul ways, "if Timotheus come, see that he may be with you without fear" (1 Cor 16:10).

e.   *"We desired Titus, that as he had begun, so he would also finish in you the same grace also"* (2 Cor 8:6)

Another reason why Titus had been sent to Corinth was to deal with the collection there for the poor saints in Jerusalem; "the same grace" refers to the grace of giving. Titus had apparently been Paul's messenger to Macedonia; he had begun a good work there and paul wanted him to finish it in Corinth. The work of Titus among the Corinthians was presumably of an exhortative character, to move so upon the hearts of the believers that they would be prepared to complete the collection satisfactorily themselves.

f.   *"God, which put the same earnest care into the heart of Titus for you"* (2 Cor 8:16)

The expression "earnest care" means diligent zeal, watchful interest and earnestness. What a commendable feature in a servant of the Lord! Titus himself had originally manifested such care when he was among the Macedonians; it was of God.

g.   *"Titus, he is my partner and fellowhelper concerning you"* (2 Cor 8:23)

"Partner" (*koinōnos*) indicates one who is partaker of the same circumstances; Titus had a common outlook with Paul. As Paul's fellowhelper, he followed on in the apostle's ways and thus the two were marked by common deeds. These terms show how much Paul valued the fellowship of Titus in the work of the Lord.

h.   *"I desired Titus, and with him I sent a brother. Did Titus make a gain of you?"* (2 Cor 12:18)

This verse with itis two references to Titus points to the transparency of Titus in his service. It is a good thing when brethren who work together have the same convictions on matters relating to christian liberty. So Paul goes on to say, "walked we not in the same spirit?" — again emphasising their common outlook, — and, "walked we not in the same steps?" — pointing again to their common deeds; their steps were steps of fellowship, they were equally yoked together.

We next see our character, Titus, associated with the work on the island of Crete. Paul speaks of Titus as "my genuine child (literally) after the common faith" (Titus 1:4). It has already been pointed out that Paul had evidently been instrumental, under the hand of God, in the conversion of Titus, but the expression "my genuine child" implies dearness. It was their mutually-held faith that placed them into accord with one another and with the elect. The twofold duty of Titus (Titus 1:5) will be considered in the exposition of the epistle.

In the letter addressed to him, Titus had received Paul's exhortation "be diligent to come unto me to Nicopolis" (Titus 3:12), but Scripture is silent as to whether Titus was able to fulfil it. The final reference to Titus is found in Paul's last epistle where he says pointedly and without elaboration, "Titus (is departed) unto Dalmatia" (2 Tim 4:10). It can only be assumed that his move to Dalmatia (possibly the Illyricum of Rom 15:19) was for the furtherance of the work of God.

5. Purpose of Writing

Titus had been left by the apostle Paul on the island of Crete with a two-fold charge

a.   to set in order the things that were wanting and
b.   to ordain elders in every city (Titus 1:5).

The main purpose of this letter, inspired by God, was to give Titus written apostolic authority for carrying out the commission and to give him guidance in these very matters.

In particular Titus was encouraged to rebuke sharply (1:13) those in the assemblies on Crete who had been adversely influenced by false teachers and their doctrine, that they might be sound in the faith. In contrast to the activities of those errorists, Titus was to speak those things which befitted sound teaching (2:1), for the conduct of all was to be consistent with what was taught and believed. He was to speak and exhort and, if occasion demanded, rebuke authoritatively; he was to conduct himself in such a way that none would despise him (2:15). Indeed Paul's fellow-labourer was to be an example to the believers both in his walk and his words (2:7-8).

The recipient of the epistle was to remind those in his care of their responsibilities not only towards those in political and civil realms, but towards men in general (3:1-2). In the letter Titus is informed of what his attitude should be towards spiritual error, whether it be false teaching or the factious individual (3:9-11).

Thus this epistle, "given by inspiration of God, is profitable (to us) for doctrine . . . that the man of God may be perfect, throughly furnished unto all good works" (2:7,14; 3:8,14).

6. Bibliography

Bentley, T.W. *Christianity in Crete*. 7 articles in Truth and Tidings. Assemblies of Christians Publishing Office, Jackson. MI 49203, June-Dec. 1980.

Cooper, H. *The Epistle to Titus*. 7 articles in Believer's Magazine. John Ritchie Ltd. Kilmarnock, Oct. 1982-Apr. 1983.

Darby, J.N. *Synopsis of the Books of the Bible, Vol. V*. Stow Hill Bible and Tract Depot, Kingston-on-Thames, 1958.

Douglas, J.D. (Ed.). *The New Bible Dictionary*. Inter-Varsity Fellowship, London, 1967.

Ellicott, C.J. (Ed.). *The Pastoral Epistles of St. Paul*. Cassell and Company, Ltd., London.

Guthrie, D. *The Pastoral Epistles*. Tyndale New Testament Commentaries. The Tyndale Press, London, 1969.

Hervey, A.C. *Titus, The Pulpit Commentary*. Kegan Paul, Trench, Trüler and Co. Ltd., London, 1901.

Hiebert, D.E. *Titus and Philemon*. Moody Press, Chicago, 1957.

Ironside, H.I. *Timothy, Titus and Philemon*. Loizeaux Bros. Inc., Neptune, New Jersey, 1947.

Kelly, W. *An Exposition of the Epistle of Paul to Titus and of that to Philemon*. C.A. Hammond Trust Bible Depot, London, 1968.

Rodgers, W. *Bible Notes and Expositions*. R.M. Press Ltd., High Street, Lurgan.

Rogers, E.W. *Paul's Pastoral Epistles, Titus*. 3 articles in Precious Seed Magazine, Nov. 1974-Mar. 1975.

Sadler, M.F. *Titus, Philemon and the Hebrews.* George Bell and Sons, London, 1890.

Unger, M.F. *Unger's Bible Dictionary.* Moody Press, Chicago, 1980.

Vincent, M.R. *Word Studies in the New Testament, Volume IV.* W.B. Eerdman's Printing Company, Grand Rapids, Michigan, 1980.

Vine, W.E. *The Epistles to Timothy and Titus.* Oliphants, Ltd., London. 1965.

Wuest, K.S. *The Pastoral Epistles in the Greek New Testament for the English Reader.* W.B. Eerdman's Publishing Co., 1952.

7. Outline

Text and Exposition

I. The Salutation (1:1-4)

> v.1 "Paul, a servant of God, and an apostle of Jesus Christ, according to the faith of God's elect, and the acknowledging of the truth which is after godliness;
> v.2 In hope of eternal life, which God, that cannot lie, promised before the world began;
> v.3 But hath in due times manifested his word through preaching, which is committed unto me according to the commandment of God our Saviour;
> v.4 To Titus, mine own son after the common faith: Grace, mercy, and peace, from God the Father and the Lord Jesus Christ our Saviour."

The salutation here is much longer than that in 1 Timothy or 2 Timothy. This opening paragraph of the epistle is noteworthy not only for its length (only that found in the epistle to the Romans compares in this respect) but also for the wealth of truth stored within its four verses.

In this opening section, Paul tells us that his apostleship is

1. "according to the faith of God's elect" — this latter expression takes our minds back to the *past*;
2. "and the acknowledging of the truth which is after godliness" — this focuses our attention upon the *present*, and
3. "in hope of eternal life" — this projects our thoughts on to the *future*.

Note the association of these profound statements with the titles "God our Saviour" (1:3) and "the Lord Jesus Christ our Saviour" (1:4).

1 On other occasions in salutations Paul uses the expressions "a servant of Jesus Christ" (Rom 1:1) and, linking himself with Timothy, "the servants of Christ Jesus" (Phil 1:1 RV), but nowhere else does he designate himself as "a servant of God". It is interesting to note that James, the Lord's brother, thus refers to himself (Jas 1:1) as he addresses "the twelve tribes scattered abroad". Although here Paul applies the term to himself, it is nevertheless true of all believers; "become servants to God" (Rom 6:22).

In using the word "servant" (*doulos*) Paul employs the most abject servile term in use among the Greeks; it carries with it the idea of one who serves another to the disregard of his own interests and refers to one who regulates his life not according to his own will but according to that of his master. Though as Saul of Tarsus he was "born free", yet Paul gladly accepts this bondservice.

The name "God" (rather than "Father") is characteristic of Paul's writings to Timothy and Titus; here in this epistle, we find such expressions as:

1. "God's elect" (1:1);
2. "God, that cannot lie" (1:2);
3. "God our Saviour" (1:3; 2:10; 3:4);
4. "God the Father" (1:4);
5. "the steward of God" (1:7);
6. "they profess that they know God" (1:16);
7. "the word of God" (2:5);
8. "the grace of God" (2:11);
9. "the great God" (2:13);
10. "they which have believed in God" (3:8).

Hence "bondman of God" is a most appropriate designation.

Paul also speaks of himself as "an apostle of Jesus Christ" (certain less important manuscripts have "Christ Jesus"). Although a personal letter to Titus, it nevertheless bears the stamp of apostolic authority, for it treats of doctrinal matters of great import and Titus was in fact to act as an apostolic delegate.

Paul's apostleship is said to be "according to (*kata*) the faith of God's elect", an expression peculiar to this passage (cf. 1 Tim 1:1, where it is "according to the commandment of God" and 2 Tim 1:1 "according to the promise of life"). The exact force of the word *kata* is not easy to determine here; it certainly signifies more than conformity, it conveys the idea of direct purpose and maybe rendered "for, in regard to", or "in order to bring about". "Faith" (*pistis*) here is used subjectively, i.e. faith which accepts the truth, and is to be contrasted with "sound in the faith" (1:13), the latter being used objectively and referring to what is believed, namely, the body of christian doctrine.

"God's elect" (*eklektos*, used elsewhere by Paul in Rom 8:33; Col 3:12) refers to those whom He has chosen and with regard to whom He has a certain purpose. The term is not employed by any other NT writer, although it is a well-known OT phrase, used especially in describing Israel as Jehovah's servant. We thus meet the truth of election at the beginning of this epistle as we do in that to the Ephesians (1:4); this brings in the idea of divine sovereignty. To summarise, Paul is saying that one object of his apostleship was that, through his instrumentality, those chosen of God should believe.

Indeed the opening verse states a twofold purpose of Paul's ministry, to produce not only faith, but also the knowledge of truth manifested in a godly life. The rendering "acknowledging" (*epignōsis*) is not to be dismissed out of hand since the idea of confessing is not absent from the thought here. The word literally means "full knowledge", that precise, experiential knowledge of the truth (*alētheia*) which (in turn) corresponds to (*kata*) godliness (*eusebeia*), literally, "god-likeness". Thus Paul's apostleship is in entire agreement with a full, inner apprehension of the divine truth as presented in the gospel.

There is an intimate connection between truth and godliness. On the one hand there can be no true godly living that is not based upon the sound doctrine of the word of God, whilst, on the other, a profession of the truth which allows an individual to live in ungodliness is a spurious profession. The theme of this epistle could well be defined as "the truth which is after godliness."

2 The preposition *epi*, translated "in", signifies upon or upon the basis of, that upon which something rests or is based. Thus the basis upon which Paul's apostleship rested was the "hope of eternal life" (an expression also found in 3:7). "Hope" (*elpis*), as used in the NT, does not imply uncertainty as to fulfilment, but rather the expectation of something future, incorporating the thought of *actuality* as well as *anticipation*.

It must be stressed that eternal life is the present possession of all who put their faith in the Son of God; this thought is emphatically prominent in the writings of John (e.g. John 3:36; 1 John 5:11,12). Paul, however, frequently treats it according to its future display; thus eternal life in all its fulness is yet future and the "hope of eternal life" embraces all that lies in the future when the believer is glorified. The term "eternal life" (*aiōnios zōē*) expresses not only the duration but the quality of that life.

The remainder of this verse and the opening part of v.3 tell us more concerning this eternal life; we learn that it was the subject of divine promise. God is here presented as the One "that cannot lie" (*apseudēs*, only used here in the NT), literally, the "un-lie-able" God. He is One who cannot know falsehood; this brings out the absolute trustworthiness of the hope mentioned. The writer to the Hebrews says "it was impossible for God to lie" (Heb 6:18); Paul expresses the idea positively when he writes, "let God be true" (Rom 3:4). By way of contrast here in this passage, we note the characteristic vice of the Cretans, "The Cretians are alway liars" (1:12). The following words might well have been directed to the natives of this island, "ye are of your father the devil, and the lusts of your father ye will do. He . . . abode not in the truth, because there is no truth in him. When he speaketh a lie, he speaketh of his own: for he is a liar, and the father of it" (John 8:44). In the phrase "God . . . promised" (*epangellō*) literally means to announce or proclaim. This promise was not made to any man; it was necessarily a promise given within the Godhead and it therefore had a far higher character than promises made in time to the fathers. It was made "before the world began" (*pro chronōn aiōniōn*), literally, "before the times of the ages", i.e. before time began to be reckoned by aeons, indeed before there were any periods marked off by time. Thus the promise which the believer lays hold upon goes back, not merely beyond the prophets or the human race, but back into eternity. Note that Paul also speaks of grace being granted to us according to the purpose of God, "before the world began" (2 Tim 1:9). The apostle here spans the whole range of what we call time; he takes our thoughts back to eternity in the past and reflects upon the promise which God made; he then projects our minds into the eternal future and speaks of eternal life as being the subject of that promise.

3 There is a contrast between the "eternal times" of the promise and the "due times" (*idios kairos*) of its manifestation. The expression literally means "in His own seasons", i.e. in the periods appointed by God in His wisdom as appropriate for such a manifestation; cf. "to be testified in due time" (1 Tim 2:6) and "which in his times he shall shew" (1 Tim 6:15).

God "manifested" (*phaneroō*) means that He made visible that which had previously been hidden; now is the time for bringing all out plainly. Note that "his word" (*logos*) becomes the object of the verb "made manifest" instead of "eternal life" as would have been expected. "His Word" refers to the gospel in which the promise was embodied; this eternal life has been made known in the glad tidings. Thus the eternal thoughts of God Himself in Christ are communicated in time. His word was manifested through preaching (*kērugma*), literally "in the message"; the word employed stands here not simply for its proclamation, but for contents of the message. Paul is seen here as God's herald or public crier making an official announcement, cf. "that by me the preaching might be fully known" (2 Tim 4:17).

Indeed Paul now speaks of his own relationship to this message. Paul's ministry in the gospel was not a matter of his own choice, it was divinely committed to him: "which is committed (*pisteuō*) unto me". This statement is expressed forcibly in the original by the transposition of the verb and subject and by the use of the emphatic personal pronoun; it may be rendered "wherewith I was entrusted", a trust from which he could not escape.

To Peter the gospel was committed more as the fulfilment of the promises made to the fathers, "as the gospel of the circumcision was (committed) unto Peter" (Gal 2:7). But Paul's ministry was unique, "the gospel of the uncircumcision was committed unto me" (Gal 2:7). The idea of having such a responsibility entrusted to him was a constant source of wonderment: indeed it is reiterated in each of the Pastoral Epistles: "the glorious gospel . . . which was committed to my trust" (1 Tim 1:11) and "whereunto I am appointed a preacher, and an apostle, and a teacher of the Gentiles" (2 Tim 1:11). The responsibility of presenting Christ in the gospel is now entrusted to us.

As far as Paul was concerned, this trusteeship was not according to any legal constraint but "according to (*kata*) the commandment (*epitagē*) of God our Saviour (*sōtēr*)"; *epitagē* stresses the authority of the command. This expression is exactly paralleled with reference to Paul's apostleship in 1 Timothy, "an apostle of Jesus Christ by (*kata*) the commandment of God our Saviour" (1 Tim 1:1).

The title "Saviour" is used six times in this short epistle, more frequently than in any other NT letter; it is employed on three occasions of God (1:3; 2:10; 3:4) and three times of Jesus Christ (1:4; 2:13; 3:6). Indeed the title "Saviour God" is almost peculiar to the Pastoral Epistles, the only other occurrences being "God our Saviour" (Jude 25) and "God my Saviour" (Luke 1:47), the latter being the only time the expression "my Saviour" is found in the NT. Although we, as believers, often speak of Christ as Saviour, it is perhaps surprising to find that in all of the writings of the apostle John, he employs the title on only two occasions and in both instances he speaks of "the Saviour of the world" (John 4:42; 1 John 4:14), the true *Zaphnath-paaneah* (Gen 41:45).

4 The letter is addressed to "Titus" (see Introduction 4 for a biography of the recipient of the letter). It is evident from the phrase "mine own son after the common faith" that Titus had been converted through the instrumentality of Paul.

The apostle addresses Timothy in a similar manner, "my own son in the faith" (1 Tim 1:2). The word rendered "own" (*gnēsios*) here means "legitimately born" or "genuine"; it is translated "true" in such expressions as "true yoke-fellow" (Phil 4:3) and interestingly is exclusive to Paul's writings in the NT. In the present verse it conveys the thought that Titus was running true to his spiritual parentage. "Child" (*teknon*) is a better rendering than "son", for it gives prominence to the fact of birth and indicates dearness.

In this opening salutation, Paul is thus seen as

1. a bondservant (1:1),
2. an apostle (1:1),
3. a trustee (1:3) and now
4. a father (1:4).

But Titus was Paul's genuine child "after the common (*koinos*) faith". One of the meanings of *koinos* is "that which belongs to several", thus "held in common"; it is employed in such expressions as "all that believed . . . had all things common" (Acts 2:44) and "the common salvation" (Jude 3). The relationship of Paul and Titus is in the realm of their "common faith"; it is their mutually-held faith (not "the faith" as the body of christian doctrine) which places them, one a Jew and the other a Gentile, into accord with each other and with all the elect who share this faith.

The most usual form of address in a Greek letter of that era may be seen in Acts 15:23 or Acts 23:26. Here Paul replaces the commonplace "greeting" with an expression which points to the heart of the christian faith. It is to be observed that although "mercy" is spoken of in the salutations to Timothy in 1 Tim 1:2 and 2 Tim 1:2, according to the oldest (and supposedly best) manuscripts, it should be omitted in this verse.

Paul's desire for Titus is present grace, the grace that sustains. There is, as far as the believer is concerned, a past aspect of God's grace, that which saves, "for by grace are ye saved through faith" (Eph 2:7), whilst Peter speaks of future grace, namely, "the grace that is to be brought unto you at the revelation of Jesus Christ" (1 Pet 1:13). Note that this epistle begins with grace for Titus, but concludes with "Grace be with you *all*" (3:15).

Titus had "peace with God through our Lord Jesus Christ" (Rom 5:1), but he needed to enjoy "the peace of God" (Phil 4:7). These blessings were not only for Titus, we can also share in them; our hearts are kept in peace as we realise that the unmerited favour of God has been bestowed upon us in Christ.

Both grace and peace relate to God the Father, as the source, the ever-flowing fountain, and "Christ Jesus our Saviour" (the correct rendering) as the channel. Scripture does not use the phrases "God the Son" or "God the Spirit," as it does "God the Father"; instead the names employed are "Son of God" and "Spirit of God". It is interesting to observe that Paul does not use the term "God the Father" outside the Pastoral Epistles. Here in this verse, the one preposition "from" (*apo*) governing both "God the Father" and "Christ Jesus our Saviour" declares the co-equality of the persons referred to and thus stresses the deity of Christ Jesus. This is the only place where the title "Christ Jesus our Saviour" is used of Christ in a salutation. He is not only the Saviour of Paul and Titus, He is *our* Saviour!

II. Concerning Elders and Errorists in Crete (1:5-16)

1. *The Recognition of Elders in the Cretan Assemblies*
1:5-9

v.5   "For this cause left I thee in Crete, that thou shouldest set in order the things that are wanting, and ordain elders in every city, as I had appointed thee:

v.6   If any be blameless, the husband of one wife, having faithful children, not accused of riot, or unruly.

v.7   For a bishop must be blameless, as the steward of God; not self-willed, not soon angry, not given to wine, no striker, not given to filthy lucre;

v.8   But a lover of hospitality, a lover of good men, sober, just, holy, temperate;

v.9   Holding fast the faithful word, as he hath been taught, that he may be able by sound doctrine both to exhort and to convince the gainsayers."

a. The Responsibilities of Titus (1:5)

5 This verse gives to us both the geographical and the historical setting of the letter (see Introduction 4 for a consideration of the destination of the epistle, viz. Crete). Here we have a strong pointer to the fact that Paul had been released from his first imprisonment and had been able to continue with his work of evangelising and planting NT assemblies. In this verse Paul alludes to the time when he and Titus had laboured together on Crete (just how long cannot be ascertained), for he had evidently left his companion there, no doubt the demand for his own presence elsewhere compelling him to depart.

The word rendered "left" (*apoleipō* — some texts read *kataleipō*) is a compound form of verb and implies that the being left behind was *temporary* rather than *permanent*. Indeed towards the end of the epistle (3:12) Paul speaks of his intention of sending another servant (either Artemas or Tychicus) to replace him; this is proof that Titus was to leave Crete for another quarter and a different work.

When Paul says "For this cause" (*toutou charin*), he is not simply stating his reason, but is pointing out that his leaving of Titus was in favour of the latter fulfilling a two-fold charge to

1.   "set in order the things that are wanting" and
2.   "ordain elders in every city",

for it is this verse that underlines the *responsibilities of Titus.*

The Greek word *epidiorthoō* (used only here in the NT and translated "set in order") is made up of three parts, viz. *epi* (upon), *dia*(through), and *orthos* (straight). It was used by secular medical writers for the setting of broken limbs or the straightening of bent limbs; thus, by implication, it may refer here to the setting right again of that which had become defective.

In one sense, Titus was to continue the work of setting in order that Paul had begun; this is suggested by the use of the expression "the things that are wanting" (*leipō*), literally "were wanting" (also used in 3:13). Owing to the necessary curtailment of Paul's stay, there were many things remaining to be accomplished in the assemblies on Crete. However, in another respect, he was not to add to what the apostle had succeeded in doing, but to restore what had fallen into disorder since the apostle had left the island. The use of the verb in the Greek middle voice indicates that Titus was to give himself diligently to accomplish what was necessary.

There are in assemblies today many things that need to be "set in order"; we have the authority of God's Word for doing so, but grace and wisdom from God are needed for the doing of it.

The second part of Paul's two-fold charge to Titus was "to ordain elders in every city". Assemblies had already been established, but there was as yet no recognised leadership. We must bear in mind that the appointment of elders is, in the first place, the work of the Holy Spirit, as Paul says to the Ephesian elders "the Holy Ghost hath made you overseers" (Acts 20:28). It is well to remember that if the Holy Spirit has made a man an overseer, then nothing and no one can prevent him from being one; conversely if the Spirit has not made a man an overseer, then no influence and no body of men can make him one. Here in these early days of the church, Titus is acting in the capacity of an apostolic delegate; we do not believe in apostolic succession — there is now no apostolic delegation.

The word rendered "ordain" ("appoint", RV) is *kathistēmi*, from *kata* meaning "down, or over against", and *histēmi*, "to cause to stand, or to set". As far as Titus was concerned, this appointing would consist first in discerning which men in each assembly manifested the features of vv.6-9; there the necessary qualifications are made known to him to enable him to decide according to apostolic wisdom. Titus would then exhort the believers in each assembly to recognise these men as divinely-raised up elders.

The men are referred to as elders (*presbuteros*), thus indicating the maturity of christian experience; it is noteworthy that the word "elder" does not appear in Paul's writings until the Pastoral Epistles are penned.

The results of the gospel were widespread among the cities of the island; this is implied by the expression "in every city", literally "city by city". We must not read this verse as if Paul was authorising elders to have responsibility in several churches in one particular city; plurality of elders in any given assembly was the general pattern and this is in evidence both in the book of the Acts and in the epistles.

The commission being given to Titus in this inspired epistle had already been communicated to him by word of mouth, "as I (emphatic) had appointed (*diatassō*) thee"; the word simply means "to give a charge" and is generally rendered "command".

The question is often asked, "How should an elder be recognised today?" The following approach might well be considered. As in all matters relating to the local assembly, the present overseers should take the lead. When they see a brother manifesting the features required in an overseer and witness that he is, within his own capacity, endeavouring to shepherd the flock, they should take him aside and express their confidence in him. They would not "invite him to join the oversight" (an expression commonly used), but would suggest to the brother in question that if he himself felt exercised to join with them (for it is scriptural that overseers should regularly meet together), then they would express their confidence in him in a more public way and, on behalf of the brother, call for the support and encouragement of the assembly.

b. The Qualifications of Elders (1:6-9)

6 The parallel passage in 1 Tim 3:2-7 should be read. In the epistle to Timothy the qualities are presented for the benefit of one who is aspiring to take up the work of an overseer, "If a man desire the office of a bishop, he desireth a good work" (1 Tim 3:1); however, here the features set forth are to be a guide to those in an assembly for the recognition of elders.

The first qualification is general, "If any be blameless" (*anenklētos*); deacons, i.e. ministering servants, must also be found blameless (1 Tim 3:10). The word signifies that which cannot be called to account. The elder must have nothing laid to his charge; he must be a man about whose past or present, accusations are not being circulated.

The next two are what might be termed domestic qualifications. "The husband of one wife" implies that preferably an overseer should be a married man. Although other interpretations have been suggested, the expression literally means "a one-wife husband", i.e. a one-woman sort of a man; as far as the elder is concerned, there is most decidedly to be only one women in his life, viz. his own wife. This interpretation is far higher in its moral requirement than the suggestion that an elder is disqualified if he should remarry after his wife's death. An elder needs to exercise great care in his conduct towards and his conversation with sisters in the assembly; he must be most circumspect.

"Having faithful (*pistos*) children" suggests that ideally an overseer should be a family man (this is strongly supported by 1 Tim 3:4-5). Circumstantially it is a man's family that will test his fitness for responsibility in God's assembly. The word *pistos* may mean trustworthy, reliable or dependable, as in the expression "faithful word" (Titus 1:9), or, alternatively, believing. It is to be noted that in 1 Tim 3:2-7 nothing is said of the spiritual condition of the children; so it is perhaps better to take the meaning here as "trustworthy" rather than to demand that for a brother to be recognised as an overseer, all of his children must have reached a point in their lives when they are clearly believers of the gospel (though it is hoped that they would become such).

As to the children, whether saved or not, they must be well behaved. *Katēgoria* ("not accused") means literally "not under accusation" — they must not lay themselves open to charges of misconduct. Two specific faults are cited:

1. "riot" (*asōtia*) which is properly the inability to save and hence implies wasting of money on one's own pleasures; it denotes prodigality, an abandoned, dissolute life. The corresponding adverb is used in the familiar parable of the so-called prodigal son who wasted his substance "with riotous living" (Luke 15:13);

2. "unruly" (*anupotaktos*) which means that which cannot be subjected to control, insubordinate; it is employed later in the expression "unruly and vain talkers" (v.10) and in 1 Tim 1:9 where it is rendered "disobedient".

Thus, on the one hand, the elder must be known as one who insists on good behaviour in the household, whilst on the other, a responsibility rests upon his children to conduct themselves in such a way as to commend his ministry.

7 From v.5 ". . . elders" and v.7 ". . . for a (literally, the) bishop . . ." it is evident that the designations "elder" and "bishop" refer to the same person (indeed in the exposition of vv.5 and 6, the terms have been employed interchangeably). The word "bishop" (*episkopos*) or "overseer" points to the character of the work undertaken; the use of the singular, "the bishop", merely indicates what kind of person an elder must be. Although the statement appears to be a repetition of that in the preceding verse, it is not redundant since it gives the reason why a bishop *must* be blameless, viz. he is God's steward. We acknowledge the importance of the word "must" in such well-known texts as "ye must be born again" (John 3:7), but we do not always lay such stress upon the word when used in its present context.

A steward (*oikonomos*) was a manager of a household or an estate; the Greek word, being derived from *oikos*, house, and *nomos*, law, signifies the law by which a household was administered or governed. The bishop is seen here as an administrator of God's house, identified with its interests, and as such he is to take care of the church of God. The possessive case "God's" is emphatic by its position; this indicates that the overseer is directly accountable to Him in the discharge of this stewardship. Paul was a steward of the mysteries of God (1 Cor 4:1); all believers are stewards of the manifold grace of God (1 Pet 4:10); in all such cases, faithfulness is required (1 Cor 4:2).

Five negatives are then noted, marking what an overseer is not to be; these might be termed *restraints*:

Mē *authadēs* ("not self-willed") is derived from *autos* (self) and *hēdomai* (to take one's pleasure). Thus he is not to be one who, dominated by self-interest and inconsiderate of others, arrogantly asserts his own will and stubbornly presses on regardless of any advice or appeal. It is wrong to think that self-will implies courage and faithfulness. One can be "gentle" (1 Tim 3:3, RV for AV "patient") — the very opposite of "self-willed" — and yet be uncompromising with reference to the truth.

"Not soon angry" (*mē orgilos*) appears only here in the NT. An elder must not be one who is quick-tempered and cannot keep his passions under control. Perhaps there is a link with the previous restraint, for if one who is self-willed does not get his own way, he may suddenly turn angry. Scarcely anything weakens authority more than a proneness to explosions of anger. Calmness gives weight and force to a needed rebuke; firmness with placidity commands respect.

"Not given to wine" (*mē paroinos*) *para* (beside) and *oinos* (wine), primarily implies, as the negative, not tarrying long at the wine; it is, too, a figurative expression for the result of drinking wine and is used here in this secondary sense of brawling and abuse — the effects of wine bibbing. Such behaviour is shameful in any man, much more so in a believer and that an elder. In passing, and yet not altogether out of context, it is not too much to say that, apart from medical purposes (1 Tim 5:23) and at the Lord's supper (1 Cor 11:25), there is no reason, certainly in the United Kingdom, why a believer should not abstain from all alcoholic drink, if alone on the principle of not stumbling a weaker brother (Rom 14:21)

The expression "no striker" (*mē plēktēs*) is used only here and in the parallel passage in 1 Tim 3:3. The overseer is not to be quick with his fists and not to be given to acts of bodily violence. Whilst women, by nature because of the Fall, are liable to misuse the tongue and hence are exhorted not to be slanderers (1 Tim 3:9), male persons, naturally, are prone to violent actions.

Me aischrokerdēs ("not given to filthy lucre") is a compound of *aischros* (shameful) and *kerdos* (gain). He must not be eager for shameful gain; he is certainly not to use his position of responsibility as a means for acquiring such. An elder must be free of greed, for it is this very thing that results in the evils of vv.10-12, cf. "for filthy lucre's sake" (Titus 1:11).

8 Paul supplements the five negative qualifications (1:7) with six positive characteristics; these are the requisites. Christianity does not consist in a series of negatives, the absence of evil qualities is not enough; positive qualities are to be cultivated. The contrast is introduced by the conjunction "but".

"A lover of hospitality" translates the single Greek word *philoxenas*, from *phileo* (to love) and *xenos* (a stranger). The word is used in the parallel passage concerning overseers in 1 Tim 3:2 and again in the general exhortation to all believers, "use hospitality one to another without grudging" (1 Pet 4:9); there Peter warns against murmuring or complaining when the visitors have left! The elder should be one who is fond of offering hospitality, without a thought of receiving a return invitation or other recompense. As indicated, the thought of the stranger is embraced in the word, cf. "be not forgetful to entertain strangers" (Heb 13:2); "to be hospitable" does not simply involve entertaining friends to dinner or tea, but having an outgoing heart towards believers in need who are strangers. The conditions of the times made such hospitality very important, since believers on their journeys could not resort to the homes of the heathen or to the public inns without being exposed to insult or danger.

"A lover of good men" (*philagathos*) could be rendered more literally "a lover of good (things)" or "a lover of goodness" as a quality itself. Here is another word unique to the passage, but its corresponding negative occurs in 2 Tim 3:3 where Paul speaks of "despisers of those that are good", which may be rendered "no lovers of good". The appellation here points to that largeness of heart which finds room for, and sympathy with, all that is good or beneficial in its nature or its effects.

Sōphrōn ("sober") comes from *sōzō* (to save) and *phrēn* (the mind); the rendering "discreet" in Titus 2:5 expresses the meaning very well. The elder must be right-minded, balanced in his opinions and actions and certainly not light or frivolous in his attitude. A man might easily allow the love of good to degenerate into either sentimentality or enthusiasm; there is the constant need for the exercise of sobriety.

"Just" (dikaios) infers a conduct towards others that conforms to the standards of right and meets with the approval of God. The overseer must be upright in his dealings with men; a failure in righteousness would weaken his authority.

Hosios is somewhat different in meaning from hagios the more familiar word translated "holy"; more than the thought of holiness is in view, it includes the idea of being gracious, as well as unpolluted. The elder must have a bearing towards the things of God.

"Temperate" (enkratēs) is an expression much narrowed and misapplied; it is certainly wider in scope than abstinence from drink. The Greek word is not used elsewhere in the NT; literally it means "one in control of strength", and so describes the overseer's ability to control his desires and appetites: he must demonstrate that he is temperate in all things. There is a distinction between "sober" and "temperate"; a sober man is moderate in the enjoyment of what is lawful, whereas a temperate man refrains from that which is unlawful and harmful.

The elder then must be just manward, holy Godward and temperate selfward.

9 The latter part of v.7 and the whole of v.8 may be regarded as a parenthesis; thus we may link this present verse with the earlier part of v.7 and read as follows "as God's steward . . . holding fast the faithful word". His stewardship involves "holding to (antechō) the faithful word" (RV). This RV rendering correctly implies the notion of withstanding opposition, a fact which is not brought out in the AV.

The elder must not play fast and loose with holy Scripture; it is absolutely trustworthy and dependable, not unreliable like the spurious doctrines of false teachers. The faithful word is the sole authority and the final court of appeal in every dispute; that it is in full agreement with the teaching given by the apostles is indicated in the qualifying clause, "as he hath been taught" (kata tēn didachēn), literally "which is according to the teaching". The elder must be characterised by doctrinal stability; he is responsible to adhere firmly to the word of God as the guide for himself, without adding to it or diminishing from it, that he may be capable of:

1.   exhorting the believers in the sound teaching (a possible rendering);
2.   convicting the gainsayers.

Here we see the special responsibility that elders have in teaching; consequently they must be "apt to teach" (1 Tim 3:2). The emphasis is upon sound (*hugiainō*) doctrine; the word signifies "to be healthy" (our English word hygiene has its derivation here) and is to be contrasted with the sickly, unpractical teaching of false teachers. It is possible to be most particular about acquiring healthful food for the nourishment of the physical body and yet to be less concerned about healthy spiritual food for the soul. Believers need constantly to be exhorted (*parakaleō*); as the elder entreats the saints, he is calling them alongside himself; he is not asking them to occupy spiritual ground into which he himself has not entered.

Additionally, the overseer must be able to deal with opponents of the truth, referred to here as gainsayers (from the verb *antilegō*) or contradictors, i.e. those who speak against the sound doctrine. He is certainly not to condone their actions but rather to convince (*elenchō*) or to convict them. The word means more than "reprove", it signifies a presentation of evidence so that the arguments of the opponents are beaten down and proved to be baseless, and the erstwhile gainsayers are put to shame. What authority there is in the faithful word!

2. *The Refutation of False Teachers*
1:10-16

v.10   "For there are many unruly and vain talkers and deceivers, specially they of the circumcision:
v.11   Whose mouths must be stopped, who subvert whole houses, teaching things which they ought not, for filthy lucre's sake.
v.12   One of themselves, even a prophet of their own, said, The Cretians are alway liars, evil beasts, slow bellies.
v.13   This witness is true. Wherefore rebuke them sharply, that they may be sound in the faith;
v.14   Not giving heed to Jewish fables, and commandments of men, that turn from the truth.
v.15   Unto the pure all things are pure: but unto them that are defiled and unbelieving is nothing pure; but even their mind and conscience is defiled.
v.16   They profess that they know God; but in works they deny him, being abominable, and disobedient, and unto every good work reprobate."

a. The Presence of False Teachers (1:10)

10 The conjunction "for" connects vv.10-16 with what has just been said; the requirement that overseers be able to convict gainsayers was justified in view of the fact that there were already numerous false teachers in Crete. Paul uses three terms to describe them; they were:

1.   "unruly (*anupotaktos*) men"; N.B. the RV ("unruly men, vain talkers") omits the word "and"; they were insubordinate, disorderly men who refused to submit to rule.

2. "vain talkers" (*mataiologos*); the Greek word is adjectival denoting "talking idly" and is used only here in the NT. The related noun occurs in 1 Tim 1:6 where it is rendered "vain jangling"; these men engaged in empty, profitless talking which led to no constructive good.
3. "deceivers" (*phrenapatēs*); again the word is used only here in the NT, although the corresponding verb is found in Gal 6:3; they were deceivers of men's minds (as the original implies) and their teaching, although no doubt plausible, had a seductive and perilous fascination, leading its victims astray. There is no room for complacency, for such men are still with us today.

It is probable that there were very few false teachers at that time who were not of the circumcision, although such were not the only men who sought to deceive the believers. These men professed to have been converted to christianity, but being of the circumcision and having a knowledge of he OT Scriptures their teaching stemmed largely from Judaism. These Jews, even in Paul's absence from Crete, had not given up their iniquitous activities.

b. The Necessity to Silence False Teachers (1:11a)

11 These men must not be tolerated, they must be put to silence, "whose mouths must be stopped" (*epistomizō*); the word originally meant "to put something into the mouth", as a bit in a horse's mouth, and hence to bridle or to muzzle. Here it is used metaphorically of reducing to silence. This silencing of unruly men could not be accomplished merely by the outward imposition of authority, but by the power of the word of God through the Spirit. The Lord Himself silenced the Sadducees ("the Pharisees . . . heard that he had put the Sadducees to silence", Matt 22:34), by presenting the truth to them in a decidedly-powerful manner. We cannot adopt a passive attitude towards false teachers and their doctrines.

c. The Activity of False Teachers (1:11b)

As a result of these deceptive false teachings, entire families were being disturbed and turned upside down; "who subvert" (*anatrepō*) whole houses". The word is used literally in John 2:15 of the overthrowing of the tables of the money-changers and metaphorically in 2 Tim 2:18 of the overthrowing of faith. No doubt one or two members of a house (*oikos*, by the figure metonymy, stands for a household) were influenced initially; soon, however, the whole family would be affected by the subversive doctrines. We must recognise that it is far easier to spread evil than to maintain what is good and holy and true.

These men were opposing the sound doctrine of Titus 1:9, "teaching things which they ought not" or, better, "teaching things which ought not to be taught". The apostle then lays bare their motive, it was "for filthy lucre's sake", i.e. for the sake of base gain (see 1:7); mercenary considerations lay behind their efforts. The object was not the glory of the Lord, but financial profit. The majority of false teachers would cease their evil work if it no longer produced monetary gain. What a contrast is the spirit of the apostle Paul who could say, "I have coveted no man's silver, or gold, or apparel" (Acts 20:33).

d. The Character of False Teachers (1:12)

12 Paul, under divine inspiration, now appeals to the testimony of a native Cretan, "one of themselves"; this testimony would therefore be unbiased and he could quote from his writings without giving offence to the inhabitants of the island. The apostle cites from Epimenides, a native of Gnossus in Crete, a heathen moralist, who lived around BC 600. To Paul this philosopher was "a prophet" by repute only, but he uses the term since the Cretans themselves recognised and esteemed him as such. The false teachers in Crete were self-styled prophets and it is possible that Paul was alluding to this here by employing the expression.

The witness of Epimenides is, in the original, in the form of a hexameter verse and is certainly not complimentary to his own countrymen; it is presented as a three-fold accusation. "The Cretians are":

1. "alway liars". Epimenides, however, was a Cretan who for once told the truth. The word *aei* rendered "alway" means perpetually or incessantly. The Cretans were indeed notorious for their untruthfulness and this is confirmed by the fact that the Greek language contains a word *kretizō* meaning to speak like a Cretan or to lie.
2. "evil beasts" (*kaka thēria*), literally, dangerous, wild beasts. This points to their wild, fierce nature, their ferocity and their love of cruelty.
3. "slow bellies" (*gasteres argai*); *gaster* refers to the stomach (whence our English word "gastric", whilst *argos* occurs eight times in the NT and is usually translated "idle"; the RV rendering "idle gluttons" conveys the correct idea. The expression stands for the grossest self indulgence and denotes their uncontrolled greed.

These three characteristics of the Cretans are manifest in the false teachers described in vv.10-11; they were:

1. liars, cf. "vain talkers and deceivers" (v.10); this tells us of their unreliable character;
2. evil beasts; they were unruly and overturned whole houses — this emphasises their mischievous activity;
3. idle gluttons; they were greedy of filthy lucre — this points to their lazy self-indulgence.

This present verse indicates the difficulties that the elders in Crete might be faced with. We need to bear in mind that evils are not everywhere the same; certain times and places have a character peculiar to themselves, of which overseers ought to be aware.

e. The Influence of False Teachers (1:13-14)

13 Paul endorses the testimony of the poet Epimenides, affirming the description given in v.12 to be true. The apostle had had first-hand knowledge of these Cretan characteristics; he knew that they were a difficult people to deal with. According to an ancient proverb, the Cretans, the Cappadocians and the Cilicians were the worst three "C's" (anglicised) of antiquity.

As to the remaining part of the verse, contrary to most commentators, the present writer believes that whilst the accusative pronoun "them" refers to the false teachers, the nominative pronoun "they" has in view believers who were in danger of being deceived by them.

On account of the natural Cretan characteristics manifesting themselves in these false teachers, Titus is to "rebuke (*elenchō*) them"; this is the word rendered "convince" in v.9 (which see). However, the verb here is qualified by the adverb "sharply" (*apotomōs*), occurring elsewhere only in 2 Cor 13:10, "lest I should use sharpness", which the RV renders "that I may not . . . deal sharply". It comes from a verb meaning "to cut"; as a surgeon's knife cuts away diseased and mortifying flesh, so must the word of Titus sharply rebuke.

The conjunction "that" (*hina*) or "in order that" expresses the object of the reproof; this aim is stated both positively (v.13c) and negatively (v.14).

The positive objective is that the believers should "be sound (*hugiainō*) in the faith; those who listen and respond to exhortation by sound doctrine (1:9) will be sound or spiritually healthy in the faith. "Faith" here is used objectively and refers to what is believed, viz the body of christian doctrine, and is to be contrasted with its subjective use in 1:1 (which see).

14 The negative aim of the reproof is that believers should not give "heed to Jewish fables and commandments of men". The word rendered "giving heed to" (*prosechō*) means, literally, "holding to" and implies the giving of one's assent as well as one's attention. These Jewish myths probably consisted of useless speculations supposedly based upon the OT, they were simply frivolous inventions without factual basis. No doubt these fables were akin to those referred to in 1 Tim 1:4, but, bearing in mind the fact that here they are spoken of as Jewish fables, it must be concluded that these Cretan false teachers were more Judaistically inclined (cf. 1:10) than their Ephesian counterparts.

The "commandments (*entolē*) of men" (note their origin) lack divine authority and are strongly reminiscent of the ascetic tendencies in the Colossian heresy, "the commandments and doctrines of men" (Col 2:22). By reference to the following verse of our chapter, it would appear that these commandments probably relate to ritualistic observances and ceremonial rites.

The men propagating these teachings were those "that turn from (*apostrepho*) the truth"; the force of the verb (a participle in the Greek middle voice) suggests "they keep on turning themselves away from the truth" — such is their character. "The truth" (*aletheia*) refers to what is taught, whereas "the faith" has in view what is believed.

Neither imagination, nor mere human morality can be mingled with divine revelation. It is our responsibility to avoid doctrinal error and to give no heed to it. We have to do with truth and not with fables; we are under grace and are not subject to the commandments of men. We must never trust the teaching or even the moral ways of those who, having once professed the truth, turn aside from it.

f. The Condemnation of False Teachers (1:15-16)

15 Believers are not only God's chosen ones, "God's elect" (1:1), but they are also God's purified ones, "the pure" (*katharos*); one purpose of Jesus Christ giving Himself for us was that "he might . . . purify (*katharizō*) unto himself a peculiar people" (Titus 2:14), i.e. a people for His own possession. The word *katharos* signifies "pure", as being cleansed, freed from soil or stain. N.B. The figure of purification presupposes a previous defilement by sin. The purity in which the believer is seen far exceeds that which results from mere ceremony or ritual.

The statement "unto the pure all things are pure" must be understood in its context; we cannot overemphasise the importance of contextual interpretation of Scripture. The words here are an echo of those of the Lord Himself, "all things are clean unto you" (Luke 11:41) and of the apostle Paul," all things indeed are pure" (Rom 14:20). The expression here in this epistle does not mean that all things are pure in the mind of, or in the judgment of, the pure, but rather that all things are pure for their *use*. We need to bear in mind that Jewish ordinances pronounced certain things impure and restricted their use. The "all things" do not, of course, refer to things morally wrong, but to such outward things as meats and drinks, to which the distinctions of pure and impure can be applied. Paul says, "I know . . . that there is nothing unclean of itself" (Rom 14:14); he reminds Timothy that "every creature of God is good, and nothing to be refused, if it be received with thanksgiving" (1 Tim 4:4).

If "unto the pure all things are pure", then the opposite is also true; "but" introduces the contrast. Paul speaks of "them that are defiled (*miainō*) and unbelieving (*apistos*)"; the immediate reference is to the false teachers, clearly marked out here as unbelievers. The word *miainō* is really just the opposite in meaning to *katharos* and signifies stained, polluted, contaminated or soiled. These men failed to appreciate that "there is nothing from without a man, that entering into him can defile him" (Mark 7:15); to them not even one thing (for this is what the word *oudeis* conveys) is pure.

Paul then defines more precisely the spheres over which the moral defilement of these men extends:

1. "their mind" (*nous*, whence our colloquial expression, "nous", indicating common sense); this signifies not simply the thinking, but also the willing part of man; defilement of the mind means that thoughts, desires and purposes are all stained and polluted.
2. "and conscience" (*suneidēsis*), literally, "a knowing with", i.e. a co-knowledge with oneself; it points to the moral consciousness within, that faculty which enables man intuitively to discern good and evil, commending the former and condemning the latter. This conscience may become seared (1 Tim 4:2), as well as defiled (here and 1 Cor 8:7) and lose its sense of discrimination. Where mind and conscience are defiled, there can be no purity.

We as believers should have a conscience that is both "good" (1 Tim 1:5,19; Heb 13:18; 1 Pet 3:16,21) and "pure" (1 Tim 3:9; 2 Tim 1:3) and also that is "void of offence toward God, and toward men" (Acts 24:16).

16 Those propagating error were not only condemned by their character (v.15) but also by their conduct (v.16).

Open apostasy is not in question here, for "they profess (*homologeō*) that they know (*oida*) God." The word *homologeō* means, literally, to speak the same thing (from *homos*, same, and *legō*, to speak), to agree with someone as to something, thus to confess belief in it; it is used in the familiar gospel text, "that if thou shalt *confess* with thy mouth the Lord Jesus," i.e. "Jesus as Lord" (Rom 10:9). The public confession of these men was that they were fully informed about God; they openly placed themselves in the ranks of believers.

However, in the case of these Cretan claimants, profession and practice were clearly conflicting; there was a disconformity between their confession and their conduct, "but in works they deny (*arneomai*) him"; they stood in a self-contradictory position. In their acts they were practically denying the very things they were careful to affirm with their lips.

This epistle has much to tell us about works (*ergon*). It was not by *works* of righteousness which we have done, but according to His mercy He saved us (3:5). Titus himself was to be a pattern of good *works* (2:7). We should be a people for Christ's own possession who are zealous of good *works* (2:14); we are to be ready to every good *work* (3:1), careful to maintain good *works* (3:8) and to learn to maintain good works (3:14).

As far as these false teachers were concerned, in their conduct they denied God, disowning Him and showing no allegiance to Him and to His Word. Whenever there is a conflict between a man's talk and his walk, it is always his walk and not his talk that truly reveals what he is.

These men are said to be "abominable" (*bdeluktos*); this is the only place where this adjective occurs in the NT, although in the LXX of Prov 17:15 it is used of men who pervert moral distinctions by justifying the wicked and condemning the just. It is interesting to note that the corresponding noun *bdelugma*, signifying an object of disgust, is employed in Matt 24:15 and Mark 14:14 of the image to be set up in the future by antichrist. If in character these false teachers are abominable, i.e. vile and detestable before God, in conduct they are disobedient (*apeithēs*), i.e. rebellious and refusing to submit to and follow the truth of God.

We have already noted the repeated call to good works on the part of genuine believers in this Pastoral Epistle; however, these professors are said to be "unto every good work reprobate (*adokimos*)".

All who profess must be tested for genuineness and the implication here is that mere professors, if put to the test in regard to any good work (i.e. all that is truly beneficial), can only be rejected. The word *adokimos* suggests being put to the test for the purpose of being approved but, failing to meet the requirements, being disapproved or found worthless.

Although when preaching to sinners, we often emphasise that their good works will not save them, it is well to bear in mind that, in the sight of God, unregenerate men can have no *good* works.

Let us not think that such men as described in vv.10-16 were found only in the first century in Crete, for they are still abroad today and there is therefore the constant need for vigilance especially on the part of elders, lest any false teachers should find their way in among the people of God.

III. Concerning Christian Conduct (2:1-3:14)

1. *Particular Directions*
2:1-15

v.1   "But speak thou the things which become sound doctrine:

v.2   That the aged men be sober, grave, temperate, sound in faith, in charity, in patience.

v.3   The aged women likewise, that they be in behaviour as becometh holiness, not false accusers, not given to much wine, teachers of good things;

v.4   That they may teach the young women to be sober, to love their husbands, to love their children,

v.5   To be discreet, chaste, keepers at home, good, obedient to their own husbands, that the word of God be not blasphemed.

v.6   Young men likewise exhort to be sober minded.

v.7   In all things shewing thyself a pattern of good works: in doctrine shewing uncorruptness, gravity, sincerity,

v.8   Sound speech, that cannot be condemned; that he that is of the contrary part may be ashamed, having no evil thing to say of you.

v.9   Exhort servants to be obedient unto their own masters, and to please them well in all things; not answering again;

v.10   Not purloining, but shewing all good fidelity; that they may adorn the doctrine of God our Saviour in all things.

v.11   For the grace of God that bringeth salvation hath appeared to all men,

v.12   Teaching us that, denying ungodliness and worldly lusts, we should live soberly, righteously and godly, in this present world;

v.13   Looking for that blessed hope, and the glorious appearing of the great God and our Saviour Jesus Christ;

v.14   Who gave himself for us, that he might redeem us from all iniquity, and purify unto himself a peculiar people, zealous of good works.

v.15   These things speak, and exhort, and rebuke with all authority. Let no man despise thee."

a. Charge to Titus (2:1)

1 This chapter both commences and closes with a direct charge to Titus himself, cf. "speak thou" (2:1) and "these things speak, and exhort, and rebuke" (2:15).

The word "but" introduces the contrast with what has gone before in the closing section of chapter 1, whilst the emphatic "thou" (*su*) sets Titus in contrast to these false teachers. Titus was to speak (*laleō*), i.e. to be constantly speaking; the saints need diligent instruction; what value there is therefore in continual exhortation. The injunction here is not so much for Titus to teach publicly, but to speak; the work of Titus was largely pastoral in character and a great proportion of a pastor's work lies in speaking face to face with those for whom he cares. Public ministry is not of itself sufficient to meet all the needs that arise in the lives of God's people. How much instruction may be imparted personally and with far greter weight than in general exhortation given from the platform. Sadly, how few brethren there are who are competent to speak privately in accordance with the profitable teaching they may give publicly.

The vain talkers and deceivers in Crete were teaching "*things* which they ought not" (1:11), but Titus was to speak "*the things* which become (*prepō*) sound doctrine". The verb *prepō* means literally to stand out or to be conspicuous among a number, hence to be becoming, seemly or fit. Paul had a special sense of the fitness of things, cf. "is it *comely* that a woman pray unto God uncovered?" (1 Cor 11:13), "as *becometh* saints" (Eph 5:3), "which *becometh* women professing godliness" (1 Tim 2:10).

For the second time in this short epistle there is reference to "sound doctrine" (cf. 1:9); healthy in itself, it produces spiritual health in those who receive it. Once again healthiness or soundness is set in contrast to the sickliness of the fanciful and false doctrine of the misleading teachers of Crete; false teaching is spiritually damaging. It is important for teachers to see to it that what they speak is befitting to, or in accord with, healthful doctrine; only this can produce practical godliness in the lives of believers and it will prove to be the best antidote to error.

b. Guiding Precepts (2:2-10)

The apostle now turns to the subject of the practical effects of the gospel and the doctrines of the faith in the lives of those who form the assemblies of the Lord's people. The various classes of persons with whom Titus must deal are considered separately, viz. the aged men (2:2), the aged women (2:3-4a), the young women (2:4b-5), the young men (2:6) and bondservants (2:9-10). We are reminded that a happy, healthy assembly will be composed of older and younger of each sex, the maturity and experience of advanced years blending with the vigour and energy of youth.

It is not, as in the Ephesian and Colossian epistles, a direct address to each of the classes, but rather the apostle gives instruction to Titus as to how he is to carry himself in his service among the saints, according to their age and sex, in order to help these various persons to walk consistently with their profession.

Paul begins with the old as having most influence in their group relations.

2 Here we find instructions concerning the aged men (*presbutēs*), i.e. those men of ripe years in the assembly, even if they are not older spiritually. It is important to note that the reference here is not to the elders or overseers of the church; features that should mark this latter class are detailed in chapter 1. With regard to these aged men, four characteristics are insisted upon:

1. "sober" (*nēphalios*); the word literally means "not drunken" and the RV rendering is "temperate". However, there is to be restraint not only in the use of wine, but general moderation and that freedom from extravagance and excitability in word and conduct. It is sad to see this quality lacking in an elderly man.

    The word *nēphalios* is translated "vigilant" in 1 Tim 3:2; the suggestion is therefore that their mere age cannot be relied upon as putting them above the need for constant watchfulness.

2. "grave" (*semnos*); this translation does not really serve to bring out the full meaning of the Greek word which carries with it the sense of gravity and dignity combined (other suggested renderings are august, venerable, reverent); yet gravity must never be confused with gloominess.

    This present age is marked by lawlessness, but this epistle reminds believers of the need for subjection; it is also characterised by flippancy and levity, but correspondingly there is the necessity on our part for seriousness of purpose, since our association is with things that are heavenly, things that are spiritual, things that are eternal. Levity is hardly suitable in an older person and least of all in an older believer.

3. "temperate" (*sōphrōn*); this quality has been considered already in relation to overseers (see comments on 1:8, where the word is translated

"sober"). Discretion is especially needed and in none so much as an elderly man.

4. "sound (*hugiainō*) in faith, in charity, in patience". Older men are to be healthy (N.B. the word is used of doctrine in Titus 1:9 and 2:1), i.e. without internal weakness, in regard to this triad of christian virtues, viz. faith, love and patience, which are often found closely associated (see e.g. 1 Thess 1:3; 1 Tim 6:11; 2 Tim 3:10). Here in this passage each of the three is governed by the definite article in the original text, but this only serves to make them prominent and the whole expression could be rendered "sound in their faith, their love, their patience". Aged men then are to be healthy in their personal trust in God (the reference here is not to "the faith" as the body of christian doctrine), in their love to others and in the patient endurance of trying circumstances, for they may have to bear with many infirmities of the body and with declining faculties.

3 The "aged women likewise (*hōsautōs*)" must show christian traits of character, they too have a solemn responsibility; the Greek adverb brings out the closeness of the comparison with what precedes. The requirements are detailed as follows:

1. "that they be in behaviour, as becometh holiness". The phrase incorporates two Greek words unique in the NT, *katastēma* and *hieroprepēs*. *Katastēma* means demeanour and describes a state of mind; it thus suggests an outward deportment that is dependent upon an inward condition of heart and mind. *Hieroprepēs*, (itself derived from *hieron*, a sacred place, and *prepō*, to be fitting), denotes that which is suited to a sacred character, that which is becoming in persons consecrated to God. The two ideas are well expressed by the RV rendering "reverent in demeanour". So on the part of the older women there must be a dignity in manner, conversation, habits and dress, but this is to be the outward expression of an inner holiness.

    Nothing graces an assembly more than elderly women of this type; they play a major rôle in maintaining the moral as well as the spiritual tone of the company.

    There follow two prohibitions; the tongues and cravings of the older women are to be controlled:

2. "not false accusers (*diabolos*)"; this Greek adjective, meaning slanderous or accusing falsely, is here employed as a noun and as such it is used no less than 34 times in the NT as a title of Satan, the devil. The older women are especially warned against the wrong use of the tongue. As men are more prone to the snare of rough or violent actions, so women have a natural tendency to give vent to their feelings in unseemly speech. Older women are perhaps more exposed to this weakness since they might well have less to occupy their time when their families are

grown up and no longer living at home. This evil may commence with "picking holes" in other people, but it leads to the spreading of criticisms and engaging in malicious gossip. Anyone who spreads false accusations among the saints is doing the devil's work. Nothing weakens spiritual harmony in the assembly more than fault-finding or spreading slander.

3.   "not given to much wine"; the RV rendering, "nor enslaved to much wine", more accurately conveys the sense of the Greek. The perfect participle of *douloō*, meaning "to make a slave of", is used here, the tense employed pointing to a confirmed drunkard. The warning in this context no doubt reflects the general conditions found among the Cretans. Evidently in Crete the tendency to these excesses, especially among the women, was more apparent than in Ephesus. For when Paul, writing to Timothy in the latter location, reminds him that deacons, i.e. ministering servants, must not be "given to much wine" (1 Tim 3:8), he does not employ such a strong word. Instead he uses the verb *prosechō* which simply means "to turn one's mind to". Sometimes older people turn to stimulants to refresh their jaded bodies and tired minds; but aged christian women are not to be self-indulgent.

However, the apostle, through Titus, is not content with guarding them against snares and, positively, these older believers have something better to occupy them; they are to be:

4.   "teachers of good things" (*kalodidaskalos*); here Paul uses a unique compound expression derived from *kalos* (good) and *didaskalos* (teacher). The older women are therefore to be teachers of that which is upright and comely, with all the weight which experience gives. Sisters who are no longer young and who might consider that their sphere of service is restricted, still have ample opportunity to do a valuable work in the home.

4-5 The responsibility of the older sisters is to "teach (*sōphronizō*) the young women"; this is an important ministry which is to a large extent sadly neglected among the assemblies of God's people in this present day. The verb *sōphronizō* means literally "to make sane or sober-minded, to recall a person to his/her senses", hence to chasten or discipline or perhaps (better) to school or train. The training here involves the cultivation of sound judgment as to the discharging of responsibilities attaching to the daily life of the young women and would be carried out by the older sisters not only by precept but by example; there is no thought here of the public ministry of women.

We may observe that when private instruction is in view and home duties and marital responsibilities are to be dealt with, Titus is not told to speak to the young women directly but rather through the elders of their own sex. All teaching brethren, whether serving locally or in a wider sphere among the assemblies of the Lord's people, should take note of this example; there is the constant need for the exercise of discretion and the servant of the Lord must take care not to place himself in a compromising situation.

Here in vv.4-5 we have a palette of seven colours (N.B. "to be sober" is omitted in the RV). The young women are to be trained:

1. "to love their husbands", literally "to be husband-lovers" (*philandros*), an adjective not found elsewhere in the NT;

2. "to love their children," literally "to be children lovers" (*philoteknos*), again an adjective occuring only in this instance in the NT. There should be true maternal warmth and tenderness; it is wrong for a young mother to put her career before the welfare of her own children.

    The family-disturbing tactics of the false teachers then in Crete (1:11) may be one reason why the need to cultivate affection in the home circle is particularly pressed here. Christianity was never intended to enfeeble the affections. The beauty of the christian home is preserved and developed by fidelity in marital and parental relationships.

3. "discreet" (*sōphrōn*); this feature should also be seen in an overseer (1:8) and in an aged man (2:2). We can only conclude that since the elder women are to train the young women to be discreet, they themselves should be manifesting this quality. The younger women might be liable to be over enthusiastic on the one hand or to be careless on the other, but they must be self-controlled.

4. "chaste" (*hagnos*) signifies pure from carnality, modest; it is used in 2 Cor 11:2 where Paul says to the local assembly at Corinth, "I have espoused you to one husband, that I may present you as a *chaste* virgin to Christ". Timothy is exhorted to covet the same quality, "keep thyself *pure*" (1 Tim 5:22). The word *hagnos* is to be contrasted with

    a. *hagios*, meaning holy, as being free from admixture with evil, and
    b. *hosios*, holy, as being free from defilement;

    it has reference to thought, act and demeanour, whether in look, speech or even in dress. Purity is especially honourable in a woman in an ungodly age of increasing moral permissiveness, it is vital that young christian women should adhere to divine principles.

5. "keepers at home" (*oikourgos*) — from *oikos*, home, and a root word of *ergon*, work; so the Greek adjective may be rendered "working at home, or domestic". N.B. Some manuscripts read "*oikouros*" — from *oikos* and *ouros*, a keeper; hence the AV translation. However, the sense is changed very little by adopting either of the two words for, after all, those who work at home are keepers of their homes. The expression signifies the fulfilment of home duties and the avoidance of going around indulging in the habit of gossiping. Paul speaks of young widows who "learn to be idle, wandering about from house to house; and not only

idle, but tattlers also and busybodies" (1 Tim 5:13). Idleness is not conducive to holiness.

The apostle here is underlining what he has stated in principle in Titus 1:4 that a young married woman's sphere is the home. She must be devoted to domestic occupation and diligent in her work. In 1 Tim 5:14 the young women are bidden to "guide the house", i.e. to be the house-ruler (not the husband-ruler). This is a privilege of the highest order and a solemn duty that must not be neglected. It may be said that, in a wider sphere, the lack of well-ordered homes is one of the major factors for the prevalence in society of juvenile delinquency.

6. "good" (*agathos*), signifying good in character; perhaps in this context a better rendering would be "kind". It might be difficult for a women who has the care of a family and many home responsibilities, but, however much her patience is tried, her goodness (or kindness) should shine through.

7. "obedient (*hupotassō*) to their own husbands". The Greek verb is used in a military connection of a general arranging soldiers in subjection to himself. However, here it is used in the passive voice and it conveys the idea of "to subject oneself" or "to be submissive to". This attitude must be adopted whether the husband is converted (see Col 3:18, by inference) or not (see 1 Pet 3:1-6); obedience to the word of God is a far more convincing proof of the reality of christianity than mere argument or preaching. It can be very irritating to a husband if his wife is always ready to question his authority or to interfere with his plans.

It will be observed that Paul through Titus and thence through the older women has more to say to these young women than to any of the other groups. The impact of the lives of young christian women upon others is evidently of vital import; this is indicated by the added clause of purpose "that the word of God be not blasphemed". This clause does not simply qualify the last-mentioned feature, viz. "obedient to their own husbands," but rather the entire exhortation which precedes including even the aged women, since it is their responsibility by precept and example to instil these qualities into the younger women.

The word "blasphemed" is a transliteration of the Greek word *blasphēmeō* which means to talk reproachfully, to speak evil of, to revile. the "word of God" in the immediate context would have reference to that which was ministered orally; today, of course, it applies to the completed canon of Scripture. Every departure from that which is right and comely is bound to be marked by unbelievers and thereby to become a cause for scoffing at the christian faith.

It is most needful that these exhortations be heeded in this present day. Divine order in the home must be observed, for modern looseness has brought the word of God into discredit. The retort of the ungodly when they witness disordered domestic life on the past of professing christians is: "If that is what your bible teaches you, I don't think much of your Bible" — in other words, the word of God is blamed.

6 The task of influencing the young men belongs especially to Titus himself; he is to "exhort" (*parakaleō*) them, a much stronger directive than "speak" (2:1). *Parakaleō* is elsewhere rendered "beseech" (e.g. in Rom 12:1) and it literally means "to call to one's side". Titus is therefore to call the young men alongside of himself; the implication is that he is not to ask them to occupy spiritual ground that he has not entered into himself; he is to be their example (this comes out more emphatically in vv.7-8).

The young men are "to be soberminded" (*sōphroneō*), i.e. to be self-controlled; it is a comprehensive demand that covers every aspect of their lives; the verb is elsewhere rendered "to think soberly" (Rom 12:3) and "be .'. . of sound mind" (1 Pet 4:7 RV). What need there is for sobriety in the people of God! We have already noted that this feature is to be seen in overseers (1:8), in aged men (2:2), in young women (2:5) (and, by inference, in the elder women) and now in young men; no class is excluded.

7-8 The responsibility of Titus to exhort the younger men leads Paul to point out to him what his own conduct and attitude should be as an example to the people of God. The example of Titus is to be comprehensive, "in all things" he is to "afford himself" (*parechō*) a pattern (*tupos*) of good works. Here initially the spotlight is turned upon Titus' actions. The word *tupos* means literally "a blow" (it is used in John 20:25 of the "print" of the nails) or "the impress of a die" hence, metaphorically, an example. The "good (*kalos*) works" refer not simply to kindly acts, but to works that are right and honourable in the sight of God. If Titus were to fail in this matter, his ministry would lose its moral power and he himself would lose his influence particularly with the younger men.

Practical conduct, although indispensable, is not everything, so the spotlight is then transferred to the teaching of Titus. The order is significant, for example comes before precept; Luke tells us "of all that Jesus began both to do and teach" (Acts 1:1).

Paul deals first with the manner of Titus' teaching, for the word *didaskalia* rendered "doctrine" is really the act of teaching. Thus "incorruptness" (*aphthoria*) and "gravity" (*semnotēs*) refer not to the subject matter of his teaching, but to the attitude and manner of Titus as a teacher; N.B. "sincerity" is insufficiently supported by manuscript evidence and is rightly dropped in the RV.

As far as Titus is concerned, there must be the absence of all insincere motives such as deceitfulness and guile; he must certainly be above seeking for popular applause. We must bear in mind that public service can be the occasion for the enhancement of personal popularity and self-aggrandisement. He must also teach in a serious manner, if his words are to earn respect; a solemn dignity is necessary when the Scriptures are being handled. A flippant manner is quite out of character in the act of teaching the Word of God.

Paul then turns to the substance of Titus' teaching; when he mentions "sound (healthful) speech or discourse (*logos*)" he is referring to the content of what is said and it stands in contrast to the unhealthy doctrine of the false teachers in Crete. The matter of his teaching is to be that which "cannot be condemned" (*akatagnōstos*, literally "not to be condemned"). The teacher must take great care not to say anything rash or reprehensible; he must avoid fanciful interpretations and anything that would provoke others to justifiably criticise the teaching. What a searching test this puts to the teaching ministry!

The apostle now gives the moral aim to the preceding exhortation, "that (i.e. in order that) he that is of the contrary part (*enantios*) may be ashamed (*entrepō*)". We have to consider not only those who are sympathetic with the doctrine, but also those who are opposed to the truth; let us "cut off occasion from them which desire occasion" (2 Cor 11:12). The word *enantios* is derived from *en* ("in") and *antios* ("against") and may literally be rendered "over against"; it is used metaphorically of being opposed as an adversary; thus when giving his testimony before king Agrippa Paul said, "I verily thought with myself, that I ought to do many things contrary (*enantios*) to the name of Jesus of Nazareth" (Acts 26:9). The use of the singular "he" in our present passage makes the opponent the representative of the class.

The end in view is that "he . . . may be ashamed"; the verb *entrepō*, used here in the passive voice, means "to turn in" (*en*, in and *trepō*, to turn), i.e. to turn in upon oneself and so give rise to a feeling of shame. Such an one, says Paul, will have "no evil thing to say of us" (RV), literally "not having one evil thing (*phaulon*) to say concerning us"; *phaulon*, used here as a noun, is the neuter of *phaulos*, an adjective primarily denoting slight, trivial, hence paltry, worthless or bad. Note that the pronoun is not "you" (AV) — indeed if the reference had been to Titus, it would have been "thee" — but "us"; this is a reminder that any indiscretion or inconsistency on the part of the teacher may well expose fellow-believers to reproach.

9-10 In the earlier part of the chapter Paul has been giving instructions for the aged men and women and the young women and men. Here Paul turns to consider servants (*doulos*), i.e. bondslaves; this was a class which overlapped all of these groups. If the former grouping was established upon age and sex, this latter was based upon social status. Slaves seem to have formed a considerable element in the churches in those early days and no doubt this is one reason for special instructions being given to them. We need to bear in mind that although slavery as such has been abolished, the principles laid down here apply to all who would work for earthly masters.

Whilst in the Ephesian (6:5) and Colossian (3:22) epistles, Paul urges servants to obey (*hupakouō*) their masters, here through Titus he exhorts (there is no word in the original for "exhort", it is inserted in the AV to complete the sense) servants to be in subjection to (*hupotassō*; see exposition of ch. 2:5) their own masters (*despotēs*) as a matter of principle. The Greek word, from which is derived our English word "despot", denotes a lord, one who has absolute ownership of, and uncontrolled power over, another; thus in those days the slave was entirely at the mercy of his masters.

This subjection is not to be rendered to masters in a reluctant, sullen and bitter manner, but actively; servants are to seek "to please them well in all things", literally "to be well-pleasing (*euarestos*) in all things". In regard to earthly masters it is not easy to "make oneself acceptable in everything", for one's employer might be an awkward person who is hard to please, but the believer is to overcome such difficulties.

Paul, having already indicated the general nature of the behaviour of slaves, now adds further particulars, two negative and one positive, to describe their conduct:

1. "not answering again" (*antilegō*); their service is to be rendered without gainsaying or contradicting. More is implied than pert answers, rather it is a question of thwarting their masters' plans or wishes — they are not to cross them. The prohibition against answering again should probably be understood in the wider sense of opposition, whether it be in word or action. In the context of present working conditions, one way of pleasing will be to avoid disputes with an employer and not to argue with a superior or seek to undermine his authority or question his instructions.

2. "not purloining" (*nosphizō*); the particulir reference is to that form of pilfering which retains for oneself part of something which has been entrusted to one's care. The slaves of Crete might have thought they had good reason to help themselves to the property of their masters, since, unless born in slavery, they themselves had been "stolen" from their families. However, adverse circumstances can never provide justification for the lowering of moral standards. The small things are important; it would not be honourable for a believer to make use of his employer's stationery or equipment for his own purposes or to use the telephone at the firm's cost for making personal calls.

3. ". . . but shewing (*endeiknumi*) all good fidelity (*pistis*)"; "but" introduces the contrast with the two preceding negative features. The Greek verb conveys the idea of showing forth or providing proof; thus these bondservants were to show themselves faithful or trustworthy in every matter committed to them. Note that Paul places a limit on this fidelity by speaking of "all (i.e. every sort of) *good* fidelity"; it is to be shown in everything that is good and beneficial. So if being faithful to my

employer means doing something dishonest or telling a lie, then I "ought to obey God rather than men" (Acts 5:29).

Paul then underlines the motive for such conduct on the part of slaves, "that (*hina*, in order that) they may adorn (*kosmeō*) the doctrine (*didaskalia*) of God our Saviour in all things." The verb *kosmeō* means primarily to arrange or put in order, but it frequently conveys the thought of giving adornment or beauty to something; indeed it is used in secular Greek of the arrangement of jewels in a manner to set off their full beauty.

In v.5, in connection with the young women, the motive put forward was negative, "that the word of God be not blasphemed", but here it is positive. As far as the christian slave was concerned, that doctrine had brought him to a knowledge of God's salvation (perhaps this is the reason why the title God our Saviour is used here; see the exposition of 1:3) and in order to make it appear beautiful and attractive to his master, he would have to exemplify that doctrine in his service. The words *en pasin* rendered "in all things" might in fact be masculine rather than neuter, giving the sense" among all men". To take account of the teaching of this latter part of v.10 would add a new dimension to one's service, albeit in many cases menial and possibly humdrum, rendered to an employer.

c. Gracious Deliverance (2:11)

One outstanding feature of this short letter is the way in which it sets forth the gospel as a threefold-cord, including within itself a past, a present and a future aspect, in each of the three chapters.

We have already noted that Paul in the opening salutation tells us of the *past, present* and *future* aspects of his apostleship (see exposition of 1:1-2). Now here in this second chapter we are reminded that, as to the *past*, "the grace of God . . . hath appeared" (v.11); as to the *present*, this grace is said to be "teaching us that . . . we should live soberly, righteously and godly in this *present* world" (v.12), whilst "looking for that blessed hope . . ." (v.13) takes our minds on to the *future*. Then in chapter 3 we are told that "the kindness and love of God our Saviour . . . appeared" (v.4) in the *past*; our *present* position is that of "being justified by his grace" (v.7), whilst the expression "according to the hope of eternal life" (v.7) projects our thoughts on to the *future*. These passages really form a backbone for the whole epistle and they stand out all the more prominently when we notice that in association with each of them there are the titles "God our Saviour" (1:3), "Christ Jesus our Saviour" (1:4 RV), "God our Saviour" (2:10), "our great God and Saviour Jesus Christ" (2:13 RV), "God our Saviour" (3:4) and "Jesus Christ our Saviour" (3:6).

11 The conjunction "for" connects vv.11-14 with what has been brought before us already in this chapter; all the pillars of exhortation in vv.2-10 are based upon these concluding verses. The doctrine (v.10) which is to be adorned by the lives of God's servants is now given here in summary. Christian truth is not merely presented as a doctrinal statement, but the principles and motives of practical christianity are also set forth.

Looking back to the past, Paul asserts the historical manifestation of the grace of God, "the grace (*charis*) of God . . . hath appeared (*epiphainō*)." The grace of God is His unmerited favour toward men expressing itself in active love; the use of the aorist tense, "hath appeared", marks the reality as a fact in history. There has been an outshining of God's grace in the person of the Lord Jesus Christ — indeed He Himself is the very personification of the grace of God.

The manifestation of this grace commenced with His incarnation, but the reference here must not be limited to that alone, for it includes His life and His death and His resurrection.

In this section Paul speaks of two appearings:

1.   the appearing of the *grace* of God (v.11) — this relates to His first advent;
2.   the appearing of the *glory* of our great God and Saviour (v.13), at His second advent.

So there is first the appearing of *grace* and then of *glory* — this is in accordance with Ps 84:11, "The Lord will give grace and glory."

The RV rendering "bringing salvation (*sōtērios*) is, in fact, an adjective meaning "saving", hence "bringing salvation". God's grace has not in fact yet appeared to all men, but it is laden with salvation for all; this is the point of the statement.

The first mention of the grace of God in the Bible is in Gen 6:8, "But Noah found grace in the eyes of the Lord"; it brought salvation to Noah and his family. Now the grace of God has brought salvation within the scope and reach of all men, not to a single people like Israel under law. God's salvation is available for all men, from the highest to the lowest (even bondslaves; see v.10), for He is "God our Saviour, who will have all men to be saved" (1 Tim 2:3-4). Sadly not all men will be saved, "for all men have not faith" (2 Thess 3:2).

d. Great Purpose — Present Godliness (2:12-14)

12 Although God's grace brings salvation within the range of *all men*, it is said to be "teaching (*paideuō*) us", i.e. those who have been recipients of God's grace and have come into the good of His salvation.

We read of grace *coming*, "grace and truth came by Jesus Christ" (John 1:17), of grace *reigning*, "even so might grace reign through righteousness" (Rom 5:21) and of grace *strengthening*, "be strong (i.e. be strengthened) in the grace that is in Christ Jesus" (2 Tim 2:1), but here we are told of grace *educating*.

The present continuous tense "teaching" is used, reminding us that it is a continuing process; no one ever graduates from the school of God's grace in this life. The word *paideuō* literally means "to bring up a child" (it is used of parental discipline), hence "to instruct" or "to train". In this child-training activity, although instruction does play a prominent part, the process also requires rebuke and chastisement. The grace that saves is also the grace that teaches; the delivering power of the grace of God has been widely proclaimed, and rightly so, but what about the disciplining power of grace?

The aim of this educative process is then expressed, first negatively and afterwards positively; "denying ungodliness and worldly lusts" is the negative side. The tense of the verb "denied" (*arneomai*), signifying to forsake or renounce, marks the decisive character of the act, and the expression may be rendered "having denied once and for all", but this is of course, carried into effect by a daily denial. In exercising "repentance toward God and faith toward our Lord Jesus Christ" (Acts 20:21) for salvation, a person turns away from ungodliness and worldly lusts.

"Ungodliness" (*asebeia*) is the very antithesis of the frequently-repeated call to godliness in these Pastoral Epistles; it indicates a lack of reverence towards God and a disregard for His Person. An ungodly man is not necessarily an outwardly wicked sinner but one who, however morally upright his conduct may be, has no place for God in his life.

"Worldly lusts" (*kosmikas epithumias*)are those desires entirely centred in this present world system; they are not necessarily evil, but refer to all such desires as are essentially earthbound, those that are limited to and characterised by this world as estranged from God. "Worldly lusts" are defined by John in his first epistle, "all that is in the world, the lust of the flesh, and the lust of the eyes, and the pride of life, is not of the Father, but is of the world" (1 John 2:16).

Peter mentions "*fleshly* lusts" and tells us to "abstain" from them (1 Pet 2:11); Paul, when writing to Timothy, speaks of "*foolish* and *hurtful* lusts" (1 Tim 6:9) and "*youthful* lusts" (2 Tim 2:22) and in both instances he warns us to "flee" them (1 Tim 6:11; 2 Tim 2:22); now as far as "*worldly* lusts" are concerned, he says "deny them".

Then follows the positive side, "we should live (*zaō*) soberly, righteously, and godly, in this present world"; in the original these three adverbs stand before the verb and are therefore emphatic. The verb *zaō* is used here of our course, conduct and character: we are to live soberly (*sophronōs*), i.e. exercising self-restraint, in relation to ourselves; righteously (*dikaiōs*) in relation to other men; and godly (*eusebos*) as to our highest relationship. We have these three great principles brought before us in the so-called Sermon on the Mount; in Matt 5 the emphasis is upon righteousness, in Matt 6 upon godliness and in Matt 7 upon sobriety.

For the fifth and final time in this epistle sobriety is mentioned (see 1:8; 2:2, 5 and 6), but now it is not applied to a specific class, but is given as that which should be characteristic of every believer. In living righteously, i.e. justly and honourably, we acknowledge the claims of others and have due regard to our duty towards our neighbour. God's grace requires of us a life of truth and strict justice in all our dealings with our fellow men. Then we learn that it is not enough to renounce ungodliness, for our lives must be lived in a godly manner as we own the rights of God over our hearts. A godly person ever seeks to live as in the presence of God.

"This present world (aiōn)", or course of things, is the sphere where such a life is to be lived. The word aiōn denotes a period of time marked (in its NT usage) by spiritual or moral characteristics. In our present circumstances we live physically in a material world, but we are also moving through an evil age. We as believers have been delivered from this present evil age by the death of Christ, "who gave himself for our sins, that he might deliver us from this present evil world" (Gal 1:4); we are to prove the truth of this now in our own experience as we continue in this present course of things. Oh, that we might respond to the teaching of God's grace!

13 The grace that brings salvation and educates us, also gives light concerning the future, "looking for (prosdechomai) that blessed hope"; the fact that the participle agrees with the personal pronoun "we" in v.12 reminds us that those who possess this hope are the ones who are at present experiencing the discipline of the grace of God. The verb prosdechomai, meaning "to wait for", has an atmosphere of expectancy about it and an eagerness to welcome the person or thing looked for.

But what is the object of our expectation? It is "that blessed hope and (kai) the appearing of the glory of our great God and Saviour Jesus Christ" — as the rendering should be. One rule of Greek grammar is that when there are two nouns in the same case connected by kai, the first noun having the article and the second noun not having the article, then the second noun refers to the same thing as the first noun, and is a further description of it. Now this is precisely the situation here with reference to "that blessed hope and the appearing of the glory", so that Paul is not here setting forth the two phases of the second advent, viz. the rapture and the revelation, as some would suggest.

The present author wishes to make it clear that he is waiting for the imminent return of the Lord Jesus to the air to take His own blood-bought people unto Himself and that, with the editors of this present series of expositions, he believes that "the Rapture" is "the Hope of the Church" and that "Before the great Tribulation she will be raptured and God's prophetic programme will continue with Jacob's trouble, the public manifestation and the millennium of blessing."

However, here in this passage Paul is thinking of the Lord's return in glory, but considered from two different points of view. For the believer it is "that blessed (makarios) hope (elpis)"; hope is not used here subjectively, of our attitude of hope, but objectively, of the thing hoped for. When "hope" is used in the NT there is, of course, no uncertainty as to its fulfilment. The adjective "blessed" in this context means "filled with richness, benefits and good things"; it is the only occasion in the NT where *makarios* is applied to an object which does not itself enjoy the blessing, but is a source of blessing to others.

The Greek conjunction *kai*, better rendered here as "even", is explanatory and introduces the definition of the character of the thing hoped for. For the Lord Himself it will be "the appearing of the glory"; for Him it will mean the full manifestation of His glory, now unrecognised and disregarded by the world. Let us remember that the last that this world saw of our blessed Lord was Him being taken down from the tree and laid in a tomb, for He appeared only to those who were His own in resurrection. Sometimes we heartily sing "That will be glory for me!" but do we take into account what that day of manifestation will mean for Him?

The reference is to the appearing of the glory "of our great God and Saviour Jesus Christ". This phrase does not speak of two persons, since the appellations "God" and "Saviour" are governed by a single article in the Greek; it is the Lord Jesus Christ Himself who is in view in this comprehensive expression. Here we have a direct statement as to the deity of Christ; His deity will become manifest to *all* at His second advent, which will likewise demonstrate His power as Saviour.

Only here in the NT is the adjective "great" (*megas*) applied to God; this passage emphasises in a wonderful way the greatness of Christ. The word of the angel Gabriel to Mary prior to His birth was "He shall be *great*" (Luke 1:32); the Lord Himself spoke of Jerusalem as being "the city of the *great* king" (Matt 5:35). Those who witnessed His raising of the widow of Nain's son from the dead acknowledged "That a *great* prophet is risen up among us" (Luke 7:16), whilst the writer to the Hebrews reminds us that we have "a *great* priest over the house of God" (Heb 10:21 RV) and that our Lord Jesus is "that *great* shepherd of the sheep" (Heb 13:20).

According to Luke's gospel, Simeon, Anna and Joseph of Arimathaea were all eagerly waiting for the Messiah. It should be noted that "waiting for" (Luke 2:25), "looked for" (Luke 2:38) and "waited for" (Luke 23:51) are renderings of the same Greek verb *prosdechomai* translated "looking for" in the present context (Titus 2:13). Simeon was waiting for a *prophet*, "waiting for the consolation of Israel" (Luke 2:25); Anna was waiting for a *priest*, she "spake of him to all that looked for redemption in Jerusalem" (Luke 2:38); Joseph of Arimathaea was waiting for a *king*, "who himself waited for the kingdom of God" (Luke 23:51). Of Simeon it is said "the same man was just and devout" (Luke 2:25), evidently he was living *righteously* and *godly*; Anna "served God with fastings and prayers night and day" (Luke 2:37); in fasting she was saying "no" to self and was thus living *soberly*, whilst in serving God she was living *godly*. Joseph of Arimathaea "was a good man and a just" (Luke 23:50), thus living *soberly* and *justly*. What an encouragement and example is this godly remnant in Luke's Gospel to us to "live soberly, righteously, and godly, in this present world, looking for that blessed hope"!

14 The death of the Lord Jesus was *voluntary*, "who gave himself"; it was *vicarious*, "for us"; it was *purposive*, negatively to "redeem us from all iniquity" and positively to "purify unto himself a peculiar people, zealous of good works". Note that in this section of the chapter we have:

1. the *historical*, "hath appeared (v.11)
2. the *educational*, "teaching us" (v.12)
3. the *prophetical*, "looking for (v.13)
4. the *sacrificial*, "who gave himself" (v.14)
5. the *experimental*, "purify . . . a people, zealous of good works" (v.14).

The relative clause "who gave himself" evidently refers to Christ alone, but the construction leads us to take the whole preceding expression "our great God and Saviour Jesus Christ" as its antecedent; this confirms that one and not two Persons are referred to in the previous verse. The Saviour gave that which is beyond all price, "who gave (*didōmi*) himself for (*huper*, on behalf of) us" — it was on the cross that He gave Himself up for us. This expression is thoroughly Pauline, cf. "who *gave himself* for our sins" (Gal. 1:4); "who . . . *gave himself* for me" (Gal 2:20); "Christ also loved the church and *gave himself* for it" (Eph 5:25) and "who *gave himself* a ransom for (*huper*) all" (1 Tim 2:6).

The purpose of His giving Himself is first expressed negatively, "that he might redeem (*lutroō*) us from (*apo*) all iniquity (*anomia*)." It seems probable that the language is taken from the LXX of Psa 130:8 (AV rendering "And he shall redeem Israel from all his iniquities") where not only the same verb but the same phrase "from all iniquity" is found, albeit in the plural. The Greek verb *lutroō* means "to release by the payment of a ransom"; it is used here in the middle voice indicating that the Person who carries out the action has a special interest in what He does. Our condition of bondage in lawlessness (N.B. *anomia* is derived from *a*, the negative, and *nomos*, law) had to be undone. The redemption here is viewed as rescuing us from the *power* rather than from the *guilt* of iniquity; the preposition used, viz. *apo* (from), denotes the completeness of that deliverance.

The positive aim of His giving Himself for us was to "purify (*katharizō*) unto himself a peculiar people, zealous of good works". Believers are not only God's *chosen ones* (Titus 1:1), they are also God's *purified ones* (see exposition of 1:15). If in 1:15 the *people* are in view, "the pure"; here we see the *price*, "who gave himself", and the *purpose*, via. that we might be a people for His own possession; so that possession is the outcome of purifying.

The Lord said through Moses to the children of Israel, "ye shall be a peculiar treasure unto me, above all people" (Exod 19:5); we may observe that God has a purpose to have Israel as His special possession in the land when Messiah reigns, a people who should belong to Him in His own right.

Meanwhile believers in this present age are His "peculiar people" (*laos periousios*) in this world. However, as such we should be characterised as being "zealous of good works"; this epistle has much to tell us about works (*ergon*) — see exposition of 1:16.

The word rendered "zealous" is really a noun, *zēlōtēs*, used adjectivally and meaning "zealot", i.e. an uncompromising partisan; indeed Paul uses this word in Gal 1:14 of his own eagerness to maintain the traditions of his ancestors. We are to live with a burning passion for good works.

e. Charge to Titus (2:15)

15 The chapter concludes with a restatement of the responsibilities of Titus himself, "These things speak, and exhort, and rebuke with all authority" — only the first of these verbs is connected with "these things" which are presumably all of the practical exhortations found in chapter 2. The word is not exactly "teach" here (see exposition of 2:1), but the truth needs to be spoken in order for believers to know, and so these matters are to be clearly set forth.

The ministry of Titus was also to be one of exhortation; we need men who are able to apply the truth to local circumstances and call from the saints a positive response to the teaching they have received. However, self-will might be at work and evil might display itself, hence reproof is sometimes necessary; the word *elenchō* used here implies a rebuke which carries with it a conviction. Titus, as Paul's delegate, had apostolic authority (*epitagē*) to rebuke in this way should any challenge him; the word *epitagē* denotes a commandment as in 1:13. We now have all the authority of the completed Word of God.

Mindful of the difficult task confronting Titus, Paul adds "Let no man despise (*periphroneō*) thee". The Greek verb is derived from *peri*, "beyond", and *phroneō*, "to be minded", and literally means to set oneself in thought beyond, hence to contemn or despise. The life and conduct of Titus are to be such as to add weight to his words; he must see to it that he gives no occasion for anyone to despise him. What a lesson for those who seek to teach and minister to the needs of God's people!

2. General Directions
3:1-7

v.1	"Put them in mind to be subject to principalities and powers, to obey magistrates, to be ready to every good work,
v.2	To speak evil of no man, to be no brawlers, but gentle, shewing all meekness unto all men.
v.3	For we ourselves also were sometimes foolish, disobedient, deceived, serving divers lusts and pleasures, living in malice and envy, hateful, and hating one another.
v.4	But after that the kindness and love of God our Saviour toward man appeared,

> v.5   Not by works of righteousness which we have done, but according to his mercy he saved us, by the washing of regeneration, and renewing of the Holy Ghost;
>
> v.6   Which he shed on us abundantly through Jesus Christ our Saviour;
>
> v.7   That being justified by his grace, we should be made heirs according to the hope of eternal life."

a. Guiding Precepts (vv.1-2)

There is a link between vv.1-7 of chapter 3 and the second chapter of this epistle (see outline in section 7 of the Introduction). If, in the section embracing vv.2-10 of chapter 2 and headed "Guiding Precepts", Paul gives directions, warnings and exhortations to men and women of different ages with regard to personal and domestic duties, and the emphasis is upon our relationships with our fellow-believers, here in the opening verses of chapter 3 he turns to consider what the behaviour and attitude of believers should be towards government and society in general.

1-2 Indeed seven matters are dealt with in these two verses, with v.1 covering the *political* and *civil* realm and verse 2 the *social* realm.

Titus is bidden to "put them (i.e. the believers on Crete) in mind" (*hupomimnēskō*) concerning these things; the Greek verb signifies "to cause to remember", the present imperative being used here; thus Titus must continue to do so. The implication is that they already knew about these matters, but needed to have them impressed afresh upon their consciences. They must "be subject to (*hupotassō*) principalities (*archē*) and powers (*exousia*)". *Hupotassō*, used here in the middle voice, signifies "to put oneself in subjection to or under the authority of some person". The terms "principalities" and "powers" are perhaps better rendered "rulers" and "authorities" respectively; some would suggest that there is not sufficient warrant for the conjunction "and" (*kai*) — the reading would then imply "rulers who are authorities". However, these terms comprehend every kind of civil official and designate government as such without indicating any particular form or person.

The apostle Peter presses similar exhortations on believing Jews in chapter 2 of his first epistle. "Submit yourselves to every ordinance of man" (or "be in subjection therefore to every human institution"), says Peter, nor does it matter "whether it be to the king, as supreme; or unto governors (i.e. delegated responsibility), as unto them that are sent by him" (1 Pet 2:13-14). Paul does so emphatically when writing to Roman believers (in chapter 13 of his letter) who were mainly Gentiles: "Let every soul be subject unto the higher powers"; he then gives the reason: "For there is no power but of God: the powers that be are ordained of God" (Rom 13:1). Now Paul charges Titus, who was a Greek, to lay these particular injunctions on the Cretan brethren whose countrymen were notorious for their insubordination and other vices.

Never was such an exhortation more needed than in the present day as the lawlessness of the age rapidly increases, openly manifest in demonstrations, protests, hooliganism and riots; the way is only being paved for the ultimate revelation of the Lawless One. If this age is marked by lawlessness, we as believers recognise the need for subjection as is stressed throughout the epistle. Thus an elder is to have "faithful children not accused of riot or unruly" (1:6). Paul, whilst warning that "there are many unruly and vain talkers" (1:10), reminds us that our Saviour Jesus Christ has redeemed "us from all iniquity (i.e. lawlessness)" (2:14). We are neither Jews under law, nor are we lawless Gentiles.

"To obey magistrates (*peitharcheō*)", is literally "to obey one in authority"; the word seems to denote obedience to particular commands of government, such as payment of taxes and dues. The principle of government should always be on the side of what is right (see, e.g., 1 Pet 2:14), but even bad government is no excuse for disobedience. Obedience always and in every place is the duty of the believer. But, say Peter and the other apostles, "we ought to obey God rather than men" (Acts 5:29) — this is the limit of our obedience; thus we are taught how to behave if obedience to a civil power would mean disobedience to God.

We are reminded in this epistle that "we ourselves also were sometimes . . . disobedient" (3:3); those who merely "profess that they know God" are said to be "disobedient" (1:16). On the other hand, servants (i.e. bondservants) are to be exhorted "to be obedient to their own masters" (2:9).

It is possible for believers to hold a rigid theory of obedience within the assembly (e.g. stressing the Lordship of Christ, recognising government in the church of God) and yet to deny a similar responsibility in the world. But then there are many who would insist on obedience to the world's authority and yet are not prepared to acknowledge the necessity for it in the local church.

In the context "to be ready to every good work (*agathon ergon*)" means to co-operate fully with civil authorities in seeking to further all that is beneficial (*agathos*) to the state and society, nevertheless maintaining the principle that what we do must be consistent with the will of God.

V.2 brings in our *social* relationships; here there are two *negative* and two *positive* injunctions.

The exhortation "to speak evil (*blasphēmeō*) of no man," literally "of not even one person", was probably especially directed in the first place at the natural tendency of oppressed believers to speak evil of their rulers (see 2 Pet 2:10 and Jude 10 for the principle), but was then extended into a more general precept. The expression does not, of course, mean that we are never to talk of nor expose the evils of men, but we are certainly not to malign or speak injuriously of others.

In the clause "to be no brawlers" the Greek adjective *amachos* means "abstaining from fighting, not contentious". We come into contact with those whose way of life is totally opposed to that of the christian, but we should not be quarrelsome. It is very difficult for those who know and appreciate the truth not to seem contentious towards those who deny it.

The conjunction "but" is omitted in the RV. The word "gentle" (*epieikēs*) means mild or actively forbearing — the very opposite of being contentious. The same expressions rendered here "to be no brawlers . . . gentle" are translated (in the reverse order) "patient . . . not a brawler" in 1 Tim 3:3; there they are among the qualities required in an elder; here they are to mark all believers.

The Greek verb *endeiknumi* conveys the idea of showing forth or providing proof of (see exposition of 2:10). We are to exhibit this quality as something that is our own, something now within us. The meaning of *praütēs* is not readily expressed in our English language; described negatively, it is the very opposite of haughtiness and self-assertiveness. This grace of meekness is to be manifested not only in our dealings with our fellow-believers, but "towards all men", clearly demonstrating that we are true disciples of Him who could say "I am meek and lowly in heart" (Matt 11:29). These latter two positive qualities are brought together in 2 Cor 10:1 where the apostle says "Now I Paul myself beseech you by the meekness and gentleness of Christ"; Christ Himself is the perfect exemplar.

b. Gracious Deliverance (vv.3-6)

3 Note the link word "for", giving us the reason for our attitude. One thing that will help us in dealing in such ways with unbelievers is to keep in mind what we were like before we were saved. "We" — this is emphatic by its position — "ourselves also" — includes Titus and not only him, but the writer of the epistle, the Cretans and ourselves, indeed all believers.

Seven vices depicting our former state are presented; not one of us can step outside this description. We must all acknowledge the accuracy of this seven-fold catalogue of depravities. Paul, in painting this dark picture, starts with the inner condition and then shows its outward expression. The first two features are Godward, the second two are *selfward*, whilst the final three are *manward*:—

"Foolish" (*anoētos*), i.e. without understanding, lacking in spiritual discernment, signifies a spiritual blindness to the reality of God and His truth and corresponds to the expression "having the understanding darkened" (Eph 4:18). "Disobedient" (*apeithēs*) signifies "unwilling to be persuaded". We were contemptuous of God's will, spurning belief. If foolishness is evidence of a blunted mind, disobedience is indicative of a hardened heart. "Deceived" (*planaō*) means led astray, wandering in error. This is evidence of a perverted will. In our unregenerate days we were made to wander from the path of truth either by false systems of religion or by our own evil affections and appetites.

The resultant life is then described. "Serving (*douleuō*) divers (*poikilos*) lusts (*epithumia*) and pleasures (*hēdonē*)" introduces the metaphor of slavery to illustrate the believer's former servitude to all kinds of (the Greek adjective denotes particoloured or variegated) lusts (see exposition of 2:12) and pleasures; *hēdonē* is always used in a bad sense in the NT and suggests the gratification of the natural desires. "Living in malice (*kakia*) and envy (*phthonos*)" shows we were spending our lives in:

1. "malice" (*kakia*) has been defined as "vicious hard heartedness" and denotes an evil attitude of mind manifesting itself in ill-will and a desire to injure.
2. "envy" begrudges the prosperity of others. There is a distinction between the Greek words *phthonos* and *zelas*, often rendered jealousy; envy desires to deprive another of what he has, whilst jealousy wants to have the same thing for itself.

"Hateful" (*stugētos*) is used only here in the NT and means "odious" or "detestable". And (omitted in the RV) hating (*miseō*) one another" indicates mutual animosity; surely the depth is reached when even among sinners there is reciprocal hatred.

If v.3 reminds us *what we were*, vv.4-6 tell us *what God has done*. In vv.1-2 we learn of *seven* virtues expected of us; in v.3 we read of *seven* vices depicting our former state; now in vv.4-7 we learn of *seven* aspects of what we are as a result of the unmerited blessing of God.

4 "But" introduces the contrast. "But . . . God" tells us of divine intervention; man's extremity was God's opportunity. The Greek adverb *hote*, translated "after that" in the AV, is better rendered "when". We have read in this epistle of the outshining of

1. the grace of God (2:11)
2. the glory of our great God and Saviour (2:13).

Now here Paul tells us of the shining forth of the kindness of God and His love toward man. The literal rendering is "the kindness and the love to man . . . of our Saviour God"; the use of two articles in the original makes these qualities distinct, but they are so closely linked that the verb "appeared" (*epiphainō*) is in the singular. See exposition of 1:3 for a consideration of the title "God our Saviour".

The word *chrēstotēs*, rendered here "kindness", denotes goodness in action; it is used in such familiar texts as "not knowing that the goodness of God leadeth thee to repentance" (Rom 2:4) and "behold therefore the goodness and severity of God: on them which fell, severity; but toward thee, goodness" (Rom 11:22). Here we have the revelation of the goodness of His heart. The kindness of God is brought in here to support the moral point that we are to show kindness to those who are now where we once were.

But we are to distinguish between the kindness of God and the love-of-

God-toward-man (*philanthrōpia*), literally "the philanthropy of God"; the word is expressive of His feeling of pity towards man. These two attributes are set in contrast to the last two evils mentioned in v.3, viz. "hateful and hating one another."

5 If in v.4 Paul points to the *source* of our salvation, in the first part of this verse he deals with the *basis* of salvation. "He saved (*sōzō*) us" expresses the saving act of God as a past fact; the reference of course is to the spiritual and eternal salvation granted immediately by God to "us" who have believed on the Lord Jesus Christ, cf. "Believe on the Lord Jesus Christ, and thou shalt be saved" (Acts 16:31).

The basis for our salvation is stated both negatively and positively. Negatively, He saved us "not by works (*ergon*) of righteousness (*dikaiosunē*) which we have done". God could never deal with us on this principle, since all our works, apart from conversion, are unrighteous: "all our righteousnesses (i.e. righteous acts) are as filthy rags" (Isa 64:6). The "we" is emphatic; we did no works of righteousness, nor were we able to. The Greek preposition rendered "by" is *ek* meaning "out of", so the phrase is literally "not out of works of righteousness" — this expresses the source of the effort on our part.

Then follows the *positive* side; "but" — by way of contrast — "according to his mercy (*eleos*) he saved us", for God had to deal with us in mercy if we were to be saved. Our disobedience merited His wrath, but His mercy held back what we fully deserved and His grace (2:11) dispensed what we of ourselves could never obtain. The position of "his" in the original makes it emphatic — it was His own mercy — and marks the contrast with "we" in the preceding clause. The word *eleos* means "the outward manifestation of pity"; such mercy assumes dire need on the part of the one who receives it and yet adequate resources to meet that need on the part of Him who shows it.

Note that in this clear statement of gospel truth, Paul makes no reference to man's side of things at all, not even to his faith.

At the end of the verse Paul tells us the means by which this salvation was effected in us, viz. "by the washing of regeneration and renewing of the Holy Ghost". Some would suggest that *loutron* rendered here "washing" means "laver" (see e.g. RV margin), but a closer consideration of the word confirms that it refers to the act of washing rather than to the water in which the bath is taken. The reference here is, in the opinion of the present author, to the work of regeneration by the word of God, cf. "the washing of water by the word" (Eph 5:26). The cleansing is effected through the application of the word of God to the heart and conscience.

The Word is elsewhere pointed out as the instrument or means of the new birth, e.g.

1. "of his own will begat he us with the word of truth" (Jas 1:18);

2. "being born again, not of corruptible seed, but of incorruptible, by the word of God, which liveth and abideth for ever" (1 Pet 1:23).

But here the expression is "the washing of regeneration (*palingenesia*)". There is only one other occasion where this Greek word is used in the NT, viz ". . . in the regeneration when the Son of man shall sit in the throne of his glory, ye (the apostles) also shall sit upon twelve thrones, judging the twelve tribes of Israel" (Matt 19:28). Thus in Matthew's Gospel the word is used to signify the new state of things to be introduced in the coming kingdom of the Son of man.

It is evident that the terms "new birth" and "regeneration" refer to the same event, but viewed in different ways. The new birth stresses the *impartation of spiritual life* where there had been spiritual death, whilst regeneration emphasises the *introduction of a new state of things* in contrast with the old.

The preposition "through" (*dia*) governs both "the washing of regeneration" and "renewing of the Holy Ghost", so that not one but two facts are presented here. The Greek noun *anakainōsis*, meaning "renewal" or "renewing", is used elsewhere in the NT only in Rom 12:2 in the expression "the renewing of your mind" which has in view the adjustment of the moral and spiritual vision and thinking to the mind of God. The "renewing of the Holy Ghost" is the renewal effected by the Holy Spirit; it is undoubtedly once and for all; indeed it is another way of saying "old things are passed away; behold, all things are become new" (2 Cor 5:17), and yet this present passage seems to indicate the continual operation of the indwelling Spirit of God.

6 The relative pronoun "which" refers to the Holy Ghost (neuter gender in the Greek text) whereas "he" relates back to "God our Saviour" (v.4). The verb "shed" (*ekcheō*) is in the aorist, or past definite, tense, indicating one single complete act; the reference here is to what took place on the Day of Pentecost. Note the words of the apostle Peter as he stood up and preached on that momentous occasion: "Therefore being by the right hand of God exalted, and having received of the Father the promise of the Holy Ghost, he hath shed forth this, which ye now see and hear" (Acts 2:33). There is no thought of any scanty or feeble supply here, for the Holy Spirit is said to have been shed or poured forth on us "abundantly" (*plousiōs*). Peter stressed that firstly the Lord Himself received of the Father the promise of the Holy Spirit and then He sent Him forth. The source was the Father, but the Lord Jesus is seen as the agent of sending, as emphasised here, "through Jesus Christ our Saviour".

Just as the three Persons of the Godhead are mentioned in their combined operations in Acts 2:33, so here in our present verse we learn of their co-operation in this truly divine salvation. It must be stressed that to speak of the Son and the Holy Spirit as the second and third Persons of the Trinity is incorrect; to do so is to relegate the Son and the Holy Spirit to inferior positions. We believe in the co-equality of the Persons of the Godhead.

The baptism in the Spirit took place once and for all at Pentecost when all believers of this church age were baptised into the body of Christ: "For by one Spirit are we all baptised into one body" (1 Cor 12:13). The body in the mind of God was complete at Pentecost; the figure of a body impresses upon us the fact of the completeness of the baptism — it is something finished. The Lord Jesus Himself was the Baptiser, not the Holy Spirit. The Holy Spirit was rather the element in which the baptism took place, just as water is the element in which we are physically baptised.

This epistle, although brief, lacks nothing in doctrinal greatness. There are 12 references to God; as to the doctrine of Christ, direct reference is made to the Lord Himself on 5 occasions. The Holy Spirit is mentioned only once in this epistle, here in vv.5-6; nevertheless, as we have seen, it is a reference of great importance doctrinally.

c. Great Purpose — Future Glory (v.7)

7 In each of the three chapters of this epistle the gospel is set forth as a three-fold cord including within itself a *past*, a *present* and a *future* aspect. We have seen in this third chapter that "the kindness and love of God our Saviour toward man appeared" (v.4) — that is past. The present aspect is now stated, "being justified (*dikaioō*) by his grace (*charis*)".

Justification is a doctrine which is, of course, dealt with fully by Paul in his epistles to the Romans and to the Galatians. Justification is a divine prerogative, "it is God that justifieth" (Rom 8:33), "that he (God) might be just, and the justifier of him which believeth in Jesus" (Rom 3:26). God Himself is the *source* of justification. Christ is the *sphere* of justification, "while we seek to be justified by (RV, in) Christ" (Gal 2:17); we thus learn that justification cannot be found "in the law" but only "in Christ". The ground (or basis) of justification is the blood of Christ shed sacrificially at Calvary, "being now justified by (or in the power of) his blood" (Rom 5:9); whilst the *means* of justification is faith, "therefore being justified by faith" (Rom 5:1). Here, in our present passage, we see the *spring* of justification: "by his grace"; cf. "being justified freely (i.e. without a cause) by his grace" (Rom 3:24). Here in Titus it is not man's side, but God's side, that is stressed. God in grace and at infinite cost procured our justification and by the same grace bestowed it upon us. We as believers are not only God's *chosen ones*, "God's elect" (1:1) and God's *clean ones*, "the pure" (1:15), but also God's *cleared ones*, "being justified".

If one result of salvation is our justification, a further outcome is that we have been made heirs; this is a present reality and not merely a future hope. The aim, "that (*hina*, in order that) we should (or might) be made heirs (*klēronomos*)", has already been achieved; we are "heirs of God, and joint-heirs with Christ" (Rom 8:17). The Greek noun denotes one who obtains a lot or a portion (from *klēros*, a lot and *nemomai*, to possess).

All that will be ours as heirs is "according to" (*kata*) or in accordance with the hope (*elpis*) given to us as a present enjoyment. As we have noted (see exposition of 1:2), although eternal life (*aiōnios zōē*) is the present possession of all who put their faith in the Son of God, nevertheless Paul frequently treats it according to its future display; thus, for the believer, eternal life in all its fulness lies before him. This then is the future aspect of the gospel.

No wonder Paul adds in v.8: "Faithful is the saying" as he expresses his complete confidence in the comprehensive statement of the gospel given here. Thus we see that the pillars of exhortation given in vv.1,2 of the chapter are firmly based upon the doctrine of vv.4-7.

3. Particular Directions
3:8-14

v.8   "This is a faithful saying, and these things I will that thou affirm constantly, that they which have believed in God might be careful to maintain good works. These things are good and profitable unto men.

v.9   But avoid foolish questions, and genealogies, and contentions, and strivings about the law; for they are unprofitable and vain.

v.10   A man that is an heretick after the first and second admonition reject;

v.11   Knowing that he that is such is subverted, and sinneth, being condemned of himself.

v.12   When I shall send Artemas unto thee, or Tychicus, be diligent to come unto me to Nicopolis: for I have determined there to winter.

v.13   Bring Zenas the lawyer and Apollos on their journey diligently, that nothing be wanting unto them.

v.14   And let ours also learn to maintain good works for necessary uses, that they be not unfruitful."

a. Concerning the Faithful (v.8)

8 The phrase "This is a faithful saying" is characteristic of the Pastoral Epistles and is found in them only (1 Tim 1:15; 3:1; 4:9; 2 Tim 2:11 and here). "Faithful" (*pistos*) signifies trustworthy or reliable, whilst *logos* rendered "saying" means, of course, "a word", the emphasis being upon the word as a concept of thought. Here, as already suggested, the reference is to the doctrine of the gospel enunciated in vv.4-7 of this chapter.

Since these things (i.e. these truths) are fully trustworthy, Paul urges that Titus in his teaching should affirm them constantly (*diabebaioomai*); the idea is not constantly in the sense of continually, but uniformly. The Greek verb is derived from *bebaioō* meaning "to confirm", the prefix *dia* intensifying the word; it is rendered "confidently affirm" in 1 Tim 1:17 RV, where it is used of false teachers who were affirming what they themselves did not understand.

These affirmations here were to be especially directed towards "those which have believed (*pisteuō*) in God" — the expression literally means "believed God", i.e. took Him at His word. Such have set to their seal that God is true. If Titus was faithfully to bring to the attention of believers their responsibilities the specific purpose (*hina*, in order that) was that they on their part "might be careful (*phrontizō*) to maintain (*proistēmi*) good works". *Phrontizō* is found only here in the NT and means to consider, to ponder thoughtfully over a matter. We as christians must give careful consideration to the importance of fulfilling our responsibilities; the connection between belief in God and good works must be maintained. (The RV marginal rendering "profess honest occupations" would appear to be out of context).

The expression "these things" summarises the truths and responsibilities set out in this verse and those preceding. All these practical courses are "good (*kalos*) and profitable (*ōphelimos*) unto men", i.e. men in general, not only to believers. *Kalos* denotes that which is honourable, fair and virtuous; the adjective *ōphelimos* is found only in the Pastoral Epistles and is used both of physical exercise and godliness (1 Tim 4:8) and of the God-breathed Scriptures (2 Tim 3:16).

b. Concerning the False Teaching (v.9)

9 Paul now reminds Titus that he will be confronted with matters that are not of the character of the things that are "good and profitable". "But" introduces the contrast — Titus and we ourselves are to shun (*periistēmi*) certain things. The Greek verb, used here in the middle voice, literally means "to turn oneself about for the purpose of avoiding something"; the tense employed points to a continuing attitude. These warnings form a special feature of all three Pastoral Epistles and show just how widespread these evils had become, largely through Jewish influences. The things to be avoided are:

1. "foolish questions"; the word *zētēsis* rendered questions or questionings is derived from *zēteō* to seek, and means literally "processes of inquiry", hence debates. The apostle characterises them as foolish (*mōros*) because they were of an utterly impractical nature and consumed time and powers which were needed for other and better things.
2. "genealogies" (*genealogia*); wild allegorical interpretations and fanciful meanings had been assigned to the genealogies as found in the OT. The combination of "questions" and "genealogies", found also in 1 Tim 1:4, shows that there was a marked similarity between the situations on Crete and at Ephesus.
3. "contentions" (*eris*). The Greek noun denotes strife, especially rivalry; these contentions were disputes and wranglings which no doubt arose out of arguments advanced by different teachers concerning the "questions" and "genealogies".
4. "strivings (*machē*, fightings, the word is always used in the plural in the NT) about the law". These were most probably arguments suggested by

disputed and intricate points connected with the Mosaic law, in most cases to make void its application to the persons themselves.

Let us bear in mind that disagreements and arguments invariably begin with error and not with truth. Frivolous and controversial questions and discussions on intricate and trifling points are unprofitable and futile. Whilst gospel truths are "good and profitable", legal squabbles are "unprofitable (anōphelēs) and vain (mataios)", i.e. they are not beneficial and are void of producing worthwhile results; hence they are unworthy of time and serious consideration.

c. *Concerning the Factious (vv.10-11)*

10 If v.9 tells us what the attitude of Titus was to be towards false teaching, vv.10-11 set before us what his reaction was to be towards a factious person.

The English word "heretick" (AV) is simply a transliteration of the Greek *hairetikos*, itself derived from the verb *haireomai*, meaning to take for oneself, to choose or prefer. A heretic (modern spelling) does not, in the language of the NT, necessarily signify a man holding false doctrine, but rather one who has chosen an idea or a course which is not commonly acceptable to the company. He is a person who is more concerned about gathering some adherents to himself and maintaining some sectarian line of truth and, in so doing, causes strife, faction and division in the assembly.

Should anyone continue with such a self-chosen idea or course, he is to be admonished; the admonition (*nouthesia*, literally, a putting in mind) is to draw his attention to the sin. *Nouthesia* implies training by *word*, whether by encouragement or, if necessary, by reproof (as here); the synonymous word *paideia* emphasises training by *acts*.

Should he refuse the first admonition, a second is to be administered — there is to be no over-hasty action. If he still does not change his ways, he is to be rejected (*paraiteomai*), i.e. he is to be shunned, avoided or given the cold shoulder. This would certainly mean imposing restraints as far as his active and public participation in the assembly meetings is concerned. There is no suggestion here of him being put away from the fellowship of the assembly, since false doctrine opposed to fundamental truth is not in question. However, the stage might be reached when an assembly would have to withdraw from a man who persistently acted in such an unworthy manner, for the saints could be divided beyond remedy.

11 His refusal to listen to the admonitions would show Titus what the man is:

1. as to his *character*, "knowing (*oida*) that he that is such is subverted (*ekstrephō*)". The verb *oida* denotes to know or perceive from

observation, whilst *ekstrephō*, rendered "perverted" in the RV, is a very strong expression and means literally "turned inside out", indeed it was used in secular medical literature for "dislocated"; the perfect passive tense of the verb indicates that the individual is in a state of being twisted or turned out of the right way.

2. as to his *conduct*, "and sinneth" (*harmartanō*). The use of the present tense stresses the fact that he is a wilful sinner — he keeps on constantly sinning, both by his factiousness and by his refusal to listen to admonitions; through hardness of heart he persists in his course of sin. Such a person is without the excuse of ignorance, but sins on in the full consciousness of his wilful and seditious conduct.

This leaves the man guilty, "being condemned of himself" (*autokatakritos* from *auto*, self, and *katakrinō*, to condemn); by his actions he unconsciously passes adverse judgment upon himself.

d. Concerning the Fellow-workers (vv.12-13)

The apostle here adds two matters of personal concern to Titus. He indicates his proposals for the future movements of Titus himself (v.12) and lays upon him an immediate obligation to be of assistance to Zenas and Apollos (v.13).

12 The position of Titus on the island of Crete was not to be permanent; he was certainly not "the first bishop of the church of the Cretans" as the appendix to the epistle in the AV would suggest. However, Paul makes the arrival of Artemas or Tychicus the condition of the departure of Titus from his present sphere of labour, "when (or whensoever) I shall send (*pempō*) Artemas unto thee, or Tychicus"; the indefinite clause in the original (*hotan* with the subjunctive) signifies that Paul was not certain as to the time when he would send either of them. Note that the reading is "Artemas . . . or Tychicus" — the apostle did not anticipate sending both.

Nothing further is known of Artemas (a shortened form of the name Artemidoras). We learn that there were men whom the Lord equipped and honoured for use in His service whose names appear incidentally on the page of the NT; they will evidently receive their reward at the Judgment Seat of Christ.

Tychicus is first mentioned along with Trophimus as being "of Asia" (Acts 20:4) and as accompanying Paul on his last missionary journey from Corinth to Asia. If we compare the closing chapters of Paul's epistles to the Ephesians and the Colossians, we find that both were taken to their destinations by Tychicus at the same time. In both letters he is given a high commendation by Paul, e.g. three lovely things are said about him in Col 4:7, he is:

1. "a *beloved brother*" — this emphasises *true affection*;

2.   "a *faithful minister*" (*diakonos*) — this incorporates *true devotion*;
3.   "a *fellowservant* (*sundoulos*) in the Lord" — this indicates *real communion*.

From 2 Tim 4:12 we learn that Tychicus was despatched once more to Ephesus, no doubt to take the place of Timothy. Evidently Tychicus was one of Paul's most trusted fellow-workers.

The word to Titus was "be diligent (*spoudazō*) to come unto me to Nicopolis"; although there were at least three cities of this name, this Nicopolis (meaning "city of victory") was almost certainly the commercial port on the coast of Epirus. Scripture is silent as to whether Titus was able to visit this city subsequently.

The statement of Paul's determined plans for the winter ahead, "for I have determined (*krinō*) there to winter (*paracheimazō*)", reveals that he was at liberty at the time of writing, whilst the adverb "there" (*ekei*) shows that Paul was not yet at Nicopolis in spite of the appendix in the AV, "written to Titus . . . from Nicopolis".

13 What a concern for the comfort and well-being of the Lord's servants is exhibited by Paul as he exhorts Titus to "bring Zenas the lawyer and Apollos on their journey diligently, that nothing be wanting unto them". Evidently Zenas and Apollos were visiting Crete to occupy themselves in the work of the Lord; no doubt they brought this epistle to Titus with them.

Nothing more is known of Zenas. The description of him as "the lawyer" (*nomikos*, an adjective used as a noun) leaves it uncertain whether the designation is Jewish or Roman; if the term is used with the same meaning as it has in the synoptic gospels, then he was a Jewish christian who had been expert in the Jewish law and would therefore be useful in opposing the Judaising teachers. However, since he possesses a Gentile name, he may well have been a practitioner of the Roman law who became a servant of Christ.

Apollos was the eloquent Jewish preacher from Alexandria who was "mighty in the (OT) scriptures" (Acts 18:24), but he knew only the baptism of John. When he came to Ephesus, Aquila and Priscilla were able to take him into their home and expound to him the way of God more perfectly (Acts 18:26). An outstanding quality in Apollos was that, unlike many men of great ability, he was teachable and did not resent the private instruction of this christian Jew and his wife. His subsequent work at Corinth in the province of Achaia towards fellow-believers and towards those outside was distinctly blessed of the Lord (Acts 18:27-28). The evident abilities of Apollos appear to have made his name a rallying point for the party spirit at Corinth which Paul had to rebuke (1 Cor 1:12-4:6). Later he became an associate of Paul in the work at Ephesus (1 Cor 16:12); this particular reference is important in that it reveals that Paul had no feelings of jealousy in his heart or rivalry concerning Apollos.

It is interesting to observe that the names of three of these acquaintances of

Paul mentioned in these verses were derived from three of the most famous heathen deities, Zenas from Zeus, Artemas from Artemis, the famous goddess of Ephesus, and Apollos from the well-known sun-god.

Now here Titus is bidden by Paul to bring Zenas and Apollos on their journey (*propempō*) diligently (*spoudaiōs*). The Greek verb, rendered in the RV "set forward on their journey", is used quite frequently in the book of the Acts and in the NT epistles and denotes that the persons journeying were to be furnished with all things that were required. Titus was evidently in a position to provide material assistance. Zenas and Apollos were to be cared for in temporal things in order that they might not be left in need, "that nothing (literally, not even one thing) be wanting (*leipō*) to them".

e. Concerning the Faithful (v.14)

14 After these specific instructions to Titus, a more general exhortation is given, directed to "ours" (RV, "our people") — clearly the Cretan believers are intended; but the expression is "ours also", so the injunction holds good for believers everywhere.

If Titus was not to forget fellow-labourers, how incumbent it was upon the saints generally. The whole weight was not to fall alone upon the shoulders of Titus; others were to share the responsibility. Too often the practical side of the work of the assembly is left to a minority.

"Ours also" were to "learn" (*manthanō*, the thought is that of learning by use and practice, to acquire the habit of) what Titus had long learned, viz. "to maintain (*proistēmi*) good works"; the Greek verb may be rendered "to give attention to". The idea behind the expression "for necessary (*anankaios*) uses (*chreia*)", literally, for urgent necessities, is "so as to help in cases of urgent need". Indeed in the original there is the definite article before "necessary uses," suggesting such occasions and objects as are presented to us from time to time. Cases of urgent need will not be difficult to find.

This injunction needs to be heeded in a day when believers give so much of their time and energies to their own things and seem indifferent not only to lost sinners, but also to needy saints.

How practical is this epistle! Titus was to be "a pattern of good works" (2:7); we are to be "zealous of good works" (2:14), "ready to every good work" (3:1), "careful to maintain good works" (3:8) and are to "learn to maintain good works" (3:14). This practical christianity is pleasing fruit, "that they be not unfruitful (*akarpos*)" — here we have a double negative; on the positive side, we are to be fruitful, not only in meeting the needs of others, but in cultivating christian graces in themselves by acts of kindness.

IV. The Conclusion (3:15)

> v.15   "All that are with me salute thee. Greet them that love us in the
> faith. Grace be with you all. Amen."

1. *The Salutations*
   3:15a

15a All who were with Paul saluted (*aspazomai*) Titus, i.e. they sent their
greetings — this was no cold formality. There is no means of identifying the
"all" who were with the apostle; the reference is most probably to Paul's
fellow-workers at the time of writing.

Paul had a specially warm place for the believers in Crete who were
affectionate towards him and his associates; to these he sends greetings,
"Greet (*aspazomai*) them that love (*phileō*, the word indicating tender
affection) us in the faith (*pistis*)". The absence of an article in the original
before *pistis* would seem to point to the fact that "faith" here is not objective,
i.e. faith as the body of christian doctrine, but subjective, viz. faith which
accepts the truth as in 1:4 (q.v.). However, the expression "in faith" may
simply mean "faithfully" or "truly".

2. *The Benediction*
   3:15b

15b Paul's last word is not for Titus only. He will be no partisan, nor will he
acknowledge any sectarianism (with which the word "heretic" has to do); his
heart breaks forth in the desire for divine blessing towards all the saints in
Crete, "Grace (*charis*) be with you all". Note "Amen" is omitted in the RV.
Grace is needed by all and for everything.

May our experience of the free unmerited favour of God in Christ Jesus
compel us to live lives which reveal His grace and love to others.